Riviera to the Rhine
Whitman Publishing Edition

www.whitman.com

© 2012 Whitman Publishing, LLC
3101 Clairmont Road • Suite G • Atlanta, GA 30329

Correspondence concerning this book may be directed to Whitman Publishing, Attn: WWII (Riviera to the Rhine), at the address above.

ISBN: 0794837719
Printed in China

If you enjoy this book, you will also enjoy *World War II: Saving the Reality—A Collector's Vault* (by Kenneth W. Rendell).

Each of the following volumes about the European Theater of Operations can be read and enjoyed separately; at the same time, each takes a natural place in the framework of the whole history of the war. *Cross-Channel Attack* • *Breakout and Pursuit* • *The Lorraine Campaign* • *The Siegfried Line Campaign* • *The Ardennes: Battle of the Bulge* • *Riviera to the Rhine* • *The Last Offensive*. For a day-by-day study of all the war's ground actions, see *Chronology: 1941–1945*.

For a complete catalog of history, hobby, sports, and other books and products, visit Whitman Publishing at www.whitman.com.

UNITED STATES ARMY IN WORLD WAR II

The European Theater of Operations

RIVIERA TO THE RHINE

Whitman Publishing Edition

by
Jeffrey J. Clarke
Robert Ross Smith

Whitman Publishing, LLC
PUBLISHING SINCE 1934

ATLANTA, GA
2012

UNITED STATES ARMY IN WORLD WAR II

Advisory Committee

(As of 6 August 1990)

U.S. Army Center of Military History

Brig. Gen. Harold W. Nelson, Chief of Military History

. . . to Those Who Served

Foreword to the First Printing

With the publication of *Riviera to the Rhine*, the Center of Military History completes its series of operational histories treating the activities of the U.S. Army's combat forces during World War II. This volume examines the least known of the major units in the European theater, General Jacob L. Devers' 6th Army Group. Under General Devers' leadership, two armies, the U.S. Seventh Army under General Alexander M. Patch and the First French Army led by General Jean de Lattre de Tassigny, landing on the Mediterranean coast near Marseille in August 1944, cleared the enemy out of southern France and then turned east and joined with army groups under Field Marshal Sir Bernard L. Montgomery and General Omar N. Bradley in the final assault on Germany.

In detailing the campaign of these Riviera-based armies, the authors have concentrated on the operational level of war, paying special attention to the problems of joint, combined, and special operations and to the significant roles of logistics, intelligence, and personnel policies in these endeavors. They have also examined in detail deception efforts at the tactical and operational levels, deep battle penetrations, river-crossing efforts, combat in built-up areas, and tactical innovations at the combined arms level.

Such concepts are of course very familiar to today's military students, and the fact that this volume examines them in such detail makes this study especially valuable to younger officers and noncommissioned officers. In truth, the challenges faced by military commanders half a century ago were hardly unique. That is why I particularly urge today's military students, who might well face some of these same problems in future combat, to study this campaign so that they might learn from their illustrious predecessors in the profession of arms.

Washington, D.C.

HAROLD W. NELSON
Brigadier General, USA
Chief of Military History

Foreword to the
Whitman Publishing Edition

On January 26, 1945, near Holtzwihr, France, a diminutive, baby-faced American infantry lieutenant—only 20 years old, but already a combat veteran of North Africa, Sicily, Italy, and France—climbed aboard a burning U.S. M10 tank destroyer that threatened to explode at any moment. Dangerously exposed to a blizzard of enemy fire while manning the flaming vehicle's unprotected .50-caliber machine gun, he single-handedly defeated a large attacking German force of six panzers and swarms of enemy infantrymen, killing or wounding 50 of them. Although seriously wounded, the lieutenant saved his company—Company B, 15th Infantry Regiment, 3d U.S. Infantry Division—from certain annihilation. When asked what prompted him to face such daunting odds alone, the lieutenant simply replied, "They were killing my friends." For his "above and beyond the call of duty" actions that day, Second Lieutenant Audie Murphy added the Medal of Honor to his 32 other medals and citations.

Murphy's wound—his third of the war—made him one of 24,324 casualties suffered during World War II by his 3d Infantry Division—the highest number of any of the 89 American divisions during the war. From August 1944 to May 1945, 3d Division advanced from the Riviera to the Rhine—and well beyond that water barrier into Germany—as part of U.S. Seventh Army, which with First French Army comprised Lieutenant General Jacob L. Devers's 6th Army Group. Although unfairly overlooked by World War II historians, making it "the least known of the major units in the European Theater," Devers's 6th Army Group played a vital role in final Allied victory over Germany. Landing August 15, 1944, on southern France's Riviera coast—Operation DRAGOON—6th Army Group on November 19, 1944, achieved the "signal honor of reaching the Rhine first." Its greatest contribution, however, was that 6th Army Group (10 combat divisions organized into three corps forming two field armies) provided Supreme Allied Commander General Dwight D. Eisenhower a vital *third* army group anchoring the 400-mile-long front line's southern flank, while Field Marshal Bernard Montgomery's British-Canadian 21st Army Group held the northern flank and Lieutenant General Omar N. Bradley's American 12th Army Group occupied the center. Arriving in France "at a time when the two northern Allied army groups were stretched to the limit in almost every way," 6th Army Group's operations prevented the enemy from massing forces that might have "drastically retarded the initial Allied drive to the German border in the north." Clearly, 6th Army Group's participation in the battles for France and Germany—notably, its drive up the Rhone River valley, the conquest of Alsace, nightmarish combat in France's Vosges Mountains, and particularly bitter fighting at Strasbourg and the Colmar Pocket— was no "sideshow" to the main event occurring in the two northern army groups. Instead, "least known" 6th Army's battlefield accomplishments on Eisenhower's southern flank proved "critical to Allied military fortunes on the Western Front."

One explanation for why 6th Army Group has not received proper credit is due to its commander. As a field artillery branch officer, 6th Army Group commander "Jakie" Devers (1887–1979) was somewhat of an outsider among senior U.S. Army European Theater commanders—nearly *all* of them were infantry officers. Indeed, in a revealing remark to Colonel Bruce C. Clarke of 4th Armored Division, cavalryman George S. Patton Jr.—another of the exceedingly rare non-infantry senior commanders serving under Eisenhower—bitingly quipped: "Colonel Clarke, if you were an *infantry* officer, you'd have been a *Major General* by now!" Eisenhower, holding full authority to choose his senior-ranking subordinates, habitually picked fellow infantry officers—understandably, he "would prefer commanders he was already familiar with and trusted thoroughly." But Eisenhower and Devers, although both protégés of U.S. Army Chief of Staff General George C. Marshall, were also rivals. In mid-1941, while Eisenhower was still a colonel, Devers became the U.S. Army's youngest major general. From 1941 to 1943, Devers had won widespread acclaim by rapidly expanding the army's armored force from 2 divisions to 16, and in 1943–1944 he had been commanding general of U.S. Army, Europe—until succeeded in that position by Ike. Although Eisenhower admitted, perhaps disingenuously, that he "entertained serious doubts about Devers' ability," when Marshall appointed Devers 6th Army Group commander on July 12, 1944, Ike nevertheless accepted the appointment. Yet, despite that fact that Eisenhower told Marshall he "cheerfully and willingly" welcomed Devers as army group commander, Ike's treatment of him throughout the war remained cool and aloof. In February 1945, Eisenhower sent Marshall his personal rankings of 38 senior European Theater officers—Ike ranked Devers only *24th* on the list, explaining his low assessment by writing: Devers "has not, so far, produced . . . that feeling of trust and confidence that is so necessary to continued success." The real tragedy of the Eisenhower-Devers rivalry, however, was that by denigrating or ignoring Devers's accomplishments, Ike was also denying 6th Army Group the much-deserved recognition that its key role in winning the Allied victory over Germany had clearly earned.

Dr. Jeffrey J. Clarke—a longtime friend and mentor—became a historian at the U.S. Army Center of Military History in 1971 and was its chief historian from 1990 to 2006. Clarke is a Vietnam War veteran—he authored volumes in the army's official history of that war—and a lieutenant colonel (ret.) in the U.S. Army Reserve. Robert Ross Smith, who retired in 1983 as chief of the Center's General History Branch, served two years as historical officer for General Douglas MacArthur during World War II and authored two volumes on Pacific Campaigns in the *United States Army in World War II* series. Their seamless collaboration produced *Riviera to the Rhine*, a much needed and superbly written account of a vitally important campaign. It is the full story, expertly told by accomplished historians, of 6th Army's blood and sacrifice.

Published in 1993, *Riviera to the Rhine* is the final volume produced in the *United States Army in World War II—European Theater of Operations* series; but chronologically, the August 1944–February 1945 6th Army Group combat operations detailed in this book cover an extensive period, overlapping the actions of Eisenhower's two northern army groups presented in *Breakout and Pursuit, The Lorraine Campaign, The Siegfried Line Campaign,* and *The Ardennes: Battle of the Bulge.* The 6th Army Group's final push into Bavaria and its role in achieving decisive Allied victory are recounted along with those of Eisenhower's other army groups in *The Last Offensive.*

Reading *Riviera to the Rhine* makes it unmistakably clear, as the authors conclude, that "the operations of Seventh Army and 6th Army Group constituted one of the most successful series of campaigns during World War II."

Jerry D. Morelock, PhD
Colonel, U.S. Army, ret.
Editor in Chief, *Armchair General* Magazine

Jerry D. Morelock, a 1969 West Point graduate, served 36 years in uniform. He is a decorated combat veteran whose military assignments included Chief of Russia Branch on the Pentagon's Joint Chiefs of Staff and head of the history department at the Army's Command and General Staff College. After retiring from the Army, he was executive director of the Winston Churchill Memorial and Library at Westminster College, Fulton, Missouri—the site of Churchill's famous 1946 "Iron Curtain Speech"—and is adjunct professor of history and political science at Westminster College. Since 2004, he has been editor in chief of *Armchair General* magazine, the only military-history magazine selected by the *Chicago Tribune* as one of its "50 Best Magazines" in the world. Among the award-winning historian's numerous publications is his acclaimed book, *Generals of the Ardennes: American Leadership in the Battle of the Bulge.* He is married to the Russian artist Inessa Kazaryan Morelock.

The Authors

Dr. Jeffrey J. Clarke has been a historian at the U.S. Army Center of Military History since 1971 and was named its Chief Historian in July 1990. He has also taught history at Rutgers University and the University of Maryland–College Park and is currently adjunct associate professor of history at the University of Maryland–Baltimore County. Dr. Clarke holds a Ph.D. in history from Duke University, is a lieutenant colonel in the Army Reserve, and served with the 1st Infantry Division and Advisory Team 95 during the Vietnam War. He is the author of *Advice and Support: The Final Years,* a volume in the U.S. Army in Vietnam series, and has contributed many articles, papers, and essays on military history to a wide variety of professional publications and organizations. Dr. Clarke is currently preparing a combat volume on the Vietnam War.

Robert Ross Smith received his B.A. and M.A. from Duke University and later served for two years as a member of General Douglas MacArthur's historical staff during World War II. In 1947 he joined the Army's historical office, then known as the Office of the Chief of Military History, where he published *The Approach to the Philippines* (1953) and *Triumph in the Philippines* (1963) in the U.S. Army in World War II series as well as several other military studies. Later he served as historian for the United States Army, Pacific, during the Vietnam War. At the time of his retirement from the Center of Military History in 1983, Mr. Smith was chief of the General History Branch.

Preface

Riviera to the Rhine examines a significant portion of the Allied drive across northern Europe and focuses on the vital role played in that drive by the U.S. 6th Army Group, commanded by General Jacob L. Devers, and its two major components, the American Seventh Army, under General Alexander M. Patch, and the French First Army, under General Jean de Lattre de Tassigny. Had these forces not existed, Eisenhower's two northern army groups, those commanded by Field Marshal Sir Bernard L. Montgomery and General Omar N. Bradley, would have been stretched much thinner, with their offensive and defensive capabilities greatly reduced. In such a case the German offensive of December 1944 might have met with greater success, easily postponing the final Allied drive into Germany with unforeseen military and political consequences. *Riviera* thus should balance the greater public attention given to the commands of Montgomery and Bradley by concentrating on the accomplishments of those led by Devers, Patch, and de Lattre and, in the process, by highlighting the crucial logistical contributions of the southern French ports to the Allied war effort.

This work also constitutes the final volume in the U.S. Army's series of operational histories treating the activities of its combat forces during the Second World War. It covers the period from August 1944 to early March 1945 and details the Allied landings in southern France, the capture of Toulon and Marseille, the drive north through the Rhone River valley, and, following the junction of the Riviera forces with those moving east from the Normandy beachhead, the lengthy push through the Vosges Mountains and the conquest and defense of Alsace. As such, *Riviera* serves as a bridge between the already published histories of the Allied campaigns in the Mediterranean and those treating the campaigns waged in northeastern France. Within the U.S. Army's World War II historical series, this volume thus initially parallels the early sections of Ernest F. Fisher's *From Cassino to the Alps*, and to the north Gordon A. Harrison's *Cross-Channel Attack* and Martin Blumenson's *Breakout and Pursuit*. Starting in September 1944, those *Riviera* chapters treating the campaign in the Vosges act as a southern component to Charles B. MacDonald's *The Siegfried Line Campaign* and Hugh M. Cole's *The Lorraine Campaign,* all supported by Forrest C. Pogue's

The Supreme Command, and Roland G. Ruppenthal's theater logistical volumes. *Riviera*'s final chapters, detailing the German offensive in northern Alsace and the subsequent Allied elimination of the Colmar Pocket, constitute a southern companion to Cole's *The Ardennes: Battle of the Bulge,* both of which lead into MacDonald's *The Last Offensive.*

Finally *Riviera* is the study of a combined, Franco-American military effort, one which frequently saw major combat units of each nation commanded by generals of the other on the field of battle. Although outwardly similar, each national component had its own unique style, and a deep appreciation of one another's strengths and weaknesses was vital to the success of the combined force. National political considerations also played a significant role in the operations of the combined force as did personal conflicts within both chains of command, all of which had to be resolved primarily by the principal commanders in the field. Although *Riviera* often focuses more closely on the activities of American combat units, the authors have no intention of slighting those of the regular French Army or of the French Forces of the Interior, both of whose operations were vital to the success of the entire force.

The authors are indebted to a long line of officials at the Office of the Chief of Military History and its successor, the Center of Military History, who ensured the continuation of the project amid periods of reduced writing resources and rising historical commitments. Center historians who made significant contributions to the manuscript include Maj. James T. D. Hamilton, Riley Sunderland, Charles F. Romanus, and Martin Blumenson. Deserving substantial recognition is Charles V. P. von Luttichau, whose original research in German records and the resulting series of monographs on the German Nineteenth Army were invaluable. Working under the supervision of the Center's Editor in Chief, John W. Elsberg, and the chief of the Editorial Branch, Catherine A. Heerin, Christine Hardyman served admirably as both the substantive and copy editor, contributing greatly to the accuracy and readability of the account. Barbara H. Gilbert and Diane Sedore Arms then carried the manuscript through all the proofing stages. The excellent maps are the work of Billy C. Mossman, a former office cartographer and author of the Army's recently published *Ebb and Flow,* a volume in the Korean War series. Others who assisted include Gabrielle S. Patrick, who typed much of the final version; Arthur S. Hardyman, the Center's Graphics Branch chief, who muted many (but not all) of the final author's unorthodox ideas on maps and photographs; Linda Cajka, who designed the cover and mounted the photographs; Michael J. Winey and Randy W. Hackenburg of the U.S. Army Military History Institute (MHI) at Carlisle Barracks, Pa., and Ouida Brown of the National Archives who assisted the author in selecting the photographs; Dr. Richard J. Sommers and David A. Keough of MHI; Izlar Meyers of the National Archives; John Jacob of the Marshall Library; Kathy Lloyd of the Naval Historical Center; John Taylor of the National Security Agency historical and records offices; the historians and archivists at the Service Historique de l'Armee; and James B. Knight, Mary L. Sawyer, and Hannah M. Zeidlik of the Center, all of whom provided invaluable research assistance. The authors are also in debt to those colleagues at the Center who read portions of the manuscript, including Dr. Richard O. Perry, Dr. John M. Carland, Dr. David W. Hogan, George L. MacGarrigle, Dr. Joel D. Meyerson, and Lt. Col. Adrian G. Traas.

Outside readers of the entire manuscript included Professor Russell Weigley of Temple University; Martin Blumenson; and General John S. Guthrie, former operations officer (G–3) of the Seventh Army. In addition, portions of the manuscript were read by Col. Thomas Griess, the former chairman of the West Point History Department; French historians Paul Rigoulot and Georges Coudry; Col. Helmut Ritgen, former battle group commander of the Panzer Lehr Division; William K. Wyant, who is currently preparing a biography of General Patch; and Michael Hennessy, who is completing a dissertation on the ANVIL landings. Both Smith and Clarke also wish to acknowledge their debt to the many veterans of the U.S. Seventh Army and the 6th Army Group who freely discussed their experiences with the authors (and their interest in seeing the work completed), and in particular Franklin L. Gurley, the indefatigable veteran and historian of the 100th Infantry Division.

Following the completion of the volume, the final author discussed the bibliographical note and citations with the archivists at the Military Reference Branch and the Military Field Branch of the National Archives (Dr. Elaine C. Everly, Howard Whemann, Wilbert B. Mahoney, Timothy P. Mulligan, and John L. Taylor) to ensure that those interested could easily locate the material used in preparing this study. Since neither Smith nor the earlier contributing authors were able to participate in the final revision and drafting efforts, the final author is also responsible for all interpretations and conclusions as well as for any errors or omissions that may occur.

As one former infantryman remarked to the author at a veterans' meeting several years ago, "We don't expect you historians to tell us what we did—only we know that. What we want is to know why we did it—how we fit into the larger picture." It is this task that *Riviera to the Rhine* attempts to accomplish, providing a tactical, operational, and strategic story that treats the roles and missions of the Riviera-based armies, how they went about accomplishing those missions, and how those accomplishments fit into the larger framework of what another

Center historian, Charles MacDonald, once described as "the mighty endeavor."

Washington, D.C.   JEFFREY J. CLARKE

Contents

PART ONE

Strategy and Operations

PART TWO

The Campaign for Southern France

PART THREE

Ordeal in the Vosges

PART FOUR

The November Offensive

Table

Maps

Illustrations

All photographs are from the Department of Defense files except those appearing on pages 57, 58, and 67, which are the courtesy of the Militaergeschichtliches Forschungsamt.

PART ONE

STRATEGY AND OPERATIONS

CHAPTER I

The Debate Over Southern France

Although ultimately proving to be one of the most important Allied operations of World War II, the invasion of southern France has also remained one of the most controversial.[1] From start to finish and even long afterwards, Allied leaders hotly debated its merits and its results. Most judged the enterprise solely on the basis of its effect on the two major Allied campaigns in western Europe, the invasion of northern France and the invasion of Italy. Supporters, mainly American, pointed out its vital assistance to the former, and detractors, mostly British, emphasized its pernicious influence on the latter. Even many years after these events, surprisingly few have ever examined the campaign in southern France itself or added anything to the original arguments that surrounded the project from its initial inception to its execution some fourteen months later. Yet the debate over the invasion of southern France was central to the evolving Allied military strategy during that time and became almost a permanent fixture at Allied planning conferences in 1943 and 1944.

The Protagonists

President Franklin D. Roosevelt and Prime Minister Winston S. Churchill together headed the Anglo-American coalition and made or approved all political and strategic decisions. They were assisted by their principal military advisers, the American Joint Chiefs of Staff (JCS) and the British Chiefs of Staff (BCS).[2] Each

[1] This chapter is based on the following works in the United States Army in World War II series of the U.S. Army's Office of the Chief of Military History (now the Center of Military History, or CMH): Robert W. Coakley and Richard M. Leighton, *Global Logistics and Strategy, 1943–1945* (Washington, 1968); Maurice Matloff, *Strategic Planning for Coalition Warfare, 1943–1944* (Washington, 1959); Forrest C. Pogue, *The Supreme Command* (Washington, 1954); Gordon A. Harrison, *Cross-Channel Attack* (Washington, 1951); Howard McGaw Smyth and Albert N. Garland, *Sicily and the Surrender of Italy* (Washington, 1965); and Martin Blumenson, *Salerno to Cassino* (Washington, 1969). The principal British source was John Ehrman, "Grand Strategy," vol. V, *August 1943–September 1944* (London: HMSO, 1956), a volume in the series History of the Second World War, United Kingdom Military Series. Unpublished sources were the following manuscripts (MS): CMH MS, James D. T. Hamilton, "Southern France" (hereafter cited as Hamilton, "Southern France"); MTO MS, Leo J. Meyer, "The Strategic and Logistical History of MTO" (copy in CMH, and hereafter cited as Meyer, "MTO History"); and CMH draft research papers by Walter G. Hermes and Darrie H. Richards, both in CMH, for the Matloff volume cited above.

[2] The JCS members were Admiral William D. Leahy, Chief of Staff to President Roosevelt; General George C. Marshall, Chief of Staff, U.S. Army; Admiral Ernest J. King, Chief of Naval Operations

national group met separately and formulated plans and programs, but then came together in a single committee called the Combined Chiefs of Staff (CCS) to discuss matters further and arrive at joint decisions. The CCS spoke for the president and the prime minister, allocated resources among the theaters of operation, and directed Allied theater commanders. From time to time, when the two Allied political leaders came together to resolve key issues, the CCS accompanied them and sought to reconcile the often divergent views and interests of the United States and Great Britain. Occasionally, Roosevelt and Churchill conferred with other Allied leaders, such as Joseph Stalin, and on those occasions the military chiefs were also consulted.

At first the British tended to dominate the Anglo-American strategic deliberations. They had been in the conflict from the beginning, had amassed more experience, and had more military forces engaged than the poorly prepared Americans, who entered the struggle more than two years later. As the Americans committed increasing manpower and materiel to the war, they gradually became the more important partner and had correspondingly greater influence on the courses of action adopted by the alliance.

In 1942 Churchill had proposed the North African invasion, and Roosevelt, over the objections of the JCS, had acquiesced. At the Casablanca Conference in January 1943, the British had recommended and the Americans had reluctantly accepted the seizure of Sicily upon the conclusion of the Tunisian campaign. What differentiated the outlooks of the two parties was where and when to make the Allied main effort in Europe.

The Americans wished to launch an immediate cross-Channel attack from England to the Continent, followed by a massive and direct thrust into the heart of Germany. General George C. Marshall, Chief of Staff of the U.S. Army, a member of the JCS, and the dominant figure among American planners for the war in Europe, was the primary spokesman for this operational strategy, and Marshall tended to judge other ventures by evaluating their possible effect on what he thought should be the main Allied effort. In contrast, the British preferred a peripheral, or "blue water," strategy, undertaking lesser operations around the rim of Europe to wear down Germany and Italy before launching the climactic cross-Channel strike. What the British wanted in particular was to continue the offensive momentum in the Mediterranean area as opportunities unfolded.

British preference for operations in the Mediterranean, especially along the eastern shores of the sea, was motivated in part by postwar political considerations that were not shared by their American Allies. As such they were rigorously opposed by Marshall and his cohorts. But the United States, in turn, had similar political commitments in Southeast Asia and

---

and Commander in Chief, U.S. Fleet; and General Henry H. Arnold, Chief of Staff of the Army Air Forces. The BCS leaders were Field Marshal Sir Alan Brooke, Chief of the Imperial General Staff (Army); Air Chief Marshal Sir Charles Portal, Chief of the Air Staff; and Admiral of the Fleet Sir Dudley Pound (replaced in October 1943 by Admiral of the Fleet Sir Andrew B. Cunningham).

China that had little to do with British interests overseas. Differences in military strategy and postwar political concerns thus colored all discussions of future Allied operations and in the end forced the CCS to adopt a series of compromises not entirely satisfactory to either side. Such, inevitably, is the nature of coalition warfare, and the southern France invasion represented one of the major compromises of the Anglo-American partnership during World War II.

Trident, May 1943

The proposal for an invasion of southern France formally arose in May 1943 at the TRIDENT Conference, a series of meetings between the American and British staffs held in Washington, D.C. At the time, the Allies had cleared North Africa and were preparing to invade Sicily, but had not yet decided on subsequent operational objectives. In their preliminary gatherings, the JCS had their eyes firmly fixed on an assault across the English Channel, eventually codenamed OVERLORD; following a successful Sicilian campaign, they wanted to begin transferring all Allied military resources out of the Mediterranean theater to support an OVERLORD invasion sometime in the spring of 1944. But this, they realized, was hardly feasible. The campaign in Sicily promised to be over by the end of summer, and the prospect of suspending all ground operations against the Axis until the following year, a gap of possibly eight or more months, was unacceptable. Some interim operations beyond Sicily were required, and the considerable Allied establishment in the Mediterranean argued for further activity in the area, especially if it could divert German resources from northern France without greatly impeding the Allied buildup in Great Britain.

The JCS considered a number of potential target areas, including southern France, southern Italy, Sardinia and Corsica, the Genoa area of northwestern Italy, Crete and the Dodecanese Islands in the eastern Mediterranean, the Balkans, and the Iberian Peninsula (*Map 1*). The majority of American planners regarded an early invasion of southern France as extremely risky: an exploitation northward would require more strength than the Allies were likely to leave in the Mediterranean, and the operation would demand the prior occupation of Sardinia and Corsica, causing another diversion of Allied resources. As for the Iberian Peninsula, earlier fears that the Germans might move against Gibraltar had disappeared, and no one saw Spain as a potential invasion route to anywhere. In the eastern Mediterranean, air support requirements for operations appeared to depend on Turkish entry into the war on the Allied side, an unlikely event. Many also believed that operations in either the eastern Mediterranean or the Balkans would lead to a major Allied commitment in southeastern Europe, where logistical and geographical problems could preclude the application of decisive strength. Although the Italian peninsula appeared to be an immediately feasible objective, the JCS feared that the invasion would evolve into a major campaign that would divert resources from OVERLORD. Instead,

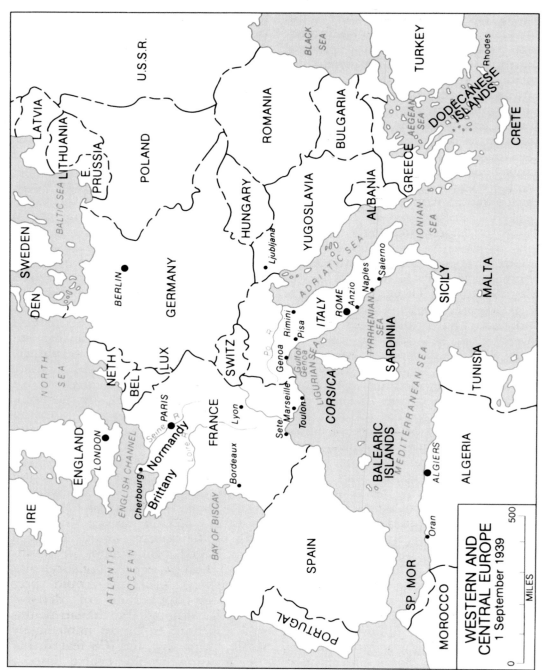

WESTERN AND
CENTRAL EUROPE
1 September 1939

MAP 1

This map is printed in full color at the back of the book, following the Index.

American planners concluded that the seizure of Sardinia, and probably Corsica as well, would prove the most desirable action in the Mediterranean. The operations would keep some pressure on the Axis, while from bases on Sardinia and Corsica the Allies could pose strong threats against both Italy and southern France, thereby pinning Axis forces in place.

British planners attending TRIDENT were better prepared. They quickly agreed with their American opposites that an early invasion of southern France would be difficult and, furthermore, doubted the value of seizing Sardinia and Corsica. Instead, the BCS proposed that action in the Mediterranean be aimed at eliminating Italy from the war in 1943. The collapse of Italian resistance would not only provide the Allies with a great psychological victory but would also, the BCS argued, compel Germany to redeploy strong forces to Italy to hold the German southern flank, thereby promoting the success of OVERLORD as well as relieving German pressure on the Russian front. As an alternative, the BCS were prepared to propose a move into the Balkans, estimating that Germany would divert strong forces from both the east and west to hold southeastern Europe. In the end, however, they persuaded the Americans that an early invasion of Italy was the best solution.

Thus the idea of an invasion of southern France attracted some attention at TRIDENT, but was dropped from primary consideration. Instead, with some reluctance on the part of the JCS, the CCS approved the concept of knocking Italy out of the war

in 1943. Almost immediately they directed General Dwight D. Eisenhower, commanding Allied forces in the Mediterranean,[3] to draw up plans for invading Italy and tying down the maximum number of German divisions in the Mediterranean area. In late July, with Allied success on Sicily assured and with the sudden collapse of the Mussolini government in Italy, the CCS, at Eisenhower's behest, agreed that an invasion of southern Italy would best achieve the ends set forth at TRIDENT; the Allied high command scheduled the invasion for early September 1943.

Another Look at Southern France

Throughout the summer of 1943 American planners continued to regard the Mediterranean theater with mixed feelings. The Joint War Plans Committee of the JCS emphasized the advantages of fighting the major western European battles in Italy if the Germans so elected, pointing out that once the Allies had cleared the Italian peninsula, the newly renovated French Army could invade southern France with relative ease. The Joint Strategic Survey Committee, thinking along similar lines, suggested that after Italy had been eliminated from the war, the Allies might well launch a major invasion of southern France in conjunction with a much smaller

---

[3] At this time Eisenhower's command consisted of Allied forces in North Africa and in the western and central Mediterranean. He was also commander of the U.S. Army's administrative headquarters, the North African Theater of Operations, U.S. Army (NATOUSA). The region east of Italy was under General Sir Henry Maitland Wilson, the commander of the British Middle East Theater.

OVERLORD effort undertaken with forces left over from the Mediterranean. Navy planners favored a major effort in Italy, believing that a southern approach would allow more amphibious resources to be switched to the Pacific.

Although the JCS easily resisted these internal arguments against the basic OVERLORD concept, they were still unable to decide how best to exploit the decline of Axis power in the Mediterranean with the resources left in the theater after OVERLORD requirements had been met. The situation was further complicated by the lack of sufficient shipping to move the bulk of Mediterranean resources to England for OVERLORD. In many cases it was easier to ship OVERLORD forces from America to England than from the Mediterranean; for example, the Allies would probably never have enough shipping to move the French Army from North Africa to England for participation in OVERLORD.

American planners thus believed that after all OVERLORD requirements had been met they would still have enough strength left in the Mediterranean to maintain strong pressure against German forces in Italy; to seize Sardinia and Corsica; to establish air bases on the Dodecanese Islands; and, in conjunction with OVERLORD, to launch some kind of assault against southern France. Even if the Allies halted all offensive action in the Mediterranean, they would still have to leave twelve to fourteen divisions in the theater to maintain security and to pose threats. Better to have these forces engage in at least limited offensives than to have them waste away from inaction. A small, multi-

division landing in southern France would obviously complement OVERLORD, representing a secondary, southern prong of the Allied attack on German-occupied France. Current OVERLORD plans in July 1943 even called for such a diversionary effort against southern France at the time of the cross-Channel assault. But American planners now began to propose that the southern landings be more than a diversion and be upgraded to a larger effort—one that would provide continued assistance to OVERLORD, would make immediate use of the French Army, and, incidentally, would preempt any British proposals to employ excess Allied strength in the eastern Mediterranean.

For these reasons the JCS decided in August 1943 formally to support an invasion of southern France, code-named ANVIL, which would be launched either before, during, or after OVERLORD as the situation permitted; they ultimately concluded that the operation would have to follow OVERLORD.[4] American planners reasoned that a successful ANVIL would probably depend on OVERLORD to deplete German strength in southern France, while the seizure of the southern ports and a subsequent drive to the north would force the Germans to defend the approaches to their own country from two directions. Still giving overriding priority to OVERLORD, the JCS thus settled on a three-phase plan for the Mediterranean: (1) eliminating Italy from the war and clearing the Italian peninsula as far north as Rome; (2) capturing

---

[4] Shortly before the invasion of southern France, the code name changed to DRAGOON, but to avoid confusion ANVIL is used throughout the text.

Sardinia and Corsica to increase the width and depth of the Allied air penetration into Europe; and (3) creating a situation in the Mediterranean favorable to the launching of ANVIL about the time of OVERLORD. Specifically, the JCS plan for southern France called for the seizure of a beachhead in the Toulon-Marseille area, the development of Toulon and Marseille into major supply ports, and an exploitation northward up the Rhone valley to support OVERLORD. This was the basic ANVIL concept on which all planning for the invasion of southern France turned for nearly another year.

The Quadrant Conference

Soon after the end of the Sicilian campaign in August 1943, Roosevelt, Churchill, and the CCS met in Quebec at the QUADRANT Conference. There the British accepted the JCS program for the Mediterranean in principle. However, the BCS also pointed out that the Allies would have to make OVERLORD a much stronger assault than current plans envisaged and that the forces already allocated to OVERLORD would require more amphibious lift than had been planned. If the United States was unwilling to make the additional lift available from Pacific allocations, it would logically have to come from the Mediterranean, inevitably threatening ANVIL. The BCS also believed that an effective ANVIL would require a three-division assault, but British projections indicated that by late spring of 1944 the Allies would have only a mixed collection of ships and landing craft left in the Mediterranean, capable at best of putting a single reinforced division ashore. Eisenhower agreed with the BCS that anything less than a three-division ANVIL would not be feasible unless Allied forces in Italy had first reached the Franco-Italian border.

The JCS admitted the necessity for increasing the OVERLORD assault echelon, but they convinced the BCS that the Allies should continue planning for at least some kind of ANVIL operation on the basis of the limited means expected to be available in the Mediterranean at the time of OVERLORD. Accordingly, a QUADRANT decision by the Combined Chiefs of Staff directed Eisenhower to prepare an ANVIL plan by November 1943. The directive was somewhat vague and did not differentiate between the British view that ANVIL should be reduced to a threat at the time of OVERLORD and the American desire to make ANVIL a major operation directly connected to OVERLORD. But obviously the pressures against ANVIL were growing. A JCS insistence on a three-division ANVIL would create a natural competition between OVERLORD and ANVIL for amphibious resources. Meanwhile, the demands of operations in Italy would generate their own momentum at the expense of both ANVIL and OVERLORD. Finally, the British, at QUADRANT, expressed continuing interest in limited operations in the eastern Mediterranean, operations that would also divert resources from ANVIL.

Eisenhower submitted his reduced ANVIL plan in late October 1943. By then the heady optimism of the summer had faded. The Allies had successfully invaded southern Italy in September, Italian resistance had col-

MEMBERS OF U.S. AND BRITISH STAFFS CONFERRING, *Quebec, 23 August 1943. Seated around the table from left foreground: Vice Adm. Lord Louis Mountbatten, Sir Dudley Pound, Sir Alan Brooke, Sir Charles Portal, Sir John Dill, Lt. Gen. Sir Hastings L. Ismay, Brigadier Harold Redman, Comdr. R. D. Coleridge, Brig. Gen. John R. Deane, General Arnold, General Marshall, Admiral William D. Leahy, Admiral King, and Capt. F. B. Royal.*

lapsed, and the Germans had evacuated both Sardinia and Corsica. But they had also quickly moved reinforcements into Italy, while the Allied buildup was slow. By late October the Germans had twenty-five divisions in Italy as opposed to eighteen for the Allies, and the Allied commanders faced a stalemate if not a serious reverse. Hopes that Allied forces might reach Rome before the end of 1943 had disappeared.

Eisenhower's ANVIL plan made it clear that the Allies would be able to mount little more than a threat to southern France at the time of OVER-

LORD, then scheduled for about 1 May 1944. There was simply not enough amphibious shipping in the European theater for two major assaults. Eisenhower himself felt that there was little chance for the Allies to be far enough north in Italy by the spring of 1944 to launch an overland invasion of southern France from that quarter; the best he could promise was the seizure of a small beachhead in southern France in the unlikely event that the Germans withdrew the bulk of their forces from the south. He concluded that the Allies might do better at spreading out German defenses by continuing the Italian offensive with all resources available in the Mediterranean. As for the eastern Mediterranean, Eisenhower, with the concurrence of the BCS, judged that no operations could be undertaken in that area until the Allied forces on the Italian mainland were at least as far north as Rome. In the end, Eisenhower recommended that ANVIL remain indefinite, as one of several alternatives the Allies should consider for the future in the Mediterranean.

The British requested that the JCS accept Eisenhower's concept as a basis for future planning, a step the JCS reluctantly took early in November. As a result, plans for an ANVIL operation in conjunction with OVERLORD were dropped from consideration before the next CCS meeting, and ANVIL was absent from the SEXTANT Conference agenda when the CCS convened at Cairo late in November 1943.

The Cairo and Tehran Conferences (November–December 1943)

The meeting of the western Allied leaders with Generalissimo Chiang Kai-shek at Cairo, code-named SEXTANT, on 22–26 November 1943, was followed by a second conference with Joseph Stalin in Tehran, 28 November–1 December, and then a final session at Cairo, 3–7 December.[5] At the initial SEXTANT meetings, the British again pressed for increased Allied efforts in the central and eastern Medi-

terranean. They proposed a schedule that called for an advance in Italy as far as Rome by January 1944; the capture of Rhodes during February; a drive in Italy as far as the line Pisa-Rimini (about halfway from Rome to the Po River in northern Italy); and increased support to Yugoslav guerrillas (including the establishment of minor beachheads on the east coast of the Adriatic). To provide the amphibious lift needed to support all these operations and to increase the amphibious allocations for OVERLORD, the BCS recommended canceling amphibious undertakings in Southeast Asia and postponing OVERLORD until July 1944. Eisenhower appeared to support the British outlook. He acknowledged the value of harassment operations across the Adriatic and suggested that after the Po valley had been reached, the French Army could move westward into southern France and the other Allied forces could advance northeast.

The reaction of the JCS was predictable. The British and Eisenhower presentations threatened the place of OVERLORD as the centerpiece of the war in Europe. Although the May target date was hardly sacrosanct, a delay until July was intolerable, and waiting until the Allies had reached the Po River valley would probably set the invasion back to August. Moreover, commitments to Chiang Kai-shek at Cairo made it virtually impossible for the JCS to cancel Southeast Asia operations. To General Marshall all these proposals posed serious threats to OVERLORD and represented a return to the British peripheral strategy or, worse, one that would have had American troops fighting in

5 For a detailed treatment of the conferences, see Keith Sainsbury, *The Turning Point: Roosevelt, Stalin, Churchill, and Chiang Kai-shek, 1943. The Moscow, Cairo, and Tehran Conferences* (Oxford: Oxford University Press, 1985).

the Balkans and the Italian Alps.

Settling nothing at Cairo, the CCS moved on to Tehran for consultations with Stalin and Russian military leaders. During preliminary conferences in Moscow among American, British, and Russian officials in late October and early November, the Americans had gathered that the Russians favored increased efforts in the Mediterranean and perhaps some operations in the Balkans to divert German strength from the eastern front. U.S. representatives had also received the impression that the Russians were no more than lukewarm toward OVERLORD.[6] However, at Tehran Russian representatives vehemently objected to further Anglo-American operations in the Mediterranean-Balkan area that might detract from OVERLORD, which, the Soviets insisted, had to be launched in May 1944. To the surprise of both the Americans and British, the Soviets also proposed an invasion of southern France in support of OVERLORD. While not insistent about ANVIL, the Russians firmly opposed other major offensives in the Mediterranean and took a stand against any advance in Italy beyond the lines the Allies had already attained. Stalin maintained that any major operation in the Mediterranean other than

ANVIL would prove strategically indecisive and could lead only to the dispersal of OVERLORD resources. He appeared intrigued with the pincers aspect of a combined OVERLORD–ANVIL campaign, but urged that not even ANVIL should be permitted to interfere with OVERLORD.

The CCS promised Stalin that OVERLORD would be launched toward the end of May 1944, a compromise between the American date of 1 May and the British proposal of 1 July. The CCS also assured Stalin that they would execute ANVIL concurrently with OVERLORD on the largest scale possible with the amphibious lift left in the Mediterranean in May, and they agreed to carry the offensive in Italy no farther than the Pisa-Rimini line, about 150 miles north of Rome, but 100 miles short of the Po valley.

Returning to Cairo, the CCS took another look at the amphibious lift available for ANVIL. Even by scraping the bottoms of all potential barrels, they estimated that sufficient lift for a one-division assault with a quick follow-up of two-thirds of a division was all that could be assembled by May 1944. As a remedy, the BCS again proposed canceling projected amphibious operations in Southeast Asia or reducing Pacific allocations. With great reluctance, Admiral Ernest J. King, Chief of Naval Operations and a member of the JCS, agreed to divert enough Pacific lift resources to execute a two-division ANVIL assault.[7] However, King's

---

[6] The principal American figures at the preliminary Moscow talks were Secretary of State Cordell Hull, Ambassador to Russia W. Averell Harriman, and Maj. Gen. John R. Deane, the U.S. military representative in Moscow. The ranking British were Foreign Secretary Anthony Eden and General Sir Hastings Ismay. A mystery still surrounds these preliminary Moscow meetings. The Americans may have misunderstood the Russians; Soviet thinking may have undergone a sweeping change between the Moscow and Tehran conferences; or the Russians may simply have been attempting to ascertain the reactions of the western Allies to various proposals.

[7] King expressed concern that the reallocation might delay the capture of Truk in the central Caroline Islands, then scheduled for July or August 1944. However, the JCS had already begun to question the necessity for seizing Truk and were also looking for other operations to cancel in order to

offer helped little, permitting only a minimum, risky ANVIL assault; making no allowance for unforeseen contingencies in the Mediterranean; and still leaving the amphibious resources for OVERLORD at a level that many planners considered inadequate.

The British were still dissatisfied and requested that even more amphibious shipping be allocated from the Pacific theater. Reminding the JCS that Russia would ultimately enter the war against Japan, the BCS argued that major amphibious operations in Southeast Asia were thus unnecessary, making it possible to transfer more such resources to the European theater. But the JCS at first refused to accept the British rationale, and the matter reached a temporary impasse. However, on 5 December President Roosevelt, changing commitments to China, agreed to cancel some of the planned operations in Southeast Asia, and the CCS thereafter began dividing the excess lift between OVERLORD and ANVIL.

Thus, at the beginning of December 1943, ANVIL was again on the agenda and, instead of a diversionary threat, was to be an integral adjunct to OVERLORD. Indeed, the CCS now went so far as to agree that OVERLORD and ANVIL would be the "supreme" operations in Europe during 1944 and that no other campaigns in Europe should be allowed to prevent the success of those two. Prospects that other operations in the Mediterranean, at least, would not interfere with ANVIL were also brightened by a

British agreement to halt in Italy at the Pisa-Rimini line and by the fact that a British condition for the capture of Rhodes—Turkish entry into the war—could not be met. The only other Mediterranean threat to ANVIL was the possibility that outflanking amphibious maneuvers in Italy, such as the one planned for Anzio in early 1944, might reduce ANVIL allocations. But most American planners foresaw that the real danger to ANVIL, if any, would come from pressures to strengthen the OVERLORD assault.

Anvil Canceled

The turn of the year saw a general reshuffling of command structures and boundaries in the European and Mediterranean theaters. The CCS appointed Eisenhower as supreme Allied commander for OVERLORD, and he left the Mediterranean in December. General Sir Bernard L. Montgomery, who was to be Allied ground commander for OVERLORD, and Lt. Gen. Walter Bedell Smith, who was to be chief of staff at Eisenhower's new command—Supreme Headquarters, Allied Expeditionary Force (SHAEF)—followed. The Mediterranean, previously divided between Eisenhower and the commander of the British Middle East Theater, General Sir Henry Maitland "Jumbo" Wilson, became unified under Wilson.

After reaching London Montgomery and Smith began reviewing the draft OVERLORD plans and pressing for major increases in the size of the OVERLORD assault, a step the preliminary planners had been urging on the CCS for months. Knowing that no other ready source but ANVIL existed

---

speed the war in the Pacific. See Robert Ross Smith, *The Approach to the Philippines*, United States Army in World War II (Washington, 1953), ch. 1.

from which to draw the amphibious lift needed to enlarge OVERLORD, they recommended that the lift be taken from ANVIL and that ANVIL be reduced to a one-division threat. The BCS supported these recommendations, reiterating their position that ANVIL should not be permitted to interfere in any way with OVERLORD.

The renewed pressure against ANVIL put Eisenhower in an ambiguous situation when he reached London in mid-January.[8] One of his last tasks as Allied commander in the Mediterranean had been to prepare a new ANVIL plan in accordance with a CCS post-SEXTANT directive. Eisenhower's plan had again been built around a three-division ANVIL assault followed by exploitation northward. Only the three-division ANVIL, Eisenhower believed, would provide strong support to OVERLORD—support that a mere threat could not provide. He reminded the BCS and his principal subordinates that the CCS had promised ANVIL to the Russians, and repeated his arguments about the most effective use of the French Army. If ANVIL were canceled, many French and even many American divisions might well be locked in the Mediterranean, wasted for lack of shipping to take them to northern France, for lack of port capacity in the OVERLORD area to support them, and for lack of room in Italy to deploy them. Eisenhower made clear his reluctance to reduce ANVIL to a threat and proposed that every other possible means of strengthening OVERLORD be sought.

The JCS generally agreed.

The next step in the debate was a highly technical argument between British and American logistical planners over the capacity, serviceability, and availability of assault shipping and landing craft already allocated to OVERLORD. Employing American figures, the JCS concluded that the Allies could significantly increase the size of the OVERLORD assault force and still provide the lift necessary for at least a two-division ANVIL. The JCS carried this argument almost to the point of insisting on a two-division ANVIL, with OVERLORD being undertaken with the means left over after the ANVIL demands were met. Perhaps happily for their peace of mind, other problems arose before the JCS were forced to push their argument to its logical conclusion—giving a two-division ANVIL priority over OVERLORD.

As had been the case earlier, the war in Italy now began to influence the fate of ANVIL. On 22 January 1944, in an attempt to outflank German defenses and speed the capture of Rome, the U.S. VI Corps surged ashore at Anzio, on Italy's west coast some thirty miles south of Rome. But the Germans reacted vigorously, and the Allied landing forces soon found themselves confined to the beachhead, unable to move toward Rome or even to establish contact with Wilson's main armies to the south. The Italian campaign had again bogged down, and the Anzio venture began to consume resources that planners had already earmarked for ANVIL.

The situation in Italy prompted Churchill to recommend immediate

---

[8] Before going to England, Eisenhower made a trip to the United States, and thus reached London after Montgomery and Smith.

reinforcement of the theater and the abandonment of ANVIL. Italy was where the Allies had the best opportunity to tie down German divisions and thus contribute to the success of OVERLORD. It was unjustifiable, he held, to deny resources to the Italian campaign for the sake of ANVIL. Far better to transfer the bulk of the scarce amphibious lift earmarked for ANVIL to OVERLORD, retaining perhaps enough shipping in the Mediterranean for a one-division threat and ultimately moving the French Army to northern France when more shipping became available. ANVIL, he contended, was too far from Normandy to give direct support to OVERLORD.

The BCS agreed. The Allies were attempting to execute three major campaigns, OVERLORD, ANVIL, and Italy, and had given none of them sufficient resources for success. The British arguments boiled down to two simple propositions: if the campaign in Italy went poorly, then it would be necessary to commit the ANVIL resources there; if the campaign in Italy went well, then ANVIL was unnecessary.

By mid-February 1944 ANVIL had lost most of its prominent supporters among Allied planners in both England and the Mediterranean. Even Eisenhower had begun to waver. He still wanted ANVIL, but thought that the Allies would be unable to disengage sufficient strength from Italy to execute a meaningful landing in the south at the time of OVERLORD. Moreover, he was still anxious to obtain additional resources for OVERLORD. Within the JCS, General Marshall felt that the Allies would probably have to cancel ANVIL as an operation more or

less concurrent with OVERLORD unless Wilson's forces in Italy reached Rome before April 1944. Marshall was willing to forego ANVIL if Eisenhower insisted, but suggested that the JCS could accept a stabilized front in Italy south of Rome if such a step would enhance the chances of executing ANVIL about the time of OVERLORD. He still believed that canceling ANVIL out of hand was unwise and still hoped that improvements in the Allied situation at some future date might make the operation again feasible and perhaps even necessary.

The CCS finally reached another compromise. The JCS agreed to allocate all Mediterranean resources to Italy temporarily for the purpose of seizing Rome by May 1944, and the BCS instructed Wilson, the theater commander, to continue planning for ANVIL to be launched as circumstances in Italy permitted. The CCS deferred a final ANVIL decision until late March, but this delay left the projected assault at the mercy of pressures from both Italy and OVERLORD.

In March Eisenhower, still attempting to increase the size of the OVERLORD assault force, recommended first postponing a decision on ANVIL and then canceling the operation entirely. Concerned over the ability of Wilson to transfer additional amphibious resources from the Mediterranean in time for OVERLORD, he wished to assume no unnecessary risks for the sake of ANVIL. At the time, launching both OVERLORD and ANVIL concurrently seemed impossible. The earliest prospect of gaining Rome was mid-June, which meant the earliest possible date for ANVIL was mid-July. Thus he proposed immediately reducing Mediterranean resources for ANVIL to a one-division lift, transferring the excess amphibious assets to OVERLORD, and reducing ANVIL to a strategic threat that might possibly be executed around the time of OVERLORD if the circumstances permitted. With the British agreeing to Eisenhower's proposals, the JCS, on 24 March, reluctantly concurred.

Late in March, however, the JCS appeared to be trying to reverse the decision and insisted on scheduling at least a two-division ANVIL for 10 July. The American staff may have been concerned at this point about a renewed British interest in the Balkans. Recently, for example, Wilson had proposed using the one-division lift left in the Mediterranean for a variety of operations, including the establishment of a beachhead at the head of the Adriatic. As might be expected, the JCS opposed this project as well as another Wilson suggestion that the offensive in Italy be pushed to the Po River. Wilson had already estimated that he would have difficulties deploying more than eight divisions north of Rome until he had seized major ports in northern Italy; the Americans thus believed that he would not be able to employ usefully all of the Allied forces left in the theater. The JCS also estimated that the Germans could hold a defensive line north of Rome for six months or more, while at the same time retaining the ability to redeploy significant strength from Italy to the OVERLORD area. To the JCS, a reasonably early and strong ANVIL still appeared to provide the best means of supporting OVERLORD and of effectively employing Allied resources in the Mediterranean.

To accomplish this, the JCS promised the British that sufficient amphibious lift would be made available from American resources to execute a two-division ANVIL in July.[9] However, the Americans also specified that the additional lift could be used only for the purpose of executing ANVIL on or about 10 July, and accompanied the offer with a proposal that Wilson halt his offensive in Italy south of Rome so that the ANVIL target date could be met.

Allied strategic discussions over the matter now reached an impasse. Reiterating old arguments against ANVIL and for Italy, the BCS submitted counterproposals assigning priority to Italy and allowing Wilson to use the additional amphibious lift as he saw fit. The JCS remained adamant, dissatisfied that the British were unwilling to accept an offer of additional resources without making any concessions in return. The BCS, in turn, believed that the JCS were attempting to force Wilson to adopt an American "strategy" in a theater for which the British had had primary responsibility since January.

Churchill, taking a hand in the discussions, proposed that the Allies again defer a final decision about the relative priority of Italy and ANVIL. He declared that unless the United

---

[9] In early March 1944 the JCS and the principal American commanders in the Pacific had agreed on an accelerated program of operations in that theater and a concomitant cancellation of previously scheduled assaults against strongly held Japanese positions. These changes led to a reexamination of Pacific requirements and enabled the JCS to release from Pacific allocations amphibious resources that could reach the Mediterranean late in June 1944. See Robert Ross Smith, *The Approach to the Philippines*, ch. 1.

States made good its offer of additional amphibious lift, there could be no choice in the Mediterranean—priority would go to Italy by default.

Marshall, replying for the JCS, pointed out that unless the Allies began immediate preparations for ANVIL, there would also be no options in the Mediterranean. Moreover, the United States could not make any more resources available for a campaign—Italy—in which the Americans had no faith. If ANVIL was to assist OVERLORD, Marshall argued, it would have to take place before the end of July. To meet such a target date, Wilson would have to release ANVIL units from Italy by mid-May. Marshall estimated that Wilson could continue the offensive in Italy without the units needed for ANVIL despite BCS concern over a projected infantry shortage there.

On 8 April Wilson, completing plans for a spring offensive in Italy, informed the CCS that he could no longer wait for an ANVIL decision. The renewed offensive in Italy would require his entire strength, including those divisions earmarked for ANVIL. The earliest he could execute ANVIL was probably late July, and late August appeared more realistic.

Without consulting the JCS, the BCS directed Wilson to carry out his planned deployments.[10] At the same time, they prepared a directive for a general offensive in Italy, employing all resources available in the Mediter-

ranean, and submitted it for JCS concurrence. Almost as a footnote, the proposed directive also instructed Wilson to prepare the most effective threat possible against southern France at the time of OVERLORD.

Unable to obtain any commitment for ANVIL, the JCS approved Wilson's new directive, but as their price they withdrew the offer of additional amphibious lift. Although Wilson was thus left with scarcely enough shipping for a one-division assault, the JCS agreed that he could use it as he saw fit. To all intents and purposes, the latitude of Wilson's directive and the withdrawal of the American offer of amphibious lift meant the end of ANVIL.

For Wilson the ANVIL deferral was a welcome relief. Aside from the question of amphibious lift, the decision ostensibly removed the competition between ANVIL and Italy for cargo shipping, combat aircraft, U.S. and French Army divisions, and logistical resources. The decision also settled months of uncertainty regarding the means Wilson would have for the Italian campaign and enabled him to make final preparations for his spring offensive, scheduled to begin about 10 May, almost a month before OVERLORD.[11]

Anvil Restored

For an operation that had so few consistent supporters, ANVIL proved to have remarkable staying power.

---

[10] Technically, the BCS did not have to consult with the JCS concerning the deployment directive, but, in light of the discussions under way, this unilateral action was unusual, especially since they followed with the request that the JCS concur with the new British directive to Wilson.

[11] For further details concerning the planning and execution of Wilson's spring offensive, see Ernest F. Fisher, Jr., *Cassino to the Alps*, United States Army in World War II (Washington, 1977).

Wilson's new directive was but a few days old when both the JCS and BCS, perhaps motivated by a desire to heal wounds left from the sometimes acrimonious exchanges of early April, took still another look at the possibilities in the Mediterranean.

After reexamining his resources late in April, Wilson informed the CCS that when his main forces had linked up with the Anzio beachhead, he could begin releasing sufficient strength from Italy for a major amphibious operation, but not with the one-division assault lift left to him. Among other alternatives, Wilson proposed an invasion of southern France or, with an ever-ominous sound to the JCS, a landing at the head of the Adriatic.

The BCS, studying Wilson's proposals, hinted at the possibility of a small-scale landing in southern France by the end of June, and Churchill suggested a descent on France's Atlantic coastline along the shores of the Bay of Biscay. Encouraged, the JCS renewed their offer of amphibious lift from Pacific allocations, but made it clear that they still favored a southern France invasion. In response the BCS suggested a number of alternative landing sites, including southern France, the Bay of Biscay, the Gulf of Genoa in northwestern Italy, or the west coast of Italy between Rome and Genoa. With obvious regard for American sensibilities, the BCS omitted any mention of a landing at the head of the Adriatic, although such an operation had recently loomed large in BCS planning discussions. Preparations, they recommended, should start immediately for participation by American and French

units in whatever operation the CCS selected. On 9 May the JCS, although still primarily interested in ANVIL, accepted the British proposals as the basis for further planning. Although the CCS had still been unable to reach a decision on the future course of operations in the Mediterranean, at least they had reopened the door to the possibility of ANVIL sometime in July.

Early in June, after the Allies had seized Rome earlier than expected and had come ashore on the Normandy beaches, the Anglo-American debate on Mediterranean strategy reopened. Five alternative courses of action seemed feasible: (1) an ANVIL landing in the Marseille-Toulon area followed by an exploitation north up the Rhone valley; (2) an ANVIL landing in the Sete area, west of Marseille, and an exploitation northwest to Bordeaux; (3) an assault in the Bay of Biscay area, but only after OVERLORD forces had advanced as far south as the Loire River; (4) an advance in Italy north to the Po, followed by a drive west into France or northeast into Hungary through the Ljubljana Gap; and (5) a landing at the head of the Adriatic with a subsequent exploitation northeast through the Ljubljana Gap. Both American and British planners agreed that the first three alternatives required halting the advance in Italy at the Pisa-Rimini line.

Wilson regarded a drive to the Po and then northeast through the Ljubljana Gap as strategically more decisive. His operational planners estimated that an advance to the Po would force the Germans to deploy ten more divisions to Italy, thereby relieving pressure against Eisenhower in Normandy. Yet reaching the Po would also probably necessitate retaining most of the divisions marked for ANVIL. Churchill and the BCS furthermore approved continuing the offensive in Italy to the Po, but deferred a decision on whether to swing west from there into France or northeast toward Hungary.

The JCS, while still firmly opposing an entry into southeastern Europe, had now become vitally interested in securing another major port to support Eisenhower's OVERLORD forces. Although strongly favoring a landing in southern France, the American chiefs appeared willing to settle for the Sete-Bordeaux or Bay of Biscay alternatives. Whatever amphibious operation the Allies selected, the JCS insisted that it should comprise a three-division assault and should take place on or about 25 July. In addition, they assured the British that the United States would make available most of the amphibious lift required for a three-division landing.

The need to secure more ports to support OVERLORD lent a new note of urgency to the debate over southern France. The JCS had been concerned about the port situation since the inception of OVERLORD planning, believing that the southern French ports would prove vital for funneling more Allied divisions into France, especially the French forces in North Africa. While discussing the problem with Wilson earlier in June, Marshall had pointed out that the Channel ports clearly lacked the capacity to support all the forces that the Allies planned to pour into France. His remarks were underlined shortly thereafter by a great storm in the Channel that severely upset OVERLORD unloading schedules and that, coupled with the tenacious German defense and eventual destruction of Cherbourg, made the need for another major port to support the invading Allied armies even more obvious.

By this time Eisenhower saw the original three-division ANVIL concept as the best and most rapid method of securing a supplementary port. While hoping for an early ANVIL operation, he believed that a landing in southern France would still be of considerable help to OVERLORD if undertaken before the end of August. If this target date proved impossible to meet, Eisenhower continued, then all French divisions along with one or two veteran American divisions from Italy should ultimately be shipped to northern France through the Channel ports.

American planners quickly came to the conclusion that the second half of August was the only practicable time to initiate ANVIL. The Channel storm made it impossible for Eisenhower to release various types of landing craft from OVERLORD supply and reinforcement runs before that time; furthermore, because of meteorological conditions, mid-August was about the latest possible date for an ANVIL assault. Naval planners in the Mediterranean estimated that Allied forces in southern France might have to be supported over the beaches for at least thirty days, that is, until the seizure and rehabilitation of the port of Toulon, if not Marseille as well. But they could not guarantee over-the-beach support after the mistral, the strong, northerly winds along the coast of southern France that would begin about 1 October. Therefore, 1 September was the latest safe date in 1944 for executing ANVIL, and any earlier date would ease potential problems.[12]

Wilson, meanwhile, had concluded that if the seizure of a major port was the primary consideration, then ANVIL was the best choice. The BCS, while reserving judgment about the need for another port, seemed to lean in mid-June toward the idea that ANVIL might prove desirable and necessary. By the third week of June, the JCS had decided that any further delay in reaching a decision could only result in another cancellation of ANVIL. Accordingly, on the 24th the JCS recommended to the BCS that the Allies halt in Italy at the Gothic Line (a German defensive network just north of the Pisa-Rimini trace) and that Wilson launch ANVIL as close to 1 August as possible.

Churchill, who still had his heart set on continuing the Italian campaign with a thrust northeast from the Po valley, now appealed directly to Roosevelt. Admitting that his proposals contained political overtones, he maintained that political objectives must be taken into consideration. Although introducing little that was new into the debate, he forcefully repeated all his old arguments against ANVIL and for Italy, pleading with Roosevelt not to wreck one campaign for the sake of starting another.

Advising the president, the JCS pointed out that Allied forces in Italy

would suffer a net loss of only three divisions if Wilson executed ANVIL and argued that Wilson still had ample strength to drive to the Po. The JCS were convinced that Churchill's real aim was to commit major Allied strength to the Balkans—although the British expressly denied such intentions—and did not even comment on the British contention that the capacity of the Channel ports could be easily expanded without recourse to the seizure of ports on the Atlantic and Mediterranean coasts.

Replying to Churchill, Roosevelt brought up political considerations of his own. He reminded the prime minister that the United States would hold national elections in November and noted rather obliquely that even a minor setback in the OVERLORD campaign would assure the president's defeat. Diverting significant American strength into the Balkans or Hungary was dangerous. Roosevelt also reminded Churchill that the Allies had promised ANVIL to Stalin; as for Churchill's reiterated geographical objections to ANVIL, Roosevelt pointed out that the terrain in the Ljubljana Gap region was even worse than that along the Rhone valley.

On 30 June the BCS backed off. They informed Churchill that, although they considered the Po valley–Hungary plan sounder, they were prepared for the sake of Anglo-American unity to approve ANVIL. Churchill, fearing another impasse in the Mediterranean, gave way, but could not resist the temptation to prophesy that Stalin would be pleased, for the execution of ANVIL would leave southeastern Europe open to Russian domination.

---

[12] For a discussion of the *mistral* factor, see H. Kent Hewitt, "Planning Operation Anvil-Dragoon," *U.S. Naval Institute Proceedings*, LXXX, No. 7 (July 1954), 730–45.

ANVIL was at last back in the Allied operational program. On 2 July the CCS directed Wilson to launch a three-division ANVIL on 15 August, reinforcing the amphibious assault with airborne units and following up with French Army divisions. The missions of the ANVIL forces were to seize the ports of Toulon and Marseille and exploit northward to Lyon to support future Allied operations in Western Europe. Wilson was to build up the ANVIL force to a total of at least ten divisions (most of them French) as soon as the tactical and logistical situations in southern France permitted. The Allies were to throw into Italy all other resources left in the Mediterranean, and Wilson was to push on up the Italian peninsula as best he could.

Churchill's Last Stand

Churchill continued to view the decision with foreboding and some pique, feeling that the Americans had forced ANVIL down his unwilling throat. Even after temporarily dropping the issue, he continued to believe that if the Allies were to employ major strength west of Italy, they should seize a port on the Atlantic coast of France. Until early August the tactical situation in the OVERLORD lodgment area was such that Churchill could make no good case for an Atlantic coast venture. However, after the Normandy breakout he resumed his struggle against the ANVIL decision, arguing that the landing should be switched to Brittany where the American ANVIL divisions could play a more direct role in OVERLORD and where American reinforcements from

across the Atlantic could be more easily introduced to the northern European battlefields.

The JCS quickly scuttled these last-minute proposals, noting that the Allies had little information about the conditions or defenses of the Breton ports; that the Atlantic beaches were beyond effective air support range of Mediterranean bases; that ANVIL would have ample air support; that the Allies had no plans for Atlantic coast operations; and that the Breton ports lay so much farther from Mediterranean staging and supply bases than southern France that insoluble shipping problems would be created for both assault and follow-up echelons. The JCS could see no merit in abandoning a carefully planned and prepared operation for the sake of securing what they considered only a hypothetically better line of supply and reinforcement for OVERLORD.

Stubbornly Churchill turned to Eisenhower, hoping to persuade him to recommend cancellation of ANVIL in favor of the Italian campaign. Judging that Churchill was still primarily interested in pursuing his Hungarian and Balkan projects, Eisenhower evaded his pleas, stating that he could speak only from the basis of military considerations and suggesting that if the prime minister wanted to ground his arguments on political premises then Roosevelt was the person to approach. Even Wilson proved of no real help to Churchill. Although supporting the Atlantic coast switch in principle, the Mediterranean commander-in-chief pointed out that the change would require at least a two-week delay in launching any assault by the forces already loading for

ANVIL. Churchill unhappily gave up his fight, but it was not until 11 August, only four days before the scheduled date for ANVIL, that the BCS issued Wilson a final directive to execute the operation.

To the end, Churchill remained unreconciled to the endeavor, termed it a "major strategic and political error," and predicted it would prove a "costly stalemate" and ultimately a "cul-de-sac," or dead-end.[13] Perhaps the British prime minister had good cause for concern. The American forces leading the assault had been fighting in Italy for over a year and had left the battle area only recently; preparations and training for the amphibious landing, one of the most complex types of military operations, had been hurried and incomplete; and there was barely enough shipping to send troops over the beach and support them. The Germans in southern France clearly outnumbered the initial attackers by a figure of three or four to one; had strongly resisted every other Allied attempt to land on the Continent; and could easily send reinforcements from Italy or other fronts if they wished. In contrast, many of the French units scheduled to follow were untested and short of trained personnel and equipment; no further Allied reinforcements from Italy or Great Britain could be expected; and air support would have to be staged out of Corsica, nearly one hundred miles away. The Americans, Churchill feared, were taking on much more than they could hope to handle. On 15 August, as the ANVIL landings began, he arrived in a British destroyer for a ringside seat at what many believed was one of the gravest Allied strategic mistakes of the war.

---

[13] Ehrman, "Grand Strategy," vol. V, 575–76.

CHAPTER II

Command and Organization

Many American leaders in the Mediterranean theater did not share Churchill's doubts over the value of ANVIL and its chances for success, and more than a few were convinced of its absolute necessity. If any effort had shown itself to be a dead end, it was clearly the Italian campaign where the difficult terrain had favored the defense and allowed a comparatively small number of German divisions to throttle the Allied advance northward for over a year. The temporary stalemate at Normandy in June and July 1944 only made the need for ANVIL more pressing. Yet, considering the demands of the other Allied theaters—including those in the Pacific—for ships and aircraft, for tanks and artillery, and above all for trained manpower, the men who would put together and lead the ANVIL assault and the ensuing thrust north toward the German heartland would have to be both daring and innovative. With the limited resources available for ANVIL, there would be little room for error or second thoughts during this most ambitious enterprise.

The High-Level Command Structure

Ultimate responsibility for planning and launching ANVIL rested with General Wilson as Supreme Allied Commander, Mediterranean Theater, whose combined headquarters was known as Allied Force Headquarters (AFHQ).[1] The land areas under Wilson's jurisdiction included northwest Africa, Italy, the Balkans, Turkey, most of the islands in the Mediterranean (except Cyprus and Malta), and

[1] Material on high-level organization for ANVIL is based mainly on the following: Hist of AFHQ, Part Three, Dec 43–Jul 44, Sec. 1, Record Group 331, Washington National Records Center (WNRC); U.S. Eighth Fleet and Western Naval Task Force, "Rpt on Invasion of Southern France" (hereafter cited as WNTF Rpt Southern France), pp. 1–8, and ibid., Annex A, WNTF Op Plan 4–44, 24 Jul 44, corrected to 14 Aug 44, both in the Operational Archives, Naval Historical Center; and Albert F. Simpson, "Invasion of Southern France," ch. 12 of Wesley F. Craven and James L. Cate, gen. eds., *Europe: Argument to V–E Day, January 1944 to May 1945* (Chicago: University of Chicago Press, 1951), vol. III of the series The Army Air Forces in World War II (hereafter cited as AAF III). Note: The official records of AFHQ and SHAEF cited in the text are in the custody of the National Archives and Records Administration (NARA) and are located in Record Group (RG) 331, and those of U.S. Army units and commands in RG 338 and 407, all under the control of NARA and stored at either the National Archives in Washington, D.C., or at the Washington National Records Center in Suitland, Maryland. U.S. Navy records cited can be found in the Operational Archives, Naval Historical Center, Department of the U.S. Navy, at the Washington, D.C., Navy Yard. To avoid needless duplication, references to RG 331, 338, and 407 and to the Navy Operational Archives have been omitted in most citations.

southern France.[2] Wilson's deputy commander was Lt. Gen. Jacob L. Devers, an American officer who was also the Commanding General, North African Theater of Operations, U.S. Army (NATOUSA), the U.S. Army's senior administrative command in the Mediterranean.[3] Devers' NATOUSA organization functioned simultaneously as a U.S. Army headquarters and as the American component of AFHQ. In his capacity as commanding general of NATOUSA, Devers supervised the Services of Supply (SOS NATOUSA), commanded by Maj. Gen. Thomas B. Larkin, which was responsible for the logistical support of U.S. Army forces in the Mediterranean. General Sir Harold R. L. G. Alexander's [4] Headquarters, Allied Armies

Italy, supported British forces in Italy, while Headquarters, North Africa District, handled British logistical functions in rear areas. Both logistical systems furnished support for other national forces—French, Polish, Greek, Yugoslavian, and Italian—with French requirements being met mainly through the Services of Supply, NATOUSA.

General Alexander also exercised operational control over all Allied ground forces in Italy, but allocated them to either Lt. Gen. Mark W. Clark's U.S. Fifth Army or Lt. Gen. Sir Oliver W. H. Lease's British Eighth Army for actual employment. Allied forces outside Italy fell under a variety of smaller national commands. The U.S. Seventh Army headquarters, which was temporarily in reserve, was tentatively scheduled to command all ground forces participating in the ANVIL assault.

The Allied naval commander in the Mediterranean was Admiral Sir John H. D. Cunningham, who bore the somewhat confusing title of Commander-in-Chief, Mediterranean.[5] For the execution of the naval and amphibious phases of ANVIL, Admiral Cunningham created the Western Naval Task Force and placed this command under Vice Adm. Henry K. Hewitt (USN), who was also the commander of the U.S. Eighth Fleet. Hewitt integrated British, French, Greek, and Polish vessels into the various subdivisions of the Western Naval Task Force, along with the

[2] General Sir Bernard C. T. Paget, who succeeded Wilson in command of a reduced British Middle East Theater, was under Wilson's control for certain operational matters. Paget's area included Egypt, Syria, Lebanon, and Palestine.

[3] The boundaries of NATOUSA and the Allied Mediterranean Theater were not contiguous, for NATOUSA also included all French Africa, Spain, Portugal, Austria, and Switzerland. On 1 November 1944, NATOUSA became MTOUSA, Mediterranean Theater of Operations, U.S. Army, and no longer had any responsibilities in southern France. MTOUSA boundaries were considerably diminished (on the north) from those of NATOUSA, and U.S. Army forces in southern France passed to the administrative control of Headquarters, European Theater of Operations, U.S. Army (ETOUSA).

[4] Alexander had commanded the British 18th Army Group in North Africa from 18 February to 15 May 1943. On Sicily and in Italy his headquarters was known as 15th Army Group from 10 July 1943 to 15 May 1944; as Allied Forces in Italy from 11 to 18 January 1944; as Allied Central Mediterranean Force from 18 January to 9 March 1944; and as Allied Armies in Italy (AAI) from 9 March to 12 December 1944. On 12 December 1944 Alexander stepped up to Wilson's position, and General Mark W. Clark (USA), previously the commander of the U.S. Fifth Army in Italy, took over command of Allied ground forces in Italy as Commanding General, 15th Army Group.

[5] Wilson was actually the Allied commander in chief in the Mediterranean, but bore the title Supreme Allied Commander. Cunningham was no relation to Admiral of the Fleet Sir Andrew B. Cunningham of the BCS.

Lt. Gen. Jacob L. Devers

ships and landing craft of his own Eighth Fleet.

Wilson's air commander was Lt. Gen. Ira C. Eaker. Eaker served both as Commander in Chief, Mediterranean Allied Air Forces (MAAF), and as Commanding General, U.S. Army Air Forces, NATOUSA, and as such was administratively responsible to General Devers at NATOUSA headquarters. Eaker's principal assistant for operations was Air Marshal Sir John C. Slessor, who was also the administrative commander of all British air formations in the theater.

Eaker's MAAF consisted of three major commands: the Mediterranean Allied Tactical Air Force (MATAF), under Maj. Gen. John K. Cannon, who was also Commanding General,

U.S. Twelfth Air Force; the Mediterranean Allied Coastal Air Force, under Air Vice Marshal Sir Hugh P. Lloyd; and the Mediterranean Allied Strategic Air Force, under Maj. Gen. Nathan F. Twining, also Commanding General, U.S. Fifteenth Air Force. Each command combined both British and American units; Cannon's MATAF, for example, consisted of the Twelfth Air Force (less elements assigned to Coastal Air Force) and the British Desert Air Force. Eaker's control over the Strategic Air Force was limited by the fact that Twining's primary operational direction came from the U.S. Strategic Air Force, based in England and commanded by Lt. Gen. Carl Spaatz.

While Eaker's MAAF headquarters had general control and coordination of air support for ANVIL, he delegated responsibility for direct air support of ANVIL to Cannon's MATAF. Cannon, in turn, appointed as tactical air task force commander Brig. Gen. Gordon P. Saville, the commander of the XII Tactical Air Command, Twelfth Air Force. British and French air units reinforced the XII Tactical Air Command during ANVIL, while the British Desert Air Force temporarily assumed most of the burden of air support for ground operations in Italy.

Although AFHQ was responsible for planning, mounting, and executing ANVIL, Allied planners knew that the ANVIL forces would ultimately pass to Eisenhower's control, thereby unifying the command of all forces in northwestern Europe. No specific date was set for the passage of command, but Wilson intended to make the change when ANVIL troops had established physical contact with

LT. GEN. IRA C. EAKER, *Maj. Gen.*
John K. Cannon, General Devers, and
Maj. Gen. Thomas B. Larkin.

OVERLORD forces or when Eisenhower
might otherwise be able to exercise
effective control over the units
coming north from southern France.

*The 6th Army Group and the First French
Army*

Allied planners envisaged that
about the time the ANVIL forces
passed to SHAEF control, an army
group headquarters would be created
in southern France to coordinate the
activities of two army headquarters,
one American and one French, which
would be operational at the time of
the transfer. At least indirectly, the
French played a significant role in es-

tablishing an army group headquarters.[6]

Under the leadership of General
Charles de Gaulle, President of the
French Committee of National Liberation and Chief of French Armed
Forces, the French military leaders
pressed for a high command position
during ANVIL.[7] De Gaulle wanted to
regain for France the prestige lost
during the 1940 debacle and also desired to enhance the importance of
the Committee of National Liberation. This last aim complicated command discussions, for de Gaulle, seeking recognition for the committee as
France's lawful government, sought
to have agreements concerning the
command and employment of French
forces consummated between the
committee and the British and U.S.
governments. But President Roosevelt
refused to extend such recognition
and persuaded the British to follow
his lead, making agreements with the
French only on the military level, that
is, between de Gaulle and AFHQ.
With little leverage at the time, de
Gaulle was forced to accept American
conditions, but the basic political controversy involving the legitimacy of de
Gaulle's French government-in-exile
remained alive throughout the war.

When AFHQ brought the French
into the ANVIL planning process, the
French learned that virtually the
entire Army of Free France would be
employed in southern France—seven
or eight divisions plus separate regi-

---

[6] The story of the French role in the formation of
the 6th Army Group is based largely on Hamilton,
"Southern France," ch. 6.

[7] De Gaulle's official rank was *General de Brigade*
(Brigadier General), which he retained throughout
the war.

ments and battalions, support and service units, and so forth.[8] Because of the size of their commitment, the French thus proposed that a senior French general serve as the ground commander under a higher American or British headquarters that also had appropriate air and naval components. To further justify the request, they pointed out that the initial American contribution to ANVIL would be limited to less than four division equivalents and cited the excellent combat record of their forces in Italy—the French Expeditionary Corps—which had operated as part of the U.S. Fifth Army. Finally, they pointed out that many of their troops had intimate knowledge of the terrain of southern France and that French guerrilla forces in the ANVIL area might rally more enthusiastically to French leadership than to American.

American military leaders, as might be expected, rejected the French proposals, and compromise came gradually. When Wilson pointed out that the French, with almost no experience in amphibious warfare, could play little part in the initial assault, de Gaulle agreed that the landings should be under American command. However, after the amphibious assault phase had ended, the French leader recommended that an army group headquarters be established to control the operations of two separate armies, one French and the other American, both advancing northward side by side. Wilson felt that this was

reasonable, but at first feared that the French would demand control of the army group headquarters. However, further talks revealed that de Gaulle and his generals were willing to settle for an independent army command, even under an American army group commander. Although favorable to such a command arrangement, Wilson felt that a second army headquarters should not be inserted so early. Instead he supported an interim phase between the end of the assault and the establishment of an army group headquarters, during which an American army headquarters would control three corps—two French and one American.

De Gaulle was not satisfied with what he considered Wilson's equivocal position, and about 20 April he unilaterally appointed General Jean de Lattre de Tassigny as the commander of all French ground forces participating in ANVIL. This step brought another army headquarters into the picture, for de Gaulle had previously made de Lattre the commander of Army B, a headquarters that the French had organized especially for ANVIL. De Gaulle also appointed de Lattre as his personal representative to AFHQ for all matters pertaining to French participation in ANVIL.

Faced with this *fait accompli*, Wilson worked out a compromise. De Lattre, he informed de Gaulle, would temporarily assume command of the first French corps ashore in southern France, but would have to take orders from the commander of the U.S. Seventh Army. When the second French corps reached France, de Lattre would then assume command of

---

[8] In the end, the French 2d Armored Division was shipped to northern France and for a time became part of Lt. Gen. George S. Patton's U.S. Third Army.

Army B, later to be redesignated the First French Army, but would remain under the direction of the American army commander. The U.S. Seventh Army would, in effect, assume a dual role as an army and an army group headquarters.

The aim of this arrangement was to keep top control of civil affairs, troop and supply priorities, and major tactical decisions in American hands, and to ease coordination with Eisenhower's SHAEF forces. The solution limited French authority and placed a French full general under an American lieutenant general. Nevertheless, late in May de Gaulle declared himself satisfied with the command arrangements as long as de Lattre could retain all other prerogatives of an army-level commander.

During the following month British and American planners elaborated further on the projected command arrangements. By this time they had also concluded that an army group headquarters separate from the Seventh Army would ultimately be needed in southern France.[9] A reexamination of command and control

problems expected in southern France indicated that the combined command of the Seventh Army and Army B, the First French Army, would eventually place intolerable burdens on the American army commander and his staff. Another thought, shared by Wilson and Devers, was that Clark's Fifth Army might ultimately drive up the west coast of Italy and swing west to join the Seventh Army in France. It was illogical to think that Patch's army headquarters could coordinate the operations of three separate armies. Finally, the establishment of an army group headquarters in southern France would parallel the command system developed in northern France, where Eisenhower had two army groups under his command. Thus, when ANVIL and OVERLORD forces joined, Eisenhower would receive another army group with generally similar command arrangements.

Early in July, Wilson took a preliminary step toward the formation of an army group headquarters when he decided to set up the Advanced Detachment AFHQ on Corsica during the ANVIL assault phase. Under the command of Wilson's chief deputy, Devers, this detachment was to provide liaison between AFHQ and the Seventh Army headquarters; aid coordination between the Fifth and Seventh Armies; and recommend priorities for air and naval support between Allied forces in Italy and those in southern France.

Devers informed General Marshall of the plans for the Advanced Detachment AFHQ, suggested that the detachment could readily be expanded into an army group headquarters, and

[9] Subsequent information on the organization of HQ 6th Army Group is from Radio Message (Rad), Devers to Marshall, B–13268, 2 Jul 44, CM–IN 2311; Rad, Marshall to Devers, WAR–59986, 3 Jul 44, CM–OUT 59986; Rad, Devers to Marshall, B–13568, 13 Jul 44, CM–IN 10443; Rad, Marshall to Eisenhower, WAR–64371, 13 Jul 44, CM–OUT 64371; Rad, Eisenhower to Marshall, S–55590, 15 Jul 44, CM–IN 12455; Rad, Marshall to Devers, WARX–66124, 16 Jul 44, CM–OUT 66124; and Ltr, Eisenhower to Marshall, no sub, 12 Jul 44. All in OPD file 381, RG 165, WNRC. Rad, Devers to Maj. Gen. Lowell W. Rooks, D/Cofs AFHQ, B–13160, 28 Jun 44, as quoted in Hamilton, "Southern France," ch. 9, p. 32; Hist Sec, 6th Army Group, "A History of the Sixth Army Group," ch. 1; and G–3 6th Army Gp, Final Rpt G–3 Section HQ 6th Army Group World War II (copy in CMH), ch. 1.

requested that he, Devers, be considered for the post of army group commander. Subsequently he added that Wilson also favored the formation of an army group headquarters and would support his appointment to command it.

Realizing that the proposed headquarters would ultimately come under the authority of SHAEF, Marshall sought Eisenhower's views on the matter. As the American chief of staff, Marshall thought highly of Devers, but knew that Eisenhower might have certain misgivings over the selection.[10] Eisenhower and Devers had, in fact, been rivals. Both had graduated from the U.S. Military Academy at West Point, and, although Devers had entered active service several years earlier than Eisenhower, the latter was now his superior in rank by one grade. Although neither had seen combat service in World War I, both had risen to high positions by the time the United States entered the current conflict: Devers as chief of the Armored Force, Fort Knox, Kentucky, and Eisenhower as the Assistant Chief of Staff for operations on Marshall's staff. Subsequently Eisenhower, as Commanding General, European Theater of Operations, U.S. Army, had commanded American and Allied forces during the invasion of North Africa and the ensuing campaigns in Tunisia, Sicily, and Italy, while Devers

had concentrated on the task of organizing, equipping, and training the vast armored force that Marshall wanted to put in the field. In May 1943 Marshall had named Devers commander of the European Theater of Operations, U.S. Army (ETOUSA), and Devers had been one of Marshall's leading candidates to head an OVERLORD army group command at some future date. Eisenhower, however, following his appointment as Supreme Commander, Allied Expeditionary Corps, in December 1944, had successfully pushed Lt. Gen. Omar Bradley for the post and had subsequently persuaded Marshall to move both Devers and Eaker, then the U.S. Eighth Air Force commander, to the Mediterranean Theater. Simultaneously he requested many other officers who had served under him in North Africa and Italy, such as Patton, for combat commands in OVERLORD. Marshall felt that Eisenhower was trying to pack SHAEF with his own supporters, but also found it natural that Eisenhower would prefer commanders he was already familiar with and trusted thoroughly.

For the moment, Marshall's concerns over the nomination of Devers appeared unjustified. On 12 July Eisenhower approved the idea of an army group headquarters for southern France as well as Marshall's appointment of Devers to head the new command. Although admitting at the time that he had entertained serious doubts about Devers' ability in the past, Eisenhower explained that they had been "based completely upon impressions and, to some extent, upon vague references in this theater . . . [which] never had any basis in posi-

---

[10] For a discussion of the command proposals and appointments, see Forrest C. Pogue, *George C. Marshall: Organizer of the Victory, 1943–1945* (New York: Viking, 1973), pp. 370–78, and especially Cbl, Eisenhower to Marshall, 25 Dec 43, in *The Papers of Dwight David Eisenhower: The War Years*, III, ed. Alfred D. Chandler, Jr. (Baltimore: Johns Hopkins, 1970), 1611–15 (hereafter cited as *Eisenhower Papers*).

tive information," and that, based on Devers' record in the Mediterranean, he would accept the decision "cheerfully and willingly." [11] But Eisenhower must also have known that Devers was eager to have a combat command and that his appointment would further ensure that ANVIL took place as scheduled, thus promising relief for the beleaguered forces under Eisenhower's command in Normandy. This matter settled, on 16 July Marshall made the appointment official and directed Devers to proceed with the formation of the army group headquarters.

In the end, Devers wore four hats at the time of the ANVIL assault. He was Deputy Supreme Allied Commander, Mediterranean Theater; Commanding General, NATOUSA; Commander, Advanced Detachment AFHQ, which was activated on Corsica on 29 July; and Commanding General, 6th Army Group, the headquarters of which Devers activated on 1 August. But at first the 6th Army Group headquarters consisted of only the personnel of the Advanced Detachment AFHQ, and, for reasons of security, retained the detachment title.

The new arrangements made little practical difference in the chain of command for ANVIL. Devers' Advanced Detachment headquarters on Corsica functioned primarily as a liaison and coordinating agency, and had no command or operational duties

during the assault phase. Initially, ground command of the ANVIL forces remained the responsibility of the Seventh Army, while the 6th Army Group headquarters went about the task of preparing itself for the day it would become operational in France.

Force 163 and the Seventh Army

From the beginning of ANVIL planning, responsibility for producing a theater-level program to coordinate the planning of subordinate headquarters rested with the AFHQ Joint Planning Staff, which included representatives of AFHQ, Cunningham's naval headquarters, and MAAF. [12] But the Joint Planning Staff became so preoccupied with Italy that, after producing draft ANVIL plans in late 1943, it left the burden of ANVIL planning to the Seventh Army staff, temporarily based on Sicily. In December 1943, at Eisenhower's request, the War Department officially made the Seventh Army headquarters available to AFHQ for planning, preparing, and executing ANVIL.

By December 1943 the Seventh Army, commanded by Lt. Gen. George S. Patton, consisted of a skeleton headquarters and a few service units. Patton was scheduled to leave for England in January 1944, and AFHQ had tentatively decided that General Clark, then commanding the

---

[11] For quotes see Ltr, Eisenhower to Marshall, 12 Jul 44, and Cbl, S55590, Eisenhower to Marshall, 15 Jul 44, both in *Eisenhower Papers*, III, 2000 and 2009–10. The second communication was actually prompted by information supplied by General Spaatz on the projected Devers appointment.

[12] This subsection is based primarily on the following: Hamilton, "Southern France," chs. 1–4, 6, and 9; Historical Section, Headquarters, Seventh Army, *Report on Operations: The Seventh United States Army in France and Germany, 1944–1945*, 3 vols. (Heidelberg: Aloys Graf, 1946) (hereafter cited as *Seventh Army Rpt*), I, 1–49; and Official Diary, Headquarters, Force 163, 10 Jan–15 Aug 44, RG 338, WNRC.

U.S. Fifth Army in Italy, would be the Seventh Army's commander for ANVIL. During ANVIL preparations, Clark would remain in Italy and leave a deputy in charge of ANVIL planning. After the capture of Rome, or during some suitable lull in the Italian campaign, he would leave Fifth Army and devote his full attention to ANVIL.

The presence of Seventh Army headquarters on Sicily probably served as a useful deception, but in view of the fact that the other major headquarters concerned with ANVIL were located in North Africa, Sicily was not the place to undertake ANVIL planning. AFHQ therefore directed Seventh Army to move a small planning staff to Algiers, where details could be worked out with air, naval, and AFHQ planners. But a large part of the Seventh Army staff remained on Sicily to continue deception operations, and AFHQ took precautions to prevent identification of the Algiers planning group with the staff on Sicily. Air and naval planners assigned to help with the activities at Algiers were also separated from their parent headquarters. Force 163, as the Algiers planning group became known, opened on 12 January 1944; and Rear Force 163, a small group of logistical planners, set up on 27 January at Oran, the location of Headquarters, Services of Supply, NATOUSA, and also of the U.S. Eighth Fleet's principal supply activity.

Force 163 soon grew into a joint and combined planning headquarters. Capt. Robert A. J. English (USN), from Admiral Hewitt's staff, was the chief naval planner; Group Capt. R. B. Lees (RAAF) represented MATAF; Brig. Gen. Garrison H. Davidson, for-

merly the Engineer, Seventh Army, was commander of the U.S. Army component; and Brig. Gen. Benjamin F. Caffey, Jr., Clark's planning deputy for ANVIL, presided over the whole assemblage. In March a small French contingent under Col. Jean L. Petit joined Force 163. Petit had virtually no powers of decision, but acted more as a liaison officer between Force 163 and various French headquarters. It was not until early June, when representatives of the First French Army, the French Air Force, and the French Navy joined Force 163, that planning for French participation became thoroughly integrated. Col. Andre Demetz, the G–3 of the First French Army, became the chief French planner, and his group absorbed Colonel Petit's staff.

Through January and February 1944, a confusion in command relationships bedeviled the planning staff. General Caffey found himself in a somewhat anomalous position—he was Clark's representative but was not a member of the Seventh Army staff. Ill health further crippled his influence. Moreover, Patton retained command of the Seventh Army until his departure for England in January. Brig. Gen. Hobart R. Gay, Patton's chief of staff, replaced Patton but left for England himself in February, as did a number of key staff officers Patton had selected to take with him. Command of both Force 163 and the residual Seventh Army staff was then assumed by General Davidson, and a few days later General Caffey was transferred to AFHQ–NATOUSA, leaving Davidson as the senior officer at Force 163.

AFHQ had expected that Clark

LT. GEN. ALEXANDER M. PATCH

Patton; served in Brig. Gen. John J. Pershing's expedition into Mexico; and then commanded an infantry battalion in the 1st Infantry Division during World War I. During the interwar years his career, like that of his contemporaries, alternated between military schools, teaching posts, and other routine peacetime assignments. But early in 1942 General Marshall selected Patch to command a hastily assembled Army task force headed for the South Pacific. Quickly transforming that force into the Americal Division, Patch took it to the island of Guadalcanal in December 1942 and, as commander of the U.S. Army XIV Corps, led a force of one Marine Corps and two Army divisions that finally rooted out the island's stubborn Japanese defenders by the following February. At Marshall's request Patch then returned to the United States to train American troops in desert warfare as head of the newly organized IV Corps. By the time Patch brought his new IV Corps staff to the Mediterranean in early 1944, the desert campaign had long since ended. Marshall, however, had a new post in mind for Patch and, with the approval of Devers, appointed him commander of the Seventh Army (and automatically of Force 163) on 2 March.[13]

would be able to take over Seventh Army and Force 163 sometime in mid-March 1944, but the difficulties in Italy following the landings at Anzio made this impossible. On 15 February, accordingly, Wilson relieved Clark of further responsibility for ANVIL. A new ground force commander was needed, and Maj. Gen. Alexander M. Patch, slated to be promoted in August, had just reached the Mediterranean theater.

By the time of General Patch's arrival, he had already compiled an impressive military career that stretched back to the American frontier wars. Born at Fort Huachuca, Arizona Territory, in 1889, the son of an officer in the 4th Cavalry, he graduated from West Point in 1913, a classmate of

Patch immediately began rebuilding the depleted army staff with officers and men from the IV Corps headquarters, and gradually enlarged the planning groups at Algiers and Oran

[13] For background, see Truman R. Strobridge and Bernard C. Nalty, "From the South Pacific to the Brenner Pass: General Alexander M. Patch," *Military Review*, LXI (June 1981), 41–47, and John Miller, jr., *Guadalcanal: The First Offensive*, United States Army in World War II (Washington, 1949).

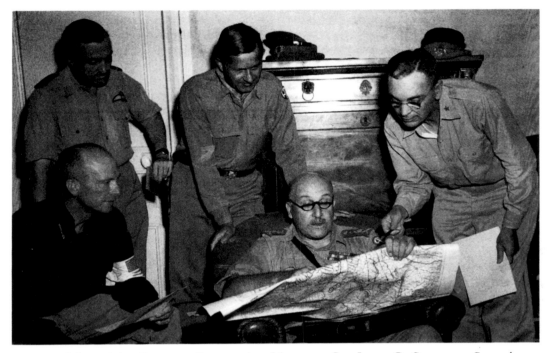

From left to right: GENERAL PATCH, AIR MARSHAL SIR JOHN C. SLESSOR, *General Devers, General Sir Henry Maitland Wilson, with map, and Maj. Gen. Lowell W. Rooks.*

with more personnel from the Seventh Army staff.[14] In May he terminated the Seventh Army establishment on Sicily and in early July moved the Oran and Algiers planners to Naples, where Force 163 dropped its *nom de guerre* and the Seventh Army headquarters made its final ANVIL preparations as a united staff. At approximately the same time, the Western Naval Task Force headquarters also moved to Naples, as did some of the air planners. The MATAF air staff divided in two, one part remaining in Italy and the other moving to Corsica, where the bulk of the XII Tactical Air Command had been concentrated during July. Meanwhile, from March to July 1944, the concerned staffs completed most of the ANVIL planning under Patch's leadership. By the end, Patch had earned the respect of his fellow commanders as a steady if quiet leader and a professional soldier's general, who was more at home with his own staff and troops than with outsiders and less concerned with the prerogatives of command than with getting the job done.

Between March and July 1944 Devers and Patch had thus become the primary movers within the theater

---

[14] The IV Corps remained in existence and fought in Italy with Maj. Gen. Willis D. Crittenberger as its commander. After Patch took over the Seventh Army and Force 163, General Davidson became the Engineer, Task Force 163–Seventh Army.

behind the continued Franco-American planning for the ANVIL assault and the ensuing drive north, even after the CCS had canceled the entire project. While Patch and his army staff devoted themselves to the more detailed planning, Devers, in his capacity as deputy theater commander and commanding general of NA-TOUSA, labored behind the scene to see that the supply buildup for ANVIL did not dissipate between April and June, when ANVIL was in all respects officially dead. As a result, its resurrection in July for implementation in August—barely one month later—was a practicable if hurried affair. Without the strong support of Devers and Patch, it is doubtful that ANVIL could ever have taken place.

CHAPTER III

Planning for Invasion

Despite the constantly changing fortunes of ANVIL in the higher Allied councils, planning for the operation continued at lower echelons almost without interruption throughout 1944. The long strategic debate, of course, created major problems. For example, in January 1944 when ANVIL planning staffs first assembled, they had no idea of the size and composition of the assault force; and the theater headquarters had allocated no troops for the endeavor, established no command organization, assigned no shipping or amphibious lift, and designated no staging or training areas. No decision had even been made concerning the specific assault area, and, without a definite operational directive, no foundation existed on which to make logistical requisitions. Moreover, as the fortunes of ANVIL waxed and waned, planners found it necessary to draw up a variety of invasion scenarios, including a one-division "threat"; a one-, two-, or three-division amphibious assault; and a semiadministrative landing—each under different estimates of German resistance in southern France. In the end, planners had to act on differing assumptions and, until July 1944, had little concrete information on which

to base detailed tactical and operational plans. Despite these difficulties the staffs associated with the ANVIL effort had done their homework well enough by this time to mesh their preliminary plans quickly with the actual requirements and assets available.

The Main Assault Force

Probably the most serious problem that Force 163–Seventh Army faced during the planning for ANVIL was ascertaining the size and composition of the assault force. Of the two, size proved the more challenging, and the inability of the Allied leaders to agree on this matter seriously inhibited detailed tactical and logistical planning and organization. For composition, planners employed the "division slice" concept—an infantry or armored division with its normal supporting combat and service force attachments. But until the number of divisions participating in both the assault and the operations that immediately followed was determined, it was impossible for tactical planners to estimate the number and type of supporting forces needed.

The earliest planning assumptions,

dating from the CCS conferences of late 1943, called for a two-division assault with an ultimate build'up to ten divisions.[1] The plan Eisenhower prepared in December 1943 called for a three-division assault and was also used by Force 163 planners. In February 1944 Wilson instructed Force 163 to assume that the main assault would consist of two divisions, with a third coming ashore in a quick follow-up. This concept governed tactical planning until July, when the CCS reinstated the three-division assault.

In December 1943 General Clark, who was then still in the planning picture, had proposed to AFHQ that the assault force include Headquarters, U.S. VI Corps, the 3d and 45th Infantry Divisions, and the 1st Armored Division, all in Italy at the time. Clark had selected units experienced in amphibious warfare, and he expected that they would be replaced in Italy by divisions scheduled to come from the United States in the spring of 1944. Headquarters, VI Corps, and the two infantry divisions remained constants in all subsequent planning for ANVIL, but Wilson decided that he would have to keep the 1st Armored Division in Italy, leaving the Seventh Army to depend on French armored divisions during the early phases of ANVIL. Force 163, which had been planning for a two-division assault with an early one-division follow-up, substituted the 85th Infantry Division for the 1st Armored Division and assigned the 85th the follow-up role. Training at the time in North Africa, the 85th Division would have combat

experience in Italy before ANVIL.

Toward late February 1944 Wilson announced that ANVIL could be launched in mid-June if the CCS approved and confirmed the selection of assault units. AFHQ began preparations to relieve the U.S. VI Corps headquarters and the U.S. 3d and 45th Infantry Divisions from the lines in Italy between 1 and 15 April, and to replace them with fresh units from the United States. However, in mid-April, the combined pressures from OVERLORD and Italy forced another cancellation of ANVIL, and tactical planning slowed until its reinstatement in June.

By 15 June, Wilson was sure that some major amphibious operation would take place in the Mediterranean and accordingly directed the VI Corps headquarters and the 45th Division to pull out of the lines in Italy at once, followed by the 3d Division on the 17th. With indications growing clearer that there would be a three-division assault, Wilson further ordered that the 36th Infantry Division, which also had amphibious experience, be relieved in Italy by 27 June and replace the 85th Division as the third major element of the assault force.

The three American infantry divisions were organized along standard wartime lines. Each division had three infantry regiments, and each regiment had three infantry battalions of about 800 to 900 men apiece. Also organic to each division were three medium (105-mm.) and one heavy (155-mm.) howitzer battalion (of twelve tubes each) and supporting cavalry (one company-sized troop), engineer, signal, quartermaster, medical, and other service elements. In addition,

---

[1]This subsection is based primarily on Hamilton, "Southern France," chs. 1–4, 6, and 9–11.

the infantry regiments had mortars, one battery of lightweight howitzers, and an antitank battery. These forces were also accompanied by the supporting combat, combat support, and service units that had for the most part long served with the divisions. Normally attached to each division were one tank battalion (of one light and three medium tank companies with fifteen tanks each), one tank destroyer battalion (75-mm. or 3-inch guns, self-propelled or towed pieces, with three twelve-gun companies), one antiaircraft artillery battalion, and one or two corps artillery battalions. The corps headquarters controlled additional supporting elements as well as its own independent mechanized cavalry squadron. Aside from the infantry battalions, all units of the corps and divisions were motorized in some fashion.

Almost all of these forces had served together for many months during the Italian campaign, and thus constituted an experienced team. The 3d Division had entered combat in North Africa in late 1942 and, along with both the VI Corps and the 45th Division, had fought in Sicily, Salerno, and Anzio in 1943, and participated in the drive on Rome during the following year. The 36th, only slightly younger, had begun its journey at Salerno in mid-1943 and arrived in Rome with the others after many grueling battles. In combat, the infantry divisions had formed closely knit regimental combat teams, each with an infantry regiment, a medium artillery battalion, and attached armor, engineer, and signal units. Tailored by the division commanders to serve as semi-independent battle

groups, these units had acquired a degree of battlefield expertise that made them potentially much more effective than the American OVERLORD forces, many of which were entering combat for the first time. Nevertheless, all of the U.S. ANVIL units were tired, fairly worn out by the continuous uphill fighting in Italy, and due for a rest. But little time was available for such pursuits. The 45th Division reached its staging area in Naples on 17 June and was soon followed by the VI Corps headquarters and the other participants. Preparations for their new mission began almost immediately.

For ANVIL, the VI Corps would be commanded by Maj. Gen. Lucian Truscott; the 3d Division, by Maj. Gen. John E. "Iron Mike" O'Daniel; the 45th, by Maj. Gen. William W. Eagles; and the 36th, by Maj. Gen. John E. Dahlquist. Of Truscott and his three division commanders, only Eagles was a graduate of West Point, and only O'Daniel had served in France during World War I. But more important, all were about the same age, forty-eight to fifty years old, and all were long-term career officers. In fact, three of the four had worked closely together for nearly a year and a half: Truscott had commanded the 3d Division from March 1943 to January 1944, when he became the deputy VI Corps commander at Anzio, taking over the corps one month later; O'Daniel had served as Truscott's deputy division commander and had taken over the 3d after Truscott's departure; and Eagles had been Truscott's assistant division commander before assuming command of the 45th Division in November 1943.

Only Dahlquist was not a member of Truscott's original team. Taking command of the 36th Division after its withdrawal from the Italian campaign, he had no combat experience and had the difficult task of turning around the 36th's reputation as a "hard luck" division, one that had suffered heavy casualties at San Pietro in December 1943 as well as during the Rapido River crossing one month later.[2]

Supporting Assault Forces

From the earliest discussions of ANVIL, Allied planners had wanted airborne support for the amphibious assault but had no idea what airborne forces would be available.[3] By May 1944, AFHQ and Force 163 had decided that nothing less than a full airborne division was needed, but Allied airborne strength in the Mediterranean was limited to a British parachute brigade group, an understrength French parachute regiment, an Ameri-

can parachute battalion, and two batteries of American parachute field artillery. Language problems and insufficient training ruled out the French unit, leaving Force 163 with only an unbalanced Anglo-American parachute regimental combat team.

In May and June airborne reinforcements reached Italy from the United States—a parachute regimental combat team, another parachute battalion, and a glider infantry battalion. AFHQ and Seventh Army also put together a full battalion of parachute field artillery; converted a 75-mm. pack howitzer battalion to a glider unit; trained two 4.2-inch mortar companies for glider operations; and transformed the antitank company of the Japanese-American 442d Infantry regiment into a glider unit. Devers' NATOUSA staff also arranged training for various small engineer, signal, and medical detachments participating in the airborne operation. In the end, the total of parachute and glider units approximated a full airborne division, and on 12 July the Seventh Army named the new organization the Seventh Army Airborne Division (Provisional), changing its formal title a week later to the 1st Airborne Task Force. Maj. Gen. Robert T. Frederick, formerly the commander of the renowned 1st Special Service Force (an American-Canadian commando unit), became commander of the new airborne force and began assembling it near Rome in July.[4]

[2] Intervs, Col Robert F. Ensslin with Gen Theodore J. Conroy, 29 Sep 77, pp. 6–7 (hereafter cited as Conroy Interv), Senior Officer Debriefing Program, Theodore J. Conroy Papers, MHI; Col Irving Monclava and Lt Col Marlin Lang with Gen Paul Dewitt Adams, 5–9 May 75, p. 54 (hereafter cited as Adams Interv), Senior Officer Debriefing Program, Paul D. Adams Papers, MHI. Adams, a former regimental and assistant division commander in the 36th Division, confirmed the problem and also noted that the 141st regiment had gone through a series of commanders in Italy and appeared to be the black sheep of the division.

[3] Additional material on the airborne force is from the following: G–3 AFHQ, Rpt on A/B Opns in DRAGOON, pp. 1–9; 2d Ind, HQ 1st ABTF, 22 Oct 44, to Ltr, CG NATOUSA to CG 1st ABTF, 8 Oct 44, sub: Rpt on A/B Opns in DRAGOON, attached to G–3 AFHQ, Rpt in A/B Opns, in DRAGOON; and 1st ABTF FO 1, 5 Aug 44. While the text employs only the code name ANVIL, the second code name, DRAGOON, is used in the footnotes, depending on the source cited.

[4] Major elements of the 1st Airborne Task Force were the British 2d Independent Parachute Brigade; the 517th Parachute Infantry (Regiment); the 1st Battalion, 551st Parachute Infantry; the 509th Parachute Infantry Battalion; and the 550th Airborne In-

MAJ. GEN. ROBERT T. FREDERICK

The next problem was finding the airlift to employ Frederick's force. In early June 1944, AFHQ had under its control only two troop carrier groups and 160 gliders. Eisenhower made available two troop carrier wings and approximately 375 glider pilots from the IX Troop Carrier Command in England; in addition, some 350 gliders arrived in the Mediterranean from the United States in July. The whole assemblage was organized into the Provisional Troop Carrier Air Division under Maj. Gen. Paul L. Williams, the commander of the IX

Troop Carrier Command, which had gained ample experience during OVERLORD.

The list of other assault units included ranger and commando forces assigned special missions. The largest was the 1st Special Service Force, approximately 2,060 men under Col. Edwin A. Walker (USA). This force, which had been in combat under the VI Corps in Italy, reached the Salerno area for final training on 3 July. There were also two French commando units: the African Commando Group of some 850 men under Lt. Col. Georges Regis Bouvet, and the 67-man Naval Assault Group, commanded by Captaine de Fregate (Commander) Seriot.

Force 163–Seventh Army also encountered problems with the major follow-up forces for ANVIL—the combat echelons of the First French Army.[5] The demands of the Italian campaign before the capture of Rome in June made it virtually impossible for AFHQ to set a date for the release of the French Expeditionary Corps from Italy. The debate over the question of command likewise helped postpone assignment of French forces until late May. In addition, a long-standing disagreement over the size and composition of the rebuilding French Army,

fantry Battalion (Glider). All were supported by the 460th and 463d Parachute Field Artillery Battalions; the 602d Field Artillery Battalion (75-mm. pack); the British 64th Light Artillery Battalion; as well as other elements.

[5] Additional information on French units is from Marcel Vigneras, *Rearming the French*, United States Army in World War II (Washington, 1958), chs. 7–10, and Jean de Lattre de Tassigny, *The History of the French First Army*, trans. Malcolm Barnes (London: Allen and Unwin, 1952), chs. 1–3 (hereafter cited as de Lattre, *History*). The original French language version, published as *Histoire de la Premiere Armee Francaise* (Paris: Plon, 1949), has also been consulted, but cited only in reference to de Lattre's key operational orders that are omitted in the English translation.

largely equipped by the United States, proved a delaying factor. Because of their limited manpower resources, the French wanted to form ground combat units exclusively, while the Americans wanted them to establish a balanced force with the appropriate number of supporting service units. Still feeling the impact of the disastrous 1940 campaign, the French generals felt that honor demanded that they put their manpower into fighting units; in addition, they believed that their army did not require what they considered the luxurious service support enjoyed by American forces. More to the point, the French military manpower consisted primarily of colonial levees drawn from north and central Africa—personnel who lacked technical skills and were often functionally illiterate. Thus until the French military were able to tap the manpower resources of the metropole, they found it extremely difficult to form the technical service organizations necessary to sustain their combat forces.

Despite these difficulties, the Allies insisted that the French establish at least a minimal combat support base. Since the entire French rearmament process depended on Allied and especially American largess, the French had little choice. In mid-February 1944, they accordingly agreed to limit their major combat units to eight divisions, including three armored, to which were added separate combat organizations such as light infantry regiments, commandos, tank destroyer battalions, reconnaissance formations, and field artillery battalions.[6] Their remaining

manpower went into service units, but the French high command was never able to organize enough to provide the First French Army with all the support it required.

Of the major French units assigned to ANVIL, the French 1st Infantry Division [7] and the 2d Moroccan, 3d Algerian, and 4th Moroccan Mountain Divisions were in Italy with the French Expeditionary Corps, as were the 1st, 3d, and 4th Moroccan Tabor (Infantry) Regiments. The headquarters of the First French Army (Army B) and the French II Corps, scheduled to be merged for the initial phases of ANVIL, were in North Africa, along with the newly formed French 1st and 5th Armored Divisions. The French I Corps headquarters, the 9th Colonial Infantry Division, the 2d Moroccan Tabor Regiment, and the African Commando Group were on Corsica. Although French unit designations differed somewhat from American nomenclature, French military organizations and their equipment—except in certain colonial formations like the Tabors—were nearly identical to that of their American counterparts in 1944. Specifically, like the American armored divisions employed in northern France, the French *division blindee* had three combat commands (instead of regiments or brigades), each with one tank, one armored infantry (half-tracks), and one armored artillery (105-

---

[6] De Lattre, *History*, p. 28, states that the French Committee of National Liberation agreed to the

eight-division program on 23 January; Vigneras, *Rearming the French*, p. 158, notes that final French agreement did not come until 16 February and, on p. 155, that the CCS did not approve the program until 2 March.

[7] Also known as the 1re Division Francaise Libre (1st Free French Division) and the 1re Division de Marche (1st Provisional Division).

mm. self-propelled) battalion; one mechanized cavalry squadron; and mechanized or motorized supporting elements. The infantry divisions were also organized on a triangular basis and used American tables of organization and equipment as well. Thus, despite differences in language, culture, and history, the two principal national components of ANVIL had an unusual degree of homogeneity.

The French forces outside Italy passed to Seventh Army control on 7 July, but Patch and de Lattre did not gain control of the units in Italy until 23 July, when the Fifth Army released them. Patch passed all of these units over to de Lattre's command with the exception of Brig. Gen. Aime M. Sudre's Combat Command 1 (Combat Command Sudre or CC Sudre) of the French 1st Armored Division. To give the assault force a mobile striking capability, Patch had detached CC Sudre from the First French Army for the assault and placed it under the operational control of the U.S. VI Corps.

French Guerrillas

The Allies expected considerable help from French partisans in southern France, and the plans of AFHQ and Seventh Army took into consideration the potential of the guerrillas for disrupting German communications and harassing German rear areas.[8] The guerrillas—or, as they were better known, the French Forces of the Interior (FFI)—had proved their value as intelligence sources long before ANVIL

took place, and the Allies also anticipated that the FFI could supply reinforcements and replacements for the First French Army.

Until the CCS issued the directive for ANVIL in July, the operations of the FFI in southern France were designed primarily to support OVERLORD. Thus, responsibility for the control and support of the southern FFI was vested in SHAEF, operating through the Special Force Headquarters (SFHQ), an Anglo-American agency in London. The Special Projects Operations Center of G–3 AFHQ only assisted SHAEF's supervision of FFI groups in southern France.

Although the Free French government had a voice in FFI operations, that voice was only as loud as the Americans and British, who controlled guerrilla supplies, allowed it to be. With their approval, de Gaulle had appointed Lt. Gen. Pierre Koenig as commander of the FFI and had made Koenig directly responsible to Eisenhower. As a practical matter, Koenig remained subordinate to SFHQ, even after SHAEF, at French insistence, approved the formation of a tripartite FFI general headquarters. Commanded by Koenig and established in London, this organization included representatives of various British, American, and French agencies.

The Allies were unable to make similar command and control arrangements for the FFI in southern France until the last moment. On 8 July, with ANVIL scarcely a month from the launching, SHAEF and Koenig transferred control of the FFI in southern France to AFHQ and Maj.

[8] This subsection is based primarily on Vigneras, *Rearming the French*, pp. 299–306, and Hamilton, "Southern France," ch. 8.

Gen. Gabriel Cochet, de Gaulle's representative for guerrilla affairs at AFHQ. Nominally responsible only to Wilson, Cochet actually had to operate through the Special Projects Operations Center at G–3 AFHQ.

The British had carefully nurtured the FFI ever since the fall of France, but by mid-1944 American support directed by the Office of Strategic Services (OSS) began to equal or outstrip the British effort. Aircraft of both nations, supplemented by French planes, delivered supplies and arms of all types to the FFI, and took an ever-increasing number of "regular" troops to France to coordinate FFI and Allied operations, to assist the FFI in organizational and supply matters, and to increase the FFI's combat potential. Such support came from OSS Operational Groups, each consisting of four officers and thirty enlisted men, and from the British Special Air Service Brigade, which included two battalions of French paratroopers.[9] The principal mission of the commando units inserted into France was usually sabotage at a particular point, after which the commandos would become part of the FFI.

Other Allied units sent into France included the Jedburgh teams, each consisting of two officers (one of them French) and an enlisted communications expert.[10] Their main missions were to establish liaison among FFI units and various Allied headquarters and to provide leadership for FFI organizations. Finally, for operations in southern France, the Allies trained a limited number of "counter-scorching" groups, which contained men from the French Navy and the OSS. The primary mission of these units was to thwart German efforts to destroy the port facilities along the coast of southern France. The groups also had secondary intelligence missions.

By 15 August 1944, the FFI in southern France could put about 75,000 men in the field, but only about one-third of them were armed. These activists, locally known as the maquis, had the support of probably thousands of part-time agents in the cities, towns, and villages. Although the guerrillas were not strong enough to engage the German Army in positional warfare, they severely limited its freedom of movement by constantly harassing German support organizations and interfering with the displacements of tactical units behind the battlefield. In addition, the sabotage activities of the maquis continually forced the Germans to employ large numbers of troops to protect and repair rail, highway, telephone, and telegraph communications. Perhaps if ANVIL had been approved sooner and responsibility for FFI operations transferred to AFHQ at an earlier date, more could have been done with the resistance forces, which were much stronger and better organized than in the north.

Organization for the Assault

The organization and responsibilities of the air, ground, and naval

---

[9] The 2d and 3d Parachute Chasseur Regiments. The French Army often employed the term *regiment* for units that the U.S. Army would designate as battalions.

[10] For a short but colorful account, see Aaron Bank, *From OSS to Green Beret: The Birth of the Special Forces* (Novato, Calif.: Presidio, 1986), pp. 14–62.

FFI Partisan Group, August 1944

components for ANVIL followed established practice in the Mediterranean
and northwest Europe.[11] The ANVIL
assault organization centered around
a joint combined command designated Western Task Force, which included the Seventh Army, the XII Tactical
Air Command, and the Western Naval
Task Force. However, although this
so-called Western Task Force was ostensibly under the joint command of
the leaders of the ground, air, and
naval components, it was actually a

notational, or fictional, organization
with no separate headquarters. Overall control of the ANVIL assault was, in
fact, vested in Wilson at AFHQ.
During the assault phase, Patch and
Hewitt theoretically would have equal
joint command responsibilities; but
from the time Western Naval Task
Force embarked Seventh Army until
the time Patch established his headquarters ashore, Hewitt was in actual
command of both the ground and
naval echelons, responsible only to
Wilson.

Air support responsibility during
ANVIL presented a rather complicated
picture. Eaker's MAAF had only general control and coordination responsibilities. Mediterranean Allied Strategic Air Force operated the heavy

---

[11] This subsection is based primarily on WNTF
Rpt Southern France; WNTF Opn Plan No. 4–44,
24 Jul 44; Seventh Army Outline Plan ANVIL, 13 Jul
44; and Annex 9, Beach Maintenance Plan, to Seventh Army FO 1, 29 Jul 44. For description of command arrangements during amphibious operations
in the Pacific, see volumes in the Pacific subseries of
the United States Army in World War II.

bombers and their escorts assigned to the support of ANVIL, while Mediterranean Allied Coastal Air Force protected the staging areas and covered the assault convoys to a point forty miles out from the assault beaches. The remainder of the air support responsibility rested with Cannon's MATAF, which undertook detailed air planning, coordinated bomber operations, supervised troop carrier aircraft operations, and provided air cover for the convoys within forty miles of the beaches in southern France. Under MATAF, Saville's XII Tactical Air Command was responsible for close air support and for air cover in the assault area. Saville had operational control over land-based and carrier-based aircraft in the assault area that were directly engaged in the close support of the invasion. The only exceptions were the aviation units of Western Naval Task Force's nine escort-carriers (CVEs), which Hewitt combined into Task Force 88 under Rear Adm. T. H. Troubridge (RN). Troubridge, in turn, formed those CVE-based aircraft not needed for local air defense into a pool available to Saville for whatever missions were within their capabilities.

Beach operations and ship unloadings were the responsibility of beach groups, one assigned to each of the three assault divisions. One Army combat engineer regiment (about 1,900 troops) and one Navy beach battalion (around 445 personnel) formed the nucleus of each beach group. The engineer regimental commander became the beach group commander, while the Navy beach battalion commander served as the beachmaster at each division beach.

Theoretically, the Army beach group commander was responsible for all beach and unloading activities, but the Navy beachmasters were responsible only to Admiral Hewitt for naval matters. Since these matters included routing and control of landing craft (including Army DUKWs [12]), beaching directions, and ship-to-shore communications concerned with unloading operations, the Navy beachmasters had responsibilities that overlapped those of the beach group commanders.

In the end, the beach control system for ANVIL produced few difficulties and little friction. The Navy beach battalions trained for ANVIL with the Army engineer combat regiments with which they were scheduled to operate during the assault. Both Army and Navy echelons of the beach groups were well versed in the responsibilities and capabilities of the other well before the invasion.

To achieve surprise, Admiral Hewitt planned to dispense with a lengthy preinvasion naval bombardment; moreover, since no interference was expected from German surface forces, he believed that a separate naval cover (or support) force was unnecessary. For the actual assault, Hewitt divided his fire support vessels among the attack forces responsible for landing the assault divisions and the commando units. For postassault operations, he intended to form his bombardment and fire support vessels into a single force that would continue to support operations ashore as necessary. This enabled him to allocate all his major

---

[12] "Ducks" are light, wheeled amphibious craft built on 2.5-ton truck chassis.

combat vessels to various bombardment, fire support, and convoy duties.[13]

Two aspects of the command arrangements for ANVIL deserve special notice.[14] First, there were no naval or air echelons in the chain of command that corresponded to the VI Corps headquarters. Second, VI Corps did not control all of the ground forces participating in the assault; for example, the French commandos, the 1st Airborne Task Force, and the 1st Special Service Force were to operate initially under direct control of the Seventh Army.

In late June, General Truscott, the VI Corps commander, reviewed Seventh Army's ANVIL plans and recommended several changes. First, he asked Patch to arrange for naval and air echelons on the same level as VI Corps for both the planning and assault phases of the operation. In addition, Truscott objected to dividing the command of ground elements during the assault. He suggested that since the main assault was a corps task, all units should be under his command as the ground assault force commander, operating on the same level as a corresponding naval commander. If the VI Corps was to be responsible for the success of the entire assault, then its commander ought to have commensurate authority.

Patch did not agree. Because Truscott's corps headquarters had been released from Italy so late, the Seventh Army, the XII Tactical Air Command, and the Western Naval Task Force had already undertaken much of the detailed planning that would normally be accomplished by the corps staff. Creating corps-level air and naval planning staffs at this late date would only result in confusion. Patch also believed that the VI Corps staff could not effectively control the operations of the airborne and commando forces during the assault as well as those of the three assault divisions. Instead, he directed that the airborne and commando units should pass to VI Corps control only when they physically joined Truscott's forces on the mainland or as otherwise commanded by the Seventh Army. Truscott accepted these judgments; the final arrangements thus embodied the Seventh Army commander's concepts, except that once the assault force was embarked, Truscott would report to Admiral Hewitt until Patch opened his Seventh Army post ashore.

The arrangement left one gap in the Army-Navy chain of command, namely, the lack of any corps-level echelon in Hewitt's organization, as noted earlier by Truscott. Hewitt had arranged for his landing force commanders to deal directly with the Army divisions, dividing his amphibious assault units into four task forces, one for each assault division with the fourth to land the commandos. There was no provision for consultations at these levels with the army corps com-

[13] For a more detailed treatment of the naval effort, see Samuel Eliot Morison, *The Invasion of France and Germany, 1944–1945*, vol. XI, History of United States Naval Operations in World War II (Boston: Little, Brown, 1959), pp. 233–92.

[14] Additional sources for the remainder of this subsection are the following: *Seventh Army Rpt*, I, 46–51; VI Corps After Action Rpt (AAR) Jul–Aug 44, Annex I, Notes on Opnl Planning for Opn ANVIL; Hamilton, "Southern France," ch. 9; and Lucian K. Truscott, Jr., *Command Missions, A Personal Story* (New York: E. P. Dutton, 1954), pp. 388–91 (hereafter cited as Truscott, *Command Missions*).

mander. During the actual landings, the commander of each Army division would be responsible to his corresponding attack force (task force) commander. When Truscott established his command post ashore, the division commanders would theoretically pass to his control; but in reality the individual naval task force commanders, acting for Admiral Hewitt, could maintain discretionary control over landing operations at the division beaches without reference to Truscott. Most of the participants were experienced and knew that the transition between naval and ground command during the assault phase of an amphibious landing was always a delicate matter, one that depended more on the close relationships between the principal ground and naval commanders than on detailed but sometimes inflexible command arrangements.

Organization for Logistics

Logistical support responsibility for American ground forces engaged in ANVIL rested with General Larkin's Services of Supply (SOS), NATOUSA, which had worked closely with Rear Force 163 during the planning phase.[15] French ground forces re-

ceived their initial supplies and equipment from the Franco-American Joint Rearmament Committee, an agency under the control of Headquarters, NATOUSA, which procured supplies and equipment from the United States for the rebuilding French Army. As a practical matter, Services of Supply had to make up many French shortages from American stocks in the Mediterranean.

Logistical support of American land-based air units assigned to back up ANVIL was the responsibility of the Army Air Forces Service Command, NATOUSA, a subordinate echelon of Eaker's U.S. Army Air Forces, NATOUSA. Most land-based aircraft directly supporting ANVIL were located on Corsican airfields and supplied by XII Air Service Command stocks provided by the Army Air Forces Service Command. Royal Air Force units attached to the XII Tactical Air Command received most of their supplies through British channels, but drew some items from the XII Air Service Command. French Air Force organizations supporting ANVIL drew initial supplies and equipment from stocks made available by the tripartite Joint Air Commission, which was responsible for reequipping the French Air Force, but the XII Air Service Command also provided some support for French air units on Corsica.

Service Force, U.S. Atlantic Fleet, was the channel through which supplies flowed to U.S. Navy forces in the Mediterranean, although Hewitt's Eighth Fleet maintained its own logis-

---

[15] This section and its subsections are based generally on the following: Coakley and Leighton, *Global Logistics and Strategy, 1943–1945*, chs. 13–15; Continental Advance Section, Communications Zone, European Theater of Operations, U.S. Army, *CONAD History* (Heidelberg: Aloys Graf, 1945), pp. 1–47; HQ, NATOUSA/MTOUSA, *Logistical History of NATOUSA–MTOUSA, 11 August 1943 to 30 November 1945* (Naples: G. Montanino, 1945), chs. 7–8; La Base d'Operations 901, *La Base d'Operations 901 dans la Bataille pour la Liberation de la France, 1944–1945* (Paris: Imprimerie Nationale, 1947), pp. 13–19; Vigneras, *Rearming the French*, ch. 10; AAF III, 330–35,

416–18; *Seventh Army Rpt*, I, 65–70; Hamilton, "Southern France," chs. 3–5 and 12; and Meyer, "MTO History," chs. 24–25.

tical base for storage and issue. Since the bulk of the French Navy had obtained its original supplies and equipment through the Joint Rearmament Commission, the U.S. Navy provided support for most French naval units participating in ANVIL. The Royal Navy supplied its own vessels, some French ships, and almost all of the shipping that belonged to the minor Allied navies (Greek and Polish, for example). All naval echelons could also draw on SOS NATOUSA stocks in an emergency.

Arrangements for supplying and distributing fuels and lubricants in the Mediterranean provided an effective system of combined and joint responsibilities and activities. All POL (petroleum, oil, and lubricants) products available in the theater came into a general pool under the control of Petroleum Section, AFHQ, which allocated stocks on a percentage basis to various national forces and civilian agencies. While each service of each nation administered and operated its own POL depots, the pool system provided that any ship, plane, or truck of any service of any nation could obtain POL supplies at any air, ground, or naval depot of any other nation or service; the amount requisitioned was subtracted from the drawer's allocation.

In obtaining, storing, and issuing supplies for U.S. Army (and to a large extent French Army) forces assigned to ANVIL, SOS operated through subordinate base sections at various ports in the Mediterranean. Of these, the Peninsular Base Section at Naples, the Mediterranean Base Section at Oran, and the Northern Base Section on Corsica bore the major

burden of supplying, equipping, and loading the ground forces for ANVIL.[16] Once the Seventh Army was ashore in southern France, supplies would continue to flow through established channels until a new organization, Coastal Base Section, could take over logistical support of the army, estimated to occur on D plus 30. SOS NATOUSA organized Coastal Base Section at Naples on 7 July and placed it under the command of Maj. Gen. Arthur R. Wilson, previously the commander of Peninsular Base Section. The staff of Coastal Base Section operated closely with Peninsular Base Section and with the Seventh Army G–4 (assistant chief of staff for logistics) during final planning and loading; Wilson made arrangements for a large part of his staff to work in appropriate staff sections of the Seventh Army headquarters in southern France until Coastal Base Section became operational ashore.

Support of French forces in southern France was ostensibly the responsibility of Operations Base 901 which, commanded by Brig. Gen. Jean Gross, French Army, was theoretically a parallel organization to Coastal Base Section. But the French lacked the technicians, equipment, and trained service troops to staff and operate Base 901 effectively; therefore, by default, Coastal Base Section became the agency actually responsible for supplying Army B (the First French Army). Base 901 essentially

---

[16] Much of Northern Base Section's work on Corsica was involved in air force support in conjunction with the XII Air Service Command, but the base section also helped supply and load some French Army units and stored emergency supplies for ANVIL ground forces.

became a French component of Coastal Base Section and served as liaison between the First French Army and the American base. To make this arrangement more effective, General Gross served simultaneously as the commander of Base 901 and as Deputy Commanding General, Coastal Base Section for French affairs; in addition, each of Coastal Base Section's principal staff sections had French deputy chiefs.

Supply and Shipping Problems

Logistical support was critical for ANVIL and the ensuing operations of the Seventh Army. When, in January 1944, Force 163 and SOS NATOUSA began to study ANVIL's logistical problems, the indefinite nature, date, place, and size of the operation made it impossible for planners to take more than preliminary steps toward obtaining supplies and equipment for the operation. Working from Eisenhower's draft ANVIL plan of December, SOS developed a rough basic plan for supporting a force of 450,000 troops for thirty days in southern France. Using this plan as a tentative guideline, SOS began forwarding supply requisitions to the New York port of embarkation (POE) as early as 18 January, and later sent a liaison officer to the POE armed with detailed requisitions and loading plans. With the cooperation of the U.S. Army Service Forces, SOS also made arrangements to have convoys sailing to the Mediterranean during the period February through April— at this time ANVIL was still projected for May—partially loaded with supplies allocated to ANVIL. At the same

time, SOS began earmarking ANVIL supplies in various theater depots, hoping to keep such items inviolate from the demands of the Italian campaign.

Loading began in New York in February, employing a process called "flatting," in which cargo was carefully packed into a ship's hold up to a certain level and then boarded over to provide space in which to stow cargo not meant for ANVIL. The flatted cargo space of these ships was filled with ANVIL materiel, while above this level (and on the weather decks) the vessels carried general supplies for the Mediterranean. SOS planned to unload the general supplies in the theater and to reload the empty space with supplies, equipment, and vehicles needed for ANVIL.

In April, after sixty-four cargo ships carrying flatted ANVIL supplies had left the United States for the Mediterranean, the CCS canceled ANVIL. U.S. agencies thereafter refused to honor further requisitions from SOS for ANVIL and likewise refused to fulfill the incomplete portions of requisitions already submitted. Army Service Forces halted further shipments of supplies to the Mediterranean over and above those required for theater maintenance and the Italian campaign.

This turn of events still left large quantities of supplies and equipment earmarked for ANVIL in the Mediterranean. The sixty-four cargo ships that had reached the theater with flatted ANVIL supplies continued to sail the Mediterranean with about half their cargo capacity still taken up by ANVIL materiel. Moreover, since January, SOS had been building up local depot stocks of materiel also allocated to ANVIL. Generals Devers and Larkin, hoping that ANVIL would be revived, now acted to freeze all materiel, both afloat and ashore, that SOS had assembled for the operation. Although General Devers was generally successful in resisting War Department pressure to have these ANVIL supplies reallocated to Italy, he also found that emergency requisitions from the Fifth Army began to eat into ANVIL supplies at an alarming rate. Nevertheless, when prospects for ANVIL brightened in June, SOS estimated that it had on hand in the Mediterranean, either afloat or ashore, about 75 percent of the supplies required for a two-division ANVIL assault, and could also see its way clear to sustain ANVIL forces ashore for some thirty days after the first landings. The most serious shortages were in certain types of engineer, transportation corps, and signal equipment.

In response to a War Department request, SOS submitted in June new requisitions to the Army Service Forces for supplies and equipment needed to make up the most critical shortages for a three-division ANVIL assault. SOS also forwarded requisitions for maintenance materiel that would be shipped directly to southern France after the assault. Since the CCS had not yet reached a firm decision on ANVIL, the War Department could make no final arrangements for loading and shipping the supplies that SOS requisitioned, but did direct Army Service Forces to start moving the materiel to embarkation ports on the east coast.

The ANVIL supply picture thus looked promising in mid-June, and prospects brightened further when, on the 13th, Devers directed SOS to switch the priority of supply operations from the Fifth Army in Italy to preparations for ANVIL. The action was not entirely effective until 2 July, when the CCS issued their ANVIL directive, which also permitted convoys loaded with ANVIL supplies to start sailing from the United States. The first ANVIL supply convoy since April left New York on 1 July—one day before the CCS directive—and the first of the new convoys reached the Mediterranean on the 15th. By this date SOS was able to report that virtually all the materiel needed for the assault and for the support of American and French forces in southern France through D plus 90 was on hand, on the way, or promised. There is no doubt that this goal was attained on such short notice largely because of Devers' generally successful efforts to freeze ANVIL supplies after the CCS had canceled the operation in April.

At least indirectly, Devers' freeze also helped solve ANVIL's shipping problems which, as the result of the on-again, off-again nature of the operation, threatened to be extremely troublesome. In general, ANVIL plans estimated that, in addition to naval assault shipping, 100 merchant-type cargo vessels were needed to carry ANVIL assault supplies and enough additional merchant shipping to provide at least 200 individual sailings through D plus 90. These requirements were over and above the shipping needed for general Mediterranean maintenance and for the support of the Italian campaign.

The first American contribution toward meeting the ANVIL requirements was the sixty-four merchant ships with flatted cargo that had reached the theater between February and April. The United States also supplied sixty more large merchant ships that arrived in fast convoys during June and July, and seventy-five generally smaller vessels from slower convoys. From June through August, the Americans also allocated additional merchant ships to the theater for general maintenance, while AFHQ scraped up the rest of the required merchant shipping from commands within the theater or borrowed it from British resources.

The shortage of amphibious assault ships in the Mediterranean for ANVIL was more serious. In June Admiral Hewitt lacked 65 landing ships, tank (LSTs); 160 landing ships, infantry (LSIs), or attack troop transports (APAs); 24 large landing craft, infantry (LCI[L]s); and 3 auxiliary troop transports (XAPs). The U.S. Navy dispatched 28 new LSTs to the Mediterranean, and Eisenhower supplied 24 more from his resources. This left a deficit of 13 out of the 96 LSTs planned for the assault. In the end, judicious juggling of shipping and units made it possible to launch the assault with only 81 LSTs. Eisenhower also sent south the LSIs, APAs, and LCI(L)s that ANVIL required, while the U.S. Navy sent the XAPs from American ports. But the newly arriving assault shipping, added to the one-division amphibious lift that AFHQ already had in the Mediterranean, was scarcely enough to carry the three assault divisions and the supporting commando units, much

less the follow-up supplies and the French troops that were to reach southern France during the first few days after the assault.

To make up for the shortage of amphibious assault vessels, various expedients were necessary. AFHQ and Seventh Army had to plan for a much earlier employment of merchant-type shipping, a risk taken largely because intelligence estimates indicated that German air and naval forces could offer little effective resistance to the ANVIL assault. In the end, the sixty-four merchant ships that had been carrying flatted ANVIL cargo around the theater since April were included in the D-day convoy. Likewise, the forces of First French Army that were to start ashore on D plus 1 were largely loaded on merchant ships.[17]

Logistics

The general supply plan for ANVIL called for VI Corps assault units to reach southern France with a seven-day supply of rations, unit equipment, clothing, and POL products.[18] Of this total, a three-day supply was to be on the backs of the troops or aboard the vehicles of the assault units, and the remainder was to be unloaded and stockpiled on the beaches. If all went well, some 84,000 troops and 12,000 vehicles would go ashore over the VI Corps' beaches on D-day. An additional 33,500 troops and another

---

[17] Additional information on merchant shipping and early convoys comes from WNTF Rpt, p. 30, and Annex 4, Convoy Plan, to Seventh Army FO 1, 29 Jul 44.

[18] Additional information on the supply plan is from Annex 6, Admin Plan, to Seventh Army Outline Plan ANVIL, 13 Jul 44.

8,000 vehicles, including the leading elements of the French Army, would unload over the same beaches by D plus 4. These follow-up units, arriving from D plus 1 through D plus 4, would carry the same amount of supplies as the initial assault units. From D plus 5 to D plus 30 troop convoys would reach southern France at five-day intervals, each loaded with a seven-day supply of rations, unit equipment, clothing, and POL products for the units carried.

Planners expected that ranger and commando units would start drawing supplies from the beach depots on D plus 1. The 1st Airborne Task Force would drop with the minimum supplies necessary to accomplish its initial missions, but would require aerial resupply for at least two days. As an added margin of safety, AFHQ put aside seven more days of supply at airfields in the Rome area, which the Provisional Troop Carrier Air Division could move to southern France for either the 1st Airborne Task Force or for any other Seventh Army unit that might become isolated. No aerial resupply was planned for D-day, but the Provisional Troop Carrier Air Division was to have 112 loaded aircraft on call and ready to fly to southern France at any time by D plus 1.

The ammunition supply plan called for all assault units to land on D-day with five units of fire for all weapons.[19] The D plus 5 convoy was to bring with it five units of fire for all

the troops it carried, plus three and one-third units of fire for all elements already ashore. The D plus 10 convoy would also carry five units of fire for its troops, plus one and two-thirds units of fire for troops ashore, and so on to ensure a steady buildup.

SOS NATOUSA and Seventh Army intended that by D plus 30, when the Coastal Base Section was to assume supply responsibility in southern France, Seventh Army units would have ten days of supply for operations in hand plus twenty days of supply in reserve. The planners estimated that through D plus 30 some 277,700 tons of cargo would have been unloaded over the beaches; roughly 188,350 of these tons would have been forwarded to units, and the remainder would be in depots.

Two closely related estimates concerning the probable course of operations in southern France had a marked bearing on the supply plan. First, intelligence information indicated to tactical planners that the advance inland would be fairly slow. As a result they did not expect that Toulon could be captured before D plus 20, or that Marseille could be secured until at least D plus 45. Logisticians estimated that the American and French ground forces would have to be supported over the beaches until about D plus 30 and that beach supply operations could not support the tactical forces much farther than twenty miles inland.

Based on these extremely conservative logistical and operational projections, Army and Navy planners saw an opportunity to make better use of the limited amount of assault shipping by reducing the amount of supplies

[19] A "unit of fire" was the estimated average amount of ammunition that a unit or weapon was expected to use during one day of combat and varied from theater to theater. See FM 9–6, Ammunition Supply (15 June 1944), p. 4.

needed for a fast-paced, mobile battle. Expecting determined enemy resistance, they instructed the logisticians to emphasize ammunition and to save shipping space by cutting deeply into early loadings of POL and rations for the period D-day through D plus 4. The planners subsequently reduced POL loadings for these days by 20 percent, lowered the amount of rations from a ten- to a seven-day supply, and cut the number of vehicles designated to haul supplies rapidly and deeply inland from the beaches. The Seventh Army was taking a calculated risk. If its forces penetrated German defenses faster and farther than expected, the reductions of POL supplies and vehicles could have a marked delaying effect on the course of the campaign. On the other hand, if the Germans offered determined resistance as they had done at Salerno, Anzio, and Normandy, then the fuel and vehicles would be a grave liability and ammunition much more vital to the troops ashore. With the limited number of amphibious ships available, the Seventh Army planners had little flexibility in this regard, and the emphasis on munitions would provide the best means of ensuring that the combat forces had the ability to secure the initial beachhead.[20]

---

[20] For further discussion of ANVIL logistics and its effects, see chapter 11, especially the sections treating munitions, transportation, and POL products.

CHAPTER IV

German Plans and Organization

Until the waning months of 1943 the Germans had focused their attention on the Russian front. Only in November of that year did the German high command come to regard an Allied invasion of western Europe as an equal if not greater threat than an invasion from the east. This realization slowly brought about major changes in German military deployments. Adolph Hitler, the politico-military leader of the German state, fully understood the dangers of an invasion of northwestern Europe. The area was not only close to the heartland of Germany's industrial base, but also lay on the approaches to the north German plains, the traditional invasion route to central Europe. He thus vowed to turn the northeastern portion of the Continent into a *Festung Europa* and resist any invasion of the northern coast as strongly as possible. With this judgment German military leaders could hardly disagree.[1]

German Organization and Operational Concepts

Before November 1943 *Oberbefehlshaber West (OB West)*, the German theater command responsible for the defense of France, had served as a reservoir of reinforcements for the eastern front and to a lesser degree for Italy and the Balkans. In November, however, Hitler and his armed forces high command, *Oberkommando der Wehrmacht (OKW)*, abandoned this practice and began strengthening *OB West* as quickly as possible to resist a predicted Allied amphibious invasion expected to strike the northern coast of France. Although unforeseen contingencies on the eastern front and in Italy forced the German high command to slow down this buildup during the opening months of 1944, *OB West* continued to prepare against the anticipated Allied cross-Channel invasion with all the local resources it could muster, hoping that somehow Germany would be able to raise the forces necessary to carry out the broad defensive policy on which Hitler and *OKW* had decided.

---

[1] German material in this volume is based mainly on a series of CMH manuscripts collectively entitled "German Operations in Southern France and Alsace, 1944," prepared by Charles V. P. von Luttichau and other historians of the former Foreign Military Studies Branch, CMH, and based on original German sources (hereafter cited as von Luttichau, "German Operations"). For more information on German operational and tactical planning, especially in regard to northern France, see the appropriate sections of Pogue, *The Supreme Command;* Har-

rison, *Cross-Channel Attack;* and Martin Blumenson, *Breakout and Pursuit* (Washington, 1961), all in the United States Army in World War II series.

Hitler's defensive policy made the coast of France the German main line of resistance (MLR) in western Europe, and *OKW* planned to fortify the Normandy shoreline so thoroughly that local reserves would be able to deal with most invasion attempts. But if the Allies succeeded in putting strong forces ashore, *OKW* wanted a powerful, mobile central reserve composed primarily of armored units, which could drive the Allies back into the sea. To create such a force, *OB West* was prepared to strip any sectors not directly affected by the invasion, although the final decision to commit the central reserve was to be made by *OKW* and ultimately by Hitler himself.

These plans, particularly making the French coast the MLR, required manpower, materiel, and time the Germans did not have. As a result, the so-called Atlantic Wall never became a true defensive line and consisted mainly of a series of semi-isolated strongpoints. In fact, well before OVERLORD began, *OB West* had reached the conclusion that it faced a virtually impossible defensive task with the means at hand and had begun tentative plans to withdraw strength from southern France to defend the northern part of the country where, most German planners believed, the main Allied invasion would come.

As early as January 1944, the Germans had developed reasonably accurate estimates of Allied intentions in regard to France. They certainly expected a major invasion and thought it would come in northern France during the first third of the year; they also believed that the invasion would coincide with a Russian spring offen-sive and that the Allies would launch strong secondary attacks at the same time as the main effort. The German high command at first interpreted the Anzio landing of late January as the beginning of a series of peripheral operations designed to pin down and disperse German forces before the cross-Channel assault. The Germans changed this estimate when they discovered that the Allies retained strong, uncommitted forces in North Africa, and decided that the Allies would launch another major attack in the Mediterranean more or less in conjunction with an invasion of northern France. In February, German intelligence even concluded that an assault into southern France would come before the cross-Channel operation. By May, however, they had taken a harder look at Allied amphibious capabilities and reduced the undertaking in southern France to the status of a threat—an estimate coinciding remarkably well with contemporary Allied decisions concerning ANVIL.

Mildly surprised when OVERLORD started without a concurrent Allied invasion of southern France (as they had been mildly surprised when the Russian spring offensive of 1944 began without a concurrent OVERLORD), the Germans kept a wary eye on southern France after 6 June. For a while *OKW* estimates fluctuated between the Italian Ligurian coast and the French Riviera as the probable sites for an Allied amphibious landing in the Mediterranean. But by early August most German planners were convinced that southern France would be the Allied target. Only *OB Southwest*, the German theater command in

Italy, still thought that landings somewhere in northern Italy were more likely. Three days before the ANVIL target date—15 August—German commanders in southern France were aware of Allied strength for the assault, of the Allies' general intentions, and of the probable date of the operation, but had not yet reached a firm conclusion as to the exact location of the assault beachhead.

Meanwhile, events in northern France had been moving toward a climax. Once the Allies succeeded in establishing a bridgehead in Normandy, Field Marshal Gerd von Rundstedt, commanding *OB West*, began to consider a general withdrawal from France. By mid-June he had become convinced that the situation in Normandy was irretrievable and that it was too late for *OKW* to do anything except pull all *OB West* forces, including those in southern France, back to the fixed fortifications along the German border. But Hitler and *OKW* vehemently disagreed, and Hitler, already dissatisfied with the course of operations in Normandy, decided that a younger, less pessimistic commander was needed in France. Accordingly, on 3 July he dismissed von Rundstedt and placed Field Marshal Guenther von Kluge in command of *OB West.*

The command change solved little. Von Kluge was unable to halt the steady Allied buildup in Normandy and the subsequent Allied breakout at St. Lo that began on 25 July. Faced with a major reversal on the battlefield, Hitler and *OKW* saw only two alternatives: a general withdrawal, as advocated by von Kluge, or a major counterattack. Breaking off in Normandy, *OKW* estimated, could lead

only to an early and deep withdrawal from northern France, forcing the abandonment of southern France and probably requiring redeployments from Italy and the Balkans as well. Instead, *OKW* recommended an immediate counterattack with all available means against the flank of the Allied breakthrough in Normandy. Hitler agreed, and what was to become known as the Mortain counterattack began on 7 August.[2]

The decision to counterattack in early August forced *OB West* to pull even more forces out of southern France. However, Hitler and *OKW* were not yet ready to openly modify the missions assigned the German armies in the south and, between 2 and 15 August, issued instructions to the German commanders in southern France confirming their mission of holding the coast at all costs. Nevertheless, *OKW* began drawing up contingency plans for a general withdrawal of all *OB West* forces to new defensive lines across northeastern France. These plans included evacuating most German forces from both western and southern France. Yet Hitler and other German leaders still hoped that the Allied breakthrough could be pinched off and contained, making such extreme measures unnecessary.

By 12 August *OKW* concluded that the Mortain counterattack had failed, and recommended a general withdrawal to the east before the remaining German forces in France became isolated and trapped. Hitler at first hesitated, feeling that his generals were too quick to withdraw. However,

---

[2] See Blumenson, *Breakout and Pursuit,* for a full account of this action.

by 15 August, the date scheduled for the Allied landings in southern France, the failure of the counterattack had become obvious to everyone, and large numbers of elite German troops were in danger of being trapped within the rapidly closing Falaise Pocket. In the north, von Kluge's chief of staff was frantically seeking new decisions from *OKW,* averring that a complete collapse of *OB West* in northern France was now imminent. Meanwhile, Hitler, once again dissatisfied with the performance of his generals, decided to replace von Kluge with Field Marshal Walter Model. Thus, as the Allied invasion fleet approached France's Mediterranean shore in the south, the German high command was in a state of general disarray, making any immediate theater-level response to the landings extremely difficult.

German Organization and Strength

At the beginning of June 1944, von Rundstedt's *OB West,* theoretically a joint theater command, was little more than an army group headquarters with minimal direct authority over local air and naval commands or even over certain other army commands in the west.[3] By that time von Rundstedt had delegated responsibility for the ground defense of northern France to Field Marshal Erwin Rommel, commanding *Army Group B,* and of southern France to General Johannes Blaskowitz, commanding *Army Group G.* The boundary line between the two units followed the Loire River

from the Atlantic to Tours and then ran southeast to the Swiss border. Von Rundstedt's command problems were complicated by the fact that Rommel also held semi-independent authority as inspector of coastal defenses and held defensive concepts not entirely in accord with those of *OB West.* In addition, Rommel had been appointed by Hitler personally and, as a field marshal, had direct access to the German leader, bypassing von Rundstedt. The *OB West* commander also had to cope with many governmental and paramilitary agencies that continually nibbled at his authority, preventing him from unifying German efforts behind the battlefield. Von Kluge, who relieved von Rundstedt on 3 July, was in a somewhat better position, having Hitler's confidence at first and developing a close personal relationship with Rommel. When Rommel was wounded in mid-July, von Kluge assumed command of *Army Group B* in addition to *OB West,* thereby consolidating the army command in northern France.

The three other major military commands in northern France were the *Third Air Force,* under Field Marshal Hugo Sperrle; *Navy Group West,* under Admiral Theodor Krancke; and the office of *Military Governor France,* headed by Lt. Gen. Karl Heinrich von Stulpnagel. Field Marshal Sperrle reported to Reichsmarschall Hermann Goering's *Oberkommando der Luftwaffe (OKL),* while Admiral Krancke was responsible to the *Oberkommando der Kriegsmarine (OKM),* under Grand Admiral Karl Doenitz.[4] As a civil admin-

---

[3] On the rolls of the German Army *HQ OB West* was actually listed as *HQ Army Group D.*

[4] Goering was the highest ranking officer of the German armed forces and as Reichsmarschall held

GENERAL JOHANNES BLASKOWITZ (center).

istrator of occupied territory, General von Stulpnagel was responsible to the German government, but as military commander of security forces in France, he reported to *OB West*. In addition, *OB West* attached most of its logistical and administrative staff sections to von Stulpnagel's headquarters, thereby making that headquarters the logistical command for German ground forces in France, somewhat analogous to Services of Supply in NATOUSA.

In southern France General Blaskowitz of *Army Group G* and General Friedrich Wiese, heading the *Nineteenth Army,* were the principal German military commanders. While Blaskowitz had been an opponent of some of the Hitlerian regime's harsher policies, Wiese had been a member of the Freikorps in 1919 and was considered a fervent Nazi by American authorities.[5] Both enjoyed good military reputations, but, like *OB West,* had limited authority over some of the military and paramilitary forces in their areas of operation. Blaskowitz,

what would correspond to a nonexistent "six star" rank in the U.S. armed forces. Doenitz's equivalent rank in the U.S. Navy was Admiral of the Fleet, five stars.

[5] For contemporary Allied evaluations of German leaders, see "G-2 History: Seventh Army Operations in Europe," IV, Annex III, Box 2, William W. Quinn Papers, MHI (copies also in Seventh Army retired records at WNRC).

GENERAL FRIEDRICH WIESE

for example, initially had direct control over only the coastal areas along the Atlantic and Mediterranean inland to a depth of about twenty miles. Prior to ANVIL, the rest of the region was under the control of Lt. Gen. Ernst Dehner's *Army Area Southern France,* a component of the *Military Governor France,* whose forces were engaged primarily in antiguerrilla and police activities.

Blaskowitz's control of local *Ost Legions* was also limited. *Ost* units were separate infantry forces made up of volunteer, drafted, or impressed soldiers from eastern Europe, mainly Poles, Russians, and Czechs; some of these organizations were attached to

army field units, and others were independent. As security forces they were considered adequate, but their conventional combat capabilities were suspect. *Headquarters, Ost Legion,* was an administrative and training command that controlled *Ost* units not specifically assigned to *Army Group G.* The *Ost Legion* headquarters was under *OB West* for operations, but reported to the German Army high command, *Oberkommando des Heeres (OKH),* for administrative matters concerning the numerous *Ost* units in *Army Group G's* area. Upon an Allied invasion of southern France, Blaskowitz was to assume greater control over both *Ost Legion* units and any tactical forces under *Army Area Southern France,* but even then his authority was not total.

In southern France, *Admiral Atlantic Coast* controlled naval units from Brittany south to the Spanish border, and *Admiral French South Coast* controlled those on the Mediterranean littoral. Both answered directly to *Navy Group West,* and the Mediterranean command was further subdivided into *Naval Command Languedoc* (west of Toulon) and *Naval Command French Riviera* (Toulon east to the Italian border). All forces under these two commands were land based and consisted of coast defense artillery, antiaircraft units, service troops, and a variety of special staffs and offices. The only surface unit in southern France was the *6th Security Flotilla,* which, with a handful of patrol craft, reported through *Security Forces West* to *Navy Group West.*

Blaskowitz's control over naval artillery was restricted. Initially all naval guns remained under naval control.

After an Allied landing had actually taken place, control was to be split, with the navy directing fire on Allied aircraft and shipping, and the army directing fire against ground targets, a division that was guaranteed to create problems.

Third Air Force responsibilities in southern France were carried out by the *2d Air Division* and *Fighter Command Southern France*. Neither had any ground support responsibilities. As of 15 August, the *2d Air Division* could muster only about sixty-five torpedo bombers and fifteen bombers equipped to carry radio-controlled missiles. *Fighter Command Southern France*, with the primary mission of air defense, had virtually no aircraft and would receive only minor reinforcements from Italy after the invasion had begun.[6]

As opposed to the weak air and naval commands, *Army Group G* was a reasonably strong and well-balanced force in early June. In the west the German *First Army*, with the *LXXX* and *LXXXVI Corps* (each with two divisions), defended the Atlantic coast from the Loire River south to the Spanish border. In the south the *Nineteenth Army* guarded the Mediterranean coast with three corps: the *IV Luftwaffe Field Corps*, with three divisions; *Corps Kniess* (soon to be redesignated *LXXXV Corps*), with two divisions; and the *LXII Reserve Corps*, also with two divisions. In addition Blaskowitz had the *LXVI Reserve Corps* which, with part of one division and various lesser units, held the Pyrenees

border area, the Carcassonne Gap land bridge between the Atlantic and Mediterranean coasts, and the Massif Central, a broad plateau region west of the Rhone valley. Behind these six corps, *Army Group G* also had the *LVIII Panzer Corps*, a reserve force controlling three panzer divisions. Finally, the *17th SS Panzer Grenadier Division*, an *OKW* reserve unit, and the *157th Reserve Mountain Division*, operating under *Army Area Southern France*, were to pass to Blaskowitz's control in the event of an Allied invasion. Thus, in June, *Army Group G* had under its command two army headquarters, seven corps headquarters, three armored divisions, the equivalent of thirteen infantry divisions, and a host of smaller combat units, while two other divisions were to pass to its control following an Allied landing.[7]

Serious manpower and equipment shortages plagued all of these units. The army group, army, and corps headquarters lacked many of the normal logistical and administrative support units and special staffs necessary for command and control, and the tactical staffs at division level and below were all greatly understrength. Despite frequent requests to higher headquarters, Blaskowitz was unable to expand even his own staff to what he felt was an adequate size, a problem that undoubtedly hampered German planning activities.[8]

---

[6] The number of planes redeployed from Italy cannot be determined, but it appears to have been less than two squadrons.

[7] Allied estimates often carried the *Ost Legion* as a separate, ready division, but these units were generally attached to existing German infantry regiments as a fourth battalion.

[8] Authorized only in late April 1944, *Army Group G* headquarters had become operational on 12 May, but was initially designated an *Armeegruppe* with an inferior status to that of *Army Group B*, which was classified as a *Heeresgruppe*. Only on 11 September

The condition of the various infantry divisions under Blaskowitz was also spotty. The long drain on German resources had left many of these units with a high proportion of ethnic Germans from conquered eastern territories, while many of the native Germans were overage or in limited service categories. Some divisions also had large numbers of *Ost* troops, and others were markedly understrength and underequipped, with little training or experience in large unit operations.

Blaskowitz classified four of his infantry divisions as static, or garrison, units with little mobility or logistical resources. One of these divisions had only seven of its nine authorized infantry battalions, and another had three *Ost* battalions attached to it. Five other divisions carried the designation *reserve*. Although supposedly in training, these divisions were engaged primarily in construction and security activities, and their conventional military capabilities had severely declined. Each had somewhere between four and nine infantry battalions, a mixed collection of light and medium artillery pieces, and a variety of *Ost* battalions.

Probably the best infantry divisions were four organized under the new 1944 tables of organization and equipment (TOE).[9] At 12,770 men, these units were substantially smaller than the 1939–43 infantry divisions

(authorized over 17,000 men), but were lighter and had greater firepower. Each 1944 division was authorized three regimental headquarters controlling two infantry battalions, as well as a seventh infantry, or fusilier, battalion operating as a reserve directly under divisional control. However, they still lacked the motor transport and logistical capabilities of the larger American infantry divisions and, by themselves, were much weaker than their Allied counterparts.

The German armored formations were a different story. Throughout World War II the German Army concentrated its best weapons, equipment, and manpower in its armored units—the panzer and panzer grenadier divisions—and left its foot infantry divisions generally neglected. The German high command regarded both types of divisions as "mobile units" and often used them interchangeably on the battlefield to stiffen the less well endowed infantry divisions and to counterattack enemy penetrations of the front lines. But assessing the precise strength of these armored formations at any given time is difficult. By 1944 the circumstances of war and Germany's low production of armored vehicles had greatly blurred the organizational distinction between panzer (armored) and panzer grenadier (armored, or mechanized, infantry) divisions. In mid-1944 each panzer division was generally authorized one two-battalion tank regiment (fifty to sixty tanks per battalion), two two-battalion mechanized infantry regiments (four infantry battalions), a mechanized reconnaissance battalion, an armored artillery regiment, and mechanized or motorized support

---

was Blaskowitz's headquarters raised to the status of *Heeresgruppe*.

[9] TOEs were published military tables listing the authorized equipment by type and the personnel by rank and specialty that a particular unit was supposed to have. Normally units in combat did well to maintain 80–90 percent of their TOE strength.

GERMAN ARMOR PASSING THROUGH TOULOUSE

units; the panzer grenadier division was normally authorized two three-battalion motorized infantry regiments (six infantry battalions), one tank or assault gun battalion, a mechanized reconnaissance battalion, and motorized support units. However, the attachment and detachment of battalion-sized units to and from these divisions was common, and the armored formations rarely went into combat with either their full authorized or existing operational strength. In addition, the use of either armored half-tracks or light trucks to carry the infantry of either type of division depended on the availability of equipment; the substitution of turretless assault guns for turreted tanks sometimes occurred for the same reason.

Thus, with a higher infantry-to-tank ratio than the standard American armored divisions (with three tank and three armored infantry battalions) and with equipment shortages further reducing their armor strength, both formations bore striking similarities to the standard American infantry division of World War II with its normal attachment of one tank battalion (sixty tanks), one self-propelled tank destroyer battalion (thirty-six pieces), and motorized support units.

Although the three armored divisions of the *LVII Panzer Reserve Corps* were in various stages of activation and training, and their infantry regiments were generally truck-mounted with few armored half-tracks, each could put at least one or two strong combat commands in the field. Moreover, their tank units were equipped with Mark IV medium and Mark V (Panther) heavy tanks, both of which were better armored and armed than their American counterparts, and their commanders, staffs, and troops were generally well experienced. Other units in reserve were less impressive. The *17th SS Panzer Grenadier Division,* for example, lacked many of its components, while the *157th Mountain Reserve Division* was hardly more than a reinforced regimental combat team. Yet these mobile reserves constituted a powerful weapon against any amphibious assault on either the Mediterranean or Atlantic French coasts.

To further beef up their combat power, the German forces in southern France also employed large quantities of captured equipment of all types. Their artillery, for example, included weapons of French, Italian, Russian, Czech, and other manufacture, all of various calibers and sizes; the variety among vehicles was even greater, ranging from models captured from the British in North Africa, to French armored machines of all kinds, to a broad collection of commercial trucks, vans, and autos drafted for military service. Although these improvisations aggravated *Army Group G*'s spare parts and ammunition resupply problems, they also enabled Blaskowitz to strengthen significantly the units under his command.

In comparison to the defenses of the Channel coast and Normandy, the fixed defensive installations in southern France were weak. Blaskowitz had been unable to obtain the materials required for strong coastal fortifica-tions, and the construction of large submarine pens at Marseille had consumed a high percentage of the defensive materiel and labor that had been made available. Civilian labor was limited, while the requirements of training, security, and antiguerrilla operations made it impossible for Blaskowitz to use military manpower extensively to bring his defenses up to the standards necessary to face a major Allied assault. Nevertheless, the German commander realized that the Allied air bases in Corsica could not begin to duplicate the air support available for a cross-Channel assault in the north, and so his freedom of maneuver in the south would be significantly greater. Thus, by concentrating his coastal defense preparations in those areas most likely to be targets of an amphibious assault and by carefully positioning his sixteen divisions, Blaskowitz could bring considerable pressure to bear against any one-, two-, or three-division ANVIL assault throughout the spring and early summer of 1944. Any Allied amphibious invasion attempt there could expect a heavy fight at the beachhead and no assurance of ultimate success.

The Effects of Overlord

After the invasion of northern France, the strength of *Army Group G* gradually deteriorated as unit after unit was ordered to the Normandy area. The *17th SS Panzer Grenadier Division* departed on 7 June, followed rapidly by the *LXXXVI Corps* headquarters, an armored division, all four 1944-type infantry divisions, four artillery battalions, and an assault gun battalion. The transfers were temporarily halted but resumed in late July with the departure of the *LVIII Panzer Corps* headquarters, another armored division, one of the static infantry divisions, another assault gun battalion, four assault gun training battalions (which had personnel but few combat vehicles), and five infantry training battalions.

Transfers from southern to northern France continued during the first half of August almost until the ships of the Western Naval Task Force were in sight of the Riviera. Major losses were the headquarters of the *First Army,* the *LXVI* and *LXXX Corps,* a regimental combat team of the *338th Infantry Division,* two more artillery battalions, another infantry replacement battalion, and one of the *11th Panzer Division*'s two tank battalions. A number of smaller units also went north between June and August, including the antiaircraft units that had protected the bridges over the Rhone and the antitank companies of four infantry divisions.

These losses greatly reduced the strength of *Army Group G,* and the reinforcements reaching southern France after 6 June provided little relief. Moving in were the *LXIV Corps* headquarters, which replaced the *First Army* on the Atlantic coast; two worn-out infantry divisions from Normandy, one of which had to be consolidated with a remaining *Army Group G* division; a battered division from the Russian front that had been merged with the cadre of a new division from Germany; two antitank battalions; and one heavy artillery battalion. By 15 August Blaskowitz had thus lost two-thirds of his armored reserve and about one-quarter of his infantry divi-

sions. Obviously he could expect no assistance from *Army Group B,* which was now in a state of near collapse, but reinforcement still might be possible from the Italian front under *OB Southwest.*

OB Southwest

The relationship of *OB Southwest* in Italy with *OB West* and *Army Group G* merits special attention.[10] German operational strategy in Italy was essentially defensive. The principal mission of the theater commander, Field Marshal Albert Kesselring, was to hold the shortest possible east-west line across the Italian peninsula and keep the Allied ground forces in Italy bottled up in the narrow peninsula as far south as possible. Although Kesselring had no responsibilities regarding the defense of southern France, he was obviously interested in any threat to his rear that an amphibious invasion might pose. But neither Kesselring nor his superiors believed that the Allied amphibious assaults against either northern or southern France posed any direct threat to *OB Southwest,* and even after ANVIL had occurred, German leaders considered a strong Allied thrust into northern Italy through the Alps highly unlikely.

Throughout the spring and summer of 1944, Hitler and *OKW* were more concerned with an amphibious assault against northern Italy along either the Ligurian or Adriatic coasts, behind the German lines. Such a landing

_____

[10] For further information on German strategy for Italy, see Ernest F. Fisher, Jr., *Cassino to the Alps,* United States Army in World War II (Washington, 1977).

could cause a complete collapse of the theater and project Allied land and air power dangerously close to the German heartland. Their fears were undoubtedly strengthened by Kesselring's estimates that the next major Allied offensive in the Mediterranean would be an assault in the Genoa area, outflanking German defenses north of Rome and forcing him to evacuate the Italian peninsula. Moreover, in June and July, Kesselring was under renewed Allied military pressure in Italy from Wilson's drives north of Rome. These multiple threats to *OB Southwest* finally prompted Hitler to send Kesselring six more divisions, including one that had been promised earlier to *Army Group G.* Furthermore, in early August *OKW* advised that, should a withdrawal from southern France become necessary, at least two of *Army Group G's* divisions should be transferred to *OB Southwest* to protect Kesselring's rear along the Franco-Italian border. In no case was there any discussion of sending reinforcements to *Army Group G* from *OB Southwest.*

In August 1944 Kesselring's continued concern about the Ligurian coast had even led him to reinforce that area. On 3 August he appointed the Italian Marshal Rodolfo Graziani to command the newly formed *Ligurian Army,* consisting of two understrength German divisions and two Italian divisions of doubtful reliability. Southeast along the coast from Genoa, but not part of *Ligurian Army,* were two more German divisions, and by 10 August Kesselring had begun assembling even more divisions in northern Italy to act as a central reserve for the entire Italian theater. However, neither *OKW* or *OB Southwest* laid even tentative plans to use these forces for a flanking attack against Allied troops landing in southern France. In fact, as the southern France campaign developed, Kesselring's only mission would be to hold the Alpine mountain passes and block any possible Allied excursion into northern Italy. Although Allied intelligence sources confirmed Kesselring's passive stand toward the invasion of southern France, Generals Patch and Truscott, the principal Allied ground commanders in the assault, continued to watch the Alpine passes on their right flank for any sign of unusual German activity.[11] The plans of the German military commanders in the past had not always been discernible, and there was no reason to believe that their operational ingenuity would disappear in the immediate future.

Perhaps a more significant factor was the preoccupation of Hitler and *OKW* with the deteriorating situation in northern France. By 15 August *OKW* was far more interested in withdrawing the bulk of *Army Group G* northward to help stem the threat of an Allied breakout from Normandy than it was in forestalling an Allied invasion of southern France. Although Hitler himself might not have let the matter drop so easily, he probably lacked the time to study the German situation along the southern

---

[11] For discussion, see Arthur L. Funk, "General Patch and the Alpine Passes, 1944," paper presented at the American Historical Association meeting in Chicago, 1987; and ibid., "Intelligence and Operations: ANVIL/DRAGOON, the Landings in Southern France," paper presented at the XIIIth International Colloquy on Military History, Helsinki, 1988 (copies at CMH).

French coast in any great detail. Thus neither Hitler, *OKW, OB West,* nor *OB Southwest* ever considered employing German forces in Italy to mount a counterattack against an Allied invasion of southern France. This critical lack of interest had been carefully noted in Allied intelligence estimates prior to ANVIL, allowing Allied planners to minimize the danger of an *OB Southwest* thrust into France through the Alpine passes after the invasion had begun.

The German Nineteenth Army

The steady transfer of *Army Group G*'s best units out of the zone and the continued deterioration of the German position in northern France may have convinced Blaskowitz that any attempt to resist a major Allied amphibious assault against the Atlantic or Mediterranean coasts was futile. In the west his coastal defenses had been so weakened that they were no more than an advanced outpost line. On 8 August *OB West* had even reduced the missions of the Atlantic forces, requiring the *LXIV Corps* to hold only three strongpoints in the event of a major landing. The corps' remaining forces—two understrength divisions, some separate regiments, and a variety of paramilitary organizations (police or security units)—were only to maintain a screen along the coast and protect *Army Group G*'s northwest flank on the Loire River. But, outside of holding local FFI forces at bay, little more could be expected from this command.

Along the Mediterranean coast, the situation was different. There Blaskowitz retained the ability to con-

test a major assault. Although greatly reduced, the forces that made up the *Nineteenth Army* were still reasonably strong, their defensive missions unchanged, and their commanders veteran soldiers. As of mid-August Wiese's forces totaled seven infantry divisions controlled by three corps headquarters. Although most of these formations were still understrength and short of equipment, many were rested and experienced units that could be expected to give a good account of themselves if well led and well positioned. Wiese's problem, like Rommel's in the north, was to decide where the Allies would land or, more accurately, how he could best deploy his forces to enable them to carry out their defensive missions under a variety of contingencies.

In early August, responsibility for the defense of the French Mediterranean coast from Toulon to the Italian border rested with the *Nineteenth Army's LXII Corps* under Lt. Gen. Ferdinand Neuling *(Map 2)*. Neuling's *LXII Corps* consisted of the *242d* and *148th Infantry Divisions* and a host of smaller units of all types. The *242d Division,* under Maj. Gen. Johannes Baessler, was deployed from the Toulon area east to Antheor Cove, a few miles north of the Argens River, and was thus responsible for a sector that would include almost all of the ANVIL assault beaches. Baessler was also designated the Toulon garrison commander, responsible for the defenses of the port. From Antheor Cove northeast to the Italian border, the coast was defended by the *148th Division* of Maj. Gen. Otto Fretter-Pico. Fretter-Pico's zone included the smaller ports of Nice and Cannes.

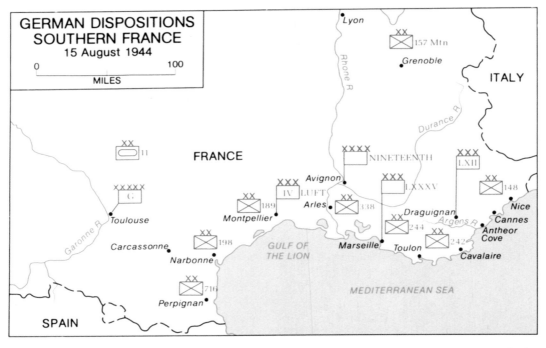

GERMAN DISPOSITIONS
SOUTHERN FRANCE
15 August 1944

0   100
MILES

MAP 2   This map is printed in full color at the back of the book, following the Index.

Guarding the German center, from Toulon west to Marseille and across the Rhone River delta, was Lt. Gen. Baptist Kniess' *LXXXV Corps*, with the *338th* and *244th Infantry Divisions*. But by 15 August the *338th Division* had already redeployed one of its regiments north and had pulled its remaining units back to the Arles area, preparing to follow. Kniess' remaining unit, the *244th Division*, was still relatively intact, but was repositioning itself to take over the *338th*'s area of responsibility. The unit commander was also charged with organizing the defense of Marseille and had no troop units to spare elsewhere.

In the west the *IV Luftwaffe Field Corps* under Lt. Gen. Erich Petersen held the area between the Rhone delta and Spanish border. His major

units were the *198th* and *716th Infantry Divisions* and the weak *189th Reserve Division*. One of the *189th*'s two infantry regiments, the *28th Grenadiers*,[12] constituted *Army Group G*'s reserve and was located north of the coast in the Carcassonne Gap area; the rest of the division was in the process of moving into the Rhone delta positions vacated by the *338th*. At the time, Wiese had also ordered Petersen to send the *198th Division* east of the Rhone where it could serve as a reserve unit behind Kniess' coastal defenses. As a further precaution, Blaskowitz was transferring *Army Group G*'s principal reserve unit, Maj. Gen. Wend von Wietersheim's *11th*

---

[12] The German term *grenadier* signified a normal infantry unit.

MAJ. GEN. WEND VON WIETERSHEIM

Panzer Division,[13] from the Toulouse area to the vicinity of Avignon, also east of the Rhone. Both Blaskowitz and Wiese considered the Marseille-Toulon region the most likely target of an Allied attack and were now hurrying forces to the threatened sector.

These movements were actually part of a more ambitious internal reorganization conceived by Wiese. Since early August the *Nineteenth Army* commander had been expecting an Allied assault at any time, but the continued redeployment of units northward forced him to alter his defensive dispositions regularly. The impending departure of the *338th Division* made yet another reshuffling necessary. But by 13 August Wiese had also concluded that the most likely area for an Allied assault lay east of Toulon, a prediction that agreed remarkably well with Allied plans. To meet this threat, he wanted to have his weaker *189th* and *198th Divisions* assume responsibility for the static defenses of Toulon and Marseille, thereby freeing his two best units, the *242d* and *244th Divisions,* to act as mobile reserves. If these units could be further reinforced by the *11th Panzer Division,* the *Nineteenth Army* might be able to give any invaders a real fight at the beachhead and buy time for a more determined defense of the larger ports and the Rhone valley. Although Hitler had ordered Wiese to have strong garrisons defend Toulon and Marseille to the death, most of the German defenses there faced seaward, and little had yet been done to fortify the land approaches to the two ports. The movement of the *189th* and *198th Infantry* and the *11th Panzers* east of the Rhone was thus the first step of this larger internal redeployment. But Wiese needed time to complete the transfers, and the involved units would need additional time to organize their new positions and deploy their components in an orderly fashion. Yet, by the night of 14–15 August, the movement of the three divisions across the Rhone

---

[13] At the time the *11th Panzer Division* had one battalion of heavy Mark V (Panther) tanks, one company of Mark IV mediums, one antitank battalion, four infantry battalions (motorized if not armored), an antitank battalion, an engineer battalion, and an artillery regiment; it was slightly larger than an American armored division except in the number, but not the size, of its tanks. "Remarks Concerning the War History of the Seventh U.S. Army," by the former operations officer of the *11th Panzer Division* (unpaginated), John E. Dahlquist Papers, MHI.

had barely begun and was being severely hampered by a lack of transportation, by FFI mines and ambushes, and by something the German staffs had forgotten to consider, the complete destruction of the Rhone bridges by Allied air attacks.[14] How soon the units could overcome these obstacles and reposition themselves was crucial to the German defense.

Whatever happened, the effectiveness of the initial German response to any Allied landings west of Toulon would depend greatly on the actions of the *LXII Corps* already in place. At first glance the state of what was to be the principal German command and control organization in the beachhead area left much to be desired. The corps headquarters had been sitting at Draguignan, about midway between Toulon and the Cannes-Nice area, since late 1942, operating generally as a training and occupation command. Although the headquarters had dropped its previous "reserve" designation on 9 August, the change in nomenclature was cosmetic, and the headquarters never acquired the staff sections and corps troops necessary for effective combat operations. *OKH* had almost retired General Neuling, the corps commander, for physical disability when his health broke down on the Russian front in the spring of 1942; and his two division commanders,

Baessler for the *242d* and Fretter-Pico of the *148th,* were also combat fatigue cases from the Russian campaign, during which both had been relieved of division commands. However, Neuling's service and his reputation as a training officer had brought him the corps command in southern France, and all three generals had a wealth of military experience between them that could not be discounted.

Of Neuling's two divisions, Baessler's *242d* was the stronger. Its *918th* and *917th Grenadier Regiments* held the coast from the Toulon area east to Cape Cavalaire, which would constitute the western edge of the ANVIL landing area. The division's third regiment, the *765th Grenadiers,* defended the coastline northwest of Cape Cavalaire, a stretch that included most of the future ANVIL assault beaches. Each regiment had the support of a battalion of the *242d Artillery Regiment,* as well as various naval artillery batteries, and each had an *Ost* unit as a fourth infantry battalion. Of the three grenadier regiments in the *242d Infantry Division,* the *765th* was by far the weakest. Having just been formed in the spring of 1944, it was only partially trained. Its fourth battalion (the *807th Azerbaijani Battalion*) was an *Ost* unit of doubtful reliability, while its other three battalions had a high proportion of ethnic Germans from the Sudetenland, Poland, Russia, and the Baltic states. At the time the only other unit in the future beachhead area was the *148th Division*'s *661st Ost Battalion,* located just north of the *765th Grenadiers.* How long these forces could effectively oppose a major assault was a question mark.

---

[14] Report of Maj. Gen. Wend von Wietersheim, 4 Jun 46, sub: 11th Panzer Division (unpaginated) (hereafter cited as "11th Panzer Division Rpt of MG von Wietersheim, 4 June 46,"), John E. Dahlquist Papers, MHI. Wietersheim commanded the panzer division at the time and noted the failure of the German command to anticipate the bridge problem in any way.

DEFENSIVE EMPLACEMENT OF A 65-MM. ITALIAN HOWITZER, *Pointe de St. Pierre, Cape St. Tropez.*

Concerned with his weakness in the expected invasion area, Wiese directed Neuling to move the *148th Division*'s reserves to the rear of the threatened zone. This reserve consisted of the division's incomplete third regiment—*Regiment Kessler*—an infantry battalion from one of the division's full regiments, and a combat engineer battalion. But for unknown reasons, *LXII Corps* was slow to carry out the order; and the *661st Ost Battalion*'s controlling headquarters, the *239th Grenadiers,* together with the *148th Division*'s other major units, the *8th Grenadiers* and *Regiment Kessler,* remained in the Cannes-Nice area farther north. In the initial defense the *765th Grenadiers* could thus expect

little assistance from the *148th Division* or anyone else.

Accurately estimating total German strength in southern France on the eve of the landings is difficult. The two *Nineteenth Army* corps primarily concerned with the assault area, Neuling's *LXII* and Kniess' *LXXXV,* reported their corps and divisional strength as approximately 53,670 troops, with an effective combat strength of 41,175.[15] These totals do not include *Army Group G* or *Nineteenth*

---

[15] In the German Army the term *effective strength* and *combat effectives* referred to soldiers serving at the combat battalion level and below. See James Hodgson, "Counting Combat Noses," *Army Combat Forces Journal,* V, No. 2 (September 1954), 45–46.

Army units not under the control of the two corps headquarters, nor do they include naval and *Luftwaffe* organizations stationed in the assault area. But even adding this non-corps elements, it is doubtful that the Germans had as many as 100,000 troops there, and the total may well have been as low as 85,000 on 15 August. In addition to the forces in the assault area, the German order of battle in the south still included the *IV Luftwaffe Field Corps* and the *LXIV Corps,* both west of the Rhone; the *11th Panzer Division* under the direct control of *Army Group G;* the *157th Reserve Mountain Division* and many police and security units under *Army Area Southern France; Ost Legion* organizations not attached to regular formations; a host of naval and air force units outside the assault area; and a large number of army administrative and logistical units. Adding all these troops to those in the assault area, German strength in southern France as of 15 August probably amounted to somewhere between 285,000 and 300,000 troops of all services and categories. By that time Wiese had been able to position approximately one-third of these forces at or near the expected invasion area west of Toulon.

German dispositions along the specific ANVIL beaches were extremely weak on the eve of the assault. Despite Wiese's reasonably accurate estimate of Allied intentions, the defenders were having severe difficulties strengthening the expected assault area and positioning their reserves for an effective counterattack. The command structure in the region still left much to be desired, and the defending troops were of a generally mixed caliber and stretched over a wide area with little depth. Much depended on how quickly Wiese could complete his current redeployment effort. Nevertheless, the evening of 14 August found all elements of *Army Group G* on full defensive alert with Wiese desperately trying to accelerate the movement of his reinforcements from the west over the Rhone River. Aerial reconnaissance at dusk had reported the approach of Allied convoys from the direction of Corsica, and, ready or not, everyone realized that an invasion was imminent.

CHAPTER V

The Plan of Assault

The choice of assault sites along the Mediterranean coast of France was in large measure dictated by the ANVIL operational concept—to land in southern France, seize and develop a major port, and exploit northward up the Rhone valley. Of these objectives, none imposed more tactical limitations on the selection of the assault beaches than the requirement for the early seizure of a major port. From the inception of ANVIL, Allied planners regarded the capture of Marseille, one of France's major port cities, as vital to the success of the operation. Sete, eighty-five miles west of Marseille, or Toulon, thirty miles east of Marseille, or the many smaller harbors dotting the French Riviera could serve as interim ports, but only Marseille could handle the projected volume of logistical operations envisaged for southern France.

Selecting the Landing Area

Washed by the waters of the Gulf of the Lion, the Mediterranean coast of France slopes on the east, along the Riviera, down to the waters of the Ligurian Sea.[1] Three major mountain masses, separated by natural corridors, rise inland from the coast (*Map 3*). On the west, the Pyrenees mountains, stretching from the Atlantic to the Mediterranean, form the traditional boundary between France and Spain; on the east, the Alps serve a similar purpose, separating France and Italy and defining the Swiss border farther north. Between these two mountain ranges and about twenty to thirty miles inland rises the Massif Central, a large mountainous plateau region that dominates southern France. The Carcassonne Gap, a valley area formed by the tributaries of the Garonne and Aude rivers, separates the Massif Central from the Pyrenees in the west; and the Rhone River valley similarly divides the central plateau area from the foothills of the Alps in the east. While the Carcassonne Gap links the Riviera with the French Atlantic coast, the Rhone valley is the historic north-south corridor of France. From Lyon, 170 miles north of the Mediterranean, the valley provides access to northern France through the valley of the Saone River and to southwestern Germany through the Belfort Gap.

---

[1] This subsection is based on *Seventh Army Rpt,* I, 3–4, 27–30; Hamilton, "Southern France," chs. 2–3; WNTF Rpt Southern France, pp. 14–15; and WNTF Opn Plan 4-44, 24 Jul 44, Annex A, Characteristics of Theater and Enemy Strength.

NORTH SEA

ENGLAND

LONDON

NETHERLANDS

GERMANY

Antwerp

BELGIUM

ENGLISH CHANNEL

LUX

Rhine R.

Cherbourg

Normandy

Seine R.

PARIS

Strasbourg

Brest

FRANCE

Brittany

Lorient

St. Nazaire

Tours

Loire R.

Dijon

Saone R.

SWITZERLAND

Geneva

La Rochelle

ITALY

BAY OF BISCAY

GIRONDE ESTUARY

Lyon

Grenoble

Bordeaux

Massif Central

Alps

Garonne R.

Rhone R.

Toulouse

Montpellier

Nice

Cannes

Marseille

Toulon

SPAIN

GULF OF THE LION

FRANCE

| | Highground |

0   100

MILES

Pyrenees

MAP 3   This map is printed in full color at the back of the book, following the Index.

South of Lyon the Rhone flows through alternating steep-sided narrow valleys and more gently sloping basins. Some of the basins give way on the east to corridors penetrating deeply into the Alps. At Avignon, some forty miles north of the Mediterranean, the Rhone enters a broad delta that, with lowlands along the eastern shore of the Gulf of the Lion, forms an arc of flat, often marshy, stream-cut ground stretching from the Pyrenees almost to Marseille.

The mountains east of the Rhone and south of Lyon consist of westward extensions of various Alpine ranges. Those close to the coastal area are loosely known as the Provence or Maritime Alps. In addition there are two non-Alpine coastal hill masses northeast of Toulon, the Massif des Maures on the west and the smaller Massif de l'Esterel on the east *(Map 4)*. The Maures massif extends inland nearly twenty miles; the Esterel scarcely seven. The Argens River valley separates the Massif des Maures from the Provence Alps to the north and forms an inland east-west corridor, about fifty miles long, between Toulon and St. Raphael on the Frejus gulf. From the town of Le Luc, in the center of the Toulon–St. Raphael corridor, another corridor leads west to Aix-en-Provence, twenty miles north of Marseille, and even farther to the Rhone delta in the region between Marseille and Avignon. Northeast of the Massif des Maures, the Massif de l'Esterel continues another ten miles to the vicinity of Cannes, east of which the rough Provence Alps drop sharply to the sea.

Allied planners knew that the best beaches for amphibious assaults and over-the-beach supply operations lay near Sete, far to the west of Marseille, and along the coasts west and east of Toulon. But the beaches between Sete and Marseille were backed by marshes, streams and canals, and land that the Germans could easily flood; those between Marseille and Toulon were generally poor and known to be most heavily defended; and the shores from Cannes to the Italian border led only into the rugged Provence Alps. Further investigation proved that the Sete area beaches would not fit all requirements. Offshore conditions were poor and port facilities limited, while the terrain eastward would inhibit military movement. In addition, all of the beaches west of Toulon were either out of range or at the extreme range of the XII Tactical Air Command's bases on Corsica.

Considering these factors, Allied planners quickly narrowed down their choices of a landing area to the coastline between Toulon and Cannes. This selection presupposed that Toulon would be the Seventh Army's first port objective, and that Toulon would have to meet Allied logistical requirements until Marseille fell. But the planners also made note of many minor ports along the coastal stretch northeast of Toulon that might supplement over-the-beach supply operations during the assault. The main ones were St. Tropez, on the narrow St. Tropez gulf about thirty-five miles northeast of Toulon; Ste. Maxime, on the same gulf five miles beyond St. Tropez; and St. Raphael, ten miles northeast of Ste. Maxime.

The ANVIL plan outlined by the AFHQ on December 1943 had origi-

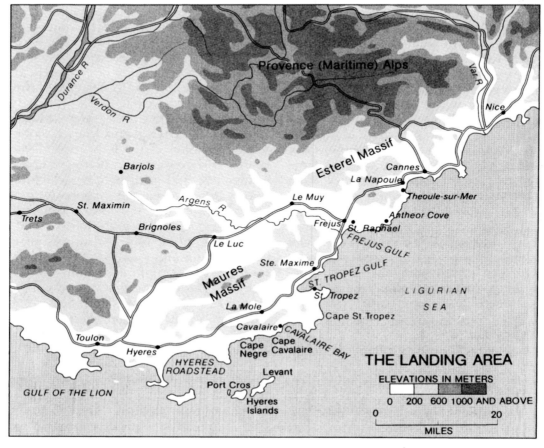

MAP 4   This map is printed in full color at the back of the book, following the Index.

nally designated the Hyeres Road-stead, about twelve miles east of Toulon, as the site for the main landings. At first glance, the AFHQ selection seemed logical. An open bay some ten miles wide, the area presented flat, extensive beaches with fine gradients and easy exits. It lay close to Toulon, and its flat hinterland was suitable for the rapid construction of airfields. One small operational field was already available only ten miles north of the beaches.

But further study convinced ground and naval planners that the Hyeres Roadstead was unsuitable. Both the roadstead and its beaches lay within easy range of German guns on the peninsulas flanking the bay or on the defended Hyeres Islands, the closest of which was only seven miles offshore. The beaches were also within range of German heavy artillery at Toulon. Moreover, the restricted waters between the Hyeres Islands and the mainland severely narrowed sea approaches to the beaches, which greatly complicated the projected naval bombardment and minesweeping operations, and in general caused a dangerous concentration of shipping in a fairly small area.

With no choice but to look farther east and northeast, planners from Seventh Army and Western Naval Task Force settled on the shoreline extending from Cape Cavalaire, thirty miles east of Toulon, northeastward almost another thirty miles to Antheor Cove, about eight miles beyond St. Raphael. Closer than the Hyeres Roadstead to supporting Allied airfields on Corsica, the Cape Cavalaire–Antheor Cove coast provided favorable approaches from the sea, contained several strands well suited to over-the-beach supply operations, included the principal minor ports, had a tidal range of only six inches to one foot, and offered potential airfield sites. The coastal region and its immediate hinterland also provided an acceptable base area from which to launch attacks westward toward Toulon and Marseille.

Despite these advantages, the Cape Cavalaire–Antheor Cove coast had several notable drawbacks. Its thirty miles of coastline, for example, translated into over fifty miles of irregular shoreline. Moreover, the potential landing sites were only moderately good to poor, and were separated by cliffs and rocky outcroppings. Almost all were backed by precipitous, dominating high ground—the highest sections of the Maures massif along most of the stretch, and the Esterel on the northeast. The Seventh Army would have to secure the high ground quickly to prevent the German Army from moving up reinforcements that might endanger the success of the landing or, at the very least, might occupy positions isolating the beaches from the interior. No planner wanted a repeat of the problems faced during the Anzio landings earlier in the year.

Beyond the beachline, more potential hazards existed. Many prospective beaches lacked good exits, and most could be economically blocked by German defenders. The approaches to Toulon were also limited, threatening to channel the advancing ground forces into two easily interdicted avenues—one along the coast and the other in the Toulon–St. Raphael corridor. The narrow coastal road could be blocked at many points, and the secondary highway between St. Raphael and Toulon was only marginally wider. Two railways—a narrow-gauge track skirting the beaches along the coast and the main standard-gauge line in the Toulon–St. Raphael corridor—added little; and the second- and third-class roads—many of which were in poor condition—that supplemented the main highways were often no more than a single lane wide and suitable for only light military traffic at best.

Operational Plans

The need to seize quickly the high ground that dominated the assault area, together with the requirement to develop supporting airfields rapidly, forced Seventh Army planners to map out a large projected beachhead area to be occupied as early as possible.[2]

---

[2] This subsection is based on the following: Seventh Army FO 1, 29 Jul 44; French Army B, Personal and Secret Memo on Opn DRAGOON, 6 Aug 44;

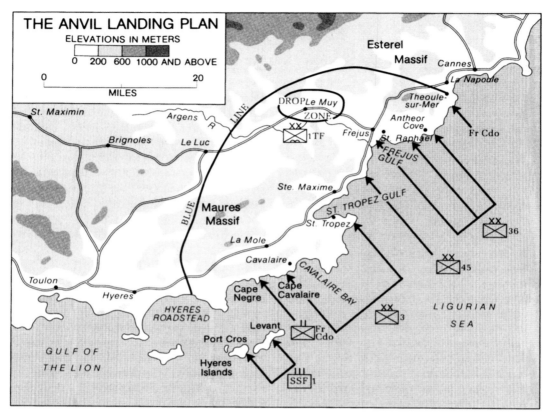

MAP 5   This map is printed in full color at the back of the book, following the Index.

The planned beachhead was to have a radius of roughly twenty miles from its center at Cape St. Tropez. On the southwest, the arc, or "blue line," began at the shores of the Hyeres Roadstead at Cape de Leoube, about eighteen miles southwest of Cape Cavalaire, curved in-land to a depth of about twenty miles, and curved back to the beach at La Napoule, eight miles north of Antheor Cove *(Map 5)*. The straight-line distance at the base of the

arc, the beachline, was roughly forty-five miles. Within the beachhead area lay three-quarters of the Massif des Maures, the entire Esterel, and the northeastern part of the Toulon–St. Raphael corridor. The blue line passed close to Le Luc, near the middle of the corridor, and included important sections of the main highways and railroads leading west and southwest toward Toulon, Marseille, and the Rhone River, as well as northeast toward Cannes and Nice.

Army planners believed that this projected beachhead had sufficient depth to protect the landing sites

VI Corps FO 1, 30 Jul 44; 3d Inf Div FO 12, 1 Aug 44; 36th Inf Div FO 53, 1 Aug 44; 45th Inf Div FO 1, 2 Aug 44; 1st ABTF FO 1, 5 Aug 44; and *Seventh Army Rpt*, I, 57–60, 106–10, 118–19.

from long-range German artillery; provided space for support airfields and adequately dispersed supply dumps; and gave the initial Allied ground combat units—the U.S. VI Corps and the leading echelons of the First French Army—enough area in which to maneuver. Seizing the terrain within the blue line would also provide the Seventh Army with high-ground anchors for its flanks as well as dominating heights along which Allied troops could prepare defenses against German counterattack. Ensconced along this high ground, Seventh Army forces could deny German access to the beachhead, while simultaneously preparing to break out in the direction of Toulon and Marseille.

After securing the landing beaches, the VI Corps had three primary missions: occupy all the terrain within the blue line as quickly as possible; protect the Seventh Army's right flank; and prepare to launch attacks to the west and northwest on order. Specific D-day tasks included capturing Le Muy, some ten miles inland along the Argens River valley west of St. Raphael; making contact with the 1st Airborne Task Force in the vicinity of Le Muy; and moving out from both flanks of the beachhead to link up with French commandos, who were to land beyond the limits of the main assault beaches.

The 1st Airborne Task Force and French commando assaults, as well as landings by the 1st Special Service Force, were to precede the VI Corps landings. Seventh Army plans had originally called for scattered paratroop drops; but, on the advice of Generals Frederick and Williams, respectively commanding the airborne

"division" and the troop carrier aircraft, Patch agreed to concentrate the drops in the vicinity of Le Muy, where the paratroopers were to begin their jumps well before first light on D-day. The 1st Airborne Task Force's main mission was to prevent German movements into the beach area from the direction of Le Muy and Le Luc through the Argens River corridor. The paratroopers were also to clear the Le Muy area, securing it for subsequent glider landings.

Colonel Walker's 1st Special Service Force was to land about midnight of 14–15 August on the two easternmost Hyeres Islands, Port Cros and Levant. Lying just south of Cape Cavalaire, the two islands were believed to shelter numerous German artillery batteries that controlled the approaches to VI Corps' westernmost beaches. Their early capture was imperative.

Shortly after the 1st Special Service Force started ashore, the French African Commando Group was to make its assault on the mainland at Cape Negre, just north of the two islands and five miles west of Cape Cavalaire. After destroying any German coastal defenses in the area, the commandos were to establish roadblocks along the coastal highway, secure high ground up to two miles inland from the cape, and forestall any German efforts to move against VI Corps' beaches from the west. Meanwhile, at the opposite end of the beachline, the small French Naval Assault Group was to land at Trayas Point, about four miles northeast of Antheor Cove, and block the coastal highway on VI Corps' right, or northeastern, flank.

H-hour for the main landings over

the Cape Cavalaire–Antheor Cove beaches was set for 0800, considerably later than had been the case during earlier amphibious operations in the Mediterranean. The hour selected represented a compromise between two conflicting demands. On the one hand, the preassault air and naval forces required sufficient daylight to permit observed and accurate bombardment of German beach defenses. But the landings also had to begin early enough to move sufficient troops and supplies ashore, establish a firm beachhead, and penetrate into the high ground behind the beaches to prevent a German counterattack.

The landing plan originally agreed to by the Seventh Army and the Western Naval Task Force called for putting the 36th Infantry Division ashore on the left, the 45th in the center, and the 3d on the right.[3] This plan also allocated all of the larger amphibious assault vessels, such as LSTs, LCTs, and LCIs, to the 3d and 36th Divisions, leaving the 45th Division to be loaded onto troop transports and landed by small craft and amphibious trucks (DUKWs) over a number of small beaches along the northern and southern shores of the St. Tropez gulf.

After VI Corps entered into the planning process, Patch's staff made several changes in the plan at the insistence of Truscott, the corps commander. Truscott wanted to land his most experienced division, the 3d, on the left so that he could quickly con-

centrate it to form an offensive spearhead for a drive on Toulon. His least experienced unit, the 36th, he felt, should be put ashore on his right, giving the division a primarily defensive mission. Furthermore, he requested that his central division, now the 45th, be landed and concentrated in the vicinity of Ste. Maxime. Truscott also asked that the amphibious resources be more evenly distributed, allowing two regimental combat teams from each division to be landed by small amphibious craft and LSTs. Finally, he wanted the blue line pulled in slightly on the west, fearing that the original beachhead area would force him to overextend to the west and thus prevent him from massing for an early drive on Toulon. Both Patch and Admiral Hewitt readily agreed to these modifications.

Truscott was less successful in persuading Hewitt to undertake operations against German underwater obstacles believed to be in the landing areas. The corps commander requested that naval forces conduct a thorough reconnaissance of all beaches before the assault, and destroy whatever obstacles might be discovered. Hewitt disagreed, judging that the great difficulties created by underwater obstacles during the OVERLORD assault would not be a factor in ANVIL. The scant tidal range along the Cape Cavalaire–Antheor Cove coast would not provide the Germans with the opportunity to construct such formidable obstacles as had the great tidal variations along the Normandy beachheads. Hewitt also felt that a detailed preassault reconnaissance would only risk revealing the projected landing sites. Thus he

---

[3] Subsequent information on the change of landing plans comes from WNTF Rpt Southern France, p. 18; *Seventh Army Rpt*, I, 46–48, 56–57; Truscott, *Command Missions*, pp. 388–91; and Hamilton, "Southern France," ch. 9.

turned down the request.

Studying all available information, VI Corps, Seventh Army, and Western Naval Task Force settled on nine separate assault beaches for VI Corps. The nature of the terrain in the assault area, combined with known or suspected German defensive installations and potential German routes of counterattack, resulted in an undesirable but necessary separation of the assault beaches. Some, for example, were as much as eight miles from their nearest neighbor. Varying from 80 to 4,500 yards in width, and from 10 to 50 yards in depth, each beach presented individual problems. Nevertheless, Allied planners believed that they had no choice but to accept the risks such separations presented.

On the left, the 3d Infantry Division was to land across beaches in the Cavalaire Bay–St. Tropez region. The division's first two regiments were to be put ashore in the Cavalaire Bay and St. Tropez areas, with the third regiment following in the Cavalaire Bay sector. Thereafter the division was to clear the St. Tropez peninsula, which separated Cavalaire Bay from the St. Tropez gulf; seize St. Tropez and the town of Cavalaire; secure the Cavalaire–St. Tropez road; and, upon corps orders, strike west toward the blue line and Toulon.

The 45th Division in the center was also to send two regiments ashore in the assault, landing them abreast about two miles northeast of Ste. Maxime. Its third regiment was to follow the others ashore, but was to be committed only with Truscott's permission. On the morning of D-day the 45th was to capture Ste. Maxime and nearby high ground, move north

and northeast to clear the shoreline and hills for two miles inland, and drive to the Argens River, about eight miles north of Ste. Maxime.

On the right, the 36th Division was to land only one regiment at H-hour, putting it ashore on a broad beachline about four miles east of St. Raphael, with one infantry battalion to make its assault at Antheor Cove, three miles farther away. A second regiment was to follow the first ashore over the beaches east of St. Raphael, while plans called for the third to land at 1400 farther west between the mouth of the Argens River and St. Raphael. Planners estimated that elements of the 45th Division would be in position south of the Argens to support the 36th Division's last regiment in the Frejus gulf region. If for some reason it proved impossible to make the afternoon assault north of the Argens, the 36th Division's third regiment would also go ashore at the main landing beaches to the east.

The 36th Division's most pressing mission was to protect Seventh Army's right flank, a task that entailed a rapid drive to the northern end of the blue line at La Napoule. The division's other missions included seizing St. Raphael; capturing Frejus, two miles west of St. Raphael; advancing inland along the Argens valley to join elements of the 1st Airborne Task Force; and, if the airborne units were unable to do so, clearing Le Muy and its environs.

Combat Command Sudre (CC Sudre) of the French 1st Armored Division was to land on D-day over 36th Division beaches, assemble in the Frejus area, and prepare to strike westward through the Argens valley. Initially, the French armor was to serve as the VI Corps' reserve and exploitation force. But before the end of July, Truscott had become dissatisfied with arrangements for his control over CC Sudre, the only homogeneous armored unit under his command.[4] The First French Army expected the return of this brigade-sized armored force as soon as significant French forces were assembled ashore, probably by D plus 3. De Lattre wanted Sudre's armor to protect the French right, or northern, flank during his subsequent attacks against Toulon and Marseille and to provide armored strength against any German panzer units that might counterattack the French. Since Seventh Army could not promise that VI Corps would retain CC Sudre past D plus 3,[5] Truscott decided on 1 August to organize a light mechanized combat command from American forces assigned to the VI Corps. The unit, later designated Task Force Butler (TF Butler),[6] included one cavalry squadron, two tank companies, one battalion of motorized infantry, and supporting artillery, tank destroyers, and other ancillary forces. Truscott placed the provisional unit under Brig. Gen. Frederick B. Butler, the VI Corps deputy commander, and initially viewed it as a substitute for CC

Sudre, assigning it the relatively limited mission of assembling in the vicinity of Le Muy and preparing to attack either west or northwest on corps orders. In addition, its late organization precluded its loading as a separate entity, and the task force was not scheduled to be assembled at the beach area until D plus 2.

If all went according to plan on D-day, the vanguard units of First French Army were to start landing over U.S. 3d Infantry Division beaches on the VI Corps' left flank on D plus 1. The early arrivals were to include the French 1st Infantry Division, the 3d Algerian Infantry Division (less one regiment), and the French 1st Armored Division (less CC Sudre and another combat command). Plans also called for the 9th Colonial Infantry Division, with two Moroccan Tabor Regiments (light infantry) attached, to arrive by D plus 9, but the rest of the French II Corps, including the last elements of the 1st Armored Division, were not to reach southern France until D plus 25.

After assembling on shore, the leading French units, strengthened by CC Sudre, were to pass through the VI Corps left wing and strike for Toulon, which Seventh Army hoped would fall by D plus 20, 4 September. Following the seizure of Toulon, the French were to move against Marseille, simultaneously preparing to strike northwest toward the Rhone at Avignon. Marseille, Allied planners estimated, would probably not be in French hands until D plus 40 to 45, or about 25 September.

A final aspect of the ANVIL ground plan concerned the French Forces of the Interior (FFI). Seventh Army,

---

[4] Additional information about CC Sudre and TF Butler in this subsection is from Truscott, *Command Missions*, pp. 403–07; and de Lattre, *History*, pp. 55, 74–75.

[5] By the same token, Patch would not promise de Lattre to return the CC Sudre to French control by D plus 3, as de Lattre had requested before the landings.

[6] The official VI Corps designation for TF Butler was Provisional Armored Group, VI Corps.

acting in concert with General Cochet, the FFI director for southern France, and with Special Projects Operations Group at AFHQ, assigned the FFI a series of missions designed to hamper German movement into the ANVIL assault area and to assist Allied advances throughout that area. First, FFI forces were to destroy bridges, cut railroad lines, and block highways. Next, they were to try to create major diversions inland in order to disperse or pin down German forces that might otherwise mass for counterattacks against the beachhead. Third, the guerrillas were to cut telephone and telegraphic communications systems throughout southern France. Fourth, the FFI was to attack German fuel and ammunition dumps, sabotage German airfields, and engage isolated German garrisons and small units. Finally, they were to prepare to conduct tactical combat operations on the flanks of whatever routes the Allied assault divisions might use in breaking out of the beachhead.

Air and Naval Support Plans

Although Allied planners were confident that German forces in southern France would be unable to prevent a successful lodgment along the Cape Cavalaire–Antheor Cove coastline, the planners also knew that the cost of the landing, as well as the speed of VI Corps' advance inland to the blue line, would depend largely upon the efficacy of the preassault air and naval bombardment.[7] The success of the French drives against Toulon and Marseille would likewise depend heavily on air and naval support. The most dangerous threat, however, was the ability of the German defenders to assemble enough forces for an effective counterattack on the beachhead. The ultimate success of ANVIL would thus hinge a great deal on the efforts of the air arm, with assistance from the FFI, to isolate the landing area.

Air attacks at least indirectly related to ANVIL had been under way for many months before 15 August as part of the Mediterranean Allied Air Forces' general program of operations. Moreover, MAAF operations in support of OVERLORD, although designed mainly to slow German redeployments to northern France, also contributed to ANVIL. However, from 2 July to 5 August MAAF was able to devote relatively little effort to southern France because of the demands of ground operations in Italy as well as the priority given to strikes against German oil and rail facilities in eastern and southeastern Europe. During July, air attacks over southern France were directed primarily against German naval installations at Toulon, various rail centers, and bridges over the Rhone and Var rivers (the latter between Cannes and Nice). At the same time, air operations in support of the FFI were stepped up.

The first phase of an air campaign more directly associated with ANVIL began on 5 August. From 5 to 9 August, MAAF's primary missions were to neutralize *Luftwaffe* units in

---

[7] This subsection is based on *Seventh Army Rpt*, I, 45–56, 60–62, 101–05; AAF III, 416, 420–28; WNTF Rpt Southern France; and Hamilton, "Southern France," ch. 9.

southern France and northwestern Italy, interdict German communications between Sete and Genoa, and attack German submarine bases. From 10 August to approximately 0350 on the 15th, MAAF was to pay special attention to German coastal defenses, radar stations, troop emplacements, and communications. This phase was to culminate on the 14th with especially heavy attacks against overland communications and selected bridges. The final phase of the preassault aerial bombardment was to begin at first light (approximately 0550) on D-day and last until 0730. During this last effort air attacks were to be concentrated against coastal guns, beach defenses, underwater obstacles, and troop installations.

MAAF had adopted the program of bombing German coastal defenses in the Cape Cavalaire–Antheor Cove area before D-day with some reluctance. Air planners felt that, to ensure tactical surprise at the assault beaches, the coastal bombardments should extend from the Spanish border all the way around to the Italian coast southeast of Genoa. General Eaker, commanding MAAF, believed that, in conjunction with the naval bombardment on D-day, air attacks could destroy all significant shore defenses in the assault area in less than two days, that is, D minus 1 and the morning of D-day.

Both Patch and Truscott, concerned that surprise not be lost, were inclined to agree with Eaker's estimate. But Navy planners were not so optimistic. Admirals Cunningham and Hewitt, for example, felt that an air bombardment limited to D minus 1 and D-day, even in conjunction with

strong naval shelling, could not effectively neutralize German coastal defenses in the area. Instead, the Navy held that a more complete destruction of German coast defenses, including radar installations, would at least partially compensate for the loss of tactical surprise. They also pointed out that concentrated air attacks on D minus 1 and D-day would probably alert the Germans to the location of the assault beaches in any case. Moreover, a concentration of air effort in the Cape Cavalaire–Antheor Cove area on D minus 1 might start forest and supply dump fires, the smoke from which could obscure targets ashore for the crucial air and naval bombardments of D-day morning.

Taking the Navy concerns into consideration, Seventh Army and MAAF agreed to stretch out the planned air campaign, with one proviso. To avoid the risk of disclosing to the Germans the selected assault beaches early in the game, Eaker insisted that his command would divide its efforts more or less equally among four potential landing areas between 5 and 13 August: Sete and vicinity, the Toulon-Marseille region, the Cape Cavalaire–Antheor Cove coastline, and the Genoa area.

The D-day air and naval attacks presented some equally complex problems for the planners. To be effective, the bombardments would have to start just after first light, but air strikes would have to cease early enough to allow smoke and dust to settle, thus providing better visibility for the final naval bombardment. In addition, the time allocated to naval gunfire could not be too long, for the naval forces in the Mediterranean possessed but limited supplies of ammunition for their larger guns. Bombardment vessels would have to conserve some ammunition to support operations ashore after the assault.

Planners ultimately decided that the last concentrated air strikes should start at 0610 and end at 0730, when the naval gunfire support ships were to begin a final, drenching shelling of the assault beaches. From 0650 to 0730 naval bombardment was to be limited to carefully selected targets in the assault area (and mainly to its flanks), and this was to be lifted when MAAF bombers were striking the beaches. Such an arrangement demanded especially tight coordination of air and naval operations. From 0610 to 0730 fighters and bombers were to give first priority to German artillery positions, and second priority to German installations that might block the advance inland. The air strikes were to give special attention to any German weapons that could not be reached by the relatively flat trajectory of naval gunfire. The half hour (0730–0800) left for the final naval bombardment was a considerably shorter period than normally needed for most amphibious assaults, especially in the Pacific, but the circumstances of the ANVIL assault left little choice. In effect, the concentrated air bombardment early on D-day would have to substitute for more extended naval gunfire.

In addition to its responsibilities for landing and supporting the assault forces, Western Naval Task Force also had the mission of conducting a series of diversionary operations. Task Group 80.4, the Special Operations Group, was to make two such efforts. Starting from Corsica on D minus 1, on a course headed toward Genoa, one section of the group was to swing northwest about midnight to create diversions in the Cannes-Nice area. MAAF planes, dropping various types of artificial targets, were to help the naval contingent to simulate a much larger force. A westerly naval unit, simulating a convoy twelve miles long and eight miles wide, was to operate meanwhile along the coast between Toulon and Marseille. MAAF was to add to the confusion by dropping dummy parachutists in the same region.

The final arrangements for air and naval bombardment, the selection of H-hour, and the type of landings thus represented marked departures from previous amphibious operations in the Mediterranean. ANVIL's H-hour was considerably later than was usual in the Mediterranean, where previous landings had taken place under cover of darkness. But earlier assaults in the Mediterranean had been directed against unfortified and virtually undefended coasts. Accordingly, for the first time in Mediterranean experience, planners had to arrange heavy, concentrated air and naval bombardment before H-hour on D-day. Finally, the air bombardment plan for D-day demanded that heavy bombers execute mass takeoffs during the hours of darkness, another first in the Mediterranean theater, in order to reach their objectives on schedule.

Beyond D-day

Until early August, the Seventh Army had no firm plans for the campaign following the seizure of the beachhead and the capture of Toulon and Marseille. The ANVIL directive from AFHQ directing Patch's forces to exploit northward up the Rhone toward Lyon was extremely vague. Estimated German resistance, together with the logistical problems involved in supporting large forces in southern France until the port of Toulon at least became operational, made it appear that Seventh Army and First French Army forces would not be ready to strike north along the axis of the Rhone much before 15 October. In early June, well before OVERLORD began, Mediterranean planners believed that it might even be mid-November before Patch and de Lattre had control over the Rhone valley from the Mediterranean north to Lyon. More detailed plans for future operations therefore were not an immediate concern.

But as June and July passed and Allied intelligence officers tallied the German withdrawals from southern France, prospects for more rapid progress grew accordingly. At AFHQ, Wilson foresaw a possibility that a weakened *Army Group G*, failing to contain Seventh Army's beachhead or to hold Toulon, would concentrate on the defense of Marseille and the approaches to the Rhone. In such a case, *Army Group G* might leave the area east of Marseille and the Rhone River valley nearly undefended. Available information indicated that the Germans had only one understrength division scattered about this eastern flank area, a region where, the Allies knew, the FFI was strong and active.

With this information, Wilson, on 11 August, proposed two new courses

of action.[8] First, he suggested that the Seventh Army could strike northwest directly from the beachhead to the Rhone north of Avignon, leaving only minimum forces in the Marseille area to secure the left and to contain German units in the Rhone delta. A second possibility was to strike generally north from the beachhead through the Provence Alps toward the Grenoble area, over one hundred miles north of Toulon.

Wilson apparently regarded the proposed thrust to Grenoble primarily as a means of protecting the Seventh Army's right flank and stimulating FFI activity east of the Rhone. But Patch and particularly Truscott saw in Wilson's suggestions an opportunity to exploit whatever weaknesses might be found in German defenses between the Rhone and the Italian and Swiss frontiers. For such purposes, Truscott already had an exploitation force available, TF Butler. Although he had originally planned to employ it only in a limited role, its missions could be easily expanded if the situation warranted.

The VI Corps commander subsequently drew up tentative plans to rush TF Butler to the Durance River as soon as the force could assemble ashore. His plans allowed for two possible thrusts: one to cross the Durance River and strike west for the Rhone near Avignon; or, alternatively, another to drive on north toward Grenoble. The latter maneuver, Truscott thought, could develop either

_____
[8] Material on final operational planning is from Memo, SACMED to CG Seventh Army, 11 Aug 44, sub: Opn DRAGOON; Min, SACMED (and AFHQ Joint Plng Staff) Mtg, 10 Aug 44 (both in AFHQ files); and Truscott, *Command Missions*, p. 407.

into a swing west to cut the Rhone valley between Avignon and Lyon, or into a drive through Grenoble to Lyon. With quick success by TF Butler, VI Corps would be in a position to outflank German defenses along the lower Rhone and to block an *Army Group G* withdrawal up the Rhone valley. But the feasibility of such projects depended on the speed with which the Seventh Army reached the blue line, the strength of opposition in the beachhead area, and *Army Group G*'s reaction to the ANVIL assault.

Allied Intelligence

Because of the prodigious Allied information collection effort, including the highly secret ULTRA intercept program, the Seventh Army had a reasonably accurate picture both of the organization and strength of the German forces in the ANVIL assault area and of German deployments all along the Mediterranean coasts of France and Italy.[9] The main problem facing intelligence personnel was to keep up to date with the constant movement of German units in and out of southern France since OVERLORD began. Due to the frequency of these movements, the Seventh Army did not have completely accurate information on the specific location of German corps and division command

posts in the assault area; and information on units at and near the assault beaches, while generally correct, was sometimes erroneous in detail. Despite these shortcomings, however, the information available was fairly complete and accurate.

Seventh Army intelligence estimates placed German strength in the coastal sector from the Rhone delta east to the Italian border at approximately 115,000 troops, a figure that was probably too high by at least 15,000. On paper, the Germans appeared to have sufficient force to put up a strong defense, but the Seventh Army knew that many German units were not up to strength and that many others were second-rate formations. German coastal defenses were known to be fairly strong in some locations but quite weak in others, and available information indicated that the defenses lacked depth. Once Allied forces pushed through the narrow belt of German coastal defenses, Seventh Army planners felt that they would encounter few other prepared defensive installations except at Toulon and Marseille. Seventh Army intelligence estimated the German Toulon garrison at 10,000 troops and the Marseille defenders at 15,000 (actually, the Germans had 13,000 men at Toulon and 18,000 at Marseille). The garrisons were known to include not only German Army infantry and artillery, but also engineer, antiaircraft, and fortress troops, communications and supply units, and various naval personnel.

The Allies also knew that there would be little danger from German air and naval forces. ANVIL planners put *Luftwaffe* strength in southern

[9] This subsection is based mainly on Seventh Army G-2 records, Jul–Aug 44; Annex 1, Intel, to VI Corps FO 1, 30 Jul 44, and Amend 1, 7 Aug 44; Annex A, Characteristics of Theater and Enemy Strength, to WNTF Opn Plan 4-44, 24 Jul 44; and French Army B, Personal and Secret Directive No. 1 on Operation DRAGOON, 6 Aug 44, in Annex II of de Lattre, *Histoire* (French language edition).

France around 250 aircraft, of which less than two-thirds would be operational on 15 August. Considering the demands of the current battles in northern France and Italy, they expected that the *Luftwaffe* would not be able to send any significant reinforcements to southern France and that its operations during the landings would be limited to scattered torpedo-bomber attacks and some night mine-laying sorties, with fighters probably used for air defense only.

Admiral Hewitt's staff considered German naval strength in southern France insignificant. With approximately one destroyer, seven corvettes, five torpedo boats, five or six submarines, and miscellaneous small auxiliaries—and it was doubtful that the destroyer or the submarines were operational—they deemed the Germans incapable of significant offensive action at sea.

The Allies had no expectation of achieving strategic surprise. Believing that German aerial reconnaissance would have discovered the obvious preparations for a major amphibious assault, they correctly estimated that the Germans would expect the attack to come along the French Riviera as opposed to the Atlantic or Ligurian coasts. On the other hand, Seventh Army hoped to achieve some degree of operational and tactical surprise concerning the exact time and place of the landings. But keeping the 15 August target date a secret was difficult. The need to coordinate FFI operations with the assault considerably increased the potential for compromising security, while the final air bombardment would also give away the time and place of the landings.

But with the many deception efforts undertaken, the Allied planners felt reasonably confident that the Germans would be unsure of the precise date and location of ANVIL until 14 August, and even then the defenders would not be completely certain until the Allied landing craft were actually sighted heading toward the shore. In addition, Seventh Army planners believed that *Army Group G* would not be able to oppose the initial landings effectively nor those of the French follow-up divisions.

The main problem facing Allied intelligence officers was ascertaining the German response once the Seventh Army was ashore. They estimated that neither *OB West* nor *OB Southwest* would be able to reinforce *Army Group G* after the ANVIL assault. Nevertheless, they believed that *Army Group G*'s most probable course of action would be to try to contain the Allied beachhead by attempting to hold the Massif des Maures. But given the current disposition of German forces, Seventh Army also believed that the defenders would be unable to redeploy enough strength into the Maures to secure the range before French and American forces could move inland and occupy the terrain. Faced with strong Allied forces in the hills above the beachline, the Germans would probably fall back on the defenses of Toulon and Marseille. From Toulon the Germans could pose a serious threat to Allied lines of communication, inhibiting all westward advances toward the Rhone valley. Moreover, the Germans undoubtedly recognized the logistical importance of the port cities to the Allies. The longer the Germans held on to Toulon and Marseille, the more difficult it would be for the Seventh Army to project its combat power far from the landing beaches.

Should the Germans fail to hold the two major ports for an extended period, Seventh Army planners estimated that *Army Group G* would withdraw up the Rhone valley, making temporary stands at successive delaying positions. However, they considered it unlikely that the Germans would start withdrawing up the Rhone valley until *Army Group G* had begun to exhaust its defensive potential in the coastal sector. This depletion, Seventh Army estimated, would probably not occur until the fall of Toulon, expected about 5 September.

The Role of ULTRA

During these discussions the Seventh Army intelligence staff undoubtedly benefited greatly from the information derived from ULTRA, code name of the now Anglo-American operation for intercepting, decoding, and disseminating the radio communications of the German high command. Raw ULTRA information would in fact be available to the principal American commanders in southern France—Generals Devers, Patch, and Truscott[10]—and to their main staff officers throughout the entire campaign. When correlated with other intelligence, this data usually gave them a fairly good idea of the opposing order of battle, that is, the

strength and location of the major German units opposing them. This picture, in turn, enabled them to have a better understanding of German military capabilities and intentions. In a few cases, ULTRA intercepts even provided Allied commanders with critical German orders almost before the designated recipients had received them in the field.

ULTRA, however, also had its drawbacks and limitations. First, raw intelligence was often of limited value until it could be correlated with other information sources—prisoner of war reports, air reconnaissance, captured documents, and observations of tactical ground units on the battlefield. Second, many key military decisions were made by the Germans during command conferences, and detailed plans were normally hand-carried by staff liaison officers, with little of this information ever being transmitted directly through wireless communications. As a result, ULTRA was often mute regarding specific German intentions. In addition, both *OKW* and *OB West,* and even Hitler, sometimes gave field commanders a wide degree of latitude in carrying out their missions (or sometimes orders were ignored), further reducing the value of ULTRA in revealing specific German operational and tactical intentions. Finally, the time between the interception of a radio transmission and its arrival in a decoded, translated format at the field commands was normally about twelve to twenty-four hours, or longer depending on the significance of the message. For this reason ULTRA information was less useful during fluid combat situations; moreover, it was often only of limited

---

[10] Although corps commanders were normally not privy to ULTRA information, Truscott had been a recipient during the Anzio campaign, and various references in his *Command Missions* indicate that he still received information via Patch.

value at division and lower echelons where highly perishable tactical intelligence often arrived too late to be significant. Thus, although ULTRA was of undisputed value in outlining the general German military situation on the battlefield, it in no way obviated the need for Allied intelligence staffs to rely on a wide variety of information sources concerning their opponents and to continue their traditional but time-consuming analysis efforts to turn that information into intelligence useful to the operational and tactical commanders on the battlefield.[11]

---

[11] For background documents on ULTRA, see the NSA/CSS Cryptologic Documents collection in Record Group (RG) 457, NARA, especially SRH–023, "Reports by U.S. Army ULTRA Representatives with Army Field Commands in the European Theatre (sic) of Operations, 1945," Part II, Tab F, Memo, Maj Warner W. Gardner to Col Taylor, Office of the Military Attache, England, 19 May 45, sub: Ultra Intelligence at Sixth U.S. Army Group (hereafter cited as Gardner ULTRA Report); and Tab G, Memo, Maj Donald S. Bussey to Col Taylor, Office of the Military Attache, England, 12 May 45, sub: Ultra and the U.S. Seventh Army (hereafter cited as the Bussey ULTRA Report). A large though incomplete collection of the messages that had first been encoded by the German ENIGMA enciphering machine and then intercepted, decoded, and translated by the Allied ULTRA intelligence-gathering program has been published by the British Public Records Office and is available at the U.S. Army Military History Institute, Carlisle Barracks, PA, on microfilm, but without any finding aids. The data does not show interception date-time groups for the original ENIGMA intercepts, and thus messages cited from this collection note only the sequential decoding number and date-time group of the transmission of the decoded, translated message to the field. However, since decoded intercepts were sent directly from England to special communications units (SCUs) in the field and passed directly to special liaison units (SLUs) on the staffs of the major commands for limited dissemination, and since the SCUs and SLUs destroyed all copies of these records almost immediately, it is virtually impossible for the historian to document the arrival of specific messages and ascertain their disposition. Interv, Clarke with Col Donald S. Bussey (Ret) (the former

Finally, to put ULTRA in perspective, the contribution of the Office of Strategic Services (OSS) intelligence networks established in southern France under Henry Hyde should also be noted. Based in French North Africa, Hyde's organizing effort began approximately one year before the invasion; the final OSS network included about 2,500 intelligence agents throughout the area held by *Army Group G.* These agents usually communicated information on German military forces to the central OSS headquarters in North Africa through an extensive and elaborate secret radio system, and smuggled maps, overlays, sketches, drawings, photographs, and similar material through Spain. Hyde himself worked closely with the Seventh Army G–2 (assistant chief of staff for intelligence), Col. William W. Quinn, and Quinn even made special arrangements so that he could receive OSS reports at sea during the voyage to the assault area. From these agent reports, the Seventh Army was able to piece together an even more detailed picture of German dispositions and strength. In fact, on 13 August, just before the actual landings, a French OSS agent, bicycling from Cannes to Hyeres, made a final survey of the landing

---

Seventh Army SLU chief), 19 Aug 87; interv, Alexander S. Cochran, Jr., with Bussey, "Protecting the Ultimate Advantage," *Military History Magazine* (June 1985), 42–47 (original draft of interview at CMH); and Funk, "Intelligence and Operation ANVIL/DRAGOON." A good secondary treatment of ULTRA is Ralph Bennett, *Ultra in the West* (New York: Scribners, 1980), which supplements the official *British Intelligence in the Second World War,* III, Part 2, by F. H. Hinsley et al. (London: HMSO, 1988). Both cite ENIGMA date-time groups for the interception of key ULTRA messages, information that is currently still unavailable to the general public.

areas; the report was quickly cabled to Quinn aboard the Seventh Army's command ship, making any last-minute surprises on the assault beaches extremely unlikely. Later, at the request of Patch and Quinn, the OSS assigned intelligence teams (from the Strategic Services Section, or SSS) to each of the American combat divisions, and the organization continued to provide order-of-battle information to the Seventh Army staffs throughout the ensuing campaign.[12] ULTRA was thus only one of many Allied intelligence sources used by the Seventh Army, and only in extremely rare instances would it provide information that could not have been obtained elsewhere.

Final Assault Preparations

Because the Seventh Army did not gain control over most ANVIL ground assault units until late June—and some French units not until late July—the time available for final training, rehearsals, loading, and logistical preparations was limited.[13] On the other hand, many of the assault units already possessed ample amphibious experience, and most of the remainder had acquired extensive

combat experience in Italy, all of which eased the compressed tactical planning, training, and loading requirements.

ANVIL training emphasized amphibious loading and unloading procedures including small craft embarkation and debarkation, ship and vehicle loading, the operations of joint Army-Navy fire control parties, the tactical command and control problems peculiar to assault landings, and other related matters. Special attention was also given to the destruction of underwater and beach obstacles. In addition, the estimated strength of German beach defenses demanded that some sort of armored support move ashore with the assault waves. Lacking "amtracks"—the armored, tracked landing vehicles that played a critical role in most Pacific amphibious assaults during World War II—the Seventh Army had to train selected elements of medium tank battalions in the operation of the floatable but less stable duplex-drive (DD) tanks available in the European theater.[14] The assault plan called for each

---

[12] On supporting OSS operations, see U.S. War Department, *The Overseas Targets: War Report of the OSS (Office of Strategic Services)*, II (New York: Walker, 1976), 166–77 183, 187–90, 200, 204–05, 223–48; MS, William J. Casey, "Up the Route Napoleon," pp. 3–10 (copy at CMH; hereafter cited as Casey MS); Casey, *The Secret War Against Hitler* (Washington, D.C.: Regnery Gateway, 1988), pp. 133–37. Bicyclers with similar tasks were undoubtedly touring all possible Mediterranean landing sites to provide a cover for the actual reconnaissance.

[13] This section is based primarily on *Seventh Army Rpt*, I, 71–89; WNTF Rpt Southern France, pp. 166–73; and TF 87 Rpt Southern France, p. 1.

[14] Amtracks included landing vehicles, tracked (LVTs), and landing vehicles tracked, armored (LVT[A]s); with their high freeboard, they were crucial for the Pacific Ocean assault beaches, which normally exhibited much greater wave turbulence than those located on the European coasts. Not as satisfactory at sea but better once ashore, the DDs were Sherman medium tanks that achieved flotation by means of heavy canvas coverings attached to the lower hull. Raised mechanically, the coverings permitted the DD tanks to disgorge from LCTs and make their way shoreward, using propellers attached to standard truck differentials (and mounted on the tank's sprocket hubs) to move the cumbersome vehicles through the water. Since these machines were especially vulnerable to underwater mines or obstacles that could put holes in the canvas coverings, their crews were trained in the use of the Monsen Lung, a submarine escape device.

45TH INFANTRY DIVISION TROOPS LOAD UP AT BAGNOLI, ITALY, *August 1944.*

division to set eight DDs ashore at the time of or immediately after the first landing waves.

Much of the training for the assault units took place at Seventh Army's Invasion Training Center near Salerno, Italy, although the 3d Division ran its own school at Pozzouli. Participating in the training and directing most of the final phases were elements of Western Naval Task Force. The three VI Corps divisions undertook final rehearsals along the Italian coast between 31 July and 6 August. Although the training of the tactical ground units was fairly complete and realistic, the lack of time made it impossible to undertake more than token unload-

ings of vehicles and cargo, while some landing ships and other vessels reached the Mediterranean so late that they could not participate in the final rehearsals. In addition, although MAAF aircraft undertook limited air support operations, training staffs were unable to incorporate naval gunfire into the rehearsals, and the nine days remaining between the completion of the rehearsals and the assault were not enough for extended critiques and remedial instruction. However, the previous experience of most VI Corps units in amphibious operations had to substitute for more extended training.

The 1st Special Service Force start-

ANVIL CONVOY EN ROUTE TO SOUTHERN FRANCE, AUGUST 1944

ed its training in early July south of Salerno, emphasizing the use of rubber assault boats, scaling of cliffs, and attacks on fixed defenses. The force undertook final rehearsals on islands off the Italian coast during the night of 7–8 August—rehearsals that, Colonel Walker later reported, were far more rugged than the actual assaults on the Hyeres Islands. The French commandos received similar training elsewhere.

Many paratroop elements of the 1st Airborne Task Force had received refresher training on Sicily during May, and thus preassault preparations focused on unit training, with special attention to ground tactical operations. A shortage of parachutes in the theater precluded final rehearsal jumps, but all glider units undertook at least one flight and landing. The entire task force limited its final rehearsal to a ground exercise near Rome, and completed its preparations for ANVIL by 12 August.

Final loading and staging for all seaborne elements began on 8 August. Most VI Corps assault units loaded at Naples and Salerno, but CC Sudre of the French 1st Armored Division came from Oran in North Africa. The French 1st Infantry Division and the 3d Algerian Infantry Division staged at Brindisi and Taranto, ports on Italy's heel, as did a few smaller French units. The 9th Colonial Infantry Division and a Moroccan Tabor regiment boarded ship from Corsica, and most MAAF units staged on Corsica. The rest of First French Army, scheduled to arrive much later, was to be shipped from Italy and North Africa.

The loading from scattered ports, the need to keep shipping within range of land-based air cover, the varying speeds of the vessels of the assault convoys, naval diversionary operations, and the pre–H-hour assaults by the 1st Special Service Force and French commandos combined to force Western Naval Task Force to set up a complex convoy schedule. Each separate group of ships and landing craft had to move along carefully prescribed routes to make the rendezvous with other groups at selected times and points. All VI Corps assault units aboard LCTs and LCIs, together with the 1st Special Service Force on American APDs and British LSIs, also had to complete their final staging on Corsica.

The final D-day convoys comprised approximately 885 ships and landing craft sailing under their own power. On the decks of this armada were loaded nearly 1,375 smaller landing craft. Exclusive of naval crews, the convoys carried roughly 151,000 troops and some 21,400 trucks, tanks, tank destroyers, prime-movers, bulldozers, tractors, and other vehicles. Included in these totals were about 40,850 men and 2,610 vehicles of the First French Army that were to start unloading on D plus 1. After a few minor problems in the final loading and departures, Admiral Hewitt was able to report that "all convoys sailed as planned without incident and rendezvous were effected as scheduled." [15]

---

[15] WNTF Rpt Southern France, p. 173.

PART TWO

THE CAMPAIGN FOR
SOUTHERN FRANCE

CHAPTER VI

Isolating the Target Area

The first task of the ANVIL invaders was in some ways the most difficult. Transporting over 100,000 men across hundreds of miles of ocean and depositing them on a small number of beaches in a specific order in the space of about a dozen hours was no small accomplishment, even if there had been no hostile resistance. Yet it was during this period that the invading force was the most vulnerable. Although German weakness at sea and in the air made the sea journey a fairly administrative affair, the diverse capabilities of the German forces in southern France guaranteed that the reception of the Seventh Army divisions would not be so passive. Mines, coastal artillery, and radio-controlled air-to-surface missiles were only the initial concerns. A determined German counterattack at the beachline could prove disastrous, while the interdiction of the beach exits and the arrival of strong German forces, including artillery, on the surrounding hills could be equally fatal.

Although Allied intelligence had pointed out the disabilities of the German defenders, there was always the chance that ULTRA or the other intelligence sources had missed some critical last-minute German troop deployment and that the assaulting force might be in for a surprise. How fast, for example, could Blaskowitz move the vaunted *11th Panzer Division* to the beachhead area? The Germans had defended all previous Allied landings on the Continent with great vigor, and there was no indication that they were about to change their policy in this regard. For this reason, the ANVIL commanders knew it was crucial to interdict German movement into the planned beachhead area with any and all means available. Without a successful lodgment, the Seventh Army would be unable to make advances toward Toulon, Marseille, Lyon, or anywhere else.

Prior to the actual landings, the primary Allied objective was therefore to neutralize the projected landing areas by making it as difficult as possible for *Army Group G* to reinforce their beach defenses or interfere with the Allied advance to the blue line. To this end the Allies sought to immobilize the German defenders throughout southern France in every way possible. This task was the common objective of the Allied air and naval campaigns in southern France, the FFI ground operations there, and, closer to the beachhead, the activities of the airborne, ranger, and naval assault forces.

The French Forces of the Interior (FFI)

OVERLORD had provided a great stimulus to the FFI in southern France, and during June and July the southern FFI grew stronger and bolder as German fortunes waned.[1] With *Army Group G* dispatching unit after unit northward to Normandy and concentrating much of its remaining strength along the coasts, the FFI took control over large areas of southern France, posing serious threats to *Army Group G*'s two most important overland lines of communication, the Carcassonne Gap and the Rhone valley. As a result *Army Group G* had to assign an increasingly large number of tactical units to keep the gap open, and had to take even more drastic steps against FFI units threatening the upper Rhone valley.

One FFI force even established an open resistance government in the rugged uplands known as the Vercors, southwest of Grenoble, and marshaled a standing army of some 6,000 armed men to defend it. Coming out of the mountains to harass German traffic along the Rhone valley, these FFI forces, acting in concert with other guerrillas north of Lyon and in the Massif Central

west of the Rhone, threatened to block the river valley. Alarmed by this threat, the Germans moved against the FFI concentration in late July with a force that included approximately thirteen battalions of infantry, a parachute battalion, a tank battalion, and supporting artillery. In the ensuing action, and in related expeditions north of Lyon and into the Massif Central, the Germans secured the Rhone valley, although they were unable to destroy the highly mobile French guerrillas. On the contrary, *Army Group G* soon found that its focus on the Rhone valley area only made it possible for the FFI to ignite countless brush fires throughout the rest of the region.

Sabotage rapidly increased far beyond the capacity of *Army Group G* to halt or control it, or even to keep up with the growing repair and reconstruction tasks. For example, between 1 and 15 August, the FFI cut rail lines in the Carcassonne Gap and Rhone valley over forty times and, during the same period, destroyed or severely damaged thirty-two railroad and highway bridges in southern France, most of them east of the Rhone. The FFI also established an almost daily schedule for cutting both underground and overhead telephone and telegraph lines; after 6 August *Army Group G*'s telephone, telegraph, and teletype communications with its forces on the Atlantic coast and with *OB West* were, at best, sporadic. Because of interference from the mountains of southern France, radio proved an ineffective substitute, and *Army Group G* often found it easier to maintain wireless communication with Berlin than with *OB West* near Paris.

---

[1] This section is based on Hamilton, "Southern France," ch. 8; and von Luttichau, "German Operations," ch. 6, "The French Resistance Movement." For detailed coverage of FFI activities throughout the southern France campaign, see Arthur L. Funk's forthcoming *Special Operations and the Invasion of Southern France: SOE, OSS, and French Resistance Cooperation with the U.S. Seventh Army, January–September 1944.*

Meanwhile, the FFI had become so aggressive that *Army Group G* was able to move only large, well-protected convoys along the highways and railroads of southern France, and had to increase the number of guards at supply dumps, bridges, and headquarters installations. By 7 August the situation had reached the point where General Blaskowitz, commanding *Army Group G,* reported that the FFI no longer constituted a mere terrorist movement in southern France, but had evolved into an organized army at his rear. By 15 August the FFI had virtual control over southern France except for the Carcassonne Gap, the Rhone valley, and narrow strips along the Atlantic and Mediterranean coasts. Although lacking the strength to stand up to the larger conventional German forces, the FFI severely limited the mobility of *Army Group G.*

Air and Naval Operations

While the FFI accelerated its activities, Mediterranean Allied Air Forces (MAAF) began a widespread air interdiction campaign against the German land communications networks, followed by concentrated attacks against specific targets in the coastal areas.[2] By 15 August the MAAF had destroyed almost all important rail and highway bridges over the Rhone, Durance, and Var rivers, leaving intact only two or three highway bridges that were incapable of bearing heavy military traffic. From 10 August to 0550 on D-day, MAAF flew some

5,400 sorties and dropped over 6,400 tons of bombs on German coastal defenses from Sete to Genoa. Beginning at 0550 on D-day, MAAF planes flew 900 fighter-bomber and 385 medium- and heavy-bomber strikes against German positions in Seventh Army's assault area. Danger to Western Naval Task Force (WNTF) vessels close to shore somewhat curtailed the pre–H-hour air strikes in the area of the 36th and 45th Infantry Divisions' assault beaches, for low overcasts that extended out to sea obscured both the beaches and the offshore shipping. Therefore, although the air interdiction effort proved highly successful, the air attacks against German coastal artillery emplacements were less effective.

The results of the naval bombardment were also mixed. Before 0730, spots of low overcast, combined with smoke and dust raised by the air bombardment, forced naval gunships to resort to unobserved fire at many points. After 0730 visual conditions improved, and the support ships were able to move shoreward, concentrating observed fire against the landing beaches. At 0750 naval fire shifted to the flanks of the beaches, thereby helping to isolate the individual landing areas. Combined with air bombardment, the final naval shelling was generally effective in neutralizing the major beach defenses and in destroying underwater and beach obstacles or cutting paths through these obstacles. On the other hand, neither air nor naval bombardments detonated most beach-laid mines or mines laid in shallow water just offshore. WNTF ocean minesweepers began operations about 0300 on D-day, but

---

[2] This section is based on Hamilton, "Southern France," ch. 11; *Seventh Army Rpt,* I, 101–05; AAF III, pp. 420–26; and WNTF Rpt Southern France.

found no mines in the deep waters off the assault beaches or off the Hyeres Islands. Shallow-water minesweepers, operating closer to the beaches, cleared only a few mines and were unable to sweep the last 100 yards to the shoreline.

Guide boats that marked the transport assembly and unloading areas began taking station offshore about 0300, followed shortly by ships and landing craft bearing VI Corps assault units. Meanwhile, transport planes carrying the 1st Airborne Task Force had long since taken off from airfields near Rome and were winging their way toward the Le Muy drop zones; subsidiary operations of the 1st Special Service Force and French commandos had been under way for nearly three hours.

Rangers and Commandos

Task Force 86, with troops of the 1st Special Service Force and the French African Commando Group aboard, left Corsica on the morning of 14 August and hove to about five miles southeast of Levant island shortly after 2200.[3] At 2300 1st Special Service Force troops began disembarking from APDs and LSIs into rubber assault boats, which LCAs and LCPRs then towed shoreward. Shortly after midnight the leading waves, carrying scouts and security detachments to serve as guides for the main echelons, started toward the islands. Cutting their tows 750 to 1,000 yards off-

shore, these detachments landed on Levant and Port Cros just after 0030, and the main assault waves arrived one hour later.

The 1st Regiment, 1st Special Service Force, went ashore near the northeast corner of Port Cros, while the 2d and 3d Regiments made their assault along the eastern shore of Levant. Despite the fact that the small garrisons on both islands expected an attack, the Germans offered no opposition to the landings, and tactical surprise was complete. In both cases the American rangers had deliberately landed under broken, rocky cliffs rising vertically forty to fifty feet above the water, which apparently the German defenders had seen no reason to secure.

Landing on Levant to the 2d Regiment's right, the 3d Regiment immediately swung northeast to take out a battery of German artillery emplaced at the island's northeast corner. Clearing its area of responsibility before 0630, the 3d Regiment found only cleverly camouflaged dummy artillery pieces. Meanwhile, the 2d Regiment had struck southwest, discovering German resistance centered in ruined fortifications and monastery buildings in the west-central section of the island. Most of the Germans surrendered during 15 August, and all fighting was over on Levant by 2030 that evening. The task had cost the 1st Special Service Force about 10 men killed and 65 wounded, for approximately 25 German soldiers killed and 110 captured.

On Port Cros, also scheduled to fall on D-day, operations did not go according to plan. Initially the 1st Regiment encountered little opposition

---

[3] Material on the seizure of Levant and Port Cros is from TF 86 Action Rpt Southern France; 1st Sp Serv Force Unit Jnl, 14–17 Aug 44; and 1st Sp Serv Force After Action Rpt (AAR), Aug 44.

and by 0630 had secured the eastern quarter of the island. But the German garrison withdrew to prepared positions in thick-walled old forts and in an old chateau at the island's northwest corner. Infantry assaults against the structures proved useless and air and naval fire support ineffective—the 8-inch shells fired by the heavy cruiser USS *Augusta* during the afternoon simply bounced off the walls, and the rockets and light bombs that MAAF planes directed against the forts early on the 17th proved equally innocuous. Finally, late on the morning of the 17th, twelve rounds from the 15-inch guns of the British battleship HMS *Ramillies* convinced the Germans that further resistance was futile. The capture of Port Cros cost the 1st Special Service Force 5 men killed and 10 wounded, while the Germans lost 10 killed and 105 captured.

At Cape Negre the French African Commando Group encountered considerably more difficulty gaining the shore than the American rangers.[4] The vessels carrying the French force broke off from the rest of Task Force 86 at 2155 on the 14th and started the commandos shoreward about 2230. Plans called for two LCAs to land some sixty commandos on a rocky, cliff-faced beach at the southeastern corner of Cape Negre at

0045. Meanwhile, a lone scout was to go ashore to mark landing sites for the main body at Rayol Beach, two miles east of Cape Negre; at 0050 two ten-man parties would follow to secure the rocky points off both flanks of Rayol Beach, and at 0100 the main force would land.

Chance and human error quickly upset these elaborate plans. A light westerly current pushed the leading Cape Negre craft off course, while a low haze made it impossible for coxswains to identify landmarks. The LCAs that followed also drifted to the west, with the result that all of the groups ended up landing a mile or so west of their objectives. But despite—or perhaps because of—the mixups, the commandos had a surprisingly easy time once ashore; several of the scattered teams caught the Germans completely unawares. The commandos on Cape Negre quickly overran some artillery emplacements,[5] cleared five or six pillboxes or bunkers, and by daylight had established a strong roadblock on the coastal highway at the inland base of the cape, turning back a German counterattack at 1100. Meanwhile, those landing to the east of Cape Negre cleared the Rayol Beach area and established a second block on the coastal road. About

[4] Material on the African Commando Group's operations is mainly from the following: Groupe de Commandos d'Afrique, Compte-Rendu d'Opns, 15–24 Aug 44; Georges R. Bouvet, "Un Debarquement de Commandos (Nuit du 14 au 21 Aout 1944): l'Operation du Cap Negre," in *Revue Militaire d'Information*, No. 152 (April 1950), 15–20, and No. 153 (May 1950), 13–20; TF 86 Action Rpt Southern France; TG 86.3 Action Rpt Southern France; 7th Inf Jnl, 15 Aug 44; 7th Inf S-3 Rpt 1, 16 Aug 44; and *Seventh Army Rpt*, I, 108.

[5] The commandos had landed expecting to find two to four coast defense guns in the 150-mm. to 167-mm. caliber range. But, as far as can be ascertained from official records and Bouvet's account, they actually found two empty emplacements that were probably alternate positions for 105-mm. artillery of the *242d Division*. Jacques Robichon's *The Second D-Day* (New York: Walker, 1969) claims that three guns were destroyed at Cape Negre, one three-inch and two six-inch (pp. 112–13); but this is based primarily on interviews and differs from official records in many details.

CAPE NEGRE

1300, troops of the 7th Infantry, 3d Division, reinforced the commandos at the roadblock.

In the meantime a third group of commandos had struck out north of the beach toward the town of La Mole, over three miles inland. Scattered German troops offered some resistance along the way, but by 1215 the commandos had cleared the town and had captured a battery of artillery emplaced on high ground nearby. Elements of the 7th Infantry reached La Mole shortly after 1630.

On the far right (northeastern) flank of the Seventh Army's assault area, the attempt by the French Naval Assault Group to complete the isola-tion of the main beaches encountered severe difficulties.[6] Carried forward from Corsica aboard PT boats, the sixty-seven men of the French Naval Assault Group started ashore from rubber assault boats about 0140, disembarking on a rocky shore at Deux Freres Point, a mile south of Theoule-sur-Mer. But as the naval troops started inland toward the coastal road, a quarter-mile away, they walked into an extensive mine-field only recently emplaced. The first detonation caused several casualties

_____

[6] Information on the French Naval Assault Group operations is from Groupe Naval d'Assault de Corse, Compte-Rendu d'Opns; TG 80.4 Opns Rpt Southern France; and 141st Inf Jnl, 16 Aug 44.

and alerted the Germans; at daylight, still trapped in the minefield, the French group was forced to surrender.[7] Nevertheless, although the naval soldiers had failed to establish a blocking position along the coastal road, their activities, along with those at Cape Negre, diverted German attention away from the main landing area.

The 1st Airborne Task Force

The paratroopers of the 1st Airborne Task Force had mixed success, and their assault was accompanied by the initial confusion that characterized most Allied airborne efforts during the war.[8] Trouble began as the leading troop carrier aircraft came in over the coast of southern France and prepared to drop pathfinder teams that would mark the drop zones for the main force of paratroopers. The pilots found the area around Le Muy completely obscured by ground fog up to 800 feet thick, forcing them to drop the teams using only rough navigational estimates. Such dead reckoning inevitably led to error and was compounded when some planes went farther off course while attempt-

---

[7] On 16 August, after elements of the 36th Infantry Division located some survivors, the roster of the French Naval Assault Group stood at 10 men killed, 17 wounded (and recovered), 28 missing (and presumed taken prisoner), and 12 unscathed (and recovered); two days later 6 of the missing turned up, leaving the total casualty list at 49 of the 67 who had landed.

[8] This section is based on AAF III, pp. 427–31; G–3 AFHQ Rpt on A/B Opns in DRAGOON; and the official records of the 1st ABTF, the 517th Prcht RCT, the 509th Prcht Inf Bn, the 550th Gli Inf Bn, and the 1st Bn, 551st Prcht Inf. For a popular treatment, see William B. Breuer, *Operation Dragoon: The Allied Invasion of the South of France* (Novato, Calif.: Presidio, 1987).

ing to find breaks in the inland fog. In the end, of the nine pathfinder teams that started dropping about 0330 on 15 August, only three, all from the British 2d Independent Parachute Brigade, landed in their proper drop zones. Two American teams landed on the northern slopes of the Esterel, thirteen miles east of Le Muy; another dropped into hill country eight miles east of the town; and three more, which landed closer to Le Muy, were unable to orient themselves on the ground until dawn.

The lack of pathfinders and the continued poor visibility over the drop zone severely hampered the main airborne assault. The pilots ferrying the 509th Parachute Infantry Battalion and the 463d Parachute Field Artillery Battalion, the first sizable American units to drop, found no signals from the ground to guide them to the proper zone, which was centered in broken, partially wooded terrain about two miles southeast of Le Muy. Again using blind navigation, one group of aircraft of the 509th's serials sent two companies of parachute infantry and two batteries of artillery groundward over the correct drop zone at 0430. A second group of planes, however, strayed off course and dropped one infantry company and two artillery batteries into the hills south of St. Tropez, nearly fifteen miles southeast of Le Muy. In toto, only about half the 509th's battalion combat team landed in or close to its proper drop zone.

As the night wore on, the confusion grew worse. None of the troopers of the 517th Parachute regimental combat team landed on their assigned drop zones, which were centered on a flat, cultivated area over two miles west of Le Muy. Exiting from their planes about 0435, most of the soldiers from the 1st Battalion, 517th Infantry, were scattered from Trans-en-Provence, four miles northwest of Le Muy, to Lorgues, six miles farther west. Much of the regiment's 2d Battalion landed one or two miles northwest of Le Muy in the vicinity of La Motte, but about a third of the battalion's paratroopers found themselves on rising ground east and northeast of the town. The 3d Battalion of the 517th dropped along an east-west line almost six miles long and about twelve to fourteen miles northeast of Le Muy, while approximately a battery of the regiment's 460th Parachute Field Artillery Battalion landed in rising ground just northwest of Frejus, some twelve miles southeast of its assigned drop zone. Still others were blown far and wide in ones and twos and, outside of a few that landed in the ocean, many had difficulty later reconstructing exactly where they had first touched down.

With two of its three pathfinder teams operating their ground radar sets to mark the drop zones, the British 2d Independent Parachute Brigade did a little better. Starting the assault about 0450, half of the 4th Parachute Battalion, one company of the 5th Parachute Battalion, and the bulk of the 6th Parachute Battalion, totaling something less than two-thirds of the brigade, landed in correct drop zones. Most of the remaining paratroopers were scattered over a wide area roughly nine miles northeast and northwest of Le Muy.

Once on the ground the paratroopers tried to regroup as quickly as possible. Most of the 1st and 2d Battalions, 517th Parachute Infantry, managed to reach their assigned assembly areas shortly after dawn on 15 August, and the British troops who had landed near Callas marched to their proper area later in the morning. But the bulk of the American and British troopers who had landed outside of the immediate Le Muy area were unable to join their parent units until D plus 1, and the 1st Airborne Task Force did not collect the last scattered elements of the parachute drop until D plus 5. A later count revealed that less than 40 percent of the paratroopers of the predawn lifts landed in the assigned drop zones, and by 0600, as dawn arrived, only about 60 percent of the men of the first parachute lifts had been assembled in the Le Muy area.[9]

Follow-up parachute and glider landings were scheduled to start at 0815 on 15 August, when gliders were to bring in artillery and antitank units of the 2d Independent Parachute Brigade. But fog still blanketed the landing areas north of Le Muy when the planes towing the brigade's gliders arrived. The aircraft, without cutting their tows, thereupon turned back to their Rome area airfields; ultimately they returned to release the gliders in the Le Muy area about 1800. The landings of other gliders carrying elements of the 1st Airborne Task Force headquarters and support troops were delayed about an hour, and did not start until about 0930. The 1st Battalion,

_____

[9] The situation described here contrasts with the statement in AAF III, p. 428, that only 20 of the nearly 400 aircraft assigned to the parachute operation missed the proper drop zones by "an appreciable distance."

AMERICAN AND BRITISH PARATROOPERS TAKE A SHORT BREAK, *D-day 1944.*

551st Parachute Infantry, jumped without incident into the 517th regiment's drop zone beginning at 1810, as planned, while the 550th Infantry Airborne Battalion came in via gliders at 1830, also on schedule. Other units that came in by glider late in the day—such as the 602d Glider Field Artillery Battalion—likewise landed on or near schedule.

The Germans had planted antiglider obstacles throughout much of the Le Muy area, mostly using stakes about twelve feet tall and six inches thick, dug at least two feet into the ground. In some cases these sticks, deliberately sunk shallow and loose by French workers, served mainly as breaking power for the gliders, but in most instances the stakes snapped off the gliders' wings, caused ground loops, and otherwise made a sham bles of the glider landing zones. More trouble stemmed from the fact that the first gliders to arrive set down in the best and clearest areas instead of in their assigned zones; as later groups arrived, they found the best spots already packed with grounded gliders, thus forcing the pilots to select less desirable, rougher areas. In the end, only 50 of some 400 gliders used in the airborne operation were salvageable. Fortunately, damage to cargo and passengers was minimal—only about 80 incapacitating casualties among the paratroopers and about 150 among the troops who came in by glider, not counting 16 glider pilots killed and 37 injured.

The total of about 230 jump and glider casualties represented only 2.5 percent of the nearly 9,000 airborne troops who arrived in southern France on D-day. Thus by 1900 on the 15th, D-day evening, about 90 percent of the troops and equipment borne by gliders were ready for action.

Fortunately for the paratroopers who landed early, German resistance was light, and, except in Le Muy proper, the troopers experienced only a few minor skirmishes as they moved to assembly areas and objectives. By the time German reinforcements began to trickle in late in the day, the paratroopers had secured high ground along both sides of the Argens River east of Le Muy, had occupied hills overlooking the Toulon–St. Raphael corridor in the vicinity of Les Arcs, five miles west of Le Muy, and had cleared several small towns of German troops. A formal juncture with the main ground forces began that night about 2030 when troops of the 509th Parachute Battalion met a patrol from the 45th Division's reconnaissance troop.

Le Muy itself remained in German hands for the time being. The commander of the 2d Independent Parachute Brigade judged that the scattered drop, together with the initial failure of the gliders to land his artillery and antitank weapons, left him insufficient strength to launch an attack against what appeared to be a strongly defended town. However, except for the seizure of Le Muy, the 1st Airborne Task Force had executed its D-day missions, establishing strong blocking positions along the Argens valley and further isolating the beach area. The scattered parachute drop had not appreciably affected the 1st Airborne Task Force's operations and may, on the contrary, have created diversions that helped confuse the German reaction to both the airborne and amphibious assaults.

Complementing the air, naval, guerrilla, commando, and parachute operations was a series of widespread deception efforts associated with almost every aspect of ANVIL. For example, in the weeks immediately preceding the invasion, the OSS and FFI had established dummy broadcast circuits and inserted an ever-increasing stream of false messages into their radio nets to mislead any German listeners regarding the focus of the Allied intelligence-gathering effort, thereby concealing the general landing area. The air attacks that were spread out along the coasts of southern France and northwestern Italy served the same purpose. On the eve of D-day, the Allies also arranged for the appearance of dummy, booby-trapped paratroopers, air-released strips of tin foil, and paraded a small boat flotilla past Marseille to simulate an invasion. To the east, another mock invasion fleet by U.S. Navy PT boats and other small craft led by Lt. Cmdr. Douglas E. Fairbanks (USNR), a well-known American cinema star, steered past Genoa and caused a ruckus near Cannes. However, although Radio Berlin later announced that the German garrison at Marseille had repulsed a major Allied invasion, neither the German radar operators nor the German commanders were taken in by these last-minute ruses.[10]

---

[10] See Morison, *The Invasion of France and Germany*, pp. 249–50; Casey MS, pp. 2–3.

The First German Reactions

For the Germans, the first confirmation that a major Allied assault was imminent came about 2330 on 14 August, when ships of the Western Naval Task Force bombarded shore installations in the Marseille area, and MAAF planes began dropping dummy parachutists in the same region.[11] Nineteenth Army staff officers first thought that the main Allied assault might come over beaches in the vicinity of Marseille, but the diversionary operations deceived the Germans for less than an hour. Next, reports filtered into the Nineteenth Army headquarters that attempted Allied landings at Cape Negre and on the Hyeres Islands had been repulsed. However, not until 0600 on the 15th did coastal defense units report that Allied troops were actually ashore on the mainland, and even these messages noted only that German forces were containing assault forces at Cape Negre.[12]

German intelligence regarding the airborne assault was not much better. News of the approach of troop carrier aircraft reached Nineteenth Army headquarters at Avignon and Army Group G at Toulouse about 0430 on the 15th from OB Southwest in Italy, and preliminary reports concerning parachute drops near Le Muy began arriving at Avignon around 0600. Meanwhile, both wire and radio communications began breaking down throughout the Nineteenth Army's area, and General Wiese, the army commander, continued to receive most of his information about the airborne operation through OB Southwest channels. Not until nearly 1030 on D-day did Wiese obtain local confirmation of the air drop.

One major reason for the delay was that the 1st Airborne Task Force had, as an unexpected consequence of its scattered drop, isolated General Neuling's LXII Corps headquarters at Draguignan, seven miles northwest of Le Muy, and the paratroopers had cut all wire communications within sight. As a result, Neuling soon lost contact with both Nineteenth Army and his two infantry divisions, although apparently he was able to direct the 148th Infantry Division to start its reserves toward Le Muy before his headquarters was completely cut off. Had Neuling carried out the Nineteenth Army's orders of 13 August to move the division's reserves into the Argens valley between Le Muy and St. Raphael, the task of the airborne force might have been much tougher.

Communications were much the same at Army Group G headquarters. Shortly after 0800 on the 15th the telephone lines between Army Group G at Toulouse and Nineteenth Army at Avignon went out, probably as the result of FFI sabotage. Radio communications between the two headquarters were also unsatisfactory during the day, and most of the information that General Blaskowitz, commanding Army Group G, obtained on the 15th

[11] This section is based primarily on von Lutti-chau, "German Operations," chs. 9 and 10.

[12] Times given in German sources are an hour later than those used in this text. In August the Germans operated on Zone A time, Central European Standard Time or British single daylight saving time, while the Allies operated on Zone B time, British double daylight saving time. The time difference sometimes causes confusion, but insofar as possible the text transliterates German times into the Allied clock.

actually came from *OB West* headquarters near Paris, relayed there from the coastal area through German naval communications.

Out of touch with both *Army Group G* and the *LXII Corps*, General Wiese of *Nineteenth Army* had to act quickly and independently. Before the sun was well up, he had decided that the main threat lay in the Le Muy–St. Raphael region. The Allied airhead at Le Muy would make it relatively easy for Allied ground units to push inland from likely assault beaches in the Frejus–St. Raphael area, and would severely hamper his ability to assemble blocking or counterattacking forces in the Toulon–St. Raphael (Argens River) corridor just north of the Maures massif. Accordingly, Wiese's first priority was to find and assemble enough forces to clear the paratroopers from Le Muy as rapidly as possible.

Early on the morning of the 15th, Maj. Gen. Richard von Schwerin, commanding the *189th Infantry Division*, had arrived at the *338th Infantry Division* headquarters in Arles, on the Rhone River some twenty miles south of Avignon. A few days earlier, when the *338th Division* was still scheduled to redeploy to Normandy, *Nineteenth Army* had directed the *189th Division* to take over the *338th's* sector astride the Rhone delta and to assume control of the *933d Grenadiers, 244th Infantry Division*, which was moving into that portion of the *338th's* sector extending from the Rhone east to the vicinity of Marseille. News of the invasion prompted *OB West* to cancel the *338th Division's* redeployment northward, an action that enabled Wiese to hand von Schwerin the task of com-

manding the *Nineteenth Army's* counterattack forces. About 0900 von Schwerin moved to the *LXXXV Corps* command post about fifteen miles east of Avignon (and about seventy-five miles west of Le Muy), with orders to take command of a provisional division that Wiese was trying to assemble for the effort.

The provisional organization was to consist of the *189th Division* headquarters (von Schwerin's original command); an understrength regimental combat team built around the *932d Grenadiers* of the *244th Division*; the headquarters of the *189th Division's 15th Grenadiers*, controlling a total of three infantry battalions from the *189th* and *338th Divisions*; the *198th Division's 305th Grenadiers*, which was still west of the Rhone; and, for artillery, the *Luftwaffe's 18th Flak Regiment*. Wiese directed von Schwerin to assemble and take charge of all or any of these units that were immediately available and mount a counterattack toward Le Muy from the vicinity of Vidauban, in the Toulon–St. Raphael corridor about eight miles southwest of Le Muy, in order to destroy the Allied airhead and to assist the presumably trapped *LXII Corps* forces at Draguignan.

The first unit von Schwerin could find was the regimental headquarters of the *15th Grenadiers*, which had arrived from west of the Rhone during the morning. He quickly dispatched the unit sixty-five miles farther west to Le Luc, some six miles west of Vidauban, to act as an assembly control command. He then drove on to Vidauban himself, where he found a few service troops of the *242d Division* as well as headquarters personnel of the *18th Flak Regiment*, but no firing batteries. Moving on to Le Luc, he found that the command elements of the *932d Grenadiers* had arrived, but the unit's infantry battalions were still straggling eastward. It was now mid-afternoon and the only effective combat unit von Schwerin had under his command in the forward area was the assault company from his own division headquarters.

Meanwhile, events had moved so rapidly that the *Nineteenth Army* was about to change von Schwerin's orders. Wiese had learned that for the time being the *LXII Corps* headquarters was safe at Draguignan. However, his fear of a quick thrust up the Argens valley toward Le Muy by Allied troops now known to have landed near St. Raphael was becoming more pressing. Wiese thus directed von Schwerin to ignore Draguignan, and instead to push through the Allied paratroopers around Le Muy and then sweep down the Argens valley to turn back into the sea whatever Allied forces might have landed in the Frejus–St. Raphael region.

By the time von Schwerin had received and digested these orders, dusk was upon him, and the only additional combat strength that he had been able to assemble near Vidauban were parts of two battalions of the *932d Grenadiers*. With little more than the equivalent of a disorganized regiment at his disposal, von Schwerin decided to ignore Wiese's new directive and continue preparing for an attack toward Le Muy and ultimately Draguignan to relieve the *LXII Corps* headquarters.

About the same time that von Schwerin started to go off on his own, the *148th Division*, evidently having received new orders from either the *LXII Corps* or the *Nineteenth Army*, finally began moving a force equivalent to an infantry battalion (probably part of *Regiment Kessler*) toward Draguignan. Near Fayence, twelve miles northeast of Le Muy, the *148th Division*'s unit ran into trouble when it was halted by strong elements of the FFI, reinforced by British paratroopers who had landed in the Fayence area by mistake.

In the end, all German attempts on 15 August to mount a counterattack against the landing area failed and, for at least the first day, the Allied beaches appeared safe from outside interference. In the interior, the Allied deception operations, the air attacks against the Rhone bridges, and continued FFI operations against German communications made a quick response to the initial Allied air and sea assault difficult. Closer to the beachhead area, the French commandos and the American and British paratroopers had positioned themselves astride the main avenues of approach leading to the landing beaches from the west, effectively isolating the beachline. Meanwhile the main assault force, which had started ashore over the Cape Cavalaire–Antheor Cove beaches about 0800 on 15 August, was encountering unexpectedly weak opposition and had begun to penetrate inland faster and with greater strength than most planners had ever dared to hope.

CHAPTER VII

The ANVIL Beachhead

On the transport and fire support ships offshore, first light on 15 August revealed a clear, calm Mediterranean day. Although cool at first, variable light surface breezes promised that temperatures ashore would rise sharply during the morning. Coastward, a bank of mist, thickening inland into the fog that had helped scatter the paratroopers, partially obscured the beaches, leaving only the forbidding peaks of the Maures and the Esterel clearly visible. As the fog began to dissipate after sunrise at 0638, smoke and dust from air and naval bombardment continued to keep the coastline hazy, and visibility dropped to as little as fifty yards off several assault beaches for a while. Despite all the information supplied by the vast Allied intelligence effort, no one could be certain of what German defenses were hidden by that late summer veil.[1]

The 3d Division Lands

The first objective of the 3d Infantry Division was to secure the squat St. Tropez peninsula on the left, or southwestern, section of the ANVIL beachline (*Map 6*). The area was defended by the fourth, or *Ost*, battalion of the *765th Grenadier Regiment* (*242d Division*), supported by two field artillery battalions and one coast artillery battery. Seventh Army planners had chosen two beaches for the 3d Division's assault: one on the southern base of the peninsula off Cavalaire Bay, and a second at the head of the peninsula just south of St. Tropez. Temporarily, the northern side of the peninsula, including the narrow St. Tropez gulf, would be avoided.

The 3d Division's southernmost beach was Alpha Red, located on the shores of Cavalaire Bay. The landing area consisted of low, mostly bare sand dunes backed by a narrow band of pines twenty to thirty yards deep. The coastal road, N–559,[2] lay beyond

---

[1] The principal sources for coverage of U.S. Army operations in this chapter are the official records of HQ VI Corps and the 3d, 36th, and 45th Infantry Divisions and their component or attached units. Naval source materials include the WNTF Rpt Southern France; N–2 Section, Eighth Fleet, Survey of Assault Beaches, Invasion of Southern France; and the AARs of TF 84, TG 84.1, TF 85, TU 85.15, TG 85.6, TG 85.7, and TF 87. Information on German activities derives mainly from von Luttichau, "German Operations," ch. 9.

[2] During the period covered by this volume, main French highways and roads had two designations, *N* for National and *D* for Departmental. The N highways correspond roughly to U.S. interstate highways and the D roads to state routes. Other classifications for lesser roads existed, but are rarely used in this work.

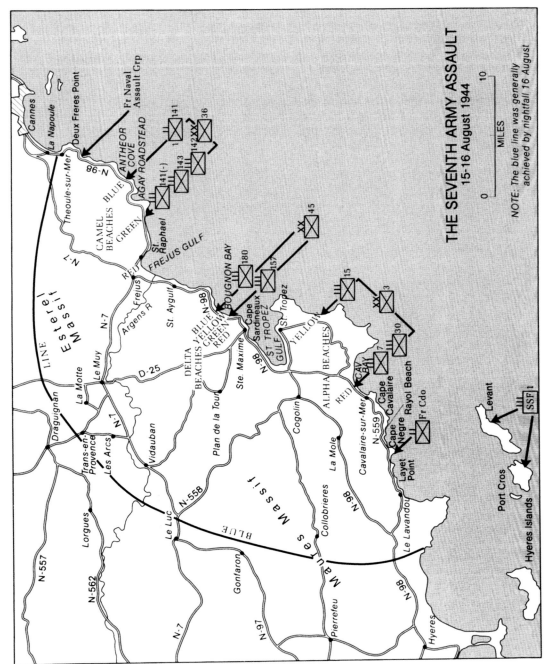

THE SEVENTH ARMY ASSAULT
15-16 August 1944

0   10
MILES

NOTE: The blue line was generally
achieved by nightfall 16 August

This map is printed in full color at the back of the book, following the Index.

MAP 6

the pines, while the narrow-gauge railroad that skirted the coast ran parallel to N–559, swinging inland near the center of Alpha Red. Cultivated fields lay beyond the eastern half of the beach; and on the west, rocky, pine-clad foothills rose just inland. On the left, Route N–559 passed by the resort town of Cavalaire-sur-Mer and wound south and southwest along the coastal hills to Cape Negre, six miles away; on the right, the coastal route turned north at the eastern edge of the beach, cutting through the lightly wooded, low hills along the inland base of the St. Tropez peninsula for about six miles to the opposite side of the cape.

About six miles northeast of Alpha Red, at the end of the peninsula, lay the 3d Division's other assault beach, Alpha Yellow. The landing area offered over two good miles of excellent beach on which the entire 3d Division could easily have landed. But exits were poor. A narrow, one-lane road that might not hold up under heavy military traffic led north to St. Tropez, and there was no direct route west across the peninsula to Route N–559.

Alpha Red was the assault beach for the 3d Division's 7th Infantry regiment. The regimental left was to drive inland about two miles to secure dominant high ground and then push southwestward along the coast via N–559 toward Cape Negre. The center was to advance north along N–599 to the junction with Route N–98 and be prepared to move southwest into the interior along N–98 about eight miles to La Mole. The right was to probe into the St. Tropez peninsula. The 30th Infantry was to follow

the 7th Infantry ashore at 0900 and advance north across the base of the peninsula to secure Cogolin, a road junction town on N–98, about three miles inland from the head of St. Tropez gulf. Subsequently the 30th Infantry was to push westward along a third-class road toward Collobrieres, about fifteen miles northwest of Alpha Red and in the heart of the Maures massif. To the 15th Infantry, landing at Alpha Yellow, fell the tasks of clearing the peninsula and seizing St. Tropez. These missions completed, the 15th was to assemble in reserve near Cogolin.

Air and naval bombardment took place generally as planned at both Alpha Red and Yellow, while minesweepers efficiently accomplished their tasks. About 0715 Apex craft—radio-controlled LCVPs loaded with high explosives—started shoreward at Alpha Red. Some hit concrete tetrahedrons armed with mines, thereby opening channels through these offshore obstacles; others went on to detonate on the beach, exploding mines. Preceded by twenty-one rocket-equipped landing craft, the leading assault wave at Alpha Red started shoreward about 0630. The rockets blasted the shoreline between 0750 and 0756, and were quickly followed by the first troops and several DD tanks. One tank hit a mine and sank, as did two LCVPs carrying men of the 2d Battalion, 7th Infantry, resulting in sixty casualties. Later waves landed generally according to schedule, although mines, both offshore and on the beach, damaged a few additional craft and forced landing control officers to close the right flank of the beach for some time. The 30th

Infantry started ashore at 0920, twenty minutes late, but by 1015 the regiment and most of the artillery scheduled for Alpha Red were ashore. General O'Daniel, commanding the 3d Division, came ashore at Alpha Red about 1045.

Opposition at the beach was negligible, but inland the 7th Infantry came under small-arms, machine-gun, and mortar fire from elements of the *242d Division*. During the morning the most stubborn opposition centered at Cavalaire-sur-Mer and nearby Cape Cavalaire, but the 3d Battalion, 7th Infantry, cleared the area by 1030. Accompanied by tanks and tank destroyers, the battalion continued west astride Route N–599 toward the area held by the French African Commando Group. Picking up part of the French unit, the 3d Battalion probed onward until dusk, halting before a German strongpoint at Layet Point, a mile southwest of Cape Negre and over seven miles southwest of Alpha Red.

In the center the 1st Battalion, 7th Infantry, struck out from Alpha Red sometime around noon, pushing northwest over rugged coastal foothills of the Maures to reach Route N–98, a mile east of La Mole, at 1630. On the right the 2d Battalion, encountering scattered resistance, moved north along N–559, marched into Cogolin during the afternoon, and then advanced southwest along Route N–98. Both 7th Infantry battalions joined the French commandos, who had already cleared La Mole, and moved into the town at dark.

The 30th Infantry, driving rapidly north from Alpha Red behind the 7th, cut across the base of the peninsula to the head of the St. Tropez gulf, where it joined elements of both the 3d Division's 15th regiment and units of the 45th Division. The 3d Battalion, 30th Infantry, passed through Cogolin about 1400 and then struck west for Collobrieres, which fell at 2000, fully twenty-four hours earlier than had been expected. The rest of the 30th Infantry started northwest across the Maures from Cogolin about 1700; by nightfall leading elements were scarcely five miles short of Le Luc, at the center of the Toulon–St. Raphael corridor.

The 15th Infantry's assault at Alpha Yellow, executed on schedule, followed the pattern at Alpha Red. Again mines rather than German fire caused the few casualties suffered. *Ost* troops of the *242d Division*, stunned by the air and naval bombardment, surrendered at the earliest opportunity. The 1st Battalion, 15th Infantry, struck directly inland and by 1400 secured the high ground in the center of the St. Tropez peninsula, overrunning a German strongpoint in the process and suffering eight casualties while capturing forty prisoners.[3]

On the right, the 3d Battalion, delayed by skirmishes with withdrawing troops of the *242d Division*, reached St. Tropez about 1500 to find that misdropped troopers of the 509th Parachute Infantry Battalion, aided by the FFI, had already cleared most of the town. Remaining resistance was centered at the Citadel, a medieval fortress on the eastern outskirts of St. Tropez. But before the 15th Infantry

---

[3] For action at this strongpoint, the much-decorated Audie L. Murphy, then a staff sergeant, received the Distinguished Service Cross (DSC).

could organize a concerted attack, the paratroopers induced the small German garrison of sixty-seven men to surrender.

The 2d Battalion followed the rest of the 15th Infantry ashore, marched overland to the St. Tropez area, and joined elements of the 30th Infantry and the 45th Division. Meanwhile, patrols of the 15th Infantry, aided by the 3d Cavalry Reconnaissance Troop, cleaned out bypassed portions of the St. Tropez peninsula. By dark the 15th Infantry was assembling at Cogolin in division reserve.

The Assault in the Center

The 45th Division's Delta beaches lay along the shores of Bougnon Bay, about eight miles north of Alpha Yellow and across the mouth of the St. Tropez gulf. The division's landing areas were again defended by only a single battalion, the *1st Battalion* of the *765th Grenadiers*, backed by one field artillery battalion and one naval battery. Delta Red, southernmost of the Delta beaches, was located about a mile and a half north of Ste. Maxime, and the others, Green, Yellow, and Blue, were a few miles farther up the coast, separated by 500- to 1,000-yard stretches of less hospitable shoreline. Behind the beaches, Route N–98, hugging the coastal contours, pointed the way southwest to Ste. Maxime and northward to St. Raphael. Rising, cultivated slopes led inland for about half a mile before giving way to the steeper, wooded hills of the Maures.

No offshore obstacles existed at the Delta beaches, and the preassault air and naval bombardment had already destroyed much of the artillery the Germans had emplaced to defend the area. On the morning of D-day, only one 75-mm. gun fired a few ineffective rounds at landing craft before an American destroyer silenced the piece. Three 81-mm. mortars on Cape Sardineaux let go about sixty rounds before they too were destroyed, while a 20-mm. automatic cannon at the northeastern limit of Bougnon Bay fired ineffectively for some time. Other German weapons in the area were in firing condition on D-day, but the weight of the air and naval bombardment, together with last-minute rocket barrages, discouraged the crews. In the end, most of the defenders at gun emplacements and other strongpoints in the Delta beach region readily surrendered to 45th Division troops.

At Delta Red and Delta Green a few rounds of mortar fire and some small-arms fire harassed the 157th Infantry's leading wave, which went ashore at 0802. The 3d Battalion swung southwest from Delta Red along Route N–98 toward Ste. Maxime, encountering only weak, scattered opposition in the area. At Ste. Maxime resistance was more determined, and the battalion had to call on naval gunfire support before securing the town about 1530. Then, led by a platoon of light tanks from the 117th Cavalry Squadron, the battalion moved on to the southwest, halting at dusk along the western shore of the St. Tropez gulf after meeting troops from the 3d Division.

The 1st Battalion, 157th Infantry, landed unopposed at Delta Green and advanced generally through the Maures along a stream valley to Plan de la Tour, about five miles inland from Ste. Maxime. The 2d Battalion followed the 3d ashore over Delta Red and moved without opposition onto high ground some three or four miles west and southwest of Ste. Maxime.

In the 45th Division's center, the 2d Battalion, 180th Infantry, started ashore at Delta Yellow about 0758, encountered negligible resistance, and at dusk was in control of high ground four miles northwest of its beach, pushing deeper into the Maures. At Delta Blue on the right the 1st Battalion encountered little opposition (although land mines disabled four DD tanks), but ran into increasingly stubborn resistance as it swung north along Route N–98. By dusk the main body was scarcely a mile and a half beyond Delta Blue, although other elements, having marched over hills just inland, had reached N–98 a mile and a half farther north. During the evening, patrols probed northward to St. Aygulf, four miles north along Route N–98 from Delta Blue, and found well-defended German strongpoints at the southern edge of town.

The 3d Battalion, 180th Infantry, drove due north and inland from Delta Blue, following a poor road over rough, semiforested hills. The battalion ran into strong resistance from elements of the *242d Division* and at dark was still maneuvering to clear high ground about two miles north of Delta Blue. Late in the afternoon a platoon of the 45th Reconnaissance Troop struck northward from Ste. Maxime along a third-class road (D–25) that led to Le Muy, twelve miles away. It was this platoon

that, about 2030, met elements of the 509th Parachute Infantry Battalion south of Le Muy. The 45th Division had not required the services of its third regiment, the 179th Infantry, on D-day, and the unit landed without incident to assemble in reserve near Ste. Maxime.

The 36th Division on the Right

As fortune would have it, the Germans had concentrated most of their defenses in the area to be assaulted by the "hard luck" 36th Division. The short stretch of coastline between the mouth of the Argens River north to Antheor Cove was defended by the *765th Grenadier Regiment's 2d Battalion*, backed by a field artillery battalion, a naval battery, and the *1038th Antitank Battalion*. The area included the small port of St. Raphael and, slightly inland, the town of Frejus. In addition, the *3d Battalion, 765th Grenadiers*, was in reserve in the Frejus region, and the fourth, or *Ost*, battalion of the *239th Grenadiers (148th Division)* held the area north of Antheor Cove for six miles to Theoule-sur-Mer.

The primary beach of the 36th Division was Camel Green, where the 2d and 3d Battalions of the 141st Infantry, 36th Division, were scheduled to land. Situated a little over three miles east of St. Raphael, the landing area was backed by a steep embankment on top of which ran Route N–98 and the main-line, standard-gauge railroad, which emerged from the Toulon–St. Raphael corridor at St. Raphael to continue along the coast toward Cannes and Nice. Beyond the embankment were stone quarries cut deep into the sharply rising, scrub-covered hills of the Esterel. Three miles northeast of Camel Green lay tiny Camel Blue, the assault beach for the 1st Battalion, 141st Infantry. Situated at the head of Antheor Cove, the beach gave way a scant ten yards inland to the Route N–98 embankment, beyond which the main railroad crossed a narrow gorge via an eight-span bridge.

To the 141st Infantry fell the task of carrying out the main part of the 36th Division's initial mission, that is, securing the right flank of the VI Corps. Once it landed, the regiment was to concentrate its efforts on clearing the shores of Agay Roadstead, between Camel Green and Camel Blue, so that the division could use an excellent strand at the top of the roadstead for general unloading. Next, the 1st Battalion was to swing northeast along the coast toward Theoule-sur-Mer and La Napoule, at the eastern end of the Army beachhead line, a little over six miles beyond Camel Blue. The rest of the regiment was to strike north across the Esterel to the Army beachhead line and Route N–7, which ran along the inland slopes of the Esterel from Frejus to Cannes.

The 143d Infantry, following the 141st ashore at Camel Green, was to drive rapidly westward in the opposite direction to seize St. Raphael and support the landing of the 142d Infantry over Camel Red, the 36th Division's third beach located at the head of the Frejus gulf. Camel Red gave direct access to Frejus, to a small airfield, and to the road net of the Argens valley sector of the Toulon-St. Raphael corridor and, in general, promised to provide the best beaches in the entire VI Corps assault area for the discharge of both troops and cargo. The Camel Red region was also the logical area in which to establish a base for a major thrust toward Le Muy and objectives farther west.

Once ashore at Camel Red, the 142d Infantry was to strike inland for about a mile to clear Frejus and then push westward along Route N–7 toward the 1st Airborne Task Force. If necessary, the regiment was to help the airborne troops seize Le Muy, ten miles up the Argens valley from Frejus. However, because of expected German opposition at Camel Red, the 142d's assault was not scheduled until 1400 in the afternoon. In the event that the 142d could not land at Camel Red, the regiment was to come ashore over Camel Green, swing inland past the 143d Infantry, and descend upon Frejus and Camel Red from behind.

The landings of the 36th Division also began on schedule. At Camel Green, the initial assault waves found no underwater obstacles and at first encountered little opposition. From 0900 to 1300 sporadic fire from German artillery on high ground to the west and northwest harassed unloading operations, but caused little damage and few casualties; it was finally halted by naval gunfire. At Camel Blue farther east some machine-gun fire had greeted the first waves, but all firing ceased by 0900. As at the St. Tropez beaches, many of the *Ost* troops began surrendering as soon as the American troops advanced beyond the shoreline.

By 1000 the 141st had secured both Camel Green and Camel Blue, but at Agay Roadstead the 1st and 2d Battalions met stubborn opposition from elements of the *242d Division,* and it was 1700 before the roadstead's shoreline was secure. The 2d Battalion then headed up a twisting road across the Esterel; by sunset, about 2030, it was less than a mile from Route N-7 and over two miles inland from La Napoule.[4] The 1st Battalion, which had to backtrack to Camel Blue after helping out at the Agay Roadstead, was two miles north of Blue by dark, having encountered only scattered opposition from *148th Division* troops along winding Route N-98. The 3d Battalion, relieved at Green in midafternoon by other division units, began moving north over the Esterel along back roads in between the 1st and 2d Battalions. The 141st Infantry's casualties for the day were approximately five men killed and twenty-five wounded, almost all incurred during the action at Agay Roadstead.

The 143d Infantry ran into more opposition to the west. After assembling at Camel Green, its 1st and 3d Battalions advanced west and northwest to secure high ground along the slopes of the Esterel and a mile or two inland. Closer to the coast, the 2d also moved west, heading directly toward St. Raphael, but encountered stubborn resistance from a series of strongpoints controlling N-98, the shore road. Mortar and artillery fire from the right also harassed the battalion, while scattered groups of German infantry on hills just inland helped slow progress. By 1400, when

the 142d Infantry was scheduled to make its afternoon assault over Camel Red, forward elements of the 2d Battalion, 143d Infantry, had not yet reached St. Raphael and could not assist; and the closest troops of the 180th Infantry, 45th Division (which VI Corps had hoped would also be able to support the 142d Infantry), were still a good four miles south of Camel Red at 1400. The 142d regiment would have to make what was expected to be one of the most critical landings alone.

Camel Red

During the morning of 15 August, after the success of the main landings was assured, naval and air echelons went forward with preparations for the Camel Red assault. Here, for the first time, the attackers met considerable opposition. The Germans, recognizing the importance of the Camel Red area, had developed a much stronger network of coastal defenses there. Static installations included a minefield across the Frejus gulf, single and double rows of mined concrete tetrahedrons at the shoreline, and, on the beach, two rows of double-apron barbed wire, a concrete antitank wall seven feet high and over three feet thick, a twelve-foot-deep antitank ditch on the seaward side of the wall, and extensive fields of land mines on the beach, on the nearby airfield, and on the roads and paths leading inland. There were machine-gun positions in the antitank wall, and pillboxes and other strongpoints just behind it. Larger emplacements, a few holding 88-mm. guns, enfiladed the beach from the harbor front at St.

---

[4] Under the double daylight saving time the Allies were using, sunset on 15 August 1944 was at 2035; it did not become completely dark for nearly another two hours.

PILLBOX GUARDS BRIDGE TO ST. RAPHAEL. *Supporting installations are behind it.*

Raphael. Inside the town the defenders had turned many buildings into lesser defensive works, and booby traps and mines were plentiful. Artillery dominating the beach included a battery of 75-mm. guns and another of 105-mm. in hills south of the Argens River; another 105-mm. battery emplaced in rising ground a mile north of St. Raphael; two batteries of 100-mm. howitzers on high ground northwest of the port; and various light antiaircraft batteries sprinkled throughout the region. Finally, the *1038th Antitank Gun Battalion* had zeroed in on Camel Red and its approaches with eight or ten of the newest model 88-mm. guns. Towed from place to place as the occasion demanded, these weapons had been

unscathed by the preassault bombardment. Infantry in the area included at least two reinforced companies of the *2d Battalion, 765th Grenadiers (242d Division)*.

The strength of the defenses was soon apparent. About 1100, minesweepers clearing the deep-water approaches came under fire from German artillery that covering destroyers were unable to neutralize, and had to retire. From approximately 1205 to 1220 over ninety B–24 medium bombers dropped nearly 200 tons of high explosives in the Camel Red area. But when the shallow-water minesweepers darted shoreward again about 1235, they found that the aerial bombardment had likewise failed to reduce the volume of German fire, and the minesweepers again retired under heavy shelling. Apex drone boats went in about 1300 and also received fire; all but three of the drones malfunctioned, and some had to be destroyed by Navy ships.

Meanwhile, four destroyers, two cruisers, and a battleship began a final 45-minute bombardment. The assault waves of LCVPs had already formed and, led by rocket craft, started shoreward shortly thereafter. At 1400 the leading wave was about 3,000 yards offshore and under fire from German artillery, when Capt. Leo B. Schulten, USN, commanding the Camel Red assault group of Task Force 87 under Rear Adm. Spencer S. Lewis, temporarily halted the landing. Initially he decided to postpone the assault on Camel Red until 1430. At the same time, he informed Admiral Lewis of the situation and requested instructions.

Schulten's message placed Lewis in a dilemma. The TF 87 commander had no desire to cancel the landing, but sending the 142d Infantry ashore as planned over Camel Red seemed a serious error. Obviously the preassault bombardment had failed to neutralize the German artillery; the minesweeping had been incomplete; and the drones had accomplished little. Admiral Lewis also believed that Schulten's postponement had already cost them whatever shock effect the air and naval bombardments might have had, thus allowing German defenders time to recover and reoccupy any vacated positions. Chances for tactical surprise had certainly been lost, and sending the assault forces in now would undoubtedly result in heavy casualties for both the ground

and naval forces involved.

Lewis first attempted to consult with the 36th Division commander, General Dahlquist. Since he and Dahlquist had prepared alternate plans for landing the 142d Infantry at Camel Green, the admiral knew he could make the switch with a minimum of confusion. Moreover, reports from shore indicated that the 36th Division could probably secure Camel Red by an overland attack, while Camel Green was proving to be a far better unloading beach than expected. On the other hand, Dahlquist, who had been ashore since 1000, might need the 142d Infantry to land at Camel Red for tactical reasons. Accordingly, between 1400 and 1415, Lewis tried to reach the division commander by radio, but, since adequate ship-to-shore communications had not yet been established, the effort was unsuccessful. Reluctant to delay his decision any longer, at 1415 Lewis directed Schulten to cancel the Camel Red assault and land the 142d over Camel Green, which had long since been secured by the 141st Infantry.

The 142d Infantry started ashore at Camel Green about 1515, and before 1600 its leading units had started north through rear elements of the 143d Infantry, which continued its push southwest along the coast, still encountering determined resistance. Two miles inland from Camel Green the 142d Infantry wheeled westward, under orders to reach positions from which it could launch an attack into Frejus by 2000. However, the distance involved, the slow movement through the steep, wooded hills, and some skirmishing with German units—probably the *765th*'s reserve battalion—combined to delay progress, and darkness found the 142d's forward elements still three miles from the town. Yet the prognosis was good. The regiment's casualties for the day were only five men wounded—certainly far fewer than there would have been if the unit had made an assault at Camel Red—and the progress of both the 142d and the 143d together with the airborne blocking force had just about sealed off the entire Frejus area. The only serious loss occurred that night when the *Luftwaffe* launched its only effective air sortie against the beachhead; JU–88 twin-engined light bombers managed to hit and sink *LST–282* off Agay Roadstead with radio-controlled bombs, resulting in forty casualties and the loss of several 36th Division artillery pieces.

The 1st Airborne Task Force

Since the British 2d Independent Parachute Brigade had failed to take Le Muy on D-day, the 550th Glider Infantry Battalion, supported by part of the 509th Parachute Battalion, undertook the task shortly after midnight on 16 August.[5] The two units launched their first attack at 0200, but, making little progress against stubborn resistance, they withdrew at daylight and returned at 0900 with artillery support. The two battalions then pushed slowly into the town. Toward midafternoon, tanks of the 191st Tank Battalion, attached to the 45th Division, rumbled up the road

across the Maures from Ste. Maxime to lend a hand; and the last defenders of Le Muy surrendered shortly thereafter.

Meanwhile, the 1st Battalion, 551st Parachute Infantry, had set out west for Draguignan, where elements of the *LXII Corps* headquarters still held out. By 2300 on the 16th, the battalion had cleared most of the town and captured part of the corps staff as well as Brig. Gen. Ludwig Bieringer, the German military governor of the Var department.

West of Le Muy, at Les Arcs, the 517th Parachute Infantry had begun to run into the first signs of an organized German response. True to his decision at dusk on the 15th, General von Schwerin had continued preparations at Vidauban to attack toward Le Muy and relieve the *LXII Corps* headquarters at Draguignan. By 0700 on the 16th, he had finally managed to assemble about four infantry battalions from the *244th Division,* two 105-mm. howitzers from the same division, and a couple of heavy weapons platoons and the assault company from his former division headquarters. Moving several miles northeast from Vidauban, the German force split at a road junction just south of Les Arcs—one group heading north for Les Arcs, and the other, intending to strike for Le Muy, temporarily holding at the junction.

The first German group entered Les Arcs about 0730, threw out a small American outpost, and gained a foothold on rising terrain north of town, while the 517th Parachute Infantry held along the hills to the northeast and east. About 0930 the 517th's paratroopers were joined by

---

[5] This subsection is based on the official records of the 1st ABTF and its components, and on von Luttichau, "German Operations," chs. 9 and 10.

MAJ. GEN. LUDWIG BIERINGER, A PRISONER OF WAR. *General Frederick is on the passenger side of the jeep.*

the 2d Battalion of the 180th Infantry, 45th Division, which had made its way over the Maures massif via back roads and trails. It had passed through Vidauban—then inexplicably empty of Germans—and, aided by a platoon from the 645th Tank Destroyer Battalion, began clearing Route N–7, which threatened the German rear. A few hours later, elements of the 157th Infantry, 45th Division, approached Vidauban from the south and found the town again occupied by Germans, but they managed to clear the area of hostile troops by 1530. Late in the day, reinforced by its 3d Battalion, the 517th Parachute Infantry launched an attack of its own, and by dusk had virtually surrounded Les Arcs.

Doomed to failure before it started, General von Schwerin's counterattack now collapsed, and the remaining Germans in the vicinity of Vidauban and Les Arcs withdrew to the west and northwest under cover of darkness. During the day's fighting, the Germans had lost not only many heavy weapons and vehicles, but also the equivalent of two infantry battalions of the *244th Division* against forces of the 1st Airborne Task Force and the 45th Infantry Division. The action at Les Arcs was also the last significant engagement of the 1st Airborne Task Force in the Toulon–St. Raphael corridor. By the morning of 17 August the airborne forces were in firm control of their objective area, including the railroad-highway junc-

TROOPS OF 45TH DIVISION WADE ASHORE NEAR ST. MAXIME

tion towns of Le Muy, La Motte, Trans-en-Provence, and Les Arcs, which both blocked the main entrances to the beachhead and secured the inland approaches to Toulon. Shortly before noon on the 17th, major elements of the 36th Division began to arrive at Le Muy from the Frejus area, and the initial mission of the airborne force ended.

The Advance to the Blue Line

German opposition during the night of 15–16 August and throughout the 16th was strongest on VI Corps' far left, beyond Cape Negre, and on the right, along the Argens valley for about five miles inland. In the southwest, the 7th Infantry, 3d Division, drove toward Toulon in two columns—the 3d Battalion and the French commandos along the coastal road (Route N–559) and the rest of the regiment about three miles inland along Route N–98.[6] The German strongpoint at Layet Point, where the Allied coastal force had been halted late on the 15th, fell early on the morning of the 16th, but the area was not entirely cleared until almost 1500. Against scattered opposition, the coastal force pushed on

[6] Additional information on 3d Division and commando operations comes from Bouvet, "Un Debarquement de Commandos . . . l'Operation du Cap Negre," *Revue Militaire d'Information*, No. 153; and Groupe de Commandos d'Afrique, Compte-Rendu d'Opns, 15–25 Aug 44.

and by nightfall had patrols in Le La-vandou, about three miles beyond Layet Point.

Starting out from La Mole about 0330 on the 16th, the 7th Infantry's inland column halted at 0730 in front of a strong *242d Division* roadblock about seven miles beyond La Mole. Defensive fire and rugged terrain de-layed progress for the rest of the day, but during the night the American units, guided by the FFI, began flank-ing marches that were to carry them past the obstacle early on the 17th.

North of the 7th Infantry, the 30th Infantry regiment also swept west-ward in two columns. About 1000 a small group started out from Collo-brieres opposed mainly by *242d Divi-sion* artillery, antitank, and mortar fire; it emerged from the mountains about 1600 at Pierrefeu in the Toulon–St. Raphael corridor. The unit had broken through a heavily wooded, easily defensible section of the Maures and was a good eight miles west of the Army beachhead line. Meanwhile, other elements of the 30th Infantry regiment had reached Gonfaron, ten miles northeast of Col-lobrieres on Route N–97, the main highway through the southwestern section of the Toulon–St. Raphael corridor. By dusk on the 16th the main body of the 30th Infantry was assembled at Gonfaron, with patrols active to the west and southwest.

North of the 3d Division, units of the 45th Division that had completed their missions along the coast marched across the northeastern por-tion of the Maures on the 16th, push-ing west and assisting the paratroop-ers at Vidauban. By the following day, 17 August, the division had cleared a wide area south of the Argens River from Frejus to Le Luc and stood astride the central portion of the Toulon–St. Raphael corridor. Above the 45th, units of the 36th Division had secured the coast on the 16th and then pushed scattered German elements off the Esterel massif before swinging west to join the airborne units at Le Muy. By the 17th they oc-cupied a broad area on the VI Corps' right flank, from Theoule-sur-Mer, at the northern end of the blue line, to the region around Draguignan a few miles northwest of Le Muy.

The 36th Division seemed to work harder for its gains. Shortly before dawn on the 16th, units of the 142d Infantry had entered Frejus unop-posed, but soon became involved in a series of minor skirmishes after day-break. They were unable to secure the town until 1330, and then met further resistance while pushing up the Argens valley that afternoon. Along the coast, the 143d had cleared St. Raphael by 0930, but, as expected, encountered stubborn resistance from *242d Division* elements in the Camel Red area. Meanwhile, north of Frejus and St. Raphael, 141st Infantry units ran into a second counterattacking force along Route N–7 in the north-eastern corner of the Esterel. A German motorized column, probably consisting of part of the reserve bat-talion of the *239th Grenadiers, 148th Division*, came rolling south along the highway early in the morning from the direction of Cannes. The infantry-men of the regiment's 2d Battalion easily dispersed these Riviera rangers, who apparently had little knowledge of the rapid American advance. How-ever, to prevent further excursion from this quarter, the 141st regiment's 1st Battalion and some divisional engineers moved up to La Napoule, destroying a local highway and railroad bridge just south of the town.

An Appraisal

On both 15 and 16 August the VI Corps had penetrated farther and more easily than planners had thought possible. Except on the far west, in the sector of the 7th Infantry, VI Corps and the 1st Airborne Task Force had reached and crossed the Army beachhead, or blue, line. By the end of D plus 1 Truscott's forces thus had a firm hold on the vital Toulon–St. Raphael corridor, making it nearly impossible for German ground forces to launch a significant attack on the Allied beachline. Although German resistance had stiffened somewhat on the 16th, it was still spotty and much weaker than expected. In fact, the Germans had failed to make any strong or coordinated attempt to contain the beachhead, and the VI Corps found no indication that the Germans had any firm front line. Resistance had been disorganized and confined to widely separated strongpoints; counterattacks had been highly localized and uncoordinated with units defending the beachline. In addition, intelligence officers at VI Corps and Seventh Army could find no indications that the Nineteenth Army was massing forces for a major counteroffensive, and could only assume that the Germans would attempt to delay further penetrations while preparing stronger defenses at Toulon.

The ANVIL commanders had other reasons to be optimistic. By the 16th they had confirmed the low caliber of the German units that were facing their forces. Captured documents and interrogation reports showed that the vast majority of the 2,300 prisoners taken by Seventh Army units were either overage Germans or members of Ost units. In addition, Allied losses had been much lower than expected on D-day, with only about 95 killed and 385 soldiers wounded.[7] Furthermore, instead of rising sharply on the 16th as many planners had expected, VI Corps casualties were somewhat lower than they had been on the 15th. Losses of equipment and materiel had also been relatively insignificant. Despite the misgivings of Churchill, the ANVIL landings, according to the U.S. Navy historian Samuel Eliot Morison, had been "an example of an almost perfect amphibious operation from the point of view of training, timing, Army–Navy–Air Force cooperation, performance, and results."[8]

Just about the only major controversy regarding this initial phase stemmed from Admiral Lewis' decision to back away from the Camel Red beach and put the 36th Division's 142d Infantry regiment ashore on Camel Green. The division commander, General Dahlquist, later approved the decision and regretted only that

---

[7] The figures on the wounded include those carried as injured in action; the killed include those who died of wounds. The figures are approximations from incomplete and contradictory information in the official Army records. For the first three or four days of the campaign, casualty figures were not adequately recorded, but as command, control, and administration procedures formalized ashore, casualty reporting became more accurate.

[8] Morison, The Invasion of France and Germany, p. 291.

the concerned regiment could not have been scheduled for Camel Green from the beginning. The delay at Camel Red had wasted six or seven hours. On the other hand, he believed that to have planned to land almost his entire division over Camel Green would have been unsound. Truscott, however, was later extremely critical of the decision, holding that the failure to carry out the assault on Camel Red forced his units to spend an extra day securing the beach from the land approaches, directly causing delays in the landing of Combat Command Sudre and ground echelons of the tactical air force, which in turn delayed the seizure and occupation of airfields near Frejus and in the Argens valley. According to Truscott, the net result was the lack of close air support for the VI Corps in the critical days that followed and his own inability to send Sudre's armored unit "northwest or north as . . . planned." Thus he termed the decision "a grave error which merited reprimand at least, and most certainly no congratulation," adding that, "except for the otherwise astounding success of the assault, it might have had even graver consequences." [9]

Truscott's criticism appears unjustified. The 36th Division did not secure the St. Raphael–Frejus area until midafternoon on 16 August, and even then the task of clearing offshore and beach obstacles proved to be so great that Army engineers and Navy demolition experts were unable to open Camel Red for discharge operations until 1900 on 17 August, D plus 2. Thus, even if the 142d Infantry, regardless of casualties, had secured Camel Red during the afternoon of 15 August, the beach would not have been ready to receive CC Sudre or any other unit until late on the 16th at the earliest.

Truscott's own plans had called for the French armored command to land sometime on the 16th, with "first priority" to Camel Red.[10] But Sudre's force actually landed over the 45th Division beaches during the night of 15–16 August, and was assembled ashore earlier than would have been the case if it had landed over Camel Red on the 16th in accordance with Truscott's original plans. From its assembly point near Ste. Maxime, CC Sudre could have started north along Route N–98 on the morning of the 16th and would have reached the Argens valley no later than it would have if the unit had landed over Camel Red on the 16th. Truscott could also have sent the unit north into the Argens valley over the Ste. Maxime–Le Muy road on the 16th. The 45th Division had already established liaison with the 1st Airborne Task Force along this road, and during the afternoon of the 16th a platoon of the 191st Tank Battalion, attached to the 45th Division, reached Le Muy over the same road. Had Sudre's armor followed that route on the 16th, it might well have reached Le Muy considerably sooner than if it had landed at Camel Red during the afternoon of that day.

But the entire matter is academic. Well before 15 August, Patch had decided that CC Sudre would have to be returned to de Lattre's control soon

[9] Truscott, *Command Missions*, pp. 414, 418.

[10] Ibid., p. 397; see also VI Corps FO 1, 30 Jul 44.

after the landings. Truscott could not have sent it "northwest or north." Realizing this, Truscott had made plans to put together Task Force Butler for a possible drive north and northwest of the beachhead area, and had expected CC Sudre to attack generally westward in the region south of the Durance River. In the end, Sudre's armor began to reach the middle of the Toulon–St. Raphael corridor during the night of 16–17 August, certainly no later than it could have if put ashore over Camel Red on the afternoon of the 16th in accordance with preassault plans.

Truscott's remarks about delays in airfield construction and lack of air support east of the Rhone are also difficult to support. Even if the 142d Infantry had landed on Camel Red as scheduled, it is doubtful that engineers could have begun work on the airfields near Frejus before the 17th, when surveys actually began. Moreover, existing and potential airfield sites in the Argens valley and in the Toulon–St. Raphael corridor were all in VI Corps' hands as soon as or earlier than anyone had expected.[11] But the rapid Allied penetration, combined with adverse soil conditions in the beachhead area, forced aviation engineers to make drastic revisions in construction plans; unloading delays at both Alpha and Camel beaches also slowed airfield progress. In the beachhead area engineers could not meet construction schedules: the crash (emergency) airstrip was

opened two days late, three of the four planned dry-weather fields were four days behind schedule, and the rapid advance inland prompted engineers to cancel the fourth. On the other hand, a field at Sisteron, sixty miles northwest of Camel Red and not planned before the assault, was open on 23 August; a field at Le Luc was ready on the 25th, a week ahead of schedule; and one at Cuers, also in the Toulon–St. Raphael corridor, was operational on D plus 12, ten days ahead of schedule. Thus it is unlikely that the failure of the 142d Infantry to land at Camel Red on the afternoon of D-day had any bearing on close air support for the VI Corps east of the Rhone.[12] Truscott's postwar contentions may signify little more than his frustrations with some aspects of the campaign that followed.

Certainly for Truscott, the evening of 16 August was filled with both elation and expectation. For all practical purposes, his forces had gained the initial objectives that the Seventh Army had assigned to them, and had done so twenty-four to forty-eight hours before most planners had thought possible. The next stage, according to the Seventh Army's invasion directive, was to reorganize the assault force and mount an aggressive drive to the west and northwest. Con-

---

[11] Additional information on air force planning and construction derives from MATAF Rpt on Opn Dragoon and XII Tactical Air Command Rpt on Opn Dragoon.

[12] Air Force reports emphasized inadequate shipping for the air buildup in southern France, unloading problems that resulted primarily from using merchant ships instead of LSTs for some supplies and equipment, and transportation problems ashore. Finally, the very success of VI Corps created a major problem for the air forces because, according to the official Air Force account, "the battle line was so completely fluid that MATAF's planes could not be used for close support." AAF III, p. 433.

sidering the apparent German weakness all along his front, Truscott was eager to begin executing this second phase as soon as possible. A strong advance inland toward Toulon and the Rhone would also keep the Germans off balance, making it increasingly difficult for them to concentrate enough forces to contain the Allied beachhead area. With Patch's approval, Truscott issued the new attack orders before dark on the 16th.

CHAPTER VIII

Breakout: 17–19 August

Eager to take advantage of the weakness of the German defenders and their slow response to ANVIL, Truscott sent his three divisions inland. He wanted the bulk of the 3d Infantry Division to continue its advance on 17 August, first pushing its left flank westward to the line of the Real Martin and Gapeau rivers, both running generally north to south under the western slopes of the Maures.[1] Once there, the division's left was to hold until the French II Corps, on or about 20 August, could move up to continue the drive toward Toulon. The rest of the 3d Division was to assemble in the Le Luc–Gonfaron area and strike westward along the axis of Route N–7 to Brignoles, thirteen miles beyond Le Luc, and to St. Maximin, eleven miles farther and twenty-five miles directly north of Toulon (*Map 7*). Meanwhile, the 45th Division was to dispatch one regimental combat team northwest from Vidauban to the Barjols area, about eleven miles north of St. Maximin. CC Sudre (CC1)[2] of the 1st French Armored Division was also to head westward to the St. Maximin–Barjols line, using both N–7 and secondary roads between the 3d and 45th Divisions.

On the VI Corps' eastern flank, scattered forces of Task Force Butler were to assemble at Le Muy on the 17th, reorganize in accordance with preassault plans, and start probing northwest on the 18th. The 36th Division was to relieve the 1st Airborne Task Force in the Le Muy–Les Arcs region and then, leaving one regiment along the coast to protect VI Corps' right flank, be prepared to follow TF Butler. After assembling in reserve at Le Muy, the airborne force was to move eastward to relieve the regiment that the 36th Division had left behind.

In brief, Truscott's plans provided for three mutually supporting maneuvers: first, a general pressure westward along the coast toward Toulon; second, an outflanking of Toulon to the north (possibly followed by an advance westward toward the Rhone); and third, a drive northwest by TF Butler and the 36th Division. On the

---

[1] Additional planning material for American units in this section is from Truscott, *Command Missions*, p. 416–19.

[2] The French 1st and 5th Armored Divisions normally used numerals to designate their combat commands—1, 2, and 3 in the 1st Armored Division and 4, 5, and 6 in the 5th Armored Division. The French 2d Armored Division, in contrast, used letters taken from the last names of the commanders.

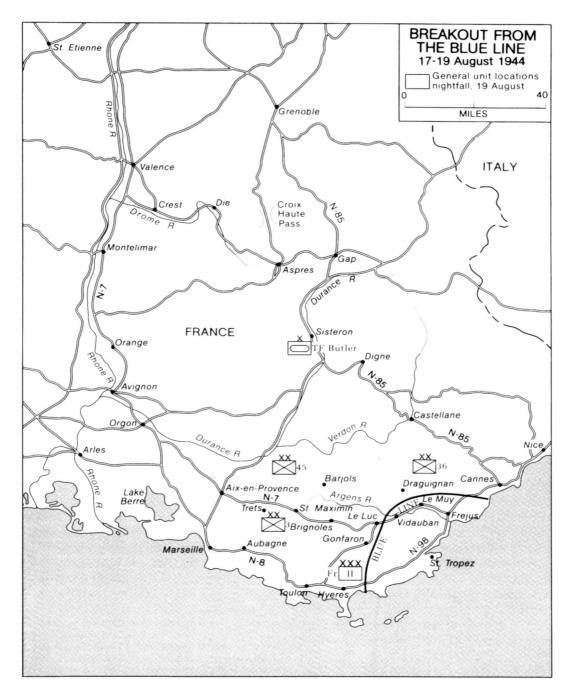

BREAKOUT FROM
THE BLUE LINE
17-19 August 1944

General unit locations
nightfall, 19 August

0   40

MILES

MAP 7   This map is printed in full color at the back of the book, following the Index.

left, the advance westward to the Real Martin and Gapeau rivers would secure a base area for the attack on Toulon and Marseille by the French II Corps. The push in the center to the St. Maximin–Barjols line would protect the French northern flank and threaten the Rhone valley. Finally, the advance northwest by TF Butler and the 36th Division would greatly complicate German efforts to hold the lower Rhone and would pose a serious threat to a subsequent German withdrawal from the area.

German Plans

The German commanders spent the night of 16–17 August assessing their options.[3] With the failure of the LXII Corps' 148th and 242d Divisions to halt or even slow down the invasion and with the collapse of the German counterattack in the Les Arcs area on the 16th, General Wiese, the Nineteenth Army commander, concluded that his major problem was no longer mounting an immediate, ad hoc assault but rather establishing a defensive line that would give his combat forces still west of the Rhone time to transfer to the east side of the river, either for defensive purposes or to build up the strength needed to launch a substantive counteroffensive. Furthermore, he decided that any new attempts to rescue the LXII Corps headquarters would be fruitless and could only disrupt orderly redeployments. However, on the basis of inadequate intelligence, Wiese also esti-

mated that the Seventh Army posed no immediate threat to the region west of Toulon, allowing him to move units east from the Marseille area for defensive purposes and replace them with forces from west of the Rhone.

Late on the afternoon of 16 August Wiese directed General Baessler, commanding the battered 242d Division, to build up delaying positions along the line of the Real Martin and Gapeau rivers from the coast inland for thirty miles northeast to Vidauban. (Wiese did not yet know that Vidauban was already lost.) To help hold this sector, he pulled three battalions of the 244th Division from positions west of Toulon and assigned the units to Baessler. About the same time, Wiese directed the 148th Division, now cut off on the eastern side of the Allied landing area, to employ whatever units it could find to halt what he believed to be an Allied drive along the coast toward Cannes. At this point, he thus had no clear idea of specific Allied objectives inland.

Pressing Westward

The rapid Allied advance westward soon made Wiese's defensive plans obsolete.[4] On the left of the 3d Division, the 7th Infantry and the French African Commando Group moved up to the Real Martin and Gapeau rivers on the 17th and 18th, encountering

---

[3] German information in this chapter is based on von Luttichau, "German Operations," chs. 8–11 and 15.

[4] The general sources of information for Allied ground operations in this and subsequent chapters are the official records of the units mentioned in the text. Continued repetition of citations to these sources becomes redundant, but planning material, controversial matters, and complex situations are fully documented, while citations are made, as appropriate, to published material, both official and unofficial.

some stubborn but scattered resistance from units of the *242d Division*. On the 18th and 19th the French commandos and elements of the French 1st Infantry Division relieved the 7th Infantry in the coastal sector and continued the drive west.

In the 3d Division's center the 15th Infantry, following the 3d Provisional Reconnaissance Squadron,[5] reached the town of La Roquebrussanne on 18 August, ten miles south of Brignoles. The 30th Infantry, charged with seizing Brignoles, started out on 17 August with a firefight at Le Luc, but part of the regiment and elements of CC Sudre cleared the town after a four-hour action. Meanwhile, the main bodies of the two Allied units continued westward along Route N–7 and lesser roads, nearing Brignoles late on the 18th. After a battle that lasted until the next morning, the area fell to the French and American attackers. Farther north, the 157th and 179th Infantry, 45th Division, headed out of the Le Luc–Vidauban area late on the 17th, encountered little resistance, and halted at dark on the 18th within striking distance of Barjols. The entire advance completely dislocated the center of the line that Wiese had hoped to establish.

Well to the east the 142d Infantry, 36th Division, cleaned out the north side of the Argens valley with little trouble and, passing through units of the 1st Airborne Task Force at Le Muy, mopped up the Draguignan area during the 18th. The 143d Infantry reassembled in the vicinity of Le Muy on the 17th and 18th, while the 141st Infantry and the 636th Tank Destroyer Battalion spread out to secure the region extending east from Le Muy to the coast as well as the slopes of the Esterel. During the 18th the 636th Tank Destroyer Battalion sent reconnaissance troops north about fifteen miles from Frejus in an effort to rescue a group of misdropped paratroopers that the Germans had cut off. The first attempt failed, but after hard fighting on the 19th, elements of the 141st Infantry and the tank destroyer battalion extricated many injured paratroopers.

Meanwhile, the 36th Division's Cavalry Reconnaissance Troop had been indulging itself in a series of long-distance scouting patrols to the north. Rapidly moving twenty-five to thirty miles north and northeast of Le Muy as far as Route N–85, which is the main highway from the Riviera to Grenoble, the light cavalry units encountered no significant resistance on 17 and 18 August. The patrolling, together with information received from ULTRA sources,[6] reflected the general weakness of the German forces along the Seventh Army's eastern flank. Once TF Butler and the 36th Division started north and northwest, they apparently would face no significant threat on their right, or northeastern, flank.

The German Defense

In the early afternoon of 17 August, *Nineteenth Army* officers

---

[5] The squadron consisted of the 3d Cavalry Reconnaissance Troop, the 3d Division Battle Patrol (itself a provisional unit), the Reconnaissance Company of the 601st Tank Destroyer Battalion, and Company D (light tanks) of the 756th Tank Battalion.

[6] Bussey ULTRA Report.

TROOPS AND TANK DESTROYERS MOVE THROUGH SALERNES

learned that VI Corps' center and right wing had passed through the defensive line they had planned to establish from the coast to Vidauban. Seeking some way to hold back Allied forces until more German units, especially the *11th Panzer Division,* could move to the east side of the Rhone, General Wiese decided to establish two new defensive lines. The first would extend northward from the eastern defenses of Toulon through Brignoles to Barjols. The second line, about fifteen miles farther west, would anchor on the south at Marseille, stretch eastward about twenty miles along Route N–8 (the Toulon-Marseille highway), and then swing north to the Durance River about fourteen miles northwest of Barjols.

These two lines represented Wiese's last effort to tie the defense of Toulon and Marseille to that of the Rhone River valley, which was still fifty miles farther west.

Wiese assigned responsibility for holding the two new lines to Lt. Gen. Baptist Kniess, commanding the *LXXXV Corps.* Kniess would have what was left of the *244th Division* (guarding Marseille), the *338th Division* (less one regimental combat team), the remnants of the *242d Division,* and part of the *198th Division,* which was still trying to cross the Rhone. Wiese also gave Kniess General von Schwerin and his *189th Division* headquarters, along with the miscellaneous units that von Schwerin had already assembled. Kniess, in turn, directed Baessler of the *242d Division* to hold Toulon and the southern part of the first line with whatever units the division commander could round up; he ordered von Schwerin to hold the center at Brignoles and Barjols with the *15th Grenadiers* of his former division and the battered *932d* and *933d Grenadier Regiments* of the *244th Division*. The *198th Division*, reinforced by elements of the *338th Division*, would man the second line as quickly as possible, for Kniess had little confidence that he could hold the first line past nightfall on 18 August. If all went well, the delay along the first line would provide enough time for the *11th Panzer Division* and the remaining elements of the *198th* and *338th Divisions* to cross the Rhone.

The German plans were again overtaken by events. Except on the immediate Toulon front, General Kniess was unable to establish the first line, and the Brignoles-Barjols area fell before any *LXXXV Corps* units could establish a coherent defense. Accordingly, during the afternoon of 18 August, Wiese directed a general retirement to the second line. Here Kniess planned to have the *198th Division*, which so far had been able to deploy only two infantry battalions, hold the northern section of the second line near the Durance River; the *242d Division*—now so reduced in strength as to be redesignated *Battle Group Baessler*—defend the center with the equivalent of a regimental task force; and two battalions of the *244th Division* anchor the line in the south at Marseille. The garrison at Toulon would have to fend for itself.

The Allied push westward was, however, again relentless. By the morning of 19 August, the 30th Infantry, 3d Division, had cleared Brignoles, and Sudre's CC1 had pushed to St. Maximin, eleven miles farther west. The 15th Infantry joined the French armor at St. Maximin later in the day and by the evening had traveled another nine miles west to the town of Trets. The general advance met only minor German resistance, but had breached the center of Kniess' second line of defense before it could be established.

Meanwhile, north of Brignoles, the 179th Infantry of the 45th Division had cleaned out Barjols on the 19th, while still farther north the 157th Infantry had pushed west and by dusk was nearing the Durance River. It began to appear to jubilant operations officers at all echelons of command that the east-west highways and byways between the coastal ports and the Durance River might be undefended all the way to the Rhone. If so, the *Nineteenth Army* might be in for a major disaster if the American drive west continued at its current pace.

For General Patch, the Seventh Army commander, the capture of Toulon and Marseille was more pressing. Until the ports were in Allied hands, the success of the invasion could not be confirmed. Thus, as Sudre's armored force was preparing to continue its drive west, Patch ordered Truscott to return the unit to French control for the assault on Toulon. Reluctant to lose the force and arguing that its return east would create traffic jams, which would seriously inhibit the westward progress of the 3d Division, Truscott rushed to the Seventh Army's command post at St. Tropez to dispute the decision.

Patch was unmoved and refused to reverse the long-standing arrangement. Although sympathetic, he reminded Truscott that the Seventh Army had promised General de Lattre to return CC1 by dark on the 19th to a position from which it could move forward on the 20th with the rest of the French forces heading toward Toulon. General Sudre of CC1, who disliked the redeployment order as much as Truscott, had no choice but to move his command back east along Route N–7, thus creating the traffic jams Truscott had feared and, more important, depriving the VI Corps of its most powerful mobile striking force. In its place, Task Force Butler would have to suffice.[7]

Task Force Butler

By evening on 17 August, almost all of TF Butler had assembled just north of Le Muy.[8] A brigade-sized unit, the force included the 117th Cavalry Reconnaissance Squadron; the 753d Tank Battalion (with two medium tank companies); the motorized 2d Battalion of the 143d Infantry, 36th Division; Company C, 636th Tank Destroyer Battalion; and the 59th Armored Field Artillery Battal-

ion.[9] Support forces included Company F of the 344th Engineer General Service Regiment; a reinforced company from the 111th Medical Battalion, 36th Division; the 3426th Quartermaster Truck Company; and a detachment of the 87th Ordnance Company (Heavy Maintenance).

Butler's mechanized task force started out early on 18 August, first following the 45th Division's trail west to the Barjols area, and then striking north on its own. By noon the force had reached the Verdon River, ten miles above Barjols, but found the highway bridge destroyed and was unable to cross until about 1600, despite assistance from the FFI and local French civilians. Then, with only about four hours of daylight left and five hours of fuel, Butler decided to wait for his resupply column, due to arrive that night. Meanwhile, one element of the force, Troop C, which had taken a slightly different route north, bumped into a portion of the *LXII Corps* staff that had eluded the airborne units, and captured the unfortunate General Neuling.

The next day, 19 August, the main body of the task force struck out northwest, crossing to the west bank of the Durance River to take advantage of better roads there, and continued north to Sisteron. Troops A and B of the 117th Cavalry remained on the eastern side of the river and, after a few minor skirmishes with isolated German units, entered Sisteron unop-

---

[7] See also Truscott, *Command Missions*, pp. 422–23.

[8] In addition to official records, material in this chapter on the operations of TF Butler derives from Frederick B. Butler, "Task Force Butler," *Armored Cavalry Journal*, LVII, No. 1 (Jan–Feb 48), 12–18, and No. 2 (Mar–Apr 48), 30–38 (hereafter cited as Butler, "Task Force Butler"); and John A. Hixon, "Analysis of Deep Attack Operations—U.S. VI Corps: Task Force Butler, August 1944," MS, U.S. Army Combat Studies Institute, Fort Leavenworth, Kansas, 1987 (hereafter cited as Hixon, "TF Butler").

[9] The 117th Cavalry Squadron consisted of three reconnaissance troops (A, B, and C), a self-propelled assault gun troop (E), and a company of light tanks (F) (there was no Company or Troop D). The 753d Tank Battalion left behind Company A, medium tanks, and Company D, light tanks.

posed about 1800 hours. The main column, its march north disturbed only by a mistaken strafing attack from friendly aircraft, reached the town shortly thereafter. The only sizable action took place at Digne, fifteen miles southeast of Sisteron, where armored elements of Butler's force helped an FFI battalion convince about 500 to 600 German defenders—mostly administrative and logistical troops—to surrender after several hours of fighting.[10]

That evening Butler refueled his vehicles, established outposts north of Sisteron, and sent out several mobile patrols to the west, which scouted to within thirty miles of Avignon and the Rhone. With good radio communications established with VI Corps headquarters and several intact bridges over the Durance River in his hands, he was ready to move his task force either north toward Grenoble or west-northwest toward the Rhone River in the vicinity of Montelimar. Impatiently he awaited Truscott's orders.

Accelerating the Campaign

The campaign in southern France was quickly reaching a crisis point. Well before 19 August the unexpected weakness of German resistance in the assault area had brought about two significant changes in Seventh Army plans.[11] The first was Truscott's

exploitation order of late 16 August, which had started the 3d and 45th Divisions westward and TF Butler northward. The second, made by Patch, was to accelerate the unloading of the French II Corps.

Original plans had called for the first echelon of the French II Corps to land between 16 and 18 August, and the second between the 21st and the 25th. Seeking to exploit German weakness and speed up the move to Toulon and Marseille, Patch, in conjunction with Admiral Hewitt and General de Lattre, pushed up the schedule. The bulk of the first French echelon came ashore on 16 August, and elements of various French armored units arrived the next day. This allowed the troop transports to make a rapid trip back to Corsica, and return with troops of the second echelon on the 18th. By nightfall that day almost all troops of the II Corps (excepting those of one armored combat command and one regiment) were ashore, but scarcely half the trucks, tanks, tank destroyers, artillery, and other heavy equipment were on hand.

Meanwhile, on 17 August, Patch and de Lattre decided to move the French troops up to the line of the Real Martin and Gapeau rivers on the 19th instead of assembling all of French II Corps, including its missing equipment, near the beaches. This decision alone had the French forces

---

[10] For the interaction of Task Force Butler and local FFI, see unpublished paper, Arthur L. Funk, "Allies and Maquis: Liberation of Basses Alpes (Alpes de Haute-Provence) and Hautes Alpes—August 1944," 16 pp. (copy CMH).

[11] This section is based largely on *Seventh Army Rpt*, I, 152; Headquarters, Seventh Army, "Diary for Commanding General, Seventh Army," vol. II (of

three volumes), entries for 17–21 Aug 44 (copy in CMH, hereafter cited as Seventh Army Diary); Seventh Army G–2 Rpts 1–8 and 16–23 Aug 44; VI Corps G–2 Rpts 1–7 and 15–21 Aug 44; VI Corps War Rm Jnl 19–21 Aug 44; Seventh Army FO 2, 1200 19 Aug 44; Truscott, *Command Missions*, pp. 421–23; de Lattre, *History*, pp. 71–75; von Luttichau, "German Operations," ch. 10.

moving westward at least six days earlier than originally planned. Finally, rather than waiting until 25 August, when all the French vehicles and equipment would be ashore, de Lattre wanted to attack Toulon as soon as possible, asking only for the return of Sudre's armor on the 19th and the loan of artillery ammunition from Seventh Army stocks. With this help, he felt he could launch an effective assault on 20 August before the Germans had time to organize their defenses. Patch agreed to the acceleration, supplied the ammunition de Lattre needed, released CC1 to French control, and at noon on the 19th directed de Lattre to move immediately toward Toulon and Marseille.

Simultaneously, Patch ordered VI Corps to push westward to Aix-en-Provence, fifteen miles north of Marseille, in order to protect the northern flank of the attacking French. The American corps was also to secure crossings over the Durance River; seize Sisteron (which TF Butler reached about four hours later); continue strong reconnaissance northward; and prepare to start the 36th Division north toward Grenoble.

Seventh Army's new orders also reflected changes in Allied estimates of German capabilities and intentions in southern France. Patch's intelligence staff had originally expected that *Army Group G,* after making every effort to contain the Allied beachhead, would conduct an all-out defense of Toulon and Marseille, and, after it had exhausted its defensive potential east of the lower Rhone, would ultimately undertake a fighting withdrawal up the Rhone valley. But late on 17

August Seventh Army planners received information through ULTRA channels that forced them to revise this estimate. According to an ULTRA intercept, *Army Group G* was about to initiate a general withdrawal of its forces from southwestern France and the Atlantic coast south of Brest; if accurate, the withdrawal of the *Nineteenth Army* could not be far behind, and the success of the landing was assured.

The German Withdrawal

In Germany, *OKW* was more concerned about *Army Group B* in northern France than about *Army Group G* in the south. The Allied breakout from the Normandy beachheads at St. Lo, the failure of the German counterattack at Mortain, and the threatened Allied envelopment of the German forces in the Falaise Pocket, all pointed to a major German disaster in the north. At the same time, the ANVIL landings made it impossible for *Army Group G* to withdraw from southern France to northern Italy if German defenses in the Normandy area finally collapsed. Accordingly, on 16 August *OKW* put the issue before Hitler: either authorize the immediate withdrawal of *Army Groups B* and *G* or preside over the destruction of both. Having no real choice, Hitler reluctantly assented, and *OKW* quickly issued the necessary orders.

From the start, German execution of the orders was hampered by poor communications. The withdrawal orders for *Army Group G* were in two parts. About 1115 on 17 August Blaskowitz's headquarters received the first part, pertaining mainly to forces on the Atlantic coast and in southwestern France. This order came directly to *Army Group G* from *OKW,* and it was not until 1430 on the same day that Blaskowitz received an identical directive relayed through *OB West* channels. Presumably *OKW* dispatched the second part of the order, pertaining largely to the *Nineteenth Army,* at 1730 on 17 August, but neither *OB West* nor *Army Group G* received the second order that day. Such was the state of German communications that it was 1100 on the 18th before Blaskowitz, via *OKW* radio channels, received the second part of the order, which directed the *Nineteenth Army* to withdraw northward from southern France. Meanwhile, by early afternoon of the 18th, ULTRA sources had supplied the Seventh Army with the second part; thus Patch and Wiese were probably evaluating the new information at about the same time.[12] Both armies now had to consider how best to react to the sudden change in plans.

Upon receiving the Atlantic coast–southwestern France directive on the 17th, Blaskowitz had ordered Lt. Gen. Karl Sachs, who commanded the

[12] The first part of the withdrawal orders is ULTRA Msg XL 6753, 171408 Aug 44, and the second is XL 6919, 181356 Aug 44, ULTRA Collection, MHI. According to data presented in Bennett, *Ultra in the West,* p. 159, and Hinsley et al., *British Intelligence in the Second World War,* III, 2, pp. 274–75, the ULTRA decrypt of the first part of the withdrawal order was based on an ENIGMA intercept from *Naval Group West* to *Admiral Atlantic* at 0940, 17 August, and was dispatched to the field at 1408 that day. The second part was based on an intercept at 1730, 17 August (source not noted), and dispatched to the field at 1356, 18 August. Although both messages dealt with the withdrawal of *Army Group G* forces, each is distinct from the other and not "part" of a larger order. See also von Luttichau, "German Operations," ch. 10, pp. 1–7.

LXIV Corps on the Atlantic front, to begin moving eastward immediately. The *LXIV Corps* was to assemble most of its assigned forces—the *16th* and *159th Infantry Divisions,* miscellaneous army combat and service units, and a conglomeration of small air force and naval organizations—in the northern part of *Army Group G's* Atlantic sector. These units, representing three-quarters of *LXIV Corps'* strength and virtually its entire combat complement, were to move generally eastward south of the Loire River to a rendezvous with the main body of *Army Group G* north of Lyon. Left behind on the Atlantic coast were the garrisons of three coastal strongpoints that Hitler directed be held to the end: *Defense Area La Rochelle, Fortress Gironde North,* and *Fortress Gironde South. LXIV Corps* was also to leave a small force at Bordeaux until the German Navy could put to sea a few submarines undergoing repairs there.

In the extreme southwest, Blaskowitz wanted Maj. Gen. Otto Schmidt-Hartung of the *564th Liaison Staff,* a military government organization, to lead a motley collection of army service units and air force troops out of the Pyrenees–Carcassonne Gap–Toulouse area to join other *Army Group G* units along the west bank of the Rhone near Avignon.

The second *OKW* message—a "Hitler Sends" directive—ordering the northward deployment of the *Nineteenth Army,* called for a more carefully thought out withdrawal concept. On the western Mediterranean coast, the *IV Luftwaffe Field Corps,* with the *716th Infantry Division* as its principal combat component, was to retire up the west bank of the Rhone, picking up Schmidt-Hartung's group, some local naval units, three infantry battalions of the *189th Division,* one or two *Luftwaffe* infantry training regiments, and other miscellaneous units. On *Army Group G's* far eastern flank, the *148th Division* and the *157th Reserve Mountain Division* no longer concerned Blaskowitz because the *OKW* withdrawal orders had transferred the two divisions to *OB Southwest* in Italy, and their retirement to the Alps seemed a relatively simple affair.[13]

Extracting that portion of the *Nineteenth Army* engaged in combat was by far the most difficult undertaking. Blaskowitz's concept called for these forces to retire through successive defense lines, holding the U.S. Seventh Army east of the Rhone and south of the Durance until the *11th Panzer Division,* the bulk of the *198th Division,* and the two remaining regimental combat teams of the *338th Division* could cross the Rhone to participate in a general withdrawal up the east bank. The garrisons at Toulon and Marseille, ordered by Hitler to fight to the death, were to tie down as many Allied troops as possible and ensure that the harbor facilities did not fall into Allied hands intact.

On 18 and 19 August the staffs of the *Nineteenth Army* and *LXXXV Corps* drew up detailed plans for the withdrawal, specifying three successive

north-south delaying positions, labeled A, B, and C. The first, line A, began above Marseille and centered on Aix-en-Provence; the second, line B, was located between Lake Berre and the Durance River; and a third, line C, was just west of the Rhone. Kniess wanted his *LXXXV Corps* units to reach line A during the night of 19–20 August; line B during the night of 20–21 August; and line C before daylight on the 22d. The *Nineteenth Army* expected him to hold along line C until evening on the 23d, by which time, Wiese hoped, all preparations would be complete for a rapid, well-organized withdrawal up the Rhone valley, with the *IV Luftwaffe Field Corps* on the west bank and the *LXXXV Corps* on the east.

For the Germans, the appearance of American mechanized forces north of the Durance River on the 19th was an unwelcome surprise. As yet, *Army Group G* had little solid information concerning Task Force Butler, but Blaskowitz had learned enough by nightfall on the 19th to realize that he might have a problem securing the eastern flank of his forces withdrawing up the Rhone valley. With the *Nineteenth Army* already having trouble holding back VI Corps in the area south of the Durance River, a strong threat north of the Durance might turn a carefully phased withdrawal into a rout. On the other hand, Blaskowitz felt he had sufficient strength to deal with any immediate threat north of the Durance, and also estimated that for the time being a major thrust northward toward Grenoble and Lyon was of secondary importance in Allied planning.

On the evening of 19 August,

---

[13] Seventh Army intelligence during late August placed these two weak units, along with the *5th Mountain Division* and elements of the *90th Panzer Grenadier Division,* under the *LXXV Corps,* with a defensive mission along the Franco-Italian Alpine border, protecting *OB Southwest's* rear. "G-2 History: Seventh Army Operations in Europe," I, 15–31 August 44, Box 2, William W. Quinn Papers, MHI.

German attention thus remained focused on the critical Avignon area, the focal point for German forces withdrawing both east across the Rhone and north across the Durance. By that time substantial components of the *11th Panzer Division* and the *198th* and *338th Infantry Divisions* still had to cross to the east bank of the Rhone on a single ferry near Avignon and on two more farther south. In addition, the Germans had to hold crossings over the Durance east of Avignon until the *LXXXV Corps* as well as units coming over the Rhone south of Avignon could move north across the Durance. A strong Allied drive toward Avignon could cut off much of the *LXXXV Corps.* An additional concern was an Allied drive to and across the Rhone south of Avignon before the *IV Luftwaffe Field Corps,* withdrawing up the Rhone's west bank, could escape. If that happened, the bulk of the *IV Luftwaffe Field Corps* would probably be lost. Under these circumstances, Generals Blaskowitz and Wiese could hardly avoid the conclusion that a strong Seventh Army drive to the Rhone in the Avignon area would be the Allies' most logical, timely, and likely course of action.

In the Allied camp, however, the proper course of action was not so evident. Based on the ULTRA information that Patch had received on 17 and 18 August, the Seventh Army's best move appeared to be an immediate push toward the Rhone in an attempt to cut off the *Nineteenth Army.* But a number of factors stayed Patch's hand. Logistics had now become a major problem. A general shortage of trucks and gasoline meant that the Allied logistical system could not immediately support a major effort to cut off the *Nineteenth Army* at Avignon or farther north up the Rhone valley. For deeper operations inland, Toulon and Marseille would have to be taken and rehabilitated, a task that a strong German defense might make exceedingly difficult. In northern France, Eisenhower's forces were already suffering from a lack of operational ports, and Patch, with comparatively little over-the-beach supply capability, could not afford similar difficulties. Thus, on the 19th, he made Aix-en-Provence the western limit of Truscott's VI Corps advance, primarily to protect the Seventh Army's main effort, which was seizing Toulon and Marseille.

Toulon and Marseille

Before the invasion, de Lattre had planned to capture Toulon and Marseille in succession, but the accelerated French landings allowed him to envision almost concurrent actions against both ports.[14] He divided his forces into two groups: one under Lt. Gen. Edgar de Larminat consisting of two infantry divisions, some tanks, and the African Commando Group; the other under Maj. Gen. Aime de Goislard de Monsabert consisting of an infantry division, some tanks, and a ranger-type unit. De Larminat was to attack Toulon westward along the coast; de Monsabert was to maintain flank contact with the VI Corps on the right, strike into Toulon from the

---

[14] De Lattre, *History,* pp. 72–75, 95–97; Army B, Genl Opns Order 5, 19 Aug 44; Army B, Particular Order 8, 20 Aug 44.

north, drive to the coast to encircle the city, and, if possible, probe west toward Marseille. From the afternoon of 19 August through the night, French troops poured westward from the landing beaches to take positions for the assault against Toulon on the following day.

If the Germans had had more time and materiel, they might have turned Toulon into a formidable fortress. The local garrison consisted of about 18,000 troops, including 5,500 naval personnel and 2,800 air force men, plus naval and army artillery and anti-aircraft guns. Equally important, the port was virtually surrounded by rugged hills and mountains—those to the north rising to nearly 2,500 feet. If Toulon was strongly defended, the Allied timetable could be severely disrupted. However, from the start German command difficulties hampered the organization of a coherent defense. The senior admiral of the port had died of a heart attack several days before ANVIL, and General Baessler, the senior army officer, had been cut off from the city several days afterward. Rear Adm. Heinrich Ruhfus, who subsequently took command of the German defense, did the best he could and evacuated the increasingly restive civilian population, probably about 100,000 men, women, and children, prior to the battle. But Ruhfus needed time to reorganize his forces. The existing defenses were strongest in the wrong places. On the landward approaches, they were spotty and incomplete—in some cases no more than roadblocks—and little attention had been paid to the northern and western sectors of the city. If the Allies moved quickly, the Ger-

mans would have difficulty putting up any effective resistance.

The French attacked on the morning of 20 August, and the first results were less than promising.[15] Heavy artillery, antitank, and machine-gun fire was initially severe along the coastal road, and de Larminat's forces had to reduce, one by one, a series of major and minor strongpoints. Infantrymen clawed their way to the outskirts of Hyeres, nine miles east of Toulon, late in the day; but determined German resistance stopped the French drive from the northeast (Map 8). In the west, however, de Monsabert's units achieved spectacular success. Swinging across high rough mountains, they outflanked the German defenders and pushed through the western approaches to the city, some leading elements penetrating to within less than two miles of the Toulon waterfront. Another group, operating approximately six miles west of Toulon, cut the main highway between Toulon and Mar-

---

[15] The following account is based on de Lattre, History, ch. 5; La Premiere Division Blindee au Combat (Malakoff-Seine, 1947), pp. 32–52; de Monsabert, La 3eme Division d'Infanterie Algerienne dans la Bataille de Provence, Toulon-Marseilles, Aout 1944 (Offenburg, n.d.), pp. 21–65; Histoire de la Neuvieme Division d'Infanterie Coloniale (Lyon, n.d.), pp. 30–38; La lre D. F. L.: Epopee d'une Reconquete, Juin 1940–Mai 1945 (Paris, 1946), pp. 124–27; 3d Algerian Inf Div, Journale de Marche, 19–31 Aug 44; and French Army B, Comptes Rendus de 3eme Bureau, 18–31 Aug 44. For additional information on French units throughout the course of the later campaigns, see the Service Historique de l'Armee, Guerre 1939–1945: Les Grandes Unites Francaises, Historique Succinct, 6 vols. (Paris: Imprimerie Nationale, 1972–76), especially the daily corps situation reports in vol. V, "Campagnes de France et d'Allemagne," pt. III of three parts, or subvolumes) (hereafter cited as Historique Succinct); and interviews of Marcel Vigneras, a CMH historian, with various French commanders in 1945 (hereafter cited as Vigneras Intervs).

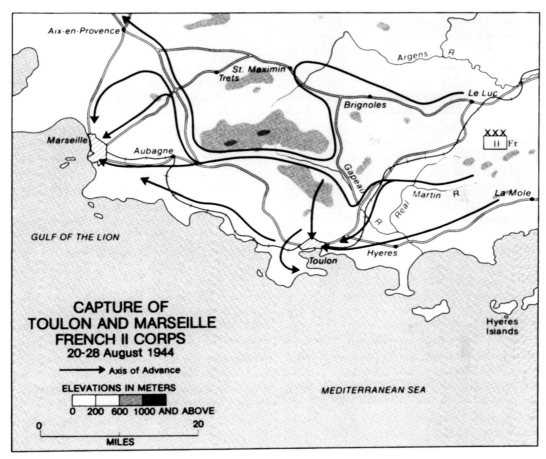

CAPTURE OF
TOULON AND MARSEILLE
FRENCH II CORPS
20-28 August 1944
→ Axis of Advance

ELEVATIONS IN METERS

0 200 600 1000 AND ABOVE

0   20
MILES

MAP 8   This map is printed in full color at the back of the book, following the Index.

seille, with elements of de Monsabert's armor approaching the strongly defended village of Aubagne, which was eight miles from Marseille and the key to the eastern approaches to that city. In addition, troops of the U.S. 3d Division, preparing to attack Aix-en-Provence, spilled into the French zone and came within six miles of Aubagne.

On the morning of the 21st the French attacked Toulon with renewed vigor. While some units hammered away toward the city along the coast, others continued to encircle the port on the north and west. Progress in the north was disappointing as German resistance stiffened. One French tank company managed to penetrate to about three and a half miles from the principal square in Toulon, but was cut off, taking heavy casualties while holding out for almost thirty-six hours.

Toward the end of the day, de Larminat, believing that the operations against the two ports demanded a unified command, requested permission to take charge of the entire operation. De Lattre turned the corps commander down and, after a lengthy argument between the two quick-tempered generals, dismissed de Larminat and took direct control of the operation.[16] The command change had little, if any, effect on French operations.

On the 23d, the French continued to exert pressure on Toulon, forcing the Germans back into their inner fortifications, overrunning German strongpoints west of the city, and opening rail and highway connections toward Marseille. As the fighting continued, the German defense lost cohesion, and negotiations opened for the surrender of isolated German groups. The last organized German resistance ended on 26 August, and a small command garrison under Admiral Ruhfus surrendered on the 28th after two days of intense Allied air and naval bombardment. The battle cost the French about 2,700 men killed and wounded, while the Germans lost their entire garrison of 18,000. However, the French claimed to have taken almost 17,000 prisoners, indicating that only about 1,000 Germans lost their lives defending the city—hardly a serious attempt to follow Hitler's order to fight to the last man. Toulon had been secured a full week ahead of Allied expectations.

Even as the French invested Toulon, part of their forces were moving on their second objective,

Marseille. From the beginning of the attacks, de Lattre had decided that the conquest of Toulon would not absorb his entire force and directed de Monsabert to probe aggressively to the west. Although reminding his subordinate of Toulon's priority, de Lattre probably expected him to interpret his instructions as broadly as possible and to exploit favorable opportunities to speed the seizure of Marseille. But de Monsabert's first objective was Aubagne.

The German force at Aubagne was part of the 13,000-man garrison of Marseille, which included several key units of the *244th Infantry Division* and 2,500 naval and 3,900 *Luftwaffe* personnel, all under the control of Maj. Gen. Hans Schaeffer, the *244th Division* commander. The landward approaches to Marseille gave the Germans significant defensive advantages, but again time and lack of materiel worked against them. Their fortifications were less extensive than at Toulon, and the half a million civilian inhabitants of the second largest city in France were becoming increasingly hostile. Schaeffer had chosen not to evacuate the city, and as the attacking French military forces drew near, the FFI became bolder, encouraged by a major civil uprising on the morning of 22 August.

Without waiting to reduce Aubagne, de Monsabert positioned his units, consisting of less than a division in strength, around the eastern and northern outskirts of the city to harass the confused defenders. Gains on the 22d put French troops within five to eight miles of the heart of the city, and they prepared to strike well into the port on the following day.

---

[16] General de Larminat later received a command on the Atlantic coast. Vigneras Intervs, p. 14.

FRENCH TROOPS IN MARSEILLE, AUGUST 1944

While approving de Monsabert's initiative, de Lattre was concerned by the dispersal of the attacking forces. Patch had informed him of the appearance of the *11th Panzer Division* in the Aix-en-Provence area, and de Monsabert's trucks and combat vehicles were running low on fuel.[17] Believing that the French lacked sufficient strength for a full-fledged battle in Marseille, should it come to that, de Lattre instructed de Monsabert to back off a bit and ring the city with his troops, but to limit his offensive operations to clearing the suburbs until more units arrived.

On the ground, de Monsabert believed that more could be lost than gained by holding back. He relayed de Lattre's orders to his own subordinates, but his instructions to Col. Abel Felix Andre Chappuis, who commanded the 7th Algerian Tirailleurs, were flexible. Spurred by calls for assistance from resistance groups inside Marseille, Chappuis' infantry prowled the eastern suburbs; in the early hours of 23 August, one battalion, encouraged by large crowds of exuberant French civilians, plunged into the city itself. By 0800, the tirailleurs had begun pushing through the city streets, and two hours later, after cutting through the center of Marseille, they reached the waterfront. Later that day the rest of the regiment entered the city from the north and

---

[17] De Lattre, *History*, p. 100. See p. 142 of this volume.

northeast. This unplanned drive decided the issue, and the fighting, like the final days in Toulon, became a matter of battling from street to street, from house to house, and from strongpoint to strongpoint, with ardent FFI support.

On the evening of 27 August, Schaeffer parlayed with de Monsabert to arrange terms, and a formal surrender became effective at 1300, 28 August, the same day as the capitulation at Toulon. The French had lost 1,825 men killed and wounded in the battle for Marseille, had taken roughly 11,000 prisoners, and had again accomplished their mission well ahead of the Allied planning schedule.[18]

West to the Rhone

Meanwhile, the general picture of German weakness along the approaches to the Rhone changed on the afternoon of 21 August when elements of the *11th Panzer Division* were reported west of the river. Patch and Truscott wondered whether the German armored movements, about which they could learn little, might indicate a counterattack. Truscott's only reserve, the 36th Division, was already on its way north on the route followed by Task Force Butler, as was a regiment of the 45th Division. Truscott had been considering sending the entire 45th Division to the north, but now tabled this idea and ordered the 3d and 45th Divisions to halt along a north-south line above Marseille.[19]

Unknown to the Allied commanders, the Germans had no intention of mounting a counterattack. Wiese's decision to send a tank-infantry task force with about ten tanks toward Aix-en-Provence was a reaction to what had been, until the 21st, a steady Allied push to the Rhone. The task force was merely to give the Americans pause, something to think about. Wiese hoped to slow American progress and buy time for Kniess' *LXXXV Corps* withdrawal. Truscott, in any case, had been ordered to hold up until Toulon and Marseille were secure. As a result, Kniess was able to withdraw the remainder of his forces without interference. His corps assembled along the second defensive line on the morning of 21 August and pulled back easily to the final line during the following night. By the morning of the 22d, almost all units scheduled to cross over the Rhone from the west were on the eastern bank, and the bulk of Petersen's *IV Luftwaffe Field Corps*, still west of the Rhone, was moving north and coming abreast of Kniess on the other side.

Deployed along the final defensive line early on the 22d, Kniess planned to hold until dark on the 23d. His defenses extended from the Rhone River at Arles, northeast to the Durance River at Orgon, and then north thirty miles to Avignon and the main Rhone valley. The focal point was Orgon, where the Durance River passed through a defile two miles wide. The Germans had to hold the gap until all of Kniess' units could cross the river to the north bank. Concerned about his eastern flank, Wiese sent reconnaissance units of the *11th Panzer Division* to probe north

---

[18] See *La 3eme Division d'Infanterie Algerienne dans la Bataille de Provence*, p. 6; de Lattre, *History*, pp. 114–15; and Seventh Army G–3 Rpts.

[19] See pp. 150–151 of this volume.

of the Durance and ascertain the intentions of the American armored forces that Wiese knew were active there; but the unit found little except assorted FFI resistance units.

Not until late in the morning of the 22d was Truscott sufficiently satisfied about German intentions in the lower Rhone. With the attacks against the ports proceeding as planned, he released another regiment of the 45th Division for redeployment northward, but decided to keep the 3d Division south of the Durance until French forces could relieve it. Both the 3d Division and the remainder of the 45th advanced westward during the day, and both units reached Kniess' abandoned second line that afternoon.

Wiese now began to worry less about his southern front. Increasingly disturbed by threats developing on the eastern flank of his withdrawal route, he ordered all elements of the *11th Panzer Division* to move immediately north; he alerted Kniess to start the *198th Division* moving up the Rhone as well, leaving him only the weak *338th Division* and miscellaneous

attached units to hold the Durance crossings at Orgon, to protect his southern flank, and to defend Avignon against an American sweep. Wiese now wanted all his units to be north of the Durance well before dark on 23 August, the time previously set for abandoning the final line below the Durance.

On the 23d, with the ports not yet secure, Patch and Truscott cautiously limited the 3d Division's movement west and thereby may have sacrificed an opportunity to cut off major portions of Kniess' corps south of the Durance or to block the withdrawal of Petersen's corps. Virtually undisturbed during the daylight hours, the remainder of Kniess' forces crossed the Durance during the night of 23–24 August. On 24 August, as French units began to relieve elements of the 3d Division, and Allied troops occupied Avignon unopposed, Kniess' *LXXXV Corps* escaped. His forces, together with those of Petersen, now marched rapidly up the Rhone valley toward Montelimar, thirty miles away, and the focus of operations quickly began to shift to the north.

CHAPTER IX

The Battle of Montelimar

As de Lattre's French forces prepared to move against the port cities with the bulk of Truscott's VI Corps on their northern flank, Patch began to consider his future course of action if all went well along the coast. His first task, to secure the landing area, had been accomplished; seizing Toulon and Marseille was his next major objective. The ports would give him the logistical base he needed for a sustained drive north to join Eisenhower's armies in northern France, his third major task. But until the ports were secure, supplying his American divisions with fuel, vehicles, and ammunition for anything so ambitious would be extremely difficult. Nevertheless, both he and Truscott were eager to exploit the rapid German withdrawal and unwilling to allow the remainder of the *Nineteenth Army* to escape intact, especially if the Germans intended to make a stand farther up the narrow Rhone valley. Truscott had created Task Force Butler for this purpose. With its motorized infantry battalion, its approximately thirty medium tanks, twelve tank destroyers, and twelve self-propelled artillery pieces, and the armored cars, light tanks, and trucks of the cavalry squadron, TF Butler represented a balanced, mobile offensive force.

Task Force Butler (19–21 August)

On 19 August, Butler's vehicles were already well on their way north. At noon, shortly before Butler reached Sisteron, Patch directed Truscott to alert one infantry division for a drive northward on Grenoble. Truscott, in turn, instructed General Dahlquist, the 36th Division commander, to be prepared to have his unit execute the order early the following day.[1] The VI Corps commander expected at least one regiment of the 36th Division to be at Sisteron on the afternoon of the 20th. Convinced of German intentions to withdraw up the Rhone valley, Truscott also radioed Butler to hold at Sisteron and await the arrival of Dahlquist's units, adding that he should continue his patrols westward to "determine the practicability of seizing the high

---

[1] In addition to unit records, the following account is based on the following: Truscott, *Command Missions*, pp. 423–34; Seventh Army FO 2, 1200, 19 Aug 44; 36th Div OI 200200B Aug 44 (note: early OIs identified only by date-time group); Msg, CofS 36th Div to CO 143d Inf, 2208 19 Aug, 143d Inf Jnl, 19 Aug 44; Butler, "Task Force Butler"; *Seventh Army Rpt*, I, 188–228; and Hixon, "TF Butler." For another participant's account of the battle, see Adams Interv (Adams commanded the 143d regiment at Montelimar), pp. 61–65, Paul D. Adams Papers, MHI.

ground north of Montelimar." [2] Montelimar, a small city on the east bank of the Rhone River about fifty miles north of Avignon and sixty miles west of Sisteron, lay astride the most probable German route of withdrawal. (See Map 7.)

Butler, whose radio communications with VI Corps headquarters had become intermittent, never received the message. [3] The only instructions arriving during the night of 19–20 August stated that the mission of his task force was unchanged. Shortly before midnight, Butler thus reported his intention to continue his reconnaissance activities the following morning, but warned that shortages of fuel and supplies would limit his advance to forty miles in any direction. He emphasized his need for further instructions that would enable him to direct his main effort either north to Grenoble or west to Montelimar and the Rhone. The general also felt uneasy remaining stationary at Sisteron, deep in enemy territory, with limited logistical support. The FFI and his own artillery liaison planes had reported a strong, mobile German force at Grenoble and a large garrison at Gap, about thirty miles above Sisteron. Both could block Butler's advance northward. Expecting Grenoble to be his immediate objective, Butler decided to establish a strong outpost at the Croix Haute Pass, about forty miles north on the

main highway to Grenoble, and to dispatch a force to Gap. Meanwhile, he sent his operations officer in a liaison plane to corps headquarters for more specific guidance.

On the following morning, 20 August, Butler grouped the main body of his task force at Sisteron and Aspres, thirty miles to the northeast, and sent reinforced cavalry troops to the pass at Croix Haute and to Gap. Both forces reached their objectives during the afternoon, the Gap patrol capturing over 900 German prisoners after a short skirmish aided by local FFI elements. By dusk Task Force Butler was thus spread over a wide area, but oriented more for an advance on Grenoble than one on Montelimar. Supply convoys brought Butler news on the approach of 36th Division elements, but his operations officer returned with no information other than that new orders would be forthcoming sometime that night.

On the evening of the 20th, Butler met with Brig. Gen. Robert I. Stack, the assistant division commander of the 36th. Stack, arriving with an advance echelon of the division headquarters and a regimental task force built around two battalions of the 143d Infantry (its third battalion was with Butler), passed on to Butler what information he could: that the 36th Division was now displacing north; that Truscott had released the division's 142d Infantry from corps reserve at noon that day, and this regiment was now arriving at Castellane, thirty-five miles away; and that the 141st Infantry had finally been relieved by airborne troops on the Seventh Army's right flank and would follow north the next morning. How-

---

[2] Truscott, *Command Missions*, p. 424.

[3] On Butler's radio and air liaison difficulties, see Hixon, "TF Butler," pp. 21–23 and Enclosure 5. Butler received an excellent SCR–299 mobile radio on the 19th, but it did not end his communications problems, possibly because of the increasingly difficult local topography.

AMERICAN ARMOR MOVES INLAND

ever, he warned Butler that all divisional movements had been slowed by a serious shortage of fuel and trucks, and that most units were moving north in time-consuming company-sized shuttles. Precisely when they would reach Sisteron was unknown. The assistant division commander further explained that he intended to have the 143d Infantry strike out for Grenoble on the following morning, 21 August, and that it was his opinion also that Grenoble was Butler's most logical objective.

Radioing Dahlquist, Stack asked whether the 143d Infantry was to use the same roads to Grenoble as Butler. Dahlquist, having talked with Truscott on the 19th but knowing little of Butler's movements, responded that

Butler was to remain in the Sisteron area until most of the 36th Division had arrived and promised to seek clarification on the matter from Truscott. Communicating with Stack several hours later, Dahlquist instructed him to hold all arriving division elements in the Sisteron region and to cancel the move to Grenoble, explaining that the division's objective might be changed to the Rhone valley. Further orders, Dahlquist continued, would come early the following morning. Stack relayed this information to Butler about 2300, 20 August.

Unknown to Stack and Dahlquist, Truscott had met again with Patch around noon of the 20th, had informed him of the decision to send the 143d Infantry northward, and had requested his approval to follow the regiment with the rest of the 36th Division and to send Task Force Butler west to the Rhone. Patch quickly agreed with these plans, which were bold undertakings considering the uncertain situation in the south and the lack of vehicles and fuel. Perhaps mindful of these constraints, Truscott did not immediately relay these orders to Butler, thereby failing to forestall the temporary dispersion of his task force. By the end of the day, however, the corps commander had become more certain of German intentions south of the Durance River and of his ability to reinforce Butler if necessary. Thus at 2045, 20 August, Truscott finally radioed specific instructions to Butler, directing him to move to Montelimar at dawn with all possible speed. There Butler was to seize the town and block the German routes of withdrawal. The 36th Division would follow the task force as quickly as possible.

Butler received the message that night and acknowledged receipt early the next morning. Nevertheless, Truscott also sent Lt. Col. Theodore J. Conway of his G–3 section to Butler's headquarters with more specific written instructions. Reaching Butler's command post at Aspres in the early hours of 21 August, Conway delivered the letter from Truscott instructing Butler to seize the high ground immediately north of Montelimar, but not the city itself, before dark that day. Two battalions of corps artillery were on their way to reinforce the task force, but initially only a single regimental combat team from the 36th would support the effort; the rest of the division would follow later.

Dahlquist would take control of Butler's task force when he arrived in the forward area.

The new orders presented several problems. First, neither Stack nor Dahlquist had been informed of the switch in the main effort from Grenoble to Montelimar. Second, Butler's movements on the previous day had oriented his advance north toward Grenoble, and he needed considerable time to reassemble his scattered forces. At the same time, he felt compelled to leave a small blocking force at Gap to secure his rear and, as directed by supplemental orders from Truscott, to retain the block at the Croix Haute Pass until 36th Division units could take over.

By daybreak of 21 August, Butler had regrouped the bulk of his task force at Aspres. Leaving a small detachment at the pass and a larger one at Gap, he started the rest of his command rolling westward. Moving without interference a good twenty-five miles, the task force reached Crest on the Drome River in the late afternoon, about thirteen miles east of the Rhone. Before it lay the Rhone valley and the setting for the eight-day battle of Montelimar.

The Battle Square

Almost twenty miles northeast of Montelimar, the town of Crest was at one corner of what became known as the Montelimar Battle Square, bounded by the Drome River on the north, the Rhone River on the west, and the Roubion River on the south (*Map 9*). With sides varying from nine to seventeen miles, the square, or rectangle, encompassed an area of about

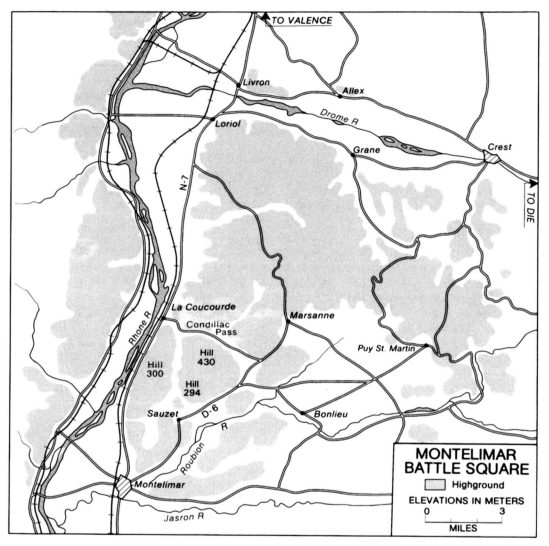

MAP 9   This map is printed in full color at the back of the book, following the Index.

250 square miles on ground that alternated between flat, open farmland and rugged, wooded hills, which rose, often steeply, to more than 1,900 feet.

Montelimar itself is on a small, flat plain extending along the north bank of the Roubion River, a little over two miles east of the Rhone. Route N–7, the main north-south artery along the Rhone, passes through the city and then runs almost due north to the Drome. A secondary road, D–6, runs northeast from Montelimar about two miles to the small village of Sauzet and then turns east, skirting the northern bank of the Roubion. On Route N–7, about six miles above Montelimar, is the small town of La Coucourde. Between Montelimar and La Coucourde the eastern side of the Rhone valley narrows considerably, squeezing both N–7 and a parallel railway line between the Rhone and a high ridgeline, which the American troops labeled Hill 300. The ridgeline easily dominated Route N–7, as well as a parallel road on the west bank of the Rhone and the railways on both sides. Two other hills to the east, Hill 294 and Hill 430, provided additional observation of both banks of the Rhone and, to the south, overlooked the approaches to Sauzet and D–6. In all, this high ground dominated the Rhone valley for a distance of roughly fifteen miles. All retreating German forces would have to pass through the bottleneck that Task Force Butler was about to squeeze.

Initial Skirmishes (21–22 August)

Late in the afternoon of 21 August, Butler's men moved south from Crest to Puy St. Martin, and then west to Marsanne in the center of the square, probing farther west through the Condillac Pass toward La Coucourde and south down Route D–6 toward Sauzet and Montelimar. Lt. Col. Joseph G. Felber, commanding the advance party, immediately recognized Hill 300 as the key terrain feature and established his command post nearby at the Chateau Condillac. Unable to secure the entire ridgeline of Hill 300, Felber set up outposts, roadblocks, and guard points and posted accompanying FFI soldiers in Sauzet.

German forces were already traveling north along the main highway, and, as soon as an artillery battery could unlimber its pieces, Felber had it open fire on the German traffic. A second battery and several tanks and tank destroyers soon added their fire, while a cavalry troop and some infantry placed a roadblock across the main highway, until a German attack at dusk drove the small force back into the hills. On the north bank of the Drome River, another cavalry troop, after moving west from Crest, fired on a German truck column fording a stream, and then advanced and destroyed about fifty German vehicles.

Upon reaching the forward area, Butler ordered the troop operating on the Drome back to Crest to protect the roads to Puy St. Martin, but left a platoon on the north bank of the Drome as flank protection. After establishing his command post at Marsanne, he sent a message to Truscott's corps headquarters at 2330 confirming his unit's arrival at the objective area. His forces, Butler reported, were thinly spread, but with the expected reinforcements—a regiment of the 36th Division and more artillery—he was confident he could deal with a determined German reaction and launch a successful attack against Montelimar the following afternoon. However, until he was resupplied with ammunition, his artillery and tank destroyers would be unable to halt all the German traffic along the highway.

The morning of 22 August found Butler still waiting for supplies and reinforcement. Meanwhile the Germans moved first, mounting what was to be the first of many efforts to dislodge the Americans. Grouped around the reconnaissance battalion of the *11th Panzer Division* and elements of the *71st Luftwaffe Infantry Training Regiment*,[4] an *ad hoc* force attacked north from Montelimar about noon, took Sauzet, and forced an American outpost and the FFI back into the hills. The action, however, proved to be a feint. The main German force reassembled south of the Roubion River, advanced nine miles east, and then swung north, crossing the river and advancing on Puy St. Martin and Marsanne, behind Butler's defenses. Almost unopposed, the Germans occupied Puy that afternoon, cutting the American supply line to Crest and Sisteron.

The German success was short-lived. By chance, Butler's detachments at Gap and the Croix Haute Pass had been relieved by some of Stack's forces on the 21st, and both had been traveling to rejoin Butler. The Gap group had just turned south from Crest on the afternoon of the 22d, and its commander, realizing the implications of the German advance, quickly organized a tank-infantry counterattack into Puy. While Sherman tank fire blocked the roads leading from Puy to Marsanne, the unit from Gap cleared Puy that evening, destroying ten German vehicles but suffering no casualties.

---

[4] The *Luftwaffe* unit, which had been leading Petersen's withdrawing columns on the west bank of the Rhone, outdistanced the rest of the retreating German forces before losing most of its transportation to Allied air attacks and FFI ambushes. Some of the regiment's troops then crossed the river near Montelimar and, in disarray, hitched rides on vehicles of the *11th Panzer Division*. The *Luftwaffe* unit commander was later court-martialed for his role in the regiment's flight northward and for deserting his troops.

Butler believed that the German attack was only a probe to determine his strength, and he expected a much stronger assault on the following day, 23 August. Still no units of the 36th Division had arrived during the day. The only forces joining him on the 22d were his own detachments from Gap and the pass and two 155-mm. battalions of VI Corps artillery. Equally important, his own artillery and armor were dangerously low on ammunition, with about twenty-five rounds per gun. To preserve his position, he needed both reinforcements and resupply.

Reinforcing the Square

Around 2200 on the evening of the 22d, as Butler was beginning to despair, a single battalion of the 141st Infantry arrived along with the regimental commander, Col. John W. Harmony. Harmony quickly brought Butler up to date on the situation in the rear. Throughout the previous day, 21 August, he explained, General Stack had been waiting at Sisteron to learn whether to move the 143d Infantry to Grenoble or Montelimar. Dahlquist, the 36th Division commander, had not yet been able to determine where Truscott wanted the Rhone blocked. Although ready to push the 143d north to Grenoble or west to Montelimar, he had also ordered the 142d Infantry to Gap to protect his eastern flank and had sent Harmony's 141st regiment initially to Sisteron to serve as his reserve. Unconfirmed intelligence reports still placed the *157th Reserve Mountain Division* in the Grenoble-Gap region, and an attack on the 36th Division's northeastern flank thus remained a possibility. Dahlquist had then altered these plans on the evening of the 21st, judging that the 143d was too oriented on Grenoble to assist Butler and giving the mission to the 141st. Harmony related that his regiment, the last major unit of the 36th Division to displace north, had arrived in the Sisteron-Aspres area only on the morning of the 22d and, due to the general shortage of vehicles, had not been able to advance much farther. Using captured German fuel stores, he had finally managed to bring the one battalion with him to Marsanne, but did not expect the rest of his units to reach the Montelimar area until the following day. In the meantime, Butler would have to make do with this limited reinforcement.

The lack of reinforcements reflected American indecision. Throughout the day and evening of 21 August neither Patch nor Truscott had been willing to make Montelimar the major effort. They were still unable to predict when Toulon and Marseille would fall or confirm the beginning of a complete German withdrawal up the Rhone valley. On the morning of the 21st, Truscott had ordered one regiment of the 45th Division—the 179th Infantry—to Sisteron, but had canceled the movement abruptly at 1330 when an ULTRA intercept informed him that units of the *11th Panzer Division* had crossed the Rhone and were south of the Durance River.[5] Although the radio

intercept was accurate, the armored threat was just a ruse, for the *11th Panzers* had been able to ferry only a few of their imposing machines across the Rhone.[6] Nevertheless, the move apparently succeeded, for Truscott stayed his hand; it was not until 2300 that evening that he finally ordered Dahlquist to move on to Montelimar, and the next day before the 179th regiment resumed its movement north.

When Truscott's orders arrived, late on the 21st, Dahlquist sent the rest of Harmony's 141st regiment on its way west and, through the 22d, tried to reorient the rest of his scattered division on Montelimar. To secure his northern flank, he decided to allow the 143d Infantry to resume its advance on Grenoble, which Americans entered that afternoon, and then have it swing west and south, through the city of Valence, into the battle square.[7] Transportation problems, however, hindered his efforts to accelerate the movement of the 141st to Montelimar, and to follow it with the 142d regiment from Gap and the rest of the division. Impatient with these delays, Truscott arrived at the 36th Division command post near Aspres shortly before noon

[5] ULTRA Msg XL 7178 201029 Aug 44, ULTRA Collection, MHI; Truscott, *Command Missions*, p. 426. The message was also supposedly confirmed by POW reports according to "G-2 History: Seventh Army Operations in Europe," I, 15-31 Aug 44, 5, Box 2, Quinn Papers, MHI, but the POW item may have been only a cover story by Quinn, the Seventh

Army G-2, to allow Patch to pass the information on to Truscott's subordinates and to the French without revealing the true source (see p. 124 of this volume).

[6] See "11th Panzer Division Rpt of MG von Wietersheim, 4 June 46," and G-3, *11th Panzer Division*, "Remarks Regarding the War History of the Seventh US Army," 20 Jun 46 (both unpaginated), in John E. Dahlquist Papers, MHI.

[7] For a treatment of the FFI and American actions in the Grenoble area, and the withdrawal of the weak *157th Reserve Mountain Division* east to the Franco-Italian border region, see unpublished paper, "United States and Resistance Cooperation in the Liberation of Grenoble" (copy CMH).

and, finding Dahlquist absent, made his dissatisfaction clear to the division chief of staff, Col. Stewart T. Vincent. Noting the 143d advancing on Grenoble, the 142d at Gap and points east, and elements of the 141st just pulling into Aspres, he demanded that the entire division move to the Rhone "forthwith," and attached the 179th regiment (45th Division) to the division for employment at Grenoble.

Upon returning to his own command post, Truscott composed a letter to Dahlquist with detailed instructions. Indicating his displeasure with the division's deployments, he emphasized that "the primary mission of the 36th Division is to block the Rhone Valley in the gap immediately north of Montelimar." [8] Dahlquist was to push the entire 141st regiment to Montelimar as soon as possible; move the 179th to Grenoble and shift the 143d from Grenoble to Montelimar; and march the rest of the 142d west to the Montelimar-Nyons area to protect Butler's southern flank. He also suggested that Dahlquist screen Butler's northern flank by reconnoitering toward Valence above Montelimar. The 45th Division, he explained, would ultimately assume responsibility for the entire Grenoble-Gap-Sisteron region. Truscott appreciated Dahlquist's logistical difficulties, however, and arranged to have the Seventh Army headquarters rush a special truck convoy of fuel to the north during the afternoon. This resupply, together with captured gasoline, allowed the bulk of the 141st, following Harmony, to resume its march west at 0330 early on the 23d.

---

[8] Truscott, *Command Missions*, p. 427.

Late on the evening of the 22d, about 2100, Truscott and Dahlquist hashed out their differences over a recently opened telephone line. Dahlquist recommended moving the 179th, rather than the 143d, to Montelimar and even suggested sending the entire 45th Division there while the 36th dashed up to Dijon, 150 miles farther north. Truscott brushed aside these proposals, showed increasingly less sympathy for Dahlquist's transportation problems, and again emphasized the need to block the Rhone valley near Montelimar, telling him to get his men there even if they had to walk. His one concession was to allow Dahlquist to move the 179th Infantry to the west in lieu of the 143d.

Throughout the rest of the night and into the early morning hours of 23 August, Dahlquist continued to shuffle the growing number of units under his command into some kind of order. Lack of fuel and transportation rather than lack of manpower remained his key problem. Soon after conversing with Truscott, he directed the 142d Infantry to start westward at once, traveling at night, not to the Nyons region southeast of Montelimar as Truscott had recommended, but rather to Crest and Butler's area. Several hours later, however, Dahlquist countermanded the order and sent the 142d to Nyons, where the leading elements arrived about 0730 on the morning of the 23d.

Meanwhile, as the 179th Infantry was leaving Sisteron at 2230, 22 August, Dahlquist changed its objective from Grenoble to Montelimar, but, as the unit rolled into Aspres around midnight, he changed its destination back to Grenoble. Once there, the unit was to relieve the 143d Infantry, which would then move west to Valence and south to Montelimar. Again, the availability of fuel and vehicles dictated these troublesome changes, and Dahlquist and his staff labored to keep them to a minimum.

Dahlquist's final orders for 23 August appeared to put his house in order at last. Pushing the 143d to Montelimar through Valence would safeguard Butler's northern flank, and deploying the 142d into the Nyons area would cover Butler in the south; meanwhile, the movement of the 141st directly to Montelimar would receive priority, and the divisional units could follow as transportation became available. Truscott approved these final dispositions and also ordered the 180th Infantry, another 45th Division regiment, to the Gap area from where it and the rest of the division could follow the 179th to Grenoble and points north at some future date. As a result, the 45th Division was soon able to relieve the last 36th Division units in these areas, leaving Dahlquist free to devote his attention to the Rhone. But Truscott was still uneasy. To make sure that his operational concept was clearly understood by Dahlquist, he telephoned him once again at 0200 hours, 23 August, and reminded him that his task was to halt the German withdrawal. Not a single German vehicle was to pass Montelimar.

The German Reaction

The German commanders were quick to appreciate the dangerous situation. Late on 21 August German in-telligence reports had convinced Wiese, the *Nineteenth Army* commander, that the Allied forces that had suddenly appeared above Montelimar posed a serious threat to his northward withdrawal.[9] He responded by sending his most powerful and most mobile force, the *11th Panzer Division* under Maj. Gen. Wend von Wietersheim, toward the troubled area. It was the division's reconnaissance battalion that had probed Butler's positions on the 22d, while the rest of the *11th*, less the force feinting toward Aix-en-Provence, began blocking the major roads to the Rhone coming from the east. But the action around Puy that afternoon, when Butler's armor pushed light elements of the *11th Panzers* back across the Roubion, further alarmed Wiese, who then order von Wietersheim to speed his entire division northward. The panzer division was to clear the high ground northeast of Montelimar and secure the main highway from Montelimar north to the Drome. Wiese also directed General Kniess, the *LXXXV Corps* commander still at Avignon, to reinforce Wietersheim's unit with the *198th Infantry Division* within twenty-four to forty-eight hours.

Fortunately for Butler, von Wietersheim found Wiese's orders hard to execute. Fuel shortages, the presence of service and administrative traffic on the roads, and the difficulties of marching at night under blackout

---

[9] For the account that follows, von Luttichau, "German Operations," chs. 13–14, has been supplemented by materials in the 36th Division and VI Corps G–2 Journals and the daily G–2 Periodic Reports of Task Force Butler, the 36th Division, and VI Corps, as well as prisoner-of-war interrogations and translations of captured documents.

conditions all delayed the movement of his division north. *Groupe Thieme*, the first major element of the division, reached Montelimar only at noon, 23 August, with a battalion of infantry, ten medium tanks, and a self-propelled artillery battery; the rest of the division was not expected to arrive before the 24th. Yet the Germans were determined to take the initiative. Although they were unsure of the exact strength of the American forces, they realized that every delay gave their enemy more time to build up his strength along their unprotected line of withdrawal.

In the Square (23–24 August)

On the morning of 23 August, Dahlquist dissolved Task Force Butler as a separate entity, but allowed Butler to remain in command of those forces in the battle square area. Butler planned to have the 141st Infantry, with the motorized battalion of the 143d attached (one of the original components of Task Force Butler), take control of the Rhone front from the Drome River south to the Roubion. Initially he tasked one battalion to secure Hill 300; another, with tanks and tank destroyers, to strike southwest from Sauzet to seize Montelimar; and the two remaining battalions to serve as a reserve near Marsanne, helping to secure Hill 300 as necessary. Small forces were to patrol the main supply route from Crest to Puy, guard both banks of the Drome, and secure Butler's southern flank on the Roubion. Butler also dispatched cavalry elements to the north and south in order to link up with 36th Division units on their way to Valence

and Nyons. However, German activities and the late arrival of the 141st Infantry put most of these plans in abeyance.

Shortly after dawn on the 23d, the Germans again attempted to take the initiative. Above Montelimar elements of the panzer division's reconnaissance battalion, supported by a few tanks and self-propelled guns, infiltrated into Sauzet only to be thrown out by an American counterattack several hours later. About noontime, another small German armored column, repeating the maneuver of the previous day, struck across the Roubion River toward Puy St. Martin, but was also pushed back, this time by concentrated American artillery fire. Finally, *Groupe Thieme* entered the fray, moving from the Sauzet area toward the Hill 300 ridge, but again American forces resisted the pressure and held.

Uncertain of German strength and dispositions, the American counterattacks fared little better. About 1630 that afternoon Butler sent an infantry battalion, some service troops, and a few tanks southward through Sauzet to seize Montelimar. But the German defense was far too strong, and a counterattack halted the American drive at 1800 scarcely a mile short of the city. Thus neither side had accomplished a great deal during the 23d.

Since the German withdrawal through the Montelimar area had not yet begun in earnest, Butler had not made a strong effort to interdict Route N–7 physically. Some ammunition had come up during the night, and the artillery units had engaged several German convoys on the highway, destroying nearly one hundred vehicles. But the need to conserve

shells for defensive fire and the uncertainty of resupply limited the
effort. The Germans, for their part,
had begun to sort out a potentially
monumental traffic jam at Montelimar
and had started some administrative
and service organizations moving
northward again. However, they had
made little progress clearing the
danger area, especially the all-impor-
tant Hill 300. Both sides required
more strength at Montelimar, and
both expected stronger actions by
their opponents on the following day.

Outside of the battle square, Dahlquist inexplicably had shown little urgency in moving the rest of his division to the Montelimar area on the
23d. In the north, the 143d Infantry
did not leave Grenoble until 1730
and, although encountering no opposition, had stopped above Valence,
more than twenty miles north of the
Drome, that evening. In the south,
the 142d Infantry had two infantry
and one artillery battalions in the vicinity of Nyons—twenty-five miles
southwest of Montelimar—by midafternoon, but made no effort to move
up to the battle square. Perhaps Dahlquist felt that the coming battle would
not be limited to the square, and was
thus wary of pushing his entire division into an area that might become a
German noose. The earlier German
attacks on Butler's flank at Puy St.
Martin supported this concern.

Dahlquist's plans for 24 August
were conservative. He ordered the
143d to seize Valence and the 142d
to extend its covering line from
Nyons to within ten miles southeast
of Montelimar. Only later, sometime
during the night, did he order the remaining battalion of the 142d that

had been left at Gap to move to Crest
as soon as the 180th Infantry of the
45th Division relieved it. In the Montelimar Battle Square, Dahlquist
wanted Butler to secure all the
ground dominating the valley between Montelimar and the Drome
River and, if possible, to capture the
city itself. But without the direct support of the 143d and 142d regiments,
Butler's ability to block the Rhone
valley physically and to handle
German counterattacks at the same
time was becoming questionable.

Wiese was more realistic. Throughout the 23d, he repeatedly urged von
Wietersheim to rush his panzer division up to Montelimar, and pressured
Kniess to have the *198th Division*
follow as soon as possible. He recommended that the *198th* relieve *11th
Panzer Division* outposts and roadblocks at least as far north as Nyons,
and have a regiment at Montelimar by
the morning of the 24th. Then Wiese
wanted von Wietersheim to clear all
American forces from the area using
the entire *11th Panzer Division,* the
regiment of the *198th,* and the *63d
Luftwaffe Training Regiment,* which was
then assembling at Montelimar.

Wiese's subordinates had their own
problems. At the time, Kniess was
more concerned with having his corps
across the Durance River that night,
and made no provisions to deploy a
regiment of the *198th* up to Montelimar; von Wietersheim had to contend
with crowded roads and shortages of
fuel, and his armor arrived in the
battle square area in dribs and drabs.
Nevertheless, German strength in the
Montelimar region on 24 August was
enough to give Task Force Butler and
the 36th Division considerable trou-

ble. Another American attack that morning by a battalion of the 141st Infantry from Sauzet toward Montelimar again ended in failure when German troops, striking from the west, first drove a wedge into the American flank, and then infiltrated a maze of small roads and tracks to threaten the unit's rear. That evening, as Harmony attempted to withdraw the battalion, a second series of infantry-armor counterattacks struck the unit's front and flanks, cutting the battalion off from Sauzet and dispersing many of the troops. American artillery broke up further German efforts, and the battalion managed to fight its way back to Sauzet, but, as German pressure renewed, the Americans again pulled out of the village and took positions on the southern slopes of Hill 430. The battalion lost about 35 men wounded and 15 missing, captured 20 Germans, and estimated killing 20.

Meanwhile, a few miles farther north, a second German attack had cleared several early morning American patrols from Route N–7, and then had slowly pushed scattered elements of the 141st Infantry off most of the Hill 300 ridgeline. By dark the American position had received a serious setback. Pleased, Wiese ordered von Wietersheim to finish the job on the following day with the rest of his units plus several battalions of the *198th Division*, which the army commander had personally dispatched north.

Both Sides Reinforce

Behind the battlefield on the 24th, Dahlquist now directed the rest of his units into the battle square, still with less dispatch and more confusion than was called for. That morning, for example, he ordered the 2d Battalion, 142d Infantry (relieved of its defensive assignment at Gap), first to Crest, then to Nyons, and finally, as it entered Nyons at 1500, back to Crest. He then directed the rest of the 142d regiment, still in the Nyons area, to follow and take up positions in the battle square along the Roubion River guarding the American southern flank. Meanwhile, between 1300 and 1830, Dahlquist dispatched no less than four contradictory directives— three by radio, one by liaison officer—to the 143d Infantry still above Valence. The regiment started to receive them at 1600 in the wrong sequence. Not until 1900 did the regiment, reinforced by FFI units, get under way toward Valence only to be halted by German defenses on the outskirts of the town; and, as the American units reorganized for a second effort, another order arrived directing its immediate movement to Crest. Breaking contact, the 143d left Valence to the FFI and the Germans, but were unable to reach Crest and the battle square until early the following morning, 25 August.

By this time Dahlquist was becoming more concerned with defending his own positions than in attacking Montelimar or blocking the Rhone highways. Expecting larger German attacks on the 25th, he tried to organize his forces into a tight defensive posture, with the 141st and 142d regiments on line (the 141st on the high ground and the 142d along the Roubion) and the 143d and Task Force Butler, now reconstituted, in reserve. The only offensive action planned for the next day was to have elements of the 141st attempt to cut Route N–7 at La Coucourde, several miles farther north of the previous day's battles. Truscott, who had visited Dahlquist's forward command post near Marsanne that day, wanted a more offensive role for Butler, but had approved Dahlquist's plans, allowing the division commander to deploy his forces as he thought best.

The confusion in American command channels was far from over. About 2330 that night, 24 August, Dahlquist, concerned about protecting his flanks and rear, asked Truscott to send a regiment of the 45th Division to Crest early the next day. Although he had already instructed the 45th Division to move the 157th Infantry to Die, twenty miles east of Crest, Truscott refused the request, feeling that Dahlquist's strength in the battle area was adequate. A few hours later, perhaps feeling that the division commander's defensive concerns might lead him to abandon his main mission, Truscott reminded him that he still expected his division to block the main highway as soon as possible. His troops, Dahlquist radioed in reply, had been there during the day, and he assured Truscott that they were "physically on the road." [10] However, although small groups of American soldiers may have reached the highway from time to time, the implication that they controlled any portion of N–7 was inaccurate; at best, Dahlquist's knowledge of his own troop dispositions may have been faulty.

On the German side, the fog of war had begun to dissipate a little. On the evening of the 24th a detailed copy of Dahlquist's operational plans for 25 August had fallen into their hands, giving the German commanders their first clear picture of the forces opposing them at Montelimar. [11] As a result, Wiese now decided to move the entire *198th Infantry Division* to the north and form a provisional corps under von Wietersheim, consisting of the *11th Panzer* and *198th Divisions,* the *63d Luftwaffe Training Regiment,* the *Luftwaffe 18th Flak Regiment* (with guns ranging from 20–mm. to 88–mm. in caliber), a railroad artillery battalion (with five heavy pieces ranging from 270-mm. to 380-mm. in caliber), and several lesser units. With these forces he expected von Wietersheim to launch a major attack before noon on the 25th and sweep the American units away. At the same time, Wiese continued to urge Kniess to move his corps north as fast as he could. Having withdrawn the last of the *LXXXV Corps* across the Durance during the night of 23–24 August, and having executed another withdrawal the following night without pressure from the south, Kniess was about fifteen miles north of Avignon but still more than thirty-five miles south of Montelimar on the morning of the 25th. Success at Montelimar would be for naught if Kniess' units were destroyed in the south.

While the rest of the 36th Division

---

[10] Rad, Dahlquist to Truscott, 0130 25 Aug 44, 36th Div G–3 Jnl, 25 Aug 44.

[11] Dahlquist later confirmed the loss, attributing it to a "very stupid liaison officer" who fled from his jeep when fired on by a small German roadblock, leaving the operational plans behind. Dahlquist Ltr (to wife), 29 Aug 44 (hereafter cited as "Dahlquist Ltr" and date), John E. Dahlquist Papers, MHI.

entered the battle square that night, von Wietersheim, with Dahlquist's order in hand, issued detailed instructions for his attack. He divided the units under this control into six separate task forces, four from the *11th Panzer Division—Groupes Hax, Wilde,* and *Thieme* and the *11th Panzer Reconnaissance Battalion*—and two from the *198th Division* built around the unit's *305th* and *326th Grenadiers.* The *198th Division,* reinforced with armor, would conduct the main effort. The *305th Grenadiers,* attacking northeast of Montelimar, were to seize the eastern section of Hill 430, seal the western end of the Condillac Pass, and then move northwest to Route N–7. Slightly to the east, the *326th Grenadiers* would support this effort by striking across the Roubion near Bonlieu, marking the weakly held boundary between the 141st and 142d Infantry, and then driving north. In the west, *Groupe Hax,* consisting of two panzer grenadier battalions and two battalions of the *63d Luftwaffe Training Regiment,* reinforced by artillery and tanks, was to support the *198th Division*'s attacks by clearing the area north and northeast of Montelimar, the rest of Hill 300, and the western slopes of Hill 430. Meanwhile, *Groupe Thieme,* with one panzer grenadier battalion supported by tanks and the *119th Replacement Battalion,* was to assemble at Loriol in the north and strike eastward along the south bank of the Drome River to Grane, five miles short of Crest; at the same time *Groupe Wilde,* consisting of another panzer grenadier battalion, an artillery battalion, and a few tanks, would relieve elements of *Groupe Thieme* outposting Route N–7 around La Coucourde. Von Wietersheim

hoped that the *305th Grenadiers* would be able to isolate the American infantry and artillery in the Hill 300–Condillac Pass area, while the *326th Grenadiers,* coming up from the south, swept behind them and linked up with *Groupe Thieme* in the north, thus surrounding the entire 36th Division. *Groupe Wilde,* at La Coucourde, would act as a reserve, able to reinforce any of the various efforts or strike into the Condillac Pass on its own. Finally, the *11th Panzer Reconnaissance Battalion* was again to push into the Puy St. Martin area, further disrupting American lines of communication. Taking advantage of the dispersion of Dahlquist's units, his logistical difficulties, and the temporary numerical superiority of the German forces, the armored division commander hoped to destroy completely both Task Force Butler and the 36th Division. With this impediment out of the way, the German withdrawal could be easily accelerated and all delaying action could be focused on the U.S. 3d Division slowly moving up from the south.

The Battle of 25 August

The German plan of attack was ambitious but exceedingly complex and depended greatly on the ability of the participating units to arrive at their assembly areas on time and ready for action. From the beginning, difficulties in communications and transportation made a coordinated attack, as envisioned by von Wietersheim, impossible. *Groupe Thieme,* setting out from Loriol around 1130, was the first unit under way. Pushing back outposts of the 117th Cavalry Squadron, the attackers reached Grane before 1400, while other German forces seized Allex, on the north side of the Drome, at approximately the same time. Alarmed, Dahlquist sent Task Force Butler, now little more than a weak battalion combat team, north from Puy St. Martin about halfway to Crest to protect his main supply route; Butler, in turn, dispatched a tank platoon northwest over a mountain road toward Grane. Unable to retake Grane, the tank unit established a blocking position just south of the town, while a heterogeneous collection of infantry, reconnaissance, armor, and engineer units hurriedly set up roadblocks west of Crest on both sides of the Drome. Although this mixed force expected a major German effort against Crest to follow, no further German advances along the Drome took place that day. *Groupe Thieme* had accomplished its mission and was content to defend its gains.

Elsewhere German attacks accomplished much less. *Groupe Hax,* for example, did not start out until 1400, and then succeeded only in consolidating earlier gains above Montelimar. *Groupe Wilde* did not reach its assigned positions in the Hill 300–La Coucourde area until 1500, and the planned attacks of the *305th Grenadiers* and the *11th Panzer Reconnaissance Battalion* never even began. The only serious German threat in the south that day was the attack of the *326th Grenadiers* in the Bonlieu area late in the afternoon. Although the grenadiers easily routed a company of the 111th Engineer Battalion which was holding the area, American artillery quickly broke up their advance and again

forced the Germans back across the Roubion. The 1st Battalion, 143d Infantry, part of Dahlquist's reserve, entered Bonlieu at 2100 hours that night without opposition.

The American effort that day to cut Route N–7 turned out to be the most promising offensive action. Due to the early departure of *Groupe Thieme* and the late arrival of *Groupe Wilde,* the Germans had left the Hill 300–La Coucourde area nearly unprotected for much of the day. However, Harmony's 141st Infantry was stretched thin along a six-mile front, and the regimental commander was unable to put together an attacking force until late afternoon. Finally, around 1600, while units of the 2d Battalion, 143d Infantry, secured the northern slopes of Hill 300, the 1st Battalion, 141st Infantry, moved west out of the Condillac Pass supported by some tanks and tank destroyers and struck out for La Coucourde. Despite the arrival of *Groupe Wilde* elements, the attack succeeded, and by 1900 one and later two rifle companies, four tanks, and seven tank destroyers were blocking the highway.

Whether the Americans could keep the block in place was critical. Until darkness halted observed fire, American artillery prevented the Germans from assembling forces for a counterattack, but Harmony doubted that he could hold the roadblock through the night. Increased German pressure across his entire front made it impossible to reinforce the blocking force, and he had considerable difficulty keeping it supplied. Accordingly, he suggested that the force retire into the pass for the night, blowing up several small bridges in the area before leaving, and return in the morning. But Dahlquist, complying with Truscott's orders, told him to maintain the block as long as possible.

At this juncture, von Wietersheim took a personal hand in affairs. Disgusted with the failure of his plans and especially with the inability of his forces to keep at least the highway open, he organized an armored-infantry striking force from units scraped up in the Montelimar-Sauzet area and led a midnight cavalry charge against the American roadblock. By 0100 on the 26th, German armor had dispersed the blocking force, knocking out three American tanks and six tank destroyers and driving what was left back into the Condillac Pass. After reopening the highway, Wietersheim swung some of his forces east to seize the high ground on the northern side of the pass to prevent the Americans from resuming their ground attacks on the highway in the morning. At the time, Harmony still had two rifle companies on the northern section of the Hill 300 ridgeline, but nothing strong enough to counter this new German force.

Once again the action at Montelimar ended in a stalemate. Dahlquist had still committed little of his strength in La Coucourde area, and most of his 142d and 143d Infantry had seen no action. With so much American strength held in reserve or in supporting defensive positions, the inability of Dahlquist and Harmony to interdict the highway—their main mission—was not surprising. But Wietersheim had done little better. His grandiose attack plans had gone nowhere and, in the end, had only spread his forces out over the periphery of the battle square, nearly leading to his defeat in the center where it counted.

More Reinforcements

Additional American troops were on their way to the Montelimar sector. When Truscott learned of the German push toward Crest on the 25th, he directed the 45th Division to send the 157th Regimental Combat Team and the 191st Tank Battalion north to the battle square area. Taking a southerly route via Nyons, one battalion and most of the tanks reached Marsanne about 2200 on the 25th; the rest of the regiment along with one tank company began closing on Crest early the following morning. Truscott attached the units at Marsanne to the 36th Division, instructing Dahlquist to use them as his reserve, and ordered the rest of the force to remain at Crest as the corps reserve.

Meanwhile, late on the 25th, Dahlquist began planning for a limited offensive on the following day. He wanted Task Force Butler to attack first west from Crest along the south bank of the Drome and then south along Route N–7 to the Condillac Pass. At the time, Harmony's 141st Infantry was still maintaining its roadblock near La Coucourde, and it appeared that no more Germans would reach the Drome. Nevertheless, expecting stronger German counterattacks on the 26th in the southern sector of the battle square, Dahlquist continued to deploy his main strength, the bulk of the 142d and 143d regiments, and the recently arrived battalion of the 157th with its attached tanks in reserve or in defensive positions along his northern and southern flanks.

In the early morning hours of 26 August, American tactical plans again underwent a major revision. The dispersion of the 141st regiment's roadblock at La Coucourde prompted Dahlquist to change Butler's mission, and he subsequently directed the task force to launch an attack at daylight from the western exit of the Condillac Pass to restore the roadblock. Butler's attack was still the only offensive action that Dahlquist planned for the 26th.

The Germans were also changing their plans. Late on the 25th von Wietersheim directed the *110th Panzer Grenadiers,* previously split between *Groupes Hax* and *Thieme,* to displace north of the Drome and protect the routes of withdrawal beyond the river. At the same time he notified Wiese that he felt unable to retain command of the provisional corps and devote sufficient attention to his own division. Wiese, unhappy with the conduct of operations that day, agreed and assigned most of the remaining forces in the Montelimar sector to the *LXXXV Corps,* directing Kniess to continue the attacks against the American forces in the area on the 26th. For this purpose, he allowed Kniess to employ *Groupes Hax* and *Wilde,* both reduced to a single panzer grenadier battalion but each reinforced with tanks.

On 26 August Kniess planned to renew the attacks north and northeast of Montelimar between Hill 300 and the Bonlieu area with the *198th Division's 305th* and *326th Grenadiers.* He expected *Groupe Wilde* to keep Route N–7 open and placed *Groupe Hax* in

reserve near Montelimar. He also wanted the withdrawal of the rest of his corps speeded up. Still well south of Montelimar were the *308th Grenadiers* plus other elements of the *198th Division;* the *338th Division,* less one regiment traveling up the west bank of the Rhone; several field artillery and antiaircraft battalions; some combat engineer units; and a host of lesser combat and service units of both the army and air force. Kniess had good reason for concern. Late on the 25th the U.S. 3d Infantry Division had caught up with several *LXXXV Corps* elements north of Avignon, and he had no way of predicting the speed of the American advance north. Accordingly, he canceled existing plans for a phased withdrawal and directed the *338th Division* to begin a forced march that, he hoped, would bring it to Montelimar early on the 26th. The *669th Engineer Battalion,* reinforced, was to man rear-guard blocking positions to cover the corps' withdrawal and delay the 3d Division.

In the south, the 3d Division had started north on the 25th after receiving orders from Truscott to push reconnaissance patrols across the Durance and prepare for a drive on Montelimar. But the progress of the division was continually delayed by general transportation problems and the necessity of waiting for French units to take over American positions south of the Durance. Leading elements of the 3d Division reached Avignon about 1400, 25 August, and, finding the Germans gone, moved fifteen miles farther north to Orange where, about 1730, they ran into the German rear guard. Under pressure from Truscott to strike northward with all possible speed, General O'Daniel, the division commander, planned to bring his main strength up to the Orange-Nyons area on the 26th, and continue northward with two regiments abreast—the 15th Infantry along the Rhone and the 30th Infantry to the east. But, like Dahlquist, he lacked the fuel and transport to move quickly.

Battles on the 26th

Well before the 3d Division resumed its march north on 26 August, Task Force Butler, after a grueling night march, assembled in the Condillac Pass, ready to drive west toward the highway. The new American attack developed slowly against scattered but determined German resistance. After a few initial patrols toward La Coucourde failed to reach Route N–7, Butler sent two rifle companies of the 3d Battalion, 143d Infantry, over the northern nose of the Hill 300 ridgeline around 1330; and as they started down the northwest slope toward the highway, he reinforced them with a platoon of medium tanks and a few tank destroyers moving directly out of the pass. Skirmishing with German infantry most of the way and harassed by German artillery fire, these forces butted into *Groupe Wilde*, which had moved up from the south and swung east toward the pass. Simultaneously, other German forces attacked from the north, and indeterminate fighting continued throughout the entire area until dusk when the American armor finally pulled back into the pass for the night, leaving the two infantry companies clinging to the northern slope of Hill 300. An-

other attempt to cut Route N–7 had failed, and again the primary reason for the failure was the inability of the 36th Division to commit sufficient strength at the crucial point.

The German attacks on the 26th were even less successful. In the Montelimar corner of the battle square, Kniess' offensive began at 1130 with a lone battalion of the *305th Grenadiers* moving toward Hill 430 and was quickly repelled by American artillery and tank fire. A second German attack at 1530 in the Bonlieu area, again hitting the crease between the 141st and 142d regiments, penetrated a little over a mile north of the Roubion, but was also stopped by American artillery, and the position was restored by counterattacks of the 1st Battalions of the 142d and 143d regiments, both pulled out of reserve. In the northern sector of the square, the *11th Panzer Reconnaissance Battalion* broke through American roadblocks to come within two miles of Crest, but was too weak to press home the attack; during the afternoon, units of the 157th Infantry helped restore American blocking positions near Grane and Allex.

The German Withdrawal (27–28 August)

During the 26th, American artillery managed to block the road and rail lines along the Rhone intermittently, but, still short of ammunition, was unable to halt the steady stream of German foot and vehicle traffic that continued up the valley and across the Drome. Although much of the movement consisted of artillery, antiaircraft, and service units, it also included major combat units. Dawn on the 27th found all of the *110th Panzer Grenadiers*, the *11th Reconnaissance Battalion*, the *119th Replacement Battalion*, most of the *119th Panzer Artillery Regiment*, and part of the *15th Panzer Regiment (Groupe Thieme)* safely north. Guarding the Drome crossings were *Groupe Wilde* and units of the *305th Grenadiers*, while south of the Hill 300 bottleneck were *Groupe Hax*, the bulk of the *198th Division*, the *338th Division*, and—mainly on Hill 300—the *63d Luftwaffe Training Regiment.* The *338th* had not moved north as rapidly as Kniess and Wiese had hoped, and it had only begun to arrive at Montelimar after dark on the 26th. However, the pursuing 3d Division proved even slower and, beset by severe fuel shortages, was ten miles short of Truscott's objective by dusk of the 26th and still fifteen miles south of Montelimar.

Although not surprised by Dahlquist's failure to block N–7, Truscott had about lost patience with the division commander. Arriving at Dahlquist's headquarters on the morning of the 26th, Truscott intended to relieve him, complaining that his situation reports had proved erroneous and that he had failed to carry out his main objective, interdicting the German withdrawal.[12] According to Truscott, Dahlquist explained that in the confusion of battle his subordinate units had sometimes misinformed him regarding their locations and progress, and that continuous German attempts to strike at his supply routes at Crest and Puy had occupied much of his reserve force.

Shortages of transportation, fuel, and ammunition were also constant problems, and the net result had been the impossibility of concentrating sufficient combat power to hold the ridgeline on Hill 300 or to establish a permanent block across the highway in the face of several desperate German divisions. Somewhat mollified by a firsthand look at the terrain, Truscott decided not to take any action against Dahlquist for the moment, but remained unhappy with the state of affairs.

At the conclusion of the conference Truscott directed Dahlquist to employ Task Force Butler once again to establish a roadblock near La Coucourde and then, if possible, move the force north across the Drome and then east to Crest to close all of the Drome crossing sites. He also suggested that Butler could then head north, bypass Valence, and take Lyon, thereby preventing the *IV Luftwaffe Field Corps* from crossing to the east side of the Rhone north of Montelimar. For this purpose, he gave Dahlquist permission to use the 3d Battalion, 157th Infantry, and its attached armor as he saw fit, but Truscott retained the main body of the 157th Infantry under his own control, directing it to move west on the north side of the Drome to help Butler close the crossing sites. Truscott also hoped that O'Daniel's 3d Division could push substantial strength into the Montelimar area on the 27th to relieve some of Dahlquist's units.

Much to Truscott's disappointment, the fighting on 27 August was inconclusive. Butler, strengthened by the 3d Battalion, 157th Infantry, again pushed west from the Condillac Pass

---

[12] Truscott, *Command Missions*, p. 430.

toward Route N–7, starting a battle that seesawed back and forth all day and that ended in failure for the Americans. During the afternoon, mixed elements of the 141st and 143d Infantry managed to push the Germans off the eastern slopes of Hill 300, but German infantry held on to the remainder of the ridge for the rest of the day. To the south, further German attacks against 141st Infantry units on Hill 430 were repulsed but, worried about another German attack on his southern flank, Dahlquist kept most of the 142d Infantry idle in defensive positions along the Roubion. Meanwhile, in the north, American elements entered Grane late on the 27th without opposition and the 157th Infantry cleared Allex; but neither force was able to move any closer to the Livron-Loriol area that day. South of the battle square, the 3d Division's northward advance was still hampered by continued transportation problems as well as by roadblocks of mines, booby traps, felled trees, destroyed bridges, and other obstacles, and by evening the unit was still four miles short of Montelimar.

On the German side Wiese had become increasingly nervous at the steady northern progress of the 3d Division and the slow speed of the *LXXXV Corps* withdrawal. He had expected to have all his units across the Drome by nightfall, except the *198th Division.* Instead Kniess had kept *Groupes Hax* and *Wilde* south of the Drome and had committed part of the *338th Division* to what the *Nineteenth Army* commander felt were fruitless attacks against Hill 430 and the Condillac Pass. Meanwhile, German materiel losses in the battle square were

mounting at a rate that Wiese considered alarming. Route N–7 was littered with destroyed vehicles, guns, and dead horses; the railroad was blocked with wrecked engines and cars, including those of the railway artillery battalion. Personnel losses had also risen sharply on the 27th, not only from American bombardments but also as a result of Kniess' unprofitable attacks.

At dusk on the 27th Wiese directed Kniess to pull the *338th Division* and *Groupes Hax* and *Wilde* across the Drome at all costs on the 28th. The *198th Division* and the rear-guard engineers were to continue to hold back the 3d and 36th Divisions and, once the other units were across the Drome, to escape as best they could.

If Wiese was pessimistic, Truscott was still optimistic. On the basis of overly enthusiastic messages from Dahlquist on the 27th and erroneous intelligence reports, Truscott believed that major portions of the *LXXXV Corps* had been destroyed south of the Drome and that only remnants of three German regiments remained in the Montelimar area. Equally significant, he knew that the French had now cleared nearly all of Toulon and Marseille without much of a fight, and the remaining German forces in both ports were expected to surrender formally at any moment. It was time to begin the drive to northern France in earnest. He therefore gave orders for the 3d and 36th Divisions to mop up the area between the Drome and Roubion rivers on 28 August, for Task Force Butler and the 157th Infantry to occupy Loriol and Livron, and for units of the 45th Division to begin moving north from Grenoble toward Lyon. He expected both banks of the Drome to be in American hands by noon, and hoped that the 36th Division could start one regimental combat team north before dark.

Truscott soon discovered that he had greatly overestimated the speed of the German withdrawal and underestimated the strength of their forces still south of the Drome. When units of the 141st Infantry, now commanded by Lt. Col. James H. Critchfield,[13] tried to advance toward Montelimar on the morning of the 28th, they were quickly repelled by the *198th Division's 308th Grenadiers* supported by heavy artillery and mortar fire; Critchfield spent the better part of the day trying to extricate two of his attacking infantry companies that had been surrounded. Task Force Butler's drive on Loriol was equally unsuccessful. Now built around the 3d Battalion, 157th Infantry, the task force ran into heavy German tank and antitank fire at Loriol, losing three medium tanks and two tank destroyers within a few minutes, which forced Butler to pull back at once. North of the Drome the 157th Infantry did little better when stubborn resistance from the *110th Panzer Grenadiers* reinforced with tanks stopped their attack just short of Livron.

Meanwhile, in the center, the 2d and 3d Battalions, 143d Infantry, spent most of the day defending American positions in the area of

Hills 300 and 430 and the Condillac Pass. Although American artillery continued to shoot up German traffic along the road, the effort to block the highway with ground troops in the area of La Coucourde was not resumed. To the south, units of the 3d Division, which had conducted a daylong running engagement with the German rear guard, entered the southern outskirts of Montelimar that evening, but were unable to secure the city until the following morning, 29 August.

Although the Germans had again frustrated American attempts to cut their route of withdrawal during the 28th, their losses in men and materiel continued to multiply. South of Montelimar the 3d Division overran a column of some 340 German vehicles and took almost 500 German prisoners. Moreover, although *Groupe Hax,* part of the *933d Grenadiers,* and elements of the *338th Division's* artillery and special troops had arrived safely across the Drome, Kniess was unable to move either the *338th Division* or *Groupe Wilde* northward. Instead he was forced to commit *Groupe Wilde* and the *338th's 757th Grenadiers* at Loriol to hold back Task Force Butler; to use a battalion of the *933d Grenadiers, 338th Division,* and another from the *305th Grenadiers, 198th Division,* to secure the high ground between the Condillac Pass and Loriol; and to retain other elements of the *305th* and the *63d Luftwaffe* to hold at least a portion of Hill 300. At dusk these units were still in place, while the main body of the *198th Division* was concentrated a few miles north of Montelimar, just above what was left of the rear-guard engineer battalion.

---

[13] Colonel Harmony had been wounded on the 27th, and Critchfield, commander of the unit's 2d Battalion, headed the regiment until Col. Clyde E. Steele took over on the 29th.

End of the Battle

With *Groupe Wilde* and elements of the *338th Division* protecting the Drome crossings near Livron and Loriol, Kniess ordered Brig. Gen. Otto Richter,. commanding the *198th Division,* to break out of the battle square during the night of 28–29 August and the morning of the 29th. For the escape, Richter decided to divide his forces into three tactical columns, each built around one of his grenadier regiments and each moving north during the early hours of the 29th by a separate route. On the west a column led by the *305th Grenadiers* was to move directly up Route N–7; two other columns, one centered around the *308th Grenadiers* and the other around the *326th Grenadiers,* were to push up separately through the valley between Hills 300 and 430 and try to swing back to the highway near La Coucourde.

Meanwhile Dahlquist, intent on resuming his clearing operations that night, ordered the 141st regiment to again strike south against Montelimar, supported by the 143d Infantry, which was also to advance toward the city through the valley between Hills 300 and 430. In addition, he ordered Task Force Butler to make another attempt against Loriol at first light, and directed the 142d Infantry, which had replaced the 157th north of the Drome, to continue west through Livron to block the Drome fords. Inevitably the opposing forces would clash head on.

As units of the 143d Infantry moved south through the Hill 300–430 valley in the early hours of 29 August, their leading elements ran into the two columns of the *198th Division* moving north. In the violent night melee that followed, some of the German soldiers managed to break through the American lines and, under constant fire, reach Route N–7 by morning; most, however, were either killed or captured during the lengthy skirmish, just about ending the effectiveness of at least two of the three *198th Division* regiments. Meanwhile the *305th*'s column, which was supposed to wait until the other groups had cut back onto the highway, left early during the night and made good its escape directly up Route N–7 without opposition.

As daylight broke on the morning of the 29th, the 141st Infantry resumed its drive on Montelimar, policing stragglers of the *198th;* capturing General Richter, the division commander; and joining forces with the 3d Division's 7th regiment coming up from the south. During the final fighting of 28–29 August, the three converging American regiments captured over 1,200 Germans (including about 700 by the 143d Infantry in the area of the Hill 300–430 valley) while suffering 17 killed, 60 wounded, and 15 missing. The 15th Infantry, 3d Division, clearing Montelimar, captured another 450 Germans; and the 3d Division's 30th Infantry, which continued mopping up during the day, took several hundred more. On the 30th, those 3d and 36th Division units remaining in the battle square swept the entire area, taking nearly 2,000 additional prisoners.

To the north, along the Drome, the 142d Infantry cleared Livron by 0930 on the 29th, and, despite stiff German opposition, Task Force Butler secured

Loriol during the afternoon. However, neither force could make a final push to the Rhone that day to stop Germans who were still crossing at a few small fords. These eleventh-hour German escapees still had some punch left, and during the night they swallowed up two American roadblocks, capturing 35 American troops. Total casualties during the 29th for the two attacking American forces on the Drome were about 13 killed, 69 wounded, and 43 missing, but approximately 550 more German soldiers were prisoners.

For the *Nineteenth Army*, 29 August was the last day of cohesive action in the battle square. As long as they could, German soldiers continued to flee over the Drome River in ones and twos and disorganized groups. *Groupe Wilde* pulled out during the early afternoon, as did what was left of the *338th Division*, followed later in the day and into the evening by those elements of the *198th Division* that had managed to break through from the south. This last-minute success, however, came at the expense of other German units, such as the *757th Grenadiers*, that were virtually destroyed during the day trying to protect the Loriol-Livron crossings.

The battle officially ended on the morning of 31 August when the 142d regiment finally reached the Rhone River, clearing the north bank of the Drome and capturing 650 more Germans in the process. Although exhausted and thoroughly disorganized, the *Nineteenth Army* had managed to save the bulk of the *11th Panzer Division*, Kniess' *LXXXV Corps* with two greatly weakened infantry divisions, and a host of miscellaneous units, parts of units, and individual groups of army, air force, navy, and civilian personnel. West of the Rhone, the bulk of the *IV Luftwaffe Field Corps*, including the understrength *716th Infantry Division* and an assortment of units under the *189th Division*, had pulled abreast of Montelimar as early as 26 August and had also continued north, led by the *71st Luftwaffe Infantry Regiment*, which, fleeing in disarray, had already reached Lyon. At Vienne, fifty miles north of the Drome, the corps crossed the Rhone, joining the *LXXXV Corps'* flight northward with elements of the *11th Panzers* constituting a new rear guard. The battle of southern France was over, and the race for the German border had begun.

Montelimar: Anatomy of a Battle

Was Montelimar an Allied victory, a German victory, or something in between? Casualty figures tell part, but by no means all, of the story. American units involved in the battle suffered 1,575 casualties—187 killed, 1,023 wounded, and 365 missing. These losses, representing well under 5 percent of the American strength ultimately committed, hardly seem heavy considering the size of the forces engaged, although the concentration of casualties in a few infantry battalions of the 141st and 143d regiments attests to the bitterness of some of the fighting and the length of the conflict.

German losses were considerably higher. American forces engaged in the attempt to cut the Rhone valley escape route captured some 5,800 Germans from 21 through 31 August.

Of these, about 4,000 were from *LXXXV Corps* units and most of the remainder from assorted *Luftwaffe* elements. In addition, the withdrawal along the east bank of the Rhone cost the German Army about 600 men killed, 1,500 wounded, and several thousand others missing during the same time period. West of the river, the *IV Luftwaffe Field Corps* lost approximately 270 killed, 580 wounded, and 2,160 missing, mostly due to air attacks, FFI operations, and the general disorganization that characterized the movement north.

Taking into account all available information, the German Army units moving up the east bank of the Rhone suffered about 20 percent casualties. More important, most of these losses came from front-line combat units, greatly reducing their effective combat strength, which was defined by the German Army as fighting troops forward of the infantry battalion headquarters. For example, the *338th Division* (omitting the attached *933d Grenadiers*) was down to 1,810 combat effectives by the 31st, and the *198th Division* was reduced to about 2,800. In addition, both units had lost much of their artillery as well as substantial quantities of other equipment, such as vehicles, radios, crew-served weapons, and small arms. Thus, although the total manpower, or "ration," strength of these units might have been considerably more than their combat effective strength— as determined by German accounting—they could assemble little more than a single, weak regimental combat team apiece for action. At the end of the month, the U.S. Seventh Army intelligence thus rated the *338th Division*

as only 20 percent effective but, over-generously, put the equally damaged *198th* at 60 percent.

In contrast, the *11th Panzer Division,* the "Ghost Division," survived the Montelimar withdrawal in relatively good condition, suffering no more than 750 casualties and arriving at Vienne with about 12,500 effectives. The unit also brought out 39 of its 42 artillery pieces, over 30 of its 40-odd heavy tanks, and 75 percent of its other vehicles. With accuracy, the Seventh Army G–2 rated the panzer division as 75 percent effective. However, the *11th* had not really done much during the campaign. While serving as the *Nineteenth Army*'s reserve, it had only been committed to battle briefly and had led, rather than followed, the main German withdrawal, with disastrous consequences for the less mobile infantry divisions.

Despite the heavy German losses in personnel and equipment, the escape of the *Nineteenth Army* was a disappointment for Truscott, Dahlquist, and Butler. Truscott, looking back on his experiences in the Italian campaign, was acutely aware of the need to destroy or at least damage the retreating German forces as severely as possible. From the beginning, the oblique advance to the Grenoble-Montelimar area had been a gamble, one that attempted to take advantage of the hasty German withdrawal as well as the failure of Wiese to protect the flanks of his narrow route of retreat. The courageous assistance of the FFI—harassing German detachments, providing valuable local intelligence to the advancing Americans, and augmenting their combat forces whenever possible—was another advantage enjoyed by the Allies that is often overlooked. But the inability of the Allied commanders to concentrate their limited forces early enough at a single point—at Montelimar or, had circumstances dictated otherwise, perhaps Loriol, Valence, or even farther north—made it extremely difficult to stop the withdrawal, especially considering the strong German response once the danger was perceived. Allied logistical problems in the north—particularly the shortage of transport—caused by the rapid success of the landing itself, also reduced the flexibility of the northward thrust and made an earlier decision on a focal point necessary. Had this been done, the Seventh Army might have been able to push more fuel and ammunition up to the battle square in support, and Butler and Dahlquist might have been able to throw much more of their strength in the Hill 300–La Coucourde area sooner. But until a firm decision was made to focus on Montelimar and was communicated to all participants, the tactical commanders could not begin to close the Rhone valley escape route. As a new division commander and one who was unfamiliar with Truscott's methods of operation, Dahlquist was unsure of himself and needed more guidance. At the time, he blamed himself for allowing the Germans to escape, feeling that he had had "a great opportunity" and had "fumbled it badly." [14] But, operating on a logistical shoestring, the so-called hard-luck 36th Division had at least given a beating to almost every retreating German division,

forcing them to run a gauntlet they would not quickly forget.

The Seventh Army's logistical problems were not mysterious. Its rapid progress inland had created a gasoline shortage as early as D plus 1; by 21 August the three American divisions alone required approximately 100,000 gallons of fuel per day. At the time there was a surplus of ammunition in the beachhead area, but the three beach fuel dumps had only about 11,000 gallons of gasoline left between them. Using captured fuel stores at Draguignan, Le Muy, and Digne (26,000 gallons) helped somewhat, as did severe rationing, but there was no easy solution. Employing the 36th Division's trucks to motorize Task Force Butler only compounded both the fuel and vehicle shortage within the Allied command. As a result, the Seventh Army and the VI Corps lacked the wherewithal to assemble Task Force Butler and the 36th Division quickly at Montelimar and support the force with adequate rations, fuel, and munitions from the beach depots 200 miles to the rear. Although the ammunition expenditures of American artillery units in the Montelimar area were approximately three times higher (about ninety 105-mm. and thirty 155-mm. rounds per tube per day) than elsewhere, there was never enough to support these infantry and armored units adequately or to interdict the highway by fire alone. [15]

From Patch's broader perspective, the results were more satisfying. His

[14] Dahlquist Ltr, 25 Aug 44, John E. Dahlquist Papers, MHI.

[15] U.S. Seventh Army, *Report of Operations*, I, 316–18. For further discussion of logistical conditions at the time, see ch. 11.

army's main objective—securing the ports of Toulon and Marseille—had been accomplished in record time, but it was a task that had kept most of the Allied combat power—including vehicles, fuel, and munitions—well south of the Durance. Patch's priorities forced first Butler and then Dahlquist to grapple with the more powerful German units at Montelimar with little direct support. Although they subsequently failed to halt the German retreat, both Task Force Butler and the 36th Division acquitted themselves well against often superior German forces that continually attempted to outflank their blocking positions. The ensuing battle greatly sapped the strength of the remaining German units, while having little effect on the American forces involved. The action also forced Wiese to use his most mobile force, the *11th Panzer Division,* at Montelimar rather than as a rear guard. As a result, the 3d Division had a relatively easy time following the Germans up the Rhone, while the capture of Grenoble and its subsequent occupation by 45th Division units that were poised to strike even farther northward was an added bonus.

On the German side, General Wiese had managed to save much of his army, in part due to the early decision of *OKW* to withdraw German forces from southern France. However, he could not have been too happy over either the Montelimar episode or the rapid fall of the Mediterranean ports. His own failure to secure the flanks of the *Nineteenth Army's* withdrawal was the result of poor planning and poor intelligence. Aside from the capture of the 36th Division's order of 24 August, similar difficulties beset the German commanders throughout the battle. As a result, they rarely had a clear idea of the strength and dispositions of the forces opposing them at Montelimar and were unable to take advantage of weak points in the American lines. Like the Americans, the Germans suffered from an inability to concentrate sufficient strength at the crucial time and place, and were thus unable to exploit local tactical successes. Piecemeal commitment of battalions, small task groups, and hastily assembled provisional units characterized German efforts throughout the battle. Moreover, the German commanders often spread out these forces over a broad front on terrain that generally favored the defense. Had they concentrated on holding the Hill 300 ridgeline and directing the remainder of their available strength at one of the American flanks—Crest or Puy, for example—they might have been able to extract much more from the south and, at the same time, deal a severe blow to their pursuers. Thus, while Montelimar was certainly not the victory that Truscott had hoped for, it highlighted serious German military weaknesses as well as demonstrated the willingness of Allied commanders to undertake a certain degree of risk and initiative at the operational level of war.

CHAPTER X

Pursuit to the North

With its rear area secure and the Germans in full retreat, the Seventh Army's next objective was to move northward as rapidly as possible and join Eisenhower's SHAEF forces by linking up with General Patton's Third Army, which was operating on Eisenhower's right, or southern, wing. While French units policed up the port cities, Patch's staff began pushing more supplies to Truscott's VI Corps units to support the trek north. At the same time, the influx of troops, supplies, and equipment over the original landing beaches continued, with the remainder of the French combat units gradually coming ashore along with the rest of the American logistical and administrative support units. As all these forces sorted themselves out, it was evident that the Seventh Army had become almost inadvertently involved in a race to northeastern France against what remained of Wiese's *Nineteenth Army*, as well as the rest of *Army Group G*'s forces fleeing from western France. The German goal was to reach the area in front of the Reich border before the Allied advance, join with *Army Group B*, and present a unified front to the invaders. As a result, from the last days of August to mid-September, the

two opposing armies in southern France raced up the Rhone valley and proceeded northward, one after the other—each often more concerned with reaching its objective than in impeding the progress of the other. Clashes between the two forces were, however, unavoidable.

Allied Plans

On 25 August, as the battle of Montelimar was reaching its climax, Patch was already issuing orders that outlined his plans for future Seventh Army operations.[1] In accordance with preassault concepts, he intended to have Truscott's VI Corps drive rapidly northward, first to the city of Lyon, 75 miles up the Rhone from Montelimar, and then to Dijon, 110 miles farther. Subject to later arrangements with Eisenhower, VI Corps would then strike northeast from Dijon 160

---

[1] Information on Allied plans in this section is based on the following: *Seventh Army Rpt*, I, 220–21; de Lattre, *History*, pp. 121–23; Truscott, *Command Missions*, pp. 430–33; Seventh Army Diary, 25–28 Aug 44; Seventh Army FOs 3 and 4, 25 and 28 Aug 44; Seventh Army OI 8, 30 Aug 44; First French Army Genl Opns Orders 17 and 24, 26 and 29 Aug 44; First French Army Preparatory Order, 28 Aug 44; Rad, de Lattre to Gen Alphonse Juin (CofS, French Natl Def), 1 Sep 44; VI Corps Fld Msgs, 241000 and 281200 Aug 44.

miles to Strasbourg on the Rhine. The tasks assigned to de Lattre's French forces were more complex. The French would first complete the seizure of Toulon and Marseille; second, screen the area west of the Rhone, pushing reconnaissance elements north along its west bank; and third push north and northwest on the right of the VI Corps, moving into Alsace and the upper Rhine valley through the Belfort Gap, about 90 miles east of Dijon. Finally, the 1st Airborne Task Force would continue to screen the Franco-Italian border area assisted by French forces when available.

For the immediate future Patch's orders of 25 August specified that the airborne force, continuing to operate under the direct control of the Seventh Army, would secure the army's east flank from the mouth of the Var River near Nice, north into the Alps about 60 miles to the Larche Pass. The VI Corps, in addition to fighting it out at Montelimar, was to push east, northeast, and north to a line extending about 130 miles northwest from the Larche Pass through Grenoble to Lyon. The French units would receive their own operational sectors as their forces became available for the drive north.

On 28 August, with the Montelimar episode nearing an end, Patch issued more specific guidance, repeating his desire to have the VI Corps start its drive north to Dijon as soon as possible and confirming Lyon as Truscott's immediate objective. West of the Rhone the French were to reconnoiter 100 miles west and southwest of Avignon, while pushing forces northward in support of the Lyon attack.

East of the Rhone, de Lattre's forces, Army B, were to support the right flank of the VI Corps by moving north through Grenoble and east of Lyon, before turning their advance toward the Belfort Gap and the Rhine. In addition, Patch instructed de Lattre to relieve the airborne units and any other American forces in the area of the Franco-Italian border.

General de Lattre was understandably upset with these instructions. If followed, they would divide what was to become the First French Army into several parts—two protecting the Seventh Army's extreme eastern and western flanks, and two others on either side of the VI Corps supporting its drive to Lyon. With such dispersion de Lattre doubted whether he could project much of a force into the Belfort Gap area, especially with his weaker logistical organization. He put these arguments to Patch, and the two subsequently reached a compromise. The 1st Airborne Task Force would continue to hold the area from the Mediterranean to the Larche Pass, but de Lattre would accept responsibility for the border region north of the pass. West of the Rhone, Patch conceded that the "reconnoitering" of southwestern France could be done by a small reconnaissance force assisted by FFI elements; de Lattre agreed to send both the French 1st Armored Division, now unified under Maj. Gen. du Touzet du Vigier, and the 1st Infantry Division up the west bank of the Rhone as soon as they were available. East of the Rhone other French units would secure the VI Corps' right flank, pushing north from Grenoble. However, after the fall of Lyon, the two French divisions coming up the west bank of the Rhone would redeploy east of VI Corps and join the rest of the French forces, thereby uniting de Lattre's army for a stronger drive on the Belfort Gap.

During the planning process, Patch viewed the capture of Lyon primarily as a stepping stone to the German border rather than as another chance to trap the retreating *Nineteenth Army,* and he paid relatively little attention to the German forces retiring across the Alps into northern Italy. But the *Nineteenth Army*'s line of withdrawal and Truscott's aggressive temperament made it inevitable that the pursuing Americans would exploit every opportunity to destroy their retreating foe. Lyon represented the first focal point of such an effort. Situated at the juncture of the Saone and Rhone rivers, Lyon was the third largest city in France and an important road and rail center, whose seizure would have important logistical as well as propaganda value. The city also controlled the two most logical German routes of withdrawal. One route led northeast through the towns of Bourg-en-Bresse and Besancon to the Belfort Gap. Another went almost due north up the Saone valley to Dijon, from where *Army Group G* forces could continue north to join other German commands facing Eisenhower's armies or could swing back east, either through Besancon or routes farther north, to the Belfort Gap. The longer Lyon-Dijon route was much easier and faster, while the Lyon-Besancon route, although shorter, offered many natural defiles that French and American forces could attempt to interdict as they had at Mon-

telimar.

The Seventh Army's G–2 section believed that the *Nineteenth Army*'s main body would follow the Lyon-Bourg-Besancon route of withdrawal because the Lyon-Dijon route would put the enemy forces in an area that was becoming a major battlefield. In contrast, Truscott's corps staff estimated that Wiese's forces would take the northern route to Dijon and then simply swing east, heading for the natural defenses of the Vosges Mountains. From the Vosges the *Nineteenth Army* could anchor its left, or southern, flank on Belfort and the Swiss border, while stretching its right out to *Army Group B* forces north of Dijon. French intelligence estimates generally agreed with this second assessment.[2]

The German Situation

The VI Corps' projection proved accurate, for the bulk of the *Nineteenth Army* was indeed to head north from Lyon to Dijon. *OB West* ordered *Army Group G* to extend what would become its right wing northeast of Dijon toward the retreating *Army Group B* forces and establish a strong defensive line from Dijon through Besancon to the Swiss border. Such a line would not only secure the approaches to the Belfort Gap, but would also create a German pocket, or salient, west of the Vosges. At the insistence of Hitler and *OKW, OB West* intended to launch an armored counterattack from this salient against the

---
[2] Seventh Army G–2 Rpt, 29 Aug 44; VI Corps G–2 Daily Rpts, 29–31 Aug 44; First French Army G–2 Daily Rpt, 29 Aug 44.

southern flank of Patton's eastward-moving Third Army. Blaskowitz, the *Army Group G* commander, also wanted to hold the salient until the *LXIV Corps,* withdrawing from the Atlantic coast, could reach Dijon and strengthen the new line.[3]

With the Montelimar episode on their minds, both Blaskowitz and Wiese were also concerned with the possibility of the Seventh Army executing a wide envelopment northeast of Lyon in another attempt to trap their retreating forces. Erroneous reports that strong Seventh Army formations had already pushed east of the city increased their alarm. Almost equally worrisome was the news that the FFI had started a major uprising within the city, a development that could further retard the German withdrawal. On 26 August Blaskowitz accordingly had sped units north from the Montelimar sector to put down the Lyon uprising and suggested that Wiese pull the *11th Panzer Division* out of the Montelimar battle to protect the *Nineteenth Army*'s flank east of Lyon. At the time the armored division was still fully engaged, however, and the best Wiese could do was direct the *IV Luftwaffe Field Corps* to accelerate its withdrawal all the way to Lyon and protect the *LXXXV Corps'* route of withdrawal up the east bank of the Rhone.

---

[3] Sources for German planning and operations in this chapter include von Luttichau, "German Operations," chs. 10–11 and 14–15; Seventh Army G–2 History, Opns in Europe, Part I and Annex V, Part II and Annex III; Hugh M. Cole, *The Lorraine Campaign,* United States Army in World War II (Washington, 1984), ch. 1 (hereafter cited as Cole, *The Lorraine Campaign);* and official records of the G–2 sections of the Seventh Army, VI Corps, and the 36th and 45th Infantry Divisions.

Following the *LXXXV Corps'* escape past Valence and Vienne during 29–30 August, Wiese arranged for a phased withdrawal through Lyon, assigning the *IV Luftwaffe Field Corps* the task of holding the city and controlling traffic through it. He intended to withdraw all of the rear-guard forces into the city on the night of 31 August, and have the bulk of the army start north up the Saone valley toward Dijon the following evening; he then intended to pull his rear guard out of Lyon on the night of 2–3 September after it had destroyed all bridges across the Rhone and Saone rivers in the area. During the exodus, the *11th Panzer Division* was to guard the army against any flanking attack from the east—a threat that Wiese knew by the evening of 30 August had again become imminent.

North to Lyon

The Allied drive on Lyon was not as far advanced as the German commanders at first feared. On 25 August both Truscott and de Lattre were hard-pressed to round up any combat units for the thrust north. The bulk of the French forces were still clearing Toulon and Marseille, while most of Truscott's VI Corps was deeply involved in the Montelimar battle. Nevertheless, on 26 August Truscott directed General Eagles, the commander of the 45th Division, to initiate reconnaissance toward Lyon from Grenoble, and on the 27th the two commanders agreed to start the 45th Division's 179th regiment moving north on the next morning. To strengthen the effort, Truscott also ordered the 157th regiment, then in the Crest-Livron area, to join the drive; for the same reason, he relieved the 180th regiment from the mission of securing the corps' eastern flank. Now regarding any threat from the Franco-Italian border area as remote, he replaced the 180th Infantry with a small provisional task force made up of reconnaissance, mortar, and antitank units.

Patch's directive of 28 August confirmed the VI Corps' new objective, Lyon. Since the first French units were not due to arrive at Grenoble until the 30th, Truscott decided that his American units would have to make the drive alone. Speed was essential. Accordingly, he ordered Eagles' 45th Division to seize Bourg-en-Bresse, lying northeast of Lyon, as soon as possible, while Dahlquist's 36th Division, advancing directly north along the east bank of the Rhone, moved against Valence, Vienne, and finally Lyon. O'Daniel's 3d Division would follow the 45th, ready to reinforce either leading division if necessary. Truscott hoped that the dual drive would make the advance more flexible, would enable VI Corps units to sidestep German rearguard defenses along the Rhone, and would ultimately offer him another opportunity to trap the retreating enemy if the Bourg-en-Bresse area could be taken early enough.

On 29 August, as the *Nineteenth Army's* survivors trundled past Vienne, 15 miles south of Lyon, leading elements of the 45th Division bypassed the retreating Germans on the east and came abreast of the city. Encountering negligible resistance, the 45th Division forces captured two intact bridges over the Rhone 15 to 20 miles east of Lyon, and on the following days, 30 and 31 August, advanced 15 miles farther north to the town of Meximieux and then another 15 miles to Pont d'Ain on the Ain River (*Map 10*). Thus far, there had been no sign of the *11th Panzer Division* or any other German security forces.

As Eagles struggled to bring the bulk of his division up to the Meximieux area, the rest of the VI Corps followed as rapidly as possible. By 31 August the 36th Infantry Division, closely followed by two regiments of O'Daniel's 3d, had also avoided the German rear-guard defenses by using roads east of the Rhone valley and was only about thirty miles from Lyon. In addition, the 3d Algerian Division started north from Grenoble on the 31st, following in the wake of the 45th Division and reporting that there were no Germans on the VI Corps' eastern flank. On 1 September the Allied concentration against Lyon continued, but early in the day the commanders of the leading American divisions began to sense the first German reactions to their rapid pursuit. At Dahlquist's command post, FFI reports indicated that the Germans were constructing heavy rearguard defenses just south of Lyon; meanwhile at Eagles' headquarters subordinate commands notified the 45th Division staff that its outposts in the Meximieux–Pont d'Ain area were being probed by German armor. Obviously the Germans were more sensitive to threats to their rear or flanks than they had been before the battle of Montelimar.

Wiese had hoped that the *11th Panzer Division* would have secured or destroyed all the Rhone and Ain river

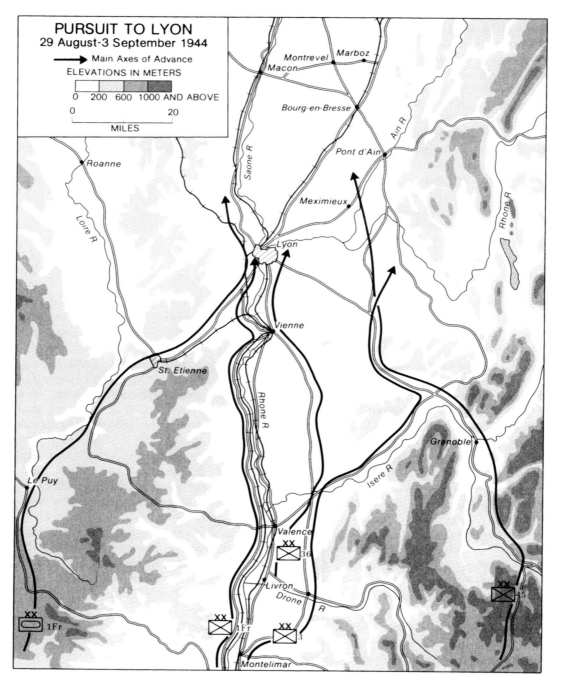

MAP 10   This map is printed in full color at the back of the book, following the Index.

bridges east of Lyon before the Americans could reach the area. This done, the task of covering the withdrawal of his two corps north to Dijon would have been fairly easy, with the panzer units slowly retiring directly to the northeast toward the Belfort Gap. But the early arrival of the 45th Division (or the late arrival of the *11th Panzers*) complicated these designs. To protect his eastern flank, Wiese now ordered General von Wietersheim, the panzer division commander, to make a major effort to dislodge the American forces from the Meximieux area and to strengthen German outposts at Bourg, about fifteen miles above Pont d'Ain. His actions would have to be closely coordinated with *Group von Schwerin*, composed of remnants of the *189th Division* and the *71st Luftwaffe Training Regiment*, which had been charged with defending the southern and eastern approaches to Lyon itself.

Meanwhile, units of the 45th Division began assembling north of Meximieux on 1 September in preparation for a major attack on the 2d, and the 117th Cavalry Squadron moved out to secure their right flank. The result was a series of disorganized engagements between elements of the *11th Panzers* and 45th Infantry Division that lasted throughout the day. At Meximieux, a strong German infantry-tank force bypassed the American troops advancing north—probably by accident—and penetrated to the center of town. There, a desperate defense by two reserve companies of the 179th Infantry and the regimental headquarters, including clerks and kitchen personnel, managed to repulse the persistent German attackers several

times, using bazooka, tank destroyer, and artillery fire against the enemy armor. Fighting continued in the town until dusk, when units of the 179th and 157th Infantry began returning to Meximieux from the north. With their withdrawal routes threatened, the German attackers finally broke off the action, but 45th Division troops were unable to clear the area completely until 0350 on the following morning.

As counted by the 179th Infantry, German casualties during the Meximieux affair totaled 85 men killed and 41 captured. In addition, 45th Division units destroyed 8 medium and 4 light tanks, 3 self-propelled guns, and 7 other vehicles. The *11th Panzer Division*, with more enthusiasm than truth, reported to the *Nineteenth Army* that it had destroyed an entire American regiment. Actually, casualties of the 179th Infantry and supporting units numbered 3 men killed, 27 wounded, and 185 missing and probably captured. Materiel losses included 2 tank destroyers, 2 armored cars, 1 halftrack, and 2 jeeps destroyed with about 20 other vehicles damaged. The most the German effort accomplished was to disrupt preparations by the 179th Infantry to participate in the 45th Division's attack on 2 September. This, however, was von Wietersheim's primary mission. Nevertheless, by the end of the day the threat to Lyon had grown even greater as both the 3d and 36th Divisions as well as the French forces moving up west of the Rhone all arrived within striking distance (some five to ten miles) of Lyon.

Despite the growing Allied threat to Lyon, Wiese felt more confident by the evening of the 1st. On the following day, 2 September, he expected that the bulk of the *Nineteenth Army* would be well north of the city screened in the south and east by the *11th Panzer Division*, now reinforced by a regiment of the *338th Division*. Yet Truscott still had hopes of catching Wiese's forces off-guard. With Patch's consent, he decided to allow the French the honor of formally occupying Lyon, while he had the 36th Division sidestep past the eastern edge of the city. To the northeast, he still expected the 45th Division to launch a major attack toward Bourg on 2 September, while the 117th Cavalry Squadron probed east and west of the town. With luck, he still might be able to penetrate the German flank defenses at some point and strike at their northward withdrawal columns.

This time the American units found the German security forces more solid and better organized. Between 2 and 3 September the 45th Division's 157th and 180th regiments encountered strong German resistance south and east of Bourg-en-Bresse, and were unable to pierce the German flank defenses there. Meanwhile, seeking less difficult routes through the German lines, Truscott had the 117th Cavalry Squadron send out a series of reconnaissance patrols from the Meximieux area toward Macon, about thirty miles north of Lyon and fifteen miles west of Bourg. Although making little progress in the west, the squadron was able to slip one of its scout troops north through the German defensive lines and past Bourg without encountering any resistance. At 1730 that evening, B Troop entered the small town of

Marboz located on a secondary road, ten miles north of Bourg. The cavalry force lost Marboz briefly to a small German counterattack, but reentered the town at dusk to stay the night.

Truscott immediately saw the tiny troop, with only armored cars and light trucks, as a lever that might unhinge the entire German flank security force. But speed was essential. Before the situation could be completely clarified, he directed the cavalry unit to push westward seven miles from Marboz and occupy Montrevel on Route N–75, the main highway northwest from Bourg. Since the new objective lay squarely on the *11th Panzer Division*'s main supply route, the isolated cavalrymen expected trouble. One platoon of Troop B even managed to work its way into the eastern edge of Montrevel that night, but was abruptly thrown out by the German garrison and forced to retire to Marboz.

Meanwhile, the 117th Cavalry commander, Lt. Col. Charles J. Hodge, tried to concentrate the rest of his widely scattered forces in the Marboz area as quickly as possible. Troop A reached the town during the night along with a forward squadron command group, which immediately began planning for a second attempt at Montrevel early on the 3d. Much, however, still depended on the arrival of more reinforcements, especially the squadron's Troop C, Troop E (assault guns), and Company F (light tanks).[4] But when these forces, which

---

[4] Troops A, B, and C consisted mainly of six-wheeled armored cars (twelve each) and quarter-ton "jeeps" (forty-five each); Troop E of M8 self-propelled guns (modified light tanks with 75-mm. how-

had been scouting the area east of Bourg, failed to show, the squadron commander decided to attack anyway with only his two reconnaissance troops.

On 3 September Troop B started into Montrevel shortly after dawn followed quickly by Troop A. After scattering about 300 German service troops, the small force secured the town by 0930, but lacked the strength to occupy the entire area. Looking over the objective in daylight for the first time, the cavalrymen found that Montrevel stood on a low ridge surrounded by open farmland with few defensive possibilities; the two troops lacked the manpower even to occupy the entire town. But expecting a violent reaction from the German armored unit—the tiger on whose tail they now sat—the two troops tried to prepare a creditable defense of the eastern section of Montrevel as best they could.

Upon learning of the threat to his main route of supply and withdrawal, von Wietersheim immediately pulled his *11th Panzer Reconnaissance Battalion* out of Bourg, reinforced it with a battery of self-propelled artillery, six medium tanks, and an engineer company, and dispatched the task force northwest to clear Montrevel. The German force reached Montrevel at 1100 and began a fight that lasted well into the afternoon. The Americans called for reinforcements, while holding on as best they could and mounting counterattacks to keep the Germans off balance. But the light armored vehicles of the cavalry were

not intended for heavy combat, and the contest was uneven; by 1330 the American force was surrounded and in disarray. The self-propelled guns of Troop E, a mile or so to the west, could provide little support because of the confused nature of the fighting, and the arrival of Troop C and Company F was delayed by traffic problems as the units tried to backtrack through the 45th Division's area of operation.

At 1430, with the Germans completely encircling the town, Company F attacked from the east and Troops A and B tried to break out. The results were disappointing. German artillery and tank fire easily destroyed or drove off the American light tanks, and only a few troopers within Montrevel managed to escape. By 1630 the American situation in the town had become hopeless.[5] The number of wounded made other breakout attempts impracticable, and the ammunition of the cavalry force had just about run out. Shortly thereafter, all of the troopers who were left in the town surrendered. Half an hour later Troop C and the 2d Battalion of the 179th Infantry began reaching the scene, but were too late to help. The remaining American forces in the area retired to Marboz for the night, leaving the German panzer division with its escape route intact.

When the cavalry squadron could take a count, it found that Troop A

---

itzers); and Company F of light tanks with 37-mm. cannons.

[5] The Congressional Medal of Honor was awarded to 2d Lt. Daniel W. Lee, commanding Headquarters Platoon, Troop A, 117th Cavalry Squadron, for heroic action, despite severe wounds, at Montrevel. (The date of the action was mistakenly cited as 2 September since almost all of the fighting actually took place on the 3d.)

had lost only 12 men, but only 8 soldiers from Troop B could be found.
In addition, Troop B and one platoon
of Troop A had lost all their vehicles—20 jeeps and 15 armored cars—
while Company F had 2 light tanks
destroyed and 3 damaged. The Germans captured 126 men, including 31
wounded, while 5 troopers had been
killed during the fight. About 10 of
those captured escaped during the
next few days, and the Germans left
behind 12 of the most seriously
wounded when they evacuated Montrevel. German personnel losses are
unknown, but the cavalry force accounted for at least 1 German tank, 2
armored cars, and 4 other vehicles.

Truscott later determined that the
117th Cavalry troopers at Montrevel
had been careless and were caught
napping by elements of the *11th
Panzer Division* withdrawing from
Bourg. However, given German and
American strength and dispositions in
the area, it is hard to escape the conclusion that Truscott simply assigned
missions to the 117th Cavalry Squadron that were beyond its capabilities.[6]
If Truscott expected more of the reconnaissance unit, then he ought to
have reinforced it with tanks and tank
destroyers. But Truscott and his staff
may have underestimated the recu-
perative powers of the *11th Panzer Division* and its strength in the Bourg
area. As later noted by von Wietersheim, the *11th* often went into action
with about 50 to 60 percent of its
available strength, in order to avoid

heavy losses from Allied air and artillery if the tactical units were caught
out in the open.[7] This policy also
made it easier to reconstitute damaged units fairly quickly, even after
they had been in heavy action as at
Montelimar, and may explain the division's seemingly great staying power
on the battlefield. Nevertheless, at
both Montrevel and Meximieux as
elsewhere, von Wietersheim's actions
were rarely decisive, even at the small
unit level; and Truscott's persistence
in using every opportunity that presented itself to turn his opponent's
flank and strike at his rear was to
slowly wear the *11th* and its sister infantry divisions down to the bone.

While his forces were reoccupying
Montrevel, von Wietersheim learned
that the bulk of the *Nineteenth Army*
had escaped north up the Saone
valley past Macon and that only the
IV Luftwaffe Field Corps rear guard remained in the area. His primary mission, protecting the retreating army's
flank, had thus been accomplished,
and the panzer division commander
now began planning his own escape.
Faced with the certainty that the VI
Corps would renew its attacks on 4
September, he ordered his armored
elements to vacate their delaying positions in the Meximieux-Bourg-Mon-
trevel area on the night of 3–4 September. But rather than heading
north with the rest of Wiese's forces,
von Wietersheim turned the *11th
Panzer Division* to the northeast, planning to pull it back along the approaches to the Belfort Gap.

On the morning of 4 September,

---

[6] See Truscott, *Command Missions*, p. 439; and the
account in the squadron commander's draft autobiography, pp. 133–35, Charles J. Hodge Papers,
MHI.

[7] "11th Panzer Division Rpt of MG von Wietersheim, 4 June 46," John E. Dahlquist Papers, MHI.

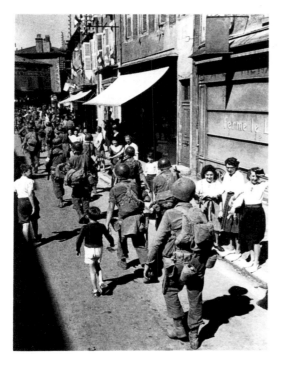

157TH INFANTRY, 45TH DIVISION, *passes through Bourg, September 1944.*

Truscott's forces found that their foes had once again escaped. Units of the 45th Division occupied Bourg-en-Bresse, while those of the 36th Division moved into Macon. There was no opposition. In the west, French units of the 1st Infantry Division, after overcoming scattered German roadblocks and their own logistical problems, had entered Lyon earlier, on the 3d, and also found the Germans long gone. However, bypassing the city on the west, CC Kientz of du Vigier's 1st Armored Division, reinforced with the 2d Algerian Spahis, achieved a signal success by trapping and destroying the *IV Luftwaffe Field Corps'* rear guard twenty miles north

of Lyon, taking nearly 2,000 prisoners. Meanwhile, on the other side of Patch's spearhead, the French 3d Algerian Division, out of Grenoble and now abreast of the leading VI Corps units, probed the Jura Alps toward the Swiss border, finding nothing but assorted FFI units. Behind the Algerians, O'Daniel's 3d Division finally rumbled up to the front lines, eager to get on with the drive north and with what many American GIs in the rear had begun to call "the champagne campaign."

A Change in Plans

Patch's original plans of 28 August had called for VI Corps to continue its drive directly north, moving up the Saone valley to Dijon in order to join Patton's eastward-moving Third Army. Simultaneously, de Lattre's forces on Truscott's right were to begin a concentrated thrust to the northeast, aiming for the Belfort Gap and the Rhine.[8] However, events had continued to move faster than many Allied planners predicted, and Truscott now believed the earlier plans were impractical. On 2 September, in view of the rapid German withdrawal to Dijon and the still-scattered deployment of the French divisions, he proposed several major revisions to these instructions. Pointing out that

[8] This section is based on the following sources: *Seventh Army Rpt*, I, 258–59; Truscott, *Command Missions*, pp. 434–40; de Lattre, *History*, pp. 133–36; Seventh Army Diary, 3–5 Sep 44; Seventh Army Directive (no number), 3 Sep 44; VI Corps Fld Msg, 031000 Sep 44; G–3, Army B, Note Concernant le Developement des Operations apres la Prise de Lyon, 2 Sep 44; G–3, Army B, SO 31–A, 2 Sep 44; Army B, Genl Opnl Order 32, 3 Sep 44; Army B, SO 33, 4 Sep 44.

de Lattre would need at least a week to concentrate his forces in the Bourg-en-Bresse area for the drive on Belfort, he suggested that his VI Corps undertake the mission instead. His three mobile infantry divisions were already massed east of Lyon and could begin to move northeast toward the Belfort Gap within a day or two. In front of them, he felt, were only scattered elements of the *11th Panzer Division*, also moving northeast, but with very little armor left. More important, a rapid thrust to the northeast, taking the shortest route to the Vosges–Belfort Gap area, would give the Seventh Army yet another chance to trap the *Nineteenth Army*, catching the Germans between Dijon and the Vosges as they ultimately tried to withdraw eastward. The French, Truscott added, were already well north of Lyon and were therefore in a better position to pursue the bulk of the retreating German forces and then swing east through the Vosges passes to Strasbourg.

Patch formally agreed to Truscott's proposals early on the morning of 3 September, but de Lattre was angry and objected strenuously to the changes. In part, his irritation stemmed from his belief that the two principal American commanders, Patch and Truscott, were making major decisions without consulting him or his staff. The fact that the French army would soon deploy more than twice as many divisions as the Americans on the battlefield lent weight to his position that the French divisions, as agreed upon, should be united on the Seventh Army's right and, after joining with Eisenhower's forces, become an independent army.

If the French forces remained split, obviously this would be impossible.

De Lattre admitted that it would take several days to transfer the two French divisions, the 1st Armored and 1st Infantry, to the area east of Lyon, and probably a few more to bring up one or two additional infantry divisions from southern France. But he also pointed out that the 3d Algerian Division, on VI Corps' right, had already sent strong armored reconnaissance elements of its own fifty miles east of Bourg to scout out the routes to Belfort; moreover, the division planned to send an infantry regiment reinforced with a tank destroyer battalion toward the Belfort Gap on the following day. Starting even more forces east at this point was dangerous, he felt; and de Lattre questioned Truscott's ability to support a corps-sized drive logistically.

In the end de Lattre compromised. On the afternoon of 3 September the French commander unilaterally announced the formation of two French corps-level commands—the I Corps under Lt. Gen. Emile Bethouart and the II Corps under General de Monsabert.[9] De Monsabert's II Corps was to control the French 1st Armored and 1st Infantry Divisions west of the Rhone and Saone, pushing north toward Dijon; Bethouart's I Corps was to operate to the right of VI Corps with the 3d Algerian and 9th

---

[9] Headquarters, French II Corps, actually became operational on 1 September, with de Monsabert, then commander of the 3d Algerian Division, taking over on the 2d. Before 1 September French forces west of the Rhone had operated as a provisional *groupement* under General du Vigier, commander of the 1st Armored Division. For the present, de Lattre's staff continued to call itself simply Army B.

Colonial Divisions and later the 2d Moroccan Division. In compliance with the revised Truscott-inspired plans, the French II Corps was to push north toward Dijon and then swing east toward Strasbourg; the French I Corps was to push east and northeast toward Belfort, presumably supporting Truscott's drive northeast. The 2d Moroccan Division would take over the northern sector of the Franco-Italian Alpine front and be replaced by the 4th Moroccan Mountain Division in early October (while the American 1st Airborne Task Force and the 1st Special Service Force continued to secure the southern sector). His forces thus remained split, but de Lattre had asserted himself as at least a provisional army-level commander of two French corps, easing the eventual establishment of a French army command, the First French Army, sometime in the near future.

Not wishing to make an issue of the matter, Patch accepted de Lattre's amendments to his plans and issued supplemental orders on 4 September. Bethouart's II Corps was to advance northeast toward the Belfort Gap on an axis that would take it south of Belfort city, and Truscott's VI Corps was to aim for the northern shoulder of the gap. Truscott, although at first fearing that this solution would restrict his freedom of movement, agreed to the compromise and set to work hammering out the details of the operations with both his own and Bethouart's new staff.

Creation of the Dijon Salient

On 3 September, as the Seventh Army leaders adjusted their plans,

Hitler personally reminded Blaskowitz of *Army Group G*'s primary responsibilities: establishing a common front with *Army Group B*; defending the approaches to the Belfort Gap; and holding the salient around Dijon. This last was obviously the most difficult task, but the German political leader still had visions of launching an armored counterattack from an assembly area west of the Vosges. Blaskowitz, aware of the German Army's limited capabilities in the west, was more concerned with holding on to the Dijon area until the remainder of his forces from the Atlantic coast could escape. However, he also knew that his pursuers from the south would not give him much time to pause and regroup. Taking all these factors into consideration, he completed plans to accomplish his diverse missions by 4 September.[10]

To protect his southern flank, Blaskowitz decided to establish delaying positions along and just south of the Doubs River, a small watercourse flowing generally west and southwest from the Montbeliard area through the small city of Besancon and joining the Saone River about thirty miles south of Dijon. The *11th Panzer Division*, still operating under the *Nineteenth Army*'s direct control, was to defend the eastern section of the new line with a thirty-mile front from Mouchard to the Swiss border. From Mouchard the *LXXXV Corps' 338th*

---

[10] For additional information on German activities, see also Cole, *The Lorraine Campaign*, chs. 4 and 5; Detmar Finke, "Nineteenth Army, 4–15 September 1944," CMH MS R–161; Dean H. Krasomil, "German Operations in Southern France," ch. 6, "The Dijon Salient, 1–15 September 1944," CMH MS R–51.

and *198th Infantry Divisions* were to extend the line westward to the town of Dole on the Doubs River, thirty miles west of Besancon, and from Dole twenty miles farther west along the Doubs to the Saone. Backstopping the *LXXXV Corps* was a second line along the Doubs east of Dole, centering on Besancon and consisting of various ad hoc combat formations under *Corps Dehner*, which was a provisional headquarters under General Ernst Dehner, who had previously commanded the administrative and security organization *Army Area Southern France.* The main task of all these forces was to guard the approaches to Belfort.

Blaskowitz intended to hold the Dijon salient with three corps: the *IV Luftwaffe Field Corps* in the south; the *LXIV Corps* in the west, if it ever arrived intact from the Atlantic coast; and the *LXVI Corps*, which *OB West* had assigned to *Army Group G* on 27 August, in the north. At the time the *IV Luftwaffe Field Corps* had only the *716th Division* and the remnants of the *189th Division*; the forces that might be available to the other two corps were uncertain. Nevertheless, Blaskowitz thought it possible to hold for at least three or four days a loose cordon of strongpoints from Givry in the south, northwest to Autun, then north past Dijon to Chatillon-sur-Seine, and back east to Langres. The western section would be no more than an outpost or screening line through which retreating *LXIV Corps* elements could pass on their way to Dijon. The missing corps had incurred few losses on its way across central France, delayed only by FFI harassment, MAAF air attacks on

march columns and bridges, and its own lack of transportation. By the time it arrived, Blaskowitz expected that he would be forced to fall back to the Saone and even farther east, depending on how much pressure the Allies brought to bear on his flanks.

At the time, elements of the *LXIV Corps* were already beginning to straggle into Dijon. The corps had begun its withdrawal with about 82,500 troops, of whom some 32,500 were members of ground combat units; the remainder belonged to various units from all branches and services assigned or attached to the Atlantic coast garrisons. Leading elements of the *LXIV Corps*' vanguard, the weak *159th Infantry Division*, reached the Saone River on 4 September; the *16th Infantry Division*, which lacked three of its nine organic infantry battalions, entered the salient on the following day. The *360th Cossack Cavalry Regiment* (horse cavalry) and the *950th Indian Regiment* (infantry) arrived about the same time, as did the *602d* and *608th Mobile Battalions* (light, motorized infantry). These organizations represented almost all of the "regular" combat strength for which the *LXIV Corps* had been able to find any transportation. Another 50,000 troops were still on the way, including rear elements, afoot, of the *16th* and *159th Divisions*; army, air force, and navy supply and administrative units; and a number of security, or police, battalions and regiments armed as auxiliary infantry. Some units and equipment were entrained but unable to move due to Allied air attacks on rail bridges and switching sites. The *LXIV* headquarters, which established a command post at Dijon on the 4th, felt that the chances of bringing many of these troops into the salient were slim.[11]

Army Group G's problems were all intensified by the increasingly rampant disorganization and depletion of units under its control, especially those now being positioned to defend the salient. All of these forces had suffered heavily from the almost inevitable straggling inherent in retrograde movements, and combat casualties had only increased the confusion. The result was a defensive order of battle so complex that its effectiveness was extremely doubtful. For example, north of Dijon, the *LXVI Corps* held the northern edge of the salient was an assortment of forces that Blaskowitz had been able to scrape together: the tankless *Group Rauch* of the *21st Panzer Division;* the *608th Mobile Battalion* and the bulk of the *16th Division* just arriving from the Atlantic coast; *Group Ottenbacher*, a provisional brigade composed mainly of police and security units; and a host of smaller combat, quasi-combat, and service units of all types. The mixed force did little to allay Blaskowitz's fear of an armored attack led by Patton toward Nancy on the boundary between *Army Groups G* and *B*.

In the west, screening the Givry-Chatillon outpost line, the *LXIV Corps* boasted *Group Browdowski*, consisting of the *615th Ost Battalion*, the *4th Battalion* of the *200th Security Brigade*, a heavy battery of the *157th Antiaircraft Battalion*, a provisional machine-gun platoon, and little more. Defending

the southern edge of the salient, the *IV Luftwaffe Field Corps* had two major commands, the *189th Division* and *Group Taeglichsbeck*. The remnant *189th*, temporarily renamed *Group von Schwerin*, had two weak infantry battalions, a four-piece artillery "battalion," and some miscellaneous attachments, altogether totaling less than 1,200 combat effectives. *Group Taeglichsbeck* included the *602d Mobile Battalion*, the *3d Battalion* of the *198th Security Regiment*, an engineer company from the same unit, three batteries of the *990th Artillery Battalion*, and an antitank company from the *16th Division*.

To the southeast, Blaskowitz regarded the threat posed by Patch's aggressive Seventh Army as equally worrisome, and the defenses in front of the Belfort Gap as little better than those outposting the salient. In answer to Wiese's pleas for reinforcements there, he dispatched the *159th Division* to *Corps Dehner*, which at the time had only a few police and security units, a couple of undependable *Ost* battalions, and a few pieces of light artillery. But to the south and east, the worn-out *11th Panzers* and the *338th* and *198th Infantry Divisions* could not have been in much better shape. In fact the composition of the *Nineteenth Army*'s various *gruppen* changed from day to day as more elements of the *LXIV Corps* came into the Dijon salient and others arrived from the immediate army rear. Wiese, for example, tried to beef up the *189th Division* in the south by adding to it the *726th Grenadiers* of the *716th Division* and the *2d Battalion* of the *5th Cossack Regiment*. Finally Hitler himself gave Blaskowitz permission to reorganize his forces more or less as he saw

---

[11] See Krasomil, "German Operations in Southern France," ch. 5, "The Withdrawal of the LXIV Corps (18 August–4 September 1944)," CMH MS R–47.

fit, bringing up to strength all of *Army Group G*'s regular formations by infusing them with "suitable" personnel from all branches of the armed services within the army group's area of operation. Only certain specialists and technicians were excepted. The result was a slow but steady rise in the paper strength of the German divisions, but the effectiveness of the filled-in units remained to be seen. Without more training, Blaskowitz believed that units composed of such fillers had little offensive capability and could only be expected to defend in place for about two or three days. The German defenders would have to continue relying more on Allied supply problems than on their own military strength to keep the attackers at bay.

The Seventh Army Attacks

Given the weak German defenses, the Seventh Army's advance northward continued almost at will between 4 and 8 September. In the west, the French II Corps' 1st Armored Division slammed into the ragged line that the *IV Luftwaffe Field Corps* was trying to improvise between Givry and Chalons-sur-Saone *(Map 11)*. It cleared both towns by the 5th and continued northward another ten to fifteen miles before halting on the 6th to await fuel supplies. During the night of 6–7 September responsibility for defending the sector passed from the *IV Luftwaffe* to the *LXIV Corps*. The change made no difference to the French, however, who continued pushing north on the 7th, nearing Beaune and rounding up hundreds of stragglers from the German *16th* and

159th Infantry Divisions who were still trying to make their way to Dijon. In light of the rapid French advance, Wiese had already decided to begin abandoning the salient, and on that day ordered the *LXIV Corps* to pull its forces back to an area within a ten-mile radius of Dijon. Thus while CC Sudre occupied Baume unopposed on 8 September, the other units of the French II Corps were busy capturing the growing number of German forces unable to reach safety. These included six railroad trains—one of them armored—full of *LXIV Corps* troops, vehicles, guns, and supplies, and some 3,000 troops from *Group Bauer,* another ad hoc march group from the Atlantic.[12] Meanwhile, Wiese had become increasingly concerned over the widening gap between the *LXIV Corps* and the rest of the *Nineteenth Army*, as Allied forces east of the Saone River began their drive on the Belfort Gap–Vosges area.

After regrouping and resupplying its forces on 3 September, VI Corps had begun its drive northeast on the 4th, heading in the general direction of Besancon on the Doubs River about fifty miles away. Initially O'Daniel's 3d Division led the attack with Dahlquist's 36th Division on the left and Eagles' 45th in the rear. On the corps' right, or eastern, flank, the 3d Algerian Division, the only French I Corps unit to have moved up to the

---

[12] *Group Bauer* started out of southwestern France as part of the larger *Group Elster*, which had originally numbered around 30,000 troops. About two-thirds of *Group Bauer*, mainly administrative and service personnel, escaped past Dijon, but the 19,000–20,000 troops of *Group Elster*'s main body surrendered to the U.S. Ninth Army far west of Autun on 16 September.

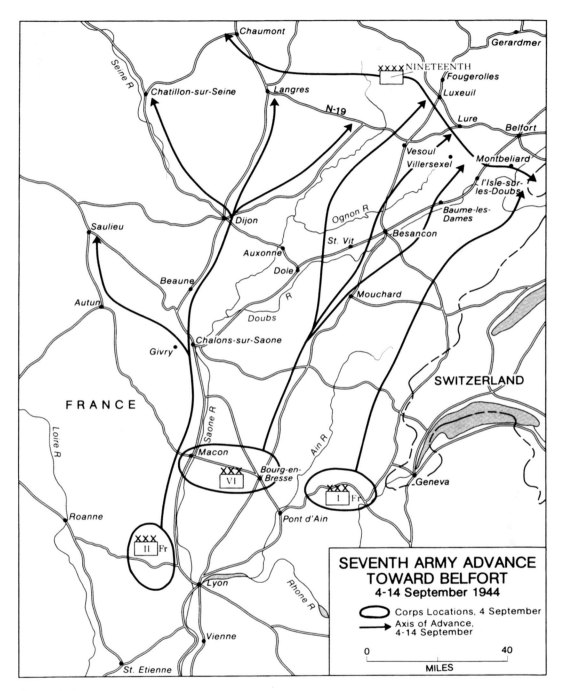

Chaumont

Gerardmer

Seine R

Chatillon-sur-Seine

Langres

XXXX NINETEENTH

Fougerolles

Luxeuil

N-19

Lure

Belfort

Vesoul

Villersexel

Montbeliard

l'Isle-sur-
les-Doubs

Ognon R

Baume-les-
Dames

Saulieu

Dijon

St. Vit

Besancon

Auxonne

Beaune

Dole

R

Mouchard

Autun

Doubs

Chalons-sur-Saone

Givry

SWITZERLAND

FRANCE

Loire R

Saone R

Macon

XXX
VI

Bourg-en-
Bresse

Ain R

Geneva

XXX
I Fr

Roanne

XXX
II Fr

Pont d'Ain

Lyon

Rhone R

Vienne

**SEVENTH ARMY ADVANCE
TOWARD BELFORT
4-14 September 1944**

Corps Locations, 4 September

Axis of Advance,
4-14 September

St. Etienne

0   40

MILES

MAP 11   This map is printed in full color at the back of the book, following the Index.

Lyon area, kept abreast of the American units. The rapid Allied advance gave Wiese no time to establish any kind of defensive line forward of the Doubs River, and the *LXXXV Corps* had to struggle to construct even a thin defensive screen there.

Approaching Besancon on the morning of the 5th, lead elements of the 3d Division began probing German defenses and seeking suitable water crossings east and west of the town. *Corps Dehner,* responsible for defending the Besancon area, still had little more than a few security units under its control, but Wiese had reinforced it with a battalion-sized task force, including a company of tanks, from the *11th Panzer Division* and was currently hurrying the *159th Infantry Division* into the sector from Dijon.[13] Wiese intended to make a stand here, if only to give the rest of his forces more time to move into their defensive sectors. However, on the 5th the supporting units of the *11th Panzer Division* were about to depart the area, leaving Besancon defended by a few 88-mm. guns and crews from an antiaircraft unit, some engineers, a naval artillery unit, one security battalion, and elements of two reconnaissance battalions.

As the 3d Division brought up its strung-out forces for a major effort against Besancon on 6 September, Truscott considered having the 3d and 45th Divisions bypass the town on the east and allowing units of the 117th Cavalry and the 3d Division to

screen any German forces there. Later on the 5th, after 3d Division troops had discovered an intact bridge west of the town, he discussed the possibility of outflanking Besancon from the opposite side. However, trouble late in the day farther east caused him to abandon the entire idea of bypassing the German defenses. At Baume-les-Dames, eighteen miles east of Besancon, the 3d Algerian Division's 4th Tunisian Tirailleurs had rushed over the Doubs using a damaged bridge, but were then severely mauled in a German counterattack by the *11th Panzer Division.* With its other elements scattered south and southeast of Baume, the French requested immediate American assistance.

Meeting with Bethouart and the commander of the 3d Algerian Division on the morning of the 6th, Truscott decided that it was too risky to simply bypass the German strongpoints and that they would have to be taken by force. To accomplish this he proposed that his 3d Division seize Besancon, the 45th Division move against Baume, and the 3d Algerian—its front somewhat narrowed—launch a concentrated thrust toward Montbeliard.

Meanwhile, during the night of 5–6 September, Wiese had again been busy reorganizing his defenses. First, he placed the *LXXXV Corps* headquarters, which had been controlling the sector west of *Corps Dehner,* in charge of the Belfort Gap defenses, leapfrogging it to the east and replacing it with the *IV Luftwaffe Field Corps* from the southern border of his now collapsing salient. Second, he moved all *11th Panzer Division* elements out of

---

[13] *Army Group G* had reassigned the *159th Division,* with five infantry battalions, from the *LXIV Corps* to the *Nineteenth Army* on the evening of 5 September, after it had arrived in the Dijon area from the Atlantic coast.

30TH INFANTRY, 3D DIVISION, CROSSES DOUBS RIVER AT BESANCON, *September 1944.*

the Besancon-Baume region, shifting them well east of the winding Doubs and onto the most direct approaches to the Belfort Gap. At the same time, he attempted to fortify *Corps Dehner's* weak defenses with the arriving *159th Division.*

Along the Doubs River these shifts did the Germans little good. O'Daniel managed to move his 3d Division troops across the Doubs and occupy the wooded hills around Besancon, thereby surrounding the town before the German defenders could react effectively. Despite a garrison that now totaled about 4,200, the strongpoint fell late on 8 September after about two days of desultory fighting, during which over half the defending troops were captured or made casualties.

Subsequently Wiese had to withdraw what remained of the *159th Division* for a complete overhaul.

West of Besancon, Dahlquist's 36th Division reached the Doubs River line on the 6th, pushed aside the weak *338th Division* elements defending the area, and, while advancing northeast of the Doubs on 8 September, bumped into the *IV Luftwaffe Corps'* *198th Division* as it was attempting to move across the rear of the German front to launch a counterattack against Besancon. A day-long battle between the two units around St. Vit, ten miles west of Besancon, saw the German forces routed, convincing Wiese that another general withdrawal was in order.

East of Besancon, Allied operations

TANKS OF 45TH DIVISION ADVANCE IN VICINITY OF BAUME-LES-DAMES, *September 1944.*

proceeded more slowly. Lack of strength in the forward areas because of transportation and supply problems were the major culprits, and there was little that Patch or Truscott could do to solve these difficulties quickly. On 7 September the 45th Division's 180th regiment crossed the Doubs southwest of Baume with no opposition, forcing *11th Panzer Division* elements to evacuate the town on the evening of the 8th to avoid encirclement. To the southeast, the 3d Algerian Division made some progress toward Montbeliard, but was firmly halted eleven miles short of the city by the bulk of the *11th Panzer Division,* which had finally been infused with some new equipment. By then it was also evident that the French could not

really pose a strong threat to Belfort until Bethouart's I Corps could bring more of its divisions up to the front line. For now, a successful drive on Belfort would depend entirely on Truscott's VI Corps.

To the Belfort Gap

By the evening of 8 September the *Nineteenth Army* had begun another major withdrawal along with the rest of *Army Group G's* forces. The Seventh Army's advances through St. Vit, Besancon, and Baume in the south made a continued stand along the Doubs River pointless; and, in the west, the French I Corps drive on Dijon was rapidly puncturing the German salient. Moreover, *OKW* had changed the proposed counterattack assembly area from the vicinity of Dijon to that of Nancy, much farther north. Thus, with just about all of the units arriving from the Atlantic coast that could be expected, the so-called salient had outlived its usefulness. However, Blaskowitz could not order too deep a withdrawal. Patton's Third Army was still moving east, and *OB West* had just transferred control of the German *First Army*—formerly on *Army Group B*'s left, or southern, wing—to *Army Group G*. The change made Blaskowitz responsible for launching the Hitler-proposed armored counterattack from the Nancy area against the Third Army. Although the army group commander could now afford to have the bulk of Wiese's *Nineteenth Army* pull back to the Vosges, a certain portion of it plus the entire *First Army* would have to remain west of the mountains to defend Lorraine.[14]

To effect these changes, Blaskowitz directed the *LXVI Corps* to withdraw its forces east thirty-five miles from Chatillon-sur-Seine to Langres, fifty miles north of Dijon. From Langres the *LXVI Corps'* new front was to stretch north some twenty miles to Chaumont, where it would then swing northeast to Nancy. He also instructed Wiese to pull the *LXIV Corps* back to the Saone, abandoning Dijon, and even farther east should French advances make it necessary; at the same time, Blaskowitz gave him permission to withdraw his forces from the Doubs River back to the northeast. Wiese, in turn, began pulling the di-

verse elements of the *LXIV Corps,* the *IV Luftwaffe Field Corps,* and *Corps Dehner* back to the east and northeast in an attempt to establish a new defensive line centering around Vesoul, a road and rail hub at the base of the Vosges some thirty miles northeast of the Doubs River line. Only in the far southeast, where the *11th Panzer Division* and assorted battle detachments held the Allied forces at bay before the Belfort Gap, did the *Nineteenth Army's* front appear relatively stable.

During 7 and 8 September the *LXIV Corps* redeployed the weak *716th* and *189th Divisions* to the Auxonne–St. Vit area, and prepared to move back even farther east on the 9th. In what had now become the *Nineteenth Army's* center, Petersen's *IV Luftwaffe Field Corps* began falling back ten miles to the Ognon River. There Wiese wanted Petersen to establish an intermediate defensive line with the *198th Division* and *Corps Dehner* (now little more than a regimental-sized task force of the *159th Division*) in the center; the *338th Division* on its right, or western, wing; and a new formation, *Group Degener,* on its left, or eastern, wing.[15] Composed of several odd police and security units, some provisional infantry companies organized from stragglers assembled at Belfort, and a couple of 88-mm. antiaircraft batteries, this patchwork organization was reinforced with a battalion combat team from the *11th Panzer Division* and later by a new provisional security regiment. With *Group Degener*

---

[14] The ensuing contest between the U.S. Third Army and the German *First Army* is the subject of Cole's *The Lorraine Campaign.*

[15] The group commander, Brig. Gen. Joachim Degener, had formerly commanded the *997th Feldkommandantur* and had led one of the *IV Luftwaffe Field Corps* columns out of southern France. *Group Degener* had initially operated under *LXXXV Corps* control.

anchoring the corps' left wing at l'Isle-sur-les-Doubs, and the *338th Division* holding the corps' right at Ognon, about ten miles north of St. Vit, Wiese hoped that he could tie his center defenses into those of the *LXIV Corps*, retreating from the salient. However, before the new positions could be firmly established, Truscott's VI Corps was again on the move.

On 9 September Truscott ordered his three divisions to wheel to the east, pivoting on the 45th Division in the l'Isle-sur-les-Doubs region. O'Daniel's 3d Division, in the center of the VI Corps line, had the mission of taking Vesoul, while Dahlquist's 36th, on the corps' left, was to swing wide to the north, keeping east of the Saone River, and end up in the Vosges foothills. Above the 36th Division, the 117th Cavalry was to screen the corps' northern flank and tie into the French II Corps as it pushed east from Dijon.

Resuming its advance on the 10th, the 3d Division encountered strong resistance along the approaches to Vesoul by *Corps Dehner* and the *198th Division*, but, just to the west of the 3d, Dahlquist's 36th Division penetrated the defending *338th Division*'s positions before the unit had time to deploy all its forces. Regarding Vesoul as critical, Truscott considered sending the bulk of the 36th to assist the 3d. However, on the night of 10–11 September, Wiese decided to pull both the battered *338th Division* and *Corps Dehner* out of the line, and again move the boundary between the *LXIV Corps* and the *IV Luftwaffe Field Corps* eastward, thereby leaving Vesoul defended only by the weak *198th Divi-*

sion. Apprised of these changes, Truscott held back the 36th Division, but finally approved its reinforcement of O'Daniel's units when the 3d Division proved unable to wrest the town from a German garrison that was larger than expected.[16] Finally, about noon on the 12th, with units of both the 36th and 3d Divisions beginning to surround Vesoul, the *LXIV Corps* ordered an immediate evacuation, and by 1500 that afternoon General O'Daniel pronounced the town secure.

Southeast of Vesoul, the 45th Division had less distance to travel, but the hilly terrain in its area favored the defense, and *Group Degener*, reinforced with armor, gave little ground without a fight. The German failure to hold at Vesoul finally forced Wiese to pull *Group Degener* back, but he quickly used it to form a new line defending the northern approaches to the Belfort Gap under the *LXXXV Corps*, and further reinforced the area with the *159th Division*, somewhat reorganized and strengthened after its ordeal at Besancon. Below the 45th Division, I Corps' 3d Algerian Division still lacked the strength to make much of an impression on the *11th Panzer Division*, now reinforced by *Regiment Menke*, a provisional infantry force operating in the more rugged terrain near the Swiss border.

During 13 and 14 September, Truscott's three divisions completed their wheeling movement against the Bel-

---

[16] The exact composition of the Vesoul garrison is unknown, but it apparently consisted of the *602d Mobile Battalion* (formerly with *Group Taeglichsbeck* at Dijon), elements of the *189th* and *198th Divisions*, and two understrength security regiments, all now controlled by *LXIV Corps* after the boundary shift.

THE CHAMPAGNE CAMPAIGN COMES TO A CLOSE

fort Gap, moving up to the towns of Fougerolles, Luxeuil, Lure, and Villersexel. To the north, units of the French II Corps from Dijon began to arrive above the 36th Division, and in the south leading elements of the French I Corps occupied the sector from the 3d Division's southern flank to the Swiss border. In the German center the *LXIV* and *IV Luftwaffe Field Corps* appeared nearly broken; neither was capable of deploying more than a confusing medley of ill-trained and poorly armed provisional units in the path of the American advance. Truscott felt that the *Nineteenth Army* was close to collapse and, on the 14th, planned to launch what he expected would be a final push into the Belfort Gap. However, early on 14 September he received new orders from General Patch canceling all current operations. Both the Seventh Army and the VI Corps had now come under the authority of Eisenhower's SHAEF headquarters, whose operational priorities and objectives did not envision possession of the Belfort Gap as especially significant. Up to now Patch, Truscott, and de Lattre had operated almost independently, with only loose supervision on the battlefield from General Wilson, the Allied commander-in-chief of the Mediterranean theater, through his deputy, General Devers. After 14 September, however, the plans of Patch and his principal commanders would have to conform to a larger operational framework dictated by

SHAEF. For all purposes the campaign of southern France was officially over and a new one begun, one in which the Mediterranean-based Allied army would obviously play a lesser role than before.

An Evaluation

By this time the Seventh Army had chalked up an impressive record. The success of ANVIL from an operational, tactical, and technical point of view was obvious. Despite the shortage of amphibious shipping and the constraints on planning and training, the execution of the operation had been almost flawless. From the German perspective, Blaskowitz and Wiese probably could not have prevented the Allied lodgment, but their response had been more disorganized than warranted, and the timely withdrawal orders saved them further embarrassment. Once ashore, Truscott had no intention of remaining within the beachhead—as had his ill-fated predecessor in the Anzio debacle barely six months earlier—and neither did Patch and de Lattre. Despite subsequent speculation over the possibilities of the battle at Montelimar, any extra fuel and vehicles that Patch might have been able to bring ashore under a different loading configuration would probably have gone to the French divisions driving on the vital ports, and not to Truscott's VI Corps. An even greater reshuffling of the ANVIL assault force would probably have changed little as well. The two French armored divisions were inexperienced, and the three mobile American infantry divisions could not have moved very far north whatever

additional support units were brought ashore until at least Toulon had been secured. Nor could Patch or Truscott have foreseen the complete disorganization of the German defenses in northern France prior to the start of ANVIL. The Allied commands were unable to confirm the breakout from Normandy until the failure of the Mortain counterattack on 10 August, and by the time that the American and Canadian forces in the north were beginning their attempt to close the Falaise Pocket on the 13th, all 500 or so ANVIL invasion ships were loaded and ready to sail. Moreover, a German collapse in the north did not guarantee a German withdrawal in the south, however logical that course of action may seem in retrospect.

Clearly Truscott's efforts to trap the *Nineteenth Army* and speed up the advance of the VI Corps northward along the Besancon-Belfort axis to within striking distance of the Rhine River had not succeeded. Nor had his forces been able to split the front of the rapidly retreating *Nineteenth Army* or to isolate those units in the Dijon salient. The Germans had repeatedly been able to shift their forces more rapidly and defend key areas more tenaciously than either Truscott or Patch had believed possible. Nevertheless, it was equally clear that the French would not have been able to concentrate their forces east of Lyon quickly enough to have undertaken a similar drive, especially since any delays would have made the advance toward the Belfort area even more difficult. As at Montelimar and Lyon, Truscott and Patch had once again shown a willingness to take a calculated risk, taking full advantage of the campaign's momentum and ready to capitalize on any errors their opponents might make. Had they attacked toward Belfort on a narrower front, they might have had more success, but such a maneuver would also have exposed the VI Corps' left, or northern, flank to a German counterattack and in addition would have allowed Wiese to concentrate more of his own forces along the immediate and more defensible approaches to the gap. In any case, a rapid seizure of the gap itself would not have necessarily opened up the Alsatian interior and the Rhine valley, since the Seventh Army's logistical problems would have multiplied even further.

Logistical problems, mainly fuel and transportation shortages, played a major role in slowing down the Allied advance in both northern and southern France. Increasing the allocations of fuel and trucks to the initial assault force might have helped somewhat at Montelimar, but could not have substituted for the seizure and rehabilitation of the larger ports, especially Marseille. Their early conquest by de Lattre's aggressive French units gave the Seventh Army an important supply edge over the Normandy-based Allied armies, although this advantage would dissipate as the distance between the Mediterranean harbors and the battlefield grew ever longer. By the time the Seventh Army had reached the Moselle, American engineer units had restored the ports, but they were just beginning the frantic effort to repair and expand the French north-south railway system. Other critical factors slowing the progress of the Seventh Army during early September included the lack of close air support, worsening weather, and general troop fatigue. The first problem was a logistical and engineering one solved by the gradual displacement of airfields north, but answers to the other two were more elusive.[17]

Troop fatigue, affecting both officers and men, was difficult to quantify. On 9 September General Butler, who had returned to his post as assistant VI Corps commander after Montelimar, noted the declining aggressiveness of the front-line troops and a tendency to rely more often on artillery and mortar fire in small combat engagements.[18] This reluctance to close with the enemy—to rely more on firepower than on maneuver on the battlefield—was, he felt, a sign that the combat troops and especially their leaders were beginning to tire, psychologically if not physically. By that time the VI Corps had advanced some 300 miles from its ANVIL assault beaches in just twenty-six days (Eisenhower's SHAEF forces had taken ninety-six days to cover a similar distance) and the actual travel mileage was obviously much greater. The 3d Division's command post, for example, had moved along some 400 miles of French roads on its way north from Alpha Red to Besancon, and many other units, such as the 117th Cavalry Squadron, had covered even more ground. According to one participant, the VI Corps headquarters units became so adept at moving that "those fellows could knock it down

---

[17] For a more detailed treatment of logistics and air support, see chapter 11.

[18] Msg, Butler to Truscott, 091900 Sep 44, Entry 100, VI Corps War Rm Jnl, 9 Sep 44.

and, just like Ringling Brothers [Circus], set it up again" at a moment's notice.[19] In the rear areas, the American and French advance northward had indeed been somewhat of a circus. Most Seventh Army soldiers had come on foot because of the critical shortage of trucks, which was aggravated by the continuing need to divert almost all vehicles to support the lengthening supply lines. In the French formations, de Lattre's officers drafted civilian autos, river boats, horse carts, and any type of functioning captured vehicles that could further the movement of troops and supplies north. Finally, although the SHAEF troops had certainly seen more fighting, they were also a larger force, able to distribute the rigors of the campaign over many more divisions; while in the case of the Seventh Army, most of the advance had been accomplished by a smaller number of units operating without respite. Thus, after pushing an average of ten miles per day, normally on foot, through German-defended territory, the forward infantry units of the Seventh Army had understandably begun to wear out as they approached the Belfort Gap and the Vosges Mountains.

Casualties also began to influence VI Corps' effectiveness. As of the evening of 9 September the corps had suffered over 4,500 battle casualties (including 2,050 killed, captured, or missing) and some 5,300 nonbattle casualties. Of the nearly 9,900 losses, about 2,900 men had been returned to duty; although the corps received

around 1,800 replacements, it was short about 5,200, mostly infantrymen. French casualties were slightly higher, although spread out over a greater number of units.[20] With most of the Allied armies in both France and Italy in the same situation, there was general competition for infantry fillers that, for the time being, could not be fully satisfied except by cannibalizing new units or turning support units into rifle formations—solutions that had only adverse effects in the long run.

Weather was another important consideration. Inclement weather almost always penalizes the attacker by reducing the mobility of military forces. By 9 September the French autumn rains had begun in earnest; streams were rising, and cross-country movement was becoming progressively more difficult. Trails and dry-weather roads turned into quagmires, forcing most vehicles to rely on paved routes, many of which were deteriorating rapidly under heavy military traffic. In addition, the overcast weather reduced the amount of air support available, greatly limiting its ability to interdict German movements during September. Terrain was also a factor, for by 9 September both

---

[19] Robert F. Ensslin (a former VI Corps G–2 staff officer), "SOD Program," MS (29 Sep 77), in Theodore J. Conroy Papers, MHI.

[20] The figures cited are only estimates based on conflicting statistics from Seventh Army G–1, G–3, and G–5 sources; HQ, VI Corps, records; and the records of VI Corps' major subdivisions. French casualty figures are especially difficult to arrive at, and in both armies the attachment and detachment of various units and the accounting of FFI losses greatly complicated all strength and casualty summaries. Officially, VI Corps records indicate that it had an assigned strength of 64,430 troops and an effective, or present-for-duty, strength of 62,145, for a shortage of 2,285; but the "assigned" strength may not reflect "authorized" strength or even the strength of the units when they first landed.

the VI Corps and the French I Corps were well into hilly, often wooded ground that gave many advantages to the defense. The combination of all these factors—transportation, supply, fatigue, weather, and terrain—thus began to blunt the edge of the Seventh Army's combat power, especially in the final drive toward the Belfort Gap.

An accurate appraisal of the German actions is difficult. Finally forced to make a stand between Dijon and Belfort, Wiese and Blaskowitz had managed to hold the area for a few critical days before retiring to the Vosges and the gap. If the conduct of the defense had lacked a certain grace and finesse, at least it was handled well enough to avoid a catastrophe. Despite the makeshift character of the successive defensive lines, Wiese was becoming more skillful at presenting a continuous front to his pursuers, thus guarding his own flanks and, by persevering, keeping the Seventh Army well away from the German border. The losses of both *Army Group G* and the *Nineteenth Army*, however, had been staggering, and Truscott's estimate that Wiese's forces were close to a total collapse was correct. Between 3 and 14 September the Seventh Army had captured another 12,250 Germans, about 6,500 of them taken by VI Corps troops. Adding the nearly 20,000 men of *Group Elster*, which had been cut off west of Dijon, the Allies had now captured roughly 65,250 men that *Army Group G* had tried to extricate from southern and western France. To this figure must be added the 31,000 German prisoners taken at Toulon and Marseille by the French, the 25,000 left hopelessly isolated in Atlantic coast garrisons,

and some 10,000 prisoners taken by the U.S. Third Army from units that *Army Group G* had dispatched north of Dijon to protect its weak right flank. The grand total of prisoners alone (plus the troops isolated on the west coast) came to 131,250, over 40 percent of *Army Group G*'s original strength on 15 August.

From available sources it is impossible to ascertain with any degree of accuracy the losses in killed and wounded among the units employed by *Army Group G* through 14 September. Estimates run as high as 7,000 killed and three times that number wounded. If so, *Army Group G*, as of the evening of the 14th, had incurred at least 143,250 casualties, over half of its strength a month earlier.[21]

The German units that survived both the arduous trek out of southern and southwestern France and the fighting against Seventh Army's French and American forces certainly did not resemble cohesive combat organizations by 14 September. All units were grossly understrength and underequipped; not one of the *Nineteenth Army*'s divisions deserved the title. The German troops were tired— even more than the VI Corps infantrymen—and their logistical system was a shambles. The *338th Division* had fewer than 3,200 men left on its

---

[21] The percentage loss is somewhat greater if the two divisions with about 10,000 troops, transferred to *OB Southwest*, are left out of consideration. Difficulties arise when factoring into the strength and loss figures the many provisional units, such *Regiment Menke*, and the many other police units turned into light infantry. The figures in the text thus reflect only the losses of *Army Group G* as it existed on 15 August, including *Luftwaffe*, naval, and *Army Area Southern France* troops. The figure of 143,250 does not include the Atlantic coast garrisons.

rolls, and of these only 1,100 were combat effectives. The *159th Division* had less than 3,500 effectives left; the *716th Division* probably had 3,250; the *198th* not more than 2,400; and the *189th* less than 1,000. And many of these "effectives" were not experienced infantrymen at all, but a mixture of police, administrative, and logistical support, navy, and other fillers thrown into depleted units as cannon fodder. The *11th Panzer Division,* which had reached Lyon almost completely intact, had suffered heavy losses between 3 and 14 September, ending up with only 6,500 men, of whom only 2,500 were in line combat battalions. In addition, the panzer division had lost all but a dozen of its tanks and was down to two operating self-propelled guns. Furthermore, the *Nineteenth Army's* many provisional *kampfgruppen* had lost up to 30 percent of their strength during the same period, but no one could tell exactly.

The good news for *Army Group G's* soldiers was the increasingly favorable defensive terrain into which their units were now withdrawing as well as the reduced frontage they would have to defend. Already, German support units were constructing hasty defenses in the Vosges Mountains and

repairing and reorienting old fixed French fortifications in the Montbeliard-Belfort area. Reserves were building up in and around Belfort, while a steady flow of better trained replacements and newer equipment had begun to arrive from Germany for the units facing VI Corps. Between 14 and 19 September, for example, the *11th Panzer Division's* operational tank strength more than doubled, even though the unit lost more tanks during that period. *Army Group G's* supply lines had also grown much shorter, making the almost traditional logistical problems of the German Army less pressing. The approaching winter weather promised to decrease even more the effectiveness of Allied air attacks and to hide German military movements and dispositions from Allied observation. On the other hand, the German Army had just about run out of space to trade for its survival in the west. If the Allied armies could engineer a major breakthrough in the weakly held German lines before the defenders had a chance to recover, the collapse that Truscott had hoped for might well follow. Nevertheless, for both sides one major campaign had ended and a new one was about to begin.

CHAPTER XI

Supporting the Campaign

Military support operations were vital to the campaign in southern France, strongly influencing both the operational course of the Allied armies and their rate of advance. Of the many aspects of military support, logistics was by far the most critical to the ground combat forces. Like most contemporary land armies, the Seventh Army needed to provide an almost continuous supply of fuel and ammunition to its various fighting, or tactical, components in order to be successful on the battlefield. The availability of such supplies often determined whether the army would conduct defensive or offensive operations as well as the nature and duration of these operations. This supply capability, in turn, depended on the establishment and maintenance of a land and sea logistical pipeline that began in the American industrial heartland and wound its way through many intermediate bases as well as through various transport modes to ports in Europe, and from there to the users in the field. At each of the many way stations along the route to the front lines, such supplies might encounter administrative or physical difficulties, or bottlenecks, which could threaten the operation of the entire pipeline, whether on the production line, at sea, or during the complex transferral of cargoes from ocean-going to ground depots and land transportation facilities at one of the European ports. With the battle of the Atlantic won by 1944, the next logistical campaign took place on the beachheads and in the ports of Europe, with Allied military success on the Continent heavily dependent on the transfer of men, materiel, and supplies from ship to shore as quickly as possible.

At this stage, the availability of amphibious vessels was critical for the initial deployment of Allied ground tactical units in Europe, and the acquisition of continental ports was crucial for maintaining these forces logistically. Early in the war Germany's logistical difficulties in North Africa and on the Russian front demonstrated the folly of giving such matters inadequate attention. The American and British high commands, more familiar with the difficulties in supporting overseas campaigns, were better prepared, although their own logistical problems often seemed to belie their greater experience.

Tactical air support was less critical given the weakness of the *Luftwaffe* at this stage of the war, but certainly the absence of support would have retarded the Allied advance, especially if German air capabilities had been greater. But, to be effective, the tactical air arm—that is, those air units dedicated to providing direct support to ground combat forces—also required an elaborate system of bases and depots, especially as the front lines moved deeper inland, and this network, in turn, was dependent on the overall Allied logistical effort.[1]

Logistical Problems

With unhappy memories of Sicily, Salerno, and Anzio in mind, ANVIL planners had expected strong German resistance and, consequently, had loaded the assault and early follow-up convoys heavily in favor of combat units and munitions. As a result, the early cargo and personnel

[1] More detailed treatment of logistics can be found in other volumes of the United States Army in World War II series, including Roland G. Ruppenthal, *Logistical Support of the Armies*, II (Washington, 1959), pp. 38–40, 118–23, 156; Joseph Bykofsky and Harold Larson, *The Transportation Corps: Operations Overseas* (Washington, 1957), pp. 290–98; William F. Ross and Charles F. Romanus, *The Quartermaster Corps: Operations in the War Against Germany* (Washington, 1965), pp. 119–21, 140–47, 169; and Alfred Beck et al., *The Corps of Engineers: The War Against Germans* (Washington, 1985), pp. 436–60. Other published sources included *Seventh Army Rpt*, I, 125–34, 144, 315–22; *CONAD History*, pp. 21–69; Hewitt, "Executing Operation ANVIL–DRAGOON," *U.S. Naval Institute Proceedings*, LXXX, No. 8 (August 1954), 897–925.

CMH manuscript sources were Lida Mayo, "The Corps of Engineers in the War Against Germans," chs. 16 and 18; and Meyer, "MTO History," chs. 26–28. Official record sources were Seventh Army Engr AAR, Jan–Sep 44; 3d Inf Div AAR, Aug 44, sec. IV, Supply; TFs 84, 85, and 87 after action reports for southern France; WNTF Rpt Southern France; and N–2 Section, Eighth Fleet, Survey of Assault Beaches, Invasion of Southern France.

landings included far less vehicles, POL stocks, troop rations, cargo-handling equipment, and service units and personnel than an army would normally need to support a mobile offensive. However, the relatively ineffective German resistance, the accelerated arrival of First French Army units, and the unexpectedly rapid penetration northward by all Allied forces quickly led to a serious shortage of vehicles and fuel. After Montelimar, the continued acceleration of the Seventh Army's operational timetable—caused primarily by its aggressive pursuit of retreating German forces—made it nearly impossible for the army's logisticians to solve the Allied supply problems satisfactorily. On 14 September, D plus 30, the Seventh Army's French and American units had reached an operational situation that most ANVIL planners had not expected until around D plus 120.

On the assault beaches, good weather, low tidal differentials, weak surf, and the absence of strong German resistance combined to minimize unloading problems. Although the delay in seizing the 36th Division's Camel Red beach postponed the discharge of some assault shipping for about thirty-six hours, the unexpected usefulness of Camel Green, together with the other favorable conditions, easily overcame this handicap. Camel Green not only substituted for Camel Red for three days, but also took much of the discharge traffic scheduled for Agay Roadstead. After some bulk cargo went ashore over the Agay beach, Agay was closed on 19 August, and its operations were transferred to Camel Red, which had opened the evening of 17 August.

Although some of the 45th Division's Delta beaches did not have good exits to the interior, they proved generally adequate on D-day. Late on the 16th, unloading began over new beaches at the head of the St. Tropez gulf, which allowed the Delta beach group to close out some less desirable strands. The Seventh Army had planned to make some use of minor harbor facilities at St. Tropez and Ste. Maxime, but the two ports were employed mainly by naval and air force units; Seventh Army cargo there was limited largely to medical supplies.

Only over the 3d Division's Alpha beaches, especially Alpha Red on Cavalaire Bay, were there serious discharge problems. At Alpha Red, beach and underwater mines forced a shutdown for a considerable period, delaying the landing of some artillery and armored units for over eight hours before paths could be cleared. At Alpha Yellow on Pampelone Bay, offshore sandbars made for wet landings, causing a number of vehicles to drown on the shoreward side of the bars and requiring the construction of long pontoon causeways for LST discharge. In addition, lateral movement across the soft sand was impossible for vehicles, and the few good beach exits quickly became jammed. Finally, using logs left behind by the Germans, the beach group was able to put together makeshift roadbeds and continue unloading; but the beach was closed on 17 August in favor of a new site a mile or so to the east. Had there been strong resistance at these beaches, the delays might have proved serious.

On D-day, approximately 60,150

Allied troops and 6,735 vehicles went ashore over Alpha, Delta, and Camel beaches, as opposed to a preassault schedule of 84,000 troops and 12,000 vehicles.[2] The beaches also handled about 50,000 long tons of supplies (excluding cargo aboard vehicles) on D-day. The shortfall from the original schedule was more than made up by 17 August, when discharge operations became centralized under the Beach Control Group, a subordinate agency of Seventh Army G–4. Established a day earlier than planned, the centralized control permitted tighter organization of discharge operations, as well as the more expeditious transfer of landing ships and landing craft among beaches as the need arose. Coastal Base Section took over both beach operations and the Beach Control Group from the Seventh Army on 9 September, about a week earlier than planned, and continued the centralized control.

The early capture of Toulon and Marseille made it possible to close out beach operations sooner than expected—namely, except for one unseasonable storm, before the mistral weather began. The Alpha beaches stopped handling cargo on 9 September; the Delta beaches closed out on the 16th; the last Camel beach shut down on the 28th. Planners had estimated that the beaches could take in 277,700 tons of cargo through D plus

---

[2] The records do not disclose if the higher figures were for the original supply plan or for the revised combat-heavy loading plan. All logistical statistics set forth in this chapter are the authors' estimates and are based on sources difficult to reconcile. In some cases these (and other figures) are carried through to the end of September because there were no mid-month statistics.

30. Actually, they accepted over 280,000 tons (excluding POL, vehicles, and cargo aboard vehicles) through 14 September and more than 20,000 additional tons through the 28th.

The high rate of discharge over the beaches created its own problems. From the beginning the capabilities of landing ships, landing craft, and DUKWs to put cargo ashore outstripped the ability of the Beach Group to handle the material and clear the beaches. The principal reasons were inadequate transportation, lack of service troops and units, shortage of beach matting, and insufficient heavy equipment such as cranes, tractors, and bulldozers—deficiencies that resulted from the planners' decision to load the early convoys heavily for combat. By D plus 5 the beach clearance and supply forwarding problems had reached a critical stage. Seventh Army and NATOUSA had already begun to seek ways to speed the arrival of service units and their equipment, especially truck units. But it proved difficult to change the schedule or the cargo of convoys and ships already loaded or partially loaded, and the decision to accelerate the arrival of French troops temporarily diverted shipping that might have brought service units from Africa, Italy, and Corsica. Moreover, what benefits were derived from hurrying forward service units were soon outstripped by the Seventh Army's continued rapid and deep penetration. These problems, especially in regard to transportation, were by no means solved by D plus 30, 14 September, nor even by the end of the month.

Hiring civilian labor did little to al-leviate the service troop shortage in the assault area. Many able-bodied men in the region had been deported to labor camps or prisons elsewhere, while others had joined the FFI or fled to North Africa. By D plus 5 Seventh Army agencies had hired only 1,000 Frenchmen, mostly old men and teenagers; by mid-September only 7,000 French civilians were working directly for the U.S. Army on the Mediterranean coast.

The Seventh Army made an effort to use German POWs (mainly *Ost* troops) in the beach area, but this practice was limited by the rules of land warfare, local antipathy to German uniforms, and language and security problems. Of even more importance was the urgent need to evacuate most German prisoners from southern France in order to forestall further complications of supply activities, especially concerning rations.[3] Some relief came in the general labor category when, late in August, three company-sized Italian service units reached the beach area, and by the end of September about 7,000 Italians were at work under U.S. Army supervision in southern France. Nevertheless, shortages of U.S. Army service troops and indigenous French labor continued to create difficulties, while the Seventh Army's rapid advance increased the problems of resupply, not only from the beaches but also from the ports as they were rehabilitated.

---

[3] Some 33,000 POWs were evacuated by 8 September alone.

FRENCH CIVILIANS RESTORING RAILWAY IN SEVENTH ARMY AREA, *Nevers, France, September 1944.*

Base Development

Viewed from the Allied preassault estimate that Toulon would not fall until D plus 20 and Marseille no earlier than D plus 45, the collapse of German resistance at both port cities on 28 August, D plus 13, represented an acceleration of about four weeks in the expected progress of the campaign in southern France. This early success was as important logistically as it was operationally, for port and base development could begin much sooner than planners had thought possible.

Initially, planners had envisaged that Coastal Base Section (CBS) and its French affiliate, Base 901, would set up an interim headquarters and facilities at Toulon, which would be used for most port and base operations until Marseille became available. But the unexpectedly early seizure of Marseille prompted a broad change in plans. Toulon was basically a naval base, and most of its facilities were ill-suited to the discharge of commercial-type shipping. On the other hand, Marseille, the foremost port and second city of France, had much better facilities for handling commercial vessels, provided better access to highways and railroads, and was better located to support the advance northward. In the end, Western Naval Task Force took over responsibility for the rehabilitation of the port of Toulon, which remained primarily a naval base, and was turned over to French control in October 1944.

For the ground and air forces, Toulon's major contribution was the employment of improvised docks for unloading vehicles that had been deck-loaded on cargo ships. This procedure allowed such vessels to move on to Marseille with hatches open and ready to discharge general cargo, thereby saving considerable time in the final unloading. Ultimately, Toulon became the principal discharge point for Civil Affairs cargo coming into southern France. The first quayside ship unloading at Toulon began on 5 September, and commercial unloading—as opposed to naval base activities—was fully under way by 20 September.

At Marseille, an advance party of CBS entered the city on 24 August, while German demolitions were still in progress. The destruction was extensive: jetties, quays, cranes, and related discharge facilities and equipment were destroyed or severely damaged; all port and channel entrances were blocked by sunken ships; both the inner and outer harbors were sown with mines; explosive demolitions, including booby traps and time bombs, had been planted throughout the onshore port area; railroad tracks had been ripped up; and warehouses, transient sheds, and other buildings along the waterfront were badly damaged. Minesweepers, mostly U.S. Navy vessels, cleared some 5,000 mines of various sizes and types from the main harbor and contiguous waters, while U.S. Army engineers removed well over thirty tons of explosives from the dock areas.

The day after Marseille fell, the 36th Engineer Combat Regiment began moving over from the beach area to start land-mine removal and other cleanup projects. On 1 September the U.S. Army's 6th Port (a terminal service command) and the 1051st Engineer Port Construction and Repair Group came ashore aboard lighters from three Liberty ships anchored offshore to assist the effort. Later in the month the 335th Engineer General Service Regiment took over many of the repair tasks, while Army engineers and U.S. Navy salvage units began clearing shipping lanes into the inner harbor. On 15 September the first Liberty ship came into the port of Marseille for direct ship-to-shore discharge; and by the end of the month eighteen quayside unloading berths were in use.

During September the port of Marseille took in approximately 113,500 long tons of general cargo, 32,800 vehicles, and 10,000 barrels of POL. In contrast Toulon, in the same month, handled about 3,440 long tons of general cargo, 19,000 tons of Civil Affairs supplies, 23,630 vehicles, and 80,000 barrels of POL.

Port-de-Bouc, a satellite port about twenty-two miles west of Marseille, served primarily for the discharge of POL products. The FFI had secured Port-de-Bouc and three nearby oil refineries, which the Germans had not destroyed. Part of the 335th Engineer General Service Regiment moved over from Marseille to undertake the repair of port facilities, aided by local French contractors, while elements of the 697th and 1379th Engineer Petroleum Distribution Companies (EPDs) rehabilitated the lightly damaged refineries, aided by oil company employees. On 10 September U.S. Army engineers began constructing a pipeline for 80-octane gasoline from the Port-de-Bouc area, but it was early November before the line was working as far as Lyon.

An unplanned, bonus supply base, Port-de-Bouc came to handle about 70 percent of the Allied POL requirements as well as a substantial amount of general cargo. By the end of September it had discharged approximately 36,840 long tons of general supplies and 240,000 barrels of POL from twenty-three ships. Total discharge for the beaches and ports through September came to about 500,000 long tons of general cargo, over 25,000 tons of Civil Affairs supplies, 325,000 troops, 69,000 vehicles, and 331,600 barrels of POL.

On 8 September Coastal Base Section formally opened its headquarters and became operational at Marseille. The command was redesignated Continental Base Section (also abbreviated CBS) on 10 September. Already the press of events had made it necessary for CBS to start assuming logistical responsibilities from the Seventh Army G–4 logistics staff on 1 September, two weeks earlier than planned. At the same time that the CBS headquarters opened at Marseille, CBS became administratively responsible for noncombat activities from the coast north to the Seventh Army's moving rear boundary, initially defined as the area south of Lyon.

Meanwhile, the Seventh Army's rapid drive northward also made it imperative for supply agencies to send representatives forward to maintain close liaison with the army G–4

staff. On 5 September a small advance office of CBS opened at Grenoble, and then moved on to Dijon by 18 September. SOS NATOUSA sent an advanced echelon of its headquarters to Marseille on 12 September, which continued on to Lyon on the 14th. During the same period Seventh Army, VI Corps, and CBS were making every possible effort to move supplies, dumps, depots, and supply points northward. On 10 September the Seventh Army opened its main supply station at Amberieu. Engineer and Signal Corps depots were set up near Bourg-en-Bresse, and a major medical supply depot was moved up to a point near Besancon on 13 September. The forward movement of depots and supply points continued throughout the month.

Fuel and Transportation

Whatever other logistical difficulties Seventh Army and CBS faced, all were overshadowed by the transportation problem. This developed not only because of combat-heavy loading of the assault convoy, but also because of a theaterwide shortage of truck and railway units as well as Seventh Army's unexpectedly rapid and deep penetration and, finally, POL shortages. Truck requirements escalated at an alarming rate as combat units drove farther north and west, forcing trucks to make time-consuming, long round trips to beach dumps, which simultaneously increased gasoline consumption. The rate of consumption immediately surpassed planning estimates. The 3d Division began to develop severe shortages as early as noon of 16 August, D plus 1;

the rest of VI Corps started to feel the pinch the next day; and by dark on 19 August the gasoline supply situation had become critical.

To assist, beach officials diverted LCTs and DUKWs from general unloading to bring ashore about 50,000 gallons of packaged gasoline from a ship in an early convoy. This measure proved only a temporary expedient, however, as the VI Corps' three divisions alone were consuming about 100,000 gallons of gas per day, and as of 21 August only 11,000 gallons were left in beach dumps. Captured German POL dumps at Draguignan, Le Muy, and Digne helped, as did gasoline found at damaged French refineries in the Marseille and Port-de-Bouc areas. But the immediate, critical shortage was not alleviated until a six-million-gallon tanker arrived on 27 August. The 697th EPD Company, which had landed on D-day, unloaded this fuel at St. Raphael, where the unit had already constructed storage tanks, emplaced tanker discharge equipment, and organized fuel canning facilities. More help for the forward area came on 9 September when the VI Corps captured another German POL dump near Besancon containing about 183,000 gallons of high-octane gasoline and 36,500 gallons of diesel fuel. The gasoline had to be cut with 80-octane fuel before it could be used in American vehicles, but the cutting process boosted the total amount of fuel available.

Obtaining POL, however, did not mean that such products could be delivered to the right units at the right time and place. The same held true for rations, ammunition, and other supplies. There still remained the

problems of truck shortages, time, and distance. To help alleviate the general transportation problem, the Seventh Army G–4 assumed centralized control over all separate truck units as soon as possible and, on occasion, took charge of transportation organic to the infantry divisions (which hardly pleased the tactical commanders). The Seventh Army also found it necessary to impose rigid movement and traffic controls, which CBS continued to exercise after taking over traffic responsibility from the Seventh Army on 9 September.

Other expedients became necessary as well. For example, by the end of August all units coming into France over the beaches were required to reload their organic vehicles with supplies for the forward combat units and make one round trip to the forward area. On the other hand, trucks and drivers organic to service units scheduled to move northward were sometimes retained in the port and beach areas for general supply operations, thereby slowing forward movement. At one point during the battle of Montelimar the Seventh Army G–4 formed a thirty-truck ammunition convoy from organic 3d Division vehicles to haul ammunition to the 36th Division—an action that, however necessary, retarded the 3d Division's own progress northward. In addition, the G–4 imposed restrictions on the consumption and shipment of some items of supply in order to gain transportation to move others that were more sorely needed by units in the north. Thus, during one period of the battle, the combat troops were put on two-thirds rations so that vehicles normally used to haul food could be diverted to bring up fuel and ammunition.

Truck shortages forced logisticians to undertake railroad rehabilitation much earlier and on a grander scale than had been contemplated during ANVIL planning. Sections of the narrow-gauge coastal railroad in the beachhead area were operational—with French civilian crews—as early as 17 August and contributed significantly to beach clearance operations. The main line, standard-gauge railroad opened from Frejus west to Ste. Maxime on 23 August, and was extended to the west and north as tactical circumstances permitted.

Although the Germans and MAAF had destroyed many railroad bridges, damage to railbeds and rolling stock was more limited, and sufficient rolling stock and French trainmen were soon rounded up to allow sections of railroad to become operational.[4] Sometimes rail movements required truck assistance. For example, breaks in the main easterly railroad line between Meyrargues and Sisteron made it necessary to transfer cargo from trains to trucks at Meyrargues and then shift the cargo again to trains at Sisteron. By mid-September temporary bridges were in place at major breaks, and the eastern line was open as far as Bourg-en-Bresse, 220 miles from the assault beaches. Before the end of the month, the line had been extended to Besancon with an initial capacity of 1,500 tons of cargo per day. By 25 September the double-

track line up the east bank of the Rhone was open from Marseille to Lyon, with a capacity of 3,000 tons a day. Before the end of September the repaired western line was pushed out to Dijon, Vesoul, and Besancon, and the easterly line, which passed through more rugged terrain, was stretched to the First French Army area opposite the Belfort Gap.

The urgent need for early rehabilitation of the railroads prompted changes in the arrival schedules of U.S. Army railroad units. The 703d Railway Grand Division (originally scheduled for 25 September) and the 713th Railway Operating Battalion (set for 5 September) began unloading at Marseille on 29 August. The parent headquarters of these two units, the 1st Military Railway Service, also arrived early and opened an advanced echelon at Lyon on 14 September.

The accelerated railroad rehabilitation program in this area progressed faster than a similar effort in Normandy, where German demolitions had been more thorough. Nevertheless, the railroads were unable to carry their full share of the supply burden for many weeks, and French and American units had to continue to depend largely on highway transportation. The supply statistics for September tell the story: during the month trucks moved some 220,000 tons of general cargo northward from the beaches and ports, while the railroads hauled slightly more than 63,000 tons. One inhibiting factor in railroad operations was a general shortage of high-grade locomotive coal in southern France; another was a lack of sufficient rolling stock to

[4] Additional information on railroad rehabilitation comes from Carl R. Gray, Jr., *Railroading in Eighteen Countries* (New York: Charles Scribner's Sons, 1955), pp. 195–201.

meet all demands, and it was well into October before any new rolling stock came into Marseille.

One potential transportation problem was less troublesome than expected. Until bad weather began about mid-September, the roads in southern France, especially the main highways, proved to be adequate for military traffic. Moreover, in the assault area, the combat units found intact bridges or easy fords; and again, until the autumn rains began, forces were able to cross most streams with little difficulty as far north as Vesoul. On the other hand, Seventh Army's rapid penetration created an early bridging problem for logistical support operations. Not anticipating such a quick breakout from the beachhead line, the Seventh Army had initially brought only one treadway bridge company and had scheduled no more such units until after 5 September. But as early as 19 August urgent requirements for heavy bridging arose, and the demand steadily increased as the Allied advance reached the Durance, Rhone, Drome, Doubs, and Saone rivers. Again the problem of rescheduling the arrival of support units—this time, engineer bridge units and equipment—proved difficult, necessitating the use of field expedients and the exploitation of local resources by engineer units to solve the more pressing bridging problems. By the end of September, U.S. Army engineers had constructed eighty-eight highway bridges, largely from locally available material, and had also erected twenty-eight Bailey bridges. Since Bailey bridge material was in short supply, these spans were replaced as soon as possible by heavy timber structures.

Another solution to the bridging problem involved curtailing air strikes. By the end of the battle of Montelimar, as VI Corps was starting north toward Lyon, Seventh Army planners estimated that the MATAF–XII Tactical Air Force bridge destruction program, if continued, would do more to slow the Allied advance than to impede the German withdrawal. Accordingly, XII Tactical Air Force and Seventh Army agreed that after 28 August bridge strikes would cease along the Rhone and Saone river valleys as well as on the streams to the east. Thereafter the tactical air command conducted only limited operations against bridges, directing most of its strikes west of the Rhone-Saone line along the main routes of withdrawal of the *LXIV Corps* from western France into the Dijon salient.[5]

Rations

While no American or French troops suffered from malnutrition during the drive north, supplying full rations to the forward units became an occasional problem that first developed early in the over-the-beach supply phase. Again the general transportation shortage was the main culprit, although the fact that ammunition and defensive materials had been loaded on top of rations on many cargo vessels of the assault convoys also impeded the timely discharge of food. In fact, such loading, undertaken in accordance with the combat-heavy concept, served to com-

---

[5] For material on air strikes against bridges, see AAF III, pp. 434–35.

plicate beach operations, because ammunition and defensive material had to be hurried ashore in order to obtain rations. This practice led to some helter-skelter stockpiling at the beaches and further slowed beach clearance, especially when it became necessary to hand-sort ammunition and other supplies. In the end, many units, as during the battle of Montelimar, had to exist on short rations from time to time—two K-rations per day as opposed to the normal three—while other packaged rations were often unavailable.

Through the first month and a half of the campaign, both the Seventh Army and the First French Army had to depend primarily on packaged rations. Local procurement could do nothing to ease the problem, for most of the area to the north as far as Lyon was not self-sufficient in basic foodstuffs. In fact, a general food shortage existed in southern France, and what little local surplus could be rounded up was urgently needed for civilian consumption. German "requisitioning" during the withdrawal further complicated the problem, and, until transportation links could be set up with major food-producing areas, a shortage of fresh food persisted in southern France. To remedy the situation, the entire schedule of shipments of civilian relief supplies was moved up, but little could be done immediately to improve distribution on the mainland. Meanwhile, a few lucky soldiers occasionally received donations of fresh eggs or other food from French farmers; other troops illegally purchased fresh food either from farmers or from a rapidly developing black market.

From their own supply system, American combat troops received no fresh bread until 26 September. By the end of September only 5,000 tons of cold storage space was available in southern France. No reefer trucks or railroad cars had yet arrived, and by the month's end legal fresh meat was still unavailable.

At least one unit—the headquarters of the 55th Ordnance Group stationed at Bourgoin, some twenty miles southeast of Lyon—solved its fresh food problem in a highly questionable manner. Somehow, during the week following the capture of Lyon on 3 September, the 55th Ordnance Group slipped two trucks loaded with war souvenirs across the Rhone and headed north through no-man's-land (some German troops, mostly stragglers, were still trying to reach Dijon) to make trading contacts with elements of the U.S. Third Army. After a risky three-day trip, the two trucks returned to Bourgoin loaded with fresh beef and pork, candy, tobacco products, and packaged rations of types not yet available to most Seventh Army's forward units.[6]

Manpower

U.S. Army replacement activities in southern France were the responsibility of Col. Wilbur G. Dockum, commanding the 2d Replacement Depot, which had previously operated in

[6] This incident is described in Lida Mayo, *The Ordnance Department: On Beachhead and Battlefront*, United States Army in World War II (Washington, 1968), pp. 289–90.

Italy.[7] The first components of the depot—one replacement company for each of VI Corps' three divisions—began landing on D-day and were ashore with 1,800 replacements by 18 August. By 9 September the 2d Replacement Depot had brought into southern France approximately 13,900 replacements of all specialties, including troops designated as RTUs (returned to unit), personnel being returned to their previous units.

Like most other units, the 2d Replacement Depot suffered from an acute lack of transportation. For example, two of the first three replacement companies ashore had to leave their vehicles and most of their equipment behind in Italy. These two units (with a total of 1,200 replacements) had to march on foot, mostly at night, northward behind the divisions they supported. When the companies reached forward divisional supply dumps, they sent replacements onward aboard divisional trucks carrying rations to the front. Ultimately, Colonel Dockum was able to secure fifty trucks from stationary antiaircraft units, and he used the railroads as much as possible; but his transportation problem was by no means solved as of mid-September.

By mid-September the 2d Replacement Depot had in France twelve replacement companies under four replacement battalion headquarters. The depot headquarters itself set up near Grenoble; and, except for one battalion headquarters and four replacement companies left in the

"THE LONG AND THE SHORT AND THE TALL": *70th Quartermaster Base Depot stocks.*

beach and port area, all components of the depot were well forward. By the end of September only one replacement company, at Marseille, was left in the rear area.

Since the casualty rate in southern France was lower than expected, no critical replacement problems arose, although a shortage of infantry replacements had begun to affect VI Corps by mid-September. The absence of any major replacement problem is demonstrated by the fact that 1,800 replacements due in on D plus 30 were not urgently needed, and the group was combined with another arriving on D plus 35.

Of the 13,900 replacements and

[7] For information on replacements, see Norton MS, "History of the Replacement Command NATOUSA," II, ch. 2 and Annex I, CMH.

RTUs that had reached southern France by mid-September, less than 4,000 were assigned to the Seventh Army, leaving a balance of about 9,500 troops available in the replacement system. The 13,900 total did not include about 500 RTUs sent directly to their units without being accounted for in the replacement flow, nor approximately 5,100 rotational replacements, that is, troops replacing men rotated to the United States on leave or on temporary duty elsewhere (most of whom never returned to the theater). Thus, by mid-September some 19,500 U.S. Army replacements from all categories had landed in southern France. Most of these troops were not needed to replace casualties, but were employed to flesh out units—such as the 45th Division and many service organizations—that had arrived in France understrength.

The French had their own replacement system, but relatively few of their replacements came from North Africa or Italy. Instead, French Army units absorbed FFI personnel by the thousands, either individually or by unit. The result complicated logistical problems, for French commanders were soon submitting requisitions for rations and equipment that far outstripped their authorized requirements. In addition, the politico-military character of the resistance made the incorporation of some FFI organizations into the armed forces a political as well as a military matter for the French command.

Medical Support

The story of medical support in southern France was like that of other support activities, with the Seventh Army's rapid drive north upsetting carefully laid plans and schedules.[8] During D-day, three separate medical battalions began coming ashore, and each one supplied a collecting company and a clearing platoon to reinforce the organic medical battalions of VI Corps' three divisions. Three 400-bed evacuation hospitals, each supporting a division, were operational by 19 August, the same day that the first U.S. Army nurses arrived in southern France.

Moving the evacuation hospitals forward behind the supported divisions proved difficult, for frequent changes of location created the inevitable transportation problems. Having arrived in France without all their authorized transportation, medical units had to borrow trucks and use ambulances to move their equipment, and even then they found it difficult to keep up with the combat units. For example, the evacuation hospital supporting the 3d Division closed down near Avignon on 7 September, but then had to wait ten days to obtain enough transportation to move north to the Besancon area. Likewise, part of the 2d Convalescent Hospital reached Besancon on 17 September, but the rest of the unit had to remain at Marseille, where its organic transportation was diverted to general supply operations. Meanwhile, the lengthy lines of communication caused forward area hospitals to become overcrowded and evacuation

[8] Additional information on medical support derives from Charles M. Wiltse, *The Medical Department: Medical Service in the Mediterranean and Minor Theaters*, United States Army in World War II (Washington, 1965), pp. 370–411.

hospitals to hold patients for extended periods of time.

Fixed-bed hospitals, totaling 14,250 beds, were not scheduled to begin arriving until 25 September. When deployed ahead of schedule, they also faced the familiar transportation problems. The 36th General Hospital, for example, started unloading on 9 September, but could not open at Aix-en-Provence until the 17th. Similarly, the 46th General Hospital reached France on 8 September, but was not operational at Besancon until the 20th.

On D-day, casualties were evacuated by LST to Corsica, from where serious cases were flown to Naples. Hospital ships arrived on D plus 1, and through 21 August transported all patients to Naples. Thereafter, hospital ships carrying predominently French patients sailed to Oran in North Africa. But after the fall of Toulon and Marseille, French casualties remained in the metropole. This change, together with the initiation of air evacuation to Italy on 22 August, the low combat casualty rate, and the accelerated buildup of medical facilities in France, made it unnecessary to employ hospital ships after 30 August. As more medical facilities became available and as weather conditions worsened in mid-September, air evacuation steadily diminished.

Through the end of September, U.S. Army hospitals in southern France admitted roughly 20,775 American troops. Of this total, 160 men died in hospitals, 8,380 were evacuated to Italy or North Africa, 8,525 were returned to duty, and, at month's end, 3,710 were still in various hospitals in France.

During the first month or so of the campaign no unusual medical problems arose. Neuropsychiatric (combat fatigue) cases were of little moment during the first month ashore, but by mid-September bad weather, stiffening resistance, and tiring troops combined to begin a marked increase in the rate of such cases among combat units. By the end of September trench foot was beginning to develop as a significant problem, one largely brought about by increasingly wet and cold weather as well as by some shortages of suitable clothing and equipment.

Signal Support

Like the Medical Corps, the Signal Corps had its problems with transportation and in supporting the Seventh Army's rapid advance.[9] The general truck shortage forced signal units to overload communications vehicles with their own supplies, but they still found that moving wire, batteries, and radio tubes forward to support combat forces was difficult.

The pace of Seventh Army's progress also made it futile to employ even the most advanced techniques of rapid pole setting and wire stringing. Instead, until mid-September, the Signal Corps devoted its efforts to rehabilitating about 1,715 miles of French wire, while stringing no more than 150 miles of its own. Fortunately, most of the area over which the Sev-

_____

[9] Additional material on Signal Corps problems comes from George Raynor Thompson and Dixie R. Harris, *The Signal Corps: The Outcome (Mid-1943 Through 1945)*, United States Army in World War II (Washington, 1966), pp. 130–31.

enth Army traveled after Montelimar was well-suited to radio communications. However, as the combat units moved into more rugged terrain during the latter part of September, radio communications had to yield to wire for both telephone and teletype circuits. By the end of the month no critical wire shortages had yet developed, but the demands for wire were beginning to exceed expectations. As was the case for almost all other commodities, forward shipment of Signal Corps supplies had already been rescheduled.

Another shortage that stemmed from the Seventh Army's rapid penetration concerned maps. As early as D plus 5, many units of the VI Corps had begun to advance beyond the area covered by the large-scale (1:25,000 and 1:50,000) tactical maps they had brought ashore. By 19 August Task Force Butler was operating mainly with 1:200,000 tourist guide maps, while during the battle of Montelimar most units had to maneuver on the basis of 1:100,000 U.S. Army maps. Before the end of August enough 1:100,000 maps were available, but as of late September the supply of the more desirable 1:50,000 maps was still inadequate.

Air Support

General Saville's XII Tactical Air Command (TAC), which was responsible for supporting Allied ground operations in southern France, initially had under its command 38 squadrons of aircraft, all based on Corsica, including 19 fighter-bomber (P–47), 4 light bomber (A–20), and 4 recon-

naissance squadrons.[10] Until 20 August the XII TAC also had under its control 6 A–20 light bomber squadrons from the Fifteenth Air Force, while 7 British and 2 American escort carriers (CVEs) provided reinforcement with 72 more combat aircraft. The British CVEs withdrew on 27 August; the American carriers on the 29th. Heavy bombers of the Mediterranean Allied Strategic Air Force, which had played a major role in preassault bombardment, flew their last missions over southern France on 16 August, D plus 1. Mediterranean Allied Tactical Air Force (MATAF) medium bombers—two wings of B–25s and B–26s supported by two groups of P–38 fighters—from Sardinia and Corsica were available through 29 August to support the XII TAC, but they normally operated outside the XII TAC's area of responsibility. This area initially ran from the Rhone River east to the Alpine divide and from the coast north to the Isere River, flowing into the Rhone from the northeast near Valence.

The Seventh Army's rapid penetration also had a serious impact on Allied air support. By 28 August, coincident with the decision to halt the MATAF and XII TAC bridge-destruction program, few lucrative targets could be found in southern France within range of MATAFs medium

[10] The XII Tactical Air Command strength consisted of the following: 15 USAAF P–47 fighter-bomber squadrons, 11 RAF Spitfire fighter squadrons, 4 USAAF A–20 light bomber squadrons, 3 FAF P–47 fighter-bomber squadrons, 1 RAF Beaufighter night-fighter squadron, 1 USAAF P–51 tactical reconnaissance squadron, 1 FAF Spitfire tactical reconnaissance squadron, 1 RAF Spitfire tactical reconnaissance squadron, and 1 USAAF P–38 photo-reconnaissance squadron.

bombers, and the mediums ceased operations over the area after the 28th. The XII TAC, taking over responsibility for all air support in southern France, faced its own range problems. The command moved three P–47 groups and a reconnaissance squadron to France during the period 23–29 August, but by the 28th one group was already complaining that its airfield in the coastal sector was out of range of the forward combat zone. By the same date virtually all targets in France, except for a few German troop columns west of the Rhone, were beyond the range of XII TAC air bases on Corsica. As of 3 September the XII TAC had airfields operational as far north as Valence, and during the period 6–15 September the command's units in France moved up to fields in the Lyon area, within range of the Seventh Army's front lines. But this force still represented less than half of the XII TAC's original strength.

The demands of the Italian campaign also reduced the availability of air support in southern France. For example, on 20 August MATAF had to divert two P–38 fighter groups (used over France primarily for bomber escort duties) to operations in Italy, while on 21 and 22 August all MATAF medium bombers allocated to support ground operations in France were diverted to Italy. Requirements in Italy, range problems, and weather further limited the XII TAC's operations over France. During the week of 23–29 August XII TAC's interdiction sorties were split almost evenly between France and Italy, and during the period 1–14 September the XII TAC flew 1,045

interdiction sorties over Italy, as opposed to 946 over France. The sorties over Italy included some flown by XII TAC planes based in the coastal sector of southern France, out of range of the Seventh Army's front.

The tactical air units in France faced supply and transportation problems similar to those of the ground forces, with transportation shortages again creating the most difficulties. The supply of air ordnance, especially at forward area fields, was rarely adequate, while transportation shortages further slowed the forward movement of both XII TAC units and airfield construction equipment. The transportation difficulties were complicated by the constant requirement to push units northward, which in turn reduced the availability of timely air support. Fortunately, the bomb supply problem did not become critical, since strafing missions proved more appropriate for most air support operations in southern France, especially after the fall of Toulon and Marseille. Of the 1,045 interdiction sorties that XII TAC pilots flew over Italy during the period 1–14 September, 1,021 were bombing missions. In contrast, the 946 sorties over France during the same period consisted of 673 strafing and 273 bombing missions.

On 15 September control of the XII TAC passed from MATAF to the U.S. Ninth Air Force, based in northern France. At the same time, the XII TAC lost control over the units that had remained on Corsica, mostly British fighter squadrons; and these forces, together with the MATAF units originally allocated to the support of ANVIL, moved to Italy.

Close Air Support

Perhaps the most remarkable feature of air operations in the southern France campaign was the total absence of normal close air support activities involving the use of air-ground liaison teams—or at least forward air observers in light aircraft, conducting air strikes in direct support of ground combat units. However, with the problems of range, airfield preparation, and continuous redeployments, the XII TAC could not respond effectively to direct support requests from tactical units. By the time aircraft were able to arrive on the battlefield at the proper location, the tactical situation had often changed and the targets were no longer present.

Because of these difficulties, the XII TAC limited its direct support to area concentrations using simple bomb-line methods, a system whereby aircraft bombed or strafed just forward of a map line that marked the forward elements of the Allied ground units. To be effective, the line obviously had to be changed continuously; furthermore, the process took considerable time and occasioned some argument between ground and air commanders. Often bomb lines were so far from the ground combat front that bombing or strafing missions were of no direct help to the ground forces. At other times the ground combat units had to be cautious about exploiting a drive for fear of overrunning the bomb line, thus exposing themselves to strikes from their own air support. Toward mid-September the VI Corps staff made arrangements with the air command to close the distance between the bomb line and the infantry's front line, but the improvement was one of degree rather than kind.

The problem was brought home most forcefully during the battle at Montelimar. Before the Allied build-up there, the XII TAC had achieved excellent results in bombing and strafing German columns moving up the Rhone valley from Avignon north across the Drome River. But establishing bomb lines after 20 August in the Montelimar area greatly restricted the use of Allied air power along Route N–7, the main Rhone highway, and provided the American tactical commander with little assistance once the situation on the ground became fluid. For example, during the German breakthroughs in the Bonlieu area it was impossible for ground force commanders to obtain air support, because Bonlieu lay south and east of the existing bomb line. Without better air support methods, the XII TAC was forced to concentrate on targets west of the Rhone and north of the Drome, all well outside the immediate ground battlefield; meanwhile the ground commanders would doubtlessly have preferred a few tactical air strikes against German infantry and armor in the Hill 300 and Bonlieu areas.

Lacking any arrangements or capabilities for providing true close air support, XII TAC operations were devoted almost entirely to interdiction sorties against retreating German columns well forward of the Seventh Army's ground front (and, until about 10 September, against *LXIV Corps'* columns west of the Rhone). But even these operations became more limited in scope and number as weather conditions began to deteriorate toward mid-September.

Despite these difficulties, both XII TAC and the attached MATAF bombers performed their interdiction missions successfully, destroying large quantities of German equipment, dispersing German troop columns, and retarding German deployments. However, that interdiction program could not by itself prevent the movement of the *Nineteenth Army* northward, and Allied airpower failed to influence significantly the outcome of any single ground engagement, except perhaps at Toulon and Marseille. The campaign in southern France thus convincingly demonstrated that interdiction operations cannot substitute for true close air support, which might have supplied the firepower needed by ground units when other support assets were lacking.

Civil Affairs

Civil Affairs (CA) operations are efforts conducted by a military command to ensure the safety and well-being of the civilian population in its area of operation. These measures are based on the legal and humanitarian obligations of the command.[11] Responsibility for conducting CA operations in southern France was vested in AFHQ, which delegated most of its CA responsibilities to Seventh Army,

while retaining technical supervision of the effort. Since the forces in southern France were ultimately to pass to SHAEF control, CA plans and operations in southern France had to be carefully attuned with those in the north; AFHQ and the Seventh Army thus closely modeled their CA directives after those of SHAEF. In both the north and the south, the Allies established no military government. Rather, local French civilian agencies conducted and controlled the civil administration within France, except for matters concerning Allied military security. The principal Allied CA contributions were in the fields of supply and coordination.

Within the Seventh Army, two officers controlled CA activities, Col. Harvey S. Gerry, the Seventh Army G–5 staff officer, and Col. Henry Parkman, Jr., who was the senior officer of Civil Affairs Headquarters, Seventh Army (CAHQ). Gerry was the adviser to General Patch on all CA matters, and monitored and coordinated CA field operations in southern France. In the field, CA operations came under the control of Parkman, who was both Chief Civil Affairs Officer, Seventh Army, and the commanding officer of the 2678th Civil Affairs Regiment, the headquarters of which functioned as CAHQ. The 2678th CA Regiment had an initial authorization of 196 officers and 398 enlisted men. Planners estimated that this strength would prove unnecessary during early operations in southern France, and so 50 officers and 75 enlisted men were temporarily returned to Italy, only to be quickly recalled when the Seventh Army's unexpectedly rapid advance increased the

---

[11] The civil affairs section is based on Harry L. Coles and Albert K. Weinberg, *Civil Affairs: Soldiers Become Governors*, U.S. Army in World War II (Washington, 1964), pp. 697–706, 751–92; *Seventh Army Rpt*, I, 69–70; *CONRAD History*, pp. 48–50; Robert W. Komer, CMH MS, "Civil Affairs and Military Government in the Mediterranean Theater," ch. 21; and miscellaneous documents and reports of the ACofS G–5 Seventh Army.

need for CA personnel. The command was thus at full strength in France by the end of September.

Ostensibly, CAHQ and the CA regiment's component teams and detachments operated under broad policies established by the Seventh Army G–5, but CAHQ had a technical channel of communications to G–5 AFHQ and sometimes received orders directly from this headquarters. Colonel Gerry at Seventh Army headquarters complained that CAHQ also established policy on its own initiative, while Colonel Parkman at CAHQ felt that the Seventh Army G–5 sometimes unduly intruded into field operations. Inevitably, discord arose between the two staffs, and the problems were not entirely solved until both policy and operational responsibilities became centralized under the 6th Army Group's G–5 late in September. Even before that time, the AFHQ G–5 had to take an active CA coordinating role in southern France in order to tie Seventh Army's civil affairs activities forward of the Army's rear boundary to those of logistical agencies south of the boundary.

Civil Affairs Operations

Despite some conflicts of interest and divided responsibilities, direct military control of civil activities was limited. As the Allies expected, local French civilian government officials were quickly able to reestablish the civil administration necessary to handle the distribution of relief supplies that CAHQ furnished through Allied military channels. So rapid and thorough was the turnover to the French that CA teams and detachments of the 2678th CA Regiment were quickly eliminated in favor of small liaison offices with French governmental agencies in key geographical locations. This transition also reflected basic U.S. Army CA doctrine.

In the field, CA operations in southern France represented an Allied effort carried out by American, British, and French military personnel. SHAEF supplied many of the American and British personnel, while other American troops, experienced in military government, came from Italy. The First French Army provided CA liaison officers for Seventh Army's combat units, CAHQ's various detachments or offices, and French local governmental agencies. As the French were unable to supply enough of these liaison officers, all those assigned were markedly overworked for the first month or so of CA operations in southern France.

Food, CA planners estimated, would be the principal civil relief necessity in the ANVIL assault area, which was a deficit food-producing region. Nevertheless, the combat-heavy loading concept for early convoys prompted planners to delay major CA food imports until the D plus 40 convoy. Preassault plans called for three Liberty ships (or the equivalent) full of CA supplies to reach southern France in five-day increments with the convoys from D plus 40 through D plus 80. Initially, relief supplies were to come from theater stockpiles, with the French furnishing edible oils from North Africa. Later shipments were to arrive directly from the United States.

The Seventh Army's rapid drive

northward created the same problems for CA units and personnel that faced all logistical support agencies in southern France. Although it was obvious that the scheduled arrival of CA personnel, supplies, and transportation could not cope with requirements, accelerating the arrival of CA troops and, to a lesser extent, supplies proved difficult. Emergency food supplies, hastily loaded as additional cargo on ships from Italy and North Africa, began arriving on D plus 10; and the first civil relief Liberty ship began unloading over a St. Tropez gulf beach on 10 September (D plus 25 as opposed to the original schedule of D plus 40). By the end of September approximately 35,000 tons of food earmarked for civil relief had reached southern France.

Meanwhile, CA officials on the ground helped alleviate the more serious distribution problems, assisting, for example, in organizing and distributing food stocks taken from the Germans and other stocks that the FFI had secretly assembled. Seventh Army resources were normally used only in an emergency, or when the American units had excess supplies, labor, or transport. Although CA personnel were reluctant to tax the hard-pressed U.S. logistical agencies during the first part of the campaign and were able to obtain most necessities from local French sources, the Seventh Army did release 100,000 cans of condensed milk and about 3,450 pounds of dried milk from its own stocks to meet a critical milk shortage among small children in the coastal areas.

Transportation required for effective CA relief operations remained critical through September. Neither the Seventh Army nor the logistical agencies could provide many trucks, and, for purely tactical reasons, the Seventh Army sometimes found it necessary to retain control of trucks allocated to CA activities. In other areas, a lack of coordination hampered the most effective use of available transportation for CA purposes. For example, although the Allies found a general surplus of food in the Lyon region, it was hard to arrange transportation to move foodstuffs south; often empty truck convoys and later empty trains moved back to the beaches and ports with their capacity for moving food to the coastal region unused. The problem was not solved until enough CA officials were available in the forward area to coordinate the movement of food stocks south with Army transportation units and commands.

The Nice-Cannes area, east of the assault beaches, was an especially troublesome region. Here, at the end of transportation lines, near famine conditions existed for some time, compounded by FFI and Allied troop misconduct such as looting and robbery. The disorderly conditions were largely under control by mid-September, but Nice especially remained a hungry area until well toward the end of September.

Nice was also a center of black market activities, which plagued CA agencies throughout the coastal area. American troops were guilty of contributing to black market operations, for even common army supplies (especially rations) as well as Post Exchange items brought high prices. By the end of September the black market was generally under control at Toulon, but remained significant at Marseille and Nice despite the best efforts of CA personnel, in conjunction with other concerned American and French agencies, to contain it. The port of Marseille became infamous as a center of traffic in stolen and pilfered goods, and some officials estimated that for a time roughly 20 percent of all supplies unloaded at the port were subsequently stolen. Here and elsewhere the theft of gasoline became a major problem, and contributed significantly to the Seventh Army's POL shortages.

Outside of food and transportation, the only major civil relief shortage involved certain types of medical supplies. Food and medical supply deficiencies were largely overcome before the end of September, while other relief problems did not materialize on the scale expected by CA planners. The rehabilitation of civilian communication and power facilities proved a much easier task than initially estimated; no significant problems with refugees or displaced persons developed; and clothing shortages were localized and overcome without undue trouble. Hospitals, hospital equipment (except for some medical supplies), and civilian medical personnel were generally adequate; school buildings were undamaged, although teacher shortages existed.

Like logistical support activities in southern France, CA operations through the end of September constituted a shoestring success, achieved after somewhat hectic beginnings. But the successful Allied CA effort would not have been possible without the universal and wholehearted cooperation of French civilian officials and agencies.

Conclusions

In summary, logistical constraints severely limited operations of the Seventh Army, the XII TAC, and many other Allied units and agencies through late September. The unexpectedly rapid and deep Allied penetration was the direct cause of most of these problems, while a theaterwide scarcity of service units and an unanticipated shortage of French civilian labor, especially at the beach and port areas, were contributing factors. Commanders and planners at all levels did their best to overcome these difficulties, but the lack of vehicles and fuel was felt throughout the campaign. Using captured German supplies and stripping vehicles from ancillary units were only short-term solutions, which were sometimes achieved at the cost of overworking the few troops and equipment that were available. Only the vigorous Allied pursuit and the German pell-mell withdrawal northward prevented the logistical situation from being more detrimental to the expanding Allied campaign.

Basic to the whole issue of logistical support was the planning concept. The expectation of a strong, protracted German resistance and possibly major German counterattacks in southern France proved incorrect. With hindsight, the Seventh Army planners might have anticipated that *Army Group G* would be more interested in withdrawing its forces northward intact than in defending the beaches and ports of southern France to the last man. Thus, overly conservative intelligence estimates had an obvious impact on logistical planning, loading, and scheduling. The resulting combat-heavy loading program for both assault and early follow-up convoys left little or no room for logistical flexibility once the situation ashore turned out differently than expected. The shortage of shipping, especially amphibious vessels, also reduced logistical flexibility as did the decision to accelerate the arrival of French combat units. Efforts to change unit and shipping schedules turned out to be only partially successful since many support units and much cargo were locked in to preassault schedules. The air units were subject to the same planning constraints. From their bases in Corsica they were prepared to support a lengthy battle on a carefully defined beachhead, but were ill-equipped for more mobile operations on the mainland.

Yet, given the complicated nature of amphibious operations and the priorities of the Allied high command, especially the precedence given to the OVERLORD forces in northern France, the ANVIL planners probably did the best they could with the means available. And while the Seventh Army may have rated German capabilities too high, the Allied armies would find in the months ahead that the German defenders would not always retreat so rapidly, even when their manpower and materiel situation indicated that withdrawal was the wisest course of action. In short, Hitler and *OKW* might easily have taken a completely different course of action, ordering the *Nineteenth Army* to defend in place and reinforcing it with units from western France and Italy. Had this been the case, the Allied combat-heavy logistical loading would have seemed a wise decision, and any proposal to structure the ANVIL assault force for a more mobile campaign highly premature.

PART THREE

ORDEAL IN THE VOSGES

CHAPTER XII

Strategy and Operations

While Truscott's divisions wheeled toward the Belfort Gap, de Monsabert's French II Corps, on the Seventh Army's western flank, had continued north toward Dijon, periodically delayed by fuel shortages. The French northern drive from Lyon had been opposed ineffectively by a medley of odd-sized German forces—*Groups Browdowski, Taeglichsbeck,* and *Ottenbacher* and what was left of *Group Bauer* and the *716th Infantry Division,* all under the occasional supervision of the *LXIV Corps* in the south and the *LXVI Corps* in the north. On 11 September the French 1st Armored Division rolled into Dijon unopposed and, scarcely pausing to join the celebration of the city's populace, headed north for Langres, about forty miles farther. Approximately fifteen miles to the west, the French 1st Infantry Division matched its pace, moving north and northeast led by the 13th Foreign Legion Demibrigade, the 2d Dragoons (tank destroyers), and the 1st Naval Fusiliers. Intermittently throughout the day both of de Monsabert's divisions had telephone contact over local lines with the French 2d Armored Division, part of Patton's U.S. Third Army that had already reached Chatillon-sur-Seine. Finally, later in the afternoon of the 11th, the 2d Dragoons met a small patrol from the U.S. 6th Armored Division at Saulieu, twenty-five miles north of Autun, which formally marked the physical union of the OVERLORD and ANVIL armies in northern France. As the II Corps moved east, the French and American forces cemented the juncture between Dijon and Chatillon, giving the Allied armies in France a common front from the English Channel in the north to the Mediterranean in the south. The time had now come to implement existing plans that would unify the Allied command structure in France and place the Allied forces from southern France under Eisenhower's SHAEF command. Henceforth Seventh Army's operations would conform to strategic and operational concepts determined by SHAEF for the prosecution of the war against Germany. The "champagne campaign" was officially over.

SHAEF's Operational Concepts

Patch's approval on 3 September of Truscott's plan for a concerted VI Corps drive on the Belfort Gap, with the French divisions of Army B split between the attacking American forces, was a purely opportunistic measure that only temporarily altered the Seventh Army's general campaign plans. Whatever the results of Truscott's drive, Patch fully intended to implement the deployment concept he had promulgated late in August—concentrating de Lattre's French forces on the Seventh Army's right and Truscott's VI Corps on the left. The VI Corps was then to advance northeast across the Vosges Mountains to Strasbourg and the Rhine, while the French divisions would push through the Belfort Gap to the Alsatian plains.[1] General Eisenhower himself had outlined this deployment plan as the Seventh Army moved toward Lyon, and it had been approved by General Wilson as well as by General Devers, the commander-designate of the 6th Army Group. Shortly thereafter Eisenhower and Devers confirmed the concept during coordinating conferences at SHAEF headquarters between 4 and 6 September.[2]

Eisenhower had always held that command of the ANVIL forces should be transferred to SHAEF soon after the Seventh Army started moving in strength north of Lyon, an advance VI Corps had initiated on 3 September. The date of transfer received consideration during the 4–6 September conferences, and on the 9th, after additional long-distance consultation, AFHQ and SHAEF finally agreed that

Eisenhower would assume operational control of the forces in southern France on 15 September. At that time Headquarters, 6th Army Group, would become operational in southern France, and simultaneously control of the XII Tactical Air Command would pass from the Twelfth to the Ninth Air Force.

Eisenhower, Wilson, and Devers agreed that the transfer of operational responsibility need not wait until SHAEF assumed logistical and administrative control except in the field of civil affairs. At the time, SHAEF was having logistical problems of considerable magnitude and was in no position to assume the added burden of controlling logistical operations in southern France. Thus the Allied commanders decided that the 6th Army Group would administer its own semi-independent logistical system through Mediterranean channels, using supplies arriving directly from the United States as well as excess stocks not needed in MTO reserves.

Eisenhower and Devers also determined that the activation of the 6th Army Group would be accompanied by the transformation of French Army B into the First French Army, an organization that would be operationally, logistically, and administratively independent of Patch's Seventh Army. Until more American forces became available, the change would leave Patch with little more than Truscott's VI Corps to control. Although Devers decided that Patch would continue to direct First French Army operations until the redeployment was completed, this somewhat anomalous situation lasted only until 19 September.

Devers was understandably dis-

---

[1] Seventh Army FO 3 and 4, 25 and 28 Aug 44.

[2] The planning sections are based on the following sources: *Seventh Army Rpt*, I, 279–86, 327–32; Cole, *The Lorraine Campaign*, pp. 1–13, 20–25, 52–56; Charles B. MacDonald, *The Siegfried Line Campaign*, United States Army in World War II (Washington, 1973), chs. 1 and 2; Truscott, *Command Missions*, pp. 441–44; Pogue, *The Supreme Command*, pp. 228–29, 249–56, 265–66, 288–98; Seventh Army Diary, Aug–Sep 44.

turbed over leaving the Seventh Army with just a single corps. Such an understrength army command could play only a minor role in future operations against Germany. Devers, in fact, had been concerned by the lack of American strength since the beginning of ANVIL. Once the landings in southern France were successful, he would have preferred transferring the entire U.S. Fifth Army as well as the rest of the Twelfth Air Force from the Italian to the southern France front. Realizing that such a large redeployment was both politically and operationally impossible, Devers had sought to have at least the Fifth Army's IV Corps shipped from Italy to southern France. But early in September Wilson had blocked the move, convincing the CCS and the JCS that the transferral would ruin any chance for the success of operations then under way in Italy. Devers next requested that one of SHAEF's American corps be transferred to the Seventh Army, a proposal that Wilson also made. At the time, Gen. Sir Bernard Montgomery's 21st Army Group had five corps and Lt. Gen. Omar N. Bradley's 12th Army Group had seven. But Eisenhower stated that he could not spare a corps at that time and believed that the three fresh American divisions scheduled to arrive through southern French ports during October and November would greatly strengthen the Seventh Army, even if no additional corps headquarters were available. In the end, the 6th Army Group received no reinforcements, and the Seventh Army was left with only a single corps headquarters and three infantry divisions in its order of battle.

SHAEF's Operational Strategy

General Devers, now in the process of assuming direct control of both the U.S. Seventh Army and the First French Army, had never commanded a unit on the battlefield. However, along with Generals Eisenhower, Lesley J. McNair, and Brehon B. Somervell, he had been one of the principal officers used by General Marshall to train, equip, and direct the efforts of the American Army in the European theater.[3] As commanding general of ETOUSA in 1943 and of NATOUSA in 1944, Devers had vigorously represented the views of Marshall and the JCS and knew the importance that they attached to a direct thrust at Germany through northern France. This background had given the new army group commander a good feel for the political and personal dimensions of the Allied high-level command, an area where Patch and de Lattre had little experience. Now, as one of the major Allied field commanders, the energetic and sometimes outspoken Devers would have the opportunity to put his ideas and knowledge into action.

Like Patch, Devers was well aware that realigning the Seventh and First French Armies was part of Eisenhower's larger plan for the use of Allied military power in northeastern France. American forces, Eisenhower had long since decided, would occupy the center of a broad Allied advance in northern France toward the German border (*Map 12*). For this

---

[3] McNair served as Commanding General, Army Ground Forces, and Somervell as Commanding General, Army Service Forces.

reason he wanted Bradley's 12th Army Group in the middle of the Allied line, between Montgomery's 21st Army Group in the north and Devers' 6th Army Group in the south. In mid-September Bradley's center command had three armies, but only two were on line, the First and the Third, with the Ninth Army still clearing the Brittany peninsula in the west. Montgomery's 21st Army Group, consisting of the First Canadian and Second British Armies, constituted the left, or northern, wing of the Allied line, and Devers' 6th Army Group was its right, or southern, wing. The eventual arrival of the Ninth Army in Bradley's center and the redeployment of Patch's Seventh Army to the left of the 6th Army Group would complete the concentration of American combat power in the center of the Allied line.

Eisenhower would have preferred transferring the entire Seventh Army to Bradley's central army group, but feared that the First French Army might not be ready to undertake total responsibility for the Allied right wing. Moreover, without Patch's Seventh Army, the 6th Army Group's American contingent would have consisted of little more than some artillery and service units directly supporting the First French Army; various logistical and administrative units along its line of communications to the Mediterranean; and the 1st Airborne Task Force, still outposting the Franco-Italian border area. Under such circumstances de Gaulle would certainly have pressed for French command of the army group or at least the elimination of the army group and an expanded role for the

First French Army. The result would have forced Eisenhower to deal with both French and British national interests personally, further multiplying his command problems. Eisenhower thus believed it necessary to preserve a significant American complexion in the 6th Army Group, and so he left the existing command arrangements in place.[4]

Having accepted the need for the 6th Army Group headquarters on his southern wing, Eisenhower was still uncertain regarding the role he would assign to it. The northern boundary of Devers' command, as established by SHAEF, stretched northeast from Langres past Epinal, about forty miles north of Vesoul, to Strasbourg on the Rhine. Although its southern flank technically rested on the Swiss border, the army group also inherited the Seventh Army's responsibility for outposting the Franco-Italian border in the far south. Initially Eisenhower assigned the 6th Army Group three general missions within its main area of operations: destroy the opposing German forces; secure crossings over the Rhine River; and breach the Siegfried Line—the generic term SHAEF applied to the German-built West Wall fortifications just inside the German border. How these objectives fit into SHAEF's larger operational plans is difficult to discern.

Following the breakout from the Normandy beachhead, the opening eastern movement of Eisenhower's OVERLORD forces had been characterized by rapid pursuit, and the ensuing period by even more narrow axes of

---

[4] See Ltr, Eisenhower to Bradley, 15 Sep 44, in Eisenhower Papers, IV, 2146–47.

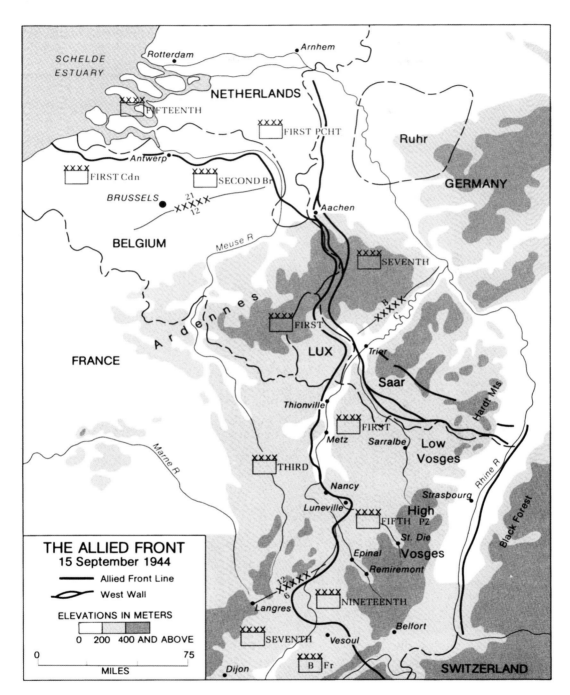

SCHELDE ESTUARY

Rotterdam

Arnhem

NETHERLANDS

XXXX FIFTEENTH

XXXX FIRST PCHT

Ruhr

GERMANY

Antwerp

XXXX FIRST Cdn

XXXX SECOND Br

BRUSSELS 21 XXXXX 12

Aachen

BELGIUM

Meuse R

A r d e n n e s

FRANCE

XXXX SEVENTH

XXXXX B C

XXXX FIRST

LUX

Trier

Saar

Hardt Mts

Thionville

XXXX FIRST

Metz

Sarralbe

Low Vosges

Marne R

XXXX THIRD

Nancy

Strasbourg

Rhine R

Luneville

XXXX FIFTH PZ

High

Black Forest

St. Die

Epinal

Vosges

Remiremont

12 XXXXX 6

Langres

XXXX NINETEENTH

Belfort

THE ALLIED FRONT
15 September 1944

━━━ Allied Front Line

⬡ West Wall

ELEVATIONS IN METERS

0   200   400 AND ABOVE

0 ——————————— 75
MILES

XXXX SEVENTH

Vesoul

Dijon

XXXX B Fr

SWITZERLAND

MAP 12   This map is printed in full color at the back of the book, following the Index.

advance because of SHAEF's inability to support a more general offensive logistically. Eisenhower had therefore never been able to implement his so-called broad front strategy. By mid-September logistical concerns had in fact made the seizure and rapid rehabilitation of a major port, Antwerp, an overriding military objective. Although Antwerp had fallen to Montgomery's 21st Army Group on 4 September, the Germans still controlled the approaches to the port from the Schelde Estuary; the estuary would have to be cleared before the port could be opened. A complementary development was the desire to concentrate the Allied ground advance against specific objectives that would seriously impair Germany's ability to wage war. The closest and most obvious target was the Ruhr industrial area of northwestern Germany, a region whose capture would also provide a wide invasion route into the heart of Germany. All these factors dictated that the main Allied effort should be focused along a narrow front in the zone of the 21st Army Group, an idea that General Montgomery as well as many high-ranking British political and military leaders vociferously advocated.

Faced in September with the continued logistical impossibility of supporting a broad offensive, Eisenhower adopted Montgomery's operational concept as the most suitable course of action. In doing so, however, he abandoned the flexibility of the broad front strategy and made terrain the main Allied objective rather than enemy forces. The failure of the Allied armies to close the Falaise Pocket earlier had already demon-strated a certain operational rigidity as well as a tendency to measure success totally in terms of terrain, a problem that had also beset the Italian campaign. Moreover, SHAEF's inflexibility in this area was further aggravated by the difficulties Eisenhower continued to have in controlling the independently minded Montgomery. Such, perhaps, was the inevitable nature of coalition warfare, and Eisenhower's ability to manage his sometimes quarrelsome subordinates, as well as to fend off their political chiefs and preserve the alliance, may have been the most accurate measure of his success in the art of generalship.

To gain his objectives in the north, Eisenhower intended to employ Montgomery's 21st Army Group and most of the 12th Army Group's First Army. He also planned to use the bulk of his available airborne forces—now in reserve and organized into the First Allied Airborne Army—in the 21st Army Group's Operation MARKET-GARDEN, an attempt to envelop the Ruhr basin from the north. If Montgomery's daring offensive succeeded, Eisenhower hoped to drive across the north German plains and finish the war by the end of the year.

With close to half its strength supporting the northern effort, the rest of Bradley's 12th Army Group was relegated to a secondary role. Patton's Third Army, Eisenhower told Bradley, was to confine itself to limited advances, pushing east to secure bridgeheads over the Moselle River in the Metz-Nancy region, thereby threatening the Saar basin, an industrial region second only to the Ruhr. This action would also fix German units in place that might otherwise be deployed north. Once the Third Army had its forces firmly across the Moselle, the 12th Army Group was to concentrate its remaining resources to help the First Army seize crossings over the Rhine immediately south of the Ruhr. Then the Third Army could begin moving against the Saar. Although the resulting SHAEF campaign plan appeared somewhat rigid, it was perhaps complex enough to confuse the Germans and still allow SHAEF some flexibility if a change in the main effort became necessary.

Despite these arrangements, disagreements over operational strategy still plagued the Allied high command. Eisenhower felt that his plans followed the principles of the broad front strategy as much as was practicable; Montgomery believed they adhered too closely to the concept, fearing that the Third Army's secondary thrust against the Saar might undermine his single concentrated thrust in the north. But in this matter, Eisenhower strongly disagreed, believing that ceasing all offensive operations in the central and southern Allied sectors would allow the Germans to transfer more forces north or to initiate a major counterattack elsewhere. The projected efforts of Bradley in the center also enabled Eisenhower to retain at least the semblance of a broad front strategy. In this, however, he was mistaken. His new offensives were now closely tied to fixed terrain objectives, while the aim of a true broad front offensive was the destruction of enemy forces, either by attrition or by maneuver once weaknesses in the enemy defenses became apparent.

Having discarded a flexible oper-

ational strategy, SHAEF had no real role to assign the newly created 6th Army Group. From a theater point of view, a major effort in the south seemed pointless. Devers' forces faced a daunting array of obstacles, starting with the Vosges Mountains, followed by the Rhine River and the West Wall, and finally the Black Forest, another thirty miles of almost impenetrable terrain, all highly favorable to the defense. And even if his Franco-American forces were somehow able to push through these barriers, which was extremely unlikely, the seizure of Nuremburg or Munich—just about the only prizes on the other side—did not seem especially worthwhile objectives. However, there were alternatives that neither Eisenhower nor his SHAEF planners ever considered: for example, sending a reinforced 6th Army Group north through the Rhenish plains in a vast enveloping maneuver against the flank or rear of the German forces defending the Saar and Ruhr regions; or sending it north as far as Frankfurt and then northeast, following the famous Napoleonic route toward Berlin through the critical Fulda corridor. Instead, both Eisenhower and his major subordinates remained preoccupied with their existing plans which called for a drive into Germany by two army groups, one operating north of the Ardennes forest, and the other to the south. Developing the port of Antwerp and designating the Ruhr and Saar as strategic objectives had been given some thought earlier during OVERLORD planning and now meshed easily with the operational concepts already in place. But SHAEF planners had never taken into consideration a major force coming up from the south, and SHAEF concepts had not changed after the CCS approved ANVIL, or even after the Seventh Army had landed and sped northward faster than anyone expected.

Finding no role for it in the northern offensive, Eisenhower appeared to give Devers' 6th Army Group a somewhat independent status. With only three American divisions and a French army composed primarily of colonial troops, Devers' command must have seemed insignificant despite its imposing army group designation. Nevertheless, although small, the group had its own independent line of communications and its own logistical base; the French forces could, in fact, recruit and train replacements immediately behind the battlefield. For the present then, the force appeared capable of sustaining itself without making any demands on SHAEF's overtaxed logistical system in northern France. This situation, in turn, enabled the group to conduct its own, more or less separate offensives that could tie down German divisions, without detracting from the more important operations in the center and north of the Allied line. But Eisenhower still expected little from the 6th Army Group, believing that even the most successful advances in the south had little strategic potential.[5]

What independence thereby fell to Devers' command was the product of circumstance—the simple geographical distance between SHAEF's northern and southern wings and the per-

ception that the southern sector of the Allied line was a dead end. But officially at least, 6th Army Group operations were part of the larger Allied concept. On 15 September, for example, Eisenhower promised Bradley that the Seventh Army, even though it remained part of the 6th Army Group, would always be maneuvered to support the 12th Army Group.[6] To the CCS and Montgomery, Eisenhower maintained that 6th Army Group operations would be designed primarily to support the more important drives farther north and to protect the 12th Army Group's southern flank. Possibly SHAEF approved 6th Army Group's offensives toward Strasbourg and the Rhine only because they did not appear to interfere in any way with the northern effort; furthermore, Eisenhower must have hoped that the southern army group's separate line of communications might enable him to increase the 12th Army Group's logistical support at some future date once the capacity of the Mediterranean supply system had been sufficiently expanded. But as long as Devers remained logistically independent, Eisenhower was apparently willing to give him a certain freedom of action.[7]

[5] For example, see Ltr, Eisenhower to Montgomery, 24 Sep 44, SHAEF File 381, Post-OVERLORD Plng I.

[6] Ltr, Eisenhower to Bradley, 15 Sep 44 Eisenhower Papers, IV, 2147.

[7] See Rad, SHAEF to 21st Army Gp, 12th Army Gp, et al., SHAEF Fwd–14764, 13 Sep 44, in SHAEF File 381, Post-OVERLORD Plng I; Min, SHAEF Special Mtg, 22 Sep 44, in HQ, 12th Army Gp AF File 371.3 Mil Objs, I; Rads, SHAEF to 12th Army Gp and 6th Army Gp, SHAEF Fwd–15934 and Fwd–15981, 26 Sep 44; Rad, SHAEF to CCS, SHAEF Fwd–16181, 29 Sep 44. The last three in SHAEF File 381, Post-OVERLORD Plng II.

LT. GEN. LUCIAN K. TRUSCOTT, *General Patch, and General Devers, October 1944.*

Patch and Truscott

Within the 6th Army Group, the reactions of the senior commanders to SHAEF's plans were mixed.[8] General Devers was undoubtedly disappointed. Hoping ultimately for a greater role for his command, he continued to press SHAEF for an additional American corps to strengthen Patch's Seventh Army. Patch was also understandably unenthusiastic upon receiving word that his forces would be rel-

egated to a minor supporting role, and Truscott was obviously displeased that his current offensive would have to be halted and his front moved north opposite the Vosges Mountains. In contrast, General de Lattre, unhappy with the current division of the First French Army between Patch's Seventh, was generally satisfied with the concentration of the French on the Allied right wing.[9] For both political and military reasons that decision, fully supported by Devers and Patch, was to prove sound.

Based on Eisenhower's guidance, Devers issued new orders calling for the French II Corps to move from the sector west of the Saone River, on VI Corps' northern flank, to the area south of the VI Corps, taking over the territory currently occupied by the 45th Infantry Division. The 36th Division would simultaneously stretch to the north, taking over the area vacated by the II Corps. These changes would put all of de Lattre's forces opposite the Belfort Gap, with the II Corps in the north and the I Corps in the south and Patch's three-division "army" opposite the rugged Vosges Mountains. Within its zone, the First French Army was to drive through the Belfort Gap and then head north to clear the Alsatian plains; to the north, the VI Corps was to march northeast across the Vosges, with its axis of advance between Vesoul and St. Die, and aim at Strasbourg, some 120 miles from Vesoul.

After fully digesting the Seventh Army's new orders, Truscott wrote a strongly worded letter to Patch

[8] This section is based on Truscott, *Command Missions,* pp. 441–45; Seventh Army FO 5, 14 Sep 44; Seventh Army Diary, 13–17 Sep 44; Rad, Devers to Eisenhower, B–16370, 13 Sep 44, in SHAEF File 381, POST-OVERLORD Plng I.

[9] De Lattre, *History,* pp. 167–69.

making strenuous objections to the change in plans.[10] Believing that the *Nineteenth Army* was close to total collapse and that the VI Corps was on the verge of breaking through the northern shoulder of the Belfort Gap to the Rhine, he reminded Patch that the Army commander himself had just approved the continuation of his offensive against Belfort and, he felt, had agreed that the Belfort Gap was one of the primary gateways to the German heartland. By the time the Allies regrouped their forces, the Germans would have slammed the gate shut. Truscott had had his fill of winter fighting in the mountains of Italy, and neither he nor any of his troops desired to repeat the experience in the Vosges. The terrain and weather, he pointed out, would allow the Germans to control the pace of any Allied offensive there and, in his opinion, would waste three fine American divisions with little benefit either to SHAEF's efforts in the north or to the First French Army's drive against Belfort. Rather than tying German divisions down to defend the area, a mountain offensive would allow them to deploy more resources elsewhere. In Truscott's opinion the greatest assistance that the Seventh Army could provide SHAEF was to send the VI Corps directly through the Belfort Gap to the Rhine. If, he concluded, the VI Corps could not be employed properly in France, then it should be returned to Italy under AFHQ control to mount an amphibious operation against Genoa. Such an operation, Truscott was convinced,

would at least break the stalemate in Italy, whereas an attack through the High Vosges Mountains would accomplish nothing.

Patch tried to soothe Truscott as best he could, relaying the news that the U.S. Senate had recently confirmed his promotion to lieutenant general. Nevertheless, he could offer little hope that SHAEF's operational concepts could be altered or that the VI Corps would be allowed to continue its offensive against the Belfort Gap. In this area Patch could do little more than affirm his confidence in Truscott and hold out hope that the Germans might also have discounted an Allied attack over the Vosges and thus maintained only a thin defensive shell there.

Tactical Transition

On 15 and 16 September Truscott's forces resumed their drive east, meeting stiff German resistance on the 15th but only scattered opposition on the following day as the 3d Division occupied Lure, the 36th Division secured Luxeuil, and the 117th Cavalry Squadron reached St. Loup. Late on the 16th, however, Truscott ordered a halt to the advance and, in compliance with Patch's directive of the 14th, issued instructions reorienting the corps for an immediate drive northeast across the Moselle River and into the Vosges Mountains toward St. Die and Strasbourg.[11] He hoped that the French II Corps, redeploying from the north, could relieve the 45th Division on his southern wing by the 17th. Ever the opportun-

---

[10] The letter is quoted in full in Truscott, *Command Missions*, pp. 441–43.

[11] VI Corps FO 3, 16 Sep 44.

ist, Truscott wanted to begin as quickly as possible before the Germans had time to recover. But Devers decided that the northern French corps would be unable to complete its redeployment until 21 September, forcing Patch to direct Truscott to hold his units in place until the transfer of area responsibilities could be completed. Truscott, temporarily frustrated, used the next several days to have his units bring up supplies and secure forward assembly areas for the Moselle crossing. During this period the 45th Division also began deploying from the VI Corps' right to its left, or northern, wing, replacing the departing French. By 18 September, Truscott thus had his three divisions oriented on the Moselle and the Vosges, ready to advance northeast on command.

To Truscott's surprise, preliminary probes toward the Moselle between 16 and 18 September found German opposition again stiffening in the southern part of his sector close to the Belfort Gap, but almost negligible resistance in the north, especially in the Remiremont-Epinal area along the Moselle. Again the irrepressible Truscott sought Patch's permission for an immediate attack to exploit the situation. This time the reaction was more positive. Although SHAEF had not yet officially approved the plan to push the Seventh Army across the Vosges, Devers and Patch agreed with Truscott that further delays would only allow the Germans to become more entrenched along the Moselle and the western slopes of the Vosges. So, with the French II Corps' redeployment nearly complete, Patch, with Devers' blessing, gave Truscott the

green light to start this new offensive the following morning. Thus, at 1630 on the 20th, the three VI Corps infantry divisions began their advance toward the High Vosges.[12]

German Plans and Deployment

Once the Allied armies had broken out of their OVERLORD beachheads, the basic German operational objective in northern France was to hold along a defensive line as far west of the Franco-German border as possible. Ostensibly, this defensive line was to originate at the Schelde Estuary in the Netherlands and cross into Germany near the city of Aachen (Aix-la-Chapelle). From the vicinity of Aachen south to the confluence of the Sarre and Moselle rivers near Trier, the line corresponded to the neglected prewar West Wall, sometimes known as the Siegfried Line. The Trier area also marked the boundary between *Army Groups B* and *G* as of 8 September.[13]

From Trier southwest thirty-five miles to Thionville, the line followed the Moselle River and was therefore designated the Moselle position. At Thionville the main defensive line was to swing sharply back southeast for about fifty miles to Sarralbe, corre-

---

[12] Msg, G–3, VI Corps, to G–3, 36th Div, 191025 Sep 44, in VI Corps War Rm Jnl, 19 Sep 44; VI Corps Fld Msg 191200, 19 Sep 44; Seventh Army Diary, 19 Sep 44. Available record files contain no written authorization permitting Truscott to reactivate his Field Order 3 of 16 September, and SHAEF did not officially approve the new offensive until 22 September, when Devers and Patch attended a conference at SHAEF headquarters.

[13] The principal sources for this section are von Luttichau, "German Operations," chs. 16 and 17; and Krasomil, "German Operations in Southern France," ch. 6, CMH MS R–51.

sponding for the most part with the French prewar Maginot Line. From Sarralbe the line was to continue generally south and southwest across the Vosges, through the approaches to the Belfort Gap, and on to the Swiss border. In the area north of Devers' 6th Army Group, the German high command also wanted to establish a western salient at Metz, on the Moselle twenty miles south of Thionville, and, in addition, a buffer line along the Moselle from Metz through Nancy, Epinal, and Remiremont, all the way south to the vicinity of l'Isle-sur-les-Doubs.

In mid-September this projected line, named the *Weststellung,* or West Line, existed largely on paper. North of Aachen, for example, construction of permanent fortifications and obstacles had barely begun, and south of the city the old West Wall defenses needed to be completely rebuilt. Between Thionville and Sarralbe, the Maginot Line defensive works, although more formidable, would either have to be altered to face westward or demolished. South of Sarralbe and opposite the 6th Army Group, the only activity on the trace of the proposed line was the hasty construction of some field fortifications in the Vosges by civilian forced labor and a few pioneer battalions.

As the VI Corps was about to begin its attack, the opposing German forces were desperately trying to buy time to turn the *Weststellung* into a solid defensive position. *Army Group G's* most immediate concern was not the Belfort Gap or the Vosges defenses, but defenses in the area around Metz and Nancy. There the progress of Patton's Third Army had

kept the German *First Army* off balance, making it impossible for Blaskowitz to assemble and direct a strong armored counterattack with Lt. Gen. Hasso von Manteuffel's *Fifth Panzer Army* against Patton's southern flank, as Hitler had ordered. The Third Army had continually forced the *First Army* back, and Blaskowitz's concerns had been almost entirely defensive. At the insistence of von Rundstedt, whom Hitler had brought back to command *OB West* in early September, he finally launched a counterattack with one panzer corps on 9 September, but by the 14th these forces had been shattered by Third Army units assisted by the Seventh Army's French II Corps driving east of Dijon.

To gain additional strength for a renewed effort, Blaskowitz requested authorization to pull the bulk of the *Nineteenth Army* back to the Moselle River, keeping some forces west of the river in front of the Belfort approaches. Von Rundstedt referred the matter to *OKW,* and Hitler approved the withdrawal on the 15th, with the proviso that *Army Group G* launch the new counterattack no later then 18 September. To ensure its success, *OB West* ordered Blaskowitz to send both the *11th Panzer Division* and the *113th Panzer Brigade* from the Belfort Gap area north to von Manteuffel.

By 17 September *Army Group G* had completed most of the redeployments and command shufflings necessitated by the scheduled counterattack. In the far north the *First Army* held *Army Group G's* right wing with two corps between Trier and Nancy. In its center, the *Fifth Panzer Army* occupied a thirty-mile front from Nancy to the

Rambervillers area just north of Epinal. Both armies faced units of Bradley's 12th Army Group. South of Rambervillers, the *Nineteenth Army* stood opposite Devers' small 6th Army Group along a front stretching for about ninety miles (*Map 13*). Along the Moselle, from Charmes ten miles south to Epinal, the *Nineteenth Army*'s *LXVI Corps* held the river line with a motley collection of *16th Division* and *Group Ottenbacher* remnants, stragglers from other *kampfgruppen* chopped up in the Dijon salient, two battalions of the *19th SS Police Regiment,* and some *Luftwaffe* and *Kriegsmarine* "retreads."

From Epinal southeast eleven miles along the Moselle to Remiremont and another eleven miles southwest to La Longine, the *Nineteenth Army*'s *LXIV Corps* took over with the *716th Division* on its right and the *189th Division* (*Group von Schwerin*) on its left. Next was the *IV Luftwaffe Field Corps* with the *338th* and *198th Divisions* deployed on a line, north to south, along a fifteen-mile front west of the Moselle from La Longine south to La Cote, about four miles east of Lure on Route N–19. Below La Cote to the Swiss border, a distance of about thirty miles, was the *LXXXV Corps*, guarding the Belfort Gap with the *159th Division* on its right, *Group Degener* in the center, and the *11th Panzer Division* on the south. Wiese had somehow managed to retain the panzer division until the night of 18–19 September, but its departure was imminent. Only the headquarters of *Corps Dehner,* currently based inside Belfort city, remained uncommitted.

From 15 to 19 September Truscott's final eastward advance had pushed back the *Nineteenth Army* units holding positions west of the Moselle from Remiremont south to the Doubs River. The German withdrawal to new defensive lines was well under way across most of the front by the morning of the 19th, which accounts for the diminishing resistance experienced by the VI Corps and the French II Corps. By the evening of 19 September the II Corps French troops were within two miles of La Cote; elements of the 3d Division were scarcely three miles from La Longine; the 36th Division had a reinforced infantry battalion two miles from Remiremont; and the 117th Cavalry Squadron had closed within four miles of Epinal. Thus, although Patch and Truscott feared that the Germans might have reestablished a firm defensive line by the 19th, both Blaskowitz and Wiese were concerned whether their units could make much of a showing south of Charmes with the Allied forces seemingly still in hot pursuit.

How close the *Nineteenth Army* was to collapse at this juncture is hard to estimate. Due to the command and administrative confusion throughout the force, even determining its general strength and actual dispositions is difficult. Employing the German practice of counting only troops under the combat battalion headquarters as combat effectives, Wiese's infantry strength numbered about 13,000 men on 19 September, with the total strength of the divisions deployed across the *Nineteenth Army*'s front perhaps three to five times as high. But these figures are conjectures only, and even these estimates leave out the numerous *kampfgruppen*, security

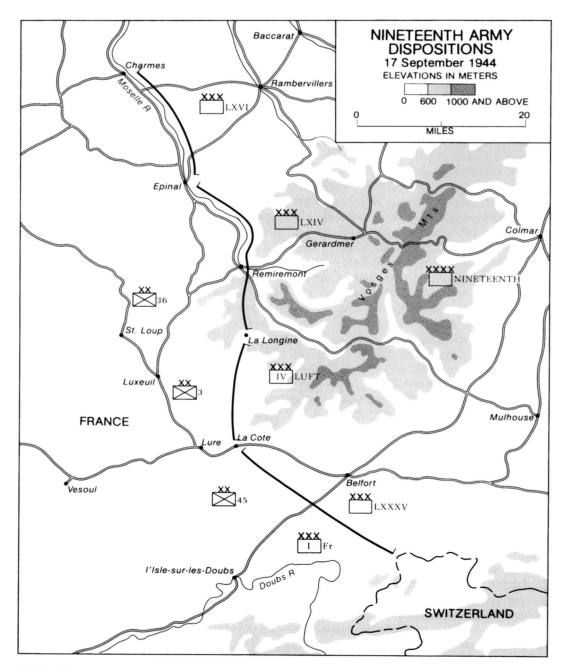

MAP 13 This map is printed in full color at the back of the book, following the Index.

and police units, Army service units, and *Luftwaffe* and *Kriegsmarine* troops filling in here and there as infantry, some of which may have been counted in with the total infantry division effectives. Other organizations in the *Nineteenth Army's* area included security, fortress, and engineer units, which were generally associated with the construction of the *Weststellung* defenses and were thus under *Army Group G* control, but could pass to the *Nineteenth Army* in an emergency. Also included in this category were the four-regiment *405th Replacement Division* and various static artillery units. Under direct army control, Wiese had about 90 pieces of field artillery, roughly 30 infantry light howitzers (75-mm.), and around 25 dual-purpose 88-mm. guns. The *11th Panzer Division,* reduced to about 25 tanks as of 19 September, was beginning to receive some replacements and new equipment, but was still only marginally effective. In sum Wiese would have an increasingly difficult time holding back a general 6th Army Group offensive, or even a smaller one if it was concentrated in the right area.

Meanwhile, events north of the *Nineteenth Army's* front had begun to threaten its right flank. Von Manteuffel's *Fifth Panzer Army* launched an attack toward Luneville on the 18th and Nancy on the 19th, but both of-fensives were too weak to have any chance of success. Von Manteuffel's left wing was quickly forced back by the advance of the U.S. Third Army's XV Corps across the Moselle, and, in the process, Wiese's northernmost force, the *LXVI Corps,* was pushed back farther east. The evening of 19 September thus found it in disarray, trying to regroup its forces south of Rambervillers and hold the *Nineteenth Army's* northern flank between the Moselle and Baccarat, situated on the Meurthe River about ten miles northeast of Rambervillers.

Not surprisingly, Hitler had become increasingly critical of Blaskowitz's performance. The failure of the *Fifth Panzer Army's* counterattack against the U.S. Third Army and the continuous withdrawal of the *Nineteenth Army* in the face of little more than Truscott's three divisions had predictably angered the German *Fuhrer*. Hitler had never established a close relationship with the apolitical Blaskowitz and, unwilling to take any action against von Rundstedt, relieved the *Army Group G* commander on 21 September. Blaskowitz was replaced by Lt. Gen. Hermann Balck, formerly the commander of the *Fourth Panzer Army* on the Russian front. But whether Balck or any other German general could greatly influence the coming battles along the German frontier was problematic.

CHAPTER XIII

VI Corps at the Moselle

When Operation MARKET-GARDEN—the Allied airborne-led offensive against the extreme northern sector of the German defensive line—began on 17 September, Truscott's VI Corps had been approaching the hasty German defenses in the Belfort Gap. But in the ensuing days, as the Allied attack in the north played out its part, Devers, the new 6th Army Group commander, reorganized the Allied forces from southern France into two armies, Patch's Seventh Army in the north (with only one corps, the VI) and de Lattre's First French Army in the south (with two corps, the I and II). The shift pushed Truscott's sector of advance to the north, and his further movement eastward toward the German border was now blocked by the formidable High Vosges Mountains. During World War I the Germans had seized the area in 1914, and the French had never bothered to penetrate there in strength. The heavily forested, rising mountainous terrain gave too many obvious advantages to the defenders. However, as the inability of Montgomery's 21st Army Group to bring the northern operation to a successful conclusion became evident by the 25th, Patch and Truscott hoped that a thrust through the Vosges might surprise the Germans and provide a back door to the German border.

Allied Plans and Alignment

Truscott's plans for the assault against *Nineteenth Army*'s re-forming defenses called for the VI Corps to push generally northeast across the Moselle River and into the Vosges foothills with three divisions abreast.[1] The 3d Division was to be on the right, or southern, wing with its open flank tied to the French II Corps; the 36th Division was to occupy the VI Corps center; and the 45th Division was to take the left, with the 117th Cavalry Squadron screening VI Corps' northern flank, adjacent to the Third Army's XV Corps. Responsibility for the left flank was ultimately to pass to the 45th Division when it completed its displacement north,

---

[1] Planning information in this section is generally from VI Corps FO 3, 16 Sep 44; VI Corps Fld Msg 191200A, 19 Sep 44; VI Corps Fld Msg 201900A, 20 Sep 44; *Seventh Army Rpt,* I, 289–90, 299; First French Army Personal and Secret Instruction 2, 17 Sep 44 (in Annex IV of de Lattre, *Histoire,* French language edition); II French Corps, Directive for the Relief of VI Corps, 18 Sep 44; de Lattre, *History,* pp. 182–83; II French Corps, Instruction Personal and Secret for the Commanders of the 1st DMI, 1st DB, 2d DIM, 20 Sep 44.

and the cavalry squadron was to move over to the right flank of the VI Corps where it would provide close liaison with the French II Corps.

The VI Corps' front for the drive across the Moselle was about thirty miles wide northwest to southeast, approximately twice the width along which contemporary U.S. Army field manuals expected a three-division corps to deploy. The corps' northern boundary with the Third Army's XV Corps crossed the Moselle about two miles north of Epinal and continued northeast thirteen miles to Rambervillers and then another nine miles to the Meurthe River at Baccarat. North of Epinal, Rambervillers, and Baccarat, Maj. Gen. Wade H. Haislip's XV Corps faced the *XLVII Panzer Corps* of *Army Group G's Fifth Panzer Army.* By 20 September the XV Corps was well beyond the Moselle in its sector and was moving into Luneville, on the Meurthe River about twenty-eight miles north of Epinal. Elements of the XV Corps crossed the Meurthe near Luneville on the 20th, and the corps' French 2d Armored Division had scouting elements within seven miles of Baccarat.

At the other end of its new front, the VI Corps' southern boundary extended from Lure northeast eighteen miles to cross the Moselle at Le Thillot, and continued northeast into the Vosges past Gerardmer, fifteen miles beyond. Route N–486, a secondary highway connecting Lure and Gerardmer, marked the boundary between the VI Corps and the French II Corps.

While Truscott's VI Corps advanced generally northeast to Strasbourg on the Rhine, de Monsabert's

II Corps was to head in a more easterly direction. General de Lattre planned a two-corps attack to breach the Belfort Gap, with the II Corps outflanking Belfort on the north while General Bethouart's I Corps undertook to drive directly through the gap to Mulhouse, twenty-three miles beyond. De Lattre hoped that the First French Army could begin its attack on or about 27 September, but Generals Devers and Patch were not so optimistic, believing that French logistical and redeployment problems would push the starting date of the French offensive back to mid-October. Until then, the most Devers and Patch expected from the French were some limited attacks in the II Corps' sector to support the VI Corps' assault.

As was his custom, Truscott established a series of phase lines for the new VI Corps offensive, which was to begin at 0630 on 20 September. Phase Line I lay generally ten miles west of the Moselle and included the forward assembly areas needed for the Moselle crossing. Phase Line II included the Moselle River, the rail and highway center of Epinal on the Moselle, and the rising ground east of the river. After crossing the Moselle, Truscott planned to have the attack move in a more northerly direction, pivoting on the 45th Division at Epinal while the 3d and 36th Divisions swung north to Phase Lines III and IV, which included Gerardmer and Rambervillers. An advance to Phase Line V would carry the corps' center and left flank across the Meurthe River between Baccarat and St. Die. From the corps' forward positions on the morning of 20 September, it was twenty-five to thirty miles to St. Die and another forty miles from St. Die to the corps' long-range objective, Strasbourg on the Rhine.

On the eve of the new offensive, substantial portions of VI Corps were already on or beyond Phase Line I and were in position to start crossing the Moselle. The 3d Division was to cross in a zone that stretched from Le Thillot northwest eleven miles to a point a mile or so south of Remiremont, also on the Moselle. Once across the river and on Phase Line II, the 3d Division was to continue northeast, cross the Moselotte River, seize Gerardmer on Phase Line III, and drive on to Phase Line IV, supporting a 36th Division attack toward St. Die.

In the center, the 36th Division's crossing zone along the Moselle extended northwest about ten miles from the vicinity of Remiremont to Arches and Archettes. The division's ultimate objective was St. Die. The 45th Division, which had to redeploy from VI Corps' right to its left, was going to be a day or two behind the other divisions in moving up to the Moselle. The division's sector along the river was about eight miles wide, and the first important objective was Epinal. After seizing Epinal and crossing the Moselle, the 45th was to continue northeast to secure Rambervillers and Baccarat.

The High Vosges

The High Vosges mountain chain is about seventy miles long, north to south, and some thirty to forty miles wide. After crossing the Moselle, Truscott's two northern attacking di-

visions would begin entering the foothills of the mountain range, while O'Daniel's 3d Division, attacking in the south, would already be running into hilly terrain as it approached the upper Moselle. In the north, along the line Epinal-Rambervillers-Baccarat, the terrain consisted generally of open but hilly farmland, with the higher elevations usually thickly wooded *(Map 14)*. Here the 45th Division would have some of the only good offensive terrain in the VI Corps sector. Elsewhere the ground would become progressively more difficult and more thickly forested. From the Moselle to St. Die and farther east, the elevation of terrain slowly rose and was increasingly broken up by large hills and mountains whose valleys served as watersheds for the region. Here the prevailing winds from the north and west brought moisture-laden clouds that fed the dense forests and almost tropical vegetation. Once across the crest of the Vosges, the attackers would find the eastern slopes of the range steeper but more sparsely wooded because of the reduced amount of rainfall. Here, after defending the broader mountain forests on the west side of the Vosges, the Germans could be expected to put up a final resistance along the great eastern passes that led to the plains below.

The road network through the High Vosges was barely adequate for military operations. Most roads ran along stream valleys dominated by sharply rising, usually forested, high ground. The roads traversing the High Vosges from east to west eventually left the stream valleys to cross over high, easily defensible mountain

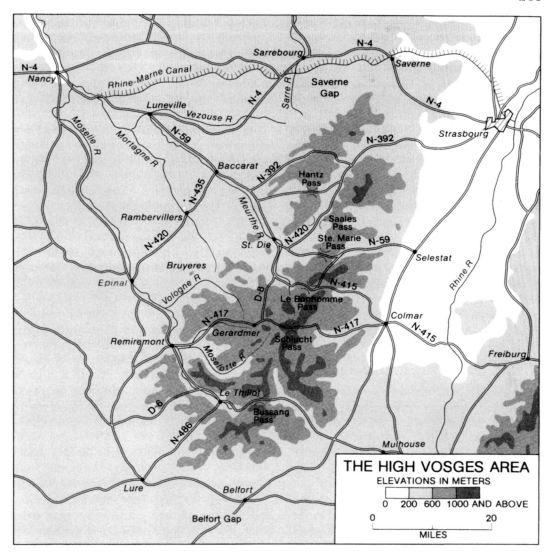

MAP 14   This map is printed in full color at the back of the book, following the Index.

passes. The few railroad lines generally ran north to south and were used
by the Germans to strengthen their
interior lines of communication.

Everywhere in the High Vosges the
rough terrain, first gradually rising
and then falling away to a deteriorated escarpment overlooking the Alsatian plains to the east, would provide
the Germans with every possible defensive advantage. The weather, too,
would help the Germans. The Allied
forces expected heavy rains to begin
throughout the mountains during late

September—and in September 1944 the rains began earlier than usual. Rain and fog would reduce visibility at ground level, while fog, rain, and thick overcasts would drastically curtail Allied air support. Throughout the coming winter, as Truscott and many other VI Corps soldiers well knew from their experiences in Italy, the weather would grow steadily worse as rain gave way to snow. In summary, the terrain of the High Vosges Mountains, the expected weather conditions, the locations and routes of the main roads, and the broad front assigned to the VI Corps would make it difficult to concentrate American offensive strength for a decisive breakthrough; and the defending Germans would find it fairly easy to block the limited number of avenues through the Vosges. However, if the Moselle could be crossed and the Vosges attacked before the Germans had the opportunity to solidify their defenses, and before the weather became significantly worse, the prospects of reaching the Rhine at an early date would be greatly enhanced.

The 45th Division at Epinal

On the morning of 20 September, when the VI Corps' attack began, the 45th Division was still in the process of moving north and had no troops in position to strike for the Moselle. But throughout the day the 117th Cavalry Squadron, roaming up and down roads west of Epinal, secured assembly ground for regiments of the arriving division, and during the late afternoon the 179th Infantry began moving into high ground west of the Moselle three to four miles south of

Epinal *(Map 15)*. The leading units encountered only scattered resistance from outposts of the *716th Division, LXIV Corps.* [2]

During the following day, 21 September, the 157th and 180th Infantry regiments deployed north of the 179th, and all three began probing for intact bridges, fords, or at least crossing sites where assault boats could be employed or treadway bridges installed. The 157th and 180th Infantry, both closing in on Epinal, encountered the stiffest resistance. North of Epinal—the 157th's sector—the Moselle was generally fordable for infantry, but the German defenders had positioned roadblocks on the approaches to the river, destroyed most of the bridges over the Moselle, and covered likely crossing sites with artillery and mortar fire from the opposite bank. At Epinal, the 180th regiment's specific objective, the river, was unfordable and, eighty feet wide, flowed swiftly northward between twenty-foot-high banks. South of Epinal the unit found only marginal fording and small boat crossing sites, and the Germans had blown up the main highway bridge at Archettes, on the regiment's right.

Unable to find suitable crossing and slowed by German roadblocks, mines, and artillery, the 157th Infantry began extending northward to Chatel, where the Third Army's XV Corps already had a forty-ton bridge

---

[2] German information in this chapter derives from Mosenthal, "German Operations in Southern France: The Establishment of a Continuous Defensive Front by *Army Group G,* 15 Sep–1 Oct 44," pp. 16–50, CMH MS R–68; Cole, *The Lorraine Campaign,* pp. 205–08, 233–35; VI Corps and 36th Div G–2 Per Rpts, 19–30 Sep 44.

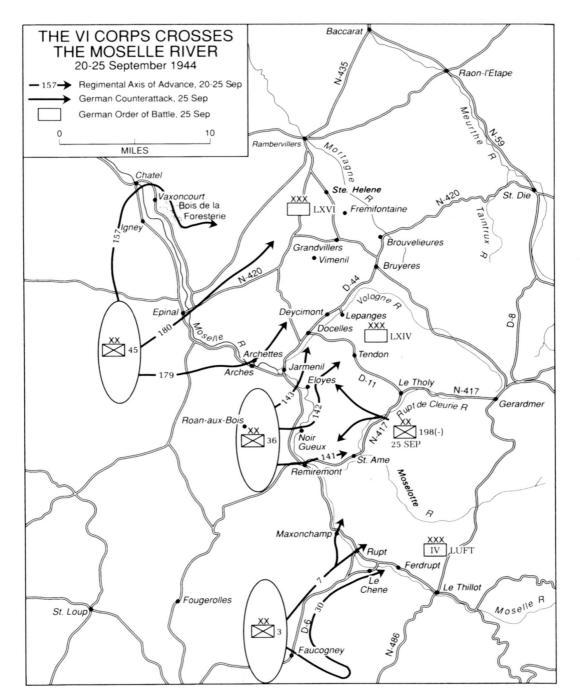

THE VI CORPS CROSSES THE MOSELLE RIVER
20-25 September 1944

- —157→ Regimental Axis of Advance, 20-25 Sep
- → German Counterattack, 25 Sep
- ☐ German Order of Battle, 25 Sep

0   10
MILES

Baccarat

N-435

Raon-l'Etape

Meurthe R

N-59

Rambervillers

Mortagne R

Ste. Helene

Fremifontaine

N-420

St. Die

Chatel

Vaxoncourt
Bois de la
Foresterie

Igney

157

XXX LXVI

Grandvillers

Vimenil

Brouvelieures

Bruyeres

Taintrux R

D-8

N-420

Epinal

Moselle R

180

Deycimont

Lepanges

Docelles

Vologne R

D-44

XXX LXIV

Tendon

XX 45

179

Archettes

Arches

Jarmenil

Eloyes

D-11

Le Tholy

N-417

Gerardmer

143

142

Rupt de Cleurie R

Roan-aux-Bois

XX 36

Noir
Gueux

N-417

XX 198(-)
25 SEP

Remiremont

141

St. Ame

Moselotte R

Maxonchamp

Rupt

Ferdrupt

XXX IV LUFT

Le
Chene

Le Thillot

Moselle R

Fougerolles

7

St. Loup

30

D-6

XX 3

Faucogney

N-486

MAP 15   This map is printed in full color at the back of the book, following the Index.

in place. General Eagles, the 45th Division commander, recommended sending the 157th regiment over the Chatel bridge to descend on the Epinal area from the north, while the 180th Infantry continued its frontal assault from the west. Truscott quickly made the necessary arrangements with the XV Corps headquarters, and, beginning about 2100 on the 21st, the bulk of the 157th began crossing at Chatel, with one infantry battalion wading across the Moselle near Igney, several miles south, on the 22d. Most of the regiment then assembled near Vaxoncourt, about eight miles north of Epinal, and began to advance south.

Facing the 157th south and southeast of Vaxoncourt was the Bois de la Foresterie, four square miles of forest heavily defended by German infantry, supported by artillery, mortars, and machine guns emplaced along the slopes to the east. On 22 and 23 September the 157th Infantry struggled south through the woods, while staving off German counterattacks against the bridgehead. General Eagles had expected the 157th to make much faster progress, thereby easing the 180th Infantry's frontal assault. Instead, at dark on the 23d, the 180th was still having trouble at Epinal, and the 157th had not yet fought its way south out of the Third Army's sector. The two-day effort had cost the 157th Infantry 10 men killed and 103 wounded.

The 180th Infantry had spent 21 and 22 September inching its way toward the Moselle in the area west and southwest of Epinal, encountering an intricate series of roadblocks, minefields, barbed-wire entangle-

ments, and booby-trapped buildings. German rifle and machine-gun fire covered many of the obstacles, while German artillery, armor, and rocket batteries east of the river harassed the attackers. Late on 22 September the Germans began withdrawing their troops to the east bank of the Moselle, vacating the western section of Epinal; but with small arms and mortar fire they repulsed several attempts by the 180th Infantry to cross the river before dark. By nightfall the regiment had reached the Moselle only at Epinal's northern outskirts.

During the morning of 23 September the 180th mopped up most of the section of Epinal west of the Moselle, but could not prevent the Germans from blowing up the last intact bridge within the small city. In the afternoon the 2d Battalion, 180th Infantry, crossed on the north and, after battling various *LXVI Corps* elements, drove laboriously up rising ground north and northeast of the city. On the southern edge of Epinal, German artillery and tank fire twice repulsed crossing attempts by the 3d Battalion. Finally, behind heavy supporting fires and the cover of darkness, the battalion successfully crossed the river that evening.

So far, the motley collection of forces under *LXVI Corps* had managed to stall both the 157th and 180th regiments, but on 24 September German resistance in front of the 45th Division's center and left began to collapse. The 157th cleared the Bois de la Foresterie, made some progress against the high ground to the east, and pushed troops south to within four miles of Epinal. The 180th Infantry, after repulsing an early morning German counterattack, finally secured Epinal during the day and probably could have driven well beyond the city, but delayed further advances pending the completion of a forty-ton Bailey bridge over the Moselle. Engineers finished the bridge about 1600 on the 24th, and supplies and vehicles started to roll through Epinal almost immediately.

On the 25th, the 157th and 180th Infantry regiments advanced six miles northeast of Epinal into the Vosges, opposed mainly by German artillery and assault gun fire. By dusk the German defenders were thus in full retreat all along the 45th Division's front. But the division's main prize was Epinal itself, a key rail and highway center that gave the Seventh Army and VI Corps an excellent supply base from which to support future drives into the High Vosges. The capture of the city, which *Army Group G* and *Nineteenth Army* considered a most important defensive bastion, had cost the 180th Infantry 55 men wounded and 30 missing, while the 157th Infantry, technically in a supporting role, had lost 15 men killed, 170 wounded, and 30 missing during the attack.

To the south, the 179th Infantry, after several false starts, managed to shuttle its troops across the Moselle in rubber assault boats during the night of 21–22 September, and secured an unopposed bridgehead just below Archettes, six miles south of Epinal. On the following day the 179th took Archettes and, only lightly harassed by German mortar and small arms fire, secured the town until the engineers had thrown a forty-ton Bailey bridge over the river by 1330.

From Archettes, the 179th pushed northeast into the Vosges toward Grandvillers and by dark on the 25th was roughly parallel to its sister regiments to the north. Casualties during 20–25 September for the 179th numbered approximately 15 men killed, 40 wounded, and 10 missing.

The 36th Division in the Center

On the morning of 20 September the 3d Battalion, 142d Infantry, started toward the river at Remiremont, a mile east of its forward position, while the rest of the regiment moved toward the same objective from the southwest. As the 142d moved out, the 141st passed northward through its rear, covering the flank of the 142d and striking for the town of Eloyes, on the Moselle River about six miles north of Remiremont. Dahlquist kept his best unit, the 143d Infantry, in reserve to exploit any crossing sites secured by the two attacking regiments.

Almost immediately the leading 36th Division units heading for both Eloyes and Remiremont met unexpectedly heavy opposition from *189th Division* forces, causing Dahlquist to adjust the division's plan of attack. Initially, he ordered his northern element, the 141st, to send its two unengaged battalions across the Moselle between Eloyes and Remiremont, with one battalion then attacking north and the other south in order to loosen up the German defenses in both areas. If suitable crossing sites could be secured, he could follow with the 143d; if not, the 143d would have to be used to reinforce one of the main efforts frontally.

Thus alerted, the 141st began scouting for likely crossing sites in its sector—which extended about six miles southeast along the Moselle from Archettes—and during the afternoon found an excellent ford at Noir Gueux, a tiny hamlet-cum-church on the far (east) bank about three miles north of Remiremont. On the west bank opposite Noir Gueux a narrow neck of woods extended to the river, affording the only covered approach to the water in the 141st Infantry's sector. As the site appeared undefended, Dahlquist decided to send the 141st Infantry's 1st and 3d Battalions across at Noir Gueux that night, with the two battalions separating thereafter, one striking for the rear of the German lines at Eloyes, and the other for Remiremont.

The units started out from their assembly areas at Raon-aux-Bois about 0100 on 21 September, marching off into a pitch-black night punctuated by cold, intermittent rain. As dawn approached, fog blanketed the Moselle valley near Noir Gueux, which helped the 141st Infantry's leading troops achieve secrecy and surprise. The men of the 1st Battalion waded through the Moselle's cold waters, meeting no opposition; but shortly after 0700, as the fog began to lift, small arms fire started to harass the attackers. Nevertheless, the leading unit completed its crossing and headed north for Eloyes. Meanwhile, General Dahlquist himself had arrived at the Noir Gueux crossing site about 0945, and found that the 3d Battalion had been unable to follow the 1st because of increased German fire. Subsequently an attempt to cross about a mile south resulted in the death of

the battalion commander, Maj. Kermit R. Hanson. Hanson had led the first two platoons across the river and then had been ambushed by a company-sized German force that had withheld their fire until the crossing began. The battalion lost 8 men killed, including Hanson, 7 wounded, and about 20 believed to have been captured. Dahlquist, who remained determined to force a crossing and convinced that the German defenses were extremely spotty, reorganized the battalion and finally pushed it across the river at the original site; he then followed it with his entire reserve, the 143d regiment, on the afternoon of the 21st.

As the 143d moved across, Dahlquist learned that his other two regiments were still stalled, the 141st around Eloyes (with one battalion still west of the river and one battalion east) and the 142d outside of Remiremont (with one battalion of the 141st west of the river and the entire 142d regiment still on the east bank). Quickly he ordered the entire 143d regiment north to Eloyes where it blocked the exits to the town on the east, and on the 22d it proceeded to clear the town house by house. Between 23 and 25 September the 143d consolidated the rest of the Moselle area in the 36th Division's northern sector and began pushing into the Vosges foothills.

While the 143d worked over Eloyes, Dahlquist regrouped the somewhat lackluster 141st and sent the regiment south to Remiremont. There the 142d had started its attack on 20 September from a point barely two miles from the town, but after two days of fighting the regiment had

TROOPS OF 36TH INFANTRY DIVISION CROSS THE MOSELLE, *near Longuet, September 1944.*

no more than a foothold in the western section of Remiremont. However, on the 22d, as the arriving 141st threatened the German rear, resistance began to fall apart and the 142d was finally able to secure the town the following morning. The four-day battle for Remiremont had cost the 142d Infantry 42 men killed, 111 wounded, and 40 missing.[3]

On 24 and 25 September, the 141st and 142d regiments realigned themselves and began advancing into the Vosges, with the 142d shifting northward into a new sector between the

143d and the 141st. The 141st Infantry, which had started out as the 36th Division's northernmost element and was now on the division's right, advanced to St. Ame; the 142d approached Tendon, and the 143d neared Docelles. Behind them corps engineers quickly erected a Bailey bridge at Remiremont and a heavy platoon bridge at Jarmenil. So far, the VI Corps had crossed the Moselle with relatively few casualties and was now ready to move into the mountains.

The German Reaction

Until 25 September the *Nineteenth Army*'s *LXVI* and *LXIV Corps* had tried to contain the 36th and 45th Divi-

---

[3] Later it was learned that the Germans had captured about 35 of the troops classified as missing. Most were taken prisoner on 21 September when Company E, attempting to infiltrate through thick woods to outflank a roadblock, ran into an ambush.

sions' penetrations across the Moselle by means of static defenses and local, small-scale counterattacks. These efforts had proved futile, and by dark on 23 September General Wiese of *Nineteenth Army* had decided that such tactics would continue to be ineffective unless strong armor and infantry reinforcements could quickly be brought to bear. His main concern was an Allied drive directly east from the Remiremont-Eloyes area along Route N–417 through Gerardmer and the Schlucht Pass to Colmar. A possible American drive northeast to St. Die was a secondary concern since it would have to pass through some of the worst and most easily defensible Vosges terrain. Wiese also reckoned that he had sufficient strength in the Epinal area to contain the 45th's bridgehead at least temporarily. Nor was he greatly worried about the area south of Remiremont, where, on the evening of the 23d, elements of the *LXIV Corps* and the *IV Luftwaffe Field Corps* were still holding O'Daniel's 3d Division units west of the Moselle. Furthermore, Wiese knew that French forces had taken over the entire region south of the VI Corps, and he correctly estimated that it would take the First French Army many days, if not weeks, to gather enough strength to launch a concerted offensive toward Belfort.

Seeking reinforcements for the Remiremont-Gerardmer area, Wiese decided to throw in the *198th Division,* which *Army Group G* had already directed him to ship north to the *Fifth Panzer Army.* Wiese prevailed upon *Army Group G* to allow him to employ the *198th* for a counterattack in *LXIV Corps'* sector. The division was to as-

semble near Le Tholy, strike west and northwest toward Tendon and Eloyes, and drive the 36th Division back across the Moselle. In addition, a small armored group of the *11th Panzer Division,* left behind when the rest of the division moved to the *Fifth Panzer Army*'s area, was to make a number of feints to occupy other American units in the area. The time when American commanders were affected by such obvious chicanery, however, was long over.

The attack began shortly after 1200 on 25 September in the hills southwest of Le Tholy and consisted of two understrength grenadier regiments of the *198th Division* with artillery support. Misty rain and intermittent fog allowed the Germans to move through the mountains unobserved, and they were able to infiltrate between the 142d and 141st regiments. The first German strikes hit the right rear of the 142d Infantry, overrunning roadblocks along the regiment's tenuous, cart-path lines of communication, while farther south the German attack threatened the rear of the 141st Infantry around St. Ame. Confused fighting continued until dusk, forcing the leading units of the two American regiments to pull back, but blunting any serious German advance toward the Moselle. As both sides regrouped during the early hours of the 26th, *Army Group G* directed the *Nineteenth Army* to call off the attack. During the previous day, 25 September, contrary to Wiese's estimates, the 45th Division had begun to break out of its Epinal bridgehead, advancing toward Rambervillers and threatening to drive a wedge between the *LXVI* and *LXIV Corps.* Moreover, on the 25th the 3d Division had finally established a bridgehead over the Moselle south of Remiremont. It had thus become obvious that even a successful attempt by the *198th* to reach the river would leave both of its flanks vulnerable to American counterattacks.

The 3d Division on the Moselle

With the 3d Division eight to ten miles short of the Moselle on the morning of 20 September, General O'Daniel, the division commander, planned to advance toward the river with two regiments abreast—the 7th Infantry on the left and the 30th on the right—and the 15th Infantry in reserve. The 7th Infantry was to cross at Rupt-sur-Moselle, seven miles south of Remiremont, and the 30th Infantry at Ferdrupt, three miles south of Rupt. The boundary between the two attacking regiments was Route D–6, a mountain road that also marked the boundary between the defending *LXIV* and *IV Luftwaffe Field Corps.*

In the 3d Division's zone of attack, the Moselle was extremely narrow and did not constitute much of a barrier, but the terrain along the approaches to the river was much more rugged than in the north. West of the Moselle, the German defenses were concentrated in sharply rising ground that was densely forested on the higher slopes and overgrown with thick underbrush on other slopes where available maps indicated open ground. The division's advance would also have to be keyed somewhat to the progress of the French II Corps on its southern flank, which was

facing even more difficult terrain.

Starting out from positions near Faucogney on 20 September, with its main effort north of Route D–6, the 7th Infantry encountered resistance of varying intensity and took three days to move within half a mile of Rupt. However, during the night of 23–24 September some of its troops surprised a German garrison guarding a bridge over the Moselle at Rupt and managed to capture the span before the Germans could destroy it. Throughout the rest of the night the American infantry staved off several German efforts to retake or destroy the bridge and, with reinforcements, secured the area at daybreak.

During the 24th and 25th the 7th regiment, reinforced by a battalion of the 15th Infantry, pushed its left flank north toward Remiremont and in the process seized another Moselle bridge at Maxonchamp, two miles northwest of Rupt. By dark on the 25th, therefore, the 7th Infantry had established two bridgeheads over the Moselle, expanded them east of the river, and come more or less abreast of the 36th Division units at Remiremont in the face of only sporadic opposition by *338th Division* elements.

To the south, the 30th Infantry had begun its attack on 20 September, advancing south and southeast of Faucogney toward Melay and several other towns on the left flank of the division's axis of advance. Initially it hoped to outflank German positions along the easily defensible Route N–486, the Lure–Le Thillot highway. But Route N–486, marking the boundary between the VI and the French II Corps, was in the French zone of responsibility, and the 30th

Infantry was forced to traverse thickly forested ground dotted with numerous small lakes, but few good roads. The *198th Division,* which employed N–486 as a main supply route, readily recognized the threat of the 30th Infantry's advance, and defended the area stubbornly.

The American regiment, in three separate columns, spent 20–21 September pushing south and east, but without much success. By the evening of the 21st, the inability of the French II Corps to deploy any significant strength northward along N–486, together with the 30th Infantry's failure to secure the division's southern flank, began to worry O'Daniel. The 3d Division commander, fearing that the Germans would soon exploit the growing gap between his forces and those of de Monsabert, urged Truscott to persuade the French to take over the area so that he could concentrate his entire division across the Moselle and toward Le Tholy and Gerardmer. But for the moment Truscott demurred, and instead directed the 117th Cavalry Squadron—which the 45th Division had relieved on VI Corps' northern flank—to move to the 30th Infantry's right in order to help protect the exposed southern flank.

On the morning of 22 September, as the American cavalry unit took over the Melay area aided by the 3d African Chasseurs (the reconnaissance squadron of the French 1st Armored Division), the 30th Infantry reassembled near Faucogney to strike northeast across rugged hill country toward Le Chene and the Moselle. But despite redeployment of the bulk of the *198th Division* north for its counterat-

tack against the 36th Division, the 30th could make no progress in its new avenue of advance. Rain, fog, miserable roads and trails, minefields, defended roadblocks, mortar and artillery fire, and determined German infantry resistance combined to slow progress. By dusk on the 25th, the 30th Infantry was still short of the Moselle and halted, pending relief by French forces.

Results

The Americans' progress in enlarging their bridgeheads and pushing east of the Moselle had convinced Wiese by 25 September that another withdrawal was necessary. Accordingly, he proposed to *Army Group G* that he pull the *LXVI* and *LXIV Corps* back about ten miles to positions between Rambervillers and Le Tholy. General Balck, commanding *Army Group G,* agreed with Wiese's proposals, but von Rundstedt at *OB West* felt that the recommended withdrawal would take the *Nineteenth Army*'s right and center back too close to the southern, forward section of the *Weststellung,* a section that had come to bear the designation *Vosges Foothill Position.* Hitler had already personally directed *Army Group G* to hold the Allied forces west of the *Vosges Foothill Position* in order to gain time to improve its main defenses, and von Rundstedt was reluctant to challenge the directive without due cause. However, continued pressure from Patton's Third Army against the *Fifth Panzer Army* north of the *Nineteenth Army*'s *LXVI Corps* had already forced the embattled *XLVII Panzer Corps* back to Rambervillers, and *OB West* doubted that its withdrawal would stop there. Considering the situation at Rambervillers, von Rundstedt agreed only to authorize a limited withdrawal in the Vosges, allowing the *LXVI Corps* and the northern wing of the *LXIV Corps* to pull back formally to the Rambervillers–Grandvillers–St. Ame area, but insisting that Wiese hold on to the more easily defensible Vosges terrain farther south.

On 26 September Wiese accordingly ordered the withdrawal of both the *LXVI Corps* and the *LXIV Corps'* right flank element, the *716th Division*. The two understrength regiments of the *198th Division,* already operating under *LXIV Corps* control, were to remain and back up the *716th* and *189th Divisions*. The rest of the *198th Division* was to hold the right flank of the *IV Luftwaffe Corps* south of Rupt. There the *IV Luftwaffe* was to continue its successful efforts to jam up the American and French attackers in the hills southeast of Le Thillot. On his northern flank, Wiese hoped that the more difficult terrain that the *LXVI Corps* was backing into between Baccarat and Bruyeres would ease its defensive tasks. The American offensive could not continue indefinitely, and when it did stop, the Germans could sink into their Vosges strongholds and perhaps survive the coming winter intact.

Wiese's hopes could not disguise the fact that the Germans had already been summarily ejected from good defensive terrain almost without a fight. What might have been a major combat operation for the VI Corps turned out to be an almost routine affair for Truscott's forces. The speed of the attack had caught most of the German defenders still west of the river in scattered, hastily prepared positions, while the more easily defensible Moselle River was left completely unguarded in many places; VI Corps engineers had easily erected bridges over the river in a matter of hours with little interference from German artillery fire. Given time, perhaps as little as a few days, the defending German corps might have easily improved their defensive screens west of the river, covered the river line itself with more mobile patrols, reserves, and artillery fire, and turned the river towns into strongpoints with stronger reserve forces in the hills to the east able to counterattack any VI Corps bridgeheads. But only in the far south was the American advance significantly retarded—as much by the terrain and French inactivity as by German defensive strength. Yet the Americans had only begun to approach the formidable Vosges Mountains, and the northern redeployment of Truscott's energetic VI Corps had been duly noted by the German high command. Once it entered the mountains, Wiese had good reason to believe that he could begin to channel the forward progress of his relentless pursuer and finally slow down the tempo of its advance.

CHAPTER XIV

Approaching the Gaps: Saverne

Despite Truscott's success in forcing the Moselle, the natural and man-made obstacles between the 6th Army Group and the German border were formidable. For this reason Devers was not nearly as confident as Truscott that the Vosges could be easily forced. Facing the German *Nineteenth Army* in mid-September, the 6th Army Group had only six divisions on line—Truscott's three American infantry divisions and the equivalent of three French divisions under de Lattre's control, all that he had been able to bring up from the south so far. Like the divisions in the two northern Allied army groups, these forces were overextended logistically, while the real battle for Germany had just begun. Without substantial reinforcements, it was doubtful that the 6th Army Group could play a major role in this struggle.

Regarding a sustained offensive over the Vosges with serious misgivings, both Devers and Patch considered alternate routes to the German border. The Vosges barrier could be bypassed in the north through Saverne or in the south at Belfort. The Saverne Gap was a generally narrow defile that separated the High Vosges from the Low Vosges, a somewhat lesser range that

angled off to the east into Germany, where it became known as the Hardt Mountains. The much wider Belfort Gap separated the High Vosges from the Jura Mountains and the Swiss Alps. But Truscott's initial drive for the Belfort Gap had fallen short in early September, and Patton's Third Army had been stopped at Metz many miles west of Saverne and the Sarre River valley to the north. Since then the German defenses in both areas had grown stronger, as de Lattre's French and Patton's American units soon discovered. Until the First French Army could put most of its seven divisions on line, the Belfort Gap would be difficult to force, and the more narrow Saverne Gap lay in the zone of the Third Army's XV Corps above Rambervillers and Baccarat. Devers thus had no choice but to send Truscott's weary forces into the mountains. At the very least the effort might weaken the German defenses in the gap areas, and, if employed carefully, the better-equipped and better-supported American infantry might wear the hastily assembled German "grenadiers" thin. Nevertheless, a battle of attrition in the mountains was not a mission that the American commanders or their troops relished, and Devers and Patch continued to study the possibility of bypassing the Vosges Mountains to the north through the Saverne Gap.

Allied Planning

By late September, Allied offensive activities throughout the northern European theater had ground to a halt. Montgomery's drive against the Ruhr had been stopped at Arnhem, and Patton's drive on the Saar had been halted in Lorraine. Both northern Allied army groups had outrun their supply lines, and the 6th Army Group was not in much better shape.[1] Other factors contributing to the general slowdown were poor weather, which complicated both tactical and logistical problems, and increasingly determined German resistance. In Eisenhower's mind the only real solution to the logistical problem was an early opening of the port of Antwerp in Belgium. Yet he had postponed concerted action to open Antwerp in favor of MARKET-GARDEN, the 17–24 September attempt to envelop the Ruhr industrial area from the north. But the support demands of the operation only made the already serious logistical situation of the two northern Allied army groups worse.

On the afternoon of 22 September, with the success of MARKET-GARDEN already in doubt, Eisenhower met with his major subordinate commanders, including Generals Devers and

Patch, to consider new plans. For the immediate future, Eisenhower told his subordinates, the logistical situation as well as tactical considerations would continue to make it impossible to implement a broad front strategy. Instead, the main Allied effort would have to remain in the north, in the sector of Montgomery's 21st Army Group. There, he pointed out, the principal Allied objective was clearing the seaward approaches to Antwerp. But Eisenhower also agreed to allow the 21st Army Group's offensive to continue against the Ruhr. The Ruhr effort, in turn, would still require the direct support of a companion offensive by the U.S. First Army, on the 12th Army Group's left, or northern, wing; and the logistical support needed for the entire offensive meant that the rest of Bradley's forces, mainly Patton's Third Army, would have to remain in place. The same restrictions would apply as well to the U.S. Ninth Army, which on 29 September began moving eastward from Brittany to take over a sector between the First and Third Armies in the middle of the 12th Army Group.

As for the 6th Army Group, the 22 September conference specified that Devers, with his separate line of communications north from the Mediterranean, could continue his offensive toward Strasbourg as well as his efforts to push through the Belfort Gap. Although Eisenhower still considered that the 6th Army Group's primary mission was to protect the 12th Army Group's southern flank, the conferees recognized that a rapid Seventh Army drive to Strasbourg on the Rhine would best satisfy that requirement.

During the conference Devers reit-

---

[1] Planning material in this section derives largely from Pogue, *The Supreme Command*, ch. 16; Cole, *The Lorraine Campaign*, pp. 257–59; MacDonald, *The Siegfried Line Campaign*, chs. 6, 8–9; Devers Diary, 21–22 Sep 44; Seventh Army Diary, 21–23 Sep 44; 12th Army Gp LI 9, 25 Sep 44; Martin Blumenson, ed., *The Patton Papers, 1940–1945* (Boston: Houghton Mifflin, 1974), pp. 552–57.

erated his request for another U.S. corps for the Seventh Army and specifically asked for the Third Army's two-division XV Corps, which was operating just north of the 6th Army Group and opposite the Saverne Gap. Noting that his army group could easily support both the XV Corps and at least one more division for that corps, over its existing line of communications from the south, he pointed out that such a transfer of logistical responsibility would considerably ease the burden on Eisenhower's northern supply system and would also allow Bradley to narrow the 12th Army Group's wide front.

At the time, Devers' proposals were especially appealing to the harried SHAEF tactical and logistical planners. Thus, after some consideration of alternatives, Eisenhower, on 26 September, decided to transfer the XV Corps to the 6th Army Group on the 29th and to add a third division to the corps sometime in October. He also decided that three more American divisions, which had been scheduled to join the 12th Army Group after landing in northern France, were to be diverted to Marseille for the 6th Army Group. All told, six divisions either in or scheduled to join Bradley's 12th Army Group would be transferred to the 6th Army Group during September and October. However, Eisenhower informed Devers that these would be the last transfers of this nature, and he apparently did not expect them to change the role of the 6th Army Group in future Allied operations.[2]

Although General Bradley could hardly view the loss of six divisions to the 6th Army Group with pleasure, he saw the logistical advantages involved in the immediate transfer of the XV Corps to Devers' command. Patton, however, was less complacent and, upon learning of the negotiations regarding his corps, told Bradley that "if Jake Devers gets the XV Corps, I hope his plan goes sour."[3] When the transfer was formally announced, Patton wrote "May God rot his guts" in his diary. But the armored commander's colorful remarks often obscured his more serious side. Patton was obviously content to let the 6th Army Group's infantry handle the fighting in the Vosges and was more concerned over the decision to halt the forward motion of his own army in favor of continuing Montgomery's offensive in the north.

A Change in Command

On 29 September 1944, control of the XV Corps officially passed to the 6th Army Group and the Seventh Army. Patch thus gained a second corps with a total effective strength of approximately 50,500 troops. The main maneuver elements were the 79th Infantry Division, with about 17,390 troops including attachments; the French 2d Armored Division, with roughly 15,435 troops including attachments; and the 106th Cavalry

---

[2] Additional details concerning the results of the 22 September conference come from the following: HQ, 6th Army Group, "A History of the Sixth Army

Group" (ca. June 1945), pp. 14–16 (hereafter cited as "Hist, 6th Army Gp"); Rad, B–16654, 6th Army Gp to SHAEF, 25 Sep 44; Rad, SHAEF Fwd–15934, SHAEF to 6th Army Gp et al., 26 Sep 44; 12th Army Gp LI 9, 25 Sep 44.

[3] Blumenson, *The Patton Papers, II, 1940–1945,* p. 553.

Group, consisting of the 106th and 121st Cavalry Squadrons and the 813th Tank Destroyer Battalion. Corps troops, exclusive of the two divisions and their attachments, numbered around 17,680. More important, the principal commanders in the XV Corps had earned excellent reputations in the fighting from Normandy to the Moselle. The XV Corps commander, General Haislip, and the commander of the 79th Division, Maj. Gen. Ira T. Wyche, had both done well under Patton's demanding eyes; and the head of the French 2d Armored Division, Maj. Gen. Jacques Leclerc,[4] was considered by most American leaders to be one of the finest tank commanders in the Allied army. Haislip, a West Point contemporary of both Patton and Patch, had commanded the XV Corps since February 1943, bringing it through the Desert Training Center in the southwestern United States and then, via Northern Ireland and England, to Normandy and through northern France. In the process he had put together a corps staff and supporting organization that would rival Truscott's VI Corps in excellence. Another plus was Haislip's close relationship with the sometimes difficult Leclerc, who was a close associate of de Gaulle and a long-time veteran of the Free French military forces. Although the French armored division commander's temper rivaled that of de Lattre, his experience and expertise would prove invaluable in the coming battles.

The acquisition, despite General Devers' enthusiasm and optimism, was not without its problems. Like the VI

MAJ. GEN. WADE H. HAISLIP

Corps, the XV Corps was exhausted, and its logistical situation was even worse than that of de Lattre's French units in the south. After over one hundred days of combat and pursuit, the infantry units of the 79th Division were tired, and the division was short many items of supply and equipment. All three infantry regiments were well below their authorized strength of 3,348: the 313th by about 575 troops, the 314th by 360, and 315th by 600. The division's artillery battalions were short of well-trained personnel and ammunition as well. After visiting the 79th, General Devers estimated that Wyche's command needed at least two weeks out of the line for rest and replenishment of both personnel and

---

[4] *Nom de guerre* of the Vicomte Philippe Francois Marie de Hauteclocque.

supplies.[5] For the moment, however, the unit could not be withdrawn from its current operation.

The 2d French Armored Division was hardly in better shape. Reviewing the division's status on 28 September, General Leclerc pointed out that the division was operating largely with equipment issued in North Africa over a year ago.[6] The division's 4,000-odd vehicles were in need of thorough overhaul, without which maintenance problems would soon become unmanageable. Moreover, much of the nearly twenty-mile front that the division was currently holding north of Rambervillers was rough, wooded, and ill-suited to armored operations, especially in wet weather. Such terrain, Leclerc pointed out, required strong infantry forces; his unit, organized along the standard lines of a U.S. armored division, had only the three armored infantry battalions and could not be expected to hold the same frontage that an infantry division with nine infantry battalions could. In addition, the division's armored infantry companies were down to about eighty effectives, approximately one-third of their authorized strength. Leclerc therefore requested that his defensive sector be reduced as soon as possible.

Although Haislip accepted Leclerc's evaluation, neither he nor Patch had any infantry to spare. The 79th Infantry was fully occupied in the northern sector of the XV Corps' front, and all of Truscott's infantry was committed

in the Vosges. He could only hope that German inactivity would allow Leclerc to pull his units out of the line, one by one, for rest and maintenance.

Meanwhile, Haislip struggled to remedy his own logistical problems. Beginning on 29 September, the Seventh Army started to provide the XV Corps with some supplies, notably gasoline and ammunition, which alleviated the corps' most urgent requirements. Despite Devers' promises, however, it was not until the third week of October that rail deliveries at the Seventh Army's main supply centers, established in and around Epinal, were able to meet all the army's needs, including those of the XV Corps.

With the transfer, the 6th Army Group also became responsible for carrying out tactical missions already assigned to Haislip's corps. Devers and Patch clearly understood that these missions included securing the Luneville area and continuing to protect the right, or southern, flank of the Third Army—both of which required the XV Corps' 79th Division to continue clearing the area east of Luneville. Furthermore, supplementary Seventh Army orders specified that Haislip's corps was ultimately to seize Sarrebourg, about twenty-seven miles beyond Luneville and some ten miles short of the Saverne Gap, and in its southern sector, to assist VI Corps units in capturing and securing Rambervillers. For these operations the boundaries of the XV Corps were virtually unchanged. In the north, its border with the Third Army's XII Corps followed the southern bank of the Rhine-Marne Canal to Heming,

---

[5] Devers Diary, 1 Oct 44.

[6] General Leclerc's views derive from a document entitled "General Leclerc's Opinion on the Possibilities Offered to the 2d French Armored Division in a Defensive Situation and in the Present Zone of Operations," in XV Corps G–3 Jnl File, 28 Sep 44.

GENERAL LECLERC *(in jeep)* AND STAFF AT RAMBOUILLET

and from there continued northeast along Route N–4 to Sarrebourg; in the south its boundary with Truscott's VI Corps followed a line between Rambervillers and Baccarat. Within these confines Haislip would fight his most notable battles during the coming months.[7]

VI Corps Attacks (26–30 September)

On 26 September Truscott resumed the VI Corps' drive to the northeast, with the 45th Division on the left pushing out of its bridgehead at Epinal *(Map 16)*. At the time, the division's sector closely corresponded to the area defended by the German

LXVI Corps, and, in fact, the effective combat strength of the defending corps was about the same as the attacking American division. But with the German defenders pulling back on Wiese's orders and with the terrain being generally open and rolling farmland, the 45th had little trouble advancing. The 157th regiment, with elements of the XV Corps' French 2d Armored Division on its left, covered the fifteen miles to Rambervillers by the 29th against scattered resistance and found that the Germans were beginning to pull back even farther east toward Baccarat. South of the 157th, the 45th Division's 180th and 179th Infantry had a tougher time, especially in the slopes and woods west of Bruyeres, but managed to reach the

[7] Seventh Army FO 6, 29 Sep 44.

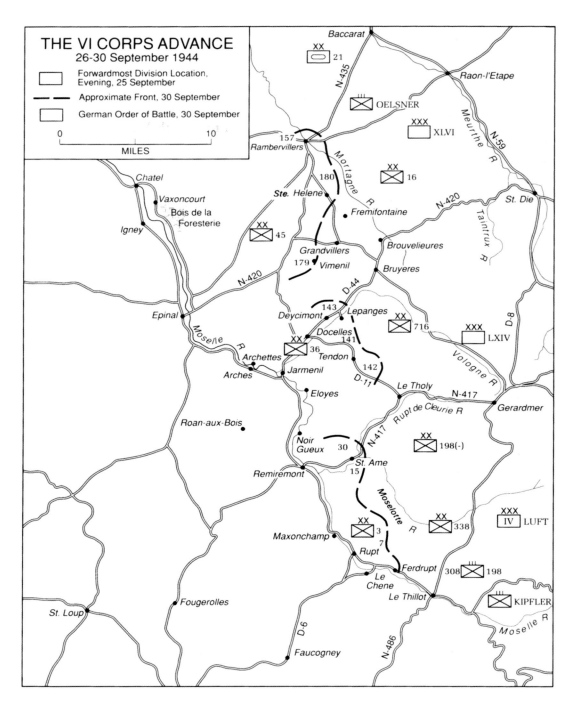

THE VI CORPS ADVANCE
26–30 September 1944

☐ Forwardmost Division Location, Evening, 25 September

▬▬ Approximate Front, 30 September

☐ German Order of Battle, 30 September

0 ——————————————— 10
MILES

Baccarat

XX
21

Raon-l'Etape

N-435

⊠ OELSNER

XXX
XLVI

N-59

Meurthe R

157
Rambervillers

180

XX
16

N-420

St. Die

Ste. Helene

Fremifontaine

Taintrux R

Chatel

Vaxoncourt

Bois de la
Foresterie

Igney

XX
45

Grandvillers

179 Vimenil

Brouvelieures

Bruyeres

N-420

D-44

143

Lepanges

D-8

Deycimont

XX
716

XXX
LXIV

Epinal

Docelles
141

Moselle R

XX
36

Tendon

142

D-11

Vologne R

Archettes

Jarmenil

Le Tholy

N-417

Arches

Eloyes

Rupt de Cleurie R

Gerardmer

Roan-aux-Bois

Noir
Gueux   30

N-417

XX
198(-)

St. Ame

15

Remiremont

Moselotte R

XX
338

XXX
IV LUFT

Maxonchamp

XX
3
7

Rupt

Ferdrupt

308 ⊠ 198

Le
Chene

Le Thillot

⊠ KIPFLER

Fougerolles

Moselle R

St. Loup

D-6

N-486

Faucogney

MAP 16   This map is printed in full color at the back of the book, following the Index.

Ste. Helene–Vimenil area by the 29th abreast of one another. The month thus ended with all three of the 45th Division's regiments on a north-south line below Rambervillers facing the Vosges Mountains.

In the middle and southern sectors of the VI Corps' offensive, the progress of the 36th and 3d Divisions through the Vosges foothills was much slower. Aiming directly for Bruyeres, the 36th Division's 143d Infantry took two days to break through units of the *716th Division* defending the area west of Tendon, while the 142d, with the 141st securing its right flank, did little better against elements of the *198th Division* to the south. On the 27th the 142d managed to advance over the Tendon–Le Tholy road, Route D–11, the main lateral German communications line in the region; and on the 28th the 141st regiment, relieved of its flank security mission by units of the 3d Division, moved in between the 143d and 142d regiments at Tendon for a concerted push on Bruyeres. But the prognosis for a rapid breakthrough was poor. The terrain was now channeling the 36th Division's upward advance into narrow, easily defensible corridors where the Germans were attempting to concentrate their defensive strength.

South of the 36th, the 3d Division found itself in a similar situation. There O'Daniel had finally brought the 30th regiment as far as Rupt on the Moselle, allowing the 15th and 7th to begin moving into the Vosges east of the river on 27 September, but leaving the area south of Rupt under German control. Once inside the Vosges, the experienced 3d Division infantrymen also found the going tough. Although the attacking units tried to bypass

German defenses on the roads to Gerardmer by side-stepping behind the 141st regiment in the St. Ame region and striking northeast toward Le Tholy, the results were the same. Thus by the end of September Truscott's forces in the north had easily reached Phase Line IV, but those in the center and south, the units that had actually begun moving into the mountains, were hardly beyond Phase Line II. Obviously a quick thrust over the Vosges was unlikely, and Devers and Patch became even more convinced that their strength might be better used reducing the German defenses in the Saverne Gap area north of the High Vosges.

XV Corps Before the Saverne Gap (25–30 September)

By 25 September General Patton, the Third Army commander, had already set in motion a XV Corps operation that was to continue well after the corps had been transferred to the 6th Army Group. News that the Third Army would have to go on the defensive had aroused Patton's innate opportunism, and he had prevailed upon General Bradley to permit the Third Army to undertake some "local" operations to straighten out his lines, securing better defensive terrain and better positions from which to launch future Third Army offensives. In this process, Patton wanted Haislip's XV Corps to expand its control of Luneville, a railroad and highway hub close to the confluence of the Meurthe and Vezouse rivers and some eighteen miles north of Rambervillers (*Map 17*).

Although elements of the Third Army's XII Corps had first entered

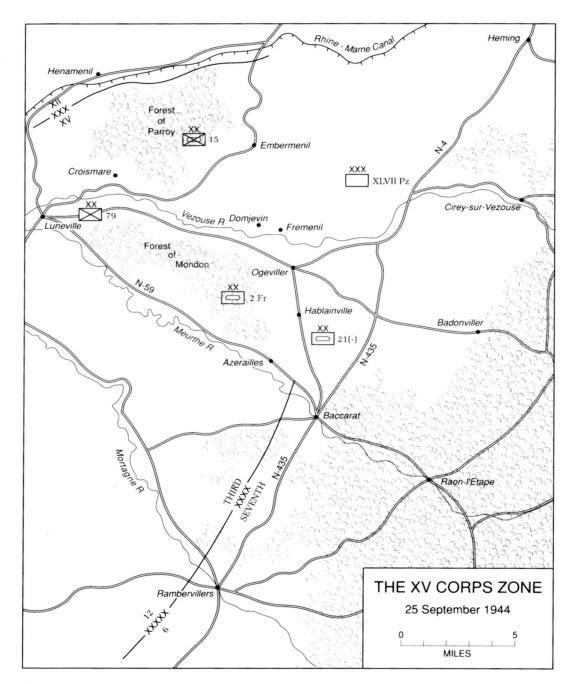

Rhine - Marne Canal

Heming

Henamenil

XII
XXX
XV

Forest
of
Parroy

XX
15

Embermenil

N-4

XXX
XLVII Pz

Cirey-sur-Vezouse

Croismare

XX
79

Vezouse R

Domjevin

Fremenil

Luneville

Forest
of
Mondon

Ogeviller

N-59

XX
2 Fr

Hablainville

Badonviller

Meurthe R

XX
21(-)

N-435

Azerailles

THIRD
XXXX
SEVENTH

N-435

Baccarat

Mortagne R

Raon-l'Etape

Rambervillers

12
XXXXX
6

THE XV CORPS ZONE

25 September 1944

0   5

MILES

MAP 17   This map is printed in full color at the back of the book, following the Index.

Luneville on 16 September, they had been unable to clear the city completely by the 20th when Haislip's XV Corps took over the sector. Haislip immediately tasked Wyche's 79th Division with rooting out the last German defenders and securing two thickly wooded areas to the east, the Parroy and Mondon forests. The two forests flanked the main roads to Sarrebourg, providing cover and concealment for German forces guarding the approaches to the Saverne Gap, and would have to be cleared before the XV Corps could move farther east.

While the 79th Division's 315th regiment mopped up the Luneville area, Wyche's other two regiments, the 313th and 314th Infantry, moved into the Mondon forest, sweeping through most of the woods by 23 September. Then, while Leclerc's French units finished policing the light German resistance at the southern edge of the forest, all three 79th Division infantry regiments moved up to forward assembly areas on the southern bank of the Vezouse River and prepared to move into the Parroy forest on the 25th.[8]

The German Situation in the Luneville Sector

As the 79th Division massed on the Vezouse River, General Balck, the *Army Group G* commander, was facing a rapidly deteriorating situation.[9] On his northern wing, from Luxembourg to Vic-sur-Seille, fourteen miles north of Luneville, *Army Group G's First Army* was heavily engaged across most of its 75-mile-wide front. Along *Army Group G's* center, the *Fifth Panzer Army*, with a thirty-mile front from Vic-sur-Seille to Rambervillers, had been roughly handled by Patton's Third Army and was currently capable of little more than defending in place. South of Rambervillers, the *Nineteenth Army* continued to occupy its ninety-mile front to the Swiss border, but was having increasing problems holding back the 6th Army Group as the Seventh and First French Armies brought more of their forces into the front lines. However, for Balck, a penetration of *Army Group G's* center presented the gravest danger: a drive through the Saverne Gap could split his armies, isolating the forces in the High Vosges; a drive north of Saverne into the Saar industrial basin would have about the same military effect but would also severely damage Germany's strategic war-making capabilities. From his perspective then, Truscott's advance into the Vosges or de Lattre's demonstrations outside of the Belfort Gap were relatively unimportant.

Balck viewed the center of his defensive line with great concern. The Rhine-Marne Canal, running east and west about six miles north of Luneville and just off the northern edge of the Forest of Parroy, divided the *Fifth Panzer Army's* sector into two parts: *LVIII Panzer Corps* operating north of the canal and *XLVII Panzer Corps* to

---

[8] For details on the Mondon forest operation, see Cole, *The Lorraine Campaign*, pp. 233–35.

[9] German material in this chapter is based largely on John W. Mosenthal, "The Establishment of a Continuous Defensive Front by *Army Group G*, 15 September–1 October 1944," CMH MS R–68; and ibid., "The Battle for the Foret de Parroy, 28 September–17 October 1944," CMH MS R–74 (both incorporated into von Luttichau, "German Operations," as chs. 17 and 18). See also Cole, *The Lorraine Campaign*, chs. 4 and 5.

the south. (The canal also marked the boundary between the Third Army's XII and XV Corps.) Since 12 September the *Fifth Panzer Army,* under General von Manteuffel, had been engaged in a series of costly armored counterattacks against the Third Army's right flank. Although these operations had slowed Patton's advance, they had also virtually decimated the armor available to von Manteuffel. As of 25 September both the *Fifth Panzer Army* and its two corps were panzer in name only. At the time, the *LVIII Panzer Corps* was continuing its fruitless counterattacks against the XII Corps, but the *XLVII Panzer Corps* had abandoned its attempts to recapture Luneville on the 23d, apparently when General Balck learned from *OKW* that the *108th Panzer Brigade,* until then slated for commitment in the Luneville sector, was to be transferred farther north. This unexpected loss of armor may have also influenced the German decision to abandon the Forest of Mondon and to withdraw the *XLVII Panzer Corps'* right flank north across the Vezouse River.

The new line that Lt. Gen. Heinrich Freiherr von Luettwitz, commanding the *XLVII Panzer Corps,* was to hold originated at Henamenil, on the Rhine-Marne Canal about six miles northeast of Luneville, passed south across the western face of the Forest of Parroy to the north bank of the Vezouse near Croismare, and then ran southeast along the Vezouse about seven miles to the vicinity of Fremenil. Here the defenses—which were hasty in nature—crossed back over the Vezouse and followed a ridge line south past Ogeviller and

Hablainville for about seven miles to Baccarat. The corps also maintained a salient at Azerailles, three miles northwest of Baccarat, to block Route N–59, leading southeast from Luneville. For the moment Balck and von Manteuffel decided to leave the defensive dispositions of the *Fifth Panzer Army* unchanged in the south, from Baccarat to Rambervillers, but both commanders remained concerned about the possibility of a VI Corps drive on the Saverne Gap from the vicinity of Rambervillers.[10]

Defending the new line from the Rhine-Marne Canal to Fremenil was the responsibility of the *15th Panzer Grenadier Division.* The rest of von Luettwitz's sector was held by the virtually tankless *21st Panzer Division*; *Group Oelsner,* a provisional infantry regiment; and part of the *113th Panzer Brigade.* Some troops of the *16th Division* were also in the *XLVII Panzer Corps'* area, while in reserve was the *112th Panzer Brigade,* reduced to less than ten tanks.[11] In case of a dire emergency, General von Luettwitz could call on several fortress battalions digging in along forward *Weststellung* positions about fifteen miles east of Luneville.

Understrength to begin with, the *15th Panzer Grenadier Division* also

---

[10] Baccarat was also on the army boundary, with Route N–435, which ran north-northeast from Rambervillers to Baccarat, marking the intra-army border.

[11] Most of the rebuilding *16th Division* was in the sector of *LXVI Corps, Nineteenth Army,* to the south of *XLVII Panzer Corps.* But during the latter part of September, units and parts of units shifted rapidly back and forth between the zones of the *XLVII* and *LVIII Panzer Corps* and other areas, making an accurate order of battle for the *Fifth Panzer Army* difficult to establish.

lacked some of its organic units.[12] For example, a regimental headquarters, a panzer grenadier battalion, an anti-tank company, and a battery of artillery were deployed well to the north with the *First Army,* while a battalion of artillery and a tank company were operating north of the Rhine-Marne Canal with the *LVIII Panzer Corps.* Shortages were especially acute in the infantry (panzer grenadier) elements, where most battalions had fewer than 350 troops, less than half their authorized strength. On the other hand, von Luettwitz had been able to beef up the division with several provisional forces—units with limited offensive capabilities, but adequate for defense. In the Parroy forest the division had deployed the *1st* and *3d Battalions,* of its *104th Panzer Grenadier Regiment; Blocking Detachment Berkenhoff,* an infantry battalion largely made up of *Luftwaffe* personnel; seven to ten tanks or self-propelled assault guns; and more mortars, artillery, and antitank pieces. Additional artillery emplaced on rising ground east of the woods had likely targets within the forest carefully registered. Effective German infantry strength in the forest was initially about 1,200, with total troop strength probably less than 2,000.

The Forest of Parroy

Well before the XII Corps entered Luneville on 16 September, the *Fifth Panzer Army* had established bases and depots deep in the Forest of Parroy, using its cover as an assembly area

for troops and armor mounting counterattacks against the Third Army's right flank. Subsequently, the forest had served the same purpose during German attempts to recapture Luneville, and German artillery hidden in the forest had continued to harass XV Corps' positions and lines of communication in the Luneville area. Von Luettwitz knew he would have to make a stand in the forest, not only to hold back American progress toward the *Weststellung* and the Saverne Gap, but also to protect the southern flank of the *LVIII Panzer Corps* as the latter continued its armored counterattacks in the sector north of the Rhine-Marne Canal.

Roughly ovoid in shape, the Forest of Parroy extends about six miles west to east and over four miles north to south, covering an area of nearly thirty square miles (*Map 18*). Much of the forest area is flat, but thickly wooded with mostly secondary growth of hardwoods, a few stands of older, bigger timber, and an occasional patch of conifers. Unlike most European forests, the Parroy was also characterized by a thick undergrowth that drastically limited observation and visibility. One third-class east-west route, the Haut de la Fait Road, passed through the center of the forest where it bisected the equally poor north-south Bossupre Road. In addition, the forest was crisscrossed with fire lanes, logging tracks, and beds of abandoned narrow-gauge railroads of World War I vintage, most of which could accommodate armored vehicles, but on a strictly one-way basis. Other features included deteriorated trenches and minor defensive installations dating back to World

---

[12] As of about 25 September the division had an authorized strength of 16,140, but an on-duty strength of approximately 11,930.

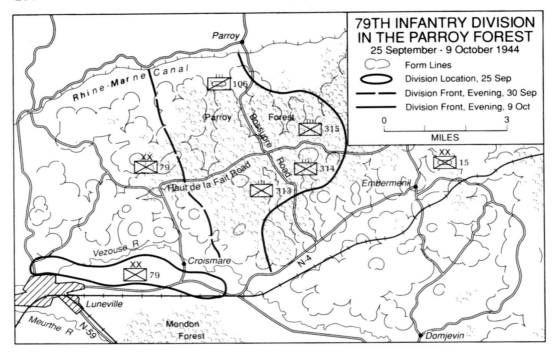

**79TH INFANTRY DIVISION
IN THE PARROY FOREST**
25 September - 9 October 1944

Form Lines
Division Location, 25 Sep
Division Front, Evening, 30 Sep
Division Front, Evening, 9 Oct

0   3
MILES

MAP 18   This map is printed in full color at the back of the book, following the Index.

War I. To these the defenders had
added mines, barbed wire, road and
trail blocks, new trenches, and
timber-roofed dugouts; while the
poor September weather produced
cold and often torrential rains, fog
and mist, mud, and swampy spots—all
of which made the Forest of Parroy
an unpleasant place in which to
travel, let alone fight a pitched battle.

In the fluid combat conditions that
had existed earlier in September
1944, the bulk of XV Corps might
well have bypassed the Forest of
Parroy, leaving follow-up forces to
surround, isolate, and clear any Germans that remained. But with the
limits imposed on offensive operations, General Patton decided to
secure the area by force in order to

acquire better positions for subsequent XV Corps attacks. If undisturbed, German infantry, artillery,
and armor in the forest could control
the main highway (N-4) leading to
Sarrebourg and the Saverne Gap, severely hampering a rapid advance
eastward.

General Wyche, with Haislip's approval, had originally planned a frontal attack from the west combined
with a single envelopment on the east
side of the forest. After meeting little
German opposition in the Mondon
forest, the two commanders expected
the same here, hoping that the 106th
Cavalry Group and one infantry regiment of the 79th Division could
sweep through the forest, while an armored task force of the French 2d Ar-

PARROY FOREST

mored Division struck northeast across the Vezouse River to isolate the woods on the east. The operation was to begin on 25 September after heavy Allied air strikes.

From the start, little went according to plan. Poor flying weather forced postponement of the air strikes, and Wyche was unable to start his attack until the 25th. In the interim, Leclerc had sent a small force over the Vezouse, but German artillery fire broke up the French infantry formations and the soggy ground confined the French armor to the roads, leading Leclerc to pull his units south, back across the river, before the 79th Division had even begun its assault into the forest.

Continued inclement weather caused Wyche to postpone air and ground attacks on the 26th and 27th, and finally Haislip decided to relieve Leclerc's division of its part of the operation and leave the entire task to Wyche. Meanwhile, American patrols into the forest had discovered that the Germans were preparing to defend the woods in strength. Accordingly, Wyche revised his plans, deciding to send two infantry regiments into the forest from the west while the cavalry group screened the area to the north along the Rhine-Marne Canal. Abandoning the whole concept of isolating the forest on the east, both Haislip and Wyche probably felt that a less complex approach—concentrating their superior artillery and infantry resources in one sector—was the best solution considering the terrain and weather.

The American attack into the Parroy forest finally began on 28 September, one day before the XV Corps was to pass to 6th Army Group control. The air attack began at 1400 followed by the ground assault of the 313th and 315th Infantry at 1630 that afternoon. However, of the 288 bombers and fighter-bombers scheduled to participate in the preparatory strikes, only 37 actually arrived, again because of poor flying conditions; and the results of the 37-plane attack against a target covering some thirty square miles were negligible. In addition, the two-hour interval between the last air strikes and the beginning of the 79th Division's ground attack gave the Germans ample time to recover from whatever shock effect the limited bombardment may have had. As a result the 79th Division infantrymen found themselves locked in a bitter struggle with the German defenders as soon as they began to penetrate the forest.

Even as the 79th Division began its attack, General Balck was again reassessing the situation in the area. North of the Rhine-Marne Canal the LVIII Panzer Corps' counterattacks had ground to a halt with more heavy losses in German armor and infantry. With no reinforcements, Balck instructed the Fifth Panzer Army to go on the defensive all across its front. To protect the Saverne Gap, he regarded both the Forest of Parroy and the Rambervillers sector as critical. Be-

lieving the latter to be more vulnerable, however, he instructed von Manteuffel and Wiese on the 29th to give defensive priority to the Rambervillers area, where the French 2d Armored Division and the VI Corps' 45th Infantry Division threatened the boundary between the two armies. To assist von Manteuffel in this task, he moved the boundary of the Fifth Panzer Army eleven miles south of Rambervillers, making the XLVII Panzer Corps responsible for the area. Von Manteuffel, in turn, moved his internal corps boundary south, allowing the LVIII Panzer Corps, under Lt. Gen. Walter Krueger, to direct the defense of the Parroy forest, while the XLVII Panzer Corps concentrated its efforts in the Rambervillers-Baccarat region.

Simultaneously Balck and von Manteuffel reorganized the Fifth Panzer Army in order to simplify command and control problems, consolidating battered units and strengthening existing divisions. In the process, the 11th Panzer Division absorbed what was left of the 111th Panzer Brigade; the 21st Panzer Division took over the 112th Panzer Brigade (less a battalion of the 112th Panzer Grenadier Regiment, which went to the 16th Infantry Division); and the hard-hit 113th Panzer Brigade was incorporated into the 15th Panzer Grenadier Division. This left Army Group G with only one panzer brigade in reserve, the 106th, which had not yet arrived from the First Army's area, and Balck and von Manteuffel made tentative plans to commit this brigade in the Rambervillers area.

Balck ended the month of September by admonishing his three army commanders not to surrender any ground "voluntarily." Every penetration of the forward lines was to be restored by an immediate counterattack. Too often, Balck informed them, reserve forces had been frittered away by premature commitments to weak points and to sections of the front only presumably threatened. In the future, all withdrawals would need his personal approval and would only be authorized if they improved current defensive positions. The Hitler order still stood—to hold west of the *Weststellung* in order to allow completion and garrisoning of fortifications there. The defense of the Parroy forest would represent the first test of Balck's orders.

The Forest and the Fight

During these deliberations the U.S. 79th Division and the German *15th Panzer Grenadier Division* had been battling throughout the western section of the Parroy forest. The 79th had attacked from the west with two regiments abreast—the 315th Infantry north of the Fait Road and the 313th Infantry to the south. Both regiments made painfully slow progress against determined German resistance, and, by evening on the 30th, the attacking infantry had penetrated scarcely over a mile into the dense forest. During this period the fighting quickly fell into a pattern that continued throughout the battle. Abandoning any attempt at a linear defense, the Germans maintained a thin screening line opposite the Allied advance and concentrated their troops at various strongpoints. By day, German forward artillery observers, hidden in prepared positions, called down predetermined artillery or mortar barrages on advancing American troops; and the concentrations were often followed by small infantry-armored counterattacks moving at an oblique angle down one of the firebreaks or dirt tracks. During the night, smaller German infantry patrols attempted to infiltrate the flanks and rear of the attacking American forces, disorganizing them and interfering with resupply efforts. Often when one American unit was forced back, the others stopped their forward progress to avoid exposing their flanks to further German attacks. Poor visibility in the forest compounded American command and control problems, and the frequent German counterattacks put the attackers on the defensive much of the time. Again and again disorganized American units were forced to fall back, reorganize, and launch counterattacks of their own to regain lost ground.

On 1 October both sides sent reinforcements into the battle. The *LVIII Panzer Corps* deployed two battalions of the *113th Panzer Grenadier Regiment, 113th Panzer Brigade*, into the forest accompanied by additional armor. On the American side, Wyche sent his third infantry regiment, the 314th, into the fray. The division commander wanted the 314th Infantry to move into the forest from the south, just east of the main penetration, and push against the flank of the defenders facing the 313th Infantry, allowing that regiment to drop back in a reserve role.

Although well executed, the maneuver did not seem to shake loose the German defenses. The 79th Division's progress remained painfully slow and it was not until 3 October that the last battalion of the 313th Infantry was relieved. On the same day the Germans once again reinforced their troops in the forest, this time with the *2d Battalion* of the *104th Panzer Grenadier Regiment, 15th Panzer Grenadier Division,* and a few more tanks and self-propelled guns. Wyche, meanwhile, with Haislip's approval, shortened the front line of the 315th Infantry by making the 106th Cavalry Group responsible for the northern part of the American advance and allowing the 315th to concentrate its forces just above the Fait Road. Between 4 and 6 October, American infantry units renewed their attacks, pushing eastward through the middle of the forest and overrunning several German strong-points near the juncture of the Fait and Bossupre roads. The Germans then counterattacked with the understrength *11th Panzer Reconnaissance Battalion* (from the *11th Panzer Division*), forcing elements of the 315th Infantry back from the crossroads. But elsewhere the Americans held their ground. Temporarily exhausted, both sides spent 7 and 8 October patrolling, reorganizing, and resupplying their forces and, in the American camp, preparing to resume the offensive on the morning of the 9th.

The new attack began with a diversionary demonstration at daybreak by the 1st Battalion, 313th Infantry, reinforced with tanks, south of the forest. Evidently, the ruse met with some success, for the Germans shelled the roads along the Vezouse throughout the morning and provided little direct fire support to their troops in the Parroy forest. There XV Corps and 79th Division artillery laid down the heaviest preparatory barrage of the entire operation, clearing the way for the main attack which began at 0650, with ample artillery support on call. Initially two battalions of the 315th Infantry drove eastward north of the Fait Road, while the 3d Battalion, 315th Infantry, and the 2d Battalion, 314th Infantry, concentrated against the German strongpoint at the central crossroads, finally overrunning that position about 1800. Meanwhile, two battalions of the 313th Infantry moved into the line south of the 2d Battalion, 314th Infantry, and pushed eastward south of the crossroads; still farther south the rest of the 314th Infantry aggressively patrolled through the southern third of the forest. At dusk the 79th Division's center had advanced only a mile and a half beyond the central crossroads, but the infantry commanders hopefully noted that German resistance was beginning to diminish.

During the evening of 9 October Krueger outlined the status of his forces to von Manteuffel and reported that he was unable to restore the situation with the forces available. The loss of the interior roads and the central strongpoints made further defensive efforts costly, especially if the Americans began to threaten the *15th Panzer Grenadier Division's* routes of withdrawal. The only uncommitted forces were two battalions (with an aggregate strength of about 550 troops) of the division's *115th Panzer Grenadier Regiment* and two fortress battalions,[13] but using these units would deprive the defenders of their

---

[13] The *1416th Fortress Infantry Battalion* and the *51st Fortress Machine Gun Battalion.*

last reserves and leave no maneuver units for operations east of the forest. Accordingly, the *LVIII Panzer Corps* commander requested permission to withdraw from the Parroy forest to a new defensive line, and the *Fifth Panzer Army* and *Army Group G* had no choice but to approve the request.

Except for some rear-guard detachments, the main body of German troops in the forest withdrew during the night of 9–10 October to a new defensive line several miles east of the woods, tying in with the *XLVII Panzer Corps' 21st Panzer Division* at Domjevin, with the intercorps boundary later moving a few miles south to Ogeviller. German losses during the fight for the Forest of Parroy, 28 September through 9 October, numbered approximately 125 men killed, 350 wounded, over 700 missing (most of them taken prisoner), and about 50 evacuated for various sicknesses.[14] More significant, however, they had now lost their principal forward defensive position along the approaches to the Saverne Gap.

More Reorganizations

During 11 and 12 October, the 79th Division and the 106th Cavalry Group cleared the remainder of the forest and pushed on to the new German defensive lines to the east. A final advance by all the 79th's regiments on the 13th managed to secure

Embermenil, in the center of the German line, but elsewhere the division made only limited progress in the face of heavy German artillery and mortar fire and flooded ground. Thereafter the dispositions of the division remained essentially unchanged.

The subsequent inactivity of the XV Corps was due in part to the redeployment of many Third Army support units, which had to be returned by the 15th. At the request of General Devers, Bradley agreed to allow Haislip to retain two heavy field artillery battalions, but the XV Corps lost four field artillery battalions, four antiaircraft gun battalions, a three-battalion engineer combat group, a tank destroyer battalion, and some lesser units, forcing Haislip to pause while he redistributed his remaining support forces.

On the German side *Army Group B* was once again to be strengthened at the expense of *Army Group G*, not only to satisfy *Army Group B*'s immediate requirements, but also in preparation for the Ardennes offensive scheduled for December.[15] The bulk of the *15th Panzer Grenadier Division* withdrew from its lines opposite the 79th Division during the night of 15–16 October, and on 17 October the sector passed to the control of the *553d Volksgrenadier Division*,[16] with an effec-

---

[14] The German casualty figures in the text are based on various figures given in Mosenthal, CMH MS R–74. A thorough search of 106th Cavalry Group, 79th Division, XV Corps, and Seventh Army files failed to produce any usable casualty figures for the 106th Cavalry Group and the 79th Division during the period 28 September through 9 October.

[15] For the planning and buildup for the Ardennes, see Hugh M. Cole, *The Ardennes: Battle of the Bulge*, United States Army in World War II (Washington, 1965), chs. 1–3.

[16] The German Army began forming *Volksgrenadier* ("people's grenadier") divisions in August and September 1944. The new divisions had a rather austere authorized strength of around 12,000 troops. Division artillery consisted of three instead of four battalions; there was no divisional antitank battalion;

tive infantry strength of no more than a few battalions. To bolster the division for its defensive mission, *Army Group G* reinforced it with the *1416th Fortress Infantry Battalion*, the *56th Fortress Machine Gun Battalion*, and the *42d Panzer Grenadier Replacement Battalion.*

Next, the *Fifth Panzer Army* headquarters passed to *Army Group B's* control on 16 October, leaving *Army Group G* with only two subordinate army commands, the *First* and the *Nineteenth.* The *First Army* assumed command of the *LVIII Panzer Corps* in the north, and the *Nineteenth Army* took control of the *XLVII Panzer Corps* in the south. A new boundary, separating the *First* and *Nineteenth Armies,* began at Ogeviller and ran northeast across the Vosges to pass a few miles north of Strasbourg. The *XLVII Panzer Corps'* attachment to the *Nineteenth Army* was short-lived, and one day later, on 17 September, *OB West* also transferred this headquarters to *Army Group B's* control, providing the *Nineteenth Army* with the *LXXXIX Corps* headquarters as a substitute.

Logistical problems, bad weather, and, apparently, slow intelligence analysis helped prevent the 79th Division from taking advantage of the German redeployments east of the Parroy forest. Moreover, the XV Corps was waiting for the 44th Infantry Division—the new third division that Eisenhower had promised Devers in September—to reach the front before the 79th Division resumed the offensive. The 44th Division, under the command of Maj. Gen. Robert L. Spragins, closed its assembly area near Luneville on 17 October and during the next few days took over 79th Division positions from the vicinity of Embermenil south to the Vezouse River, while the 79th concentrated on a narrower front for a new attack.

On 21 and 22 October the three regiments of the 79th Division, advancing abreast across a front of almost two and a half miles, gained nearly a mile and a half in a northeasterly direction from Embermenil, thus securing better defensive terrain as well as better observation of German positions. On the 23d the 44th Division started to relieve the 79th Division in place, which then began a much needed rest. Tragically, for General Patch, commanding the Seventh Army, the relief came two days too late. His son, Capt. Alexander M. Patch III, commanding Company C of the 315th Infantry, was killed by German mortar fire on 22 October, and the army commander was to feel the loss deeply for many months to come.

For the remainder of October the 44th Infantry Division played a rather static role, but one that prepared the new division for forthcoming offensive actions. Its activities were limited mostly to patrols and artillery duels, and little attempt was made to gain new ground. Elements of the 106th Cavalry Group maintained contact with Third Army units along the line

---

and service elements were greatly reduced. On the other hand the infantry elements, armed primarily with automatic weapons, had markedly more firepower than the infantry of standard divisions; furthermore, the infantry regiments and battalions of the *Volksgrenadier* divisions had their own organic antitank weapons. Most were built on the remnants of older divisions shattered during the earlier fighting in France or on the eastern front; for example, *553d Volksgrenadier Division* was formed around cadre and veterans of the *553d Infantry Division.*

of the Rhine-Marne Canal and undertook limited reconnaissance, but adopted a generally defensive attitude.

To the south, the French 2d Armored Division continued to rest and refit. From 30 September to 3 October, units of the division had supported the advance of the VI Corps' 45th Division to the Rambervillers area, culminating in several sharp engagements along the Rambervillers-Baccarat highway. On the 3d the French armor was relieved of its responsibilities in the zone by the VI Corps' 117th Cavalry Squadron, and, as planned, the division went on the defensive for the remainder of the month.

During this period the French division kept three of its four combat commands [17] in the line, rotating each

to the rear for sorely needed rest, rehabilitation, and vehicle maintenance. From 3 through 30 October the division lost approximately 35 men killed and 140 wounded, most of them as a result of German artillery or mortar fire.[18] As dusk came on the 30th, the division was preparing to launch an attack to seize Baccarat, an operation that once again would alarm the German high command and divert their attention from the more direct approaches to the Saverne Gap.

---

[17] Unlike other French and American armored divisions, the 2d French Armored Division normally operated with four rather than three combat commands. The fourth, CCR, was named after its commander, Col. Jean S. Remy, who in the division's administrative structure was also the commander of the division's organic reconnaissance squadron, the 1st Moroccan Spahis Regiment. CCR's basic organization consisted of the headquarters and one troop of the 1st Moroccan Spahis, an armored infantry company, a towed antitank company, a battery of armored field artillery, and a platoon of combat engineers. Other units were added as dictated by circumstances and missions. CCR was, in effect, a permanent reconnaissance-in-force organization, but could also be employed as a ready reserve if the tactical situation called for it.

[18] Total XV Corps casualties for the month of October, including those of the 2d French Armored Division, numbered about 365 men killed, 2,310 wounded, 165 missing, and 2,410 nonbattle. During the month XV Corps received 5,720 replacements or returnees, and the corps captured over 1,760 Germans.

CHAPTER XV

The Road to St. Die

At the beginning of October, the American commanders, Generals Devers, Patch, Truscott, and Haislip, realized that their personnel and supply problems made it impossible to launch a general offensive, even if approved by SHAEF. Before any major operations could be undertaken, their troops had to be rested, replacements brought up and trained, and supply stocks, especially ammunition and fuel, built up in the forward area. During this process, front-line infantry strength would have to be reduced by about one-third as infantry battalions were pulled out of the line for brief periods of rest and rehabilitation. For a while, no regiment could plan to have more than two of its three infantry battalions at the front at any one time. The expectation that the poor weather experienced in late September would only worsen during October made ammunition stockpiling even more necessary. Difficult flying conditions greatly reduced the amount of air support the ground troops could count on and increased the reliance on artillery and mortar fire.

Tactical considerations also militated against a hasty push to the east. All the roads from the Seventh

Army's base areas along the Moselle River led steadily upward into the thickly forested Vosges, terrain in which the Germans would continue to have every conceivable defensive advantage. The steep, wooded hills were rarely traversable by vehicles, even by the lighter American tanks and half-tracks, while the narrow mountain roads were easily interdicted; furthermore, heavy vegetation made it difficult to direct accurate artillery and mortar fire or to employ direct air support. The forests also tended to compartmentalize the battlefield, making it easy for advancing units to become widely separated and vulnerable to infiltration and enemy flanking attacks.

The VI Corps

On a larger scale, Truscott was increasingly concerned over the difficulty in securing a deep but narrow advance into the mountains. The VI Corps could not push very far east and northeast of Rambervillers without dangerously exposing its northern flank. To avoid such a situation, Patch and Truscott had hoped that Haislip's XV Corps would have been able to clear the Parroy forest rapidly and then begin a drive northeast of Rambervillers abreast of the VI Corps. The tenacious German defense of the Parroy forest, however, destroyed whatever ideas the two commanders may have entertained in that regard before October was a week old. As a result, the XV Corps was unable to launch any offensive operations in the southern sector of its zone, and the VI Corps was forced to commit sizable forces in the Rambervillers area throughout October in order to secure its northern flank.

On the VI Corps' right, or southern, flank, a similar situation prevailed. There the French II Corps had been stalled in the foothills of the Vosges, and the situation was further complicated by the diverging courses of the two Allied armies, the American Seventh moving northeast and the French First advancing east. Nevertheless, both Patch and Truscott were willing to take the risks that accompanied a unilateral VI Corps attack. Both regarded a complete cessation of offensive activity as extremely dangerous, giving the Germans too much time to build and man defenses throughout the Vosges as well as to rehabilitate their own depleted divisions.

Despite their tactical and logistical limitations, Patch and Truscott still favored a limited VI Corps offensive in October. While neither expected a quick breakthrough to Strasbourg, they believed that the city of St. Die was a reasonable objective. On the Meurthe River deep in the heart of the Vosges, St. Die was an industrial, road, rail, and communications center that VI Corps would have to seize if any drive northeast across the Vosges

was to succeed. Route N–59 and the principal trans-Vosges railroad came into St. Die from the north, through Luneville and Baccarat; Route N–420 and the railroad led northeast from St. Die through the Saales Pass, on the most direct route to Strasbourg; N–59 continued east from St. Die through the Ste. Marie Pass to Selestat, on the Alsatian plain between Strasbourg and Colmar; Route N–415 led south and then east through the Bonhomme Pass to Colmar; and Route D–8 branched off N–415 on its way south to Gerardmer, Route N–417, and the Schlucht Pass. Possession of the Meurthe River mountain town was thus vital to the Allied advance, and the Germans could be expected to defend it vigorously if allowed the time to reorganize and strengthen their forces.

VI Corps' most direct route to St. Die started at Jarmenil, on the Moselle about midway between Epinal and Remiremont. This axis followed the valley of the small Vologne River, passing through open, flat-to-rolling farmland dominated on the north and northwest by the relatively low, wooded hills and ridges of the Faite forest and on the south and east by higher, more rugged, forested terrain. Route N–59A and then Route D–44 led northeast along the Vologne about ten miles from Jarmenil to the small city of Bruyeres, a rail and road hub ringed by close-in, steep hills on the west, north, and east. From Bruyeres, Route N–420 went north about two and a half miles to Brouvelieures on the Mortagne River—here no more than a brook. Winding and hugging the slopes of heavily wooded hills, N–420 continued northeast about four miles to Les Rouges Eaux. Then the highway climbed and twisted through a dense coniferous forest to emerge in the valley of the Taintrux Creek about two and a half miles short of St. Die. The city itself lay on flat ground surrounded by wooded mountains and hills (some of the hills having a peculiar conical shape). The Meurthe River, flowing northwest through St. Die, was normally too slow to be much of an obstacle except in a few places where it ran between steep banks or manmade retaining walls.

While keeping his sights on St. Die, Truscott initially assigned the 45th and 36th Divisions the more limited goals of seizing the railroad and highway hubs of Bruyeres and Brouvelieures. Eagles' 45th was to make the main effort, striking for Brouvelieures and Bruyeres from the Rambervillers area, while Dahlquist's 36th, advancing from the south, was to keep the German frontal defenses occupied and ultimately assist in clearing Bruyeres.[1] The 45th Division's advance from Rambervillers would send it southeast, down over nine miles of forests and country roads along the southern side of the Mortagne River valley. To the south, the 36th Division would have to clear the Vologne River valley and route D–44 from Docelles to Bruyeres, a distance of about eight miles. The VI Corps attack to seize Bruyeres and Brouvelieures was to begin on 1 October, and Truscott hoped to have both objectives in hand by 8 October at the latest.

The German Defenses

The fall of Rambervillers in late September had again forced the Germans to rethink their defensive dispositions.[2] For some time the town had marked the boundary between *Army Group G*'s *Fifth Panzer Army,* which confronted the Third Army's XV and XII Corps, and the *Nineteenth Army,* which faced the Seventh Army's VI Corps and all of the First French Army. American XV and VI Corps operations in the Rambervillers sector had threatened to drive a wedge between the two German armies as early as 28 September; at that time the *Nineteenth Army*'s *LXVI Corps,* consisting largely of the rebuilding *16th Infantry Division,* lacked the strength to restore the situation. To consolidate command in the Rambervillers area, which he considered critical, General Balck of *Army Group G* had transferred control of *LXVI Corps* from the *Nineteenth Army* to the *Fifth Panzer Army.* But on the 30th, Balck had withdrawn the *LXVI Corps* headquarters from the front and passed control of the *16th Division* to the *XLVII Panzer Corps,* on the *Fifth Panzer Army*'s left, or southern, flank.[3] On the same day Balck also pushed the boundary between the *Fifth Panzer Army* and the *Nineteenth Army* south about eleven miles from Rambervillers to a northeast-southwest line passing just north of Bruyeres, a line that corresponded roughly to the

---

[1] The change in plans came in VI Corps Fld Msg 301200A Sep 44; previously Bruyeres had been the 36th Division's main objective.

[2] German information in this chapter is derived from von Luttichau, "German Operations," chs. 19–21.

[3] *LXVI Corps* headquarters took on a training mission in the vicinity of Colmar and on 6 October passed to the control of *Army Group B.*

boundary between the VI Corps' 45th and 36th Divisions.

Thus, at the beginning of October, the 2d French Armored Division of XV Corps and the 45th Infantry Division of VI Corps faced General von Luettwitz's *XLVII Panzer Corps, Fifth Panzer Army*, in the Rambervillers area. The panzer corps consisted (north to south) of the weak *21st Panzer Division; Group Oelsner*, a provisional infantry regiment made up of security troops, engineers, and *Luftwaffe* retreads, all soon to be incorporated into the *16th Division*; and the lamentable *16th Infantry Division* itself. The *21st Panzer Division* had 65 percent of its authorized strength of about 16,675 troops, but the unit had little punch left. Its *22d Panzer Regiment* was reduced to nine operational tanks, and the *125th* and *192d Panzer Grenadier Regiments* were down to about 50 percent of their authorized strengths. The division's only strong points were its high percentage of seasoned veterans and its rigorous training program for replacements. The *16th Infantry Division*, then being reorganized as a *volksgrenadier* division,[4] had an effective strength of about 5,575 ill-trained troops, and its three infantry regiments averaged about 35 percent of their authorized strength. The Germans rated the division as capable only of "limited defense."

Backing up von Luettwitz's front-line units were the fortress troops of *Group von Claer*, with a total strength of about 8,000 men. The group's principal components were *Regiment A/V*[5] and provisional *Regiment Baur*, each with five infantry battalions and some supporting artillery and antitank weapons. But von Luettwitz's control over *Group von Claer* was limited. The group's primary mission was to man *Weststellung* positions, and its troops could be employed in front-line combat only with the expressed permission of General Balck.

South of the Bruyeres–St. Die boundary between the *Fifth Panzer Army* and the *Nineteenth Army* stood the latter's *LXIV Corps*, the lines of which extended southward about twenty miles to Rupt-sur-Moselle. With the *716th Division* and the *198th Division* (less the *308th Grenadiers*) on line from north to south, the *LXIV Corps*, under Lt. Gen. Helmut Thumm, faced VI Corps' 36th Division as well as most of the 3d Division.[6]

General Wiese of *Nineteenth Army* had in reserve the small task force from the *11th Panzer Division* as well as the *103d Panzer Battalion*, just arriving at St. Die from the *First Army*'s sector. The *106th Panzer Brigade*, intended for the Belfort Gap, had not yet arrived from *First Army*, and Balck had laid tentative plans to divert the brigade

---

[4] The *16th Infantry Division* was redesignated the *16th Volksgrenadier Division* on 9 October.

[5] *Regiment A/V* was one of four fortress regiments organized by *Wehrkreis V*, an area command somewhat analagous to the U.S. Army's domestic area commands of World War II. With its headquarters at Stuttgart, Germany, *Wehrkreis V* included Alsace within its area of responsibility.

[6] At the end of September the *189th Division* (*Group von Schwerin*) was still technically part of *LXIV Corps*, but on about 28 September what was left of the division, a weak regimental combat team, passed to the control of the *198th Division*. In late October the designation *189th Division* was transferred to *Group Degener* of *LXXXV Corps*, an action undertaken to ensure that the provisional Degener organization could receive supplies and replacements through normal channels.

to the critical Rambervillers sector. There, *Fifth Panzer Army* had in reserve *Task Force Liehr* of the *21st Panzer Division* and what was left of *Regimental Group Usedom,* a unit that had launched a counterattack against units of the French 2d Armored Division northeast of Rambervillers on 2 October.[7] Badly damaged during that action, *Group Usedom* then had to dispatch one of its two panzer grenadier battalions to bolster the forces defending the Parroy forest. Losses, redeployments, and blocking commitments thus left the *Fifth Panzer Army* with no reserve worthy of the name to support the *XLVII Panzer Corps* until the *106th Panzer Brigade* arrived.

Von Luettwitz's panzer corps had other problems as well: a shortage of artillery ammunition; a lack of heavy machine guns and mortars; and, above all, a critical shortage of infantrymen. Consequently, General von Manteuffel, commanding *Fifth Panzer Army,* queried Balck on the possibility of withdrawing portions of the panzer corps to the east of Rambervillers, where it would find better defensive terrain.[8] However, the *Army Group G* commander, adhering to his policy of no withdrawals and immediate counterattacks against any and all Allied penetrations, refused permission for any retreat and likewise turned down von Manteuffel's requests for more

infantry and heavy weapons. The most *Army Group G* could promise was to increase deliveries of ammunition. At the time, Balck felt that the *Fifth Panzer Army,* whatever its problems, was still better off than Wiese's tottering *Nineteenth Army* in the Vosges and the Belfort Gap.

First Try for Bruyeres and Brouvelieures

The 45th Division's attack toward Brouvelieures and Bruyeres demanded that the Rambervillers area be secured first, in order to protect the division's northern flank. The 157th Infantry and the 117th Cavalry Squadron accomplished this task by blocking the roads leading northeast, east, and southeast from Rambervillers, while maintaining contact with the XV Corps' French 2d Armored Division in the north. These requirements, however, together with the German domination of the generally open country immediately east of Rambervillers with artillery and mortar fire, prevented the division's left from mounting any significant attacks toward Baccarat, and left General Eagles, the division commander, with only two regiments for his main effort. Nevertheless, the 45th Division commander hoped to outflank the Germans by taking an indirect approach to his objective. While pushing his 179th Infantry regiment north through the Faite forest, he wanted the 180th to make a wide swing to the left, moving up to the Rambervillers area and then heading southeast through the Ste. Helene woods, between two secondary roads (D–50 and D–47) and the small Mortagne River, to attack the German lines from the

---

[7] *Group Usedom*'s infantry consisted of two panzer grenadier battalions, one from the *21st Panzer Division* and the other from the *15th Panzer Grenadier Division,* supported by six tanks.

[8] It is not clear from available sources, but it appears that von Manteuffel wanted to withdraw *XLVII Panzer Corps'* right flank back about five miles or more to the heavily wooded hills and ridges of the Forest of Ste. Barbe, on the north, and the Forest of Rambervillers, on the south.

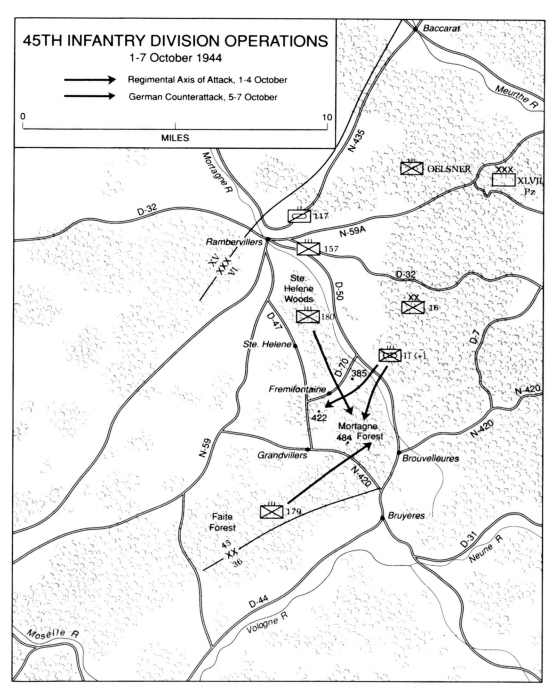

45TH INFANTRY DIVISION OPERATIONS
1-7 October 1944

→ Regimental Axis of Attack, 1-4 October

→ German Counterattack, 5-7 October

0 |————————————————————————| 10

MILES

Baccarat

Meurthe R

Mortagne R

N-435

OELSNER

XXX XLVII Pz

D-32

N-59A

117

Rambervillers

157

XV XXX VI

D-32

Ste. Helene Woods

D-50

XX 16

180

D-7

Ste. Helene

D-47

11 (+)

D-70

385

N-420

Fremifontaine

422

Mortagne
484 Forest

N-420

N-59

Grandvillers

Brouvelieures

N-420

179

Bruyeres

Faite Forest

D-31

Neune R

45 XX 36

D-44

Moselle R

Vologne R

MAP 19   This map is printed in full color at the back of the book, following the Index.

side and rear (*Map 19*).

At first the attack went as planned. While the 157th secured Rambervillers, the 180th Infantry cleared most of the mile-wide Bois de Ste. Helene by 29 September, meeting only scattered German delaying actions. German defenses, however, stiffened along D–70, a small road that bisected the 180th's advance southward and marked a general boundary between the gentle Ste. Helene woods and the more rugged Mortagne forest guarding the final approaches to both Bruyeres and Brouvelieures. To the south, the 179th Infantry emerged from the Faite forest about the same time, but found it difficult to cross the narrow N–420 valley road skirting the southern edge of the Mortagne forest. By October 2, after three days of hard fighting, the 180th managed to take Fremifontaine, a small hamlet on D–70, and the 179th secured Grandvillers; however, the stubborn *16th Volksgrenadier Division* infantry hung on to a defensive network centered around three prominent elevations—Hills 385, 422, and 489. Nevertheless, the German defenses now appeared ready to collapse.

Late on 2 October, as Eagles' converging regiments prepared to continue the offensive into the forest itself, von Manteuffel advised Balck that the *XLVII Panzer Corps* lacked the means to launch a counterattack to recapture Grandvillers and Fremifontaine, and two days later he convinced the *Army Group G* commander that the situation in the sector was becoming irretrievable. Heavily engaged in the Parroy forest battle, the *Fifth Panzer Army* had no significant resources that it could deploy south. By that time the 180th and 179th Infantry had penetrated

deeply into the Mortagne forest, bypassing German positions on Hill 385, driving a wedge between two of the *16th Division*'s regiments, and approaching to within a mile of Brouvelieures itself. Reinforcements were needed if the *16th* was to survive.

At the time Balck could do little. On 5 October he released two reserve battalions to the *XLVII Panzer Corps*, which, together with some odds and ends that von Manteuffel had been able to scrape together, the *Army Group G* commander hoped would save the situation.[9] But von Manteuffel warned that the reinforcements were inadequate, prompting Balck to allow portions of the *11th Panzer Division* north of the Rhine-Marne Canal to be pulled out of the line, despite the constant pressure there from Patton's Third Army.

The counterattacking force that von Manteuffel finally assembled thus consisted of the *111th Panzer Grenadiers* of the *11th Panzer Division*, ten to twelve Mark IV medium tanks from the same division, and four infantry battalions under *16th Division* control. Covered by German forces on Hill 385, much of the infantry and a few of the armored vehicles assembled in the Mortagne valley about three-quarters of a mile east of Fremifontaine; the rest of the tanks and additional infantry gathered at the head of a ravine about a mile to the south; and two more infantry battalions came together another mile farther south. For the northern elements of the German counterattack the most

---

[9] The reserve battalions came from *Regiment A/V*. The *Fifth Panzer Army* had already sent to the *XLVII Panzer Corps* a 100-man guard company from army headquarters, two grenadier companies of the *21st Panzer Division*, a battery of light howitzers, and three assault guns.

83D CHEMICAL (MORTAR) BATTALION, 45TH DIVISION, *fire 4.2-inch mortars, Grandvillers area.*

important objective was Hill 422, an American-held height three-quarters of a mile southeast of Fremifontaine that provided good observation in all directions. The two southern infantry battalions were to support the attack on Hill 422 and were also to strike for Hill 484, a mile and a half farther south and a similar distance east of Grandvillers, the ultimate objective.[10] If the German counterattack developed properly, it would slam into the left and rear of the 180th Infantry north-

west of Brouvelieures and sever the tenuous contact between the 179th and 180th regiments, perhaps cutting off the 180th.

The counterattack, which began about 0900 on 6 October, took the two 45th Division regiments by surprise. Although the assembly of noisy tanks and self-propelled guns was difficult to muffle, the weakening German resistance during the previous days may have given the American attackers a false sense of security; moreover, deep in the forest it was difficult to tell friend or foe by noise alone. By late afternoon the German northern wing had seized Hill 422

---

[10] Troops of the 179th Infantry had been on the northern slopes of Hill 484 since 4 October, but had not secured the entire hill.

and cut off much of the 2d Battalion, 180th Infantry, opening a wide gap between the two American regiments. In the south, however, the two attacking German battalions made little headway in the Hill 484 sector and were in turn outflanked by aggressive 179th Infantry countermaneuvers. The fighting continued throughout the night, quickly degenerating into a continuous series of violent but confused skirmishes, with neither side being able to accomplish much in the dark forests.

On the morning of 7 October, the American units began reorganizing and started eliminating the German penetrations. The 180th Infantry retook Hill 422 while the 179th isolated the German southern assault forces from the panzer grenadiers in the north and, in the process, secured all of Hill 484. Deciding that no more could be accomplished, von Manteuffel directed the *11th Panzer Division*'s task force to start disengaging during the night of 7–8 October, leaving the *16th Division* to reestablish a defensive line as best it could.

When the front finally stabilized on 9 October, the 180th Infantry had established a new line extending from the vicinity of Hill 385—still in German hands—south across Hill 422 to the regimental boundary just north of Hill 484. The German counterattack had thus forced the regiment to pull its front to the west and south about three-quarters of a mile, and had cost it 5 men killed, 40 wounded, and about 30 missing (most of these last, captured). The 179th Infantry had also pulled back and was preparing a defensive line extending southwest from Hill 484 to the northeast-

ern slopes of the Faite forest, after losing 18 men killed, 64 wounded, and about 25 missing. The 179th had captured around 30 Germans, and the 180th nearly 50.

The German attack had not succeeded in its larger objective—retaking Grandvillers and Fremifontaine—which again illustrated *Army Group G*'s inability to push any counterattack through to a decisive conclusion. On the other hand, the operations had forced the 179th and 180th Infantry regiments to take up defensive positions; the units would need nearly a week before they were ready to resume offensive operations. The *XLVII Panzer Corps* had at least bought some time for its hard-pressed left flank.

The 36th Division

Truscott had intended that Dahlquist's 36th Division only support the 45th's attack on the Bruyeres-Brouvelieures area. At the time, the division had been slowly pushing northeast up the Vologne and D–44 valley, clearing out elements of the German *716th Infantry Division* from the wooded hills on either side of its advance. By 1 October the 36th Division's 143d regiment, on the left wing, had moved through the eastern edge of the imposing Faite forest to Docelles and Deycimont, while the 141st regiment, at the division's center, had come up abreast of the 143d on the eastern side of the river, crossing first Route D–11 and then D–30 to secure the town of Lepanges (*Map 20*). To the southeast, the division's remaining regiment, the 142d, had emerged from the steep hills and valleys of the Froissard forest to

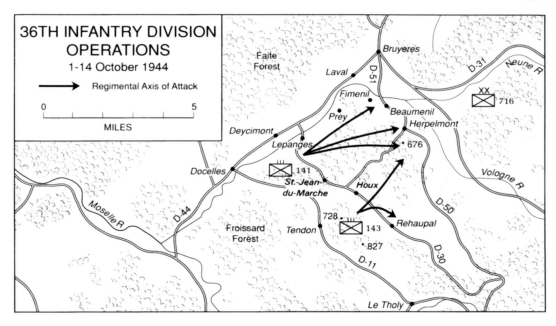

36TH INFANTRY DIVISION
OPERATIONS
1-14 October 1944

→ Regimental Axis of Attack

0   5
MILES

MAP 20   This map is printed in full color at the back of the book, following the Index.

cut D–11 near the mountain hamlet of Tendon. The regiment, reinforced by a battalion of the 141st, had then gone on to occupy two hill masses north of the road, Hills 728 and 827, cutting the *716th Division*'s lateral communications with Le Tholy and threatening Route D–30, which now became the defenders' main supply artery in the region. But despite their success, all three of Dahlquist's regiments were exhausted, and the terrain between their current positions and Bruyeres was, if anything, even more difficult. Yet any attempt to take what was obviously the easiest and most direct route to their objective area—marching straight up the Vologne River valley, with German units of unknown size in the forests on both flanks—seemed extremely dangerous.

Believing that at least one of his regiments should be removed from the line for rest and refitting, Dahlquist decided to make his main effort east of the Vologne, through a rectangular terrain compartment bounded by the towns of Laval, Herpelmont, Houx, and Lepanges—about twelve square miles of mountainous forests nearly devoid of human habitation. Possession of the area would secure his right flank for an advance up the east bank of the Vologne to Bruyeres, leaving the Faite forest to the 45th Division, with security forces along the river itself covering his left flank.

To accomplish this, Dahlquist planned to have the 141st regiment, with its two battalions and attached armor, make the division's main assault between Lepanges and St. Jean-du-Marche. The 141st would be supported by a secondary attack north from the ridge line of Hill 728–827 toward D–30 between Houx and Rehaupal, and beyond. But Dahlquist gave the latter task to the 143d Infantry, transferring it east from the Faite forest area and moving the tired 142d into reserve for a long-needed rest. During the repositioning, the 143d was even able to occupy the town of Houx on 2 October; henceforth, a small north-south road between Houx and Herpelmont would mark the boundary between the two attacking regiments.

During the planning process, Dahlquist had considered making his main effort west of the Vologne River, where his forces might have better complemented the offensive operations of Eagles' 45th Division. However, he felt that such a move, coupled with the pending redeployment of the 3d Division on his right flank from the Le Tholy area, would have given the defending *716th Division* too much room to prepare a counterattack from the southeast, and so he abandoned the idea.

One of Dahlquist's major problems was making the best use of his attached armor in this type of terrain. Like most other American divisions, he had one tank battalion and one tank destroyer battalion attached, which he habitually broke up into mixed task groupings. He had already formed one such unit, a small armored blocking force under Lt. Col. Edward M. Purdy, commanding the 636th Tank Destroyer Battalion, to secure the west bank of the Vologne River.[11]

On 2 October he created a similar grouping, Task Force Danzi, to support the 141st Infantry on the east side of the river.[12] While a small part of the force deployed in the St. Jeandu-Marche area to protect the right rear of the 141st Infantry, the main body assembled near Prey, on the Vologne a mile northeast of Lepanges, with the principal mission of assisting the infantry drive toward Herpelmont. On the 3d, Purdy assumed control of this force, while retaining command of the one west of the Vologne, but both were now subordinate to the 141st regiment.

From 1 to 4 October, the 141st, still with only two infantry battalions, made substantial progress pushing through the heavy forests, and by dusk on the 4th it had secured roughly two-thirds of the rectangle. Its left flank was on the Vologne near Prey, and the right had crossed the Houx-Herpelmont road toward the western slopes of Hill 676, half a mile south of Herpelmont. However, the regiment now began to run out of steam, casualties started to mount, and the *Nineteenth Army* began deploying reinforcements into the area.

In the 143d Infantry's sector, progress had been slower. By 4 Octo-

---

[11] 36th Inf Div OI 303100A Sep 44. Initially, the blocking force consisted of the following elements:
  Company B, 753d Tank Battalion
  Company B, 636th Tank Destroyer Battalion
  Company B, 111th Engineer Combat Battalion, 36th Division
  36th Cavalry Reconnaissance Troop.
[12] The initial composition of TF Danzi was the following:
  Company A, 753d Tank Battalion (−3 tanks)
  Company C, 636th Tank Destroyer Battalion (−1 platoon)
  Reconnaissance Company, 636th Tank Destroyer Battalion
  Antitank Company, 141st Infantry
  Company F, 141st Infantry (−1 platoon)
  One platoon, Company C, 141st Infantry.

ber the regiment had cleared the Houx area, pushed northeast a mile and a half up the Houx-Herpelmont road, and, on the right, advanced over a mile southeast from Houx along Route D–30. But the 143d quickly discovered that German artillery and mortar fire prevented them from using either of the narrow roads as a supply route or an axis of advance; like the 141st, the regiment was forced to depend on a variety of time-consuming cross-country routes for these purposes. Both regiments also found that German resistance grew stronger as their advance carried them slowly to the east-west road nets of D–51 and D–50 that the Germans were undoubtedly using to supply their forces.

Not surprisingly, armor played a minimal role in the struggle, and in fact the 141st Infantry units complained loudly about the lack of tank support.[13] The real problem, however, was the terrain, which restricted vehicles to back roads and trails that were easily interdicted by mines, demolitions, and German artillery fire. In addition, rain and fog severely limited visibility, often leaving the tanks and tank destroyers with nothing at which to fire. The rain and heavy military traffic broke up back roads and turned mountain trails into muddy quagmires that bogged down tracked vehicles; booby-trapped roadblocks, together with numerous mines along most of the better routes, slowed the armor to the pace of engineer clearing operations. Finally, in most cases, the noisy movement of

armor along the back roads and main trails, as well as across what open ground there was, immediately brought down carefully registered German artillery, antitank, and mortar fire. The *LXIV Corps* apparently did not suffer from any serious ammunition shortages.

The limited Vosges offensive produced, in fact, a serious shortage of artillery ammunition in the VI Corps, forcing Truscott to place severe restrictions on the number of daily rounds expended by each of the division's artillery battalions. Dahlquist's troops, who were perhaps the most dependent on indirect fire support because of the nature of the fighting, felt the restrictions the hardest. As a partial remedy, on 4 October Dahlquist ordered the division's tank and tank destroyer units to be attached to one of his three field artillery battalions by night in order to undertake the harassing and interdiction missions normally fired by the artillery batteries, making at least some use of his impotent armor.[14]

At about the same time Dahlquist also combined Purdy's task forces into a larger grouping, Felber Force, under Lt. Col. Joseph G. Felber, the commander of the 753d Tank Battalion.[15] At the behest of the 141st In-

---

[13] 141st Inf AAR, Oct 44, p. 8.

---

[14] Using armor in this manner was in keeping with current Army doctrine.

[15] As organized on 5 October Felber Force consisted of the following:

Company A, 753d Tank Battalion
Company B, 753d Tank Battalion
Company B, 636th Tank Destroyer Battalion
Company C, 636th Tank Destroyer Battalion
Company B, 111th Engineer Combat Battalion
Reconnaissance Company, 636th Tank Destroyer Battalion

fantry, Felber Force passed from regimental to division control, but the transfer caused some confusion, leaving the 141st with little control over its armored support. By the morning of 7 October, only two tanks and two tank destroyers were physically with the 141st Infantry. Although a request to division headquarters brought a platoon of tanks and another of tank destroyers back to regimental control, the bulk of the 36th Division's armor remained assigned to Felber Force under Dahlquist's direct supervision. Since the advancing infantry could seldom employ more than one or two tanks profitably at any one time, Dahlquist judged it best to keep the bulk of the machines in reserve for the moment.

From 4 October through the 14th, daily progress of both the 141st and 143d Infantry was measured in yards. Resistance from the *716th Division* stiffened markedly and, while the opposition was largely static in nature, German patrols constantly harassed the 36th Division's supply routes. Herpelmont fell to the 141st Infantry on 8 October, but German artillery fire rendered the road junction untenable. The 141st nevertheless secured Hill 676 south of Herpelmont, as well as the high ground immediately northwest of town. By the evening of 14 October the regiment had also cleared Beaumenil on Route D–50, a mile northwest of Herpelmont, and

Fimenil, about a mile short (southeast) of Laval.

Meanwhile, by 10 October, the 143d Infantry had secured most of the dominating terrain from the southern slopes of Hill 676 south nearly three miles to Route D–30 near Rehaupal. The regiment's gains allowed artillery forward observers to direct counterbattery fire on German positions along the upper (western) Vologne River valley west of D–50 and on rising ground east of the river.

The 142d Infantry began moving back into the line on 5 October, but made limited progress in the area south of the 143d. On 13 October the 142d took over the 143d Infantry's positions from the vicinity of Hill 676 south to Route D–30, while the 143d prepared to switch back to the 36th Division's left for a renewed attack toward Bruyeres. In fact, during the later stage of their slow advance northward, the 36th Division regiments normally deployed only two battalions on line, switching them back and forth to give each a seven- to ten-day rest. The division also began preparing to resume VI Corps' drive toward St. Die, to which the limited gains through 14 October had been a necessary, if costly, prelude. The 36th Division's infantry casualties for the period 1–14 October numbered approximately 85 killed, 845 wounded, and 115 missing, for an official total of 1,045, almost half of which were suffered by the tired 141st regiment.[16]

Antitank Company, 141st Infantry

36th Cavalry Reconnaissance Troop

The change in command from Purdy to Felber originated with a plan to transfer much of the 636th Tank Destroyer Battalion to 45th Division control, and this redeployment began on 6 October.

---

[16] Sources are the regimental records and AARs for October 1944.

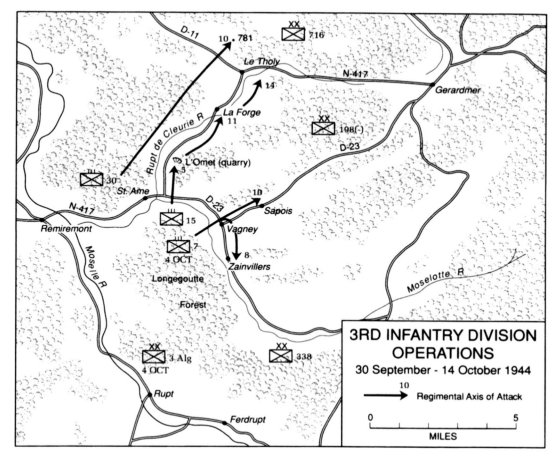

MAP 21   This map is printed in full color at the back of the book, following the Index.

The 3d Division

Immediately south of the 36th Division lay the sector of the 3d Division's 30th Infantry regiment, which had moved to its parent unit's left flank on 29 September. The 15th Infantry held the 3d Division's center around St. Ame, and on the far right the 7th Infantry held along the Moselle as far as Ferdrupt, nine miles farther south (*Map 21*). Current VI Corps plans envisaged that elements of French II Corps would soon relieve the 7th Infantry, but the division's principal objective was still Gerardmer, some ten miles northeast along Route N–417 from St. Ame, with an intermediate objective of Le Tholy, about halfway to Gerardmer. At the time, ongoing negotiations with the French to take over the area had not yet affected the division's plans.

Located at the junction of Routes D–11 and N–417 five miles northeast of St. Ame, Le Tholy had become the center of German resistance in the region. Route N-417, representing the most direct avenue to Le Tholy from the Moselle, ran through a mountain valley, along which flowed the Rupt de Cleurie River, actually a small watercourse no larger than a brook. Much of the valley, up to a mile wide, was given over to open, rolling farmland rising on both sides of the stream to rough, forested hills. For over half the distance from St. Ame to Le Tholy, Route N-417 ran along open slopes east of the river, and country lanes provided additional mobility throughout the valley, at least in good weather. However, a number of stone quarries, usually near the tree line, punctuated the upper slopes of the Cleurie valley on both sides of the river, providing the Germans with ready-made defensive positions.

At the end of September General O'Daniel, the 3d Division commander, intended to send the 15th Infantry directly up Route N-417 from St. Ame toward Le Tholy, supported by the 30th Infantry working through wooded hills along the western side of the valley. Once de Monsabert's French forces arrived in the south, O'Daniel planned to bring his third regiment, the 7th Infantry, up to the St. Ame area as well to launch a supporting, limited objective attack eastward along the axis of Route D-23, a rather difficult southerly approach to Gerardmer.

Facing the 3d Division was *LXIV Corps' 198th Division,* the unit that had earlier counterattacked the 36th Division in the same area. During the first half of October the German division opposed the advance of O'Daniel's

units with its own *305th Grenadiers,* the attached *602d* and *608th Mobile Battalions,* two battle groups built on remnants of the *196th* and *200th Security Regiments,* and a host of smaller ad hoc units that the *198th Division* was absorbing to rebuild its depleted ranks. Later the 7th Infantry would also encounter troops of the *198th Division's 326th Grenadiers* on its southern flank, while on the north the 30th Infantry would run into elements of the *716th Division,* the bulk of which was battling the 36th Division.

The attack of the 3d Division, Truscott's best and most experienced unit, ran into trouble from the beginning. By 1 October, the slowly advancing 15th Infantry had come up against a major German strongpoint at one of the largest quarries, L'Omet, on the eastern side of the valley, only about a mile and a half north of St. Ame, and there the advance of the division up N-417 halted. Unable to force L'Omet, O'Daniel switched his main effort to the 30th Infantry still advancing through the woods west of the valley, but even there progress was slow. Terrain and weather precluded both armor and air support and greatly limited the effectiveness of artillery. Not until 10 October did the regiment reach Route D-11, about a mile and a half northwest of Le Tholy, and secure Hill 781, overlooking Le Tholy on the north. There the 30th Infantry quickly discovered that the Germans had the town—which was in a shambles—well covered by artillery fire and had established strong defenses to the west, making a further advance toward Gerardmer temporarily impossible. The 30th Infantry, accordingly, made no determined effort to clear Le Tholy or to push eastward through the town. Having suffered some 600 casualties during the period 30 September–10 October, the regiment needed to catch its breath.

In the center the 15th Infantry had meanwhile found the northern and southern entrances to L'Omet quarry nearly cliff-like and covered by German automatic weapons fire, while at the eastern and western approaches the Germans had piled up impressive stone roadblocks across a narrow route through the quarry. Inside the quarry, passageways, tunnels, stone walls, and scrap piles of broken stone provided the defenders with good cover and concealment. Although the number of Germans within the quarry at first probably numbered no more than a few hundred, reinforcements arrived during the battle, while other troops manned machine-gun positions in the adjacent woods to cover most approaches to the quarry. Not surprisingly, infantry assaults on the quarry between 30 September and 2 October proved useless. On the 3d, two tank destroyers and two special M4 tanks mounting 105-mm. howitzers pumped about 500 rounds of high explosive ammunition into the German defensive works, while mortars of the 1st Battalion, 15th Infantry, lobbed in a week's allotment of ammunition. The effort had little effect.[17]

On 4 October the attack continued behind the supporting fire of three artillery battalions, but made little progress until tanks laboriously made their way up to the west entrance, knocking down the stone roadblocks and finally opening up the interior of the quarry to the infantry. The last organized resistance crumbled during midafternoon on the 5th, with some twenty Germans fleeing after most of the defenders had apparently evacuated their positions during the night.

Following the quarry fight, the 15th Infantry found the going easier as the Germans grudgingly gave way. On 6 October the regimental left reached the town of La Forge, about halfway to Le Tholy on Route N–417. German artillery and mortar fire again took command of the highway, however, and it was not until the 11th that infantry from the 15th regiment could secure the town.[18] Thereafter the regiment avoided the center of the valley, pushed more rapidly across wooded hills east of the highway, and by the evening of 14 October occupied a line from Route N–417 just south of Le Tholy west another two and a half miles along good, wooded holding ground.

On the 15th Infantry's right, the 7th Infantry regiment had begun its own infiltration of the Vosges Mountains. At the end of September the 3d Battalion, 7th Infantry, held positions on high, forested terrain south of St. Ame, which overlooked, to the east, the road junction town of Vagney on Route D–23 and the Moselotte River.

---

[17] For an account, see Donald G. Taggart, ed., *History of the Third Infantry Division in World War II* (Washington, D.C.: Infantry Journal Press, 1947), pp. 248–49. The 15th Infantry's commander, Col. Richard G. Thomas, suffered a heart attack on 4 October, and Lt. Col. Hallett D. Edson, the regimental executive officer took over the command.

---

[18] For heroic action near La Forge on 9 October, 1st Lt. Victor L. Kandle of the 15th Infantry was awarded the Congressional Medal of Honor.

4.2-INCH MORTARS HIT LE THOLY

At the time the 1st Battalion was still based at Rupt-sur-Moselle, seven miles south of St. Ame, and had projected some strength several miles up into the Foret de Longegoutte toward the Moselotte; the 2d Battalion was concentrated around Ferdrupt, three miles southeast up the Moselle from Rupt. When relieved by the 3d Algerian Division of the French II Corps, the 7th Infantry was to concentrate in the St. Ame area and then seize Vagney and the nearby forested heights.

Leaving behind small holding detachments, the regiment quietly redeployed its two battalions along the Moselle during the nights of 2–3 and 3–4 October. It began its attack on Vagney late on the afternoon of the 4th, with the 2d Battalion seizing the high ground north of the St. Ame–Sapois road, and the other units crossing D–23 to secure Hill 822, a mile west of Vagney. After a three-day battle Vagney fell on 7 October, two days earlier than the VI Corps and 3d Division had expected.

This time the Germans defended their mountain strongholds with vigor. About 2020 on the 7th, German infantry, with the support of two tanks, launched a desperate counterattack into Vagney. In the fog and darkness the 7th Infantry's troops mistook the lead German tank for a vehicle of the 756th Tank Battalion, which had a platoon of mediums in the area. The German armor then penetrated quickly into the town, taking the command posts of both the 1st and 3d Battalions under fire, which led to a wild melee before the German force was finally ejected.[19]

Brushing off the German counterattack, the 7th Infantry's right pushed up the Moselotte River on the 8th to secure Zainvillers, a mile south of Vagney, but not before the Germans blew the Zainvillers bridge. The left meanwhile reached out along D–23 toward Sapois, a mile and a half west of Vagney. After three days of stubborn resistance the Germans withdrew from Sapois, and troops of the 7th Infantry moved in, ending the regiment's last significant action in the Vagney area. Plans to push part of the 7th Infantry toward Gerardmer along Route D–23 had been abandoned by this time, and already elements of the regiment had moved out of the line as troops of the 3d Algerian Division began arriving from the south to relieve the American unit.

Relief and Redeployment

Since 28 September, discussions had been under way between the U.S. Seventh and First French Armies regarding the movement of the inter-army boundary north, which would give the French more room to maneuver against the northern approaches to Belfort and allow Trus-

cott to pull the 3d Division out of a region that had become a dead end for the VI Corps. Truscott wanted the 3d Division to spearhead a renewed offensive toward St. Die, while de Monsabert felt the St. Ame–Vagney region would give him a back door to the German defenses at Le Thillot and southward. The subsequent relief of the 3d Division caused some problems between the American and French commands, and between Truscott and Patch as well. The 3d Algerian Division, beset by supply and transportation problems and engaged in a new offensive against the Gerardmer–Le Thillot area, had been unable to move northward in strength as rapidly as the American commanders had expected. Meanwhile German resistance in the Vagney area had proved stronger than estimated, making it dangerous for the 7th Infantry to disengage until the Algerians had substantial strength on the ground. In the interim, sharp differences arose between Patch and Truscott over the scope of 7th Infantry operations in the area, and later between the French and the Americans when de Monsabert's forces were finally able to assume responsibility for the additional territory.[20]

---

[19] Fatally wounded, 2d Lt. James L. Harris, the 756th Tank Battalion's platoon leader in Vagney, demonstrated extreme heroism during the fight and was posthumously awarded the Congressional Medal of Honor.

---

[20] The boundary discussions during late September and early October were complicated, reflecting a series of misunderstandings on the part of the headquarters and commanders most concerned. See 6th Army Gp LI 1, 26 Sep 44; Devers Diary, 28 Sep–8 Oct 44; Seventh Army Diary, 30 Sep–4 Oct 44; Seventh Army Conf File, Bk 7, Confs of 1 and 3 Oct 44; Seventh Army FO 6, 29 Sep 44; *Seventh Army Rpt*, II, 359–61; Rad, CPX–14229, Seventh Army to VI Corps et al., 4 Oct 44; de Lattre, *History*, pp. 192–98; First Fr Army Personal and Secret Instr 3, 30 Sep 44; First Fr Army SO 76, 4 Oct 44; First Fr Army, "Note Concerning the Development of Opns on the Front of First French Army," 9 Oct 44.

Trouble began on 7 October when the VI Corps directed the 3d Infantry Division to be prepared to move most of the 7th Infantry out of the line after 1000 on the 8th, replacing the infantry with engineer and armored units. During the course of the 8th, however, Seventh Army informed VI Corps that such preparations were premature. Keeping close track of the French progress northward as well as their attacks on Le Thillot and Gerardmer, Patch realized that the 3d Algerian Division could not possibly take over the 7th Infantry's positions on 8 October, and instead recommended that the 7th continue its attacks eastward in support of de Monsabert's offensive. Truscott objected, fearing that the attacks would tie up the 7th Infantry for some days; furthermore, he pointed out that Patch's orders of 4 October had limited the 7th Infantry's responsibilities to the seizure of Vagney and neighboring high ground. After more discussion, Patch reluctantly agreed that it would probably accomplish little to have the 7th Infantry advance farther along Route D–34, but insisted that the regiment maintain strong pressure to the east.

Truscott and General O'Daniel interpreted the Seventh Army instructions as loosely as possible. On the 9th O'Daniel pulled the 2d Battalion, 7th Infantry, out of the front line and, by the morning of the 10th, had also assembled the 7th regiment's 1st Battalion in reserve at Vagney. Meanwhile the two commanders had agreed between themselves that the 7th Infantry would make no further efforts south; consequently, the 7th never went beyond dispatching a few

small patrols out of Zainvillers. At the time, both Truscott and O'Daniel were more interested in preserving the strength of both the 3d Division and its 7th regiment for the projected drive on St. Die and did not want to commit the regiment deeply into the Moselotte valley. In the end, the 7th Infantry left only a small holding detachment at Zainvillers, pending the arrival of French troops, and abruptly ended its advance in the north after securing Sapois on the 11th. Following the fall of Sapois, O'Daniel began redeploying the rest of the 7th Infantry, replacing them by the morning of the 12th with two companies of the 48th Engineer Combat Battalion.[21] All American pressure against the German forces in the area was thus relaxed, well before the French offensive just to the south ended.

By the 12th even Truscott, who now realized that de Monsabert's corps could initially put little more than a reconnaissance squadron and an FFI battalion in the Sapois-Vagney-Zainvillers area, began to have second thoughts about the speed of the 3d Division's disengagement; he, therefore, directed O'Daniel to leave at least one battalion of the 7th Infantry at Vagney for added security. However, two days later, on 14 October, Devers officially moved the interarmy boundary north of Route N–417 and Le Tholy, and between 14 and 17 October the French II Corps assumed responsibility for the area, relieving first the remaining 7th Infantry battalion and then the 15th regiment. It was not until 23 Oc-

---

[21] A separate, nondivisional unit attached to VI Corps and reattached to the 3d Infantry Division.

tober, though, that units of the 36th Division finally relieved O'Daniel's last regiment, the 30th, in the Le Tholy–La Forge area west of N–417. None of O'Daniel's regiments had accomplished much in any of their zones since the 11th, giving little support to de Monsabert's offensive between 4 and 17 October and allowing the Germans ample time to rebuild their battered defenses before the newly arriving French units could begin to pose a threat. All in all, the lack of coordination between the two Allied forces did not augur well for the future.

The Vosges Fighting: Problems and Solutions

As the VI Corps moved into the High Vosges during late September and early October, wear and tear on its three infantry divisions greatly accelerated. As early as 26 September General O'Daniel, commanding the 3d Division, observed a significant decline in the aggressiveness of his infantry units. Explanations that the troops were wet and tired and developing a certain caution—based on a general feeling that the war would soon be over—failed to satisfy O'Daniel, who urged his subordinate commanders to emphasize that a go-easy attitude could only prolong the war and increase casualties. Dahlquist, commanding the 36th, later noted the disciplinary problems that all VI Corps units were experiencing, especially desertions among the line infantry companies in combat (50–60 cases per division) and the ever-present straggler phenomenon that had afflicted the corps since the initial landings. In part he felt these difficulties were a product of the heavy officer and NCO casualties sustained by the fighting units in both Italy and France and the resulting decline in leadership as enlisted men were rapidly promoted to take up the slack.[22]

Other VI Corps officers echoed these concerns. The commander of the 3d Division's 15th Infantry felt that his regiment's quality was slipping. Replacements, he averred, were often inept and poorly trained. Moreover, the many veterans of the regiment's bitter fighting in the snow-drenched mountains of Italy had little stomach left for another winter's operations in French mountains. In the 45th Division the 180th Infantry reported about sixty-five recent combat fatigue cases, while at the same time skin infections were becoming endemic, largely as the result of constant wet weather and a chronic shortage of bathing facilities. Col. Paul D. Adams, commanding the 143d Infantry of the 36th Division, reported an almost alarming mental and physical lethargy among the troops of his regiment, and General Dahlquist, the division commander, had to tell General Truscott that the 36th had little punch left.

Dahlquist felt that he had been driving his troops too hard and, after privately discussing the problem with his regimental commanders, had established small division rest camps for his infantrymen. According to Colonel Adams, the troops needed to be rested continually during the late

---

[22] Ltr, Dahlquist to Brig Gen Edward C. Betts, HQ, ETO, 21 Nov 44, Correspondence, John E. Dahlquist Papers, MHI.

autumn and winter fighting in the Vosges because of the terrain and weather. "It takes about three days [of rest] with men that age," he judged.

You give them three days and they'll . . . be back in shape without any trouble. Just leave them alone, let them sleep and eat the first day, make them clean up the second day, and do whatever they want to do the rest of the time, and they'll be ready to go.[23]

Once the division headquarters became sensitive to the issue of battle fatigue, Adams felt, the 36th did much better despite the hardships it had undergone and would continue to meet in the future.

Improvements in the Seventh Army's supply situation might have alleviated some of these problems, but General Devers' optimism over the capabilities of his Mediterranean supply lines proved premature. Despite the fall of Marseille, Toulon, and the lesser Riviera ports and the best efforts of Army logisticians in the communications zone, the 6th Army Group's land supply lines were still overextended. At the end of September the Seventh Army requested daily rail delivery of some 4,485 tons of supplies and ammunition for the period 1–7 October; however, the 6th Army Group's G–4, now responsible for setting rail priorities, could allocate to the Seventh Army only 2,270 rail-tons per day, and actual receipts ran well below that figure. On 5 October, for example, the Seventh Army received only 1,655 tons by rail, and on the 6th about 1,670 tons. During the same two days the Seventh Army received by rail only 20 tons of ammunition, while its units were expending ammunition at the rate of nearly 1,000 tons per day. To make up for rail deficiencies, the 6th Army Group had to continue to rely on long truck hauls, but increasingly bad weather, deteriorating highways, vehicle maintenance requirements, and the 400-mile distance from ports to forward depots combined to make road transportation increasingly difficult and slow. In addition, moving supplies from forward depots to units in the field also proved arduous as the tactical forces moved farther into the mountains.

General Truscott had one solution to his tactical transportation problems. On 2 October, anticipating the hardships of mountain campaigning, he requested two pack trains from Italy. After numerous delays, the 513th Pack Quartermaster Company finally arrived in the Vosges area on 23 November with 300 mules and a veterinary detachment. Dividing the mule trains between the divisions still in the Vosges, the mule skinners and their charges were able to haul rations and munitions to the infantry units by night. Although providing forage for the animals was a problem, the users reported little or no interference from German artillery or mines and booby traps; and resupply, even in the most difficult terrain, was possible.[24] Had the animals and trained handlers been readily available earlier, they obviously would have been useful throughout the Vosges campaign.

Ammunition was another concern.

---

[23] Adams Interv, pp. 7–8.

[24] *Seventh Army Rpt*, I, 549.

ARTILLERY MUNITIONS: VITAL IN THE VOSGES

Even before Truscott began his limited October offensive, VI Corps was feeling the pinch of a shortage of artillery and other types of munitions.[25] On 2 October, for example, the 30th Infantry of the 3d Division reported that it was down to 300 rounds of 81-mm. mortar rounds and was approaching the exhaustion of its M1 rifle ammunition. Severe rationing was the only immediate answer. Throughout the 3d Division, for example, O'Daniel limited 60-mm. mortar ammunition expenditures to eight rounds per weapon per day and 81-mm. mortars to eleven rounds, 105-mm. howitzers to thirty-two rounds, and 155-mm. howitzers to

thirty rounds. During much of the early part of October, however, Seventh Army depots could not even furnish enough ammunition to meet these restricted rates. Even .30-caliber ammunition was sometimes critically short, and the 3d Division had to almost denude the support units of small arms ammunition to supply its rifle companies and machine-gun platoons. For several days, in fact, there was no M1 rifle ammunition to be found at the Seventh Army's expanding supply installations in and around Epinal. To preserve morale, Truscott even prohibited the dissemination of information on overall ammunition allocations below the level of infantry regiment and divisional artillery headquarters.

---

[25] On the ammunition crisis, see ibid., 540–43.

Although the VI Corps' ammunition shortages were partly overcome by mid-October, quartermaster supplies and rations remained a problem. Units often had to exist on half-rations or live off packaged, hard rations for days at a time. More serious, clothing for wet, cold weather was scarce. Winter clothing did not begin to arrive in adequate amounts until after 20 October, and even by the end of the month shoe-pacs (rubberized boots), heavy sweaters, and extra-heavy socks were available to only about 75 percent of the infantry. Heavy, long overcoats were on hand, but their usefulness was doubtful, for the field units reported that the garment was "too bulky for reconnaissance and armored units to use in their compact fighting compartments . . . [and] so immobilizing that it cannot be worn by the infantry, and, if issued to them, will be discarded the first time they attack." [26] The infantry much preferred the long, lined M–1943 field jacket, and the 3d Division gradually managed to amass enough of these jackets to outfit its infantry battalions. Other units reported shortages of signal and engineer equipment of all types throughout October, but the technical service units generally accomplished their missions through improvisation, substitution, and outright scrounging.

The solution to many of these problems was the strengthening of the logistical organizations supporting the 6th Army Group. To this end, on 18 September the Continental Base Section (CBS) at Marseille moved an advanced echelon of its headquarters to Dijon, and on the 26th, the Continental Advance Section (CONAD), under Maj. Gen. Arthur R. Wilson, became operational at Dijon, absorbing the advanced echelon of CBS. Supply agencies along the Mediterranean coast then passed to the control of a new headquarters, Delta Base Section (DBS), under Brig. Gen. John P. Ratay. Retaining some personnel from the old CBS, DBS obtained additional manpower from Northern Base Section on Corsica, which ceased to exist. At the same time SOS NATOUSA (still located at Caserta, Italy) set up an advanced echelon at Dijon under Brig. Gen. Morris W. Gilland. The French logistical agency, Base 901, divided its personnel between DBS and CONAD, with most of Base 901 moving up to Dijon with CONAD, and Brig. Gen. Georges Granier becoming the deputy commanding general of CONAD for French affairs. Although the various changes were phased in fairly rapidly and all became effective on 1 October, several weeks were necessary before the new organizations could function smoothly and support the army group's growing requirements. However, in some areas theater logisticians were powerless. The shortage of artillery ammunition, for example, was a theaterwide concern, and the solution would ultimately depend on increasing production in the United States and Great Britain. [27]

In the end, terrain and weather were the most decisive factors in defining the character of the Vosges fighting.

---

[26] 3d Inf Div AAR Oct 44, Sec IV, Supply, p. 3.

[27] Seventh Army Diary, 13 Nov 44; and for an extended discussion see Ruppenthal, *Logistical Support of the Armies*, II, 247–63.

With only ten good flying days during the month of October, Allied air power was less effective interdicting German troop movements behind the battlefield, and Allied ground units were more dependent on artillery fire support despite the shortage of ammunition. Armor, except as mobile artillery, was less useful in the mountains, leaving the bulk of the fighting on both sides to the infantry battalions; even here the compartmentalized terrain made it difficult to maneuver units that were larger than platoons and squads. In the words of one regimental commander:

The fighting during the month of October was comparable to jungle fighting, where . . . maintenance of direction was most difficult because of the dense forests. This alone resulted in many erroneous reports as to locations of units and enemy positions. Difficulties arose as orders based on the best available information, which was frequently inaccurate, miscarried, and at times resulted in bitter and unexpected fighting . . . [and he advised that] all commanders must report actual conditions carefully, avoiding all possibility of errors in locations of units and omitting entirely reports based on optimism rather than fact. Forest areas must be mopped up thoroughly. Small, well-dug-in enemy detachments if not mopped up will harass supply columns, and present difficult problems of liquidation because of our inability to use our supporting weapons inside our lines. . . . Sometimes the enemy deliberately lets us get as close as seventy-five or one hundred yards to him before disclosing his presence with fire, and on occasion lets the leading elements pass by. This reduced the fight to a small arms fight with the enemy enjoying the advantage of good cover. . . . Holding the top of a hill or even what is ordinarily termed the military crest of a wooded hill does not necessarily give us control of the surrounding terrain. We must require all units engaged in capturing a hill covered

with forests to continue down the forward slopes until the open country is under small arms fire and artillery observation.[28]

Interestingly, General Balck of *Army Group G* also likened the situation in the Vosges to jungle fighting, the key to which he considered to be having plenty of infantry on hand.[29] To this, all small-unit commanders could readily agree.

Truscott probably also would have agreed with these judgments. The weather, terrain, and lack of infantry had prevented him from putting more force in the push to Bruyeres and Brouvelieures. Nevertheless, the VI Corps was still in a better position to make a more decisive effort toward St. Die and ultimately Strasbourg and the Rhine. Securing the Rambervillers area in the north and the sector defined by Le Tholy and Route N–417 in the south gave the corps more protection on both of its flanks, while the 45th and 36th Divisions had just about cleared the way to Bruyeres and Brouvelieures in the center. At the same time, both of these divisions had managed to rest many of their infantry battalions, never putting their full strength on the line. In the south, the arrival of French units finally allowed Truscott to pull almost the entire 3d Division into reserve, where it would rest and refit for the major VI Corps offensive soon to follow. Meanwhile, on the German side, the combat strength of the *16th* and *716th Infantry Divisions* had been steadily eroded, and the two units had been regularly pushed back, giving

---

[28] Extracted from "Conclusions of Regimental Commander," 36th Inf Div AAR Oct 44, p. 2.

[29] Ltr, Balck to Jodl, 10 Oct 44, cited in von Luttichau, "German Operations," ch. 20, pp. 13–14.

them little time to improve their defensive positions and forcing their parent corps to commit what reserves they had to shore up their patchwork defensive lines. If the Seventh Army and the 6th Army Group could solve some of their more serious logistical problems and expand their unique supply routes through southern France, a more concentrated VI Corps push through the Vosges might well split the two weakening German divisions far apart.

CHAPTER XVI

Approaching the Gaps: Belfort

While the XV Corps moved out of Luneville toward the Mondon and Parroy forests and the VI Corps began its approach to the Moselle, the First French Army had marked time, waiting for the men, materiel, and supplies that would ultimately fuel de Lattre's offensive against the Belfort Gap. For the moment strong German resistance along the approaches to Belfort made any limited efforts futile, and the French had to be content with moving up the rest of their units from southern and central France and deploying them on line. Yet, perhaps even more than the American commanders, the French leaders were restless. French territory and people lay before them—towns, villages, and hamlets still under German rule and subject to the caprices of the harsh German occupation. Moreover, the German defenses still appeared to be weak in many areas, especially in the mountains where dense forests made it difficult to establish a continuous line of resistance. It was a temptation that French officers found hard to resist.

The Initial French Attacks

On the First French Army's left, or northern, wing, de Monsabert's II Corps positioned the French 1st Infantry and 1st Armored Divisions on the northern routes to Belfort; in the center and on the right, or southern, wing, General Bethouart's I Corps reinforced the 3d Algerian Division with the 9th Colonial Infantry Division and Moroccan Tabor units from southern France. General du Vigier's armored division had finally been strengthened with its third combat command, and, like Truscott, he and de Monsabert were eager to move east before the German defenses had solidified. Although many of de Lattre's units were still arriving from North Africa, American difficulties on the northern flank of the French army soon gave the French tactical commanders an opportunity for action.[1]

By 23 September both Truscott and

---

[1] French planning information is from de Lattre, *History*, pp. 182–86 and *Histoire* (French language edition), Annexe V, Extrait du Journal de March tenu au 3e Bureau de l'Etat-Major de la 1re Armee Francaise, CG II French Corps to CG VI Corps, 23 Sep 44; II French Corps, General Opns Order 18, 23 Sep 44; Ltr, CG II French Corps to CG VI Corps, 24 Sep 44; 1st French Armored Division, General Opns Order 19, 24 Sep 44; Ltr, CG 1st French Armored Division to CG 3d Infantry Division, 24 Sep 44; Memo, Lt Col G. F. Hawkens, G–3 Ops, to BG Jenkins, ACofS G–3 6th Army Gp (no sub), 24 Sep 44, in 6th Army Gp SGS File 565; 1st French Infantry Division GO 25, 25 Sep 44.

O'Daniel had also become concerned about the growing gap between the U.S. VI Corps and the French II Corps, especially considering the 3d Division's failure to make any headway on its right wing toward the Moselle. Although French and American cavalry units had tried to cover the sector between the two Allied forces, they had been stretched thin and were unable to move up Route N–486 to Le Thillot. Le Thillot itself, a key road junction town on the upper reaches of the Moselle River, lay in the French zone of advance and had become one of the major anchors of the German defenses in the mountains north of Belfort. Accordingly, on 23 September, Truscott asked de Monsabert if his forces could assume complete responsibility for Le Thillot area. At the time he suggested that the French make an armored thrust up N–486 from Lure complemented by a second French drive on Le Thillot from the north, using the crossing sites at Rupt and La Roche that O'Daniel's 3d Division had finally secured. Since the American forces were encountering only spotty defenses along the Moselle, there was no reason to believe that the French would not find the area equally permeable at some point. Enthusiastic, de Monsabert quickly passed the request on to de Lattre, who approved the proposal that evening with the proviso that the effort be limited to one combat command of the French 1st Armored Division and one regimental combat team of the French 1st Infantry Division.

Planning began immediately. De Monsabert wanted the 1st Armored Division's Combat Command (CC)

Sudre to move through the sector of the 3d Division and attack Le Thillot from the north, on the eastern side of the Moselle. CC Caldiarou, the new arrival, was to push up Route N–486 with the 3d African Chasseurs toward Le Thillot from the south; and CC Kientz and a brigade of the French 1st Infantry Division was to launch a supporting attack south of the highway. The plan obviously called for more strength than the limited forces approved by de Lattre; but both de Monsabert and du Vigier, still commanding the French 1st Armored Division, viewed the American request as an opportunity to outflank the main German defenses at Belfort between Lure and Issy-les-Doubs, and hoped that a quick strike by du Vigier's entire division might catch the Germans by surprise.

The French southern attack began early on 25 September, and the main assault on Le Thillot started on the 26th after the attacking units had moved up to forward assembly areas. De Monsabert's plans were flexible. He hoped to catch the Germans unawares and either cut a path through the southern Vosges to Belfort from the north or push directly over the Vosges via Gerardmer and the Schlucht Pass to Colmar and the Rhine. Much depended on speed, surprise, and the ability of the armor to find a weak point in the German lines—some road or pass where defenses had been neglected, poorly organized, or perhaps completely ignored.

The effort, however, proved premature. Despite the speed of the attacks, the French found the Germans better prepared than in the north. The narrow roads leading to Le Thillot jammed the attacking armor, and the battles for the heavily wooded, steep hillsides along the highways put a premium on infantry. As the attacks slowed down, the Germans were able to clog the French avenues of advance even further with reinforcements, making the quick penetration that de Monsabert and du Vigier had hoped for impossible. The fighting was similar to that encountered by the XV Corps, now attempting to clear the Parroy forest, and to that which would be experienced by the VI Corps in its drive for Bruyeres and Brouvelieures. Between 26 and 29 September progress by the French in the southern Vosges was minimal, and the attacking forces lost about 115 killed, 460 wounded, and 30 missing.

Rather than terminate the failing offensive, de Lattre chose to reinforce it. Realizing that de Monsabert had surpassed his instructions, he nevertheless approved the II Corps commander's initiative. His own estimates regarding the time necessary to bring up enough supplies and troops to launch a major frontal attack against the Belfort Gap had been too optimistic; by the end of September it was obvious that the First French Army as a whole would not be ready to resume the offensive until 20 October at the earliest. In the meantime, de Monsabert's attacks would at least put some pressure on the enemy and, at the very least, divert German attention away from the Belfort Gap. For these reasons de Lattre agreed to increase de Monsabert's infantry strength, transferring both the 3d Algerian Infantry Division and the 3d Moroccan Tabor Group to the II Corps, and promising him the 2d Tabor Group, the two-battalion French parachute regiment, and the assault battalion as soon as they arrived. In addition he increased the frontage held by Bethouart's I Corps, with the 9th Colonial Division and the recently arrived 2d Moroccan Division, by about fifteen miles, thus allowing the II Corps to narrow its focus of attack. Devers, after extensive negotiations with de Lattre, also moved the French II Corps boundary north, to encompass the entire Rupt–Le Tholy–Gerardmer area, despite the fact that the 3d Division had not yet been able to penetrate into the region very deeply.

Logistical Problems

During the boundary discussions, de Lattre took the opportunity to thrash out his logistical problems with Patch and Devers. Charging that the French had been short-changed regarding supplies and equipment, he asserted that the lack of gasoline had prevented him from bringing up enough troops and ammunition to the battle area, thus forcing de Monsabert to break off his attack before it had a chance to succeed. The "unfavorable treatment" afforded his army in the matter of supplies, he went on, was inexcusable and "seriously endangered its existence and operations." [2]

---

[2] Draft memo (no subj, no sig), de Lattre for Devers, 30 Sep 44. Apparently, this memo was never "formally" delivered to either Devers or Patch, but copies were used as a basis for discussion at both 6th Army Group and Seventh Army headquarters on 1 October. De Lattre, *History*, pp. 194–95.

GENERALS MARSHALL, DE LATTRE, AND DEVERS *visit French First Army headquarters in Luxeuil, France, October 1944.*

In a memorandum he also included statistics showing that the First French Army, with five reinforced divisions in the forward area, had received about 8,715 rail-tons of supplies between 20 and 28 September, while the Seventh Army, with three divisions at the front, had received roughly 18,920 rail-tons during the same period.

In a subsequent conference to iron out these difficulties, Seventh Army representatives initially took the position that any supplies that the army could spare from VI Corps' allocations had to be sent to the recently acquired XV Corps. They also pointed out the 6th Army Group—no longer Seventh Army—was now re-

sponsible for the logistical support of the First French Army. In private, Seventh Army logisticians believed that French supply problems stemmed largely from inadequacies in their own supply services. General Devers agreed in part, observing that the French had been slow to build up supply surpluses in the forward area. At the same time, however, he concluded that during its period of responsibility for French supply, the Seventh Army had not adequately monitored logistical operations supporting de Lattre's forces and had generally favored Truscott's units in such matters.

Based on these judgments, Devers instructed the Seventh Army to meet the most urgent logistical requirements of the First French Army. Therefore, after the conclusion of a series of conferences with First French Army representatives on 1 October, the Seventh Army G–4 recomputed requirements and stocks and allocated 65,000 gallons of gasoline, 53,000 rations, and about 280 tons of ammunition to the French. An additional 60,000 gallons of gasoline were to be turned over to them on 2 October, and the Seventh Army also agreed to make up daily shortages of rations and gasoline for the First French Army until a revised rail-supply schedule for the French went into effect on 4 October.[3]

For the moment de Lattre appeared satisfied. On 8 October, however, during a visit by General Marshall to the 6th Army Group, the French commander launched into another tirade about his supply problems, embarrassing Devers and angering Marshall.[4] Later de Lattre more or less apologized to Devers over the incident, but there were no easy answers to French logistical problems. A basic difficulty was the ability of the Seventh Army to consistently "outbid" the small French army headquarters for supplies and materiel; the larger, better-trained American staffs were simply more efficient in forecasting the logistical needs of their units and justifying those requests with detailed statistical data. In addition, the larger number of trained American supply

officers and agencies—depots, accounting offices, repair facilities, and so forth—allowed the Seventh Army to control its internal stockage and expenditure of supplies and equipment with an efficiency that the French understandably could not hope to match. As a result, 6th Army Group logisticians would have to step in at various times during the coming campaigns and approve special supply allocations to the French to make up for critical deficiencies. Until the French Army had been completely rebuilt at some future date, there was no other solution.

French Plans

Early in October new French plans called for a major assault through the High Vosges north of the Belfort Gap, continuing and expanding de Monsabert's original effort.[5] Somewhat chastened by his failure to take Le Thillot, de Monsabert believed that, despite the reinforcements sent by de Lattre, the II Corps lacked the strength to seize Gerardmer and push through the Schlucht Pass. Instead, he hoped to force a passage through the Vosges, taking a more southerly

---

[3] Devers Diary, 1 Oct 44; Seventh Army Diary, 30 Sep 44, 1 Oct 44; Seventh Army Conf File, Bk 7, Conf of 1 Oct 44; *Seventh Army Rpt*, II, 360.

[4] See Devers Diary, 8 Oct 44; and Forrest C. Pogue, *George C. Marshall: Organizer of the Victory, 1943–1945* (New York: Viking, 1973), pp. 475–76.

[5] The following analysis of the French situation and plans is based on the following: de Lattre, *History*, pp. 193–205; First Fr Army, Personal and Secret Instr 3, 30 Sep 44; First Fr Army SO 76, 4 Oct 44; II Fr Corps GO 26, 30 Sep 44; II Fr Corps GO 27, 2 Oct 44; II Fr Corps GO 29, 4 Oct 44; I Fr Corps Genl Opns Order 6, 3 Oct 44; 5th Fr Armd Div Jnl de Marche, Sep–Oct 44. In addition to official French and American records, the following secondary sources proved valuable in reconstructing the II Corps' October story: *Le IIe C.A. Dans la Bataille Pour la Liberation de la France*, pp. 28–48; *La Premiere Division Blindee au Combat*, pp. 73–82; Moreau, *La Victoire Sous le Signe des Trois Croissants* (Algiers: Editions Pierre Virillon, 1948), II, 162–92.

route between Gerardmer and Le Thillot. The 3d Algerian Infantry Division, redeploying from I Corps, was to take over II Corps' left to make the main thrust. The Algerians, covering on their left toward Gerardmer and the Schlucht Pass, were to aim their effort twenty-five miles east across the Vosges from the Longegoutte forest to Cornimont and La Bresse and ultimately to Guebwiller, at the edge of the Alsatian plain and about thirteen miles south of Colmar (*Map 22*).

In the center, du Vigier's 1st Armored Division was to support the Algerian effort by renewing its attacks in the Le Thillot area and, if successful, was to continue eastward on Route N–66 through the Bussang Pass to St. Amarin and Cernay, seven miles south of Guebwiller. On the II Corps' right, or southern, wing, the French 1st Infantry Division was to act as a hinge anchoring the eastward attack in the vicinity of Ronchamp on Route N–19. Ultimately, de Monsabert hoped that the division would also be able to push eastward just above the city of Belfort. Meanwhile, opposite the Belfort Gap, the French I Corps, with the 2d Moroccan Division on the left and the 9th Colonial on the right, was to undertake a few limited attacks to tie down German forces that otherwise might be shifted to the II Corps front.

De Lattre had initially wanted to add the strength of the French 5th Armored Division to the offensive. The 5th—the third and last of the three French armored divisions equipped by the Americans—had begun arriving in southern France from North Africa on 19 September but, because of French supply and transportation problems, would not close the front until the 20th of October and consequently could play no part in the October attacks. Its arrival in France marked the last major elements of the First French Army to reach the metropole. With only a few minor combat and service units of the approved French troop list remaining in North Africa or on Corsica, further French reinforcements would have to depend on local recruitment and training.

In any case, what de Monsabert needed was not armor, but more infantry. With de Lattre's blessing, therefore, he reinforced the attacking units with the 2d and 3d Tabor Groups, the parachute regiment, the African Commando Group, and the Shock Battalion. In reserve he left the 1st Moroccan Tabor Group, the 2d Algerian Spahis Reconnaissance Regiment (an armored reconnaissance squadron), and, when it arrived sometime after 4 October, the 6th Moroccan Tirailleurs (a regimental combat team of the 4th Moroccan Mountain Division). De Monsabert also planned to employ a number of FFI units to the full extent of their capabilities.

During the initial phase of the attack, de Monsabert wanted the 3d Algerian Division to push its left east across the Moselotte River in the Zainvillers and Thiefosse areas. Simultaneously, its right was to drive north across the Longegoutte forest ridges through the Rahmne Pass, a little over two miles northeast of the Moselle. In the center, the 1st French Armored Division, reinforced heavily with light infantry, was to outflank Le Thillot on the north via the southeastern portion of the Longegoutte

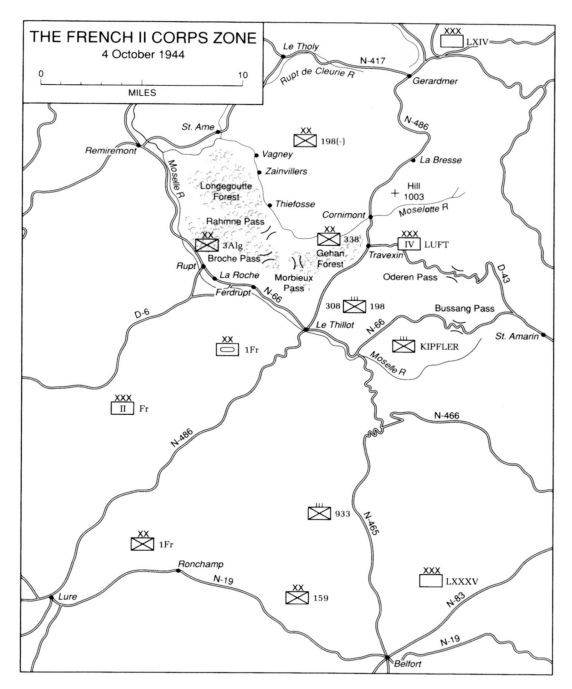

THE FRENCH II CORPS ZONE
4 October 1944

0 _____ 10
MILES

Le Tholy
N-417
Gerardmer

XXX
LXIV

N-486

St. Ame

Remiremont

Moselle R

Vagney

Zainvillers

Longegoutte
Forest

Thiefosse

La Bresse

Hill
1003

Moselotte R

XX
198(-)

Rahmne Pass

Cornimont

XX
3Alg

Broche Pass

Gehan
Forest

XX
338

XXX
IV   LUFT

Travexin

Rupt

La Roche

Morbieux
Pass

Oderen Pass

D-43

Ferdrupt

N-66

308
XXX
198

Bussang Pass

Le Thillot

N-66

St. Amarin

XX
1Fr

Moselle R

XXX
KIPFLER

D-6

XXX
II   Fr

N-486

N-466

933

N-465

XX
1Fr

Ronchamp

N-19

XXX
LXXXV

Lure

XX
159

N-83

Belfort

N-19

MAP 22   This map is printed in full color at the back of the book, following the Index.

3D ALGERIAN DIVISION MOVES UP TO THE RUPT AREA

and Gehan forests and cut the German lines of communication between the Moselotte valley and Le Thillot in a drive that would carry to Cornimont, on the upper Moselotte valley. At the same time the division was to continue pressure toward Le Thillot down Route N–66 southeast from Ferdrupt as well as along N–486 from the southwest.[6]

The 3d Algerian Division began moving into its new sector early on 3 October, and de Monsabert set 4 Oc-

tober as the date his corps would start its new attack. All in all, de Monsabert would begin his October offensive with more strength than was available to Truscott's VI Corps.

The German Defense

At the beginning of October, General Wiese's *Nineteenth Army* had two corps facing de Lattre's French forces, the *IV Luftwaffe Field Corps* in the High Vosges and the *LXXXV Corps* in the Belfort Gap, both now veteran organizations of the southern France campaign.[7] Facing de Monsabert's attacking II Corps, the *IV*

_____

[6] This description represents a great simplification of the French II Corps' General Operations Order 29 of 4 October 1944. This order, quite detailed, is replete with subsidiary tasks, supporting and covering maneuvers, and secondary routes of attack. Like most French Army orders, the II French Corps order contained far more detail than a corps-level field order of the U.S. Army during World War II.

[7] On German operations, see von Luttichau, chs. 19–21.

Luftwaffe Field Corps had on line, north to south, the *338th Infantry Division,* the *308th Grenadiers* of the *198th Division,* and *Regiment C/V.*[8] The *LXXXV Corps* extended the German front south and southeast another twenty-five miles, blocking the southern approaches to Belfort. Facing the far right of the French II Corps and most of Bethouart's I Corps, *LXXXV Corps* deployed across its front the rebuilt *933d Grenadiers,*[9] the *159th Reserve Division,* and three provisional brigades—*Groups Degener, von Oppen,* and *Irmisch*—employing an assortment of fortress units, police formations, and other odds and ends.

Balck, Wiese's superior, decided that the *Nineteenth Army* urgently needed a strong, mobile tactical reserve to supplement the small task force that the *11th Panzer Division* had left behind; he, therefore, directed the *First Army,* on *Army Group G*'s northern wing, to disengage the *106th Panzer Brigade* and the *103d Panzer Battalion* and dispatch both units south to the Belfort sector.[10]

Although primarily worried about the situation in the Rambervillers area, Balck was obviously concerned about the German defenses in the Belfort Gap. At the time he believed that French operations in late September around Le Thillot presaged a more determined effort to outflank the gap on the north, but was equally

concerned about increasing French pressure directly toward Belfort from the west and south, an error made when German intelligence mistook the troop movements of de Lattre's organizational reshuffling for reinforcements to the French forces opposite the Belfort Gap. Looking over the collection of units in Wiese's two southern corps, he characterized their effectiveness as "deplorable," and complained that "never before have I led in battle such motley and poorly equipped troops."[11] Nevertheless, he finally decided to divert the small mobile reserves from the *First Army*— the *106th Panzer Brigade* and the *103d Panzer Battalion*—to the more critical Rambervillers–St. Die area at his center, leaving Wiese with only the detachment of the *11th Panzer Division* as a reserve in the south.[12] Ultimately, the German forces in the south would have to make do with their own resources.

The II French Corps' October Offensive

The renewed offensive of the French II Corps into the Vosges began on 4 October during weather— heavy rain and dense fog—that could hardly have been worse for either infantry or armor in the forested mountains. In general the revised French dispositions pitted the 3d Algerian Division against *LXIV Corps'* *198th*

---

[8] Balck had recently given Wiese permission to commit *Regiment C/V,* another *Wehrkreis V* unit, to front-line duty. As reinforced at the front, *Regiment C/V* was also known as *Group Kipfler.*

[9] This unit was formerly part of the *244th Infantry Division,* the rest of which had surrendered at Marseille in August.

[10] The brigade was a separate, nondivisional unit; the battalion was organic to the *3d Panzer Division.*

[11] Ltr, Balck to Jodl, 10 Oct 44, cited in von Luttichau, "German Operations," ch. 20, p. 14. Although the letter was written on 10 October, there is ample evidence that Balck held the same opinions at the beginning of the month.

[12] The force now consisted of an understrength panzer grenadier battalion, six tanks, and two self-propelled assault guns.

Infantry Division in the Longegoutte and Gehan forests southeast of St. Ame; the French 1st Armored Division against the *IV Luftwaffe Field Corps' 338th Infantry Division* centered around Le Thillot and the surrounding mountains; and the French 1st Infantry Division against assorted *IV Luftwaffe* and *LXXXV Corps* units south of Le Thillot. Although all the French divisions had been beefed up with additional infantry—Moroccans, paratroopers, FFI units, and so forth—they again made little progress during the first days of the offensive. De Monsabert quickly discovered that O'Daniel's 3d Division had done little more in the Rupt-Ferdrupt area than secure the Moselle River bridgeheads, and the attacking French found that they had to fight their way into the heights above the Moselle before they could even attempt to penetrate the Vosges valleys and passes beyond.

On the 4th, the main body of the 1st Armored Division made no progress toward Le Thillot, but on the division's left the attached 1st Parachute Chasseurs, spilling over into the 3d Algerian Division's sector, found gaps in the German defenses along the southern slopes of the Longegoutte and Gehan forests, and pushed several miles north of the Moselle into the Broche and Morbieux passes. De Monsabert quickly decided to exploit the paratroopers' success and directed the armored division to concentrate all possible strength on its left for a rapid thrust northward through the two forests into the Moselotte valley. The rest of the division was to limit its operations to covering actions that would maintain some pressure on German forces along the

rest of the division's front.

Alarmed, the Germans began reinforcing *338th Division* [13] forces in the forests, but on the 5th the French armored division again made significant gains. The left drove through Rahmne Pass to the northern slopes of the Longegoutte forest, while the right pushed through the Gehan forest over a mile east of the Morbieux Pass. The *338th Division* thereupon pulled the *308th Grenadiers* [14] out of the line and assembled the regiment for a counterattack on 6 October.

At first, the German attack achieved considerable success, forcing the French to pull back from the passes and several of the surrounding hills. Confused, bitter fighting raged for two days as units on both sides became isolated or cut off, and both French and German casualties mounted rapidly. Meanwhile, to the south, French armor had managed to push its way down Route N–66 along the north bank of the Moselle, but was finally stopped one mile short of Le Thillot, again failing to take the key junction town. The Germans, however, had no intention of holding on to the two forests. The *338th Division* began to break off the action during the night of 7–8 October and the next night withdrew across the Moselotte, keeping only the northernmost section of the Gehan forest near Corni-

---

[13] On 4 October the *338th Division* sent forward its headquarters guard company and the *338th Replacement Battalion,* and on the next day the *Nineteenth Army* released two fortress machine-gun battalions to the division.

[14] This unit was a *198th Division* regiment attached to the *338th Division.* At the time the *338th* also controlled *Regiment C/V* and its organic *757th Grenadier Regiment* along its front.

mont, and leaving the French with their first foothold in the High Vosges.

The initial affray had been expensive for the Germans—the *308th Grenadiers* lost over 200 men taken prisoner alone—and the *Nineteenth Army* had to scrape up reinforcements for both *LXIV Corps* and *IV Luftwaffe Field Corps*. The army now sent forward four fortress machine-gun battalions, three fortress infantry battalions, and, demonstrating the scope of the German replacement problem, 150 troops from an NCO school at Colmar. Wiese also sent some assault guns and the small task force of the *11th Panzer Division* northward from the Belfort area to Le Thillot, which had now become the key to the German defensive line in the area under attack.

Taking up the offensive as the Germans withdrew, the 3d Algerian Division began attacking east and south from the St. Ame area between 9 and 13 October. Pushing only about six miles east of Vagney, its advance was continually hampered by foul weather and increasing supply problems. The inability of the II Corps to secure the road hub at Le Thillot forced the French to employ long, circuitous supply routes through St. Ame to support both the reinforced 3d Algerian Division and fully a third of the 1st Armored Division. Driving across or along one forested height after another, the French gained control of high ground and muddy mountain trails, but German artillery, mortar, and antitank fire made it impossible for them to use the main, paved roads through the valleys.

During the period 9–13 October

progress was limited on the 3d Algerian Division's left, where flank protection requirements and the need to take over American positions absorbed much of its strength. Heavier fighting took place at the center and especially on the right, where the Algerians assumed responsibility for the Gehan forest sector. They cleared the last Germans from the northeastern part of the Gehan forest on 13 October and the same day cut route N–486 near Travexin, a mile or so south of Cornimont, which fell to the French on 14 October after the departing Germans had burned down most of the village.

Pausing briefly to redeploy units and build up supplies, the Algerians resumed the attack on 16 October. On the left the objective was La Bresse, a road junction town between Cornimont and Gerardmer. In this sector the 6th Moroccan Tirailleurs of the 4th Moroccan Mountain Division led off.[15] Crossing N–486 north of Cornimont, the Moroccans pushed up Hill 1003 (Le Haut du Faing), dominating the upper Moselotte valley as far as La Bresse. A bloody three-day battle ensued as the 6th Moroccans—suffering about 700 casualties in the process—first seized the broad height and then secured it against strong German counterattacks. However, the 3d Algerian Division could make no substantive progress elsewhere during the period 16–18 October, and the Moroccan infantrymen found it impossible to advance beyond Hill 1003.

---

[15] The 6th Moroccan Tirailleurs had previously been de Monsabert's reserve force and had been committed only with the concurrence of de Lattre.

To the south, CC Deshazars [16] of the 1st French Armored Division drove east along the axis of Route D–43 from Travexin with the immediate objective of seizing the Oderen Pass, which would provide a rather indirect and difficult route across the High Vosges. The combat command's infantry advanced about two miles east of Travexin along high ground north and south of D–43, but the armor, in the face of German fire, could not break out of the mountain village. Beyond some isolated gains, the best the French armored division had to show after three days was possession of that portion of Route N–486 north of Le Thillot. But the achievement was of little value to the French as long as the Germans still controlled the junction of Routes N–66 and N–486 at Le Thillot itself and were able to resupply the town from the south.

By 17 October General de Lattre had had enough. Never completely enamored of General de Monsabert's plan to drive across the High Vosges in a deep, northerly envelopment of the Belfort Gap, the First French Army commander, on 17 October, decided to bring the operation to a halt. While the II Corps had made substantial gains in the area north and northeast of Le Thillot across a front of nearly twelve miles, de Lattre concluded that they had been too costly and indecisive. Moreover, south of Le Thillot, the right wing of II Corps had made no significant progress. Nowhere were de Monsa-

bert's forces ready or able to drive through the passes of the High Vosges and into the Belfort Gap or the Alsatian plains. Meanwhile, the transfer of troops and supplies to de Monsabert's forces had virtually immobilized General Bethouart's command, which, during the first half of October, had had little opportunity to begin preparations for its own offensive directly through the Belfort Gap.

Also evident to de Lattre, the forces of the II Corps had been exhausted by the slow forest fighting. The 3d Algerian Division and its attachments were spread thin in the mountains and valleys; the 6th Moroccan Tirailleurs had been chewed to bits in just three days of action; and the 1st Parachute Chasseurs (attached to the 1st French Armored Division) was operating on little more than esprit de corps. The terrain, coupled with German artillery and antitank fire, had made it impossible for the French 1st Armored Division to bring its firepower to bear; its own infantry forces, some three battalions, were equally tired. Supply problems were increasing with every yard the French gained, while unusually poor weather (exceptionally early snow had already fallen in the Vosges) complicated both logistical and tactical operations.

To resume the attack, de Monsabert would need either fresh infantry reinforcements or direct assistance from Truscott's VI Corps. De Lattre realized that both solutions were out of the question. Truscott, resting the 3d Division for his main attack on St. Die, was not about to shift the division back to Le Thillot; throwing more French strength into the Vosges

---

[16] Formerly CC Sudre or CC1. On 29 September General Sudre became assistant division commander, and Colonel Deshazars de Montgaillard, previously Sudre's second in command, took over the unit.

would probably force de Lattre to postpone his offensive against the Belfort Gap for several months. All the French infantry, except for minimum essential reserves and some poorly equipped FFI units of questionable quality, had already been committed. Moreover, Devers was pressing de Lattre to relieve the 1st Airborne Task Force along the Riviera and in the Maritime Alps, a task that could only divert more French infantry from the Vosges and Belfort sections. Even worse, de Lattre soon learned, the French provisional government was making plans to mount an all-French operation to secure the port of Bordeaux on the Atlantic coast, an effort that might force him to relinquish two of his divisions for at least several months.

De Lattre thus concluded that the tactical situation, the state of his army, and the heavy rains, snowfalls, and freezing temperatures expected in the mountains (the early harsh weather of October seemed to foreshadow a severe winter) made it impracticable for the First French Army to push strong forces into Alsace except through the relatively easy terrain of the Belfort Gap. A resumption of de Monsabert's assault in the north could well result in immobilizing the bulk of the First French Army along the western slopes of the Vosges until springtime. Instead, de Lattre decided, his offensive center of gravity would have to be shifted back to the Belfort Gap sector, and preparations to launch his long-planned offensive there would be given first priority. Henceforth, de Monsabert's activities would be limited to consolidating the gains already made, while conducting limited patrols and perhaps some minor offensive actions to keep German attention focused on the area.

General de Monsabert learned of de Lattre's decision on 17 October and formally halted the corps' Vosges offensive the next day. Although disappointed that his attacks had not made greater gains, he continued to feel, with characteristic optimism, that further reinforcements would have allowed the II Corps to regain its momentum and drive through the Vosges passes within a short time. Yet, de Monsabert could find some satisfaction in his corps' accomplishments since the beginning of October. The II Corps had freed over 200 square miles of French soil; had driven the enemy from many French towns, villages, and hamlets; had liberated thousands of French citizens; and, by French estimates, had killed about 3,300 Germans and captured over 2,000 more during the period 1–18 October—the equivalent of nine German infantry battalions.[17] The command had also forced the Germans to reinforce their front with numerous infantry and weapons battalions from the main *Weststellung* positions, thereby weakening that defensive line; it had likewise prompted the Germans to redeploy other troops from the Belfort Gap sector to bolster the Vosges front. The French offensive had even forced the German commanders to import additional reinforcements into the Vosges from other areas, including Germany

---

[17] Based on sketchy sources, French casualties totaled about 450 men killed and 2,000 wounded during the same period.

proper. Finally, under the most miserable conditions of terrain and weather and while facing shortages of artillery ammunition and other supply problems, the French II Corps had beaten back the strongest counterattacks the Germans would mount.

Perhaps de Monsabert's real problem was the inability of Devers at this stage to coordinate the efforts of the Seventh Army with those of the French and to move the full weight of the 6th Army Group against the German defenses. However, as in the north, such a unified offensive would have to wait for major improvements in the Allied supply situation. In the meantime, it remained to be seen whether Truscott's VI Corps or Bethouart's I Corps could profit from the sacrifices of de Monsabert's forces and the attention that Wiese and Balck had been forced to pay to the southern Vosges.

CHAPTER XVII

Into the High Vosges

While the U.S. XV Corps and the French II Corps undertook only limited operations during the second half of October, VI Corps resumed its drive toward St. Die on the 15th.[1] The renewed attack had several objectives. First was the seizure of Bruyeres and Brouvelieures. To sustain the offensive toward St. Die, the VI Corps still needed the rail and highway facilities in this region, lying at the center of the corps' axis of advance. Second, Truscott wanted to secure a suitable line of departure along the constantly rising, forested terrain east and northeast of Bruyeres and Brouvelieures. With these areas in hand, the VI Corps could begin its main attack—a three-division drive on St. Die—on or about 23 October, spearheaded by O'Daniel's 3d Division. Appropriately named Operation DOGFACE, the attack was to carry the VI Corps at least as far as the high ground that overlooked a ten-mile stretch of the Meurthe River valley and

Route N–59 between St. Die and Raon-l'Etape *(Map 23)*. DOGFACE, in turn, would constitute a prelude to an even larger offensive scheduled by Devers for mid-November, which would push the entire 6th Army Group over the Vosges and through the Belfort Gap.

Planning the Attack

General Truscott, commanding the VI Corps, had no illusions about the difficulties of carrying DOGFACE through to a rapid conclusion, or even of quickly executing the preliminaries of the operation against Brouvelieures and Bruyeres that were to begin on 15 October. While VI Corps' general supply situation had improved since the beginning of the month, some problems remained. The distribution of winter clothing was far from complete, critical shortages of mortar and artillery ammunition persisted, and even stricter rationing had to be imposed on artillery expenditures. The 13th Field Artillery Battalion of the 36th Division, for example, estimated that during the last half of October the unit could have fired a ten-day ration of its 105-mm. howitzer ammunition profitably in about ten minutes. Furthermore, Truscott felt that the VI

---

[1] The successive American plans are based on the following sources: *Seventh Army Rpt*, II, 363–64, 370–71; Seventh Army Diary, entries of 11, 15, and 19 Oct 44; VI Corps OI 1, 11 Oct 44; VI Corps FO 4, 13 Oct 44; VI Corps FO 5, 19 Oct 44; VI Corps OP Plan DOGFACE, 15 Oct 44; Msg, VI Corps to 45th Div, 212100A Oct 44; 3d Inf Div OI 89, 19 Oct 44; 36th Inf Div OI 12200A Oct 44; 36th Inf Div OI 191500A Oct 44; 45th Inf Div OI 1, 12 Oct 44.

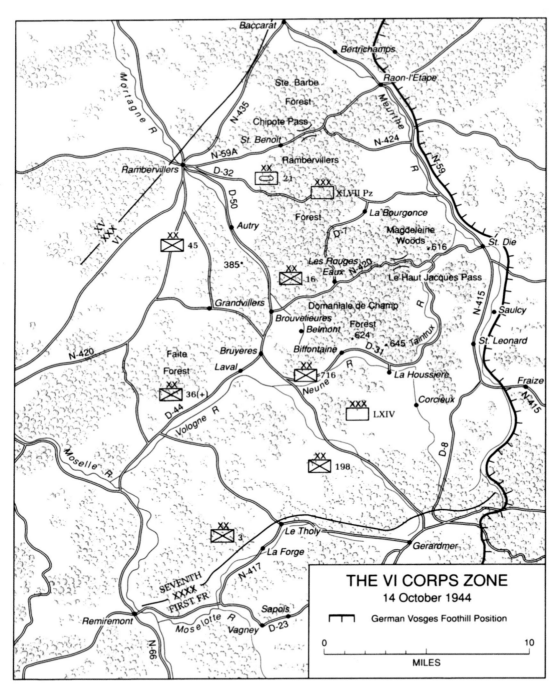

Baccarat

Bertrichamps

Raon-l'Etape

Ste. Barbe
Forest

Mortagne R

N-435

Chipote Pass

St. Benoit

N-424

Meurthe

N-59

R

Rambervillers

Rambervillers

N-59A

D-32

XX
21

XXX
XLVII Pz

La Bourgonce

St. Die

D-50

Forest

D-7

Magdeleine
Woods   •616

XV
XXX
VI

Autry

XX
45

385•

Les Rouges
Eaux   N-420

Le Haut Jacques Pass

R

N-415

Saulcy

XX
16

Grandvillers

Domaniale de Champ

Brouvelieures

Forest
Belmont   624•   •645 Taintrux

St. Leonard

N-420

Faite
Forest

Bruyeres

Biffontaine

D-31

Fraize

Laval

Neune   R

XX
716

La Houssiere

N-415

XX
36(+)

D-44

Vologne R

XXX
LXIV

Corcieux

D-8

Moselle R

XX
198

Le Tholy

La Forge

Gerardmer

XX
3

SEVENTH
XXXX
FIRST FR

N-417

Sapois

Remiremont

N-66

Moselotte R   Vagney   D-23

THE VI CORPS ZONE
14 October 1944

⊏⊐ German Vosges Foothill Position

0   10

MILES

MAP 23   This map is printed in full color at the back of the book, following the Index.

Corps lacked the heavy artillery needed for mountain fighting in the Vosges. About the only bright spot in the picture was the availability of ample ammunition for tanks and tank destroyers as well as for the cannon companies of the infantry regiments. But how much use the armor would be in the increasingly difficult terrain was very hard to predict.

Truscott also had misgivings about the condition of his infantry. For the DOGFACE preliminaries against the Bruyeres-Brouvelieures region, the picture was particularly bleak. On the north the 157th Infantry of the 45th Division and the 117th Cavalry Squadron were fully occupied with securing the VI Corps' left flank at Rambervillers and maintaining contact with the XV Corps. Until the 3d Division's thrust, which was to pass through the 45th Division's right, allowed the 45th to redeploy strength northward, the 157th and 117th could contribute little, leaving the burden of the fighting to the 179th and 180th regiments. But these two units had not yet recovered from their failure in early October to seize Bruyeres and Brouvelieures, and both were still tired and understrength.

The status of the 36th Division was mixed. The division had been reinforced for the 15 October preliminaries by the Japanese-American 442d Regimental Combat Team. This unit, composed primarily of American citizens of Japanese ancestry, had arrived in France from Italy at the end of September and was experienced and relatively fresh.[2] However, the efforts of

the 36th Division to rotate its infantry battalions in the line during the first half of October had been only partially successful in providing rest and rehabilitation. In addition, all of the division's nine infantry battalions had a serious shortage of foot soldiers, with the individual rifle companies averaging about 121 officers and enlisted men out of an authorized strength of 193 (but the 442d's companies averaged 180 men).

For the attacks on the Bruyeres-Brouvelieures area, the 36th Division would have available only the 442d and 143d Infantry regiments. The rest of the division was temporarily confined to defensive roles, covering the corps' right flank and relieving the 3d Division's 30th Infantry in the Le Tholy–La Forge sector. The 36th Division's right-flank units (and the 30th Infantry as well) were also to participate in a deception effort designed to make the Germans believe that the 3d Division, rather than redeploying, was actually concentrating for an attack eastward from the Le

---

Combat Team (Washington, D.C.: Infantry Journal Press, 1946), pp. 49–72. For previous operations of the 442d regiment in Italy, see Fisher, *Cassino to the Alps,* chs. 14–15. The last elements of the 442d had pulled out of the front lines in Italy on 6 September. In addition to the 442d Infantry, the regimental combat team's principal components were the 522d Field Artillery Battalion (105-mm. howitzers) and the 232d Combat Engineer Company. For the 15 October attack, attachments to the 442d included the 36th Cavalry Reconnaissance Troop, 36th Division; Company B, 753d Tank Battalion; Company C, 636th Tank Destroyer Battalion; Company D, 83d Chemical Mortar Battalion; and the 886th Medical Collecting Company. The regiment had a continuous problem with infantry shortages caused by the lack of qualified Japanese-American (Nisei) replacements in the NATOUSA replacement system. While still in Italy in late September the 442d had received about 675 replacements, but most arrived directly from the United States.

---

[2] Additional information on the operations of the 442d Regimental Combat Team can be found in Orville C. Shirey, *Americans: The Story of the 442d*

Tholy area toward Gerardmer in conjunction with the French II Corps offensive to the south.

Truscott expected that the 3d Division's infantry would be in better shape for the main DOGFACE offensive. While the 36th and 45th Divisions were securing Brouvelieures and Bruyeres between 15 and 23 October, O'Daniel's division would be resting at least two of its infantry regiments, the 7th and the 15th, for one week or more following their relief by French II Corps forces. However, the division's 30th Infantry, holding defensively in the Le Tholy–La Forge area, might not be available until later; therefore, the 3d Division would probably have to begin its attack toward St. Die, the main DOGFACE effort, with only two-thirds of its combat strength.

Truscott also worried about the terrain and weather his troops would be facing during both the preliminary operations and DOGFACE itself. His staff expected that precipitation would increase during the last half of October, with rain, wet snow, fog, mist, and low-hanging clouds continuing to hinder both tactical air support and airborne forward observers (artillery spotters in light aircraft). On the ground, forward artillery observers would often be unable to see potential targets or analyze the results of friendly fire. The rising, rough, and often densely forested terrain lying on the corps' route of advance would also complicate the problems of artillery registration and observation. Compared to the Vosges, the affair of the XV Corps in the Forest of Parroy would appear tame.

The rugged Vosges terrain continued to provide the Germans with various natural defensive advantages—advantages which they could be expected to improve on throughout the coming battle. To the left of Route N–420—the main road leading to St. Die—the vast, wooded ridge and mountain complex of the Rambervillers forest stretched northward over eight miles to Route N–59A, linking the towns of Rambervillers and Raon-l'Etape. The main part of the forest averaged about five miles in width, west to east; but a southeasterly portion, the Magdeleine woods, extended another five miles to culminate in heights of some 2,100 feet overlooking St. Die. Between Routes N–59A and N–420 only one second-class road, Route D–32, penetrated the difficult terrain, although many lesser unpaved roads, trails, and tracks cut through all reaches of the old forest.

To the right and south of Route N–420 lay the equally rugged and wooded terrain of the Domaniale de Champ forest, bisected only by a third-class road, D–31, which passed along the valley floor of the small Neune and Taintrux streams. East of D–31 the terrain was equally difficult until reaching the Meurthe River valley and the north-south Route N–415, which linked St. Die with Gerardmer and roughly constituted the VI Corps' right, or southern, boundary.

In the DOGFACE preliminaries, the center and right of the 45th Division, with the 180th Infantry on the north and the 179th to the south, were to seize Brouvelieures and then push north of the Mortagne River, east and west of Route N–420. The 180th Infantry would first clear the high, wooded ground that the Germans still held west of Brouvelieures, including Hill 385. At the same time, the 179th Infantry would seize Brouvelieures from the south and, in support of the 36th Division's attack on Bruyeres, clear the forested hills between the two towns. Once these tasks had been accomplished, the two regiments would secure forward assembly areas across the Mortagne River for the main DOGFACE attack.

As its share of the DOGFACE preliminaries, the 36th Division was to advance north, with the attached 442d Regimental Combat Team on the left and its organic 143d regiment on the right. The 442d, striking east across wooded hills west of Bruyeres, would seize the town, clear the surrounding heights, and then push a few miles farther to the village of Belmont, coming abreast of the 45th Division units on its left. Meanwhile, the 143d Infantry would secure crossings over the Vologne River in the Laval region and then head northeast along the Neune River valley to Biffontaine, four miles east of Bruyeres, thereby anchoring the right flank of the assembly area. The rest of the 36th Division was to hold defensive positions along high ground south of Biffontaine, ultimately relieving the 30th Infantry, 3d Division, in the Le Tholy area.

The 36th Division thus had an extended front—over ten miles from Biffontaine to Le Tholy—but Truscott evidently felt the division would have little problem with the task. The battles during the first half of October had seriously depleted German strength in the area between the Vologne River and Le Tholy, and Truscott estimated that planned deception

operations and limited French pressure would keep the Germans on the defensive in this sector. Then, when the 3d Division began its surprise attack toward St. Die, German attention would be diverted from the 36th Division's right flank to the center of the VI Corps' zone. The risks seemed acceptable.

Finally, during the DOGFACE preliminaries the 3d Division was to redeploy secretly to positions behind the center and right of the 45th Division. From there the 3d Division would eventually lead the main attack on 23 October, striking through the 45th Division and pushing toward St. Die generally on the edge of the Rambervillers forest between Routes D–32 and N–420. Once the 3d Division's surprise attack was well along, the 45th Division would shift its strength northward to clear the northern section of the Rambervillers forest from D–32 to Route N–59A, and the 36th Division would push east through the Domaniale de Champ forest, further anchoring the corps' right flank.

German Deployments

On 15 October the *Fifth Panzer Army*'s *XLVII Panzer Corps* still held a 23-mile front that included the roughly six miles between Rambervillers and Bruyeres.[3] At the time, the *21st Panzer Division* had responsibility for the northern part of the Rambervillers-Bruyeres sector, and the *16th Volksgrenadier Division* had the southern

---

[3] German information in this chapter is based largely on von Luttichau, "German Operations," chs. 19 and especially 21.

half; the small town of Autry on Route D–50 marked the boundary between the two units. Below the Bruyeres region, the *Nineteenth Army*'s *LXIV Corps* covered from Laval south through the area around Le Tholy with the *716th* and *198th Divisions*. The Germans, however, were in the midst of another command and control reorganization that was to cause some confusion during the ensuing battle. On 17 October, *XLVII Panzer Corps* headquarters was scheduled to be replaced by the *LXXXIX Corps* under Lt. Gen. Werner Freiherr von und zu Gilsa and responsibility for the corps zone would be transferred to the *Nineteenth Army*.[4] While the panzer corps was leaving for the *Army Group B* front, von Gilsa arrived on the 17th, but with only his chief of staff and little else; it would be 23 October before his corps staff was assembled and fully operational.

Additional strength available to the *Nineteenth Army* included four fortress infantry regiments and twenty fortress battalions (infantry, machine gun, or artillery). By 15 October three of the four fortress infantry regiments were fully committed to the front lines, as were all but one or two of the fortress battalions; most were in the process of being absorbed into the regular infantry divisions. Thus, according to the German system of accounting, von Gilsa's *LXXXIX Corps* had perhaps 22,000 combat effectives, and the *LXIV Corps*, under General Thumm, had as many as 18,000. Although the bulk of these troops could be considered adequate for defensive purposes only, the figures contrasted sharply with Seventh Army G–2 estimates in October, which gave the *LXXXIX Corps* only 5,200 combat effectives and the *LXIV Corps* no more than 3,000. The low American figures probably reflected the inability of Allied intelligence to track the German fortress (*Weststellung*) units and their incorporation into the line infantry divisions. During the entire month of October, for example, the Seventh Army G–2 could account for only six of the nineteen fortress battalions that the Germans committed to forward defensive roles, and by the end of the month the G–2 assessments allowed for only one of the three *Wehrkreis V* fortress infantry regiments also deployed to the front.[5]

Beyond the *Weststellung* units, General Wiese of *Nineteenth Army* could expect few reinforcements to feed into the front lines or to form any reserve. Scheduled arrivals for the last half of October included the *201st* and *202d Mountain Battalions*, light infantry units of about 1,000 men each.[6] Wiese was also to receive an understrength infantry battalion consisting of troops on probation from courts-martial and a similar unit made up of men suffering or recovering from ear ailments.

---

[4] As related earlier, von Manteuffel's *Fifth Panzer Army* headquarters also left about the same time, and its northern corps, the *LVIII Panzer Corps*, temporarily became part of the *First Army*.

[5] The German strength figures are cited in von Luttichau, "German Operations," ch. 21 (for background on the *Wehrkreis V* regiments, see ibid., ch. 19); the American estimates are from "G–2 History: Seventh Army Operations in Europe," III, 1–31 Oct 44, William W. Quinn Papers, MHI.

[6] A large proportion of the troops of these two battalions had previously been members of mountain divisions, and more than 50 percent of these troops, especially the officers and senior NCOs, were experienced.

The *Nineteenth Army*'s main armored reserve in mid-October was the *106th Panzer Brigade*, actually little more than a reduced tank battalion reinforced with supporting combat and service units that rendered the "brigade" somewhat self-sufficient. On 15 October the *106th* was stationed in the *IV Luftwaffe Field Corps'* sector south of the *LXIV Corps*. Also in reserve was the *1st Battalion, 130th Panzer Regiment*, located near Corcieux, in the *LXIV Corps'* sector, about eight miles east of Bruyeres.[7]

The *Nineteenth Army*'s artillery was in better shape. The supply of artillery and mortar ammunition had increased considerably, and the transfer of fortress artillery battalions to front-line support helped 'to augment defensive fires. Shorter and more stabilized lines of communication, developing as the Germans grudgingly fell back to the east, further eased ammunition supply problems, while inclement weather aided German efforts to move ammunition and troops on highways and railroads during daylight hours by limiting Allied air interdiction strikes. In addition, Allied artillery ammunition shortages restricted the amount of fire used to harass German supply operations, especially in the VI Corps area where Truscott was trying to build up his stocks for direct combat support missions. Finally each German division in front of the VI Corps had been reinforced by an antiaircraft battalion, the batteries of which were generally positioned at critical points, readily

available for ground support roles.

The missions and tactics of *Nineteenth Army* remained unaltered. General Balck of *Army Group G* still insisted that Wiese's units hold well forward of the main *Weststellung* positions and counterattack all Allied penetrations of their forward defensive lines. Rejecting the argument that an immediate withdrawal to the *Weststellung* would conserve both men and materiel, Balck still hoped that his delaying tactics would gain the time needed to complete the *Weststellung* fortifications and to man the defenses with newly organized fortress units from Germany. The transferral of so many fortress units to the *Nineteenth Army*'s forward defenses and the continual delays in the various *Weststellung* construction projects because of poor weather and labor shortages only increased his determination to make a stand well forward of the *Vosges Foothill Position*, the *Weststellung*'s first line of defense on the east bank of the Meurthe River.[8]

West of the *Vosges Foothill Position*, the Germans constructed only hasty field fortifications. However, from bitter experience VI Corps troops knew that the so-called hasty defenses they would encounter in the heavily forested high ground lying north and south of Route 420 could be formidable. All roads and trails would be

---

[7] Some minor elements of the *11th Panzer Division* were still in the *Nineteenth Army*'s zone on 15 October, but were soon to move north to the *First Army*.

[8] The *Vosges Foothill Position* began on the Rhine-Marne Canal at Lagarde, about twelve miles northeast of Luneville. The line ran south to the Meurthe at Baccarat, followed the east bank of the river past Raon-l'Etape and St. Die to the vicinity of Fraize, seven miles south of St. Die, and extended on south past Le Thillot to tie into the defenses of the Belfort Gap. Farther east, generally following the crest of the Vosges Mountains, lay the *Vosges Ridge Position*, the final *Weststellung* defensive line.

blocked by tangles of felled trees, and most barriers would be booby-trapped, mined, covered by machine-gun fire, or carefully targeted by German mortars and artillery. Numerous infantry strongpoints, often well concealed, covered by tree trunks, and supported by artillery and anti-tank weapons, would have to be laboriously eliminated one by one. All but the best-paved roads would break up under heavy military traffic, and wet weather would quickly turn lesser roads and mountain trails into quagmires. Elaborate minefields could be expected on critical open ground, and randomly sown mines and booby traps along roads and trails. Tree bursts from German artillery had proved especially troublesome in such terrain, and the VI Corps' infantrymen would also encounter increasing amounts of barbed-wire entanglements wherever they went.

The Preliminary Attacks

Elements of the 45th Division's 180th Infantry began the offensive early. On 14 October the regiment cleared the last Germans from battered Hill 385 overlooking the Mortagne valley and, with its rear secured, began advancing toward Brouvelieures; the 179th Infantry joined the effort on the following day. For the next four days the two regiments slowly pushed back into the wooded ridges and hills that they had abandoned after the German counterattack of 6 October, confirming that the *16th Volksgrenadier Division* had made good use of the intervening days to improve old defenses and construct new ones.

Progress against determined resistance was slow but steady. On 19 October General Eagles reinforced the 179th Infantry with a battalion of the 157th from Rambervillers, and by the 21st, after repeated attacks, the units found German resistance in the area beginning to collapse. By 1540 that afternoon the 179th Infantry had troops in Brouvelieures, where house-to-house fighting continued until dark, while advance units of the 3d Division came up from the south to secure an intact bridge over the Mortagne a mile north of Brouvelieures. The following day, 22 October, the 179th and 180th Infantry regiments mopped up west of the Mortagne; however, elements of the 180th, attempting to seize another bridge, had to fall back west of the river in the face of heavy German fire, and the defenders quickly destroyed the span. Although successful in occupying Brouvelieures, Eagles wondered if his division would still have to fight its way north over the Mortagne River to secure the assembly areas for Truscott.

The slow advance of the 45th Division was balanced by the surprisingly rapid progress of Dahlquist's 36th Division on the corps' right wing. Although fighting across well-defended forested ridges and hills, staving off numerous small German counterattacks, and subject to heavy German artillery and mortar fire, the fresh 442d Infantry had cleared the hills immediately west and north of Bruyeres late in the afternoon of 18 October, unhinging the German defenses at Bruyeres and forcing the *716th Division*'s right wing to withdraw. South of Bruyeres, Laval fell to

JAPANESE-AMERICAN INFANTRY (442D RCT) IN HILLS AROUND BRUYERES

the 143d Infantry on 15 October, and the regiment had secured several crossings over the Vologne River by the 17th. On 18 October the 143d began pushing into Bruyeres from the south, while the 442d probed into the city from the north and west; patrols from the two units began to run into one another early that evening. The next day the 143d Infantry took over the burden of clearing artillery-shattered Bruyeres, while the 442d secured the heights east of the town and began advancing farther north toward Belmont and the Domaniale de Champ forest.

The 3d Division Attacks

The slow progress of the 45th Divi-sion and the success of the 36th resulted in Truscott's modifying his plans for the main attack. By noon of 19 October he realized that a dangerous gap was growing between the two attacking divisions because of their disparate rates of advance. But he also believed that adhering to his original plan and holding the 36th Division in the Bruyeres area to wait for the 45th to cross the Mortagne River would only destroy the momentum of the 36th's attack and give the Germans time to reform their crumbling defenses. Accordingly, on 19 October, Truscott asked General O'Daniel if one of the 3d Division's waiting regiments, either the 7th or 15th, could move into the line between the 36th and 45th Divisions on 20 October from the regimental assembly areas near Remiremont. With O'Daniel's assurance that at least one and possibly both regiments could be ready by noon on the 20th, Truscott ordered the 3d Division to begin its attack at once, passing through the Brouvelieures-Bruyeres area and advancing northeast on Route N–420, while pushing into the wooded hills on both sides of the highway. When available, the 30th Infantry could be committed on the division's left. The new plan, in effect, made the 3d Division responsible for securing much of the 45th Division's portion of the DOGFACE line of departure as well as for taking over the 45th Division's mission to attack northeast along Route N–420. Nevertheless, it enabled Truscott to take advantage of the new tactical situation of the VI Corps and focused the combat power of O'Daniel's 3d Division on a narrower route of advance without any loss of momentum.

During the afternoon of 20 October the 3d Division's 7th Infantry secured a key road junction about midway between Bruyeres and Brouvelieures and cleared a steep-sided hill mass immediately east of the crossroads. Late in the day the 15th Infantry assembled near the junction, and both regiments began preparations for a major push north up Route N–420 the following morning. To all intents and purposes, the DOGFACE operation itself would commence three days earlier than Truscott had planned.

The progress of the 3d Division was rapid. By the 22d the attacking regiments were approaching Les Rouges Eaux, about halfway to St. Die, forcing remnants of the *16th*

Volksgrenadier Division back into the forests on either side of the road. At the same time the success of the 3d Division made conditions easier for the 36th, which was operating east of N–420. On 22 October the 36th Division's Felber Force, an ad hoc armored task force commanded by Lt. Col. Joseph G. Felber,[9] secured Belmont; meanwhile, the 442d and 143d regiments fought their way across the southern sector of the Domaniale de Champ forest through elements of the *716th Division*, halting only after reaching the high wooded ground above the Neune River valley just short of Biffontaine.[10] In doing so, the 36th Division had accomplished its part of the initial DOGFACE objectives and, as a bonus, had driven a wedge between the *LXXXIX Corps' 16th Volksgrenadier Division* and the *LXIV Corps' 716th Division.*

The successes of both the 3d and 36th Divisions were the product of Truscott's rapid change of plans. In addition, the deception operations of the VI Corps and the French II Corps had succeeded admirably in keeping German attention focused on the Gerardmer sector of the Vosges front. Not until the morning of 23 October did the *Nineteenth Army* learn of the 3d Division's redeployment to the VI

[9] This particular Felber Force, only one of many led by Colonel Felber, who commanded the 753d Tank Battalion, consisted of the 753d Tank Battalion (less Companies A, C, and D); 36th Cavalry Reconnaissance Troop, 36th Division; Company C (−), 636th Tank Destroyer Battalion; Company A (−), 442d Infantry; and Platoon, 111th Engineer Battalion, 36th Division.
[10] German sources state that American troops captured Biffontaine on 22 October, but American records show that the 442d Infantry did not secure the town until after a four-hour, house-to-house fight on the 23d.

Corps' center, but by then Truscott's forces had driven a deep salient into the German forward defenses in the Bruyeres sector, and the resulting confusion in the German front lines made it even more difficult to move local reinforcements to the threatened area. On the evening of 22 October, Truscott was thus justified in feeling that once again the German forces across his front were on the verge of complete collapse.

However encouraging, the developing situation forced Truscott to make further revisions in his DOGFACE plans on the 22d.[11] On his left, or northern, flank, the 45th Division was preparing to cross the Mortagne River in strength north of Brouvelieures that night. In the center, the 3d Division's surprise attack had exceeded expectations, and its two attacking regiments were well on their way to St. Die. On the right, the 36th Division had two regiments in sight of the Biffontaine objective line; in accordance with the basic DOGFACE concept, both units were ready to move on to clear the northern and eastern sections of the Domaniale de Champ.

For the moment, Truscott decided to leave the corps' current dispositions unchanged. With the 3d Division now making the main effort via N–420, he directed the 45th Division to clear the Rambervillers forest area, advancing first across the Mortagne River and then pushing north, using Route D–32 as a phase line. The 45th Division's 157th regiment would join the effort from Rambervillers, and the final objectives of the division would take it to Routes N–59, N–59A, Raon-l'Etape, and the Meurthe River valley. The 36th Engineer Combat Regiment[12] and the 117th Cavalry Squadron, both under direct corps control, would guard the 45th Division's left flank and maintain contact with the XV Corps' French 2d Armored Division north of Rambervillers.

In the VI Corps center the 3d Division's immediate mission was to seize the road junction town of Les Rouges Eaux on Route N–420. Once this town was secured, O'Daniel wanted one of his regiments to advance northeast toward La Bourgonce, taking the high ground on the north side of Route N–420; meanwhile, the rest of the division would push east down both sides of the road, securing it as the corps' main supply route and occupying the high ground in the Magdeleine woods, overlooking St. Die. The division's ultimate objective was a three-mile stretch of the west bank of the Meurthe just north of St. Die, but not the city itself, the larger part of which lay on the opposite side of the river.

Truscott's new plans also envisioned more extensive objectives for the 36th Division. On the left the 442d Infantry was to clear the northern part of the Domaniale de Champ forest and then assemble in reserve at Belmont. In the division's center, the 143d regiment

---

[11] The new plans described here developed mainly during the course of 22 October, with written orders being issued on the 23d. Sources for the new plans included the following: Telecon, CG VI Corps and CG 3d Inf Div, 220745A Oct 44; Telecon, CG VI Corps and CG 45th Inf Div, 220855A Oct 44; Telecon, G-3 VI Corps and G-3 3d Inf Div, 221105A Oct 44; Telecons, CofS 3d Inf Div and COs 7th, 15th, and 30th Inf Regts, 22 Oct; VI Corps FO 6, 23 Oct 44; 3d Inf Div OIs 90 and 94, 23 Oct 44; 36th Inf Div OI 221400A Oct 44; 45th Inf Div OI 2, 23 Oct 44.

[12] A nondivisional unit attached to VI Corps.

was to hold in place while the 141st continued the attack, pushing through the eastern section of the Domaniale de Champ and securing the high ground that overlooked La Houssiere. The regiment's final objective was the forested hills just west of St. Leonard, a railroad town on Route N–415 about five miles farther east of La Houssiere and a similar distance south of St. Die. Once in reserve, the 442d would assist the 141st as necessary. On the division's (and the corps') right flank, the 143d and 142d Regimental Combat Teams, north to south, would defend the area from Biffontaine south to the vicinity of Le Tholy; ultimately they would relieve the 3d Division's 30th regiment still in the Le Tholy area and mesh with the French II Corps' 3d Algerian Division.

Truscott, however, would never see his revised DOGFACE plans executed. Destined for a higher level command in the Italian theater, he turned over the VI Corps to Maj. Gen. Edward H. Brooks at noon on 25 October and left the Vosges front.[13] The Seventh Army

had lost its hard-charging corps commander, who had in many ways dominated the Allied campaign in southern France from the Riviera beaches to the Vosges Mountains. For over two months he had feverishly kept his three American infantry divisions on the move, forever harassing the retreating Germans and allowing them little time to rest and reorganize. His new offensive was yet another attempt to destroy the German defenses before they could solidify—an attempt that, like those before, was to be undertaken in the face of severe Allied logistical difficulties. However, the effort was also marked by much tactical and operational imagination, such as the secret massing of the 3d Division in the corps' rear. Lucian Truscott would be missed in northern France. Nevertheless, the new phase of the DOGFACE attack would begin almost immediately under the direction of General Brooks.[14]

---

[13] Truscott took command of the U.S. Fifth Army in mid-December 1944. Eisenhower's policy of holding his American corps commanders at the rank of major general (two stars) was not changed until the spring of 1945. In the Pacific, by contrast, most Army corps commanders were, like Truscott, lieutenant generals (three stars) throughout most of the war.

[14] Brooks had left the 2d Armored Division in mid-September, served briefly on the V Corps staff, and arrived at the VI Corps headquarters on 20 October where he worked closely with Truscott on DOGFACE planning.

CHAPTER XVIII

The Forests of the Meurthe

The departure of General Truscott in the VI Corps was also marked by another high-level command change affecting the 6th Army Group. On 22 October General Devers, commanding the army group, turned over his concurrent command of NATOUSA to Lt. Gen. Joseph T. McNarney, formerly Deputy Chief of Staff, U.S. Army. This rather belated shift relieved Devers of what had become nagging U.S. Army administrative responsibilities in the Mediterranean area and allowed him to devote all his time and energy to the affairs of 6th Army Group. Devers, however, unlike Bradley, continued to operate with only a small operational staff, monitoring problem areas between his two subordinate armies and SHAEF headquarters, but rarely interfering with tactical operations conducted at corps level, or with the logistical and administrative responsibilities shouldered by the larger army-level headquarters. In any case, with the XV Corps' battle of the Parroy forest and the French II Corps' attack in the southern Vosges ended, there was little Devers could do while he waited for fresh supplies and fresh units for a major army group offensive scheduled for mid-November.

Dogface Resumed

As VI Corps commander, General Brooks, a quiet New Englander with experience as an artillery officer during World War I, was to prove more reserved and less colorful than his predecessor, but equally able and innovative. Assigned to Fort Knox, Kentucky, in September 1941, he had taken over the 11th Armored Division in July of the following year; in 1944 he had commanded the U.S. 2d Armored Division in Bradley's army group during the campaigns in northern France. Although eager to do well in his first corps command assignment, Brooks would find the VI Corps infantrymen much different than his former armored troops and the Vosges terrain more challenging than the gentler ground to the north. In fact almost immediately he would inherit all the frustrations that had plagued Truscott since crossing the Moselle and gain a few new ones in the bargain.

With Devers' approval, both Patch and his new corps commander were eager to have their new drive on St. Die and the Meurthe River under way as soon as possible. Thus on the morning of 23 October, the 45th Division's two attacking regiments began crossing the Mortagne River. Despite opposition, units of the 180th Infantry were across the river by 0745 and by noon had penetrated over half a mile northeast into the Rambervillers forest, followed quickly by elements of the 179th Infantry. The crossing had cost the 180th's lead battalion nearly one hundred casualties, almost all of them suffered during the initial attempt, and the unit captured about one hundred Germans on the east bank.

Once across the river, progress was rapid. Patrols from the 45th Division soon met elements of the 3d Division; by the following day, 24 October, both of Eagles' regiments began swinging northward, making gains of up to a mile through the dense Rambervillers forest. Light resistance was less of an impediment than were the difficulties of opening supply routes on the dirt roads and trails to support further advances. The 45th Division's 157th Infantry joined the attack early on the 25th from the Rambervillers region, crossing the Mortagne near Autry and pushing east and northeast. Meanwhile, south of Autry, the 120th Engineer Battalion, 45th Division, installed a forty-ton bridge across the Mortagne to support the advance.

During the afternoon of 25 October German resistance stiffened all across the front of the 45th Division, and throughout the night German artillery and mortar fire constantly harassed the attacking units. Although forward troops braced for a possible counterattack, the morning of the 26th revealed that the night bombardment had only been a cover for a general German withdrawal. Thereafter the advance resumed. Elements of the 157th Infantry reached Route D–32 about midway across the forest during the course of the day; farther south, the 179th Infantry continued northeastward for a mile and a half, while the 180th Infantry, pinched out by the other two regiments, reverted to division reserve. By the end of 26 October the 45th Division had thus penetrated the boundary between the *21st Panzer* and the *16th Volksgrenadier Divisions* and, in conjunction with 3d and 36th Division operations to the south, had completed the isolation of most of the *16th Division* in the center of the American attack.

South of the 45th, the 3d Division had resumed its advance toward Les Rouges Eaux along the axis of Route N–420 on 23 October, with the 15th Infantry north of the road and the 7th Infantry to the south. The 7th Infantry ran into stubborn resistance in the Les Rouges Eaux sector, but made some progress south of the highway and finally cleared the hamlet on the 25th.

Just short of Les Rouges Eaux on the 23d, the 15th Infantry moved off the highway and began to advance generally northward into the rough forested terrain just west of twisting Route D–7 on 24 October. Progress was fairly steady until the vanguard ran up against a German strongpoint on the 25th, centering around a small road junction two miles within the forest; here the forward movement of the regiment halted.

Meanwhile, the 30th Infantry (moving over from the Le Tholy area) had rejoined the rest of the 3d Division and, on the 25th, dispatched its 3d Battalion northward behind the 15th Infantry. About a mile south of the strongpoint that was holding up the 15th regiment, the battalion cut east across Route D–7 and headed northeast along woodland trails for a mile and a half, encountering almost no resistance. By the time the morning was well along, the other battalions of the 30th Infantry had followed, moving undetected through a large gap in the *16th Division*'s right flank. Taking advantage of the situation, the 30th Infantry pushed one battalion north to Route D–32 while the other units moved rapidly east, heading directly for the Magdeleine woods.[1]

While the 30th Infantry's success accelerated the 3d Division's push through the Rambervillers forest, the progress of the division's 7th regiment along Route N–420—presumably the easier axis of advance—was stopped a few miles north of Les Rouges Eaux by what turned out to be the strongest opposition yet encountered.[2] The 7th Infantry had come up against the *933d Grenadiers* of the *338th Division*, representing the first major response of the German Army command to the VI Corps' offensive.

---

[1] S. Sgt. Clyde L. Choate, Company C, 601st Tank Destroyer Battalion, was awarded the Congressional Medal of Honor for action on 25 October for breaking up a German tank-infantry counterattack in the Rambervillers forest. (The date is uncertain as unit records seem to indicate that the incident occurred several days earlier.) For more information on this incident, see *History of the Third Infantry Division in World War II*, pp. 253–54, and 601st TD Battalion, "Record of Events, Oct 1–31, 1944," attached to the 601st Battalion's After Action Report for October 1944.

[2] German records state that Les Rouges Eaux was lost on 24 October, but 3d Division records show that intense fighting took place at the village on the morning of 25 October, and that Les Rouges Eaux was not completely secure until late that afternoon.

The German Response

The rapid thrust of the VI Corps threatened to split von Gilsa's *LXXXIX Corps* in the north from Thumm's *LXIV Corps* in the south. Balck and Wiese tried desperately to remedy the situation. During the night of 23–24 October, the *Nineteenth Army* thus began shifting the reinforced *933d Grenadier Regiment*[3] north from the *IV Luftwaffe Field Corps* sector in order to close the gap between the *16th Volksgrenadier Division* (*LXXXIX Corps*) and the *716th Division* (*LXIV Corps*) that had been opened by the 36th Division on the 22d. When the advance of 36th Division units southeast of N–420 continued to widen the gap on the 24th, Wiese immediately decided to commit the *602d Reconnaissance Battalion* and the *201st* and *202d Mountain Battalions*—the latter unit having detrained at St. Die during the night of 23–24 October. By the 25th at least some of these units had crossed the Meurthe River west of St. Die to assist the disorganized *16th Volksgrenadier Division* in holding on to Route N–420 and closing the gap south of the highway in the Domaniale de Champ forest. Also reinforcing the *16th Division* on 24 or 25 October were the two provisional infantry battalions made up of probationers and men with ear problems, but these units may have simply been integrated into existing divisional formations.

Although the initial German redeployments substantially reinforced the

---

[3] The principal reinforcements for the *933d Grenadiers* were the *39th Machine Gun Battalion* from the *Weststellung* and the understrength *198th Fusilier Battalion* from the *198th Division* of *LXIV Corps*.

center and left of the collapsing *volks-grenadier* division, they had done nothing to strengthen its right wing or the equally tenuous situation of the *21st Panzer Division* next door in the Rambervillers–Raon-l'Etape area. The only other backup force readily available was the *106th Panzer Brigade*, which the *Nineteenth Army* had already moved to the northeastern edge of the Rambervillers forest. But General Wiese was reluctant to commit the brigade to the direct support of either the *21st Panzer* or the *16th Volksgrenadier Division*, preferring to hold the bulk of the unit in reserve against an expected American advance into the Meurthe River valley itself via Routes D–7 and D–32. Like the American commanders, Wiese too found it difficult to employ more than a few armored vehicles effectively in the wooded terrain of the Vosges at one time.

His decision proved to be sound as the battered *16th Division* appeared to have little staying power. During 26 and 27 October, the 3d Division's 15th Infantry reduced the German strongpoint at the D–7 crossroads, cleared the road to La Bourgonce, and went on to occupy most of the town with no opposition.[4] To the north, the 179th Infantry of the 45th Division had also reached D–32, and just to the south the 30th Infantry had continued eastward through the La Bourgonce area all the way to the Magdeleine woods to secure the high ground overlooking St. Die. These last gains enabled American forward artillery observers to place the *201st*

Mountain Battalion under accurate artillery fire as it was detraining at the town, and the Germans were therefore unable to commit the *201st* along N–420 until the following day.[5]

In the sector of the *21st Panzer Division*, the German defenders had done little better. On 27 October the 45th Division's 157th and 179th Infantry regiments pushed northeast and east another mile and a half, with the 157th maintaining control over Route D–32 and the 179th drawing abreast of the 15th Infantry as it advanced into La Bourgonce. The next day, 28 October, the 180th Infantry came back into the line along Route N–59A, on the division's left wing, and all three regiments began crossing Route D–32 in force toward Raon-l'Etape.[6] Although the division encountered disorganized but determined resistance throughout the 27th and 28th, supply and support problems played the major role in slowing progress. Tracked vehicles repeatedly became mired in the muddy forest trails, while engineers had to work around the clock to keep unpaved roads and mountain trails passable for even lightweight jeeps. Bringing supplies and ammunition to forward units remained a major chore.

For the Germans, the 45th Division's advances on 27 and 28 October posed new and serious threats. Outflanked in the Rambervillers forest

---

[4] Differing from the usual reporting pattern for this period, the German records state that La Bourgonce fell on the 28th rather than the 27th.

[5] About the same time the *1st Battalion, 130th Panzer Regiment*, began withdrawing from its reserve positions at Corcieux, probably moving to the St. Die area along D–31—the Taintrux valley road—but German records are unclear on this point.

[6] With the arrival of the 180th Infantry on the division's left, most of the 36th Engineer Combat Regiment units that had been securing the division flank returned to their engineer duties.

area, the *21st Panzer Division* was forced to relinquish its positions around the town of Rambervillers, which had guarded the road approaches to both Raon-l'Etape and Baccarat. Wiese had hoped that the anemic panzer division might have been able somehow to tie its stretched defenses into those of the withdrawing *16th Volksgrenadier Division* near La Bourgonce, but both units were too weak and thinly spread to make a linear defense possible. Preoccupied with efforts to defend along Route N–420 and to close the gap south of the highway between the *LXXXIX* and *LXIV Corps,* Wiese and von Gilsa had apparently been slow to appreciate the extent and significance of a second gap that was developing between the *21st Panzer* and *16th Volksgrenadier Divisions.*

On 28 October Wiese belatedly decided to pull *LXIV Corps'* *716th Division* out of its now relatively quiet sector southwest of Bruyeres and move the division northward to positions between his ailing *panzer* and *volksgrenadier* units.[7] He also instructed these embattled units to pull back toward the Meurthe River, hoping that the *16th Volksgrenadiers* in the center of the Allied attack could hold a much smaller defensive front between the area just east of La Bourgonce and Le Haut Jacques Pass, on Route N–420 between Les Rouges Eaux and St. Die. From Le Haut Jacques Pass the *16th Volksgrenadier Division*'s main defenses were to continue south through the central portion of the Domaniale de Champ forest to the Neune valley in the vicinity of Biffontaine; south of the town, the division would tie in with *LXIV Corps* units. Now expecting an early VI Corps breakout to the east from the Rambervillers forest, Wiese also directed the *21st Panzer Division* and the *106th Panzer Brigade* to pull their remaining armor back into reserve positions, thereby denying the defending forces any armored support for the immediate future. Given the nature of the fighting and the terrain, however, it was probably a wise decision.

The *Nineteenth Army* commander's actions came somewhat late to be of much help to the *volksgrenadier* division. With the 30th Infantry's penetration of the Bois de la Magdeleine, the division's chances of establishing defenses very far north of N–420 were extremely poor, and Wiese's orders indicated that both the *Nineteenth Army* and *LXXXIX Corps* lacked accurate information about the situation along the *16th Division*'s front. Indeed, on 28 October Maj. Gen. Ernst Haeckel, commanding the *volksgrenadier* division, was in a state of confusion. As a result of nearly insoluble communications problems, he had little control of his tactical units, and many had started to fall apart. After one of his grenadier companies deserted to American lines on 27 October, General Balck came close to relieving Haeckel, but Wiese kept him on the job, mainly handling the German defenses along Route N–420. Although well aware that there were dangerous penetrations on both flanks of his unit, the harried division commander could do little about them.

---

[7] The reinforced *308th Grenadiers* of the *198th Division*, *IV Luftwaffe Field Corps*, replaced the *716th Division* in *LXIV Corps'* sector.

The Attack Stalls

Unknown to Wiese, the 45th Division was not planning to conduct any major breakout eastward from the Rambervillers forest. On the division's left, the 117th Cavalry Squadron had pushed a few miles northeast of Rambervillers with no opposition, but its flank security responsibilities prevented it from advancing more rapidly. In the forest itself, the movement of the 45th Division's three infantry regiments toward the Meurthe River was steady, but also carefully measured. The 180th Infantry crossed Route D–32 near the western edge of the forest and, on the 30th, after overcoming stubborn resistance, reached Route N–59A. In the center the 157th Infantry pushed several miles north of D–32; meanwhile, on the division's right, the 179th Infantry consolidated positions on high ground overlooking La Bourgonce, staying abreast of the 3d Division's 15th Infantry to the south, whose pace was much slower.

In the VI Corps' center the 3d Division was finding the way to St. Die more difficult. The 15th Infantry had spent its time since 27 October mopping up along Route D–7 in the La Bourgonce area, and on the 30th it began relieving 30th Infantry troops on the front lines a few miles east of La Bourgonce. While the relief was in progress, a German force—probably troops of the recently redeployed *716th Division*—attacked and drove the intermixed American units back southward about a mile; during the confusion, about twenty-five troops of the 15th and 30th Infantry regiments and a forward observer party from

the 141st Field Artillery Battalion were killed or captured. The attack, however, soon petered out, and, with its rear secured by the 15th Infantry, the 30th pressed east to assist the 7th regiment and the rest of the 3d Division in opening Route N–420.

Despite almost continuous infiltration and numerous small, intense counterattacks that probably marked the arrival of elements of the *201st Mountain Battalion* along the regimental front, the 30th Infantry was able to consolidate its positions in the Magdeleine woods area and, on 28 October, began to push elements east toward Hill 616, which dominated the highway just north of Le Haut Jacques Pass where the 7th Infantry was still stalled.[8] If the hill could be captured, the entire German defensive position in the pass would be gravely threatened, as would its line of communications to St. Die. The Germans also recognized the tactical importance of Hill 616 and strengthened the area as best they could; at dusk on 30 October they were still holding back the 30th Infantry's attacking force half a mile north of the hill's summit.[9]

Meanwhile, the 7th Infantry still had its hands full along Route N–420. Despite several days of hard fighting, the unit had been unable to clear the

---

[8] On 28 October the Germans cut the supply lines to the 3d Battalion, 30th Infantry, and set up a strongpoint behind the battalion's forward units. For destroying the position almost single-handedly, S. Sgt. Lucian Adams, Company I, was awarded the Congressional Medal of Honor.

[9] During German counterattacks at Hill 616 on 30 October, PFC Wilburn K. Ross, a light machine gunner of Company G, 30th Infantry, successfully threw back a series of German probes, remaining in an exposed position for nearly five hours, for which he was awarded the Congressional Medal of Honor.

three miles of road between Les Rouges Eaux and the entrance to Le Haut Jacques Pass, and had been equally unsuccessful in attempting to bypass German strongpoints by skirting through the edges of the Domaniale de Champ forest just south of the highway. Assistance from the 36th Division was needed, but Dahlquist's units, stretched thin over a long front, had their own problems.

The Lost Battalion

While the 45th and 3d Divisions pushed northwest toward the Raon-l'Etape–St. Die area, Dahlquist's 36th Division had moved east into the forbidding Domaniale de Champ forest south of the main attack. On 23 October the 442d Infantry, on the 36th Division's left, penetrated several miles toward the center of the forest, with one battalion clearing Biffontaine in the south. The following day the 442d was relieved by the 141st and 143d Infantry regiments, which continued the drive east. However, the hapless 141st was soon in trouble again. When the regiment's 1st Battalion occupied Hills 624 and 645 northeast and southeast of Biffontaine on the 24th, the Germans reacted at once. Near Hill 624, an artillery-supported German counterattack cut the supply lines to elements of the 1st Battalion, and a relief column of the 2d Battalion was unable to reach the isolated units, having become embroiled in several small skirmishes itself. The defenders were fresh units of the *338th Division's 933d Grenadiers,* which Wiese hoped would stem the 36th Division's penetration of the German intercorps boundary.

During the night of 24–25 October the German grenadiers overran the command post of the 1st Battalion, 141st Infantry, and completely blocked the main trail to the battalion's forward elements at Hill 645. An accounting on the morning of the 25th revealed that the Germans had cut off 241 Americans near the hill; their only contact with the rest of the regiment was the radio of an artillery forward observer.[10] As yet, the Germans were only vaguely aware of the isolated American pocket, since the situation within the densely forested hills and ridges of the Domaniale de Champ was as murky for the *933d Grenadier Regiment* as it was for the 141st Infantry.

On 25 October the 2d Battalion, 141st Infantry, gained some ground in the Hill 624 area, but fell far short of reaching the group near Hill 645. The 141st Infantry's 3d Battalion, moving into the battle area from the north, also met determined resistance and made little headway. During the afternoon the isolated group sent out a 36-man combat patrol to scout for a possible breakout route, but the detachment was subsequently ambushed. Only five men made it back to the Hill 645 perimeter and only a single soldier, after being lost five days in the woods, was finally able to reach American lines.

---

[10] The group consisted of 237 troops of the 1st Battalion, 141st Infantry, and four men from other units, including an artillery forward observer from the 131st Field Artillery Battalion, 36th Division. For detailed accounts of subsequent operations to relieve the group, see the 141st Infantry's AAR, Oct 44, pp. 26–46; Shirey, *Americans,* pp. 63–68; Seventh Army Diary, pp. 339–44; and, for color, the account in *The Fighting 36th* (Austin, Tex.: The 36th Division Association, 1946) (unpaginated).

DOMANIALE DE CHAMP FOREST (HIGH VOSGES IN BACKGROUND). *Location of "lost battalion" is noted.*

The situation remained unchanged throughout 26 October, but the trapped men were running desperately short of ammunition, medical supplies, and food. The 2d Battalion, 442d Infantry, after a two-day rest, came back into the line to allow the 141st to focus all its activities on the relief effort, but the regiment, worn thin by the long weeks of campaigning in the Vosges, was unable to clear a path to the isolated soldiers. The Hill 645 group—by now inaccurately dubbed The Lost Battalion—remained cut off.[11]

The next day, 27 October, an exasperated Dahlquist decided to bring the rest of the 442d Infantry back into the line on the 141st Infantry's left. However, the Japanese-American regiment was immediately subjected to armor-supported counterattacks launched by the *202d Mountain Battalion*, which had moved into the Les Rouges Eaux valley south of N–420.

---

[11] At the time, the American media drew an obvious parallel to "The Lost Battalion" of World War I, when some 600 troops of the 308th Infantry, 77th Division, were cut off in the Argonne Forest during the period 3–7 October 1918. In fact there were many such "lost battalions" during World War II—a common occurrence when attacking units sometimes outdistanced their companions and became isolated by enemy units infiltrating along their flanks and rear.

To the east, the 141st Infantry's progress was again negligible, and the 3d Battalion even had to give up some ground in the face of German pressure.[12] Increasingly frustrated with the performance of the 141st Infantry, General Dahlquist relieved the regimental commander and replaced him with Col. Charles H. Owens, the division's chief of staff.[13] These measures brought no immediate relief, however, to the trapped unit.

On 28 October the two recommitted battalions of the 442d Infantry moved northeast into the sector of the 7th Infantry, 3d Division, in an attempt to approach the southeastern portion of the Domaniale de Champ forest from a different angle. But again progress was painfully slow, and at dusk the 442d's leading troops were still over two miles northwest of the "lost battalion." During the day, however, the Japanese-American unit captured some ninety Germans, among them the commanding officer of the *202d Mountain Battalion.* Meanwhile, aided by clearing weather, artillery and aircraft managed to deliver some supplies to the stranded group. While howitzers fired in canisters filled with chocolate bars, P–47 fighters of the 371st Fighter-Bomber Group dropped packets of ammunition, K-rations, medical supplies, radio batteries, and water.[14] On the same day, the 36th Division's OSS detachment even sent a three-man team into the forest in an unsuccessful attempt to aid the unit.[15] All this attention undoubtedly pinpointed the location of the small force for the *933d Grenadiers,* but the Germans had become increasingly disorganized and were unable to mount a concerted attack to eliminate the American pocket.

During 29 and 30 October, at a high cost, the 442d Infantry laboriously fought its way down the southeastern arm of the forest. Finally, about 1400 on the 30th, a Nisei patrol reached the Hill 645 group, marking the end of the struggle. By 1600 the bulk of the two 442d battalions had closed around the 141st Infantry's isolated force and began evacuating the group's casualties— twenty-six wounded, including twenty-two litter cases. The next day the remainder of the group rejoined the rest of the battered 1st Battalion, and Owens quickly pulled the unit out of the line. At the time, the battalion had only 490 men left out of an authorized strength of about 870.

At the end of October, the rest of the 141st Infantry was not in much better condition. During the month the regiment had received nearly 650 fresh enlisted replacements, and another 600 enlisted men had returned to duty after being out of the line as casualties. However, both battle and nonbattle casualties had risen to the extent that the regiment was still short about 450 enlisted men, and the 36th Division as a whole was approxi-

---

[12] For heroic leadership between 24 and 27 October, T. Sgt. Charles H. Coolidge, Company M, 3d Battalion, 141st Infantry, was awarded the Congressional Medal of Honor.

[13] Col. Carl E. Lindquist had taken command of the 141st on 7 October, and Owens had been chief of staff since 12 October.

[14] See *Seventh Army Rpt,* I, 550–51.

[15] *The Overseas Targets: War Report of the OSS,* II, 248. The trio was ambushed, a French agent killed, and two Americans wounded and captured.

MEN FROM THE LOST BATTALION *(1st Battalion, 141st Infantry, 36th Division).*

mately 4,400 troops below its strength of 1 October. Coming out of the battle, the attached 442d Infantry, after only a relatively short period of fighting, was emaciated and down to little more than 50 percent of its authorized strength with no replacements in sight.

The whole affair of the lost battalion was extremely upsetting to both Dahlquist and Brooks. For five days the relief of the Hill 645 group had consumed the energies of the bulk of two infantry regiments plus a large proportion of the 36th Division's supporting artillery, armor, and engineers. The diversion had prevented the 36th Division from continuing its advances elsewhere or even starting to approach its final DOGFACE objective, St. Leonard.

In addition, fully occupied in the southeastern section of the Domaniale de Champ, the 36th was unable to provide any assistance to the 3d Division's attack up Route D–420. In fact, Brooks had to shift the 3d Division's boundary about two miles southward to cover the left flank of the troubled unit. The best that can be said of the episode was that the reinforcements sent by Wiese had also been badly damaged, as the *Nineteenth Army* once again ran up against the American hard-luck division.

The VI Corps' attack, which had seemed so promising at first, appeared to be stalled in the Vosges forests at the end of October. Troop fatigue, poor weather, difficult terrain, ammunition shortages, and fresh German reinforcements all conspired against any rapid advance to the Meurthe River. With the approach of winter, time seemed to be working against the American attackers, and the first major snowfalls in the mountains would make offensive operations even more difficult. But the Germans also had severe problems. The broad, grinding American advance was chewing up their infantry units bit by bit, never allowing them to build up their reserve for anything more than local-ized counterattacks. If the battle continued further, Wiese would have no troops to man and defend the *Vosges Foothill Positions* or any other winter defensive line. The fighting in the Rambervillers and Domaniale de Champ forests, and along Route N–420 thus seemed to be coming down to a matter of will and stamina—a war of attrition that, without assistance from the outside, only the more determined opponent would win.

CHAPTER XIX

The Gates of the Vosges

Initial DOGFACE planning had provided for limited diversionary attacks by the two Allied corps on either side of Brooks' VI Corps, namely, XV Corps in the north and de Monsabert's II Corps in the south. The lack of supplies and the general exhaustion of both units had prevented these supporting attacks from taking place. However, by late October both Devers and Patch believed that the time for launching the two secondary efforts had arrived. The gains made by the VI Corps had begun to expose its flanks, as the episode of the lost battalion had so clearly pointed out; at the same time, the concentration of the *Nineteenth Army*'s reserves on the VI Corps' front had correspondingly weakened the defenses facing the U.S. XV and the French II Corps. Moreover, both of the flanking Allied corps were somewhat rested and had been able to improve their manpower and supply situation during the past weeks. Attacks by either or both of the corps might take some pressure off Brooks' forces in the center, allowing them to reach their Meurthe River line objectives before DOGFACE ran out of steam. In addition, Devers believed that a general advance by all three corps would place them in a

better geographical position for start of the larger 6th Army Gro offensive still scheduled for m November.

Planning

In the north the objective of XV Corps' supporting attack was small city of Baccarat, a railroad a highway hub six miles northwest Raon-l'Etape. The rapid seizure the Meurthe River town before Germans could move reinforceme northward would accomplish two jectives. First, Baccarat would give XV Corps an alternate route of vance through the approaches to Saverne Gap. Second, possession the town would also give the Corps a bridgehead over Meurthe. From Baccarat, Broc could outflank the German Meurt River line (*the Vosges Foothill Positi* and send forces south through Rac l'Etape and the surrounding masses, known to the local inhab ants as "the gates of the Vosge (*Map 24*).

To accomplish this task, Gene Haislip, the XV Corps command ordered Leclerc's 2d Armored D sion to isolate the area by cutting

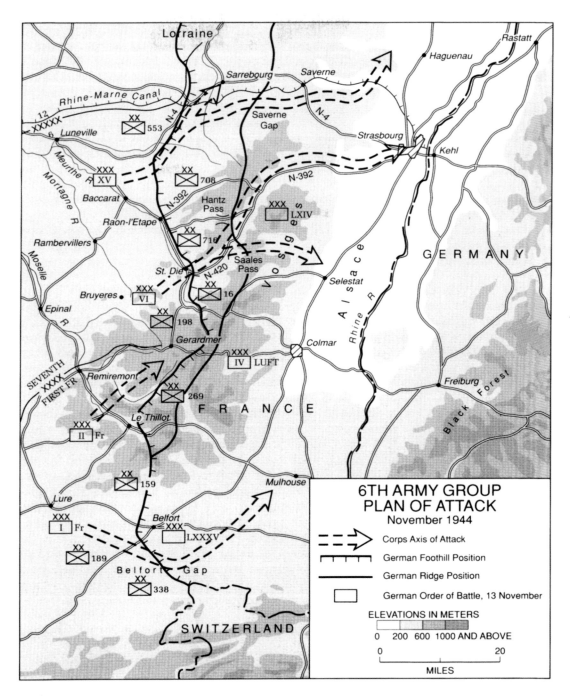

6TH ARMY GROUP
PLAN OF ATTACK
November 1944

- ▪ ▪ ▪ ➤ Corps Axis of Attack
- ⊤⊤⊤⊤⊤ German Foothill Position
- ——— German Ridge Position
- ▭ German Order of Battle, 13 November

ELEVATIONS IN METERS

0 200 600 1000 AND ABOVE

0   20

MILES

Map labels: Lorraine, Rastatt, Haguenau, Sarrebourg, Saverne, Rhine-Marne Canal, N-4, 12, XXXXX, 6, Luneville, XX 553, Saverne Gap, N-4, Strasbourg, Kehl, Meurthe R., XXX XV, Baccarat, N-392, XX 708, Hantz Pass, N-392, XXX LXIV, Mortagne R., Raon-l'Etape, Vosges, Rambervillers, XX 716, Saales Pass, GERMANY, Moselle R., St. Die, N-420, XXX VI, Bruyeres, XX 16, Selestat, Alsace, Rhine R., Epinal, XX 198, Gerardmer, Colmar, XXX IV LUFT, SEVENTH XXXX FIRST FR, Remiremont, XX 269, FRANCE, Freiburg, Black Forest, XXX II Fr, Le Thillot, XX 159, Mulhouse, Lure, Belfort, XXX I Fr, XXX LXXXV, XX 189, Belfort Gap, XX 338, SWITZERLAND

MAP 24   This map is printed in full color at the back of the book, following the Index.

main roads north and east of Baccarat, including the southeastern section of N–59 leading to Raon-l'Etape, and then to occupy the town itself.[1] Leclerc's command was to begin its offensive, planned as a short, two-day affair, on 31 October.

On VI Corps' southern flank, a French II Corps demonstration by the 3d Algerian Division was to start on 3 November and last for three days. General de Monsabert, commanding the II Corps, welcomed the opportunity to take some offensive action after having been relegated to a defensive role in mid-October. Brig. Gen. Augustin Guillaume, commanding the 3d Algerian Infantry Division, was also pleased. German artillery had been harassing his main supply routes in the Vagney-Sapois area, and a few limited objective attacks would, he felt, push German artillery observers out of the nearby hills and end the nuisance. A limited push north would also put his units on better terrain for further advances.

However, General de Lattre, commanding the First French Army, had serious misgivings.[2] Any supplies and troops consumed by the effort would obviously detract from his buildup opposite Belfort. Moreover, de Lattre doubted that much could be accomplished. The division and attached FFI units held a twelve-mile front in rough, forested, rain-sodden or snow-laden terrain; de Monsabert would have difficulty concentrating sufficient resources of his own to launch a meaningful diversion. Contributing to de Lattre's uneasiness was the knowledge that the relatively fresh and strong (14,000 troops) *269th Volksgrenadier Division* from Norway had begun to take over from the depleted *338th Division* in the area south of Gerardmer.[3] But the French Army commander hoped that a limited attack by his II Corps would at least keep the *Nineteenth Army*'s attention focused on the Vosges front and away from the Belfort Gap sector. In the end, at the urgings of Patch and Devers, he reluctantly drew upon his general reserve and provided Guillaume's division with a combat command of the French 5th Armored Division, the Shock Battalion, much of the artillery of the 1st and 5th Armored Divisions, a tank destroyer battalion, and an infantry battalion from the 4th Moroccan Mountain Division. From his own resources General de Monsabert added an infantry battalion from the French 1st Infantry Division still located south of the Algerians.

---

[1] While the orders of the Seventh Army and XV Corps did not specify the seizure of Baccarat, the 2d French Armored Division could hardly have accomplished its missions—especially cutting Route N–59—without taking the city; Leclerc obviously intended to make Baccarat his primary objective.

[2] De Lattre, *History,* p. 206, states that during a conference with General Devers on 27 October he "at once" promised French cooperation for the limited objective attack, but neither the First French Army account of the conference (copy in First French Army files and dated 30 October) nor the Devers diary of 27 October agree with this interpretation. De Lattre also appears to have been less than enthusiastic at a conference with de Monsabert and Brooks on 31 October at the French II Corps command post. See Seventh Army Diary, 31 October; and Memo, Col Joseph F. Surrat (G–3 Section, Seventh Army) to Chief of Staff, Seventh Army (no subj, but an account of the 31 October conference), 1 Nov 44.

[3] The first elements of the *269th Volksgrenadier Division* reached the front opposite the French II Corps on 26 October.

GENERAL PATCH AND MAJ. GEN. EDWARD H. BROOKS

The Attack in the North

Unconcerned with French problems in the south, Leclerc's 2d Armored Division launched the XV Corps' set-piece attack from assembly areas in the Mondon forest southeast of Lune-ville at daybreak on 31 September, supported by four battalions of corps artillery,[4] and by the artillery of the XV Corps' new 44th Division. The *21st Panzer Division,* responsible for the defense of Baccarat and environs, was caught by surprise. The Germans knew that the rolling, generally open terrain north and northwest of Bac-

carat was, in dry weather, suited to armored warfare, but on 31 October most of the area was a morass of flooded streams, water-covered roads, and mud. However, Leclerc was convinced that by keeping to the upper slopes of the low hills and ridges leading to Baccarat he could maneuver his armor in a reasonably effective manner.

Leclerc's optimism, especially in the face of weakened *21st Panzer Division* defenses, proved well founded. Moreover, the 2d Armored Division's staff had done its homework well. With bright cerise cloth panels and pennants boldly displayed for identification purposes, the French armored columns swept southeastward across a four-mile front. By early afternoon his left column had cut Route N–435 about four miles northeast of Baccarat and had then gone on to clear the town of Merviller, a few miles to the south. Meanwhile, his right-wing units had eliminated a long-troublesome German strongpoint at Aizerailles, on the Meurthe River and Route N–59 about three miles northwest of Baccarat. Late in the day French armor drove into the eastern half of the isolated town against only scattered resistance. By 1000 the next day, 1 November, CCD of the 2d Armored Division had cleared Baccarat and in the process seized an intact bridge over the Meurthe River.

On the same day CCV, attacking from the northern edge of the Mondon forest, occupied Ogeviller—on Route N–4 about seven miles north of Baccarat—which had formerly been a strongpoint on the boundary between *First* and *Nineteenth Armies.* The French pressed on another mile

---

[4] A battalion each of 155-mm. howitzers, 155-mm. guns, 4.5-inch guns, and 8-inch howitzers.

and a half along N–4 to take Herbe-viller; they then moved southeast along the west bank of the small La Blette River and cleared Montigny, on La Blette and Route N–435 about six miles northeast of Baccarat. The heaviest fighting of the day took place at Vacqueville, on a railroad spur line a mile and a half east of N–435 at Merviller. Here *21st Panzer Division* infantry, supported by five tanks, held out until 1730, withdrawing only after the French knocked out three of the German armored vehicles. Meanwhile, CCD opened Route N–59 between Ai-zerailles and Baccarat, probed south-west along N–435 toward Ramber-villers to establish contact with VI Corps' 117th Cavalry Squadron, and sent patrols out southeast of Baccarat along Route N–59.

By dusk on 1 November, the French 2d Armored Division had thus accom-plished its DOGFACE support mission. The division adopted a generally de-fensive posture and waited for VI Corps units to take over in the Bac-carat-Merviller sector. The two-day ex-ercise had cost the 2d Armored Divi-sion approximately 20 men killed and 100 wounded, while equipment losses included 7 medium tanks, 2 light tanks, 6 half-tracks, and 1 tank destroyer. The division captured about 550 German troops and estimated that it had killed over 200 more; known German materi-el losses included six medium tanks and fifteen 88-mm. guns.[5] In addition, General Spragins' 44th Infantry Divi-sion, taking advantage of confusion in the German defenses caused by the

French armored division's attack, pushed two miles farther east into the sector north of the Vezouse River, se-curing rising ground and driving back elements of the *533d Volksgrenadier Division.*

German Reorganization

Changes in Wiese's *Nineteenth Army* command structure had also contrib-uted to the German dislocation in the Baccarat area. On 28 October the *LVIII Panzer Corps* headquarters, con-trolling the southern divisions of *Army Group G's First Army*, received orders to redeploy northward to the zone of *Army Group B.*[6] To replace the depart-ing panzer corps headquarters, *Army Group G* directed the *Nineteenth Army* to transfer von Gilsa's *LXXXIX Corps* headquarters to the *First Army*. Unable to obtain a suitable replacement for von Gilsa's command, General Wiese had to shift the zone of Thumm's *LXIV Corps* northward to take over the *LXXXIX Corps* sector. The new *LXIV Corps* front was about twenty-three miles wide and extended from Do-mevre, on Route N–4 about three miles north of Montigny, to Saulcy-sur-Meurthe, three miles south of St. Die. Both Petersen's *IV Luftwaffe Field Corps* and Kniess' *LXXXV Corps* also had to extend their boundaries north-ward, leaving the *IV Luftwaffe Field Corps* with a front of over twenty-five miles from Saulcy south to Route N–66 at Le Thillot; here it tied its de-

---

[5] Most of the 88-mm. guns were on antiaircraft mounts and, once emplaced, could not be moved quickly.

[6] Von Manteuffel's *Fifth Panzer Army* headquarters and the *XLVII Panzer Corps* headquarters had already left for the north and, together with the *LVIII Panzer Corps* headquarters, would constitute the southern command and control organization of the German Ardennes Offensive in December 1944.

fenses into units of the *LXXXV Corps*, still holding in front of the Belfort Gap.[7]

These command and control changes had become effective between 30 October and 1 November, a critical period for both attackers and defenders. On 31 October, with the attack of the French 2d Armored Division well along, it became obvious that the *Nineteenth Army* could neither counterattack nor hold; Wiese therefore obtained permission from Balck to draw the army's right wing back to the general line of Montigny, Vacqueville, and Bertrichamps, conceding the loss of Baccarat. Wiese hoped that hastily assembled, weak reserves[8] could help the *21st Panzer Division* hold a new line, but on 1 November Leclerc's armor overran the line before it could be established, except temporarily, at Vacqueville. The *21st Panzer Division*'s right now withdrew east of La Blette River; the center moved into rising, wooded ground east of Baccarat and Bertrichamps; and the left, under constant pressure from the VI Corps' 45th Division, held on to the mountains surrounding Raon-l'Etape, which, Wiese was still convinced, was the VI Corps' major objective.

Uncharacteristically, Balck had acquiesced in the loss of important terrain without insisting that *Nineteenth Army* mount an immediate counterattack to regain the lost ground. Then, on 1 November, when the *21st Panzer Division* failed to hold along the Montigny-Vacqueville-Bertrichamps line, Balck reluctantly approved the withdrawal of the *Nineteenth Army*'s right and center into the forward *Weststellung* defenses, the *Vosges Foothill Position*. This withdrawal, later hastened by attacks of the French II Corps in the south, entailed a major redeployment along the *Nineteenth Army*'s entire Vosges front, from Domevre south almost 40 miles to La Bresse in the upper Moselotte River valley, which was to be finalized by 15 November. By that date Balck hoped that construction of the defensive installations of the *Vosges Foothill Position* would be completed.

Either dissatisfied with tactical preparations or frustrated by the increasingly dismal situation facing him, Balck, the *Army Group G* commander, also announced a scorched-earth policy for the areas to be vacated by the *Nineteenth Army*. Balck's orders directed that, by 10 November, all able-bodied men between the ages of sixteen and sixty were to be evacuated to the east bank of the Rhine for use as forced labor. Women, children, and men infirm or over sixty were to be herded into relatively safe areas; and each village, town, and city was to be completely destroyed as the German troops left. Apparently not trusting his regular army officers to carry out the harsh measures, or perhaps not wanting to impose the burden on tactical units, Balck arranged for the local SS[9] to undertake

---

[7] The *LXXXV Corps* boundary was also pulled north about five miles to Le Thillot.

[8] The reserves included three infantry "battalions" of little more than company strength, a weak machine-gun battalion, elements of the *106th Panzer Brigade*, and some fortress artillery. Available records do not show whether any of these reinforcements actually reached the *21st Panzer Division*'s front by 1 November.

[9] The *Schutzstaffel* (protective group) was a uniformed but lightly armed element of the Nazi Party

the necessary actions. The *SS* lacked demolitions and expertise in their use, however, and relied mainly on fire for destructive purposes, leaving the scorched-earth program subject to the vagaries of wind and weather.

The Attack in the South

Balck's orders of 1 November had scarcely been distributed when de Monsabert's II Corps launched its DOGFACE supporting attack at 0800 on 3 November, after an hour-long artillery preparation.[10] Again the Germans were caught more or less by surprise. Terrain and weather conditions were unfavorable for the attacker, but the *269th Volksgrenadier Division,* still deploying across part of the *IV Luftwaffe Field Corps* front, had been unable to organize completely the defenses of its new sector.

On the left, elements of the reinforced 3d Algerian Division gained only about a mile after fighting for three days in the dense, upland forests around Le Tholy. In the center, astride the axis of Route D–23 east of Sapois, infantry units advanced over two miles along dominating terrain north and south of the highway, penetrating some *Weststellung* positions, while supporting armor pushed a mile farther down the road. To the south, other French troops advanced only about a mile eastward from positions

held since mid-October, but they managed to occupy high ground overlooking La Bresse and the Moselotte valley, through which ran the key German north-south lines of communication.

The initial German reaction to the 3d Algerian Division's attack was limited to heavy artillery and mortar fire, but on the evening of 5 November the *269th Division* began a series of counterattacks that lasted through the 7th. The cessation of the counterattacks was probably fortunate for the French, because by the end of the day all the reinforcing units that de Lattre had made available to de Monsabert were on their way back to the Belfort Gap front. The 3d Algerian Division again went on the defensive, as did the Germans, who feared that the French were only pausing for a brief rest before renewing the attacks.

The limited French gains in the south had not come cheaply. During the attack, the 3d Algerian Division and its attachments lost approximately 150 men killed, 670 wounded, and 35 missing. Nevertheless, the effects of de Monsabert's support operations were obvious. Concerned about the threat to the sector, Balck and Wiese were forced to keep substantial strength in the southern Vosges area, which, because of the rugged terrain, probably could have been held by a much smaller force. They were thus unable to deploy more units to either the Baccarat, St. Die, or Belfort sectors. But the true measure of both de Monsabert's and Leclerc's actions was the degree to which Brooks' VI Corps could take advantage of the resulting dismay caused in the German ranks to complete its push to the Meurthe.

organization that constituted an internal political police force. Another branch, the *Waffen SS* (armed *SS*), was organized into tactical units similar to those of the German Army.

[10] In addition to official French unit records, the following material on the II Corps action is based on de Lattre, *History,* p. 206; *Le 2e C.A. dans la Bataille pour la Liberation de la France,* pp. 57–59; and Moreau, *La Victoire,* pp. 199–206.

VI Corps Resumes the Attack

With the French support operations under way, Brooks pressed his VI Corps forces forward in an effort to gain all DOGFACE objectives in time to give his three tired divisions some rest before the army group offensive began in mid-November. On the far left, during the opening days of November, the 117th Cavalry Squadron, with the aid of the 3d Battalion, 36th Engineers, completed the relief of 2d French Armored Division units in the Merviller-Baccarat-Bertrichamps area, and was soon joined by elements of the 45th Division's 179th Infantry. South of Baccarat, however, both Eagles and O'Daniel had a hard time penetrating the strengthened German defenses.

Opposite Raon-l'Etape, the 45th Division's 180th and 157th regiments continued their advance to the Meurthe River through the Rambervillers forest and along Route N–59A. By 2 November the 180th Infantry managed to reach the hamlet of St. Benoit, about halfway between Rambervillers and Raon-l'Etape, but was unable to advance much farther. A few miles northeast of St. Benoit, Route N–59A—now no more than a narrow mountain road separating the Ste. Barbe and Rambervillers forests—rose to a height of nearly 1,500 feet, passing over a divide between the Meurthe and Mortagne watersheds at the Chipote Pass. There, about four miles short of Raon-l'Etape, units of the *21st Panzer Division* made a final stand. Unable to force the pass, some elements of the 180th Infantry moved north into the Ste. Barbe forest, while the entire 157th turned south, guiding on Route N–424, a secondary road to the Meurthe. In the north, small detachments of the 180th Infantry emerged from the forest on 3 November at the west bank of the Meurthe River almost two miles above the bridge to Raon-l'Etape. But their rapid excursion proved exceptional. In the center the rest of the 180th remained stalled at the pass, and in the south the 157th Infantry progressed scarcely a mile eastward along Route N–424. With their initial energy spent, the 45th Division foot soldiers again began to show the now familiar signs of extreme fatigue that had characterized the entire Vosges campaign.

On the other side, the German defenders were in worse condition. Unable to halt the 45th Division for long and with all his reserves committed, General Wiese finally obtained permission from *Army Group G* to pull the left of the *21st Panzer Division* and the right of the neighboring *716th Division* back almost to the Meurthe River valley. At the same time, Balck reluctantly and temporarily transferred the *951st Grenadiers* of the *First Army*'s *361st Volksgrenadier Division* to the *Nineteenth Army* as a final emergency reserve. The *Army Group G* commander at first expected Wiese to use the *951st Grenadiers* to free elements of the *21st Panzer Division* for counterattacks in the Baccarat–Raon-l'Etape area. However, lack of time and means, pressure from the Americans, and muddy ground made it impossible for the panzer division to undertake any offensive measures. Nevertheless, the *951st Grenadier Regiment*, which reached Raon-l'Etape late on 4 November, immediately made its presence felt, halting renewed attacks by the 180th Infantry along Route N–59A on 4 and 5 November. But the relief was only momentary. South of N–59A, the 157th Infantry slowly continued to labor through the Rambervillers forests toward the Meurthe, while north of the mountain highway the 45th Division pushed additional forces across the Ste. Barbe wilderness. More important, since 2 November, Eagles' tired division had slowly been reinforced by troops from the fresh U.S. 100th Infantry Division—the first of the three new divisions that Eisenhower had promised Devers back in September, and also the first new American division that had reached the Seventh Army since its campaign in France began.

MAJ. GEN. WITHERS A. BURRESS

Operation Dogface Ends

On 9 November Maj. Gen. Withers A. Burress, commanding the 100th Infantry Division, formally assumed control of the zone from General Eagles. To all intents and purposes, the 45th Division had ended its role in the DOGFACE offensive. Although short of its final objective line, the division had nearly pushed the Germans out of the Ste. Barbe and Rambervillers forests, placing the few German units still on the west bank of the Meurthe River in an extremely awkward defensive position. In addition, with help from the French 2d Armored Division and the 117th Cavalry Squadron, the division had moved forces onto the far side of the Meurthe, outflanking the German defensive positions of Raon-l'Etape proper. Subsequently, the 100th Division finished clearing the forested

hills overlooking the western valley of the Meurthe north and south of Raon-l'Etape by 11 November; however, the new unit was unable to eliminate a final German strongpoint directly opposite the town.

In the VI Corps center, the 3d Division had also resumed its advance toward St. Die during the first week of November. On the division's left, the 15th Infantry moved northeast from La Bourgonce area and began a slow, methodical advance toward the Meurthe. Much of the ground was rolling and open, and the *716th Division* offered only minor resistance at various small villages and hamlets, belatedly launching only a single genuine counterattack, which proved ineffective. By 9 November the regiment reached positions along rising ground overlooking the Meurthe valley, successfully completing its DOGFACE assignments.

In the Magdeleine woods, the 30th Infantry advanced abreast of the 15th, clearing the woods and reaching the west bank of the Meurthe River only about a mile north of St. Die by 6 November. On the regiment's right, the 7th Infantry, battered and exhausted, finally broke through Le Haut Jacques Pass on 4 November, but only after having been forced to clear most of the wooded area just west of N-420. Hill 616, east of the pass, fell to the combined efforts of the 7th and 30th Infantry regiments on 5 November, after which the remaining elements of the *16th Volksgrenadier Division* began falling back on St. Die. By the evening of 9 November the 7th Infantry had also cleared the wooded area immediately south of St. Die, and had sent patrols a few miles down Route D-31 into the Taintrux valley. By that time, elements of the 30th Infantry had marched out of the southern edge of the Magdeleine woods to take responsibility for the road junction of N-420 and D-31, leaving the battered 7th to protect the division's right flank.

Relief for the tired 3d Division was on its way. Between 9 and 11 November the 409th and 410th Infantry regiments of the fresh but untried 103d Infantry Division, commanded by Maj. Gen. Charles C. Haffner, Jr., began replacing the 7th and 30th Infantry. The 103d Division was the second of the three divisions that Eisenhower had redirected from northern France to Marseille, where the 103d had begun unloading on 20 Oc-

tober. Haffner officially took over the 3d Division's sector on 12 November, allowing O'Daniel's weary forces a brief respite.

Although St. Die remained in German hands, the 3d Division, with the impetus of its early attack through the other VI Corps divisions, had reached the west bank of the Meurthe and, more important, had secured Route N-420 as a main supply route all the way from Brouvelieures almost to St. Die. But the cost had been high. From 20 October through 10 November, battle casualties within the 7th Infantry regiment alone totaled approximately 150 men killed and 820 wounded, while the unit captured about 1,100 Germans. The 3d Division's 7th and 30th regiments quickly went into reserve, resting and beginning to prepare for the main November offensive. However, since Brooks had designated the 103d Division's third regiment, the 411th Infantry, as the corps' reserve, the 15th Infantry remained in holding positions along the west side of the Meurthe valley north of St. Die.

While the two fresh divisions had arrived just in time for Eagles' and O'Daniel's tired units, Dahlquist's workhorse 36th was to have no such respite. Although the DOGFACE territorial objectives of the 36th Division had been less significant than those of other VI Corps forces—the actual task of the 36th was to secure the corps' long right flank—the terrain it had faced and the opposition it had encountered were, if anything, more difficult. Throughout early November the attached 442d and the organic 141st regiments tried to clear the central portion of the Domaniale de

Champ forest from Les Rouges Eaux on Route N–420 south to La Houssiere. The two regiments finally occupied positions overlooking the upper Neune River valley, but they still faced a medley of German forces— mixed elements of the *933d Grenadiers,* the *202d Mountain Battalion,* and various fortress units from the *Weststellung*—holding strong defensive positions in the forests between La Houssiere and St. Leonard and in the Taintrux valley. The 143d and 142d Infantry regiments, north to south, remained in holding positions along the 36th Division's right from the Neune River valley near Biffontaine south some ten miles to the vicinity of Le Tholy, a thin defensive line that was beginning to make both Dahlquist and Brooks a bit nervous.

The Germans, however, had no thought of offensive action and were more concerned about their own flanks, fearing that a major Allied penetration to St. Leonard or Corcieux might precipitate a rapid American advance along the relatively good roads that led north to St. Die, south to Gerardmer, and east across the Vosges to Colmar on the Alsatian plains. The Germans therefore defended the area stubbornly. From 1 to 4 November, determined German infantry resistance, heavy artillery and mortar fire, miserable weather, flooded streams, inadequate air support, and the now ever-present seas of French mud severely limited 36th Division advances. The Domaniale de Champ forest network had even fewer roads than its northern neighbors, and its flooded dirt avenues and trails mired vehicles and foot soldiers alike, making it nearly impossible to bring

up supplies or to maneuver troops with any degree of dispatch. The cold, wet weather took an increasing toll on the mostly Hawaiian-born 442d infantrymen; combat losses, although heavy, were greatly outnumbered by nonbattle casualties—trench foot, severe colds, flu, and pneumonia being the most common illnesses. By 7 November the 442d was down to an average of thirty effectives in each rifle company, and one battalion had to be withdrawn from the front that day. By the 9th, when the rest of the regiment came out of the forward lines, one company could muster only seventeen riflemen fit for duty, and another only four. The 442d was virtually incapable of further operations.[11]

Replacing the dissipated 442d, the somewhat rested 142d Infantry reentered the forest and by 8 November had pushed through the Taintrux valley, only about a mile and a half short of the 7th Infantry's advance from the opposite direction. During the night of 9–10 November, as part of Balck's general withdrawal, the remaining German units pulled most of their troops east of D–31, allowing units of the 142d regiment to occupy La Houssiere unopposed and to push over a mile farther east. There Operation DOGFACE ended for the tired 36th Division, well short of its final objective, the high ground overlook-

---

[11] Shirey, *Americans,* p. 71. The 2d and 3d Battalions, 442d Infantry, went back into the lines on 13 November to relieve the 142d Infantry in a quiet sector, but were taken out of the line again on 17 November and sent with the rest of the regiment to the French Riviera and the relatively quiet Franco-Italian border area. At the time the 442d Infantry left, it could hardly marshal more than half of its authorized strength.

COMPANY L, 142D REGIMENT, 36TH DIVISION, PULLS BACK TO REAR IN SNOWFALL, *near Langefosse, France, November 1944.*

ing St. Leonard. Nevertheless the right flank of the VI Corps appeared secure, and in balance the stubborn incursions of the 36th had attracted much German attention, thereby diverting major units that might have been deployed in the St. Die–Raonl'Etape area to jam up the main advance.

Operation DOGFACE gave the VI Corps strong positions opposite the Meurthe River line, the so-called *Vosges Foothill Position,* and thus the offensive had achieved its stated purpose. Balck and Wiese perhaps were also satisfied, for the stubborn German defense, coupled with adverse weather and terrain, had sapped

the strength of Brooks' infantry regiments, units that had been in almost continuous operations since 15 August. Certainly by the end of DOGFACE, none of the three "veteran" American divisions looked forward to another major offensive, especially one which might send them ten miles farther across the Vosges through even more precipitous terrain. Yet, as Truscott might have reminded them, the sooner they started, the weaker the German defense would be; and this time the VI Corps would have welcome reinforcements, including new infantry and armored formations that would almost double its size and striking power.

PART FOUR

THE NOVEMBER OFFENSIVE

CHAPTER XX

Planning the November Offensive

During October and early November 1944, the German Army had temporarily stopped the Allied offensive in northwestern Europe. In the sector of the British 21st Army Group, Montgomery's forces had secured the Schelde Estuary by 3 November, and minesweepers had cleared a path to Antwerp by the 8th. However, several more weeks would be needed to clear all of the estuary and repair the harbor before Antwerp could become a working port. Meanwhile, Allied tactical, logistical, and manpower problems had been complicated by the autumn storms and early cold weather, making it impossible for the right of the 21st Army Group or the left of Bradley's 12th Army Group to make any significant progress toward the Ruhr, Germany's industrial heartland (*Map 25*). The principal accomplishment of the U.S. First Army, on Bradley's left, had been the costly and time-consuming seizure of Aachen (Aix-la-Chapelle). There the First Army had penetrated over ten miles into Germany, but was still far short of the Ruhr. About 23 October the U.S. Ninth Army, after a brief stint as the 12th Army Group's center command, moved up to the left of Bradley's sector to provide more direct support of Montgomery's 21st Army Group. This redeployment left the First Army as Bradley's center command, with Patton's Third Army still on his right, or southern, wing.

Beset by logistical difficulties in October, the Third Army had failed to open the Metz approaches to the Saar basin which, straddling the border between France and Germany, was second only to the Ruhr as a center of German war-making capabilities. The German defense of the Aachen and Metz areas underscored the continuing ability of the *Wehrmacht* to frustrate any narrow "strategic" ground advance into Germany of the type advocated by Montgomery. As a result, Eisenhower had become convinced late in October that an all-out offensive to defeat Germany by the end of 1944 was impossible.[1] All that could be undertaken was a limited offensive program for November and probably for December as well.

Eisenhower saw nothing in the sector of the 6th Army Group that might change his views. Although Devers' armies had an independent supply line from the Mediterranean,

---

[1] For high-level discussions concerning the possibility of defeating Germany by the end of 1944, see Pogue, *The Supreme Command*, pp. 307–09.

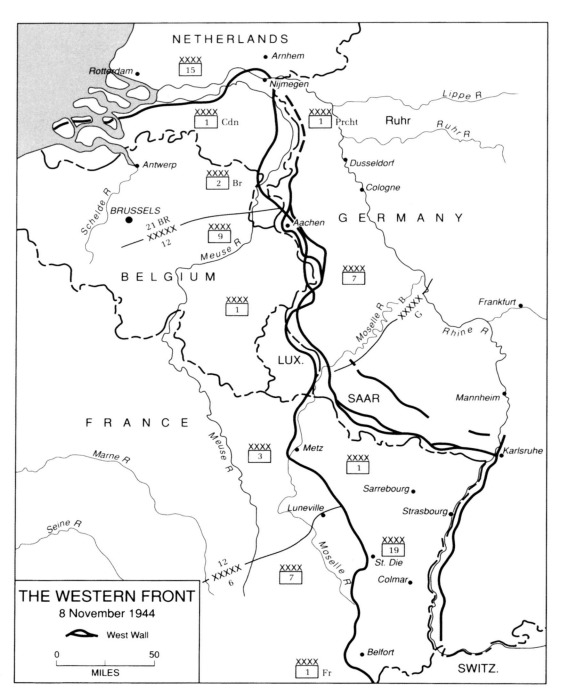

NETHERLANDS

Rotterdam •

• Arnhem

XXXX
15

Nijmegen

Lippe R

XXXX
1   Cdn

XXXX
1   Prcht

Ruhr

Ruhr R

• Antwerp

• Dusseldorf

XXXX
2   Br

• Cologne

G E R M A N Y

Schelde R

BRUSSELS
•
21 BR
XXXXX
12

XXXX
9

• Aachen

Meuse R

B E L G I U M

XXXX
7

Frankfurt •

Moselle R

B
XXXXX
G

Rhine R

XXXX
1

LUX.

Mannheim •

SAAR

F R A N C E

Meuse R

Marne R

XXXX
3

• Metz

XXXX
1

Karlsruhe •

Sarrebourg •

Seine R

Luneville •

Strasbourg •

Moselle R

XXXX
19

12
XXXXX
6

XXXX
7

• St. Die

Colmar •

THE WESTERN FRONT
8 November 1944

⌁ West Wall

0   50
MILES

• Belfort

SWITZ.

XXXX
1   Fr

MAP 25   This map is printed in full color at the back of the book, following the Index.

the 6th Army Group still needed several weeks to become logistically ready for a renewed major offensive effort. Moreover, the results of 6th Army Group operations during October led Eisenhower to doubt that Devers' command could make any major contributions to the Allied advance in November. On the southern army group's northern wing, the Seventh Army's XV Corps had done little after clearing the Parroy forest, and Leclerc's seizure of the Baccarat area at the end of the month represented only a minor action across the much larger Allied front. At the 6th Army Group's center, the picture was even less encouraging. During Operation DOGFACE the VI Corps had pushed some ten miles through the Vosges across a fifteen-mile-wide front, but the pace had been slow and costly. By November the corps' three veteran divisions were again at the point of complete exhaustion; a successful November offensive would depend greatly on the capabilities of the fresh but untried 100th and 103d Infantry Divisions and the equally inexperienced 14th Armored Division, all of which were scheduled to enter the front line as soon as possible.[2]

To the south of Devers' American forces, the First French Army had made promising gains during October and November, but had been decisively stopped by stiffening German resistance in the southern section of the High Vosges. General de Lattre, the French commander, was pleased that attacks by the French II Corps had compelled the Germans to commit strong forces in the mountains, but he had no intention of ordering more French troops into the Vosges where the terrain so heavily favored the defenders. Instead, he continued to prepare his I Corps, which had been nearly inactive during October, for a mid-November attempt to pierce the German defenses in the Belfort Gap area and then advance to the Rhine.

General Planning

From 16 to 18 October, Eisenhower held a series of conferences with his senior commanders concerning the course of operations in November.[3] All of the meetings reflected Eisenhower's continued concern with logistical problems. Conferring with Devers and Bradley at the 6th Army Group headquarters on 16 October, Eisenhower asked if the army group's line of communication from the Mediterranean could be used to increase the flow of supplies to the Third Army. At the time, Devers estimated that he could probably start passing 1,000 tons of supplies per day to Pat-

---

[2] The 14th Armored Division began unloading at Marseille on 29 October, and elements of the division were first committed to the Nice area to relieve units of the 1st Airborne Task Force. The first major increment of the division did not reach the forward area of the VI Corps until 20 November.

[3] General sources for this subsection are the following: Pogue, *The Supreme Command*, pp. 305–11; Cole, *The Lorraine Campaign*, pp. 298–318; MacDonald, *The Siegfried Line Campaign*, pp. 379–93; Devers Diary, 16–17 Oct 44; Seventh Army Diary, 16–18 Oct 44; Hist, 6th Army Gp, ch. 3; Final Rpt, G–3 Section, HQ 6th Army Gp, WWII, pp. 16–20; SHAEF Internal Memo, 22 Oct 44, sub: Decisions reached at Supreme Comdr's Conf, 18 Oct 44; Ltr, Eisenhower to Devers, 23 Oct 44 (no sub); SCAF Directive 114 (SCAF–114), 28 Oct 44; SCAF–118, 2 Nov 44. The last four documents are in SHAEF SGS 381, Post-OVERLORD Plng II. SCAF–114 and SCAF–118 also have SHAEF message numbers, respectively, SHAEF Main S–64375 and SHAEF Main S–65076. (In Pogue, *The Supreme Command*, p. 310, n14, SCAF–118 is mistakenly cited as SCAF–119.)

ton's forces after 15 November, but would be unable to provide any substantial assistance earlier. In the Supreme Commander's mind, this response only emphasized the importance of opening Antwerp for the northern Allied armies. The task would even have to take precedence over any renewed attack by Montgomery and Bradley against the Ruhr, and underlined Allied inability to launch a decisive offensive against Germany until the following year.

The conferences culminated on 18 October at Brussels, Belgium, where Eisenhower, Montgomery, and Bradley worked out plans concerning primarily the November operations of the 21st and 12th Army Groups. This meeting, in turn, led to the promulgation on 28 October of a new Eisenhower directive, Supreme Commander Allied Forces No. 114 (SCAF–114), for operations in November and, by inference, December as well.[4] SCAF–114 demonstrated that SHAEF's operational concepts had changed little since September. The document again placed the main Allied offensive effort in the sector held by Montgomery's 21st Army Group and in the part of the 12th Army Group's zone lying north of the Ardennes, an area roughly between Arnhem and Aachen. While securing the seaward

---

[4] Cole, *The Lorraine Campaign*, p. 298, incorrectly states that the directive was issued on 18 October, "complete with the 'probable' dates for new attacks." But SCAF–114, issued on the 28th, contains no target dates, and tentative timing was left to SCAF–118, issued on 2 November. The delay in promulgating SCAF–114 may have been caused by Eisenhower's desire to be certain that the 21st Army Group operations to clear the Schelde Estuary would be successful before he issued any new, sweeping orders.

approaches to Antwerp had priority, the 21st Army Group was to push its right south and southeast from the vicinity of Nijmegen to clear its sector west of the Rhine, simultaneously seeking bridgeheads across the river. Meanwhile, forces of Bradley's 12th Army Group that were north of the Ardennes were also to move up to the Rhine, swinging their left northward in conjunction with the 21st Army Group's drive south and at the same time trying for bridgeheads over the Rhine south of Cologne.

In the center—that portion of the First Army's zone lying south of the Ardennes plus all of the Third Army's sector—12th Army Group forces were to seize the Saar basin, advance generally northeast to the Rhine, and secure bridgeheads over the river opposite the Frankfurt area. Subsidiary to the main effort north of the Ardennes, these operations were to be timed to support the northern offensives.

Eisenhower's SCAF–114 called for only limited offensive actions in the Ardennes and Vosges areas. The immediate task of the 6th Army Group, Eisenhower informed Devers, was to protect the right flank of the 12th Army Group, primarily by securing the Luneville area. But since the Luneville "area" had certainly been secure since the end of the Parroy forest battle on 10 October, well over two weeks before SCAF–114 appeared, the mission seems a bit superfluous. However, SCAF–114 also directed Devers to clear the Germans from the 6th Army Group's sector west of the Rhine and ultimately seize crossings over the river in the vicinity of Karlsruhe and Mannheim, some forty and seventy-five miles north of

Strasbourg, respectively.

The directive again reflected a compromise between a rigid single-thrust strategy and a broad front operational concept. Moreover, it outlined a program that probably went beyond what Eisenhower actually had in mind for the near future. The most Eisenhower evidently expected of operations in November, if not December as well, was to clear all German forces from the area west of the Rhine River, from Nijmegen in the north to the Swiss border in the south. Although the directive included provisions for the opportunistic seizure of bridgeheads over the Rhine by all three army groups, it also specified that movement of the Allied forces in strength across the river would have to wait for considerable improvement in the logistical situation as well as for the arrival of fresh Allied divisions. Eisenhower was apparently now reconciled to the probability that major advances beyond the Rhine, including the seizure of the Ruhr, would be delayed until 1945.

From Devers' point of view, the Karlsruhe and Mannheim areas could best be considered long-term objectives, since even their approaches were currently well outside his army group's operational zone. The 6th Army Group's own river-crossing plans thus focused on the Rastatt area, about twenty-eight miles north of Strasbourg. South of Rastatt, the densely wooded mountains of the Black Forest dominated the eastern edges of the Rhine valley, greatly reducing the attractiveness of any bridgeheads over the upper Rhine. The Rastatt area thus represented the most southerly crossing point where the 6th Army Group might expect to secure good avenues

of approach leading east and northeast deep into Germany or, alternatively, north up the Rhine valley to Karlsruhe and Mannheim.

SCAF-114 set no firm timetable for the November offensive, but the army group and army commanders involved soon learned that Eisenhower expected the left of Bradley's 12th Army Group to lead off the attack against the Ruhr sometime between 1 and 5 November, with the right of the 21st Army Group following on about 10 November. The Third Army, on the right, or southern, wing of the 12th Army Group, was to begin its attack against the Saar as soon as its logistical situation permitted, but no later than five days after the left of the 12th Army Group began the offensive. Thus the latest target date for the start of Patton's Third Army offensive would also be 10 November, and it could well be several days sooner if Bradley's northern forces jumped off early.

Not surprisingly, given Eisenhower's apparent indifference to the potential of the 6th Army Group, neither SCAF-114 nor an amendment on 2 November, SCAF-118, specified a date for launching Devers' supporting offensive in November. However, after consulting with Bradley, Patton, Patch, and de Lattre, Devers set 15 November as his own target date.

Several considerations led Devers to select 15 November.[5] First, his G-4 set the 15th as the earliest date on which the army group's logistical

---

[5] Additional material on internal 6th Army Group planning is from the following: 6th Army Gp LI 2, 28 Oct 44; Devers Diary, 4 Nov 44; Seventh Army Diary, 24, 25, and 28 Oct and 3 Nov; Ltr, CG Seventh Army to CG VI Corps and CG XV Corps, 5 Nov 44.

system could support a sustained offensive to carry the Seventh Army and the First French Army to the Rhine. In addition, Devers hoped that the Seventh Army, especially its VI Corps, could secure a suitable line of departure for the main offensive by 5 November, thereby affording the army about ten days to rest some of its worn divisions and to introduce the fresh 100th and 103d Divisions into the line. Another consideration stemmed from a study by the 6th Army Group staff of German reactions to major Allied attacks, which concluded that the Germans usually started moving their general reserves either on the evening of the second day or morning of the third day of a strong Allied offensive. To take advantage of this pattern, it seemed logical to stagger the starting dates of the November offensives of the 6th and 12th Army Groups. Thus, if the 12th Army Group's Third Army attacked on 10 November, the 6th Army Group's Seventh Army should strike no earlier than three days (13 November) and no later than five days (15 November) after the Third Army moved.[6] If the attacks could be echeloned in this manner, the Germans would probably be in the process of moving reserves to the sector under attack by the Third Army, and the Seventh Army offensive would force them to reconsider their deployments, thereby causing further delays.

Accordingly, Devers planned to have the offensives of both his Seventh and First French Armies begin on or about 15 November in a series of attacks. On the Seventh Army's left, XV Corps was to launch its offensive on D-day, presumably 15 November, while on the right the VI Corps would strike on D plus 2. The XV Corps was first to head northeast for Sarrebourg, along Route N–4 about thirty miles north of St. Die. Then Haislip's right wing would swing eastward to force the Vosges Mountains via the Saverne Gap, the narrow waist of the Vosges nearly fifteen miles east of Sarrebourg and at the western edge of the Alsatian plains. Subsequently, the XV Corps would continue northeastward astride the Low Vosges in a corridor some twenty miles wide, with the Third Army's XII Corps on the left and the Seventh Army's VI Corps on the right.

The VI Corps, beginning its attack on the 17th, was to advance northeastward with its main effort along the axes of Routes N–420 and N–392 through the Saales and Hantz passes, northeast of St. Die. Breaking out onto the Alsatian plains, General Brooks' corps was then to seize Strasbourg and secure the west bank of the Rhine north and south of the city. Initially, Patch's Seventh Army planners estimated that the VI Corps attack would constitute the army's main effort during the November offensive, with the XV Corps attack drawing off the German reserves. But as D-day approached, the army staff adopted a more flexible attitude about the relative weight of the two attacks.

---

[6] Citing the Third Army Diary for 5 November 1944, Cole, *The Lorraine Campaign,* p. 302, states that on 5 November Devers told Patton that the Seventh Army's XV Corps would jump off *two* days after the Third Army's attack began, but no confirmation of this statement can be found in 6th Army Group sources.

South of the VI Corps, the French II Corps was to mount another three-day limited objective attack in the Vosges Mountains between 10 and 15 November, both to support the VI Corps' offensive and to divert German attention from the Belfort Gap. There, de Lattre's I Corps was to launch the main effort of the First French Army's November offensive on or about the 15th and attempt to breach the gap, not north of Belfort as long envisioned, but south of the city along the Swiss border.

The First French Army

By the end of the first week of November, the First French Army's logistical situation had improved considerably. Nevertheless, General de Lattre realized that it would be difficult for his forces to sustain an all-out offensive against determined German resistance for more than ten days or perhaps two weeks at most. His best hope was that the German defenses in the Belfort Gap would collapse quickly under the weight of a strong, sudden onslaught before any major logistical problems arose.

He also faced severe manpower constraints.[7] Well before the end of October de Lattre's command had begun to run out of trained replacements from its diminishing resources in Africa. Moreover, de Lattre wanted to replace at least 15,200 black troops from tropical and subtropical Africa—

most of them in the 1st Infantry and 9th Colonial Divisions—before winter weather arrived. As planned before ANVIL was launched, the First French Army had begun to tap the manpower resources of metropolitan France soon after the Riviera landings; by early October some 52,000 troops from various FFI organizations had joined de Lattre's regulars, and the number rose to over 60,000 by the end of the month.[8] Meanwhile, a concurrent program of individual recruitment and training had attained some success in filling holes in the ranks of de Lattre's regular formations.

The integration of the European soldiers into what was in reality a colonial army proved difficult, and the task was further complicated by the political differences between the often conservative North African French Army cadre, many of whom had been supporters of the Vichy French regime, and the more leftist FFI leaders, especially those who were members of the French Communist Party. Experimenting, de Lattre had first attached battalion-sized FFI units to existing organizations, a procedure that worked fairly well for commando-type units where the light infantry experience of the FFI found a compatible home. The same process also achieved some success within the armored divisions, where the FFI battalions were often welcome additions to the infantry-short combat commands. In the French infantry divisions, however, the FFI battalions, normally attached as fourth battalions to existing

---

[7] The following discussion of French manpower problems is based mainly on de Lattre, *History*, pp. 169–78; Devers Diary, 22 Dec 44; Vigneras, *Rearming the French*, chs. 18–20; *La 1re D.F.L., Epopee d'une Reconquete*, p. 148; *Historique de la Neuvieme Division d'Infanterie Coloniale*, pp. 44–47.

[8] Another 60,000 to 75,000 FFI troops, outside de Lattre's authority, served in western and southwestern France.

FRENCH NORTH AFRICAN SOLDIERS

regiments, were often misused and neglected, while at the same time creating a drain on the supplies and equipment of the parent unit.

In the case of the black African troops, de Lattre found that the best solution was to replace them company by company or battalion by battalion with Caucasian forces. In this manner some 6,000 FFI troops replaced an equivalent number of black soldiers in the French 1st Infantry Division's line battalions as well as in some artillery and service organizations, with the indigenous French troops often taking over the arms and equipment, including overcoats and helmets, of the departing Africans. Although it depended more on individual recruitment, the 9th Colonial Infantry Division ab-

sorbed three FFI infantry battalions and two FFI infantry companies during the process of replacing its 9,200 Senegalese troops.[9] Later, due to the difficulties of securing sufficient replacements from North Africa to keep all Algerian and Moroccan regiments up to strength, de Lattre replaced one regiment each of the 3d Algerian, the 2d Moroccan, and the 4th Moroccan Mountain Divisions with FFI units.

The amalgamation of FFI units into the regular formations as well as the rapid influx of hastily trained individ-

[9] On completion of the replacement process, the 4th, 6th, and 13th Senegalese Tirailleurs were redesignated the 21st, 6th, and 23d Colonial Infantry Regiments, although they were obviously no longer colonial formations.

ual replacements created serious problems. Many of the younger men recruited in metropolitan France had no military experience at all, not even with the FFI; and those recruits with prior experience were unfamiliar with the American equipment and organization used by de Lattre's forces. Complicating matters further was de Lattre's practice of maintaining numerous FFI-based battalions and regiments in addition to organizations that the Combined Chiefs of Staff (CCS) had approved for the French rearmament program.[10] Since the CCS would not, and indeed could not, provide arms and other equipment for such units, de Lattre had to juggle First French Army stocks, seek surplus American and British equipment, and use a variety of salvaged and captured materiel to keep the extra FFI units minimally equipped. The effort placed an undue strain on the First French Army's already weak logistical machinery, while at the same time adding to the stress on American supply agencies.[11]

Whatever de Lattre's logistical and manpower problems, far greater threats to the success of the Belfort Gap operation lay in proposals to strip the First French Army of some of its strongest units on the very eve of the November offensive.[12] The first of these threats involved the 190-mile front along the Franco-Italian border from Switzerland south to the Mediterranean. As of mid-October the French held about two-thirds of the sector with the 4th Moroccan Mountain Division (less one regimental combat team) and numerous FFI units that were in the process of being formed into a provisional Alpine division. The American 1st Airborne Task Force, including the Canadian-American 1st Special Service Force, held the southern third of the front. General Devers had been seeking ways to release these specialized assault troops from their essentially static defensive role, and in mid-October he alerted General de Lattre to be prepared to have First French Army units take over the southern third by 11 November, only days before the Belfort Gap offensive was to begin.

De Lattre predictably objected to the extension of his responsibilities in the far south. The task would probably have forced him to return the 4th Moroccan Mountain Division's third regiment to the Franco-Italian front, reducing his strength for the Belfort Gap offensive. As a counter, he thus suggested that a substantial number of his black African troops, those currently being replaced in the 1st Infantry and 9th Colonial Divi-

---

[10] De Gaulle and the French Provisional government followed the same policy outside of the First French Army's zone.

[11] In the end the CCS supported the formation of four new French infantry divisions in metropolitan France. See Vigneras, *Rearming the French*, ch. 20.

[12] General sources on the diversions include the following: de Lattre, *History*, pp. 203–05, 219–22; Hist, 6th Army Gp, ch. 2; Vigneras Interviews; Devers Diary, 25 Oct 44 and 4 and 7 Nov 44; Rad, Eisenhower to Devers et al., SHAEF Fwd 14223, 9 Sep 44; SCAF–93 (SHAEF Fwd 16181), 29 Sep 44;

SCAF–119 (SHAEF Main S–65164), 2 Nov 44; Memo, Eisenhower to Lt Gen Walter B. Smith (Chief of Staff, SHAEF), 22 Sep 44; Ltr, Eisenhower to de Gaulle, 25 Sep 44; Amendment 1, 31 Oct 44, to 6th Army Gp LI 2, 28 Oct 44. Copies of most high-level documents concerning the diversions are located in the 6th Army Group AG files of RG 407, in the 381 series, particularly 381.1 and 381 JPS, and in RG 331, SHAEF SGS File 475/2, France, Employment of French Forces.

sions, be reorganized and reequipped for the task; the climate in the southern third of the area was comparatively mild and would impose no undue hardship on these forces. Devers, however, believing he could not provide the necessary supplies and equipment for what would be new French units, rejected the idea and recommended that de Lattre send the 9th Zouaves, an independent regiment, to relieve the American forces in the south. But the French commander had already earmarked the Zouaves for a role in the November offensive and asked that the relief at least be delayed until the end of the month. Tentatively Devers agreed, but in the meantime he made arrangements for the 442d Regimental Combat Team, which was then redeploying south from the Vosges, and elements of the newly arrived 14th Armored Division to take over the border positions.

Of potentially greater impact on de Lattre's forthcoming offensive were plans to divert two of the strongest French divisions from the Belfort Gap front. Since early September General de Gaulle had been pressing Eisenhower to authorize an operation to open the Gironde Estuary, which was the seaward approach to the port of Bordeaux in western France. With all other Allied-controlled French ports devoted almost exclusively to military requirements, there was a pressing need for a large port that could handle civilian relief supplies as well as equipment and commerce necessary to begin restoring the French economy. The need was especially acute in the areas of western and southwestern France, which were still dependent on long overland routes for supplies. Moreover, the fact that isolated German forces in the Gironde Estuary were blocking access to France's second largest port rankled French leaders, especially since the Germans had left most of Bordeaux's facilities intact when they evacuated the port on 28 August. Finally, there was the matter of internal security. Communist agitation in southwestern France had already been highlighted by clashes between the various resistance factions, and many conservative Frenchmen like de Gaulle feared some kind of leftist revolution led by the strong Communist-dominated FFI groups. The fact that the Communists had been among the first to take up arms against the German occupiers and had borne the brunt of the early resistance struggle only increased their standing in many French eyes, which made both the conservative de Gaulle and veteran French politicians extremely nervous. In addition, there was always the possibility that the Germans might mount destructive raids out of their defensive enclaves or even attempt to reach the relative safety of Spain. Had they timed such efforts with German operations in the northeast, the weakly armed FFI, backed only by a few regular Allied units, would have had difficulty stopping them.

At first Eisenhower was firmly opposed to such diversions, and on 9 September he informed the CCS and Devers that SHAEF would commit no forces to operations in southwestern France until German pockets at Brest and at some of the lesser Brittany ports had been cleared. But de Gaulle and the French Department of National Defense insisted that the Bordeaux area had to be liberated. Feeling that his own prestige was at stake, de Gaulle proposed that the French 1st Armored Division be pulled from the line to help FFI units clear out not only the Gironde pockets, but also the Germans still occupying the smaller port of La Rochelle, about thirty-five miles to the north. He also suggested that the French 1st Infantry Division be redeployed to Paris to promote internal security and provide a training base for the new French divisions. Again Eisenhower applied the brakes. No diversions from the First French Army, he informed de Gaulle on 25 September, could be countenanced until the arrival of more American divisions in France.

Nevertheless, four days later the Supreme Commander began to give way to political considerations. Informing the CCS that internal security in southwestern France was becoming a major problem, he authorized AFHQ to send appropriate small units of the French rearmament program still in North Africa or on Corsica to southwest France to help restore order. He also told the CCS that he intended to redeploy additional forces there from the First French Army when the military situation made such a withdrawal possible. However, perhaps influenced by the cost and destructiveness of Allied operations to seize Brest, Eisenhower did not at this time propose any operations to reduce the Gironde pockets.[13]

In early October General de Gaulle, evidently encouraged by Ei-

senhower's statement, alerted de Lattre that his 1st Armored Division would be employed for operations against the Gironde Estuary and added that the French 1st Infantry Division would also be withdrawn for similar endeavors.[14] Meanwhile, SHAEF and the French Department of National Defense undertook preliminary planning for an effort to clear the Gironde Estuary, dubbed Operation INDEPENDENCE.[15] Much initial groundwork apparently took place with little or no participation of Generals Devers and de Lattre or their staffs, and it was not until 2 November that SHAEF directive SCAF–119 made the 6th Army Group responsible for the final planning and execution of INDEPENDENCE.

Devers and de Lattre were obviously upset over the prospect of losing so substantial a force, but neither appeared to have much influence over SHAEF or the French Department of National Defense regarding this issue. At the direction of SHAEF, Devers formally outlined the two-division troop requirement of Operation INDEPENDENCE for de Lattre on 31 October, and also indicated that the Gironde Estuary operation would be expanded to include the seizure of La Rochelle plus another strong German pocket at St. Nazaire, ninety miles farther north. Other actions contemplated during INDEPENDENCE included sealing off the Franco-Spanish border and restoring order throughout

---

[13] The Brest operation is covered in Blumenson, *Breakout and Pursuit*, ch. 30.

[14] See Vigneras Interviews, pp. 30–31; and de Lattre, *History*, p. 219. Lt. Col. de Camas recalled that de Lattre received the alert on 2 October, but de Lattre stated that he first learned of the proposal in a letter from de Gaulle dated 7 October.

[15] Known until 2 November as Operation HIATUS.

southwestern France, tasks that might divert even more strength from the First French Army.

After receiving SCAF–119, Devers limited the scope of the planned operation to the Gironde Estuary and, on 6 November, provided de Lattre with a final troop list for INDEPENDENCE. The operation was to take a 60,000-man bite out of the First French Army, including 45,000 combat troops. The French 1st Armored Division headed the troop list, followed by the 1st Infantry Division, the 9th Zouaves, an armored reconnaissance squadron, two tank destroyer battalions, and a three-battalion field artillery group.[16] The 1st Armored Division was to depart the Belfort front on 11 November, just days before de Lattre's offensive was scheduled to begin; the French 1st Infantry Division was to follow on the 27th. Operations against the Gironde Estuary pockets were to begin about 10 December and be completed by 1 January 1945.

Conferring with Devers on 7 November, de Lattre again registered his vehement objections to the diversion. The French commander argued that if INDEPENDENCE were to be a 6th Army Group operation, then the Seventh Army should also contribute troops to the endeavor, suggesting that the XV Corps' French 2d Armored Division be substituted for his own 1st Armored Division. In any case, de Lattre insisted, he could not

let the armored division go until he had decisively broken through the Belfort Gap defenses, and he did not expect such an event before the 20th.

Devers, knowing the key role that Haislip had planned for Leclerc's 2d Armored Division in the XV Corps' November offensive, could not agree to the switch. However, sympathetic with de Lattre's desire to keep the First French Army intact and equally eager to assure the success of the Belfort Gap operation, he made some concessions. Initially, he moved the departure date of the French 1st Armored Division back to 16 November and that of the French 1st Infantry Division to 28–30 November; he also deleted the 9th Zouaves, the reconnaissance squadron, and some service units from the INDEPENDENCE troop list. Subsequently, de Lattre's supply officers "recomputed" the logistics of the armored division's move and decided that its main body would not have to start westward until 21 November. Devers quickly approved this further delay in the armored unit's departure, but held the infantry division's redeployment to the end of November. Thus de Lattre could count on these two units for only a limited time, and on 13 November, two days before the Belfort Gap offensive was to begin, the French armored division even sent an advance party to Bordeaux to assist in the projected move.[17]

German Prospects

By the end of the first week in November, the recent Allied attacks had

---

[16] During the planning process, the projected troop list included the French II Corps headquarters, but by 6 November Devers had decided to run the operation through a provisional French command, French Forces of the West, under General de Larminat.

[17] 1st Fr Armd Div Jnl de Marche, 13 Nov 44.

again stretched the *Nineteenth Army* to the breaking point. Only the difficult terrain had slowed the Allied advance in the Vosges and staved off a complete collapse.[18] But General Wiese still had no reserves worthy of the name to contain or counterattack even a minor Allied penetration. The *Weststellung* defenses throughout the *Nineteenth Army*'s sector were in no way capable of withstanding a concerted Allied attack, and the army could not hold the *Vosges Foothill Position* much longer with the declining forces Wiese had at his disposal. Finally, although the terrain was the greatest asset of the German defenders in the Vosges, the generally wooded and mountainous 120-mile front of the *Nineteenth Army* made it difficult for Wiese to shift his forces back and forth and to supply and support his thinly spread army.

Wiese also knew that his command, like that of General Devers, held a relatively low position in the hierarchy of the western front. At *OB West* von Rundstedt's plans and decisions were strongly influenced by his preparations for the Ardennes counteroffensive, then scheduled for late November, and he had already stripped several major armored organizations from *Army Group G* for this purpose. His other major priority was countering the expected drive of the northern Allied army groups against the Ruhr. Accordingly, *OB West* gave *Army Group B*, which was responsible for holding the Ruhr, defensive priority over Balck's *Army Group G*. Balck, in

turn, was forced to give priority to his *First Army*, which was defending the Metz area and the Saar against Patton's divisions. With Patton obviously poised to strike, Balck had already decided to send any army group reserves to his northern army. The *Nineteenth Army* would thus have to fight its battles with what was left over after all other German requirements on the western front had been met.

Balck and Wiese believed that the 6th Army Group's main effort during November would be a Seventh Army attack along the general axis of Baccarat, Sarrebourg, and Saverne. Baccarat lay in the *Nineteenth Army*'s area of responsibility, and Sarrebourg and Saverne in that of the *First Army*. The most immediate danger, the two German commanders estimated, was that Patch's command would open a gap between the *First* and *Nineteenth Armies*, thereby unhinging the defenses of the Saar basin and the Palatinate. Both commanders also agreed that the First French Army would launch a secondary offensive in the Belfort Gap sector during November, but differed over where de Lattre's blow would fall. Balck thought that French operations in the gap area would constitute only a holding action to cover the main effort across the Vosges well north of Belfort; Wiese, on the other hand, believed that the French main effort would be centered against the Belfort Gap itself.

The *Nineteenth Army*'s front now coincided with that of the 6th Army Group, for during the second week of November Balck had extended Wiese's sector northward to the

---

[18] German material in this section is based largely on von Luttichau, "German Operations," chs. 21 and 22.

Rhine-Marne Canal, which also marked the boundary between the Allied 6th and 12th Army Groups.[19] Wiese's northern army flank was anchored on the canal near Lagarde, off the eastern corner of the Parroy forest. General Thumm's *LXIV Corps* held the army's right wing from the canal southeast some thirty-five miles to Saulcy-sur-Meurthe, three miles south of St. Die. The *LXIV Corps* thus faced all of the Seventh Army's XV Corps as well as most of the VI Corps.

On 7 November the *LXIV Corps* had on line, from north to south, the two-regiment *553d Volksgrenadier Division*, the *951st Grenadiers* of the *361st Volksgrenadier Division* (at Raon-l'Etape), the weak *21st Panzer Division*, the battered *716th Infantry Division*, and what was left of the nearly destroyed *16th Volksgrenadier Division*. The next day the *708th Volksgrenadier Division* began moving into the German front lines between the *553d Volksgrenadier Division* and the *21st Panzer;* it first relieved the *951st Grenadiers* and then took over for the *21st Panzer Division*, with both of the retiring units moving north of the canal to become part of the *First Army*. The weakened *106th Panzer Brigade, Army Group G*'s only significant reserve, accompanied the *21st Panzer Division* northward, representing the last of the *Nineteenth Army*'s armor except for some assault-gun units.

Although weak in infantry and artillery and lacking antitank weapons, the *553d Volksgrenadier Division* boasted seasoned troops and good leadership. To its south the arriving *708th Volksgrenadiers* was nearly up to strength, but lacked training and experienced leaders; some 70 percent of its non-commissioned officers, for example, were former members of the *Luftwaffe* or the *Kriegsmarine.*[20] Farther south the *716th Division* was reinforced by the *757th Grenadiers*, a regiment of the *338th Division* that had remained behind when the rest of the unit moved to the Belfort Gap front in late October. Although at best a marginal division, the *716th* was still better off than the badly damaged *16th Volksgrenadiers*, which was still trying to recover from the beating it had received fighting in front of the *Vosges Foothill Position* defenses around St. Die.

Defending the southern section of the High Vosges below St. Die, Petersen's *IV Luftwaffe Field Corps* had two fairly strong divisions—the somewhat understrength but experienced *198th Division*, most of which faced the VI Corps' southern wing, and the stronger *269th Volksgrenadier Division*, which confronted the French II Corps. Finally, at the southern end of the *Nineteenth Army*'s front, Kniess' *LXXXV Corps* defended the Belfort Gap area with three divisions, the *159th*, the *189th*, and the *338th*—all jerry-rigged, but well rested and relatively fresh. How well and how long this ragged defensive line could hold up depended greatly on the individual unit commanders, for neither Balck nor Wiese could do much to assist them.

---

[19] The extension was not fully effective until 13 November; previously, the German boundary had roughly followed Route N–4, about ten miles south of the canal.

[20] The *708th Volksgrenadier Division* was built on the remains of the *708th Infantry Division*, which had been virtually destroyed in Normandy.

The Final Allied Schedule

Well into the first week of November, General Bradley of the 12th Army Group still hoped to have his First and Ninth Armies launch their offensives on 5 November, with Patton's Third Army striking on the 10th. But adverse tactical developments in the sector of the 21st Army Group forced a change in plans, and on 2 November Eisenhower and Bradley decided to reschedule the First and Ninth Army attacks for the 10th. Hoping to have at least part of the 12th Army Group under way earlier, however, Bradley asked Patton to have his Third Army begin its offensive as soon as possible and have his XII Corps, just north of the Seventh Army, strike no later than 8 November.[21] As events turned out, Patton attacked on time, but the First and Ninth Army attacks were delayed even further when Bradley approved a series of day-by-day postponements because of poor flying conditions; ultimately he did not begin his offensive until the 16th.

All these changes caught the 6th Army Group by surprise. On 5 November General Devers visited Patton's command post at Nancy to be briefed on the Third Army's tactical plans and the tentative schedule of attack. Devers evidently came away from the briefing with the understanding that Patton's terminal date was still 10 November, and he did not find out about the decisions Bradley and Patton had reached on the 2d.

Thus there was considerable consternation at the 6th Army Group headquarters when, about noon on 7 November, word came that the Third Army's XII Corps would begin its attack on the morning of the 8th, whatever the weather conditions. In order to adhere to the planned, five-day maximum interval between the 12th and the 6th Army Group attacks, Devers quickly decided to move his starting date forward from 15 to 13 November if possible. A brief review of the logistical situation revealed that the two-day acceleration would create no major problems, and new orders immediately went out to Patch and de Lattre to make the change. Within the Seventh Army, the XV Corps would strike on the 13th and the VI Corps on the 15th; in the First French Army, the I Corps would launch the main effort against the Belfort Gap on the 13th, and the II Corps would begin its supporting operations the same day. With luck the new attack dates might even increase the surprise of the German defenders.[22]

With the final preparations now under way, General Devers became increasingly optimistic. He estimated that the XV Corps would cross the Vosges and break out on to the Alsatian plains by 1 December; he also thought that the French I Corps would be in the Rhine valley by the 1st, "and probably sooner."[23] If Strasbourg could be taken and the Rhine breached, the possibilities of exploiting

---

[21] Cole, *The Lorraine Campaign*, p. 301; MacDonald, *The Siegfried Line Campaign*, p. 393; SCAF–118, 2 Nov 44.

[22] Devers Diary, 5 Nov 44; Seventh Army Diary, 7, 8, and 9 Nov 44; Hist, 9th Army Gp, ch. 3; Final Rpt, G–3 Sec, 6th Army Gp, p. 20; First Fr Army Genl Opns Order 148, 11 Nov 44.

[23] Devers Diary, 11 and 12 Nov 44, with the quotation from the 12 November entry.

such a breakthrough appeared unlimited. Devers' own predeliction was for crossing the Rhine above Strasbourg and exploiting north up the Rhine valley toward Karlsruhe, thus trapping the *First Army* and isolating the Saar industrial region in one sweep. This time he would show the other Allied commanders what his underrated forces could do and in the process grind up as many Germany corps and divisions as possible.

CHAPTER XXI

Through the Saverne Gap

As D-day for the November offensive of the XV Corps approached, Haislip readied his three divisions, now constituting the smallest Allied attacking force. His left wing was still anchored on the Rhine-Marne Canal at Xures, about three miles across from the opposing flank of the German *LXIV Corps* at Lagarde. The XV Corps' 106th Cavalry Group screened the corps' left for two miles, maintaining contact with the Third Army's XII Corps north of the canal. The 44th Infantry Division held the next seven miles south to the Vezouse River near Domjevin, now in Allied hands. The French 2d Armored Division, its front bulging eastward, covered the ground from the Vezouse south another eight miles to Baccarat, on the boundary between the XV and VI Corps. The 79th Infantry Division, out of the line since 24 October and resting south of Luneville, was to play a major role in the forthcoming attack. To strengthen these forces Patch had decided to give Haislip the VI Corps' 45th Division as soon as it had completed its rest after DOGFACE. Thus, although small in numbers, the XV Corps could marshal some of the most experienced units on the entire Allied front for the assault against the narrow Saverne Gap, now defended only by three weak *volksgrenadier* divisions.

XV Corps Plans

General Haislip, commanding XV Corps, set forth the requirements for his November offensive in succinct terms: capture and secure Sarrebourg; force the Saverne Gap; and prepare to exploit east of the Vosges.[1] With the cavalry force covering along the Rhine-Marne Canal, the 44th Division was to make the main effort initially, heading northeast twenty miles to seize Sarrebourg from the west and north. The 79th Division, coming back into the line south of the Vezouse River, would pass through the 2d Armored Division and head northeast to invest Sarrebourg from the south and east. Both divisions were to be ready to continue the offensive northeast and east after securing Sarrebourg. During this time the French 2d Armored Division would remain in reserve as the XV Corps' exploitation force. When the infantry divisions began breaking through the German defenses, Haislip planned to send the armored unit through the infantry, striking for the Saverne Gap and securing a bridgehead through the Vosges somewhere in the Saverne

---

[1] XV Corps FO 11, 8 Nov 44. Sarrebourg itself was in the German *First Army*'s *XXXIV Corps*' area of responsibility just north of the *Nineteenth Army*.

GENERALS SPRAGINS, HAISLIP, AND WYCHE AT XV CORPS COMMAND POST, *Luneville, October 1944.*

area. The timing of the armored division's attack would be critical.

The designations *Saverne* and *Saverne Gap* require some explanation. The small, busy, but pleasant city of Saverne lies under the eastern slopes of the Vosges and at the western edge of the Alsatian plains. Through the city passes Route N–4, the Paris-Strasbourg highway; the main railroad line to Strasbourg; and the Rhine-Marne Canal and its contributory stream, the little Zorn River. Another rail line leads off to the northeast, while lesser highways and secondary roads come in from the north, south, and east.

The easiest approach to Saverne from the west is along Route N–4, which passes through Phalsbourg, on

the edge of the Lorraine plateau, and winds down the wooded eastern slopes of the Vosges in a gradual southeasterly descent. However, the Saverne Gap proper lies farther south, originating in the west at Arzviller, five miles east of Sarrebourg, and emerging at the southwestern approaches to Saverne itself. The gap, an almost gorgelike passage through the Vosges, is scarcely 100 yards wide at places, but accommodates the main railroad line to Strasbourg, the Rhine-Marne Canal, the upper reaches of the Zorn River (merging with the canal through much of the gap), and a narrow secondary highway. The railroad passes through a number of tunnels (one, near Arzviller, a mile

SAVERNE

and a half long); the canal drops 500 feet between Arzviller and Saverne through a series of locks; and the road hugs the base of the forested, towering hills through much of its journey.

Haislip estimated that XV Corps would encounter no strong, continuous defensive lines, but instead would run up against delaying forces at strongpoints at key road and canal junctures—a judgment that corresponded closely with *LXIV Corps'* capabilities.[2] His units would have to

force their way through elements of at least three *volksgrenadier* divisions: part of the *361st* under von Gilsa's *LXXXIX Corps (First Army)* north of the canal and all of the *553d* and perhaps half of the *708th* under Thumm's *LXIV Corps* south of the waterway (*Nineteenth Army*). Since neither of the opposing corps had any mobile reserves, Haislip expected that the defenses would be spotty, but in great depth; therefore, he instructed his division commanders to have their leading units bypass isolated strongpoints, leaving them for follow-up forces. Should the van units became entangled in such defenses, he wanted the second echelons of the attacking

---

[2] German information in this chapter is mainly from von Luttichau, "German Operations," chs. 22 and 24.

forces to bypass the action and maintain the forward momentum.

XV Corps Attacks

After the French 2d Armored Division's seizure of Baccarat and after some minor 44th Division advances during the first week of November, little change had taken place along the XV Corps' front until the night of 11–12 November. Then, under cover of darkness, the 79th Division began moving into forward assembly lines in the Mondon forest south of the Vezouse River (*Map 26*). Heavy rains had gradually turned into blizzards during the days preceding the attack, and by evening of the 12th wet snow blanketed the entire corps sector. All streams in the area were flooded, many roads and bridges were under water, and the troops described the now ever-present French mud as bottomless.[3] In fact, the weather had been so poor that General Devers contemplated postponing Haislip's attack; but about 2300 that night he decided to proceed with the offensive, hoping that the Germans might not expect a major attack under such adverse conditions.[4] The 44th and 79th Divisions, each with two regiments abreast, jumped off on schedule early the following morning of 13 November.

Behind an intensive artillery preparation, the 44th Division attacked along the axis of the railroad line to

---

[3] XV Corps AAR, Nov 44, p. 13. In mid-November, flooding along the fronts of the Third and Seventh Armies was supposedly the worst in the area since 1919.

[4] G–3 Section, HQ 6th Army Gp, Final Report, World War II, p. 21.

Sarrebourg, with the 324th Infantry on the left and the 71st Infantry on the right. At first both regiments advanced rapidly, but by 0800 the Germans had recovered from the bombardment and responded with heavy and accurate artillery, mortar, and machine-gun fire all across the division's front. By dark, disappointing gains had carried the leading battalions hardly a mile eastward, and the high point of the day was the capture of battered Leintrey, a small town at the junction of three secondary roads. Operations on 14 November were even less productive, and General Spragins, the division commander, decided to commit his reserves, the 114th Infantry, in the Leintrey area. After passing through the 71st Infantry on the south, the 114th was to swing north across the fronts of the other two regiments, sweeping through the defenses of the *553d Volksgrenadier Division* from the flank and rear.

This somewhat unorthodox—if not dangerous—maneuver proved successful; by the evening of the 15th, the 114th Infantry had gained a mile and a half to the east, northeast, and north of Leintrey, thus dislocating the German defenses in the rising, partially wooded ground. On 16 November the 114th Infantry and the 106th Cavalry Group mopped up on the division's left, and the next day the 324th and 71st Infantry continued their advance east, passing through the wake of the 114th, which reverted to its reserve status.

By 18 November the defenses of the *553d Volksgrenadier Division* began to unravel in the face of the continuing attack. During the following day

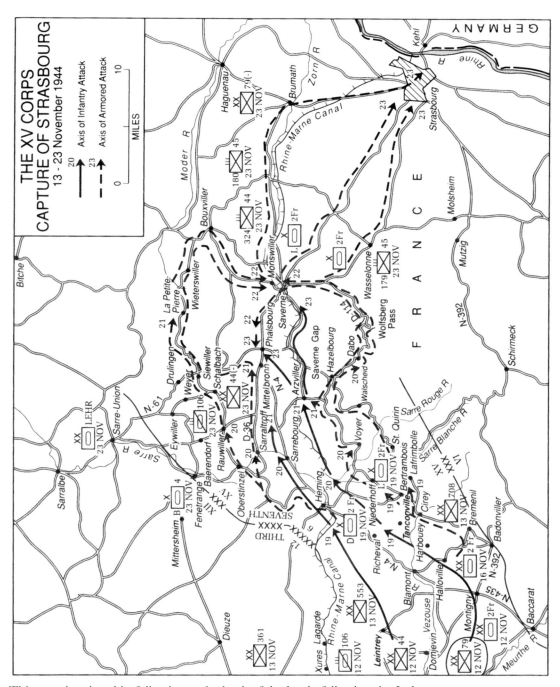

This map is printed in full color at the back of the book, following the Index.

MAP 26

the 71st Infantry undertook the division's main effort and pushed some nine miles along the axis of Route N-4, coming almost within sight of the Rhine-Marne Canal, about six miles short of the division's objective, Sarrebourg. To the north, the 324th, now in support of the 71st, kept pace, as did elements of the 106th Cavalry stretching eastward along the canal. The 44th Division had achieved at least half of the breakthrough that Haislip had hoped for.

South of the 44th Division, General Wyche's 79th Division began its attack on 13 November from a line of departure near Montigny, at the junction of Routes N-392 and N-435. By the following day the 314th Infantry on the left had reached Halloville, while the 315th on the right pushed several miles up Route N-392 toward Badonviller. The Halloville thrust threatened to drive a wedge between the *553d* and *708th Volksgrenadier Divisions* and was clearly the most dangerous penetration. As the *708th* prepared a strong counterattack, the 315th Infantry, moving up to support its sister unit, struck first and sent an infantry force backed by tanks and tank destroyers into the German assembly area east of Halloville, which dispersed the German reserves and, in the process, destroyed most of the *708th*'s assault guns.[5]

On the 15th the Germans made two more attempts to restore the situation in the Halloville sector. First, elements of the *553d Volksgrenadier Division* struck south from Blamont, along Route N-4 and the Vezouse River about three miles north of Halloville. Then another force, probably under the direct control of the *LXIV Corps,* moved up from the southeast. So ineffectual were these efforts that the 79th Division's forward units reported no unusual activity. Thus, as the 44th Division began to dislocate the *553d Division*'s defenses in the north, the 79th Division now began to penetrate the lines of the *708th Division* at will, walking nearly unopposed into Harbouey, two miles northeast of Halloville, and continuing its advance toward the southern approaches to Sarrebourg.

At the headquarters of both the *Nineteenth Army* and the *LXIV Corps,* the situation began to appear desperate as early as 16 November. Lacking any radio or telephone communications with the *708th Volksgrenadier Division,* the German commanders believed that the converging Allied attacks along Route N-4 had pushed back the *708th*'s right flank, thus cutting off the *553d Volksgrenadier Division* from the rest of the corps. Actually the situation was not yet that bleak. During the night of 15-16 November, the left of the *553d* had fallen back in fairly good order to Blamont and reestablished a defensive line on the Vezouse to Cirey-sur-Vezouse. About the same time, the rather disorganized right wing of the *708th Volksgrenadiers* began moving into line south from Cirey along rising, forested terrain dotted with installations of the *Vosges Foothill Position.* Nevertheless, the condition of *LXIV Corps'* defenses was rapidly becoming a serious problem.

---

[5] The 315th claimed the destruction of five assault guns and "some other vehicles" (315th Inf AAR, Nov 44, p. 16), while von Luttichau's "German Operations," ch. 22, relates that the Germans lost nine of the ten assault guns sent into action.

On 16 November Haislip began to commit elements of the 2d Armored Division in order to secure the flanks of both attacking divisions and to ensure that the momentum of the offensive continued. Combat Command Remy (CCR) began to push southeast from Halloville along secondary roads, clearing roadblocks and mines and generally disorganizing the *708th Division's* lines of communication. On the 17th CCV reinforced Remy, striking east about five miles along Route N–392 from Montigny to seize Badonviller and then swinging north two miles to Bremenil. Meanwhile, to the north, elements of CCL (de Langlade) began moving up to Blamont along Route N–4, as 79th Division infantry forces crossed the Vezouse River to the east, in the face of still strong opposition from the *553d Volksgrenadier Division,* and began to invest the town from the north.

On 18 November, as the 44th Division started its deep penetration of the *553d Volksgrenadiers'* front along Route N–4, the right of the *708th Volksgrenadier Division* collapsed, as Wiese had feared. CCR and elements of CCV subsequently rolled northward for four unopposed miles to capture bridges at Cirey-sur-Vezouse. The Badonviller-Cirey road had been a main supply route of the German defenders, and the French found it clear of roadblocks and mines. On the same day, the left of the 79th Division walked unopposed into Blamont. Although German artillery and mortar fire halted further progress north of the Vezouse, the effect was only temporary.

During the night of 18–19 November, the left wing of the *553d Volks-*

grenadier Division withdrew in a vain attempt to establish a new defensive line from Richeval, five miles northeast of Blamont, south and east through Tanconville to Bertrambois and Lafrimbolle. The American and French attackers never gave the *553d* time to pause. By noon on the 19th, the 79th Division's 314th regiment was approaching Richeval; the 315th had passed through Tanconville; CCL had cleared Bertrambois; and CCR units had reached out to Lafrimbolle in the mountains, a mile and a half east of Bertrambois. Haislip was now ready to begin the exploitation phase of his attack, and at 1345 that afternoon he turned the rest of Leclerc's 2d Armored Division loose.

The Exploitation Plan

Leclerc's immediate objective was Saverne, on the far side of the Vosges Mountains. Toward this end he had divided his division into carefully organized task forces, and he assigned to each complementary but independent missions, including primary and alternate routes of penetration.[6] To support the division's scheme of maneuver, his staff had also put together every available scrap of information about road conditions, German deployments, and German defenses. Leclerc planned to lead off with two combat commands, CCD (Dio) and CCL, each subdivided into two smaller task forces. After crossing the Rhine-Marne Canal, CCD units were to bypass Sarrebourg to the west and north, head east across the Low

---

[6] See 2d Fr Amd Div Preparatory Opns Order 189/3, 12 Nov 44.

Vosges well north of the Saverne Gap in two columns, and then, once on the other side of the mountains, descend on Saverne from the north and northeast. South of the canal and south and east of Sarrebourg, CCL, also with two columns, was to push rapidly east over second-class roads, crossing the Vosges well south of the Saverne Gap; push through the heavily forested mountains to the Alsatian plains; and then swing north to meet CCD. CCV would be in general reserve, ready to reinforce either CCD or CCL, while CCR, the armored division's permanent reconnaissance organization, would support CCL in the south and secure the division's extended right flank. If Leclerc's intelligence estimate was correct, the plan would allow him to avoid the strong defenses that he expected in the Saverne Gap itself and cut through the mountain passes before the Germans had a chance to block them.

Haislip's larger objectives also required that Leclerc's armor secure all eastern exits of the Vosges passes from La Petite-Pierre, eight miles north of Saverne, to Dabo, about eight miles south of the gap. To assist, Haislip wanted the 44th Division to seize Sarrebourg as soon as possible and be prepared to relieve French armor along the northern portion of the corps' objective area. In addition, the 79th Division, now relieved of its Sarrebourg mission, would be ready to exploit the French gains in the southern half of the corps' sector and secure the southern portion of the objective area. Upon relief by the 44th and 79th Divisions, Leclerc was to push his entire armored division on to Haguenau, an

important highway and rail junction on the Alsatian plains, seventeen miles north of Strasbourg. If necessary, however, the French armor was also prepared to withdraw all the way back to Weyer, on the west side of the Vosges ten miles north of Sarrebourg, in order to protect XV Corps' exposed northern flank.[7]

The so-called Weyer alternative demonstrated that Patch and Haislip were fully aware of the risks involved in a deep penetration by the French armored division. By 19 November the XV Corps' left flank was more than ten miles beyond the right wing of the Third Army's XII Corps, which was still back in the area just above Lagarde. Although currently screened by the XV Corps' 106th Cavalry Group, the gap could only grow larger as Haislip's forces drove east.[8] A similar situation existed in the south, where the lengthening boundary with Brooks' VI Corps at Baccarat was screened by CCR. Both Patch and Haislip felt, however, that the possibility of a German counterattack was minimal. The two opposing *volksgrenadier* divisions were falling apart, and the German forces on both of their flanks were too concerned with their own immediate fronts to assist the *553d* or *708th*. North of the Rhine-Marne Canal, the *First Army*'s southernmost unit, *LXXXIX Corps' 361st Volksgrenadier Division,* was fully committed to the defense of its own

---

[7] XV Corps OI 49, 19 Nov 44, as modified by XV Corps OI 50, 20 Nov 44.

[8] For XII Corps operations during the period, see Cole, *The Lorraine Campaign,* chs. 7 and 10. Units of the 106th Cavalry had entered Lagarde on 17 November, finding the Germans departed but the village thoroughly mined and booby-trapped.

sector against the attacking U.S. XII Corps. South of the XV Corps, the rest of the *LXIV Corps* had its hands full defending against Brooks' VI Corps attack, now in full swing. Only by bringing substantial reinforcements forward from outside the *Nineteenth Army*'s zone could the Germans develop any serious threat to either of the XV Corps' extended flanks, and this danger seemed remote. Such a counterattack would take time to assemble and deploy, and Haislip still had the 45th Infantry Division in reserve for such contingencies. Nevertheless, the Weyer alternative put Leclerc on notice that his forces might have to return west of the Vosges should a threat develop.[9]

Seizing the Gap

During the afternoon of 19 November CCD assembled south of the forward positions of the 44th Division near Heming, at the juncture of N–4 and the Rhine-Marne Canal. Before dawn on the 20th, Allied troops had secured several bridges over the canal, and at daylight the armored attack began. Initially the 44th Division's 71st Infantry moved northeast along Route N–4 directly toward Sarrebourg. Meanwhile, CCD and the 324th Infantry, following all passable roads, crossed the canal and headed north, delayed only by scattered elements of the *LXXXIX Corps'* *361st Volksgrenadier Division*, which for the most part lacked any artillery support.

The *361st Volksgrenadiers* were in a difficult position. During the night of 19–20 November, under pressure from the XII Corps, the division had begun withdrawing into *Weststellung* positions north of Heming, only to lose the southern portion of its new line to Haislip's XV Corps before the withdrawal could be completed. Now the division had to pull itself even farther back in an attempt to keep Sarrebourg from falling into the hands of Allied forces advancing up Route N–4 from the southwest. To assist in the effort, Balck, the *Army Group G* commander, transferred the remnants of the *553d Volksgrenadier Division* from the *Nineteenth Army*'s *LXIV Corps* to the *First Army*'s *LXXXIX Corps*; and von Gilsa, the corps commander, ordered the *361st Division* to assemble a regimental task force to reinforce the *553d* south of the canal. During the night of 19 November von Gilsa also moved the headquarters of the *LXXXIX Corps* to Sarrebourg, only to be forced to evacuate the city hurriedly on the afternoon of the 20th as the 71st Infantry approached. There was little he could do to salvage the position. By dark the 71st Infantry had secured most of the city, and other 44th Division units had overrun about half of the reinforcements sent to the area by the *361st Volksgrenadier Division*.

As these developments were taking place, CCD had continued to move north of the German lines, dividing itself into two armored columns. The southern arm, Task Force Quilichini, reached the Sarre River at Sarraltroff, over two miles north of Sarrebourg.

---

[9] On 19 November the 45th Division was in a rest area near Bains-les-Bains, over fifty miles west of the XV Corps' front lines. Seventh Army OI 14, 15 Nov 44, placed the division on general alert, with one regiment to be ready to move to the XV Corps' sector on twelve hours' notice and the rest of the division on twenty-four hours' notice; Seventh Army OI 16, 19 Nov 44, changed the alert to six and twelve hours.

Meanwhile, the northern column, Task Force Rouvillois, captured a bridge over the river at Oberstinzel, two miles farther north, and by dark had sent patrols to Rauwiller, over three miles to the east.

The French incursions abruptly forced the *361st Volksgrenadiers* backward along a new defensive line between Mittersheim, Rauwiller, and Schalbach, facing generally southward to protect the *LXXXIX Corps'* rear lines of communication. Whittled down to less than 2,000 infantry effectives, however, the hapless *361st* had little chance of holding either this new line or its main defensive positions still facing west against Third Army units.

Accurately assessing the German situation, Col. Louis J. Dio, commanding CCD, obtained Leclerc's permission to have TF Rouvillois cross the Vosges through a route farther north than the one planned, both to take advantage of German weaknesses in the area and to further dislocate any German defenses in the Vosges or in the open country north of Sarrebourg. Striking out early on the morning of 21 November, TF Rouvillois was soon past Schalbach and then swung northeast for about three miles to Siewiller, at the western edge of the Low Vosges. Crossing a main north-south artery, Route N–61, the force pushed on and by late afternoon was at La Petite-Pierre, in the heart of the Low Vosges some ten twisting road miles beyond Siewiller. Behind TF Rouvillois, the XV Corps' 106th Cavalry Group probed northward, securing Baerendorf, Eywiller, Weyer, and Drulingen on the corps' northern flank. Nowhere did the cav-

alry encounter any threat to CCD's rear.

CCD's second column, TF Quilichini, had meanwhile headed almost due east, rapidly covering the eight miles from Sarraltroff to Mittelbronn along Route D–36. After a brief clash with undermanned German defenses at Mittelbronn, the advance halted, for patrols had discovered formidable, well-defended antitank obstacles across N–4 in front of Phalsbourg, a mile or so to the east. To the rear, the 44th Division's 324th Infantry crossed the Sarre River at Sarraltroff behind TF Quilichini, and the 114th Infantry, coming out of reserve, reached out along Route N–4, two miles beyond Sarrebourg. South of Sarrebourg, units of the 79th Division now made an appearance, bypassing a CCL fight along the way and moving up to the main highway, Route N–4. The American infantry divisions along with some of the French armored units were thus rapidly converging on Phalsbourg and the immediate western approaches to the Saverne Gap.

South of Sarrebourg, CCL's northern column, Task Force Minjonnet, had left Bertrambois on the morning of the 19th and, following a third-class country road, pushed north two miles through dense forests to be halted just south of Niederhoff. The southern column, TF Massu, also made little initial progress against *553d Volksgrenadier* defenses north of Lafrimbolle, but the thinly dispersed *553d* could not hold out long. Increasingly disorganized and out of communication with its corps headquarters, the division tried to establish a new defensive line during the night of 19–20 November between

Heming, on the Rhine-Marne Canal, south and southeast along the Sarre Rouge and Sarre Blanche rivers to St. Quirin, deep in the Vosges.[10]

On 20 November the French advance in the south continued. After some brief fighting during the morning, TF Minjonnet's armor cleared Niederhoff and then swung northeast along back roads for about two miles, crossing the Sarre Rouge and forcing its way eastward another two miles to Voyer. Here it overran *553d Division* artillery positions and captured some 200 German troops. Minjonnet's flank and rear security were assured later in the day when the 314th Infantry also fought its way across the Sarre Rouge and the 313th Infantry moved up to Niederhoff.

Farther south, TF Massu spent much of the morning outflanking and breaking through last-ditch positions of the *553d* along the Sarre Blanche west of St. Quirin, which fell about 1400 on the 20th, thus marking the complete collapse of the *553d Volksgrenadier Division*'s defensive effort. Massu then sped his armor along the twisting mountain roads to Walscheid, five miles— straight line distance—northeast of St. Quirin, and continued north another three miles to pick up Route D–114, also known as the Dabo Road, which ran uphill to the southeast for eight miles through wild, forested country to the Wolfsberg Pass.

Prisoners, mostly from artillery and service units, now began to create a problem, especially for CCL task forces south of Saverne. As a remedy, the XV Corps directed the 79th Division to attach two rifle companies to the French 2d Armored Division to help handle the increasing number of surrendering Germans. About the same time, General Leclerc decided that opposition during the day warranted committing his CCV reserve in the southern sector. CCV's main effort was to be made along the Dabo Road, with TF Massu passing to its control. Task Force Minjonnet of CCL would continue north and northeast from Voyer to Arzviller, but was to double back and follow CCV through the mountains if strong opposition was encountered. CCR, which had been maintaining roadblocks along the XV Corps' right, or southern, flank, would reassemble at Walscheid, ready to secure the Dabo Road behind CCV.[11]

Amid a heavy rainstorm TF Massu, overrunning small groups of fleeing Germans, continued southeast up the Dabo Road. That evening, about 2000 on the 20th, forward elements of the task force reached the village of Dabo, three road miles short of the Wolfsberg Pass, where they halted to refuel and await the arrival of CCV. The latter force, moving out of an assembly area near Cirey-sur-Vezouse, had traveled east as rapidly as rain and road conditions permitted and, after dark, continued on with all vehicle headlights ablaze to catch up with Massu's forces near Dabo at 0200 on the 21st.

---

[10] The Sarre Rouge and Sarre Blanche rivers, ordinarily well-behaved brooks feeding into the Sarre River, had overflowed their banks in mid-November and could be forded only with great difficulty.

[11] Leclerc issued verbal orders concerning CCV about 1800 on 20 November and confirmed them with 2d Armored Division Opns Order 219/3, 21 Nov 44.

Although the Dabo Road could have been easily interdicted, the *553d Volksgrenadiers* were no longer interested. What was left of the division was surrounded and sought only to escape from the advancing Allied forces. Maj. Gen. Hans Bruhn, the division commander, assembled about 1,800 troops, some light artillery pieces, and all operable vehicles in an area just north of Voyer. Aided by a heavy downpour, Bruhn's group hugged the Rhine-Marne Canal and passed by several Allied outposts in the night, probably units of the 314th Infantry, to reach Arzviller before dawn on the 21st. Another force of some 300 *553d Volksgrenadier Division* troops farther east somehow sidled past French units along the mountain roads and also reached Arzviller during the morning of 21 November. With these two groups and miscellaneous other troops already in the area, Bruhn began to organize the defenses of the Saverne Gap proper, attempting to tie in his forces with the existing defenses at Phalsbourg. There the German defenders had received an unexpected bonus, a well-equipped battalion of troops from an NCO school at Bitche, some twenty miles north of Saverne. The defenses were thus in much better condition.

Prior to the XV Corps' attack, Bruhn had made provisions for a last-ditch defense of the most obvious approaches to Saverne, down Route N–4 and through the gorge of the Saverne Gap, but had neglected to prepare blocking positions along the narrow mountain roads north and south of Saverne, as Leclerc had surmised. The *553d* was now too weak to remedy the mistake, and the units on

both its flanks were unable to fill in. In the north the left wing of the *361st Volksgrenadier Division* had almost disappeared, while in the south the rest of the *708th Volksgrenadier Division* had been badly cut up by the VI Corps' 100th Division at Raon-l'Etape. In fact, between Arzviller and Bertrambois—the new northern boundary of the *Nineteenth Army*—a gap of about ten miles existed with no organized defense.

Starting out at dawn on 21 November, TF Massu, followed by CCV, reached the Wolfsberg Pass by noon despite spotty, but determined resistance. Two hours later its leading elements, moving as fast as possible down the steep sides of the eastern Vosges, broke through to the Alsatian plains. Massu immediately turned north, heading for Saverne, while CCV moved east, spreading out over the broad rolling terrain. Meanwhile, TF Minjonnet battled most of the day with scattered elements of the *553d Volksgrenadiers* a mile south of Arzviller; only after dark did it reverse its course and cross the Vosges via the Dabo Road, leaving the Arzviller area to the 79th Division's infantry units. During the night the German forces in the area began withdrawing into the Saverne Gap gorge for a final stand.

By 22 November, the French 2d Armored Division's penetration of the Vosges was complete. In the north, TF Rouvillois of CCD broke out of the Low Vosges at Wieterswiller, four miles east of La Petite-Pierre and, after overrunning scattered German rear units, sped south seven miles across open farmland to Monswiller, just over a mile north of Saverne, where they met elements of Massu's force. TF Massu had entered the town of Saverne earlier and, without much of a fight, had captured over 800 Germans, including General Bruhn of the *553d Volksgrenadiers*, as well as part of the *LXXXIX Corps* headquarters. General von Gilsa, the *LXXXIX Corps* commander, escaped, at least from the Allies. Dissatisfied with his performance, Balck had replaced him with Lt. Gen. Gustav Hoehne, and von Gilsa had left Saverne that morning. But Hoehne, arriving as von Gilsa left, could do little except pull the bulk of the corps headquarters out of Saverne as quickly as possible and move it into the Saverne Gap gorge. Upon learning that Bruhn had been captured, the new corps commander took over what elements of the *553d Division* he could find and, during the night of 22–23 November, led them and his remaining corps staff northward along back roads through the Low Vosges to escape a second potential trap.

While CCL (TF Massu and TF Minjonnet recombined) and TF Rouvillois of CCD cleaned out Saverne and its environs on the 22d, CCV secured more Alsatian towns and villages south and southeast of the city, meeting little German resistance. Later in the afternoon, TF Minjonnet moved northwest up Route N–4 from Saverne and by dusk, after having overrun many westward-facing German defenses, was about a mile short of Phalsbourg. Meanwhile, TF Quilichini, which had been operating north of the Sarrebourg-Phalsbourg area, west of the Vosges, crossed the mountains to rejoin the rest of CCD via the northern La Petite-Pierre

route.[12] By the end of the day only two tasks remained in order to finish securing the bridgehead that Haislip wanted into Alsace: opening the rest of Route N–4 from Phalsbourg to Saverne and clearing the Saverne Gap gorge.

West of the Vosges the 79th Division's 314th regiment had moved up to Phalsbourg on the 22d, and on the morning of 23 November the 314th and TF Minjonnet made short work of the remaining defenders. To the south, the 315th Infantry had entered the Saverne Gap gorge near Arzviller during the afternoon of the 22d, and spent all of the 23d pushing through scattered resistance from mines, roadblocks, and demolitions, finally reaching Saverne about noon on the 24th. The first phase of Haislip's XV Corps offensive was complete.

The German Response

Both Field Marshal von Rundstedt at *OB West* and General Balck of *Army Group G* quickly realized that the Allied penetration opened a dangerous gap between the *First* and *Nineteenth Armies*.[13] At the same time, pressure from the Third Army's XII Corps prompted *OB West* to warn *OKW* about the possibility of another imminent breakthrough on *First Army*'s left wing. Taken together, the operations of both the XII and XV Corps could well foreshadow a major

---

[12] General Hoehne's escaping elements apparently crossed the La Petite-Pierre road, Route D–9, between echelons of TF Quilichini.

[13] German information in the remainder of this chapter is from von Luttichau, "German Operations," chs. 24 and 25, and from Cole, *The Lorraine Campaign*, pp. 464–70.

disaster for the Germans, leading to the outflanking of the Saar basin on the south and east, the destruction of German military forces west of the Rhine, and ultimately an Allied crossing of the Rhine itself.

Von Rundstedt had already directed *Army Group H,* in the Netherlands, to dispatch the weak, rebuilding *256th Volksgrenadier Division* to the front of the *First Army.* Now, on the 21st, he had *Army Group H* start another worn-out division, the *245th Volksgrenadiers,* south to strengthen the *First Army,* and also released the four-battalion *401st Volks Artillery Corps* to *Army Group G* for the same purpose. The *First Army,* in turn, reinforced the *361st Volksgrenadier Division* with its last reserves, an understrength infantry assault battalion and the army headquarters guard company. The *361st Division,* having failed to hold the Mittersheim-Schalbach line on 21 November, was to pull its left wing northward another three miles and hold a front between the towns of Mittersheim, Baerendorf, Weyer, and Drulingen, west to east.

On 22 November von Rundstedt gave *Army Group G* a provisional corps headquarters, *Corps Command Vosges,* to consolidate defensive preparation in the Strasbourg area. To slow Allied progress there, *Corps Command Vosges* was to establish a screening line from the Moder River south to Wasselonne, eight miles southeast of Saverne. However, to accomplish this mission, *Army Group G* could give *Corps Command Vosges* only a few insignificant elements: *Feldkommandantur 987,* the occupational area command located at Haguenau; the armed forces command of Strasbourg itself; the headquarters (only) of

the *49th Infantry Division;* [14] two scratch infantry "battalions" (about 600 troops in all) from *Wehrkreis VII*; and a broad miscellany of smaller units that had begun streaming westward across the Rhine from *Wehrkreis V* and *XII.* Apparently, the *256th Volksgrenadier Division* was also to pass to the control of *Corps Command Vosges* upon its arrival in the Haguenau area, beginning about 24 November.

Von Rundstedt realized that all these defensive arrangements were largely palliative and that only a strong counterattack held out any hope of preventing an Allied breakthrough of major proportions. For this purpose he needed armored reinforcements, and for days he had been importuning *OKW* to release the *Panzer Lehr* armored division to him. [15] Currently refitting behind the battlefield, the *Panzer Lehr,* commanded by Maj. Gen. Fritz Bayerlein, had been earmarked for the Ardennes offensive, and *OKW* was reluctant to authorize its commitment. [16] However, on the afternoon of the 21st, the German high command finally approved the use of the division, and by 1800 that evening the unit had started south. However, both Hitler and *OKW* specified that *Panzer Lehr* would have to return northward by 28 November.

Passing control of *Panzer Lehr* to *Army*

---

[14] The rest of the *49th Division* had been dissolved in October.

[15] The unit's title reflected its original status as a training formation, but by 1944 its organization was identical to the other German panzer divisions.

[16] Until 20 November von Rundstedt had hoped to employ a panzer division on the Belfort Gap front, where the First French Army had already penetrated to the Rhine; but sometime on the 20th he decided that the widening gap between the *First* and *Nineteenth Armies* presented a more immediate and far-reaching threat.

Group G, von Rundstedt admonished Balck to employ the division in its entirety for an attack deep into the northern flank of the XV Corps' penetration in order to end the danger of a split between the two armies. The division was to assemble near Sarralbe, about nineteen miles north of Sarrebourg, and strike south to cut Route N–4 between Sarrebourg and Phalsbourg. Supporting the attack would be the *401st Volks Artillery Corps*, the weakened *361st Volksgrenadier Division*, and, Balck hoped, the understrength *25th Panzer Grenadier Division*. Balck wanted the *361st* and the *25th Panzer Grenadiers* to protect the eastern flank of *Panzer Lehr*'s attack, blunting any Third Army (XII Corps) thrust toward Sarre-Union, fourteen miles north of Sarrebourg.

Balck also directed the *Nineteenth Army* to organize a task force to link up with the *Panzer Lehr Division* in the vicinity of Hazelbourg, on the western slopes of the High Vosges about six miles south of Phalsbourg. To release troops for this supporting attack, Balck authorized Wiese to pull most of his right-wing units back to the *Vosges Ridge Position,* including all units between the Blamont area and the Saales Pass, a distance of about twenty miles. This last order reflected Balck's lack of information about the *553d Volksgrenadier Division,* which he thought was still holding steady in the Hazelbourg area, and about the *708th Volksgrenadier Division,* which had also fallen apart. The possibility of adding a southern pincer to Bayerlein's northern thrust was thus highly unlikely.

East of the Vosges, Balck intended to have the newly arrived *256th Volksgrenadier Division* push south and west

from Haguenau, expecting one regimental task force from the division to be available on the morning of 24 November and the rest of the division on the 26th. Finally, the *Army Group G* commander assumed that the *245th Volksgrenadier Division* would arrive from Holland by 28 November, in time to help secure the ground that the *Panzer Lehr* had taken during its armored counterattack.

With unjustified optimism, Balck promised decisive results from the complicated and decentralized series of planned operations. However, his immediate subordinate, General Otto von Knobelsdorff, commanding the *First Army*, was less enthusiastic, believing that the *Panzer Lehr* would be fortunate to hold what little of the Sarre River valley region in Lorraine his forces still controlled.

Planning the Final Stage

Although hardly privy to all these German plans and preparations, Patch's Seventh Army intelligence staff knew that something was brewing on the other side by the afternoon of the 22d. Nevertheless, General Patch had already begun to revise his plans based on the current situation in both the XV and VI Corps zones.[17] On 21 November he decided that the XV Corps was to direct its main effort after Saverne toward the capture of Haguenau and then Soufflenheim, eight miles farther

---

[17] Allied planning in this subsection is based largely on *Seventh Army Rpt*, II, 414–15; Ltr, CG Seventh Army to CGs VI and XV Corps, 21 Nov 44 (cited in Seventh Army Diary, 21 Nov 44, as Directive X–193); Seventh Army Diary, 21 and 22 Nov 44; XV Corps FO 12, 221100A Nov 44; XV Corps AAR Nov 44, pp. 29–30.

east of Haguenau and six miles short of the Rhine. Haislip was also to leave security forces in and west of the Vosges to protect his exposed northern flank and, in the south, to secure the Molsheim area, about fifteen miles south of Saverne.[18] This latter action would project XV Corps forces into the rear of German units still holding up the advance of Brooks' VI Corps in the High Vosges.

Finally, Patch ordered Haislip to "attack Strasbourg, employing armored elements to assist the VI Corps in the capture of the city."[19] Although technically Strasbourg was still a VI Corps objective, the city now appeared to be within easy reach of Haislip's forces if they acted quickly. Since Brooks' units were still fighting their way through the mountains, the new mission seemed appropriate. After the fall of Strasbourg, the XV Corps was then to reconnoiter northward along the Rhine to the Soufflenheim-Rastatt area, taking advantage of any opportunity to force a quick crossing. The VI Corps, in turn, would be prepared to cross the Rhine in its sector or, more likely, to exploit through a XV Corps bridgehead.

Issuing complementary orders during the morning of 22 November, Haislip went a step further in regard to Strasbourg. After cleaning up the Saverne area, Haislip ordered Leclerc's 2d Armored Division, previously assigned the seizure of Ha-

guenau, to strike for Strasbourg and secure the city if it reached the area before the VI Corps. He then reassigned the Haguenau-Soufflenheim mission to the 44th Division and tasked the 79th Division, also in the process of deploying east of the Vosges, to support either the 44th or the French 2d, as tactical developments dictated. The task of securing the Molsheim area was temporarily delayed and transferred to the 45th Division's 179th regiment, which was scheduled to arrive at Cirey-sur-Vezouse from its rest area before dark on the 22d. The security and liaison mission north of Sarrebourg and west of the Low Vosges would be undertaken by the 106th Cavalry Group and by the rest of Eagles' 45th Division as it came out of reserve.

Striking for Strasbourg

Starting out about 0715 on 23 November, the French 2d Armored Division's CCL rolled rapidly eastward across the Alsatian plains with TF Rouvillois on the north and TF Massu to the south.[20] Overrunning German outposts and minor garrisons in the small Alsatian farming towns, TF Rouvillois achieved complete surprise and entered Strasbourg at 1030 that morning. TF Massu, which was to have driven into the city from the northwest, encountered stronger German opposition, but ultimately followed shortly thereafter. Later, about 1300 that afternoon, CCV also began pouring into Strasbourg from the west, bringing with it a battalion

---

[18] Patch's directive actually read "occupy the Position de Mutzig," which consisted of semimodernized old stone forts on rising ground east of Molsheim and just north of the town of Mutzig along Route N–392 a few miles into the Vosges.

[19] Ltr, CG Seventh Army to CGs VI and XV Corps, 21 Nov 44.

[20] For the drive on Strasbourg, TF Rouvillois replaced TF Minjonnet in CCL.

FRENCH 2D ARMORED DIVISION MOVES THROUGH STRASBOURG

of the 313th Infantry, 79th Division.

Meanwhile, amid almost incredible scenes of German surprise and consternation, Rouvillois' armor wheeled through the streets of Strasbourg to the Rhine, seizing intact bridges over the canal-like watercourses in the eastern section of the city. Ahead lay the highway and railway bridges over the Rhine to the German town of Kehl; scarcely 650 yards short of the river, however, the French armor ran into strongly manned German defenses in apartment houses and thick-walled bunkers, buttressed by antitank barriers and antitank weapons. Soon German artillery and mortars emplaced east of the Rhine began laying down accurate fire that forced Rouvillois' troops and vehicles to pull back and seek cover. The local German commanders had apparently ignored any instructions to outpost the Alsatian plains and instead had concentrated on defending certain sections of the city, including the vital Kehl bridges.

Throughout 23 and 24 November TF Rouvillois made several attempts to reduce the German bridgehead, but the result was a stalemate. Lacking strength for an all-out assault in the urban area, the infantry-poor French armored units had to be content with isolating the German enclave from the rest of the city. The Germans, in turn, made no move to reinforce or enlarge the bridgehead and, pending orders to destroy the bridges, held on mainly to aid the escape of German troops and civilians able to infiltrate through the French vehicles to safety. In the meantime, TF Massu and CCV mopped up isolated pockets of resistance, took hundreds of German troops prisoner, and began rounding up German civilians for internment. By the time the last elements of the French armored division left Strasbourg on 28 November, the division had captured a total of 6,000 German troops—mostly service and administrative personnel—in and around the city and had taken into custody about 15,000 German civilians. From 19 to 24 November the Saverne and Strasbourg operations cost the French division approximately 55 men killed, 165 wounded, and 5 missing.

During this period, the situation in and around Strasbourg made it impossible for CCV and CCL to concentrate sufficient strength to eliminate the German enclave and seize the Kehl bridges. The disorganized but large number of German troops and civilians scattered throughout the city, including many German-speaking inhabitants who were not especially sympathetic to the French, posed a security problem that led to a wide dispersal of Leclerc's available infantry forces. Having committed the rest of his combat forces, CCD and CCR, to protect his twenty-mile line of communications across the Alsatian plains, Leclerc asked General Haislip to speed American infantry into the city. But developments west of the Vosges, together with the Seventh Army's directive to move against Haguenau, temporarily tied Haislip's hands; and Brooks' VI Corps forces would probably not be able to reach Strasbourg for three or four more days. In the meantime, Leclerc would

have to consolidate his existing gains, rest and resupply his forces, and be patient.

Haislip moved quickly to secure Leclerc's narrow supply line across Alsace. By 24 November all three regiments of the 79th Division had crossed the Vosges and begun to arrive in the Moder River area west of Strasbourg and just south of Haguenau. Behind the 79th, the 44th Division's 324th regiment and the 45th Division's 180th regiment took up station along the Alsatian plains north of Saverne, and thus the northern flank of the XV Corps' penetration east of the Vosges appeared well protected.

On the southern flank, the 45th Division's 179th regiment reached Wasselonne during the afternoon of the 23d and, as planned, struck south for Molsheim on the 24th with CC Remy, encountering little resistance. Late in the day it met elements of the 3d Division's 15th Infantry, the first of Brooks' VI Corps units to finally push through the High Vosges and onto the Alsatian plains.[21] The juncture of the two units augured the arrival of the rest of the VI Corps units to cement the southern flank of Haislip's penetration. However, CCR and CCD outposts between Molsheim and Strasbourg had already reported the absence of any German threat in the south, and thus both of Leclerc's flanks seemed secure.

However, on 23 November, as Haislip's infantry regiments were pouring across the Alsatian plains, the

---

[21] During the course of 23 November a boundary change placed Wasselonne in the XV Corps sector, but Molsheim and Mutzig remained in the VI Corps zone. Seventh Army OI 18, 23 Nov 44.

XV Corps commander suddenly learned of the arrival of the *Panzer Lehr Division* on his northern flank west, rather than east, of the Vosges. He immediately suspended movement of all XV Corps forces across the Vosges and began to reorient troops that remained west of the mountains to meet the new threat. First, he transferred the Haguenau mission from the 44th Division to the 79th, which was already positioned reasonably close to the objective area. Second, he ordered the bulk of the 44th to concentrate in the area above Sarrebourg with its 71st and 114th regiments and the two squadrons of the 106th Cavalry. Third, he kept the 45th Division's remaining regiment, the 157th, east of the Vosges as a reserve. If necessary, Leclerc's armor could also return to the Sarrebourg area, but Haislip was apparently confident that the 44th Division could handle the danger.

The Panzer Lehr Counterattack

During the evening of 21 November and all of the following day, the *361st Volksgrenadier Division* had attempted to establish a defensive line facing south from Mittersheim to Drulingen. The effort was futile, however, and the unit had slowly been squeezed between the advances of the Third Army's XII Corps from the west and assorted XV Corps units from the south. By dark on the 21st, elements of the XV Corps' 106th Cavalry Group were either in or north of Baerendorf, Weyer, and Drulingen. The following day, the XII Corps' 4th Armored Division cleared Mittersheim, and the 106th Cavalry, rein-

forced by units of the 44th Division's 71st and 114th regiments, moved up to Eywiller and several other towns— all north of what was to have been the *361st Division's* main line of resistance. Finally, on 23 November, the advance elements of the eastward-moving 4th Armored Division met units of the 71st Infantry near Fenetrange, completely disorganizing the defending *volksgrenadiers* and leaving the *Panzer Lehr Division* with no screening force on its western flank for its projected attack south.

Von Rundstedt and Balck had assumed that the *Panzer Lehr*, with about seventy tanks, would reach the Sarralbe area in time to launch its counterattack early on the morning of 23 November. However, the division deployed southward more slowly than anticipated; was not in position to attack until 1600 on the 23d, at least ten hours later than planned; and initially could muster only thirty to forty tanks, two of its four panzer grenadier battalions, and about ten assault guns for the effort.[22] By that time the XV Corps had begun to react to the German buildup, and the *Panzer Lehr* could only hope to achieve some local tactical surprise. Moreover, assistance from other German forces was negligible. The *361st Volksgrenadier Division*

---

[22] At the time, the *Panzer Lehr* had only one of its two organic tank battalions, with an authorized strength of thirty-five Mark IV and thirty-five Mark V tanks, but many had broken down on the approach march. The missing tank battalion was scheduled to be replaced by an independent Mark V *panzerjaeger* battalion, but equipment for the unit did not arrive in time for the attack. Ltr, Helmut Rittgen to Clarke, 11 Feb 88 (Rittgen commanded one of the *Panzer Lehr* task groups); and Rittgen, *Die Geschichte der Panzer-Lehr-Division im Westen, 1944/45*, ch. 11.

was too weak; *OKW* refused to release the *25th Panzer Grenadier Division* for the attack; and the *Nineteenth Army,* under strong pressure from both the VI Corps and the First French Army, lacked the means to mount any kind of counterattack from the south. Nevertheless, acting virtually alone, Bayerlein's elite unit launched its drive southward that afternoon.

The *Panzer Lehr Division* advanced in two columns: a western one with about ten to twelve Mark IV medium tanks moving south through Baerendorf, and a larger, eastern one with twenty to twenty-five Mark V heavies (Panthers) moving parallel down through Eywiller (*Map 27*). At first the German armor and accompanying panzer grenadiers rode roughshod over the scattered American advance elements. By dusk Bayerlein's forces had pushed the 106th Cavalry back to Baerendorf and Weyer, and during the night *Panzer Lehr's* western column broke through Baerendorf to reach Rauwiller, several miles to the south, taking about 200 prisoners from the 44th Division. Temporarily putting aside all thoughts of celebrating a quiet Thanksgiving holiday, elements of the 106th Cavalry and the 71st Infantry finally slowed down the German thrust just south of Rauwiller. Meanwhile, *Panzer Lehr's* eastern column pushed XV Corps cavalry forces out of Weyer and south to Schalbach, forcing the 114th Infantry to move up to cover this second threat. But despite these gains, von Rundstedt viewed the southward progress of the panzer division as too slow, and during the night he advised *OKW* that the counterattack had little chance of success.

Unknown to von Rundstedt, the situation of the *Panzer Lehr* had actually become much more precarious. While the German division was moving south, the XII Corps' 4th Armored Division, commanded by Maj. Gen. John S. ("P") Wood, had resumed its advance west toward Sarre-Union. Judging the soggy ground west of the Sarre River to be unsuitable for armored operations, Maj. Gen. Manton S. Eddy, the XII Corps commander, obtained permission from General Haislip to have the American armored unit's CCB move eastward across the Sarre into the XV Corps' zone, before swinging north toward Sarre-Union.[23] A clash between the two opposing armored formations was inevitable.

Crossing the Sarre at two points near Baerendorf on the morning of 24 November, the American combat command almost immediately ran into the *Panzer Lehr Division's* exposed western flank. House-to-house and tank-to-tank fighting ensued at Baerendorf until, during the afternoon, CCB's southern column cleared the small town, while the northern column contained German armored units attempting to outflank the embattled American forces. Elsewhere, the 71st Infantry retook Rauwiller before dark, and the 106th Cavalry Group, while losing some ground along the western slopes of the Vosges, managed to hang on to

---

[23] In Ltr, Rittgen to Clarke, 11 Feb 88, the former *Panzer Lehr* officer believed that the move by Wood's division was prompted by ULTRA information. If such was the case, the matter might have been handled discreetly by Patch and Patton, and the terrain problems used as an excuse to cover the movement of the armored force east; but available information provides no clue regarding the role of ULTRA.

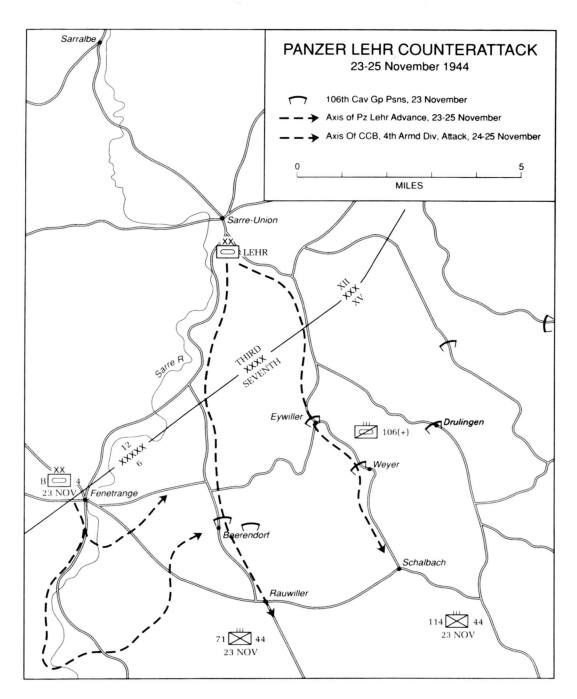

MAP 27   This map is printed in full color at the back of the book, following the Index.

Schalbach and stabilize the rest of the American line through Drulingen.

In light of these developments, von Rundstedt reduced the mission of the *Panzer Lehr* from closing the gap between Balck's two armies to just blocking Route N–4 between Sarrebourg and Saverne. The change probably reflected his realization that the *Nineteenth Army* was in no condition to launch any kind of supporting attack from the south, but the mission was still too ambitious. Although von Rundstedt also directed Balck to feed the *25th Panzer Grenadier Division* into the battle, he must have known that the understrength *25th* could not reach the Sarre-Union area until 25 November; even then it was doubtful that its addition could influence the struggle.

General Balck's evaluation of the counterattack became increasingly pessimistic throughout the 24th. He had expected the leading units of the *256th Volksgrenadier Division* to reach Haguenau that day and had planned to commit the units of the division to supporting attacks east of the Vosges as they arrived on the front. However, transportation problems continued to delay the arrival of the division, and the first units did not reach Haguenau until 26 November, with the rest of the division following on the 28th.[24] In any case von Rundstedt, who appeared to have little faith in the counterattack, now directed Balck to use

the *256th* in a defensive role around Haguenau, an order that effectively disassociated the arriving division from the *Panzer Lehr* operation. Finally, Balck learned that the *245th Volksgrenadier Division,* also arriving from the Netherlands, would not reach the *First Army*'s sector before 3 December, far too late to have any bearing on the situation he was facing in the Sarre valley.

On 25 November the battle in the Sarre River valley resumed. Just before dawn, the *Panzer Lehr*'s western column launched an attack against the 4th Armored Division's CCB elements at Baerendorf and reoccupied part of Rauwiller. Confused fighting lasted several hours, but again the Germans were forced to withdraw to the north and east with little accomplished. Meanwhile, the stronger eastern *Panzer Lehr* column was a bit more successful, overrunning part of the 2d Battalion, 114th Infantry, near Schalbach. But American artillery helped turn back further German advances south, and by afternoon all German offensive operations in the area had stopped.

The Schalbach action proved to be the high point of the *Panzer Lehr* counterattack, and on the evening of the 25th von Rundstedt, with Hitler's reluctant consent, called off the operation. The German panzer division immediately began to withdraw northward to temporary defensive lines between the Sarre River and Eywiller to lick its wounds. The movement marked the end of any danger to XV Corps' northern flank. Still relatively unscathed, Haislip's forces were ready to resume their attack to the east.

---

[24] The Seventh Army G–2 identified elements of the *256th Volksgrenadier Division* in the Haguenau area on 25 November, but they were probably only small liaison detachments reconnoitering for assembly and bivouac areas.

CHAPTER XXII

To the Plains of Alsace

The Seventh Army's plans for the mid-November offensive called for the VI Corps to launch an attack over the Meurthe River no later than two days after the XV Corps' offensive began. Thus, when Patch set the date of the XV Corps' attack for 13 November, the VI Corps' target date automatically became 15 November. But at least as early as 10 November, General Brooks, the new VI Corps commander, realized that his command as a whole would not be ready to launch a concerted, new offensive by that date. As of the 10th, the VI Corps had been able to secure the western banks of the Meurthe only in the areas of Baccarat and St. Michel-sur-Meurthe; around Raon-l'Etape and in the entire sector from St. Die to St. Leonard and south, both river-banks were still in German hands. To secure a broader line of departure for the November offensive, Brooks wanted to clear as much of the west bank of the Meurthe as possible before he launched his main attack.

VI Corps Plans

On 10 November the recently committed 100th Infantry Division, having taken over along VI Corps' left, or northern, wing from the veteran 45th Division, was moving into the high, forested hills leading to Raon-l'Etape. The "Century Division" was about four miles short of Raon-l'Etape on the northwest and west and nearly two miles shy on the southwest and south. From Etival-Clairefontaine, on the west side of the Meurthe three miles south of Raon-l'Etape, the 3d Division's 15th Infantry held about three miles of the west bank down to St. Michel-sur-Meurthe, while the rest of the 3d Division remained in reserve, resting and training for the VI Corps' new offensive. South of the 15th Infantry the untried 103d Division, less one regimental combat team in corps reserve, was taking over positions the 3d Division had previously held from St. Michel south about seven miles to the vicinity of Saulcy-sur-Meurthe. The left of the 103d Division was on high ground in the Magdeleine woods overlooking both St. Die and the Taintrux valley, but the right was still four rugged miles short of the Meurthe at Saulcy. South of Saulcy-sur-Meurthe, the left of the 36th Division was also several miles short of the high ground along the Meurthe at St. Leonard; and the center and right of the 36th stretched southwest nearly fifteen miles to the vicinity of Le Tholy, where its defenses meshed with those of the French II Corps' 3d Algerian Division.

On 10 November, after considering a number of alternatives, General Brooks settled on a plan of attack that called for refitting the 3d Division and again assigning to it the main corps effort during the November offensive.[1] O'Daniel's 3d was to lead off on 20 November with two regiments assaulting across the Meurthe in the St. Michel area to seize a firm bridgehead. Then the division would clear the forested hill masses north and northeast of St. Die in preparation for a drive northeast along N–420 through the Saales Pass and ultimately to the Alsatian plains at Mutzig, less than fifteen miles short of the division's final objective, Strasbourg.

Brooks realized that the German defenses along the Meurthe were weak and lacked depth. Furthermore, Route N–420 between St. Die and the Saales Pass was broader and in much better condition than between Brouvelieures and St. Die, the scene of the 3d Division's earlier DOGFACE advance. Nevertheless, Brooks was also convinced that a rapid breakthrough by the 3d Division hinged on the progress that the two "junior" divisions could make before 20 November in securing suitable terrain along the Meurthe River from which to launch supporting attacks. Strong efforts on the part of the 100th and

103d Divisions would divert German forces from the 3d Division's front, while a lack of progress could expose the flanks of the 3d as soon as it crossed the river. If the 3d Division spent too much of its combat power securing a bridgehead over the Meurthe, it might lack the strength to force the Saales Pass farther down Route N–420. The new VI Corps commander was especially concerned with the 100th Division's sector. If the 100th was unable to secure the Raon-l'Etape area in a timely manner and then mount a strong thrust eastward, a dangerous gap might open up between the VI and XV Corps that the 117th Cavalry Squadron would have difficulty screening. On the other hand, a sustained drive by the 100th Division would provide strong support for the advance of the neighboring XV Corps toward Sarrebourg and the Saverne Gap.

Brooks therefore wanted the 100th Division to start its attacks as early as possible, and on 12 November he directed it to proceed immediately across the Meurthe against Raon-l'Etape and the surrounding high ground (Map 28). Once this area had been taken, the division was to begin its main effort by 15 November eastward on Route N–424. This secondary highway, crossing the Vosges through the Hantz Pass, joined N–420 at St. Blaise-la-Roche, fifteen miles east of Raon-l'Etape and five miles north of the Saales Pass. If the 100th Division could begin this drive by the 15th, five days before the 3d Division's attack was scheduled to begin, Brooks felt that the success of his main effort would be assured. The early attack by the 100th would also

---

[1] The concept that the 3d Division would make the main effort dated back at least to VI Corps FO 7 of 7 November. Other alternatives were set forth in VI Corps Outline Plans A, B, and C, all dated 10 November 1944.

partially satisfy the Seventh Army's requirement that the VI Corps launch its portion of the November offensive on the 15th. Given the difficulty that the 45th Division had experienced approaching Raon-l'Etape, however, the task seemed extremely ambitious for the new division.

On the right wing of the VI Corps, Brooks wanted the 103d Division to cross the Meurthe south of the 3d Division's area, seize St. Die, and then push south and southeast toward Fraize and east to Ban-de-Laveline, thus effectively securing the southern flank of the main attack. Thereafter the division was to advance to the east and northeast abreast of the 3d Division toward the Alsatian plains. However, Brooks hoped that the 103d would be able to clear the west bank of the Meurthe River area opposite Saulcy and St. Leonard before the main attack on the 20th, and he ordered the unit to begin these preliminary operations as soon as possible.

More or less bringing up the rear, the weary 36th Division was to take over the areas vacated by the 103d Division west of the Meurthe, move forward to blocking positions along the eight miles from Anould to Gerardmer, maintain contact with de Monsabert's II Corps, and prepare to attack east and northeast across the Vosges on order.

The German Defense

The German defenders in the central Vosges would be hard-pressed to stop a determined American advance. On 10 November the *Nineteenth Army* faced the U.S. VI Corps with the *LXIV Corps* as well as part of the *IV*

Luftwaffe Field Corps. The *LXIV Corps* covered the *Nineteenth Army*'s front from the Rhine-Marne Canal south about thirty-five miles to Saulcy-sur-Meurthe.[2] The German corps' northernmost unit, the *553d Volksgrenadier Division*, confronted only XV Corps units. The next division south, the *708th Volksgrenadiers*, had just reached *LXIV Corps*' front. About half the division held lines opposite the XV Corps' sector from the Vezouse River south five miles to the vicinity of Vacqueville, on the boundary between the XV and VI Corps. The rest of the *708th Division*, standing opposite VI Corps' 100th Division, extended the German lines south another eight miles through Raon-l'Etape to Etival-Clairefontaine, which marked the boundary between the *708th Volksgrenadier* and *716th Divisions* (as well as the boundary between VI Corps' 100th and 3d Divisions). The weak *716th Division*, reinforced by the understrength *757th Grenadiers* of the *338th Division*, held along the east bank of the Meurthe River from Etival-Clairefontaine south six miles to the northern edge of St. Die. The *716th Division*'s front covered all the 3d Division's sector and about half the sector of the 103d Division. From St. Die south three miles to Saulcy-sur-Meurthe the shattered *16th Volksgrenadier Division*, with sundry attachments

---

[2] German information in this chapter derives largely from von Luttichau, "German Operations," chs. 21, 22, and 25. *Army Group G* pushed the boundary between the *Nineteenth* and *First Armies* to the Rhine-Marne Canal on 10 November, but the change was not fully effective until the 13th. Then, on 20 or 21 November, in the wake of the XV Corps' attack against Sarrebourg, *Army Group G* moved the boundary back south approximately to the Blamont-Strasbourg line.

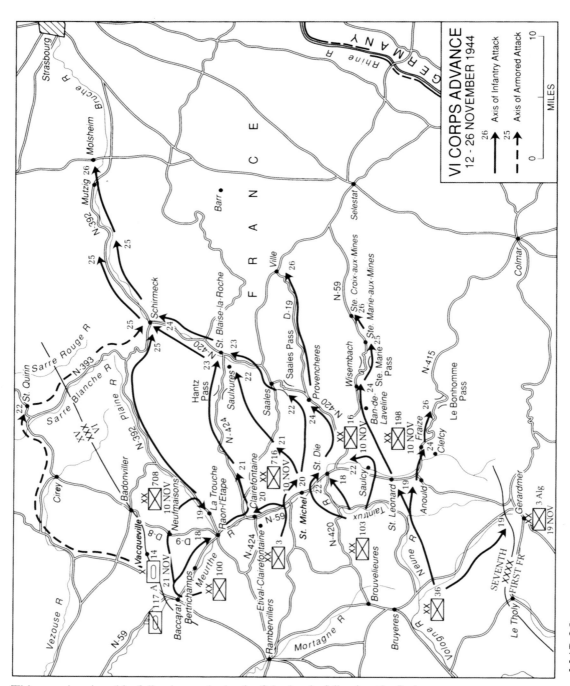

This map is printed in full color at the back of the book, following the Index.

MAP 28

such as the remnants of the *201st* and *202d Mountain Battalions*, faced the rest of the 103d Division. Saulcy lay on the boundary between the *LXIV Corps* and *IV Luftwaffe Field Corps*, with most of the latter's *198th Division* facing the 36th Division and the remainder holding in front of the 3d Algerian Division of the French II Corps.[3]

The *708th Division,* with perhaps 3,500 combat effectives, was by far the strongest of *LXIV Corps'* divisions, but no more than half of its strength faced VI Corps units on 10 November. The *716th Division,* even with the attached regiment of the *338th Division,* could muster no more than 1,500 infantry effectives, and the *16th Division,* even with nondivisional attachments, scarcely 1,000. The *IV Luftwaffe Field Corps' 198th Division* had nearly 2,500 effectives, with perhaps two-thirds of that strength in front of the 36th Division.[4] For a successful defense, the Germans would have to rely heavily on their use of the rugged terrain.

In the VI Corps' projected zone of attack, the forward defenses of the *LXIV Corps* followed the east bank of the Meurthe from the vicinity of Raon-l'Etape south to Fraize, a straight-line distance of about twenty miles. A fairly complete system of trenches formed the backbone of the line, but shoddy workmanship and lack of maintenance left older trench-

es crumbling and often half-filled with water. Virtually no hardened (reinforced concrete) positions existed along the Meurthe, while work on semipermanent positions such as bunkers of timber or sandbags fell far short of the requirements for a strong, cohesive defensive line. Barbed wire was spotty and usually thinly strung; numerous machine-gun and mortar positions had little protection; and antitank and antiaircraft ground emplacements were poorly constructed. The German defenders tried to make up for these deficiencies with the liberal use of mines and booby traps.

Lacking troops to fully man even the *Vosges Foothill Position* fortifications that had been prepared, *LXIV Corps* units deployed their forces in successive strongpoints. Between Etival and St. Die, for example, the *716th Division* merely outposted much of the eastern bank of the Meurthe with small patrols. The Germans hoped that any American river crossings could be counterattacked from the strongpoints or thrown back by artillery fire. Behind the thinly held front line, the *LXIV Corps* had no reserves, and the *Nineteenth Army* could furnish none.

Morale was generally low in the *LXIV Corps,* especially in the battered *16th* and *716th Divisions.* Many officers and men were highly skeptical of the Meurthe River defense line and were inclined to regard it as no more than a delaying position. According to such reasoning, once VI Corps units had penetrated the Meurthe line, the *LXIV Corps* would slowly fall back to the crests and passes of the High Vosges, the *Vosges Ridge Position.*

---

[3] Seventh Army G–2 estimates included the *360th Cossack Regiment,* with 375 combat effectives, in the northern part of the *IV Luftwaffe Field Corps'* sector, but no confirmation of this can be found in available German records.

[4] The figures for effectives are the authors' estimates gleaned from conflicting German and American sources.

There many Germans hoped they could settle in for the winter and enjoy the luxury of "hard" defensive installations—a hope that was to prove no more than a dream.

Despite these shortcomings, the Germans had some obvious advantages. Once across the Meurthe, the VI Corps would again be fighting its way uphill in rough, generally forested terrain that was easy to defend but hard to move through. Inclement weather, varying from torrential rains to heavy snows, could also be expected to aid the German defensive effort, sharply curtailing VI Corps' air support, making ground movement difficult, and delaying artillery support. Finally, the German corps had received artillery reinforcements in November and had an adequate stockpile of ammunition.

The Century (100th) Division

For VI Corps veterans of the 3d and 36th Divisions, the crossing of the Meurthe and projected drive through the passes of the High Vosges was painful to contemplate. The ever-worsening weather and terrain as well as the alway-improving enemy defensive techniques had become all too familiar since they had first started across the Moselle River on 20 September. The men of the 100th and 103d Divisions, entering combat for the first time, would soon learn the same lessons that had been painfully acquired by the GIs of the older divisions during the two months of slow, laborious, and costly progress that had gained the VI Corps scarcely twenty miles toward the Rhine.

For the 100th, or Century, Division, going into combat for the first time, the prospects seemed less dismal. The new troops were both nervous and excited, anxious about what the future attack would bring, yet more eager than the veteran soldiers to show what they could do.[5] General Burress, the division commander, decided against a frontal assault on Raon-l'Etape across the Meurthe River and instead, in agreement with Brooks, planned to attack the now heavily fortified area from the rear, using Baccarat—which VI Corps had inherited from the French 2d Armored Division's earlier attack—as an assembly area. Burress planned to move two of his regiments across the Meurthe at Baccarat—then secured by the 117th Cavalry—and send them south against the hopefully unfortified, but steep hills north and northeast of Raon-l'Etape. His third regiment and other division elements were to demonstrate west of the river with machine-gun, cannon, and artillery fire, drawing German attention away from the main effort. If successful, the maneuver would cut enemy supply routes to the town, forcing the Germans either to capitulate or withdraw northward in disarray. With speed and a bit of luck, the fresh division might even beat the tired 3d to the Alsatian plains and Strasbourg beyond.

On 12 November the 100th Division's 397th and 399th regiments, after an administrative crossing of the

---

[5] The following account is based on the records of the 100th Division and on the comments of Franklin Gurley, a veteran of the 3d Battalion, 399th Infantry.

398TH INFANTRY, 100TH DIVISION, IN RAON-L'ETAPE AREA, NOVEMBER 1944

Meurthe at Baccarat, attacked south-eastward toward Raon-l'Etape, about six miles away. On the right, the 397th moved along the east bank of the Meurthe toward the small village of Bertrichamps and Hill 443, a steep abutment flush against the northern edge of Raon-l'Etape. On the left, the 399th headed east for the town of Neufmaisons where it would then wheel southeast toward Hill 539, actually a steep ridge line that overlooked the Plaine River valley and the northern exits to Raon-l'Etape. As elements of both units began to reach their intermediate objectives at Bertrichamps and Neufmaisons, they quickly discovered that the German defenders, mostly *708th Division* troops, had taken advantage of the pause in the VI Corps' offensive to construct a northern extension of the Meurthe River line, using a local road, D–8/9, as a supply route.[6] On both sides of the small road and into the Wilderness forest beyond, the defenders had built extensive barbed-wire barriers, cleared fields of fire, and constructed an impressive network of trenches, foxholes, bunkers, and machine-gun emplacements, which the new American troops quickly dubbed the "winter line." They were obviously expected by the German grenadiers.

---

[6] Routes D–8 and D–9 were actually a single road, the designation of which changed as it passed French interdepartmental boundaries. The forests between Neufmaisons and Raon-l'Etape were known as the Forest of the Wilderness and the Forest of the Small Wilderness.

The attacking regiments spent the afternoon of the 12th and all of the 13th probing the hidden positions with patrols, seeking weak points while being surprised at their length and breadth.

On 14 November the 100th began a series of battalion-sized attacks against the newly constructed line and, with additional division and corps artillery support, penetrated the German positions on the 15th, the official starting date of VI Corps' offensive. After policing the remaining defenders, both regiments began pushing southeast through the forests of the Wilderness for their principal objectives. Hindered mainly by rain, snow, muddy mountain trails, and dense woods, the American forces began to arrive at the base of Hills 443 and 539 sometime on the 16th.

At the foot of Hill 539, the 1st Battalion of the 399th Infantry overran a small German force, and one company immediately climbed to the hill's relatively flat summit, the *Tete des Reclos* ("top of the wilderness"), actually two knolls connected by a short saddle. From there the American infantrymen could look down on the Plaine River valley, the back door to the *Vosges Foothill Position* defenses at Raon-l'Etape and southward. The German response was quick. From late morning until dusk the *708th Division* hurled a series of attacks at the *Tete des Reclos,* at one point routing one of the defending American platoons before the position could be restored. By the morning of 17 November, the 100th Division force on the hilltop was down to sixty-five men, but the German troops were also exhausted; with more American infan-

trymen pouring down the hills on either side, the defenders began to evacuate to the southeast. Early on the 18th, Burress thus reported that Raon-l'Etape proper, although heavily mined and booby-trapped, was clear of German troops. The gates of the Vosges were in American hands.

With the fall of Raon-l'Etape, Brooks decided to take advantage of Burress' success and proposed sweeping changes in the corps' assault plans.[7] Perhaps seeking to avoid costly assaults over the Meurthe River by the 3d and 103d Divisions, he had his staff develop plans for the other two divisions to undertake administrative crossings of the Meurthe near Raon-l'Etape, behind the lines of the 100th Division. With the 3d Division still assigned the main corps effort, the revision called for the 3d and 103d Divisions to pass through the 100th and head south and east with their missions and objectives essentially unchanged from the plan of 10 November. The 100th would assist the movement by securing the rising, wooded terrain on the far (southeastern) side of the Plaine River valley and then continuing eastward along the axis of Route N–424. Only the role of the 36th Division was unaffected.

At this point VI Corps planning exhibited some confusion. Brooks was

---

[7] The subsequent discussion of VI Corps planning changes is based on the following: Seventh Army OI 15, 18 Nov 44; VI Corps AAR Nov 44, pp. 28–30; VI Corps FO 8, 18 Nov 44; VI Corps OI 9, 19 Nov 44; VI Corps War Room Jnl, 18 and 19 Nov 44; 3d Inf Div War Room Jnl, 18 and 19 Nov; Taggart, ed., *History of the Third Infantry Division in World War II,* p. 266. However, the after action reports of the 3d, 100th, and 103d Divisions for November 1944 make no mention of the changes discussed here.

apparently under the impression both that the *708th Volksgrenadier Division* had completely folded and that the entire 14th Armored Division would be available for his main attack on the 20th. He therefore planned to use the new armored division as his pursuit force and expected to turn the unit loose early, having it pass through the infantry divisions and drive east and northeast along all passable roads to the Mutzig area. Only later did he learn that the VI Corps would obtain only one reinforced combat command from the new armored division.[8]

The new plan would not only avoid assault crossings of the Meurthe, but would also project VI Corps units behind and to the east of German defenses along the river from Raon-l'Etape south past St. Die; furthermore, it provided for rapid exploitation by mobile armored units, as Haislip had done in the north. Execution, however, would depend on the 100th Division's continued progress, and Brooks must have had some second thoughts as he watched the attacks of Burress' regiments bog down throughout the afternoon of the 18th in the face of renewed German resistance. The 100th Division troops had, in fact, quickly discovered that German reinforcements, perhaps

from the *716th Division,* had occupied a second series of hill masses across N–59 and the Plaine River; meanwhile, a German strongpoint at a quarry on the southern outskirts of Raon-l'Etape blocked any advance south along Route N–59. The 398th regiment, Burress' third regiment, crossed over the Meurthe and passed through the 399th, but could advance no farther than La Trouche, a small hamlet on Route N–392 about two miles east of Raon. Although it had undoubtedly focused German attention away from the St. Die area, the 100th Division's attack had clearly lost much of its steam. Nevertheless, that evening Brooks issued written orders putting the revised plan into effect, and the 3d Division quickly began redeploying its regiments toward Raon-l'Etape.[9] Obviously he still hoped that the 100th Division's attack would regain momentum early on 19 November, and that the division could quickly secure enough ground to allow the new plan to be carried out on the 20th.

The revised plan was short-lived. During the night of 18–19 November, Brooks learned that O'Daniel's 3d Division was trying to infiltrate patrols across the Meurthe and that a battalion of the 15th Infantry had been alerted to follow if the patrols gained a foothold on the east bank. Brooks immediately approved the initiative and informed O'Daniel that he could start his main attack with full corps support if the unit could push a

---

[8] The text (para. 3e) of VI Corps FO 8, issued at 1800 on 18 November, as well as the operations overlay accompanying the FO clearly indicate that VI Corps expected to gain the entire armored division, but Seventh Army OI 15 of 18 November attached only CCA (reinforced) to VI Corps, effective 0600 on 19 November. No time identification can be found for Seventh Army OI 15, but it must have reached the IV Corps command post *after* VI Corps' FO 8 had been issued. The principal reinforcement for CCA was a medium-tank battalion, which gave the combat command two tank battalions instead of the usual one.

[9] VI Corps FO 8, 1800 18 Nov 44. Although the FO was timed at 1800, the VI Corps War Room Journal for 18 November reveals that the commanders of the 3d, 100th, and 103d Divisions knew of Brooks' intentions by 0930 that day.

bridgehead over the river that night. The 3d Division's proposal hardly outlasted the dawn on 19 November. During the night the 15th Infantry made five attempts to send patrols across the Meurthe, but only one reached the east bank. German resistance was not the problem, for the Germans either ignored or were unaware of the crossing efforts. Rather, the swift, flooding, and rising Meurthe was the culprit, swamping rubber boats and nearly drowning swimmers. The lone successful patrol crossed near St. Michel-sur-Meurthe, but could not be reinforced; daylight finally ended the hopes of Brooks and O'Daniel for a quick, surprise Meurthe crossing in the center. Nevertheless, the absence of any German response to the effort was encouraging.

The new day brought another disappointment for General Brooks. Encountering heavy German small-arms, mortar, and artillery fire throughout the 19th, the 100th Division was again unable to secure the high ground south of the Plaine River that held the projected assembly areas and lines of departure of the 3d and 103d Divisions. By noon on the 19th, Brooks himself at last decided to abandon the revised plan and return to an amended version of the earlier 10 November plan.[10] The only substantial change was the addition of the 14th Armored Division's CCA to the VI Corps' order to battle, and assigning to it the mission given to the

entire division in his 18 November plan—passing through the 3d and 100th Divisions and striking directly for Mutzig and Strasbourg.[11] But even this rider was to be short-lived.

The Meurthe River Assault

For the 3d Division the change of plans on 19 November created few problems, and the 7th and 30th Infantry regiments concentrated for the 20 November crossings in the St. Michel area without incident. Nevertheless, O'Daniel felt that moving noisy tanks and tank destroyers forward to direct support positions near the crossing sites during the night of 19–20 November would alert the German defenders. Consequently, he kept most of his tracked vehicles well to the rear and tied them into artillery fire direction centers to provide indirect fire support. As a result only a few tanks and tank destroyers—those that had moved up to the riverbank earlier—were able to provide direct support for the crossing. However, his precautions proved successful as the evening of 19 November saw assault boats of the 10th Engineer Battalion, 3d Division, ferry several infantry platoons across the Meurthe at two points just over a mile north of St. Michel unopposed. Protected against surprise attack from the east bank, the engineers had installed two footbridges by midnight and added a light assault boat bridge before dawn on the 20th. Shortly after midnight, troops began crossing the footbridges, and by 0600 five infantry battalions of the 3d Division were assem-

---

[10] VI Corps OI 9 of 19 November, ordering the revision, was issued at 1300 that day, but entries in the VI Corps and 3d Division War Room Journals indicate that Brooks reached his decision an hour or two earlier.

[11] VI Corps OI 10, 20 Nov 44.

bled on the east side of the Meurthe waiting for the signal to attack. German opposition so far had been negligible, and surprise was apparently complete.[12]

At 0615, VI Corps and 3d Division artillery began a thirty-minute barrage directed against known and suspected German strongpoints, assembly areas, and artillery positions. Promptly at 0645 the artillery fire shifted eastward, and the infantry moved out to exploit the successful night crossing.

On the left, the 30th Infantry quickly secured a section of Route N–59 and headed north up the highway toward the Clairefontaine and Raon-l'Etape area.[13] At Clairefontaine the progress of the advancing infantry was temporarily halted by a German strongpoint; throughout the day German defenders thus continued to control the east-bank junction of Routes N–59 and N–424, between the 3d Division's 30th Infantry and the 100th Division's 397th in the north. But, sandwiched between the two American regiments, the defenders could not hold out for long. Meanwhile, to the south, troops of the 7th Infantry advanced a few miles inland and then pushed southwest, securing the area around St. Michel-sur-Meurthe, where they found few Germans but took heavy casualties from mines and booby traps. Around one small hamlet, for example, mines alone accounted for nearly 150 casualties within the regiment.

On 21 November both the 3d and 100th Divisions began to make substantial progress. The 7th and 30th Infantry regiments advanced two to four miles in a northeasterly direction, while to the left the 397th Infantry of the 100th Division secured Clairefontaine and pushed four miles east along Route N–424. German opposition was spotty and limited largely to sporadic artillery and mortar fire; as before, most delays stemmed from supply and transportation problems caused by flooding along the Meurthe, and were soon compounded by inadequate traffic control west of the river and by even more changes in VI Corps plans.

Late on 20 November, General Brooks decided to send two regiments of the 103d Division over the Meurthe at the 3d Division's crossing sites, rather than to install additional bridges farther south. Worsening flood conditions greatly complicated the effort. The 103d Division units crossed via the 3d Division's footbridges during the night of 20–21 November without difficulty until 0600 on the 21st, when one footbridge washed away. A second, its approaches flooded, had to be removed at 0800. By that time the 103d Division's two regiments had most of their troops across the river, but none of their vehicles or heavy equipment. The nearby light assault bridge had accommodated about seventy-five jeeploads of 3d Division supplies and equipment on the 20th, but shortly before midnight its approaches became impassable, leaving 103d Division units with no opportunity to use the span.

---

[12] For a detailed account, see Earl A. Reitan, "The Seventh Infantry Crosses the Meurthe (20 November 1944): The American Way of War in a Small Unit Action," MS (1986); copy at CMH and an abridged version published in *Infantry*, LXXVI, No. 5 (Sep–Oct 86), 29–33.

[13] Clairefontaine, on the east bank of the Meurthe, is not to be confused with its neighbor, Etival-Clairefontaine, west of the river.

To reinforce the two-division bridgehead, the 36th Engineer regiment had begun installing a heavy treadway bridge and a Bailey bridge to the south at St. Michel, with the treadway having priority. Initially, the engineers made good progress on the treadway bridge, but German artillery fire forced a temporary halt to the construction effort, and the treadway was not ready for traffic until 0700 on the morning of the 21st. However, after about forty heavy vehicles of the 3d Division had crossed—including eleven tanks and six tank destroyers— a tank became immobilized in the mud at the eastern exits and blocked further traffic. About 1100 on the 21st the 36th Engineers opened the Bailey bridge at St. Michel, and 3d Division vehicles again began pouring across the Meurthe. However, several hours later VI Corps gave the 103d Division priority at the Bailey bridge site so that it could support its two regiments that had crossed downstream earlier. The net result of all these delays and shifts back and forth was a monumental traffic jam on the west side of the river, made even worse by the arrival of the 14th Armored Division's CCA into the 3d Division's forward assembly areas during the day.

Another change in plans on the 21st contributed to the confusion. At 1400 Brooks again altered his plan of attack, directing CCA to cancel its projected Meurthe River crossing in the Raon-l'Etape area through the 3d and 100th Divisions. Instead, the unit was to take a wide northerly detour, moving north to St. Quirin, which had been secured by the French 2d Armored Division on the 20th; from

there it would strike out to the southeast into the wild, rocky, forested valleys of the Sarre Blanche and Sarre Rouge rivers. Its new objective was to seize the Schirmeck area at the junction of Routes N–392 and N–420, twelve miles southeast of St. Quirin and ten miles north of the Saales Pass in order to block a German withdrawal. With German troops in the north now beginning to fall back in disarray before the XV Corps' offensive, Brooks felt that the chances of CCA's making such an end run were good, including the possibility of isolating the *716th* and *16th Divisions*. The mission, once CCA moved out of its current location, would also ease the traffic problems in the corps' rear.[14]

Despite the crowded roads, the armored unit started off quickly. CCA reached St. Quirin early on 22 November, passed temporarily to XV Corps' control, and then headed southeast in two columns.[15] However, the route was more difficult than expected, and the command took over two days to reach Schirmeck. Numerous mines along narrow Route N–393 and booby-trapped roadblocks of felled trees delayed its advance. About three miles west of Schirmeck, a giant road crater proved impassable and stalled CCA for over twelve hours. Finally, on 25 November, after some intense clashes with German units, the armored command arrived

---

[14] Whether the traffic jam influenced Brooks' decision to redeploy CCA is not clear from available records. VI Corps OI 12 of 21 November, directing the redeployment, reflects only the tactical intent set forth in the text.

[15] Seventh Army OI 17, 22 Nov 44. Much of CCA's route to and from St. Quirin lay north of the boundary between VI and XV Corps.

at Schirmeck, only to find that other VI Corps units had already secured the area. CCA's advance thus had little tactical significance, serving as no more than a training exercise for the new unit.

The 100th and 3d Divisions

Late on 21 November General Brooks, convinced that the Germans were rapidly withdrawing across the entire front of the VI Corps, changed the nature of his advance from attack to pursuit. Ultimately, he sent the 100th Division northeastward along Routes N–392 and N–424, the 3d Division north on Route N–420, the 103d Division east on D–19, and the 36th Division east on N–59 and N–415. He also directed each of his four division commanders to organize fast-moving motorized task forces to strike immediately toward division objectives. Built around the nucleus of an infantry battalion, each task force was to include artillery, tank, tank destroyer, reconnaissance, and engineer units.[16] These mobile units were to bypass weak resistance and isolated strongpoints, leaving mop-up chores to the nonmotorized infantry, which would presumably follow at a slower pace.

Although the concept had considerable merit, its execution proved less than successful. Mined and booby-trapped roadblocks and craters, frequently covered by small-arms, machine-gun, and mortar fire, often halted the "highly mobile" task forces, as they had the armor of CCA. Meanwhile, the foot infantry units were normally able to bypass such obstacles and march on at a steady pace. For example, on 22 November, marching infantry of the 100th Division advanced another two miles eastward across a broadening front astride Route N–424 before the division's mechanized Task Force Fooks could catch up. On the 23d the 397th's foot infantry again spearheaded the division's drive and advanced nearly seven miles, moving quickly through the Hantz Pass and capturing St. Blaise-la-Roche, at the junction of Routes N–424 and N–420 about five miles north of Saales.[17] Frustrated, Col. Nelson I. Fooks attempted to use lesser roads south of N–424, but again encountered roadblocks and craters and could gain scarcely two miles—and that only after his infantry had left the trucks to advance on foot. The next day, 24 November, General Burress disbanded the mechanized force and turned the advance over to the 1st Battalion, 399th Infantry, which proceeded to march ten miles farther to Schirmeck by nightfall.

Meanwhile, another 100th Division task force consisting of the 1st Battalion, 398th Infantry, and the 117th Cavalry Squadron had been operating along the Plaine River valley and Route N–392 northeast from Raon-

---

[16] Typical was the 100th Division's Task Force Fooks under Col. Nelson I. Fooks, commander of the 398th Infantry: 2d Battalion, 398th Infantry; 100th Reconnaissance Troop; Battery A, 69th Armored Field Artillery Battalion; Platoon, Company B, 636th Tank Destroyer Battalion; Company A (−), 753d Tank Battalion; Platoon, Company B, 325th Engineer Battalion; Medical and Signal Detachments, 100th Division.

[17] The Congressional Medal of Honor was awarded to 1st Lt. Edward A. Silk, Company E, 398th Infantry, 100th Infantry Division, on 23 November 1944 for heroic action in clearing German infantry units from the northern section of Route N–424.

l'Etape. By the evening of 24 November, forward elements, having encountered negligible resistance, had moved fifteen miles beyond the Meurthe; and on the 25th the 117th Cavalry swung east along N–392 to make contact with CCA of the 14th Armored Division, just short of Route N–420.

The 3d Division was not far behind. With its traffic and supply problems solved, O'Daniel's forces had struck rapidly and forcefully northeast on 22 November. The division's motorized task force, TF Whirlwind, took off along narrow mountain roads north of St. Die. Meeting little resistance, it wound up the day with a six-mile advance that carried the ad hoc unit to the outskirts of Saulxures, about a mile south of St. Blaise-la-Roche. To the east, the progress of the 30th Infantry along Route N–420, the main highway, was slower, and the regiment was finally stopped half a mile short of Saales that afternoon. Meanwhile, on the far right, the 7th Infantry encountered the strongest opposition of the day, and in one intense fire fight took about 110 prisoners from the *716th Fusilier Battalion, 716th Division,* including the battalion commander.

On 23 November, 3d Division units overcame isolated opposition at Saales and Saulxures and joined forward elements of the 100th Division to clear the road junction at St. Blaise-la-Roche. All along Route N–420 both divisions found stockpiles of ammunition, barbed wire, and construction materials and passed by many incomplete, unmanned defensive installations, none of which the Germans had had the time or the manpower to use. The attacks of the 100th and 3d Divisions had shattered both the *708th* and *716th Divisions.* As the German troops fell back in small groups to the east and northeast, the American units drove through the vaunted *Vosges Ridge Position* hardly aware of its existence.

The following day, 24 November, lead elements of both the 3d and 100th Divisions set out along Route N–420 and the Bruche River valley, heading down the eastern slopes of the Vosges toward Schirmeck, Mutzig, and Strasbourg. The two units soon began to compete with one another for the lead, a rivalry fueled by rumors of a 72-hour pass for whichever division reached Strasbourg first. With the 3d on the right bank of the Bruche and the 100th on the left, the two American forces were often visible to each other as they cleared what few obstacles remained in their paths. Both divisions reached Schirmeck that evening, captured different sections of the town, and resumed the competition on the morning of the 25th. O'Daniel, complaining that the 100th was capturing towns in his sector, disbanded TF Whirlwind, which had spearheaded his drive on the 24th, and allowed the 15th Infantry to take the lead. Nightfall on the 25th finally found 3d Division troops slightly ahead of the 100th Division's infantrymen and over halfway to Mutzig. Early on 26 November a fresh battalion of the 100th's 399th Infantry, still dreaming of a three-day pass, took up the race only to be overtaken by a motorcycle messenger, who delivered the news that the division was to be redeployed north. Patch and Devers had decided to strengthen Haislip's XV Corps as quickly as possible, and

411TH INFANTRY, 103D DIVISION, IN VICINITY OF ST. MICHEL

the 100th Division was to be the first installment. The 3d Division thus continued the drive east alone, reaching the Mutzig area that afternoon and linking up with patrols from the XV Corps' 45th Division shortly thereafter. The VI Corps had finally broken out of the Vosges only to find that Strasbourg, still fifteen miles distant, was already in the hands of the French 2d Armored Division. The 72-hour passes would have to wait.

The 103d Division

Before General Haffner's 103d Division could launch its mid-November effort, it had to clear a two-mile-wide, triangular-shaped, wooded hill mass between St. Die and the Taintrux

valley. The 409th and 411th Infantry regiments successfully undertook this task during the period 16–18 November, while the 410th Infantry guarded the division's left flank. Opposition was minimal. During the night of 17–18 November, a patrol of the 410th entered the section of St. Die lying west of the Meurthe River and found the area deserted. The Germans had already sacked, burned, or otherwise destroyed the eastern part of the city and had herded well over 40,000 civilians into the western section of St. Die, which had boasted a prewar population of only 20,000.

For the November push, the 103d Division deployed the 411th Infantry on its right wing, adjacent to the 36th Division, while concentrating the regiments crossed the Meurthe over 3d Division bridges during the night of 20–21 November, immediately spreading out east and southeast and clearing high ground north and northeast of St. Die against light, intermittent resistance. On 22 November, elements of the 409th Infantry, coming in from the north, entered St. Die unopposed. Meanwhile the division's motorized task force, TF Haines,[18] circled around north of St. Die on back roads, securing much of Route N–420 from St. Die to Provencheres-sur-Fave. Provencheres fell on the 24th under the combined pressure of TF Haines, the 409th Infantry regiment, and units of the 3d Division coming up along Route N–420. Like both the 3d and 100th, the 103d Division passed many unmanned German defensive works and abandoned stockpiles of military supplies. To the south the 411th Infantry forced a crossing of the eastern section of the Meurthe near Saulcy-sur-Meurthe on the 22d against heavy small-arms and machine-gun fire and pushed north up N–59 toward St. Die.

In accordance with new VI Corps orders on the 23d,[19] the 103d Division now advanced in a more easterly direction toward Ville, a road junction town deep in the mountains about ten miles east of Saales. The division's ultimate objective was Barr, on the Alsatian plains eight miles northeast of Ville and an equal distance south of Mutzig in the 3d Division's zone. Heavily mined roads, well-defended road-

blocks, some stubborn pockets of resistance built on incomplete defensive installations, and sporadic artillery and mortar fire slowed progress, as did time-consuming marches along muddy mountain trails to outflank German strongpoints. By the afternoon of 26 November, leading elements of the 103d Division cleared Ville, but were still five miles short of the plains.

The 36th Division

The tired, understrength 36th Division, its rifle companies averaging only two-thirds of their authorized strength, made the transition slowly from its unfinished DOGFACE role into the mid-November offensive. During the period 10–19 November the division pressed east and southeast, at the same time taking over 103d Division positions west of the Meurthe. By the evening of 19 November, in the face of intermittent and rather weak resistance, the 36th Division's left had finally reached its DOGFACE objective, the high ground west of the Meurthe in the vicinity of St. Leonard, about five miles south of St. Die. The division had also gained high, forested terrain overlooking Anould, located on the flooding Meurthe two miles farther south. On the far right (southeast), 36th Division troops were already within a mile or two of destroyed Gerardmer by 19 November, and elements of the 3d Algerian Division of the II French Corps entered the town that day.[20]

So far the 36th Division, in the area

---

[18] TF Haines was built around the 2d Battalion, 409th Infantry, commanded by Maj. Lloyd L. Haines.

[19] VI Corps OI 14, 23 Nov 44.

[20] With its left held largely by weak FFI units and dangerously extended northward, the 3d Algerian Division could make little progress beyond Gerardmer during the rest of November.

from St. Leonard south about ten miles to Gerardmer, had been facing mainly the *198th Division* of the *IV Luftwaffe Field Corps*. During the night of 17–18 November, however, the *198th* began to pull out of its lines for redeployment to the Belfort Gap front. The movement was beset by confusion. To cover the withdrawal, the *Nineteenth Army* directed the weak *16th Volksgrenadier Division* to take over the *198th*'s positions in the Anould-Fraize area, an almost impossible task considering the strength of the *16th*. Although the *Nineteenth Army* had also instructed the departing *198th* to leave a rear guard south of St. Leonard, apparently the orders were ignored. Meanwhile, instead of moving up to the Meurthe River, most of the arriving *16th Volksgrenadier* troops began to occupy the *Vosges Ridge Position*, six to ten miles east of the river.

The 36th Division's boundaries and missions had also changed. When Brooks decided to have the 103d Division cross the Meurthe north of St. Die over the bridges of the 3d Division, he moved the boundary between the 103d and 36th Divisions northward over three miles. Shortly thereafter, Brooks made the 36th Division part of his pursuit and directed it to drive east and northeast across its extended front abreast of the remainder of the VI Corps. Its intermediate objective was Ste. Marie-aux-Mines, on Route N–59 about twelve miles (straight-line distance) east of St. Die and two miles east of the Ste. Marie Pass.[21] From the pass, the division was to continue eastward twelve miles

to the city of Selestat on the Alsatian plains between Colmar and Strasbourg. Brooks also instructed Dahlquist, the division commander, to launch a secondary effort along the axis of Route N–415 through Le Bonhomme Pass, about five miles east of Fraize, leading directly to Colmar.

The new tasks were onerous for the tired unit. Nevertheless, by 20 November the 36th Division had already moved in strength up to the west bank of the Meurthe, and it began crossing the river the next day between St. Leonard and Clefcy. Opposition came mainly from German artillery and mortar fire, while sodden ground, overflowing streams, and heavily mined areas also slowed progress. Gains on the 21st included the seizure of Anould and possession of a large section of Route N–415, which had been the main interior communication line of the German defenders. But as the 36th Division moved east, its main effort evolved into a battle for control of N–59, the road to the Ste. Marie Pass.

From St. Die to the vicinity of Bande-Laveline, a distance of about six miles, Route N–59 ran along an open valley, but soon thereafter it began twisting steeply upward through heavily wooded hills. Here the road, a major highway to the north between Luneville and St. Die, shrank to little more than a minor mountain byway, easily interdicted and, as the terrain became steeper, increasingly difficult to bypass. German defenses in the 36th Division's sector were the best organized and most complete in VI Corps' zone, probably reflecting the work of the veteran and well-led *198th Division*, which did much of the

---

[21] VI Corps OI 11, 20 Nov 44; VI Corps OI 13, 22 Nov 44.

GERMAN ASSAULT GUN KNOCKED OUT BY 76-MM. M4 TANK OF 36TH DIVISION, *Ste. Croix-aux-Mines area.*

groundwork in the area. Although the *16th Division*, now responsible for the defense of the region, was unable to man all the roadblocks and other defensive works, it held on to many of the prepared positions tenaciously.

German resistance on 22 and 23 November temporarily held the 36th Division in check along the Meurthe, but on the 24th the pace picked up as the defensive effort weakened. In the south, 36th Division troops seized Fraize and reached out to within a mile of Le Bonhomme Pass; to the north, other units cleared Wisembach on Route N–59 about two miles east of Ban-de-Laveline. Although German resistance stalled progress in Le Bonhomme Pass area for two days, Ste.

Marie-aux-Mines fell to the division on the 25th; on the 26th the 36th Division pushed three miles farther on N–59 to Ste. Croix-aux-Mines, seven miles short of the Alsatian plains near Selestat. Now, like the rest of VI Corps, the 36th Division was about to receive new orders changing its missions and objectives.[22]

Although the American VI Corps attack had finally suceeded in breaking through the High Vosges, the offensive had begun in a somewhat confused and uncoordinated manner. Perhaps overestimating the German linear defenses along the Meurthe River, Brooks had initially tried to

_____
[22] VI Corps OI 17, 26 Nov 44.

outflank them instead of penetrating through the scattered German strongpoints as Haislip had done. Certainly the 100th Division's determined actions around Raon-l'Etape sapped the strength of German defenders and shook the entire defensive line loose. Given the initial weakness of the German line, however, both the 3d and 103d Divisions probably could have crossed the Meurthe earlier than the 20th, thereby threatening the German forces that held up the 100th in the Plaine River valley and starting the drive east almost immediately. Of course, the full-scale offensives in the Belfort and Saverne Gap areas also helped the VI Corps' drive, making it impossible for the Germans to throw in reinforcements this time around.

Brooks' decision to begin the pursuit early in the offensive was correct, but his forces were probably unprepared to make the transition on such short notice; and many, like the 14th Armored Division, were too inexperienced. Nevertheless, like Haislip and Truscott before him, Brooks had seen some daylight and wanted to push his forces as far as he could before outrunning his supply lines or becoming mired in the difficult terrain and weather. Thus his orders gave a sense of immediacy to the entire advance and allowed the German defenders of the *708th, 716th,* and *16th Divisions* little opportunity to man the *Vosges Ridge Position.*

With Strasbourg taken by the XV Corps, Brooks found himself shifting the direction of his attack from the northeast to the east. He sent the 103d Division to Selestat and the 36th toward Colmar and, on Patch's orders, redeployed the 100th Division, on the VI Corps' northern wing, to the XV Corps. In this final effort, the VI Corps' advance was less focused and more opportunistic; its success would depend greatly on the ability of the French to make commensurate progress toward Colmar from the south. Before his forces could advance farther in this new direction, however, Brooks would need additional instructions from his superiors, Patch and Devers, regarding the ultimate destination of the VI Corps.

CHAPTER XXIII

Through the Belfort Gap

The first Allied troops to arrive at the Rhine River in the 6th Army Group's sector of the western front were French, and the signal honor of reaching the Rhine first belonged to a detachment of the French 1st Armored Division, a component of Bethouart's long-quiescent I Corps. This patrol reached the Rhine on 19 November at Rosenau, some thirty miles east of Belfort and about seventy miles south of Strasbourg. Thus, even as Haislip prepared to unloose Leclerc's 2d Armored Division against Saverne and as Brooks maneuvered his forces for the crossing of the Meurthe, de Lattre's French forces had already completed the first stage of their long-awaited Belfort penetration.

The First French Army's Front

While the First French Army began to deploy for the November offensive, the width of its front had continued to grow as Devers moved its boundary with the U.S. Seventh Army northward. In mid-November de Lattre's northern boundary thus followed the trace of Route N–417 from Remiremont on the Moselle northeast to Le Tholy and then east to Gerardmer deep in the Vosges (*Map 29*). From there, the boundary again turned northeast across the Vosges and continued to Erstein, about twelve miles south of Strasbourg, and then crossed the Rhine to Offenburg. As the First French Army's southern boundary remained fixed on the irregular but stable east-west Swiss border, every northeastern advance of the northern boundary would obviously enlarge the army's frontage as it moved east.

In early November de Lattre had both of his corps on line with two infantry divisions apiece and had withdrawn his two armored divisions for rest and refitting. On the First French Army's left, de Monsabert's II Corps faced the steep mountains and narrow passes of the High Vosges, while on the right Bethouart's I Corps stood poised before the long-prepared German defenses of the Belfort Gap. The intercorps boundary led east from the vicinity of Lure, passed south of Champagney (twenty-five miles south of Gerardmer), and stretched east again to Valdoie, just three miles north of Belfort. De Lattre tentatively intended to extend the intercorps boundary east and northeast to Mulhouse, on the Alsatian plains twenty-five miles south of Colmar.

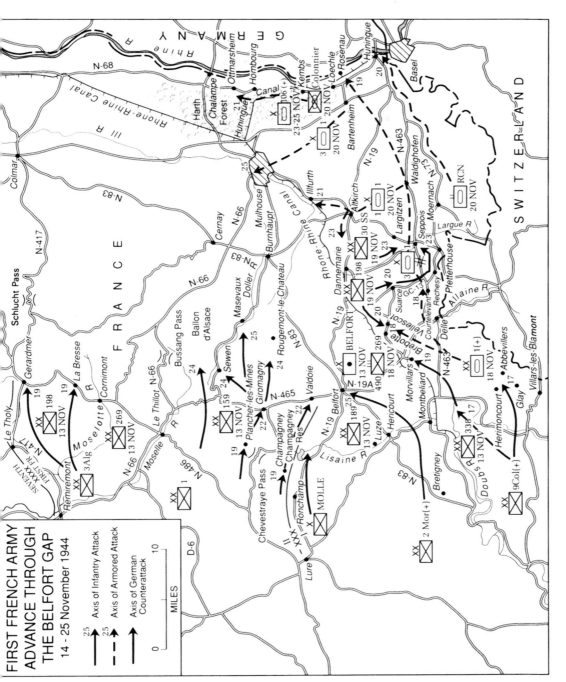

FIRST FRENCH ARMY
ADVANCE THROUGH
THE BELFORT GAP
14 - 25 November 1944

Axis of Infantry Attack

Axis of Armored Attack

Axis of German
Counterattack

MILES

0   10

This map is printed in full color at the back of the book, following the Index.

MAP 29

The French II Corps had on line, from north to south, the 3d Algerian Infantry Division and the 1st Infantry Division, both reinforced by a few regular and FFI units.[1] The 3d Algerian Division held the corps front from the vicinity of Le Tholy southeast about ten miles to Cornimont. The 1st Infantry Division extended the front south almost twenty miles farther to Ronchamp, just west of Champagney.

Below these units, the I Corps had on its left a provisional force, Group Molle,[2] holding a front that ran south about seven miles from Ronchamp. On Group Molle's right was the 2d Moroccan Infantry Division, covering a sector that stretched south ten miles to the Doubs River. South of the Doubs, the 9th Colonial Infantry Division's lines ran southeast and then east to the Swiss border at Villars, eighteen miles south of Belfort. Both divisions had more or less permanent FFI and regular attachments, while for the offensive de Lattre intended to reinforce the I Corps with the 5th Armored Division, CC2 of the 1st Armored Division, a regimental combat team of the 4th Moroccan Mountain Division,[3] two separate tank destroyer battalions, the 9th Zouaves (light infantry), and a host of lesser units. De Lattre also gave I Corps first priority for units in the First French Army's general reserve, which would be made available to the two corps as the situation dictated.[4]

Fire support for the French offensive would have an American flavor. In the I Corps, the artillery was commanded by Brig. Gen. Carl C. Banks, USA, who was also in charge of the U.S. Army's 13th Field Artillery Brigade. For the Belfort offensive, the brigade (exclusive of French units) consisted of the 1st Field Artillery Observation Battalion; the 36th Field Artillery Group; and the 575th, 630th, 697th, and 933d Field Artillery Battalions. In addition, the U.S. Army's 2d Chemical Mortar Battalion (4.2-inch) was in direct support of the 9th Colonial Division.

In general, the First French Army's forces were rested and in fairly good condition for the November offensive. The only major exception was the 3d Algerian Division, which had not been out of the front lines since it first began moving against Toulon and Marseille on 20 August. Although the division had undertaken no substantial offensive operations since the first week of November, it had continued aggressive patrolling in order to focus German attention on the High Vosges. There its units had been operating in the most rugged terrain

---

[1] Since all units discussed in the chapter are French, the national indicators are generally not used. In addition, attachments and detachments of reinforcing units within both French corps changed frequently, and no attempt is made to follow these changes in detail.

[2] Group Molle was a provisional brigade consisting largely of FFI units plus a few regular reinforcements, such as a reconnaissance squadron, a towed antitank gun company, and some artillery and mortars.

[3] The 4th Moroccan Mountain Division was being replaced in the Franco-Italian border area by the newly formed French 27th Alpine Division.

[4] Both French armored divisions in de Lattre's command had three brigade-sized combat commands: CC1, 2, and 3 in the 1st Armored Division; and CC4, 5, and 6 in the 5th Armored Division. Additional information on force structure can be found in First Fr Army Personal and Secret Instr 4, 24 Oct 44; and First Fr Army Genl Opns Order 148, 11 Nov 44.

and during the worst weather on the entire French front. The 1st Infantry Division, by contrast, had seen relatively little action since late September and, adopting a generally defensive attitude, had spent most of October absorbing indigenous replacements for its black troops. The 2d Moroccan Division had likewise engaged in mainly defensive action since taking over its sector north of the Doubs River in early October, as had the 9th Colonial Division south of the Doubs. The 1st Armored Division had not been in heavy combat since mid-October and had come out of the line on the 25th of that month. The 5th Armored Division was fresh but untried. Finally, all units were fully equipped and had devoted substantial time to training and building up their supply stocks. Although the weather conditions had somewhat dampened the spirits of the French troops for the coming offensive, most were confident that they would soon overcome the best the Germans had to offer in the Belfort Gap and the southern Vosges.

Defending the Gap

From Le Tholy south about fifteen miles to Le Thillot, the left wing of the *Nineteenth Army's IV Luftwaffe Field Corps* confronted the left of de Monsabert's II Corps.[5] South and southeast about thirty-five miles from Le Thillot to the Swiss border, *LXXXV Corps* was responsible for holding the approaches to Belfort and blocking the Belfort

---

[5] German information in this chapter is based on von Luttichau, "German Operations," chs. 22, 23, and 25.

Gap. In static defensive positions behind this corps, *Fortress Brigade Belfort* held the city of Belfort and the old stone and masonry forts that encircled it. East of these organizations, provisional *Corps Dehner* controlled other provisional units along the Swiss border and temporarily served as a reserve headquarters.

On 7 November *Army Group G* learned that *LXXXV Corps* headquarters was to be transferred to *Army Group B*, and on the 14th *Corps Dehner* took over the tactical command in the Belfort sector. Having only a skeletal staff and lacking the normal corps support units, *Corps Dehner* was ill prepared for its expanded role. Officially given the title of corps on 15 November, the organization became *LXIII Corps* on the 18th, and its former security mission along the Swiss border went to an *ad hoc* organization designated *Staff Boineburg*. The entire command change could hardly have come at a worse time for the German defenders.

Whatever the deficiencies of the corps-level commands, the *Nineteenth Army* could rely on several fairly good divisions in the Belfort area. On the north, holding a sector extending some five miles south from Le Tholy, the left of the *198th Division* faced part of the 3d Algerian Division. Understrength but consisting largely of battle-tested veterans, the *198th* could be depended on to hold its ground. The rest of the *IV Luftwaffe Field Corps* zone was held by the relatively strong and fresh *269th Volksgrenadier Division*, which had recently arrived from Norway.

From the corps' boundary at Le Thillot south about fifteen miles to

Route N–19—the main east-west highway through Belfort—the *159th Division* held good defensive terrain with three rebuilt regiments that had felt little pressure since late September. The division, with a southern boundary that corresponded roughly to the First French Army's intercorps boundary, faced most of the French 1st Infantry Division. Two regiments of the *159th* were almost up to strength, and the weaker third regiment was made up of fortress and *Wehrkreis V* troops. The division had less than half of its authorized artillery, and its antitank battalion was considerably understrength.

From Route N–19 south about ten miles stood the *189th Division*, facing Group Molle and much of the 2d Moroccan Division. The *189th* was also responsible for the defense of Hericourt, a key highway junction and railroad town about six miles southwest of Belfort. The division was truly an ersatz unit. The division headquarters had formerly belonged to the *242d Infantry Division,* most of which had been destroyed in southern France during August. One infantry regiment was built on a former police security regiment, and a second on a *Luftwaffe* infantry training regiment; the third had been pieced together from stragglers and miscellaneous small units rounded up in the Belfort area. The division lacked reconnaissance and engineer battalions, was short of both artillery and ammunition, was weak in antitank weaponry, and had scant reserves. Nevertheless, the *189th* had had time—since late September—to weld its disparate components together, and the *Nineteenth Army* rated the division as ade-

quate for defensive purposes.

From a point a mile or so south of Hericourt, the *338th Infantry Division* extended the German front south and southeast over fifteen miles to the Swiss border. The *338th,* facing the right of the 2d Moroccan Division and all of the 9th Colonial Division, was the weakest link in the German line. Pulled out of the High Vosges toward the end of October, the division had brought south just two *ad hoc* infantry regiments, both of which were suitable only for static defensive missions.[6] The division was also short of artillery and devoid of reserves, deploying all of its existing infantry on its eggshell-thin front line. In brief, the Germans had inadvertently placed their weakest division along what was to be the focal point of the French attack.

Situated slightly to the rear of the *189th* was *Fortress Brigade Belfort*, with two fortress artillery battalions and several fortress machine-gun companies. Necessity had forced the brigade to transfer some of its artillery to the infantry divisions, while a number of its remaining guns were captured French and Russian pieces for which little ammunition was available. The brigade had recently received thirty new 88-mm. antitank weapons of German manufacture, but most of them had arrived lacking vital parts, such as sights.

As a tactical reserve, the *LXIII Corps* [7] stationed two understrength infantry battalions at Belfort, while an understrength infantry battalion of

---

[6] The division's *757th Grenadiers* remained attached to the *716th Division* in the St. Die area.

[7] Although the designation *LXIII Corps* was not adopted until 18 November, this title will be used throughout the chapter to avoid confusion.

the *189th Division* was also earmarked for a reserve role. However, as was the case elsewhere along the *Nineteenth Army*'s front, there were no true reserves. All of the armored units that had once been scheduled for the Belfort Gap had been diverted either to the *First Army* or to the *Nineteenth Army*'s northern front. In an emergency at the Belfort Gap, General Wiese could call only on the NCO training center at Colmar—some 1,500 troops in all, counting students, faculty, and staff. A more remote possibility was the *30th SS Grenadier Division,* a unit of conscripted Russian nationals stationed near Mulhouse who were waiting for transportation east across the Rhine. Following a mutiny in September, the division had been reorganized, but was still considered unreliable. Nevertheless, the unit now had a substantial German cadre (one German to three Russians) and might have some defensive possibilities. Outside of these forces, however, the *Nineteenth Army* had no other reserves from Colmar south to the Swiss border.

The weaknesses of the German forces in the Belfort Gap sector reflected a fundamental difference of opinion between General Balck of *Army Group G* and General Wiese of *Nineteenth Army* regarding the intentions and capabilities of the French. After de Lattre had halted the attempt by de Monsabert's II Corps to outflank Belfort on the north in October, Wiese decided that the French would ultimately switch their main effort to a drive through the Belfort Gap itself in order to take advantage of better terrain. Balck, on the other hand, was convinced that the French

would sooner or later resume their advance across the High Vosges, aiming for Colmar on the Alsatian plains. Once this had been accomplished, the *Army Group G* commander thought that the French would then swing back south to open the Belfort Gap by attacking from the rear. Any French pressure toward the Belfort Gap from the west, he believed, was only an effort to divert *Army Group G*'s attention away from a major threat across the Vosges. For this reason Balck insisted that Wiese keep two of the *Nineteenth Army*'s best divisions, the *198th Infantry* and the *269th Volksgrenadier,* in the High Vosges, occupying the excellent mountain defensive terrain opposite the French II Corps; meanwhile, the relatively flat area south of Belfort, a region much more difficult to defend, was left in the hands of the ailing *338th Division.*

De Monsabert's diversionary attack of 3–5 November in support of VI Corps' DOGFACE offensive created a stir at *Army Group G* headquarters and undoubtedly confirmed Balck's estimate of French intentions. Meanwhile, de Lattre initiated an elaborate deception program that also focused *Army Group G*'s attention on the Vosges. Carefully prepared false or misleading orders found their way into German hands;[8] troop movements that never took place were brought to the attention of the Germans; and fake command posts for I Corps units were established in the II Corps sector. Then, as 13 November

---

[8] First Fr Army Personal and Secret Instr 3–A, 20 Oct 44; First Fr Army Orientation Directive 4, 1 Nov 44; First Fr Army Orientation Directive 5, 4 Nov 44. See also de Lattre, *History,* pp. 217–18 and 225.

approached, all attack units of Beth-ouart's I Corps began moving up to their lines of departure under cover of darkness; poor weather, although creating some problems for the French, further concealed the assembly of attacking forces.

French Plans

The role of de Monsabert's II Corps in the November offensive was at first limited to maintaining an attitude that was aggressive enough to keep the Germans worried about the Vosges front.[9] Depending on available strength and on developments in the I Corps sector, the II Corps was ultimately to drive across the Vosges along the axis of Route N–66 and the Bussang Pass in order to join I Corps forces in the vicinity of Mulhouse. On the I Corps' left side, Group Molle was to maintain contact with the II Corps and seize the dam at the Champagney reservoir, about three miles southeast of Champagney, to prevent the Germans from flooding the Lisaine River valley between Hericourt and Montbeliard.

South of Group Molle, the 2d Moroccan Infantry Division was to launch the I Corps' main effort, first driving eastward north of the Doubs to the Lisaine valley, and then seizing Belfort city with the surprise attack from the south. Failing that, the division was to encompass Belfort on the north and south, attacking the metropolitan area and the surrounding forts from the rear. Initial reinforcements for the 2d Moroccan Division included two combat commands of the 5th Armored Division, CC4 and CC5, and four or five FFI infantry battalions.

Below the Doubs River, the 9th Colonial Infantry Division was to drive generally northeast, its left flank on the Doubs and its right on the Swiss border. Continuing across a north-south stretch of the Doubs (which makes a great loop near Montbeliard), the division would press northeastward to the general line of the Allaine River between Morvillars and Delle, on the Swiss border. The 9th Colonial Division's reinforcements included CC2 of the 1st Armored Division, the 6th Moroccan Tirailleurs (a regimental combat team) of the 4th Moroccan Mountain Division, the 9th Zouaves, a tank destroyer battalion, and four FFI infantry battalions. Both the main and secondary attacks were to begin simultaneously on 13 November.

The I Corps Assault

During the night of 9–10 November I Corps' leading attack units began moving up to their lines of departure for the assault on the 13th. The weather had been rainy and overcast for several days, and on the 9th continued heavy rains increased the flooding along the Doubs and its tributaries. During the next few days, problems caused by inclement weather mounted. Many of the corps' tem-

---

[9] Information on French plans and operations in the rest of this chapter is based mainly on de Lattre, *History*, pp. 224–82; *Historique de la Neuvieme Division d'Infanterie Coloniale*, pp. 51–59; *La Premiere Division Blindee au Combat*, pp. 87–97; Service Historique de l'Armee, *Guerre 1939–1945, Les Grandes Unites Francaises, Historiques Succincts, Campagnes de France et d'Allemagne, (1944–1945), 3e Partie* (Paris: Imprimerie Nationale, 1976), pp. 541–92 (hereafter cited as *Historiques Succincts*).

porary bridges were washed out or seriously damaged; lesser roads became impassable for wheeled or even tracked vehicles; wire communications failed; radio transmissions were sporadic; and low visibility made the registration of artillery fire almost impossible. On the 11th, General Bethouart, the I Corps commander, suggested postponing the attack until the weather improved. At first de Lattre refused to countenance any delay, but approved some changes, agreeing with Bethouart's proposal to have the 9th Colonial Division lead off the attack. Since the so-called colonial division was now made up mostly of younger troops from metropolitan France, the French generals thought that these soldiers might be better able to contend with the mud, rain, snow, and increasingly cold weather than the men of the 2d Moroccan Division. Accordingly, the generals moved the date of the 9th Colonial Division's attack up to the 13th and pushed that of the 2d Moroccan Division back to the 14th. De Lattre also instructed Bethouart to move his armor forward on the 14th, somewhat earlier than planned, so as to be ready to exploit any success the two infantry divisions might achieve. Finally, the French army commander directed de Monsabert's II Corps to launch diversionary attacks in the Champagney area on 13 and 14 November.

For both sides, dawn of 13 November revealed what de Lattre later described as a "Scandinavian landscape." [10] Heavy snow had been falling for hours, and the almost com-

plete lack of visibility forced the French to cancel the attack. The next morning, 14 November, low, dark clouds continued to cover much of the sector, but some clearing took place north of the Doubs. After another quick change of plans, de Lattre and Bethouart ordered the offensive to begin, with the 2d Moroccan Division attacking at 1200 behind a two-hour artillery preparation, and the left wing of the 9th Colonial Division joining in at 1400. Elsewhere on the 9th Colonial front, fog, sodden terrain, and additional snowfall held the division in place.

As the French were preparing their attack, Maj. Gen. Friederich-August Schack, the newly appointed commander of the defending *LXIII Corps,* decided to take a personal look at his unfamiliar front. Schack drove to an observation post near Bretigney, on the north side of the Doubs River about eight miles west of Montbeliard, and on the way picked up Maj. Gen. Hans Oschmann, commanding the *338th Infantry Division.* Suddenly French artillery began a devastating barrage that immobilized the observation party—the two generals, each with an aide; it was over two hours before the small group could start groping eastward through woods that artillery fire had turned into a shambles. Running into small groups of Moroccan infantrymen, Oschmann was killed and the two aides captured, but Schack somehow made his way past the Moroccans and reached his command post at Belfort before dark.

In the midst of the melee in the woods, a detailed map of the *338th Division*'s dispositions fell into French hands, along with notes revealing that

---

[10] De Lattre, *History,* p. 228.

Oschmann, far from expecting a major attack, had concluded that the French across his front were digging in for the winter. For the *338th Division*, the attack of the 2d Moroccan Division had thus come as a complete surprise, and the response of the defenders was further hampered by the absence of both the corps and division commanders during the early stages of the attack. To make matters worse, the French artillery fire had also disrupted German wire communications, making it impossible for the *LXIII Corps'* staff to obtain an accurate picture of the situation at the front.

During the first day of the attack, 14 November, the left wing of the 2d Moroccan Division gained little ground against the relatively strong *189th Division*, but in the center and on the right the Moroccans broke through *338th Division* positions across a front of nearly six miles and advanced over two miles into the German lines. With its attack delayed until 1400, the 9th Colonial Division found *338th Division* units south of the Doubs on the alert, yet pushed forward on the left a mile and a half across a three-mile front.

French armor played only a minor role in the early gains, but de Lattre, hoping for a breakthrough on the 15th, immediately released the headquarters and CC3 of the 1st Armored Division to the I Corps, leaving only the division's CC1 as the First French Army's main reserve (as well as the only element of the division immediately redeployable to the Atlantic coast). General Bethouart, the I Corps commander, intended to retain both the 1st Armored Division's CC3 and the 5th Armored Division's CC6

as his own reserve, while allowing the 9th Colonial Division to retain CC2 and the 2d Moroccan Division to keep CC4 and CC5. If the armored units advanced ahead of the infantry, they could begin operating independently under the control of the armored division headquarters.

Despite French advances, no alarm bells rang on 14 November at *Army Group G*, where Balck continued to regard all activities on the Belfort front as a ploy to divert attention from the Vosges. More concerned with the situation on the *Nineteenth Army's* northern front and with the *First Army's* sector, *Army Group G* had even begun preparations to move the *338th Division* north by rail during the night of 14–15 November. The result was a tug of war that evening between *Army Group G* and the *Nineteenth Army*. While Balck was directing the *Nineteenth Army* to pull the *338th Division* out of the Belfort lines, Wiese, the *Nineteenth Army* commander, was instructing the *LXIV Corps* to disengage the division's missing regiment from the St. Die area and speed the unit south to the Belfort front. At the same time, Wiese ordered the *IV Luftwaffe Field Corps* to move two field artillery battalions (one of them organic to the *338th Division*) south to Belfort, along with two light antiaircraft battalions. Pending the arrival of these units, General Schack of *LXIII Corps* committed his three reserve infantry battalions in the *338th Division's* sector early on the 15th.

Schack's reinforcements had little immediate impact. On 15 November the center and right of the 2d Moroccan Division gained another three miles in the *338th Division's* sector; to the south, the 9th Colonial Division overran some of the *338th Division*'s strongest positions and seized a number of important road junctions. By dark the *338th Division*'s front was thus completely disorganized, and General Wiese directed the *LXIII Corps* to pull the division back a mile or two in an attempt to stabilize it along a new line. Then—and only then—did Wiese seek permission from *Army Group G* to execute the withdrawal. Lacking accurate information regarding the situation on the Belfort front, however, Balck continued to call for the complete disengagement of the *338th* from the south, leaving Wiese with little choice except to procrastinate, thereby creating a temporary stalemate over the matter.

On 16 November French armor, previously slowed by mud, disintegrating roads, and extensive minefields, began to play a more decisive role. With their left flank along Route N–83, the Hericourt-Belfort highway, elements of the 5th Armored Division and the 2d Moroccan Division reached a point scarcely a mile short of Hericourt and the Lisaine River. To the south and along the Doubs, the Moroccans and attached armor advanced another two miles to the east and northeast. Even farther south the 9th Colonial Division's attack finally gathered momentum, with the support of the 1st Armored Division's CC3, and advanced up to three miles. On the far right, close by the Swiss border, French troops reached the vicinity of Glay, seizing more road junction towns and further disrupting local German tactical communications, which depended heavily on the

telephone and teletype lines of the German-controlled French civil communications system.

During the course of 16 November, General de Lattre released CC1 of the 1st Armored Division from army reserve. This move came as something of a surprise to General du Vigier, who commanded the armored division, for he had been prepared to start CC1 toward the Atlantic coast on the 18th, with the rest of the division following on the 21st. On the 17th, however, de Lattre officially halted further deployments for INDEPENDENCE and told du Vigier that departures for the Atlantic coast would be postponed a minimum of four days.[11]

De Lattre's action must have had at least the tacit approval of General Devers, who was having increasing doubts about removing any major units from the First French Army at such a crucial point in the Belfort Gap offensive. On the 16th Devers told Lt. Gen. Sir Frederick E. Morgan, the SHAEF Deputy Chief of Staff, who was visiting the 6th Army Group command post, that no French units would be withdrawn from the Vosges and Belfort fronts as long as they continued their current drive; he believed that Morgan agreed with his position.[12] Thus, for at least a few more days, Bethouart's attacking

---

[11] De Lattre, *History*, p. 221; 1st Fr Armd Div Jnl de Marche, 15–16 Nov 44; *La Premiere Division Blindee au Combat,* pp. 90–91; First Fr Army Warning Order 156, 16 Nov 44; Msg, 72/OP/3.8, First Fr Army to I Fr Corps et al., 17 Nov 44. Initially, de Lattre intended to use CC1 in the II Corps sector, but he returned the command to 1st Armored Division control on 19 November; *Historiques Succincts, 2e Partie,* pp. 883–89.

[12] Devers Diary, 16 Nov 44.

corps could look forward to employing two full armored divisions against the weakening German forces on the Belfort front.

On the other side, the German commanders had been unable to resolve their differences. All day long on the 16th, Wiese continued to argue with *Army Group G* over the redeployment of the *338th Division,* which by dark was becoming so disorganized that its disengagement would have been extremely difficult. By that time even *OKW* was becoming perturbed about the situation and informed *OB West* that a French breakthrough at the Belfort Gap had to be prevented at all costs; *OB West* quickly relayed these instructions to *Army Group G.* About 2000 on the 16th, General Balck, now under pressure from his superiors to reevaluate the entire situation, decided to leave the *338th Division* in place and to send instead the much better *198th Division* of the *IV Luftwaffe Field Corps* to the *First Army.* At the same time Balck directed that the shattered *16th Volksgrenadier Division* and the weak *716th Division,* both still deployed in the St. Die area, be moved south to replace the *198th Division* in the southern Vosges.

After absorbing these orders, General Wiese of *Nineteenth Army* must have felt that he had won a battle but lost a campaign. He had intended to redeploy the *198th Division* to the Belfort Gap and the *16th Volksgrenadier Division* to his northern flank, leaving only the *716th Division* in the St. Die area. In retrospect, he probably would have been content to lose the *338th,* if he could have retained the *198th.* The decisions, however, were

not his to make, and Balck's orders made the German situation in the south even more precarious.

Finally, during the evening of 16 November, Balck gave Wiese permission to undertake a limited withdrawal. The *LXIII Corps* was to pull back to the Lisaine River, between Hericourt and Montbeliard, and the southern elements of General Schack's *338th Division* were to make a parallel withdrawal between Montbeliard and the Swiss border. But Wiese, acting on his own, had already approved a similar withdrawal on the previous evening, so Balck's new directions had little bearing on the situation around Belfort.

Breakthrough

On 17 November the German front began to fall apart. The 2d Moroccan Division and its armored attachments overran *189th* and *338th Division* positions and pushed bridgeheads across the Lisaine River between Luze, Hericourt, and Montbeliard. To the south, the center of the 9th Colonial Division pushed east about five miles to Herimoncourt. Its left wing joined the Moroccans at Montbeliard, and its right wing, led by CC2, reached out to Abbevillers, three miles northeast of Glay, encountering only spotty resistance.

Sensing an imminent breakthrough, General Bethouart issued new orders, which de Lattre tentatively approved. Du Vigier's 1st Armored Division (reinforced)[13] was to assemble in the Ab-

_____

[13] At this juncture the reinforcements included the 6th Moroccan Tirailleurs (a regimental combat team of the 4th Moroccan Mountain Division), the 9th Zouaves, the separate tank destroyer battalion, and a nondivisional reconnaissance squadron.

bevillers-Herimoncourt area in order to strike east between the Rhone-Rhine Canal and the Swiss border. His main effort was to take place on the left with the first objective being Morvillars, seven miles northeast of Montbeliard and close to the south bank of the canal. Then du Vigier was to push on to Dannemarie, a rail and road center along Route N–19 on the south side of the canal about twelve miles east of Belfort. Behind the 1st Armored Division the 9th Colonial Division was to mop up, secure the armored division's left flank, and seize bridgeheads along the Rhone-Rhine Canal between Montbeliard and Morvillars.

In part, the bridgehead mission was designed to support attacks against Belfort by the 2d Moroccan Division and the attached combat commands of the 5th Armored Division. However, indications are that de Lattre and Bethouart felt that Belfort could be secured in a few days primarily by infantry forces and that the combat commands of the 5th Armored Division could be returned to division control by noon on 19 November. Then, de Lattre envisaged, the entire armored division could begin an exploitation along the general axis of Route N–83 from Belfort northeast to Cernay and ultimately to Colmar. To accomplish this, the division was first to move south and then east, crossing the Rhone-Rhine Canal at or near Morvillars and continuing north to N–83, bypassing all of the urban Belfort region on the east.

Meanwhile, a new struggle between *Army Group G* and the *Nineteenth Army* had developed over the deployment of the *198th Division*. About noon on

17 November General Balck decided to leave the *198th* under Wiese's control, but specified that he move the division to the *Nineteenth Army*'s northern flank, where the attack against Sarrebourg by Haislip's XV Corps was beginning to have an effect. For the moment Balck approved the transferal of only one regimental combat team of the *269th Volksgrenadier Division* south, from the *IV Luftwaffe Field Corps'* Vosges front to the Belfort area. That evening, probably because of pressure from *OKW* and *OB West*, Balck finally decided that the French operations around Belfort were more significant than he had first believed, and he approved the movement of the *198th Division*, along with the regiment of the *269th Volksgrenadiers*, to the Belfort Gap. About the same time he also gave Wiese permission to pull the *LXIII Corps* back to the *Weststellung*—actually, a southeastern extension of the *Vosges Ridge Position*—from Hericourt southeast to the Swiss border.

Once again the German reaction come too late to affect the situation on the ground. The withdrawal, which concerned primarily the *338th Division*, began after midnight, and dawn on 18 November found *338th* troops still retreating east. To avoid French roadblocks and to take advantage of the best roads, most of the units south of the Rhone-Rhine Canal withdrew through Morvillars with the intent of reforming along the Allaine River and Route N–19A. There the northern trace of the Swiss border would greatly reduce the frontage that the survivors of the *338th* would have to hold. However, the withdrawal plans required the division first to

FRENCH LIGHT TANKS AT HUNINGUE

reassemble in the Allaine River valley and then to move into the *Weststellung* positions, many of which were little more than symbols on a map.

Again the French gave the Germans no respite. Long before the German redeployments could be completed, units of the 1st Armored Division had penetrated the *Weststellung* positions from Morvillars southeast to Delle, having encountered mainly service troops and security detachments. Only in the Morvillars area did the *338th Division* successfully defend a *Weststellung* location, but French armor broke into the Allaine valley well south of Morvillars and pushed north across the river for about three miles. At Delle, two miles beyond the *Weststellung* southern anchor, another armored force seized a bridge over the Allaine; meanwhile, closer to the Swiss border, other armored units probed eastward four miles beyond Delle to Courtelevant without encountering significant opposition. This last advance took place along Route N–463, a good highway that led toward the Rhine, less than twenty-five miles away.

The French advance continued the next day, 19 November, but with little success on the left wing where the Germans held on to part of Morvillars. There CC2 of the 1st Armored Division and elements of the 9th Colonial Division were unable to secure any crossings over the Rhone-Rhine Canal and, in the face of stiffening opposition, made scant progress toward Dannemarie. French losses now began to mount, and casualties in the armored command alone included 30 men killed, about 60 wounded, and 11 tanks destroyed.

To the south CC3, starting out from Courtelevant before dawn, headed eastward in three columns. Pushing along Route N–463 through Seppois and over the Largue River, the advancing armor reached Largitzen north of the highway, Moernach south of the road, and Waldighofen in the center, located on N–463 eleven miles east of Courtelevant and only twelve miles from the Rhine River. During the afternoon of the 19th, an advance detachment of the command swung off along back roads; it avoided almost all German defenses and reached the Rhine at Rosenau, twelve miles northeast of Waldighofen, a little after 1800 that evening.[14] Reinforcements soon came forward, and the 2d Battalion of the 68th African Artillery, 1st Armored Division, lobbed a few shells across the Rhine—the first French artillery fire to fall on German soil since the spring of 1940. The breakthrough had been achieved.

As de Lattre received word that his forces had reached the Rhine, General Devers had more good news for the French commander. Devers had again been able to postpone the departure of the 1st Armored Division for Operation INDEPENDENCE on the Atlantic coast, this time until mid-December. However, the redeployment of the 1st Infantry Division remained set for the end of November. Having already postponed the start of INDEPENDENCE from 10 December to 1 January, Devers now pushed the starting date back even further to 10 January, a delay that SHAEF approved.[15]

The Battle of the Gap

However promising the Rosenau penetration, the French situation in the Belfort Gap at dusk on 19 November was by no means secure. The operations of the 2d Moroccan Division against Belfort had not progressed as rapidly as hoped, and de Lattre found it necessary to leave the 5th Armored Division's CC6 attached to the Moroccan unit, while the rest of the armored division moved south. In fact, the 2d Moroccan Division, even with the support of CC6, was unable to clear the Belfort area until 25 November.[16] A second major problem was the failure of the 9th Colonial Division and CC2 to secure crossings over the Rhone-Rhine Canal, thus making it impossible for the 5th

---

[14] The detachment consisted of a platoon of medium tanks and a platoon of armored infantry and was under the command of 1st Lt. Jean Carrelet de Loisy of the 2d African Chasseurs, a tank battalion organic to the 1st Armored Division. Lieutenant de Loisy was later killed at Mulhouse on 23 November.

[15] De Lattre, *History*, p. 221; Vigneras–de Camas Intervs; Devers Diary, 21 Nov 44. The exact chronology of the decision to postpone the 1st Armored Division's redeployment is a bit vague. De Camas indicates that the decision was made on 19 November; de Lattre's work cites 20 November; and the Devers diary shows that Devers did not reach a firm decision until the 21st, when he received SHAEF approval to postpone INDEPENDENCE to 10 January.

[16] On 20 November the 2d Moroccan Division and CC6 passed to de Lattre's direct control, and on the 22d they came under the command of de Monsabert's II Corps. CC6 remained with the II Corps until late December; the 5th Armored Division never operated as a complete division until late April 1945.

Armored Division to begin its drive toward Cernay. Instead the armored division was temporarily immobilized in the Montbeliard region, where its long columns of vehicles clogged the supply routes of the 9th Colonial and 1st Armored Divisions.

A third danger was the nature of the French penetration. The 1st Armored Division's CC3 had poked out a very slender salient to the Rhine, and its supply routes east from Delle were extremely vulnerable. In order to secure the armored command's lines of communication eastward, Bethouart's forces would have to clear and hold the cut-up, hilly, and largely wooded terrain south of the Rhone-Rhine Canal from Morvillars to Dannemarie, as well as similar terrain south of Route N–19 from Dannemarie to Altkirch. Although de Lattre was not an ULTRA recipient, he knew from his own sources that the German *198th Infantry Division* had moved out of the Vosges and must have expected it to arrive in the threatened area shortly.[17]

De Lattre gave the task of securing the French penetration to the 9th Colonial Division. He ordered the 1st Armored Division, joined by its CC1 on 20 November, to clear the west bank of the Rhine from Huningue (on the Swiss border) north seventeen

miles to Chalampe, where several major bridges crossed the Rhine. However, Dannemarie on Route N–19 was still an objective of the 1st Armored Division, which indicated that de Lattre felt the muscle of both divisions would be needed to hold the broad area north of the French penetration. Finally, de Lattre remained confident that the inexperienced 5th Armored Division (less CC6) would somehow find a way to breach the Rhone-Rhine Canal on the 20th and launch a drive north toward Colmar, which would parallel the 1st Armored Division's projected advance north along the Rhine. A second breakthrough by the 5th Armored Division would also greatly hamper any German efforts to interdict the supply lines of the 1st Armored Division along Route N–463 and would complete the German rout.

On the other side of the front, General Wiese of *Nineteenth Army*, at dusk on 19 November, was considering another major withdrawal, abandoning Belfort and pulling his army's southern flank all the way north to Mulhouse. At *OB West*, however, von Rundstedt was adamantly opposed to giving up Belfort without a protracted fight. Instead, he directed *Army Group G* to hold at Belfort and, at the same time, to mount a counterattack south of the city, cutting off the French penetration and pushing their forces back south and west of the Allaine valley.

Finding the means to hold Belfort and simultaneously mounting a counterattack posed major problems for Wiese. During the period 17–19 November the German command had shifted four battalions of the *189th*

---

[17] The 3d Algerian Division had quickly noted the unit's departure, while Devers had learned of the movement from ULTRA Msg HP 7173, 200213 Nov 44, copy in ULTRA Collection, MHI. This piece of ULTRA information was also inadvertently passed down to the VI Corps on the 20th which caused great consternation among ULTRA officers because of a possible security breach. All ULTRA information had to be confirmed by some other source before it could be released and acted upon. Bussey, ULTRA Report.

Division to the *338th Division*'s sector, a step that weakened the defenses of Belfort city but did little to stay the French advance.[18] By November, the *490th Grenadiers* of the *269th Volksgrenadier Division* had also reached the front with orders to push down the Allaine valley south of Morvillars. Before the *490th* could attack, however, the French had driven past the valley and attacked Morvillars in strength. The *490th* had then deployed defensively in the vicinity of Brebotte, on the Rhone-Rhine Canal three miles northeast of Morvillars, at least blocking further advances along the canal to Dannemarie. On the same day, two *Wehrkreis V* infantry battalions, hurriedly brought across the Rhine, deployed along the canal to the northeast of the *490th Grenadiers*; it was these forces that prevented the French from crossing the waterway, which would have allowed the 5th Armored Division to begin its drive to the northeast. Additional reinforcements on the way included another infantry battalion, a small armor-infantry task force with ten tanks, and an antitank company, all from *Wehrkreis V*; meanwhile, *Wehrkreis VII* was preparing two regimental combat teams for deployment west of the Rhine. Other units that would arrive in the Belfort Gap sector within a day or two included the *280th Assault Gun Battalion* and the *654th Antitank Battalion*, the latter unit equipped with thirty-six new 88-mm. guns mounted on Mark V (Panther) tank chassis.

---

[18] Counting the *189th Division* battalion that *LXIII Corps* had committed to the *338th Division*'s sector on 15 November, the *189th* lost five battalions, representing well over half its infantry strength.

Casting about for additional forces, Wiese secured permission to employ the unreliable *30th SS Division*. Initially, the division's role was to be limited to a holding mission along the Largue River, which Route N–463 crossed at French-held Seppois. However, the redeployment of the *198th Division*, which was scheduled to launch an attack toward Delle and the Allaine valley during the night of 19–20 November, was so slow that Wiese assigned to the *30th SS* a supporting offensive role. While the *198th Division* struck for Delle, the *30th SS Division* was to retake Seppois and block the Largue valley north and south of Route N–463.

It was almost dark on 19 November before the *198th Division* had assembled sufficient forces (actually, hardly more than a regimental combat team) in the Dannemarie area for its counterattack south. With little or no prior reconnaissance, the division moved southward through terrain characterized by poor roads, swamps and lakes, and many stands of thick woods. Early on the 20th, its leading elements reached Brebotte, Vellescot, and Suarce, about halfway to the final objective, Delle; but they were finally halted after running into French armor and infantry deploying for an attack in the opposite direction, toward Dannemarie. The result was inconclusive fighting throughout the afternoon of the 20th centering around Suarce. Meanwhile, to the east, elements of the *30th SS Division* advanced to a point just over a mile north of Seppois, but had to withdraw under French pressure. The French then set up blocking positions in the Largue valley to protect the Seppois bridges, across which a steady stream of French military traffic passed throughout 20 November.

While CC2 and elements of the 9th Colonial Division turned back the *198th Division*'s first counterattacks, the 1st Armored Division was ready to begin its part of the drive north. By 1000 on 20 November, CC3 had assembled in the area of Bartenheim, three miles west of the Rhine at Rosenau; CC1, coming forward through Delle and Seppois, began pulling into Waldighofen about noon. Meanwhile, an armored reconnaissance squadron, speeding northeast along Route N–73 from Moernach, reached Huningue on the Rhine River near the Swiss border, but was unable to eliminate a strong bridgehead that the Germans had established on the west bank of the Rhine, nor could it create a bridgehead of its own on the east bank.

At this juncture, French operations also began to exhibit some confusion. Like Patch, de Lattre had no clear idea of his army's long-range objectives once the Rhine had been reached and Belfort cleared. The formulation of more specific plans to clear the entire Alsatian plains or force a crossing of the Rhine had not yet begun. Although de Lattre's general plans had called for the early seizure of Mulhouse, he began to attach more importance to a deep drive north along the Rhine to the Chalampe bridges as the offensive progressed; between 18 and 20 November, he had conveyed these ideas to Generals Bethouart and du Vigier. De Lattre was, in fact, ready to let the 1st Armored Division bypass Mulhouse on the east in order to speed the

drive north.[19] His field commanders, however, may have viewed an early seizure of undefended Mulhouse as necessary to secure the flank of a major drive north. In addition, the lure of historic Mulhouse, the second most important city of Alsace after Strasbourg, may have influenced the French officers. Whatever the case, about 1330 on 20 November, CC3 struck northwest toward Mulhouse from Bartenheim. Encountering only scattered resistance, the armored task force achieved considerable surprise as leading units pushed into that portion of Mulhouse lying south of the Rhone-Rhine Canal. On the following day, the 21st, CC3 crossed the canal and cleared most of Mulhouse north of the waterway; but it was 25 November before the last Germans evacuated the city—the same day that the last Germans left Belfort.

Du Vigier's other major unit also converged on Mulhouse. CC1, which could have swung eastward past the rear of CC3 on 20 November to initiate a drive toward Chalampe, instead headed for Altkirch, ten miles southwest of Mulhouse. By dark, leading elements were within three miles of Altkirch. After a sharp clash with *30th SS Division* troops, the task force cleared the small city on the 21st and advanced four miles farther north along the Rhone-Rhine Canal to Illfurth.

The commitment of CC1 and CC3 at Altkirch and Mulhouse left only a

---

[19] In contrast, I Corps orders dating back to 17 November provided that the 1st Armored Division would, if possible, seize Mulhouse by surprise attack, thus giving priority to Mulhouse rather than Chalampe.

small 1st Armored Division element, Detachment Colonnier, along the Rhine. Consisting of an armored infantry company and a tank destroyer platoon, it nevertheless undertook the task of driving north to Chalampe and seizing the Chalampe rail and highway bridges across the Rhine. On 20 November Detachment Colonnier moved out from Kembs, four miles north of Rosenau; reached Hombourg, five miles farther north that afternoon; and arrived at the southern outskirts of Ottmarsheim, just three miles short of Chalampe, on the morning of the 21st. But, this was as close as any French formation would come to Chalampe for two and a half months. On 23 November German counterattacks forced the detachment to withdraw to the west side of the Harth forest between the Rhine and Mulhouse. Meanwhile, the Germans were able to retain and reinforce their west bank bridgeheads at Chalampe and Huningue and, in between, establish new bridgeheads at Rosenau, Loechle, and Kembs. De Lattre's hopes for an early drive north up the Alsatian plains at least as far as Chalampe had begun to fade away and, given the First French Army's limited strength along the Rhine, may not have had great potential anyway.

The German Counterattacks

The inability of du Vigier to secure the western banks of the Rhine between Chalampe and Huningue was undoubtedly disappointing for General de Lattre. However, the continued German resistance in the area southwest of Dannemarie and the failure of Bethouart to free the 5th Armored

Division for the planned drive on Cernay must have been even more frustrating. Now, as the rest of the *198th Division* and other reinforcing elements arrived, the French situation became more precarious. Perhaps inevitably, since it had been de Lattre's forces that led off the 6th Army Group's November offensive, it was these attacking forces that first captured the attention of the German high command and were now about to feel the consequences of their early success.

By 20 November, with the arrival of German reinforcements both north and south of the Rhone-Rhine Canal west of Dannemarie, Bethouart's I Corps forces were unable to make any significant progress east of Morvillars. Now leading the corps' attack in this area, the 1st Armored Division's CC2 had been unable to advance over the canal or move along its southern side any farther than Brebotte and Vellescot. Thus, Task Force Miquel,[20] leading the 5th Armored Division from Montbeliard east along N–463 to Delle and then north through Morvillars, soon learned that the division would have to fight its own way across the canal. By midmorning TF Miquel reached Brebotte, where the unit took over from elements of CC2 and managed to advance northeast another two miles, constantly under fire from German weapons north of the canal. Forward elements attempted to cross the canal, but were thrown back with heavy losses. This

---

[20] TF Miquel consisted of a reconnaissance squadron, a company of armored infantry, a company of medium tanks, and a combat engineer platoon, all organic to the 5th Armored Division.

INFANTRY-TANK TEAM OF FRENCH 5TH ARMORED DIVISION, *Belfort, November 1944.*

check left TF Miquel with its vehicles strung out back to Morvillars and then south on Route N–19A in the Allaine valley. Forward movement was further impeded by CC2 vehicles in the Brebotte area as well as by convoys bringing supplies up to CC2 and elements of the 9th Colonial Division. Behind TF Miquel, the 5th Armored Division's next column, CC5, began just north of Delle and stretched back all the way to Montbeliard, where the 5th Division's CC4 could not even move out of its assembly areas because of the crowded road conditions. Efforts to bypass roadbound units and push more strength up to the Brebotte-Vellescot area came to naught, for both wheeled and tracked vehicles quickly bogged down in rain-soaked terrain. Soon a large traffic jam twelve miles long blocked the narrow roads all the way back to Montbeliard, and the French were unable to untangle the confused situation for about thirty-six hours.

Late in the evening of 20 November de Lattre directed CC2 to move out of the Brebotte–Vellescot–Allaine valley area in order to give the 5th Armored Division room to maneuver its stalled components. De Lattre then wanted the 5th, with its two combat commands on line, to cross the Rhone-Rhine Canal, push one task force north toward Cernay, and swing the other eastward to seize Dannemarie, previously an objective of the 1st Armored Division. If the armored units were still unable to force their way across the canal, de Lattre intended to make more changes in his plans, by having the 1st Armored Division strike out for Cernay from the Mulhouse area and by giving the 5th Armored Division the task of pushing north along the west bank of the Rhine to Chalampe. However, he realized that such a switch would absorb many precious hours, dangerously slowing the momentum of his attack. In either case the bulk of the 9th Colonial Division would have to protect the northern flank of I Corps' penetration above Route N–463, leaving no more than one detached regiment to support a more determined advance north along the west bank of the Rhine.

Sorting out all of the involved units understandably proved difficult. Somehow, during the night of 20–21 November, CC2 extricated itself from the Brebotte-Vellescot area, backtracked through Delle, and began reassembling its components in the Waldighofen area on Route N–463 by noon of the 21st. Along the Rhone-Rhine Canal, however, CC5 of the 5th Armored Division, remained partially entangled in the traffic jam and could make no progress in either crossing the canal or advancing northeast toward Dannemarie. At the same time, CC4, under local orders to secure the Suarce area and then strike north for Dannemarie, bypassed the traffic jam and reached Delle about 0930, shortly after most of CC2 had passed through on its way to the Rhine. Events now took a turn for the worse, however, from the French point of view. At Delle, CC4 learned that the Germans were holding Suarce and had cut the vital Route N–

463 near Courtelevant, behind CC2. The 1st Armored Division operating to the east was thus isolated, cut off from its sources of supply.[21]

With supply convoys of the 1st Armored Division and rear elements of CC2 already backed up at Delle, the arrival of CC4 created another traffic jam. But clearing N–463 east of Delle had immediate priority. Moving as fast as it could, CC4 managed to work its way around the confusion and overrun the German roadblock by noon. But at 1430 the Germans again cut the road, and CC4 was not able to reopen the highway until 1700. Meanwhile, elements of CC2 had returned from Waldighofen to help out near Courtelevant and to clear secondary supply routes south of N–463. Scattered German elements, however, continued to block the lesser roads below N–463, and the highway itself was still threatened by German forces operating in the forests north and south of the highway.

Redeploying part of CC2 to protect the supply routes heading east from Delle immobilized the rest of the combat command in the Waldighofen area. As a result, de Lattre's efforts to push more French strength north up the west side of the Rhine River were again frustrated. He had hoped that CC2 could continue northward from Waldighofen to take over the task of securing the Mulhouse area while CC3 regrouped for the push northward. By dark on the 21st, however, his latest hopes for the seizure of the Chalampe bridges had evaporated in

---

[21] The German roadblock apparently lay at the junction of Routes N–463 and GC–13 (leading north to Suarce), a mile or so east of Courtelevant.

the face of increasing German pressure.

Much of that pressure on 21 November came from the *198th Division*, which, by the end of the day, had finished deploying its main body from Vellescot to Courtelevant.[22] The *30th SS Division* added some pressure in the Altkirch region and along the Largue valley north of Seppois. The following day, 22 November, Wiese of *Nineteenth Army* intended to push a large part of the *198th Division*, reinforced by elements of the *654th Antitank Battalion*, south to the Swiss border near Rechesy, a mile or so south of Courtelevant. Another force, built on elements of the *30th SS Division* and the rest of the antitank battalion, was to strike south for Seppois and then continue south and southeast to help *198th Division* units cut any secondary French supply routes south of N–463. Wiese hoped that the *106th Panzer Brigade*, the *280th Assault Gun Battalion*, and a *Wehrkreis V* infantry regiment would reach the Seppois sector during the day to assist.

On the morning of 22 November the *308th Grenadiers* of the *198th Division*, again cutting Route N–463, reached Rechesy and Pfetterhouse on the Swiss border, but French forces halted a northern thrust from Pfetterhouse to Seppois. Above Seppois the attack of the *30th SS Division* came to a quick halt in the Largue valley a little over two miles north of Route N–463; to the west, French forces finally captured Suarce and pushed the

Germans back several miles toward the canal and Dannemarie. Obviously the reinforcements that Wiese expected had not arrived at the *198th Division*'s front.

Throughout the 22d the Germans continued to threaten Route N–463 east of Courtelevant and blocked the highway intermittently, but at least one 1st Armored Division fuel convoy broke through to the east.[23] The unstable situation along N–463 continued to stall traffic at the Delle bottleneck, however, and the one regiment of the 9th Colonial Division that was to have deployed to the Rhine could not move past Delle. Meanwhile, waiting at Mulhouse deep inside the German lines, CC3 had to bring in its outposts and reconnaissance units as German reinforcements, many of them crossing the Rhine over the Chalampe bridges, began moving toward the city.

During 23 November Wiese wanted the *198th Division* to continue blocking Route N–463 as well as all secondary east-west roads in the area, moving some of its forces all the way down to the Swiss border.[24] The *Nineteenth Army* commander expected that the *106th Panzer Brigade* and the *280th Assault Gun Battalion* would reach the *198th Division*'s sector during the day, but he directed the *198th* to move out on the 23d without waiting for the armor to arrive. In addition, he or-

---

[22] The organized remnants of the *338th Division* had withdrawn north of the Rhone-Rhine Canal on 19 or 20 November, and only stragglers remained to the south.

[23] The German situation at this point is briefly outlined in ULTRA Msg HP 7440, 221702 Nov 44, but the decoded intercept does not reveal any information that was not available to the French through their own intelligence sources.

[24] In part, the insistence on sealing the Swiss border stemmed from a German suspicion that the French were using Swiss roads to bypass German roadblocks.

dered the *30th SS Division,* with elements of the *654th Antitank Battalion* in support, to resume its attack southward against Seppois.

On 23 November it was the German deployments that were beset by confusion and disarray. North of Seppois, the *30th SS Division* was again unable to make any progress south and instead had to pay considerable attention to the 1st Armored Division's CC1, which had started to push west and north from Altkirch, heading for Dannemarie and threatening its rearward supply lines. To the south, the German counterattack reached its high point in the morning, when the *198th Division's 308th Grenadiers* established a strong roadblock on Route N–463 about two miles west of Seppois; secured most of the Rechesy-Pfetterhouse-Seppois road south of the main highway; and patrolled routes in and out of the Swiss border to the south. The regiment was clearly overextended, however, and could not be expected to hold these positions without reinforcement from German armor arriving that afternoon.

Again the German reinforcement effort was late, and the constant switching back and forth of units may have almost exhausted the *Nineteenth Army's* staff and transportation capabilities. Transportation problems virtually halted the southward movement of the *280th Assault Gun Battalion,* and confusion in the German high command prevented the *106th Panzer Brigade* from reaching the critical area. Apparently, the armored brigade's leading elements had moved over the Rhine River bridges at Chalampe and motored south, reaching

Ottmarsheim on Route N–68 about 1000 on 23 November. There they prepared to move farther south along the Rhine and then directly west to assist the *198th Division.* But as the panzer unit reached Ottmarsheim, Wiese informed Balck that other units had recaptured a key bridge across the Huningue Canal in the middle of the Harth forest about five miles east of Mulhouse. Acting on this information, Balck directed the *106th* to cross the bridge, bypass Mulhouse on the east, and feint toward the area between Altkirch and Mulhouse. Then the brigade was to swing back to the Huningue Canal, turn south and then west to bypass Altkirch, and drive directly toward Seppois. The entire maneuver was exceedingly complicated, and Balck only made the situation worse by directing that the armored brigade be committed piecemeal as its various components reached the front. Instead of concentrating the tank brigade for a rapid, powerful thrust, Balck invited the unit's destruction in detail.

Not surprisingly, the maneuver was a total failure. During the afternoon of 23 November, as the *106th Panzer Brigade* moved toward Mulhouse reinforced by several weak infantry battalions, it ran up against units of the 1st Armored Division and quickly became engaged in a day-long armor duel with the French. The next morning, 24 November, the battle continued with CC2 plus the artillery of the 1st Armored Division repulsing a series of attacks by forces assigned or attached to the *106th* in the area immediately east and southeast of Mulhouse. At the same time, French fire made it impossible for the German brigade to move southward.

The lack of expected armored support sealed the fate of the *308th Grenadiers* of the *198th Division.* During the afternoon of 23 November, French units regained control of Route N–463 through Seppois, isolating the *308th Grenadiers* from the rest of the *198th Division* north of the highway; the next day French forces swept the Rechesy-Pfetterhouse area, destroying most of the regiment. What was left of the *308th*—less than 300 troops—crossed the border into Switzerland to be interned. The French breakthrough at the Belfort Gap was now complete, and the German counterattack a failure.

The Belfort Gap Secured

When Bethouart's I Corps initiated its drive through the Belfort Gap on 14 November, the immediate mission of de Monsabert's II Corps was to maintain sufficient pressure across its mountainous front to keep some German attention focused on the High Vosges.[25] On 15 November, at the request of VI Corps, the II Corps had mounted a limited attack on its left flank in conjunction with the 36th Division, pushing southeast through Le Tholy toward Gerardmer. The French effort, undertaken largely by FFI units attached to the 3d Algerian Infantry Division, passed through Le Tholy and advanced along Route N–417; in doing so, the French discovered that the Germans had burned

many hamlets and farms along the way. The diversionary effort had ended quickly around the 16th, but on 19 November the 3d Algerian Division noticed that the *198th Division* was pulling out of its lines and lost no time in following up. The left wing of the division reached destroyed Gerardmer, while five miles to the south other troops of the division entered burned-out La Bresse.

On the same day, 19 November, the 1st Infantry Division, on the II Corps' right, or southern, wing, began a series of attacks to support the I Corps' 2d Moroccan Division, which was having considerable difficulty clearing the city of Belfort. Holding its position on the left in order to maintain contact with the 3d Algerian Division, the 1st Division planned to push its center east along the axis of the Chevestraye Pass and Plancher-les-Mines toward Giromagny, on Route N–465 about eight miles north of Belfort. Its leading forces would then exploit seven miles farther east to Rougemont-le-Chateau and Masevaux, at the southern edge of the Vosges; meanwhile, the division's right would push east from Ronchamp to seize Champagney and nearby high ground and then head generally east and northeast. The plan was, in effect, a modified revival of the attempt to outflank Belfort on the north that de Lattre had called off in mid-October.

The attack began on 19 November. In the center, the 1st Division found that the once-strong German defenses in the Chevestraye Pass area had been vacated, and the attackers pushed on to a ridge overlooking Plancher-les-Mines. On the right, Champagney,

---

[25] Information on II Corps operations in this section is based on de Lattre, *History,* pp. 259–60; *Le 2e C.A. dans la Bataille pour la Liberation de la France,* pp. 59–71; *Historiques Succincts, 3e Partie,* pp. 127–53.

where the French encountered extensive minefields and liberally sown booby traps, fell the same day with only spotty resistance, and troops of the 1st Division met elements of the 2d Moroccan Division near the Champagney reservoir to the south.

The Moroccans, meanwhile, had penetrated farther into the city of Belfort and had slowly begun to eliminate the remaining German defenders. On the 20th, in order to allow the I Corps to concentrate on operations to the east, General de Lattre took direct command of the 2d Moroccan Division and two days later passed control of the unit to de Monsabert.

While the 3d Algerian and 2d Moroccan Divisions progressed slowly in the northern and southern sectors of the widened II Corps zone, the 1st Infantry Division in the center continued to forge ahead and moved into Giromagny north of Belfort nearly unopposed on the 22d. The division's left flank then pressed toward the great bulk of the Ballon d'Alsace, six miles north of Giromagny, as the right, keeping in touch with the Moroccans to the south, reached Valdoie, two miles north of Belfort.

Impressed by the 1st Division's progress and concerned over the German counterattacks south of the Rhone-Rhine Canal, de Lattre issued new orders on 22 November, calling for a general exploitation across the First French Army's entire front. Bethouart's I Corps was to advance north and de Monsabert's II Corps move generally east, thereby squeezing the German forces in the middle. A northern advance in strength to Mulhouse, which was already in

French hands, would obviously threaten the rear of the German counterattacking forces around Dannemarie, as well as those defending along the Rhone-Rhine Canal to the west. Each side would thus be attempting to attack the rear of the other.

De Lattre's new orders called for the II Corps to push its center through Rougemont-le-Chateau and drive for Burnhaupt on the Doller River. The Moroccans on the corps' right would secure Belfort, and the Algerians on the left would push east across the Vosges through the Bussang and Schlucht passes. This accomplished, de Monsabert's forces were to take Cernay, ten miles west of Mulhouse, and join Bethouart's I Corps forces, now reinforced by the rest of the 4th Moroccan Mountain Division from the Italian Alpine front. The two corps would then begin a concentrated push north to Colmar and eventually Strasbourg, thus liberating all of Alsace.[26]

On 23 and 24 November the 1st Infantry Division again made significant progress, reaching the crest of the Ballon d'Alsace on the left, the outskirts of Sewen on the Doller River in the center, and a point just two miles short of Rougemont-le-Chateau on the right. Despite these gains, however, de Lattre decided on the 24th that his plans were too ambitious. In the Vosges, the 3d Algerian Division continued to meet determined German resistance and made little progress; on the corps' right the 2d Moroccan Division remained stalled by some German-held strongpoints in and

---

[26] First Fr Army Genl Opns Order 163, 22 Nov 44; de Lattre, *History*, p. 269.

around Belfort. To the east, I Corps faced steadily increasing German pressure in the Mulhouse region, while the *198th Division,* now with some armored support, still had sufficient strength north of Route N–463 to threaten I Corps' main supply route in the Courtelevant-Seppois area. Also influencing his thoughts was the imminent loss of the 1st Division, which would be pulled out of its lines within a few days to redeploy to the Atlantic coast for Operation INDEPENDENCE.[27] The 2d Moroccan Division (plus CC6) and the 3d Algerian Division would then have to take over the 1st Division's sector, greatly diluting the combat strength of the II Corps. Finally, de Lattre had to take into consideration the losses of men and equipment that the First French Army had suffered over the past ten days (14–24 November) as well as his declining stocks of ammunition, fuel, and other supplies.

Recognizing the limitations of his strength and realizing that a major operation to clear all of Alsace was at least temporarily out of the question, de Lattre issued new orders on the 24th outlining a more conservative plan.[28] The primary objectives of the revised plan were securing the entire Belfort Gap area and destroying the remaining forces of the *LXIII Corps* as far north as the Doller River—roughly

the region south of Sewen, Masevaux, Burnhaupt, and Mulhouse. For this purpose de Lattre's orders called for a double envelopment by the I and II Corps, with the pincers to close at Burnhaupt. Bethouart's I Corps, holding firmly at Mulhouse, was to push part of its strength west from Mulhouse and northwest from Altkirch toward Burnhaupt, and de Monsabert's II Corps was to strike for Burnhaupt from the west. In the II Corps' sector the main effort would have to be made by the 2d Moroccan Division and its attached CC6, but de Monsabert intended to keep the 1st Infantry Division in the line pushing eastward as long as possible.

At dawn on 25 November de Monsabert's forces were surprised to find that the German troops facing them in the gap area had withdrawn during the night, and both the 1st Infantry and 2d Moroccan Division immediately accelerated their drives east. On that day the 1st Division pushed to within half a mile of strongly defended Masevaux; to the south, the Moroccans were not even able to regain contact with the retreating Germans. On the other hand, de Monsabert realized that the Germans were probably trying to build up some sort of defensive line along the trace of the Doller River in order to hold up the French advance and extract their remaining forces from the Dannemarie-Suarce area. Both he and Bethouart would have to move their forces as rapidly as possible if their trap was to close before the Germans could escape.

De Lattre received a needed boost on the 26th when General Devers announced yet another postponement of First French Army redeployments

---

[27] As of 24 November the 1st Infantry Division was still scheduled to move westward during the period 28 November–7 December, with the 1st Armored Division following a week or so later.

[28] De Lattre discussed the basics of the new plan with Generals de Monsabert and Bethouart during the afternoon of 23 November, and he issued the plan in directive form about noon on the 24th as First French Army General Operations Order 167. De Lattre, *History,* p. 272.

FRENCH TROOPS RAISE TRICOLOR
over Chateau de Belfort, November 1944.

for INDEPENDENCE. Now the 1st Infantry Division would not have to be pulled out of the lines and reassembled until 2 December, and the 1st Armored Division not until the 5th.[29] This delay enabled both French corps to resume their envelopments with confidence, and on the afternoon of 28 November, after much bitter fighting, the pincers closed at Burnhaupt.

The completion of de Lattre's "Burnhaupt Maneuver" marked the end of the First French Army's November offensive. By seizing both Belfort and Mulhouse, the French had completely outflanked the German defenses in the Vosges Mountains

and, in the process, further eroded the German forces facing the 6th Army Group. The Burnhaupt Maneuver, taking place from 25 through 28 November, had bagged some 10,000 German prisoners, most of them from the *LXIII Corps,* which had lost at least another 5,000 prisoners earlier during the period 14–24 November.[30] However, French manpower losses from 14 through 28 November were also serious and numbered 1,300 killed, 4,500 wounded, 140 missing, and over 4,500 nonbattle casualties. French materiel losses included about 55 medium tanks, 15 light tanks, 15 tank destroyers, 15 armored cars, and 50 half-tracks, while many more combat vehicles had been damaged, and all were in need of overhaul. Moreover, the task of clearing all of upper Alsace was only half completed.

De Lattre's inability to achieve all his objectives reflected some of the inherent weaknesses of his army. Although de Lattre himself had personally supervised the actions of both corps, giving de Monsabert and Bethouart considerably less freedom than Patch had afforded Truscott, Haislip, and Brooks, his span of control was limited, especially as the advance began to stretch French staff and communications capabilities thin. In addition, many of his key units, such as the 5th Armored Division, were relatively inexperienced, and many of

---

[29] 6th Army Gp LI 3, 26 Nov 44.

[30] De Lattre, *History,* p. 282. On p. 284 de Lattre adds another 10,000 Germans killed during the period 14–28 November, for a total of some 25,000 killed or captured; but von Luttichau, "German Operations," ch. 25, gives *Nineteenth Army's* total losses during the period 10–30 November only as "in excess of 10,000 men."

his infantry units were made up of recently recruited soldiers with little more than the rudiments of military training. The trained military technicians necessary to fill out the First French Army's ordnance, signal, engineer, and other support units were in extremely short supply, making it difficult for French forces to sustain an extended armywide battle for any length of time. The projected losses to support Operation INDEPENDENCE were another major factor that hampered French planning, causing confusion and hesitation. Thus, although de Lattre was unable to drive all the way up the Rhine valley, he probably did the best anyone could have with his existing resources and constraints. In this respect, Wiese's insistence that the *198th Division* be brought south and deployed as quickly as possible across the 1st Armored Division's line of communications probably saved the day for the *Nineteenth Army*. However, given the confusing orders from Balck, the Germans were fortunate not to have suffered even heavier losses in the Belfort Gap.

Whether an early seizure of the Chalampe bridges would have affected the situation is moot. French control of Chalampe might have left Mulhouse in German hands and stretched du Vigier's slender supply lines even thinner. A stronger drive north along the Rhine might also have made it easier for Wiese, if he had the nerve, to concentrate the *198th Division* and other early reinforcements for a more intensive counterattack south of Dannemarie, obviously with undesirable

consequences for du Vigier's armor. The arrival of reinforcements such as the *106th Panzer Brigade* might have been delayed if they were forced to cross the Rhine north of Chalampe, but the lag would have been of no consequence. In short, the German infantry counterattack south of Dannemarie, which temporarily interdicted the French 1st Armored Division's supply lines, was the primary factor behind de Lattre's inability to project more strength along the Rhine throughout the offensive.

The end of the battle on 28 November saw the French consolidating their gains in and around Belfort, while the Germans continued to pressure I Corps units in the Mulhouse area and in the region between Mulhouse and the Rhine, building up new defenses along the line of the Doller River west of Mulhouse and holding tenaciously to the mountainous terrain north of Masevaux. Although Wiese still controlled a large portion of the Alsatian plains in the region around Colmar, General Devers now believed that those units of the *Nineteenth Army* still west of the Rhine would soon withdraw across the river. Furthermore, he estimated that once the forces of the First French Army had caught their breath, they would be able to police up the rest of the German troops between Mulhouse and Strasbourg, with the help perhaps of one or two American divisions. However, considering the winter weather and the exhaustion of his own troops and supplies, de Lattre was by no means so hopeful.

CHAPTER XXIV

Lost Opportunities

By the end of November, Devers' 6th Army Group had shattered Wiese's *Nineteenth Army* in a series of hammering blows. Haislip's XV Corps had led off on 13 November in the north, followed one day later by Bethouart's II Corps in the south. In the center, Brooks' VI Corps had already begun the first of several preliminary attacks to set up his main thrust over the Vosges. Nowhere did the initial Allied assaults meet any effective German resistance. By 19 November, the day that de Lattre's forces reached the Rhine, the 3d Algerian Division had finally occupied Gerardmer deep in the Vosges; Brooks' 100th Division had taken Raon-l'Etape; and Haislip's infantry had advanced nearly to Sarrebourg. Two days later, on the 21st, Leclerc's armor had begun exploiting north and south of both Sarrebourg and Saverne nearly unopposed; Brooks had ordered his infantry divisions to begin a pursuit across the High Vosges; and du Vigier's French 1st Armored Division had taken Mulhouse and Altkirch deep in the German rear. All this had been accomplished in cold and extremely wet weather over terrain that was either heavily forested and mountainous or laced with innumerable rivers, canals, and other small but flooded waterways.

The two major German counterattacks, the excursions of the *Panzer Lehr* in the north and the *198th Division* in the south had been *ad hoc* affairs, poorly planned and never reinforced. The German high command and control system was incapable of keeping pace with the tempo of the Allied operations and was unable to respond effectively. As a result, the U.S. Seventh Army and the French First Army were slowly squeezing the German *Nineteenth* in a giant vise: Haislip's XV Corps reached the Rhine on the 23d, and Brooks' VI Corps began pouring down the other side of the Vosges on the 25th; de Lattre's First French Army occupied Belfort and the entire gap area during the same period. In the process, six of the *Nineteenth Army*'s eight infantry divisions were nearly destroyed: the *553d* and *708th* on the approaches to Saverne; the *716th* and *16th* in the High Vosges; and the *338th* and *198th* around Belfort. Only the *269th* and the *159th* remained in fair condition, ensconced in the heart of the Vosges Mountains immediately west of Colmar. For the moment it appeared that only these two divisions (to be joined shortly by two more from the Netherlands) and a large mishmash of personnel and units—the sweepings from both the Vosges-Alsatian battlefields and the German trans-Rhine military regions—were left to defend the borders of the German Reich against the still relatively undamaged 6th Army Group.

The Colmar Pocket

By 24 November the German high command was constantly reevaluating the rapidly deteriorating situation of Wiese's *Nineteenth Army*. Both it and *Army Group G* faced severe difficulties. In the north, the Allied breakthrough to Strasbourg had opened a gap of fifteen to twenty miles between the *First* and *Nineteenth Armies;* in the south, French forces had made a similar penetration, thus threatening Wiese's army with a double envelopment. Isolated and beset by major attacks from the Seventh Army's VI Corps in the center, Wiese knew that his forces were once again close to complete collapse. Fresh units as well as more replacements, and more equipment were desperately needed if the *Nineteenth* was to survive this new crisis intact.[1]

Initially both the *Nineteenth Army* and *Army Group G* had lacked timely, accurate information about the situation in the south, especially the status of the *198th Division* in the Seppois area. Early on the 24th the two headquarters apparently assumed that the *198th* still held blocking positions from Suarce to the Swiss border, not realizing that the area had been lost to the French that morning. However, even without full knowledge of the *198th Division*'s operations, General Wiese, commanding the *Nineteenth Army*, understood that the situation in the south was rapidly deteriorating. The last defenses in and around Belfort were about to collapse, and the operations of the *106th Panzer Brigade* in the Mulhouse area were achieving little. With no more reserves and no reinforcements expected, Wiese recommended to Balck that *Army Group G*'s southern boundary be pulled back to the east and north immediately.

Balck agreed with Wiese's assessment. The *Army Group G* commander judged that the attacking Allied army group would probably attempt to encircle and destroy the *Nineteenth Army* as quickly as possible by means of concurrent drives south from Strasbourg and north from Mulhouse. During the morning of 24 November, he therefore suggested to von Rundstedt at *OB West* that the *Nineteenth Army* withdraw on its southern front to the line Ballon d'Alsace–Dolleren–Rougemont-le-Chateau–Montreux. Although the proposed withdrawal would surrender the city of Belfort as well as the last German strongpoints in the region, it would also shorten and consolidate the *Nineteenth Army*'s southern front.

Apparently *OB West* made no immediate reply to this recommendation, which was probably just as well because, during the course of the day, Balck learned that French troops had seized the Ballon d'Alsace[2] and were

---

[1] German information in this chapter is based on von Luttichau, "German Operations," chs. 23–25.

[2] Actually, troops of the French 1st Infantry Division reached the crest of the Ballon d'Alsace on 24

nearing Dolleren. This news, together with more information about the worsening situations in the Belfort and Seppois sectors, evidently impelled Balck, during the afternoon of 24 November, to suggest an even deeper and more extensive withdrawal along *Nineteenth Army*'s southern flank. Balck recommended to von Rundstedt that a new, southward-facing defensive line be established ten miles farther back, anchored at Thann and extending through Route N–66 and Mulhouse and then east across the Harth forest to the Rhine. With such a withdrawal, Balck concluded, the *198th Division*, the *106th Panzer Brigade*, and the *654th Antitank Battalion* could be released from the Mulhouse-Seppois area and dispatched northward to deal with the Saverne Gap–Strasbourg penetration of the U.S. Seventh Army.

Balck's second recommendation created some consternation at *OB West* and *OKW*, for it clearly implied that Balck was proposing to give up the *Nineteenth Army*'s presumed hold on the Swiss border as well as a considerable chunk of German-controlled real estate in southern Alsace. Reflecting a lack of accurate information, von Rundstedt still believed that the major threat to the *Nineteenth Army* came from the Allied drive through the Belfort Gap; he could not understand how *Army Group G* could consider redeploying the *198th Division* northward, when all indications were that the *Nineteenth Army*'s southern flank needed reinforcement. The situ-

ation in the north, he felt, could be better handled by the *Panzer Lehr Division* and other units already in the Sarrebourg-Saverne-Strasbourg area.

During the course of the late afternoon, as information on the situation in the Saverne area arrived at *OB West*, von Rundstedt began to reconsider the matter. With the apparent failure of the *Panzer Lehr* to accomplish its mission, he became pessimistic and notified *OKW* that only immediate reinforcements—at least two panzer divisions and one infantry division, all fully up to strength—could salvage the situation in northern Alsace. But *OKW*, husbanding all German reserves for the Ardennes counteroffensive, had little to offer, as von Rundstedt must have expected. That being the case, the *OB West* commander informed his superiors that further efforts to close the gap between his two armies would have to be abandoned, and that the *Nineteenth Army* would have to fall back to avoid destruction.

Although von Rundstedt still hoped that Wiese's endangered army could hold at least temporarily along its southern flank, both he and Balck had come to the obvious conclusion that the only solution to the *Nineteenth Army*'s difficulties was a complete withdrawal across the Rhine, and they passed that evaluation on to *OKW*. As they expected, however, Hitler had no intention of voluntarily giving up reannexed Alsace to the French and refused to discuss the matter; the German political leader even ordered his army planners to assess the possibility of canceling the Ardennes counteroffensive in favor of a major counterattack in Alsace and Lorraine.

November, but they lost much of it to a German counterattack on the 25th. The Germans then held the Ballon until the afternoon of 26 November.

Although he quickly abandoned this idea, Hitler remained adamant in his refusal to authorize a withdrawal to the east bank of the Rhine in the south, and he insisted that the areas of Alsace still under German control be held at all costs. However necessary or logical from a purely military standpoint, the Fuhrer would countenance no withdrawal across the Rhine. Wiese's army would either survive or die.

In the face of Hitler's decision, von Rundstedt had difficulty authorizing any withdrawals for Wiese's reeling forces. Between the evening of 24 November and the afternoon of the 26th, he approved a series of local boundary changes based on individual tactical situations, but felt he could go no further. Forbidding Balck and Wiese to redeploy the *198th Division* northward, he emphasized that southern Alsace was to be held at all costs and that only minor adjustments within their defensive zones would be considered.

With Hitler's reluctant consent, *OB West* issued orders late on 24 November authorizing the *Nineteenth Army* to fall back on a new defensive line that more or less reflected the gains the Allies had made. The boundary between the *First* and *Nineteenth Armies* was again moved south, this time to Erstein, on the Ill River about twelve miles south of Strasbourg and four west of the Rhine. The defenses were to extend westward nineteen miles past Barr to Le Hohwald, located in a particularly rugged section of the Vosges. From Le Hohwald, the new westward defensive line was to slant southwest thirteen miles to Ste. Marie-aux-Mines on Route N–59 and

then south about thirty-five miles, generally following the *Vosges Ridge Position*, to Dolleren, deep in the upper reaches of the Doller River and five miles east of the Ballon d'Alsace. The realignment would generally affect only the *LXIV Corps* and the *XC Corps*, the redesignation given the *IV Luftwaffe Field Corps* on 22 November. The situation on *Nineteenth Army's* southern flank still remained vague, as did the positions of the *First Army* above Erstein. Until the battlefield became clearer, little more could be done.

In the Vosges and north of Colmar, the German units that were still intact began occupying the new line on the night of 24–25 November without incident. Meanwhile, on the *Nineteenth Army's* northern and southern flanks, the situation continued to deteriorate. By late afternoon of 26 November von Rundstedt, with accurate and up-to-date information finally at hand, concluded that the southern flank of the *Nineteenth Army* had to be withdrawn immediately, and he finally persuaded *OKW* to approve a new defensive line somewhat short of the trace that General Balck had originally proposed. The new southern main line of resistance was to begin at Masevaux, about six miles southwest of Thann, and extend generally eastward along the axis of the Doller River to Mulhouse and then on to Hombourg and the Rhine. Further discussion between *OB West* and *OKW* provided for the redeployment of the *198th Division* and *106th Panzer Brigade* to the *Nineteenth Army's* northern flank, not for Balck's avowed purpose of striking at XV Corps' penetration to Strasbourg, but rather to help hold the new Erstein–Barr–Le Hohwald line north of Colmar. Von Rundstedt's earlier decision to halt further attempts to close the gap between the *First* and *Nineteenth Armies* went unchallenged.

During the night of 26–27 November Hitler gave his reluctant assent to the withdrawal in the south, and about 0200 on the 27th von Rundstedt issued the necessary orders. At the time, Wiese retained some faint hope of driving the French out of the Mulhouse area, and German troops near Seppois were still threatening the French supply route on N–463. But time was running out. The German forces holding out in the Belfort city area had already withdrawn during the night of 24–25 November; during the 26th, French forces reached the outskirts of Masevaux, threatening the *Nineteenth Army*'s new Doller River line before it was firmly established. Wiese had no time to consider further attacks against the French flanks or rear.

The Hitler-approved directives of 24 and 27 November committed the *Nineteenth Army* to the defense of a vast bridgehead west of the Rhine, a bridgehead that soon became known in the Allied camp as the Colmar Pocket. Initially, the salient had a base along the Rhine River forty-five miles long between the Erstein and Mulhouse areas; in the center it extended more than twenty-five miles westward from the Rhine into the High Vosges. Both *OKW* and *OB West* estimated that, without major reinforcements, the *Nineteenth Army* could hold the Colmar Pocket bridgehead for about three weeks, a time span probably dictated by the date set for the launching of the Ardennes offensive.

Even this task, however, was dependent on the influx of thousands of replacements for the army's eight hollowed-out infantry divisions and at least some antitank, artillery, and assault guns. If successful, the bridgehead would keep the Allies at arm's length from the German border and would threaten both flanks of the 6th Army Group's two penetrations. But the creation and maintenance of the pocket would also consume steadily diminishing German military resources that might be used more profitably elsewhere.

A Dubious Decision

On 24 November, the Allied high command initiated a series of decisions that would have a major impact on the course of the war in Europe. At the time, Patch's Seventh Army, elated by the success of its advance through the Saverne Gap to Strasbourg and the Rhine, was planning more ambitious undertakings. Despite some uncertainties regarding the security of XV Corps' flanks both east and west of the Vosges, and despite the fact that forward elements of the *Panzer Lehr Division* were scarcely six miles away from the XV Corps' command post at Sarrebourg, planners from the 6th Army Group, Seventh Army, and XV Corps staffs were speeding preparations for a Rhine crossing in the Rastatt area north of Strasbourg. Rather than move south, Devers still preferred to have the Seventh Army strike north across the Rhine against all German expectations. Orders had already gone out alerting specialized river-crossing units to start moving to forward assembly areas, and by the afternoon of 24 November, amphibious truck (DUKW) companies were rolling toward the Rhine from rear area depots and training centers.[3]

As yet no firm date had been set for the Rhine River assault. Before the November offensive, however, Devers and Patch had looked forward to a Rhine crossing between 10 and 20 December, and they now accelerated the projected effort to the first week of December. A VI Corps exploitation north through a XV Corps bridgehead would begin no later than the second week of the month. The project, however, immediately ran up against serious opposition within the Allied camp.

On 24 November, as the German high command debated its options, Eisenhower and Bradley began a tour of the Allied southern front. The two American generals first visited the Third Army command post at Nancy, where they found Patton's attacking forces roadbound and nearly halted. Abominable weather, flooding, and military traffic were breaking up what few good roads remained passable in Patton's sector, and elsewhere the ground had turned into a sea of mud. Additional factors delaying Patton's troops just to the north of the Seventh Army included a high rate of nonbattle casualties (with trench foot predominating), lack of infantry replacements, extensive German minefields, a growing shortage of artillery

ammunition, and miscellaneous other supply problems.[4]

During the brief stopover, Patton urged that either a portion of his seventy-mile front be assigned to Devers or the XV Corps be returned to Third Army control, preferably the latter.[5] Bradley was also anxious to have his main effort against the Saar basin gather some momentum, but judged that a transferal of forces would be too time-consuming. Instead he favored narrowing Patton's front so that the Third Army commander could concentrate his attacking forces against a smaller number of objectives; reassigning the southern portion of Patton's zone to Patch's Seventh Army would best satisfy this requirement. Although Eisenhower was apparently noncommittal, he also seemed to have made up his mind that something drastic had to be done to assist Patton.

Eisenhower and Bradley next traveled to Luneville. There, after joining Devers and Patch, they proceeded first to Haislip's new XV Corps headquarters at Sarrebourg and then to Brooks' recently opened command post at St. Die.[6] At Sarrebourg the energetic Haislip proved an anxious host, exuberant over the capture of Strasbourg but concerned over the

---

[3] See Ltr, Engr Seventh Army to CO 40th Engr Regt, 21 Nov 44 (as cited in Seventh Army Diary, 21 Nov 44); Seventh Army OI 19, 24 Nov 44; *Seventh Army Rpt*, II, 418–19; comments of John S. Gutherie, former G–3, Seventh Army, on draft MS, Oct 88 (hereafter referred to as "Gutherie comments").

[4] For further details see Cole, *The Lorraine Campaign*, ch. 12.

[5] For an account, see Hansen Diary, 24 Nov 44, Chester B. Hansen Papers, MHI. (Hansen was one of Eisenhower's aides.)

[6] The account of the Eisenhower-Bradley visit to the 6th Army Group is based on the following sources: Devers Diary, 24–25 Nov 44; Hansen Diary (first draft), 24–25 Nov 44, Chester B. Hansen Papers, MHI; Intervs, Thomas Griess with Devers, 29–30 Dec 69 and 17–20 Aug 70 (copy CMH); Seventh Army Diary, 24–25 Nov 44; and XV Corps AAR, Nov 44.

southward progress of the *Panzer Lehr* through the Sarre River valley. At St. Die, the usually serious Brooks was more relaxed, elated over his success in finally pushing his command over the Vosges and urging all of his scattered forces to continue the pursuit. Within both headquarters Eisenhower and Bradley found the corps staffs busily planning to push their forces farther east, seize bridgeheads over the Rhine, and cross into Germany itself. Eisenhower, however, quickly ended these preparations. Concerned about Patton's flagging offensive, he wanted the Seventh Army's axis of attack reoriented from the east to the north, through the Low Vosges and against the *First Army*'s southern flank. At Haislip's command post, he even issued verbal orders on the 24th directing the XV Corps to halt all preparations for a Rhine crossing, change direction immediately, and advance generally northward astride the Low Vosges Mountains in close support of the Third Army. Supporting Patton's advance into the Saar basin was to have first priority.

Somewhat stunned by the new orders, Devers was determined to challenge them. Returning to the 6th Army Group headquarters at the Heritage Hotel in Vittel that evening, the three principal American ground commanders had a late formal dinner and then retired to Devers' private office to talk over the entire matter. The ensuing discussion lasted until the early hours of the following day and saw a heated argument between Eisenhower, Bradley, and Devers.[7]

Eisenhower continued to insist that Devers halt all preparations for a Rhine crossing and turn the Seventh Army north to assist Patton's forces as quickly as possible. Although current SHAEF directives had provided for the opportunistic seizure of bridgeheads across the Rhine during the November offensive by all participants,[8] the Supreme Commander now ruled firmly against a Seventh Army crossing. Furthermore, he proposed transferring two divisions from the 6th Army Group to Bradley's 12th and extending the boundary of Haislip's XV Corps to the northwest. Devers objected bitterly to each of these measures, arguing that the Seventh Army was the force that ought to be strengthened and not the Third. If assisting Patton was the primary objective then, he contended, a Seventh Army Rhine crossing at Rastatt followed by a drive north to envelop the Saar basin was the best solution. On this point, however, Bradley strongly disagreed: attempting to force the Rhine against the prepared defensive positions of the West Wall was foolhardy and would only lead to failure. Exasperated, Devers countered that the Germans currently had few if any troops in front of the Seventh Army and that Patch's reconnaissance patrols across the Rhine had found the defenses there completely unmanned. Eisenhower was unmoved. He instructed Devers to use whatever strength was necessary to clean up the area between the Vosges and the

---

[7] The Hansen diary only notes that the meeting took place, and the author has reconstructed the

discussion from information in the Devers diary, the Griess-Devers interviews, and Memo, Bradley to G–3, HQ, 12th Army Group, 26 Nov 44, Bradley Papers, MHI (copy CMH).

[8] SCAF–114, 28 Oct 44; SCAF–118, 2 Nov 44.

Rhine but to turn the Seventh Army north as quickly as possible, attacking west and east of the Low Vosges. There would be no Rhine crossing. Eisenhower did compromise, however, promising Devers he would allow the 6th Army Group to keep its two divisions and even obtain a second armored division, if Devers agreed to keep his troops on the west bank of the Rhine. In the end, the 6th Army Group commander had no choice but to go along with the new directive, suggesting only that the XV Corps take over part of Patton's sector west of the Low Vosges in order to give Haislip more room to maneuver (not wishing him to be limited to the mountains). But none of the three commanders was fully satisfied with the results of the meeting, and all were stung by the tenor of the discussions. The Supreme Commander reportedly came out of the conference "mad as hell" over Devers' open criticism of his operational strategy, while Devers emerged equally angry, wondering if he was "a member of the same team." [9] Thus, instead of abating, the tension between Eisenhower and Devers seemed only to have grown.

The following day Eisenhower and Bradley concluded their visit, touring the French front before returning north via Vittel on the morning of the 26th. Nothing Eisenhower saw in the southern sector of the 6th Army Group altered his decisions. Therefore, between 25 and 26 November, Patch's Seventh Army staff drew up new plans based on Eisenhower's instructions. As quickly as possible the XV Corps was to advance generally northward with its right on the crest of the Low Vosges and its left along a boundary between the 6th and 12th Army Groups, which would be pushed westward and northward in order to narrow Patton's front. Ultimately, the Seventh Army's VI Corps would also head northward on the eastern side of the Vosges, clearing the area from the Low Vosges Mountains to the Rhine. [10] Satisfied that they had no alternative, Patch and Devers wanted to turn the Seventh Army north as rapidly as possible before the Germans could move reinforcements into the area, especially in the sector west of the Low Vosges along the German border.

The new army group boundary, effective 26 November, ran north roughly along the Sarre River, from Fenetrange to Ramstein in Germany; there it turned east to cross the Rhine near Mannheim, about seventy-five miles north of Strasbourg (*Map 30*). Both Devers and Patton were displeased with the arrangement. The 6th Army Group commander felt that the natural boundary was the Saar River itself between Fenetrange and Saarbrucken, while Patton believed that the Vosges chain was the more logical dividing line. Both were un-

----

[9] This final material is based on notes taken by Brig. Gen. Daniel Noce, the AFHQ Assistant Chief of Staff for Operations (G–3), who visited the SHAEF theater 2–7 December and spoke with both Brig. Gen. Walter Bedell Smith, Eisenhower's chief of staff, and Brig. Gen. David G. Barr, Devers' chief of staff, regarding the Vittel meeting. See Notes of 4 Dec 44, Daniel Noce Papers, U.S. Military Academy, West Point, N.Y.

[10] Seventh Army Diary, 25 and 26 Nov 44; 6th Army Gp LI 3, 26 Nov 44; Rad, 6th Army Gp to SHAEF, BX–20454, 26 Nov 44; Ltr, CG Seventh Army to CGs XV and VI Corps, subj: Directive, dated 27 Nov 44; and SCAF–136, 27 Nov 44.

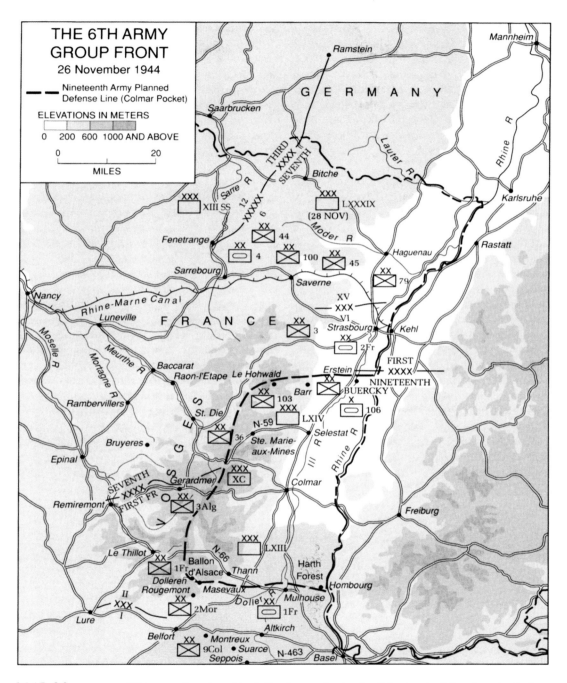

THE 6TH ARMY
GROUP FRONT
26 November 1944

- - - Nineteenth Army Planned
Defense Line (Colmar Pocket)

ELEVATIONS IN METERS

0   200 600 1000 AND ABOVE

0   20
         MILES

Mannheim

GERMANY

Ramstein

Saarbrucken

Lauter R.

Rhine R.

Karlsruhe

THIRD
XXXX
SEVENTH

Sarre R.

Bitche

Rastatt

XXX
XIII SS

12
XXXX
6

XXX
LXXXIX
(28 NOV)

Moder R.

Fenetrange

XX
44

Haguenau

Sarrebourg

XX
4

XX
100

XX
45

XX
79

Saverne

Nancy

Rhine-Marne Canal

Luneville

FRANCE

XV
XXX
VI

Strasbourg

Kehl

Moselle R.

Mortagne R.

Meurthe R.

Baccarat

XX
3

XX
2Fr

Raon-l'Etape

Le Hohwald

Erstein

FIRST
XXXX
NINETEENTH

Rambervillers

St. Die

XX
103

Barr

XX
BUERCKY

XXX
LXIV

X
106

Bruyeres

Epinal

XX
36

N-59

Ste. Marie-
aux-Mines

Selestat

Rhine R.

III R.

SEVENTH
XXXX
FIRST FR

Gerardmer

XXX
XC

Colmar

Remiremont

XX
3Alg

Freiburg

Le Thillot

N-66

XXX
LXIII

Harth
Forest

XX
1Fr

Ballon
d'Alsace

Thann

Masevaux

Dolleren
Rougemont

XX
2Mor

Dolle
XX

Mulhouse

Hombourg

XX
1Fr

II
XXX
I

Lure

Belfort

XX
9Col

Montreux

Suarce

N-463

Altkirch

Seppois

Basel

MAP 30   This map is printed in full color at the back of the book, following the Index.

doubtedly interested in the politics of the matter: Patton's XII Corps might have been transferred to Devers if the Sarre River boundary had been chosen, and Devers' XV Corps could have been lost to Patton had the Vosges been selected. The 26 November boundary was thus a SHAEF-imposed compromise that satisfied no one.[11]

Whatever the influence of the boundary arrangements, Eisenhower's basic decision against an early Rhine crossing by the Seventh Army had a profound effect on the course of operations along the western front. The specific results are, of course, debatable. At the time, however, Devers, Patch, and Haislip were certain that the XV Corps could seize a bridgehead in the Rastatt area with relative ease and that the VI Corps would soon be ready to exploit northward through that bridgehead, thereby outflanking German fortifications west of the Rhine. Devers was also confident—mistakenly, as it turned out [12]—that the First French Army, with the aid of one or two Seventh Army divisions, would make short work of the battered *Nineteenth Army* in the Colmar Pocket. At the time neither he nor his staff appears to have been aware of Hitler's determination to hold on to

lower Alsace.

Devers was clearly upset over the results of the meeting with Eisenhower and Bradley. The 6th Army Group commander regarded Eisenhower's decision as a major error, holding that he ought to have reinforced success—that is, the Seventh Army's breakthrough to the Rhine—and that Eisenhower was more concerned with territorial objectives than with destroying the enemy. Devers judged that Patton had started his armored exploitation too early and without due regard for the terrible weather conditions.[13] Furthermore, he believed that Patton's Third Army logically belonged in the 6th Army Group and that the Third and Seventh Armies working closely together could easily crack the German Saar basin defenses, if that was what Eisenhower wanted.[14]

Obviously these sentiments were not shared by Eisenhower and Bradley. The Supreme Commander appeared extremely reluctant to capitalize on the Seventh Army's unexpectedly rapid breakthrough to Strasbourg and the Rhine, and he seemed to attach little or no significance to the concomitant First French Army drive through the Belfort Gap to the Rhine and the possible collapse of the *Nineteenth Army*. Instead, Eisenhower held to his policy that called for destroying all German forces west of the Rhine, from the Netherlands south to the Swiss border, before initiating any major operations east of the river. His operational concept also dictated that the main Allied effort take place in

---

[11] In addition to sources previously cited, the boundary material is based on the following: George S. Patton, Jr., *War As I Knew It* (Boston: Houghton Mifflin, 1947), p. 177; Devers Diary, 24 and 26 Nov and 19 Dec 44; Blumenson, *Patton Papers, I, 1940–1945* (Boston: Houghton Mifflin, 1974), p. 582.

[12] Indicative of Devers' early optimism about the reduction of the Colmar Pocket was the fact that 6th Army Group LI 3 of 26 November called for the 36th Division to be withdrawn from Colmar Pocket operations by 30 November. LI 4 of 2 December removed that restriction.

[13] Devers Diary, 23 Nov 44.
[14] See Devers Diary, 24 Nov and 5 Dec 44.

the north. Perhaps no one at SHAEF had expected the comparatively small 6th Army Group to achieve so much, especially in the tough Vosges terrain. Furthermore, a Rhine crossing by the Seventh Army might well have demanded that Eisenhower switch his main effort from the sector of Montgomery's 21st Army Group to that of Devers' 6th Army Group, an extremely difficult task. With these considerations in mind, Eisenhower may have simply concluded that he was having enough trouble dealing with Montgomery and the British without trying to force through such a major change of direction in the main Allied ground thrust. The political demands of waging a coalition war could not be denied.[15]

In balance, Devers was fortunate to escape from the conference with his command intact, having only narrowly averted the loss of at least two experienced divisions, and perhaps the entire XV Corps as well, to Patton's Third Army. Far from being reinforced, Devers had to face the extension of the army group boundary to the west and north, which would only limit the power that the Seventh Army, without reinforcements, could bring to bear. The Seventh Army, in turn, was to lose three more experienced divisions temporarily: Leclerc's French 2d Armored Division and Dahlquist's 36th Infantry Division to help de Lattre's forces clear the Colmar Pocket; and O'Daniel's 3d Infantry Division, which was tasked to guard Strasbourg and cover the gap

between Devers' two widely separated armies. As a result, Patch had even fewer forces with which to continue his general offensive. Finally, Devers still faced the loss of two French divisions for operations on the Atlantic coast. Thus, just when he felt most strongly that his command should be heavily reinforced, Devers could foresee only a net dilution of his strength. His gloom was at least partially dispelled by the expected arrival of the remainder of the 14th Armored Division and all of the new 12th Armored Division in early December, although both units needed additional training before they would be ready to fight.[16]

The influence of Patton on Eisenhower's decision may have been incidental, and the threat of transferring two divisions from the Seventh to the Third Army may have been only a means to keep Devers in line. Subsequently, Patton confided his belief that Patch's Seventh Army should have pushed the VI Corps across the Rhine,[17] indicating that he did not share the worries of his superiors regarding the security of the Third Army's right flank. Even if the VI Corps had crossed the Rhine, Patton would still have had the bulk of Seventh Army's XV Corps on his right flank west of the river,[18] a point that Eisenhower and Bradley seem to

---

[15] For Eisenhower's relations with Montgomery in November 1944, see Pogue, *The Supreme Command*, ch. 17.

[16] SHAEF reassigned the arriving 12th Armored Division from the U.S. Ninth to the Seventh Army on 27 November 1944.

[17] Blumenson, *The Patton Papers*, 1940–1945, p. 583.

[18] This assumes, as did Seventh Army plans, that no more than two XV Corps divisions would be needed to establish a bridgehead near Rastatt, and that these two would be returned to the west bank once the VI Corps had passed through the bridgehead.

have ignored. Another possibility, apparently dismissed with little consideration, was to have Patton's armor-heavy Third Army supply the exploitation force that would drive northward out of the XV Corps' projected bridgehead. Although the redeployments necessitated by cranking Third Army forces into the Rastatt bridgehead equation would have created difficult logistical and tactical problems, such a maneuver was not impossible.

Discussing the matter thirty years after the event, Lt. Gen. Garrison H. Davidson, the Seventh Army Engineer in 1944, who would have been largely responsible for moving Seventh Army units across the Rhine, still felt that Eisenhower's Sarrebourg decision was, to say the least, open to question.[19] At the time, Seventh Army engineers were prepared to support an assault crossing of the Rhine on a two-division, or eight-battalion, front. Citing the thorough preparations undertaken by the Seventh Army engineers to support the effort, General Davidson wrote:

It is interesting to conjecture what might have been the effect of the exploitation of an unexpected crossing of the Rhine in the south in late November or early December and an envelopment of the Ardennes to the north along the east bank of the Rhine. . . . I have often wondered what might have happened had [Eisenhower] had the audacity to take a calculated risk as General Patton would have instead of playing it safe. Perhaps success would have eliminated any possibility of the Battle of the Bulge; 40,000 casualties there could have been avoided and the war shortened by a number of months at

the saving of other thousands of lives.[20]

The Seventh Army, Davidson concluded, had "provided [Eisenhower] with an opportunity to depart from his broad front strategy . . . and make a lightning thrust across the Rhine in the Strasbourg-Rastatt area."[21] Indeed, a strong push up the east bank of the Rhine toward Mainz and Frankfurt might have forced Hitler to commit his carefully husbanded reserves in order to prevent the complete destruction of *Army Group G*; and in the south the remnants of the *Nineteenth Army* could hardly have been expected to increase their strength in the Colmar Pocket in the face of such dangerous penetration.[22] Almost thirty-five years to the day after Eisenhower's fateful decision, Col. Donald S. Bussey, then the ULTRA officer at Seventh Army headquarters, retained as his "most vivid recollection of that event . . . the long faces around the headquarters when we were denied the opportunity to exploit [the] breakthrough to the Rhine. . . ."[23]

For General Patch and all his staff the abrupt changes must have been particularly disappointing. Eisenhower's decision meant that the Seventh

---

[19] In November 1944 Davidson was a brigadier general.

[20] Garrison H. Davidson, *Grandpa Gar: The Saga of One Soldier As Told to His Grandchildren* (privately reproduced, 1976), pp. 94–95; also Ltrs, Davidson to Brig Gen Hal C. Pattison (Chief of Military History), 23 Jul 68, and to Robert Ross Smith, 20 Dec 80 (copies at CMH).

[21] Ibid., p. 95.

[22] According to the Griess-Devers interviews, Devers and his staff were well aware that the Germans had placed the *Fifth* and *Sixth Panzer Armies* in reserve and were concerned that these forces might be used against the Seventh Army following the failure of the *Panzer Lehr* counterattack.

[23] Ltr, Donald S. Bussey to Smith, 27 Nov 79 (copy CMH).

Army's principal effort was not to be directed at Germany east of the Rhine, but rather against German territory west of the river. The direction of Patch's main push would thus have to be changed from east and northeast to generally north, a switch that forestalled any chance to develop a shortcut into the heart of Germany east of the Rhine. In addition, the Seventh Army would lose most of its priceless momentum. Eisenhower's orders required major regroupings within both of the army's corps; as a result, neither corps would be ready to launch another major offensive until 5 December. These delays, in turn, would provide the *First* and *Nineteenth Armies* with a much needed respite, during which they would be able to rest and reorganize their units and absorb replacements and materiel.[24]

In the end, Eisenhower's Sarrebourg decision also reinforced Hitler's own plans. First, it confirmed the German leader's decision to adhere to a counteroffensive in the Ardennes instead of switching the main effort to Lorraine and northern Alsace. Second, the decision gave the Germans a free hand to continue the Ardennes buildup, which could proceed without facing the crisis that a Rhine crossing by the Seventh Army would have created. Finally, it allowed the *Nineteenth Army* to reorganize while continuing to maintain the Colmar

bridgehead. Had the Seventh Army begun crossing the Rhine in strength, the reserves that were later poured into the Colmar Pocket would have been needed elsewhere, and Hitler might have been more amenable to a general withdrawal back across the upper Rhine if the Reich heartland were under a more immediate threat.

Explaining his decision in a letter to General Marshall on 27 November, Eisenhower once more revealed that he had only a limited role in mind for the 6th Army Group. All current 6th Army Group operations, Eisenhower told the American Chief of Staff, "are, of course, merely for the purpose" of cleaning up Devers' area before turning the bulk of Seventh Army northward to undertake, in conjunction with Patton's Third Army, "a converging attack upon the great salient in the Siegfried Line west of the Rhine." If only Devers could "hurriedly throw his weight north," then Patton's chances of success would be greatly improved, and he was "anxious," he admitted, "to get the thing speeded up."[25] Once again Eisenhower had opted for an operational "strategy" of firepower and attrition—the direct approach—as opposed to a war of opportunistic maneuver. The Seventh Army was to have no opportunity to fully exploit the hard-won successes of the Saverne Gap and Strasbourg.

---

[24] *Seventh Army Rpt,* II, 418, 455–59.

[25] Quotes from Ltr, Eisenhower to Marshall, 27 Nov 44, *Eisenhower Papers,* IV, 2320–21.

PART FIVE

THE CAMPAIGN FOR ALSACE

CHAPTER XXV

A Change in Direction

By evening on 26 November 1944, Patch's Seventh Army had begun to redeploy its forces in compliance with General Eisenhower's decision to send the army northward. West of the Low Vosges and north of Sarrebourg, its new Fenetrange-Ramstein boundary with the Third Army defined the future axis of advance of the Seventh Army. In the far south, however, its old Gerardmer-Selestat-Erstein border with de Lattre's First French Army was unaltered and would remain so until Brooks' VI Corps finished pushing its way east and northeast through the High Vosges. At the time of the new orders, only elements of O'Daniel's 3d Division had actually reached the Alsatian plains, while the 103d and 36th Divisions were still fighting through the high mountain passes. Thus, temporarily at least, the Seventh Army would be advancing in two different directions—east through the High Vosges and, in the area between Sarrebourg and Strasbourg, north toward the German border. The northern effort was initially to be conducted by Haislip's XV Corps alone; consequently, Patch made the boundary between his XV and VI Corps an east-west line from Wasselonne, at the base of the Vosges, to La Want-

zenau, about five miles northeast of Strasbourg (*Map 31*). On the 27th, Patch intended to transfer the French 2d Armored Division, which was currently securing the Strasbourg area, to the VI Corps, and give Brooks' 100th Infantry Division to Haislip to make up for the loss. The XV Corps would thus have four infantry divisions—the 44th, 45th, 79th, and 100th—to make the initial assault north. Although the Seventh Army's subsequent deployment was rather awkward, the continued German weakness in the center of Patch's command—the gap between the *First* and *Nineteenth Armies* of *Army Group G*—allowed him to split his forces in this manner without running too great a risk.

The XV Corps Sector

West of the Low Vosges,[1] in the Saar River valley, 26 November found the *Panzer Lehr Division* and elements of the *361st Volksgrenadier Division* pulling northward to a delaying line between Wolfskirchen, Eywiller, and

_____

[1] The Low Vosges are generally considered to be the section of the Vosges Mountains that extends northeast from the Saverne Gap about thirty miles to the Lauter River.

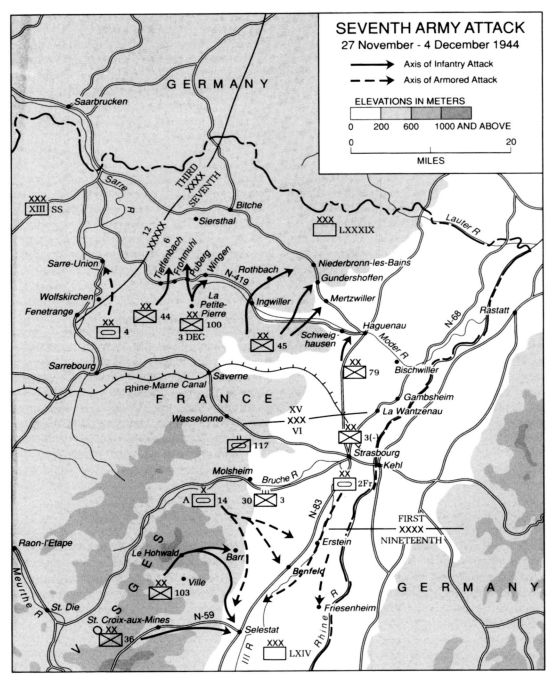

MAP 31 This map is printed in full color at the back of the book, following the Index.

Durstel. About the same time, the *25th Panzer Grenadier Division* was closing on Sarre-Union, about five miles to the north, intent on stemming any further American advance. Pursuing the German units were CCB of the 4th Armored Division, part of the Third Army's XII Corps operating in the XV Corps' zone, and two regiments of the XV Corps' 44th Division—the 71st and 114th—assisted by the corps' 106th Cavalry Group. During the day, the rest of the 4th Armored also entered the XV Corps' sector, pressing for Sarre-Union and bypassing the 44th Division's slower-moving infantry.[2]

As their forces retreated north, *Army Group G* and the *First Army* began to develop plans for establishing a more substantial east-west defensive line in front of the German border. Not expecting their forces to hold the Wolfskirchen-Durstel area for long, General Balck and General von Knobelsdorff, who commanded the *First Army*, hoped to establish a new series of positions that stretched east from Sarre-Union, through the Low Vosges and along the Moder River, past the small city of Haguenau, and on to the Rhine—as straight-line distance of nearly forty-five miles. Contrary to earlier plans, *Panzer Lehr* was to remain in the *First Army*'s rear area for the time being, while the *25th Panzer Grenadier Division* would hold along the new main line of resistance from Sarre-Union east about nine miles to

Frohmuhl, on Route N–419 in the Low Vosges.[3] The weak *361st Volksgrenadier Division*, which had been of little help securing *Panzer Lehr*'s counterattack, was to redeploy eastward and, after absorbing remnants of the *553d Volksgrenadier Division*, hold over ten miles of the new front along N–419 and the Moder River from Frohmuhl to Ingwiller, across the Low Vosges Mountains.[4]

East of the Vosges the *245th Volksgrenadier Division*, which had yet to reach the *First Army*'s area of operation from the Netherlands, was to cover the front from Ingwiller southeast twelve miles along the Moder to Schweighausen. Pending the arrival of the *245th*, the sector would be held by miscellaneous units under *Corps Command Vosges*, reinforced by the reconnaissance battalion of *Panzer Lehr*. The *256th Volksgrenadier Division*, the leading regiment of which reached Haguenau on 26 November, would hold the final sixteen miles of the new line, from Schweighausen past Haguenau to Gries and then to the Rhine River at Gambsheim, about ten miles northeast of Strasbourg.

Responsibility for establishing and defending the new Sarre-Union–Gambsheim line would be vested in

---

[2] Information on German operations in this chapter is from von Luttichau, "German Operations," chs. 25 and 26, and for the delaying action ch. 23. The operations of the U.S. 4th Armored Division in late November are covered in Cole, *The Lorraine Campaign*, ch. 10.

[3] The directive of 21 November that released the *Panzer Lehr* for its abortive counterattack had stipulated that the division would return northward by 28 November to prepare for the Ardennes offensive. Apparently this restriction was lifted on or about 24 November, when Hitler postponed the Ardennes operation to mid-December.

[4] The *553d Volksgrenadier Division* had been almost eliminated while defending Sarrebourg against the XV Corps' Saverne Gap offensive. Apparently not all remaining troops of the *553d* went to the *361st Division*, however, for a reconstituted *553d Division* appeared in the German order of battle of January 1945.

the *LXXXIX Corps*, currently reorganizing north of Haguenau after having lost much of its staff and almost all of its equipment in the Saverne area. The corps became operational again on 28 or 29 November, taking over the missions and units assigned to *Corps Command Vosges*.

At first, the German defenses were extremely weak east of the Vosges. The *361st Volksgrenadier Division*, for example, was still greatly understrength: one regiment had only two battalions, one of which could muster only 150 troops; another regiment consisted of a single infantry battalion with 300 effectives; and a third had two battalions of 300 men each. The two divisions coming from *Army Group H* in the Netherlands were not in much better condition. The *256th Volksgrenadier Division*'s three regiments had only two half-strength battalions each, and the *245th Volksgrenadier Division*'s six infantry battalions were even weaker. Furthermore, the *245th* contained a large percentage of former navy and air force personnel that had been shoveled into the army, and its artillery consisted of captured Russian guns with little ammunition.

On 26 November General Haislip, the XV Corps commander, had elements of three infantry divisions intermixed across his northern front to deal with these German forces. In the XV Corps sector west of the Vosges was the 44th Infantry Division with its 71st and 114th regiments reinforced by another regiment, the 157th from the 45th Division, and elements of the 106th Cavalry Group. East of the Vosges and directly north of Saverne was the 44th Division's third regiment—the 324th—and the rest of the 106th Cavalry. Farther east, outposting the Alsatian plains and protecting the northern flank of the French 2d Armored Division from Saverne to Strasbourg, was the 45th Division's 180th regiment; on its right was the 79th Infantry Division, with all three of its organic regiments holding the sector south of Haguenau.

Haislip intended to reorganize and beef up these forces before attacking. During the next two days he relieved the 45th Division's 179th regiment of its security responsibilities in the Wasselonne area south of Saverne and sent it north to the right of its sister unit, the 180th. Next, when the 100th Infantry Division passed to his control on the 27th, he began deploying it north of Saverne, as he moved the 324th regiment back to its parent unit on the other side of the Low Vosges and returned the 157th regiment to the 45th Division on the other side. The net result of this complicated switching would give each of his four northward-facing divisions their three organic infantry regiments, while presenting a continuous front to the German defenders and allowing the divisions to attack in strength as soon as possible. The XV Corps thus had on line, west to east, the 44th, 100th, 45th, and 79th Infantry Divisions. The gradual arrival of the rest of the new 14th Armored Division, which Patch had earmarked for the drive north, would also help. However, the process of reorienting his entire command north, to include the corps' logistical, fire support, engineer, and intelligence elements, proved time-consuming, and it would be several days before all of Haislip's forces could test the new German line.

The VI Corps Sector

While the XV Corps aligned itself for a drive north, Brooks' VI Corps continued to push through the Vosges, intending to clear the entire area from the mountains to the Rhine of all German forces in its sector. On 26 November, Leclerc's 2d Armored Division held the Strasbourg area with CCL and CCV, but was scheduled to be transferred to the VI Corps on the 27th; the tired 3d Division would take over responsibility for Strasbourg. Brooks wanted the armored unit to drive south toward Erstein, Selestat, and Colmar, which would complement the advance of his infantry divisions from the west. To that end, CCV captured two east-west bridges over the Ill River on the 26th, several miles south of Strasbourg; CCD, in reserve, prepared to lead the drive south; and CCR continued to patrol along the Bruche River and Canal west of Strasbourg, maintaining contact with the 3d Division in the vicinity of Molsheim. The 3d Division had entered Molsheim on the 26th and pushed four to five miles farther north and south into the vineyards of the Alsatian plains, meeting little resistance. As the rest of its components arrived on the plains, leading units of the infantry division began moving into Strasbourg on the night of 26–27 November, freeing the rest of Leclerc's armor for the drive south.

Other VI Corps elements positioned themselves to assist. CCA of the 14th Armored Division, still part of Brooks' corps, moved into Molsheim in the wake of the 3d Division; to the south, leading elements of the 103d Infantry Division reached Ville on the 26th, five miles short of the Alsatian plains and about fifteen miles southwest of Molsheim. The 103d Division's immediate objectives were Le Hohwald and Barr, both focal points on the defensive line that the *Nineteenth Army* was trying to establish north of Colmar.

Farther south, the 36th Infantry Division's leading unit, the 142d Infantry, had reached St. Croix-aux-Mines, on Route N–59 about seven miles south of Ville as well as seven miles short of the Alsatian plains. St. Croix had been another projected defensive focal point of the *Nineteenth Army,* but the 142d infantrymen had taken the town before the Germans could deploy enough strength there for a protracted defense. South and southwest of St. Croix, however, the rest of the tired 36th Division was strung out for about twenty miles, encountering stubborn resistance in the High Vosges west of Fraize, as had its neighbor, the 3d Algerian Division, which was still stuck in the vicinity of Gerardmer.

The *Nineteenth Army* had not yet been able to form a solid defensive ring around its Colmar bridgehead. In VI Corps' sector on 26 November, Thumm's battered *LXIV Corps* held the area between Selestat and Barr, guarding the approaches to the Alsatian plains with bits and pieces of the *708th Volksgrenadier* and *716th Infantry Divisions.* East of Barr to the Rhine, the northern edge of the bridgehead was screened by a provisional unit, *Division Buercky,* assisted by a melange of *SS* elements, security police, ambulatory hospital patients (including a company of VD cases), and some engineers, all backed by an 88-mm. antiaircraft battalion and a few assault guns. During the 26th, the *106th Panzer Brigade,* redeploying after its abortive and costly counterattack against French I Corps forces around Mulhouse, closed *Division Buercky*'s sector to take up positions in the vicinity of Erstein. The *280th Assault Gun Battalion* accompanied the brigade, and both promised to give some concrete form to the German defenses north of Colmar.

Southwest of the *LXIV Corps,* Petersen's *XC Corps* (formerly the *IV Luftwaffe Field Corps*) continued to hold out in the High Vosges, defending the western approaches to Colmar and facing part of the U.S. 36th Infantry Division as well as the 3d Algerian Division and other elements of the French II Corps. The *XC Corps* had the barely viable *16th Volksgrenadier Division* on its right and the *269th Volksgrenadier Division,* now the *Nineteenth Army*'s best unit, on its left; both divisions occupied excellent defensive terrain. Farther south Schack's *LXIII Corps,* facing the bulk of the First French Army, defended the southwestern and southern portions of the Colmar Pocket with what was left of the *159th, 189th, 338th,* and *198th Infantry Divisions* and the problem-ridden *30th SS Division.* The next day, 27 November, as de Lattre's forces completed their double envelopment at Burnhaupt, Wiese began transferring the battered *198th Division* northward to strengthen the *LXIV Corps.* Initially he planned to concentrate the *198th* in the area of Selestat, a critical rail and road junction city on the Alsatian plains ten miles south of Barr and less than fifteen miles north of Colmar.

Seventh Army's plans for this sector were in a state of flux on 26 November. Patch wanted the VI Corps' two southernmost divisions, the 103d and the 36th, to complete their push over the Vosges and, assisted by CCA of the 14th Armored Division, to secure Barr and Selestat as quickly as possible. As noted above, on the 27th Patch formally transferred Brooks' 100th Division to Haislip and Haislip's French 2d Armored Division to Brooks, with the VI Corps' 3d Division assuming all security responsibilities for the Strasbourg area. Once Barr and Selestat had been secured, however, Patch intended to turn the entire VI Corps northward, leaving only Leclerc's armored division in the area north of Colmar. At the time, he estimated that Leclerc's division, reinforced by a few regiments of VI Corps infantry that stayed behind, could easily mop up the German forces left between Selestat and Colmar, a distance of about ten miles, joining units of the First French Army as they drove north from Mulhouse. Furthermore, Patch expected all American forces supporting the effort to be redeployed northward by 30 November. Clearly both he and Devers still believed that the Germans would not make a strong effort to hold the Colmar bridgehead. Constrained from advancing across the Rhine, they were thus anxious to turn the bulk of the Seventh Army north to support the attack of Patton's Third Army into the Saar, perhaps beating him to the German border.[5]

Based on Patch's initial guidance,

[5] 6th Army Gp LI 3, 26 Nov 44; Ltr Directive, CG, Seventh Army, to CGs, XV and VI Corps, 27 Nov 44; de Lattre, *History,* pp. 280–81.

Brooks gave more specific instructions to his VI Corps units on the 26th. First he ordered CCA of the 14th Armored Division to move quickly from the east in multiple columns in order to secure the section of Route N–83 south of Erstein behind the main German defensive line. Once the French 2d Armored Division had taken Erstein, it was to pass through that portion of the road secured by CCA and advance rapidly to the Selestat area. CCA was then to regroup in the vicinity of Benfeld, five miles south of Erstein, and be prepared to reinforce other units as necessary. The 103d and 36th Infantry Divisions were to continue pushing east to the Alsatian plains and then secure the area behind the French armored division as Leclerc's forces moved south. Finally, the 36th Division was to earmark one regimental combat team to reinforce the French 2d Armored Division as far as an east-west line through Colmar. Presumably the 36th Division would also redeploy north by 30 November, as specified by Patch.[6]

The VI Corps Advance (27 November–4 December)

On 27 November the bulk of the 3d Infantry Division moved into the Strasbourg sector and by 1 December had cleared the city of the bridgehead that the Germans had been able to maintain. Southwest of Strasbourg the 3d Division's 30th regiment policed the area south of Molsheim and temporarily provided an infantry battalion for Leclerc's initial drive south. At

the same time, the VI Corps' 117th Cavalry Squadron moved from Wasselonne to the Gambsheim area north of Strasbourg and subsequently, on 29 and 30 November, attempted to occupy Gambsheim. The light mechanized unit lacked the strength, however, to handle the growing German forces in the area and fell back to La Wantzenau, thus screening the VI Corps' northern boundary.

With these forces securing his northeastern flank, Brooks continued to direct the 103d and 36th Divisions through the remaining German Vosges defenses in the VI Corps sector. South of the 30th Infantry, the 103d Division's 411th Infantry reached Le Hohwald on the 27th and, despite determined local resistance, sent one column through to the Alsatian plains at the western edge of Barr, about twenty miles south of Molsheim. Barr, however, turned out to be well defended, and a two-day fight ensued that involved much of the 411th Infantry as well as elements of the 14th Armored Division's CCA.

As units of Haffner's 103d Division struggled through Le Hohwald to Barr, the French 2d Armored Division and CCA of the U.S. 14th Armored Division began the drive south. Initially CCA split into three columns; one approached Barr from the north, while the other two moved against the German strongpoint at Erstein. Of these, the first column pushed east directly toward Erstein while the second moved southeast, swinging behind the strongpoint in the vicinity of Benfeld. Meanwhile, the bulk of the French 2d Armored Division began to advance on Erstein from the north, directly down Routes N–83 and N–68.

---

[6] VI Corps OI 17, 26 Nov 44.

As the French and American armor advanced, they encountered a series of difficulties that were to plague mobile operations on the southern Alsatian plains for many months. All waterways, regardless of size and purpose, were running high, and many were at flood stage as a result of heavy rains. The soft, water-soaked ground restricted vehicles to the main roads, which were often mined and blocked by all types of barriers. The Germans had destroyed almost all of the bridges in the area, however small, and targeted the most significant crossing sites with mortar and artillery fire. Rain and sometimes snow continued to curtail Allied air support operations and also interfered with radio communications. All these factors reduced the mobility of the Allied armored units, making it difficult for them to operate with speed and efficiency.

Throughout 28 November heavy fighting took place at both Barr and Erstein. At Barr the 411th Infantry battled into the town from the west, attempting to clear each house and building one by one; meanwhile, the supporting CCA column entered the city from the north and east. This proved a costly mistake. With little accompanying infantry, the armor found itself out of place in the narrow streets and lanes; it lost eighteen tanks in the course of the day, eight of which were abandoned when Company B of the 48th Tank Battalion was forced to withdraw from the town, leaving behind most of its equipment and many of its dead, wounded, and missing. The following day, 29 November, the 103d Division's foot soldiers finally cleared Barr, and the armored unit was fortu-

nate enough to recover all eight of the abandoned medium tanks, still in serviceable condition, as well as nineteen of Company B's tankers.[7] The men of the 14th Armored Division were acquiring their experience the hard way.

The new American armored unit had difficulties in the Erstein area as well. German defenses and counterattacks forced the southern column out of Benfeld, about five miles south of Erstein, on the 27th, while the Erstein defenders unceremoniously threw back the northern column on the 28th. Finally relieved by elements of the French 2d Armored Division, CCA regrouped its scattered units on the night of 28–29 November just south of Barr, and prepared to resume operations south. Meanwhile, late on the 28th, Leclerc's CCD pushed into Erstein from the northeast against strong resistance and, after a pitched battle, occupied most of the city by dark. Here the French tactical experience paid off, enabling them to wield their tank, artillery, and armored infantry forces more efficiently than the novice American formation.

The next day, 29 November, the 2d Armored Division's CCD mopped up at Erstein and, against steady resistance, slowly spread out to the west, southwest, and south. As the rest of Leclerc's division rolled up to the Barr-Erstein area, CCA of the 14th Armored Division, still game, began advancing south of Barr, but was prevented from moving more than a mile or so toward Selestat because of a

[7] *Seventh Army Rpt*, II, 448–49; and Capt. Joseph Carter, *The History of the 14th Armored Division* (Atlanta: Albert Love Enterprises, n.d.), n.p. These two sources offer greatly differing accounts of the same episode.

series of destroyed bridges.

While the fighting was taking place at Barr and Erstein, the rest of the 103d Division had pushed slowly through the Vosges, bypassing Barr on the south, and had reached Dambach-la-Ville, five miles north of Selestat, on 30 November in the face of only scattered German resistance.

South of the 103d, Dahlquist's 36th Division had continued its slow, ragged advance directly on Selestat, all the while pushing laboriously over some of the highest and most rugged hill masses of the High Vosges. While the 141st regiment operated off to the southwest in the Bonhomme Pass area, the 142d and 143d Infantry, pressing generally eastward, found some towns and villages unoccupied and passed many unmanned roadblocks. Nevertheless, progress was slow because of time-consuming, cross-country marches to outflank manned German strongpoints; the difficulties of pushing armor through the narrow, easily interdicted mountain roads; and the continual problems of resupply. Moreover, as the 36th Division neared the Alsatian plains, German resistance, although still somewhat disorganized, continued to stiffen. The first major element to reach the plains, the 3d Battalion, 142d Infantry, emerged from the mountains on 30 November, five miles south of Dambach-la-Ville and only two miles west of Selestat.

Patch had expected that by 30 November both Barr and Selestat would have been secured and that the French 2d Armored Division would have reached Colmar, making it possible to redeploy the rest of Brooks' American forces north. Obviously the

American timetable had been upset. Yet, until the morning of 29 November, General Patch and his G–2 appeared to believe that the increasing German resistance in the northern section of the Colmar bridgehead was only a temporary condition, representing an effort to cover a phased and orderly *Nineteenth Army* withdrawal east across the Rhine.[8] If so, the Seventh Army and VI Corps staffs must have been surprised when, during the 29th, the French 2d Armored Division reported encountering troops of the *198th Division,* and the 36th Division reported capturing members of the *106th Panzer Brigade.*[9] Obviously a *Nineteenth Army* withdrawal across the Rhine would not have required redeploying these two units north from the Belfort-Mulhouse sector. With this new information, Devers, Patch, and Brooks began to reevaluate their own plans. Initially, however, their only change was to rescind the 30 November deadline on the redeployment of the involved American forces north. The VI Corps would have to continue its offensive south against Selestat, and for the moment Haislip's XV Corps would have to carry out the northern offensive alone.[10]

On 30 November VI Corps began its advance on Selestat. The 14th Ar-

---

[8] Seventh Army Conference File, 29 Nov 44; *Seventh Army Rpt,* II, 448.

[9] The two German units had started northward on 27 November in accordance with *OKW* and *OB West* orders. If ULTRA warned Patch of this move, he may have withheld the information from his subordinates until it could be confirmed by other sources. There is no evidence, however, that ULTRA helped out here.

[10] Amendment, 30 Nov 44, to Ltr Directive, CG, Seventh Army, to CGs, VI and XV Corps, 27 Nov 44.

SELESTAT, CENTRAL CITY AREA WITH ILL RIVER IN FAR BACKGROUND

mored Division's CCA, after an intense fight, captured St. Pierre on Route N–422, thus opening the road south of Barr; the next day it reached the towns of Scherwiller and Ebersheim, both just a few miles north of the city. However, CCA began redeploying north on 2 and 3 December to join its parent unit in the XV Corps, and units of the 103d Infantry and French 2d Armored Divisions quickly took over its positions.

As American forces slowly converged on Selestat from the west and north, Leclerc expanded his hold on the central and eastern portions of the Alsatian plains. CCR took Benfeld on 1 December and cleared Route N–

83 all the way to Selestat. To the east, a CCD column pushed south along the Rhine from Kraft to Friesenheim, while CCV moved into line for the first time between CCR and CCD. On 3 December the French division halted, awaiting new orders, along an east-west line roughly between Ebersheim and Friesenheim, with the Germans still entrenched close to the Rhine on the unit's left flank.

While the French armor moved south, avoiding the larger urban areas, the 103d Infantry Division entered Selestat on 1 December, accompanied later in the afternoon by units of the 36th Division. By the 2d, the two divisions had four battalions of infantry—well supported with armor and artillery—inside the city as well as other units surrounding it on the outside. But despite the overwhelming Allied strength in the area, it took nearly three days to clear the city of German defenders, with the last resistance ending only on the afternoon of 4 December.[11]

With the fall of Selestat, the VI Corps' mission officially ended. Patch had decided to leave the 36th Division, half of which was still in the Vosges, to help Leclerc's 2d Armored Division make the final push south to Colmar. Accordingly, the rest of Brooks' VI Corps forces including the 103d Infantry Division began moving north. However, the matter of Colmar was obviously not settled. Progress against the northern edge of the pocket had been extremely slow, and advances in the west and south by the tired and undersupplied First French Army had been even less successful. Now, with Devers pulling forces out of the Colmar region and Wiese constantly reinforcing the defenders within, closing down the pocket was becoming increasingly difficult.

The XV Corps Moves North
(26 November–4 December)

In the northern sector of the Seventh Army's area of operation, the objectives of Haislip's XV Corps were tied to the Third Army's rate of advance. Although terrain objectives were clearly unappetizing to Devers and Patch, they gave the effort their full support, directing Haislip to start his redeploying forces north as soon as possible. On 26 November, while the rest of the XV Corps reorganized and prepared for the new mission, Haislip ordered the 44th Division, currently the only unit facing north, to continue its operations west of the Low Vosges in support of the Third Army's 4th Armored Division in the Saar River valley. At the time, the 4th Armored was attempting to penetrate the German Wolfskirchen-Eywiller-Durstel delaying line just south of Sarre-Union; Haislip attached the 44th Division's 71st regiment to the armored unit in order to speed up the effort, while sending the 44th's other regiment in the area, the 114th, north across the western slopes of the Vosges.

The 4th Armored Division, weary and roadbound by heavy rains and flooded streams, made slow progress, but reached Wolfskirchen and Eywiller on the 27th, Durstel on the 29th, and Sarre-Union on 1 December, although it took four more days to secure the city. By that time the 4th had passed out of the XV Corps' sector, and the 71st regiment had returned to 44th Division control.[12]

East of the 4th Armored Division, the 114th regiment kept pace, taking Tieffenbach on 28 November and thus penetrating the planned German main line of resistance before it could be established. However, as the regiment moved east along Route N–419

---

[11] The Congressional Medal of Honor was posthumously awarded to Sgt. Ellis R. Weicht, Company F, 142d Infantry, 36th Division, for heroic action at St. Hippolyte southwest of Selestat; his was the first of several such awards to American soldiers in this area during December 1944 and January 1945, attesting to the bitterness of the fighting.

[12] For details of 4th Armored Division operations during the period 26 November–4 December, see Cole, *The Lorraine Campaign,* pp. 469–71, 521–25, and 530–31.

into the mountains, it came up against more organized defenses and was unable to reach its new objective, Frohmuhl. South of Tieffenbach and Frohmuhl, the 121st Cavalry Squadron of XV Corps' 106th Cavalry Group pushed reconnaissance elements into the Low Vosges, where they encountered increasing numbers of German patrols and reported German armor and infantry moving east along N–419. The traffic may have marked the redeployment of the *361st Volksgrenadier Division* and *Panzer Lehr's* reconnaissance battalion. Meanwhile, the 44th Division's third regiment, the 324th Infantry, had just returned from the other side of the Vosges, and moved up to the N–419 area to help consolidate the division's hold on the key roadway. By 2 December the 114th Infantry had finally seized Frohmuhl, while the other two regiments of the 44th Division pushed a few miles north of N–419; progress, however, was still extremely tedious.

On the other side of the mountains, east of the 44th Division's sector, units of the 45th Infantry Division had already joined the assault on the German Vosges defenses. On 28 November the 45th Division's 157th regiment had taken Ingwiller, but the 100th Division's 397th regiment, temporarily attached to the 45th, had been able to push only about a mile or so along N–419 northeast of the town by the evening of 2 December. On both sides of the Low Vosges the *361st Volksgrenadiers,* realizing that the N–419 mountain road was the key to its defensive position, had begun to defend the highway with more determination.

Not wanting to channel his attacks along the easily defensible roadway, Haislip planned to bring the rest of the 100th Division up the crest of the Low Vosges, have it attack through the center of the German positions between Frohmuhl and Ingwiller, and then continue north with the 44th Division on its left to seize several key Maginot Line positions about twelve miles away. Specifically, Spragins' 44th Division was to strike northeast for the fortified high ground at and near the town of Siersthal, and Burress' 100th Division, with two regiments, was to head for Bitche, four miles east of Siersthal and the center of some of the strongest Maginot Line fortifications. The 100th's other regiment, the 397th, was to outflank and overrun the German defenses on Route N–419 west of Ingwiller and then join the rest of the division. The two-division attack would begin on 3 December across a front of about twelve miles through rugged, heavily wooded terrain that greatly restricted armored support.[13]

Now it was the turn of Haislip's forces to try their skills at mountain fighting. The XV Corps' attack through the width of the Low Vosges began on the 3d as scheduled, but neither of the two participating divisions was able to push more than a few miles north during the first two days. All across the front, the defending Germans used observed artillery and mortar fire to slow American progress, while demolitions, roadblocks, minefields, and a series of minor counterattacks contributed to

---

[13] XV Corps FO 14, 2 Dec 44.

the delays. The central Vosges area proved particularly difficult. Attacking from the vicinity of La Petite-Pierre deep in the mountains, units of the 100th Division managed to advance four miles northward by 3 December, reaching the hamlet of Puberg just south of Route N–419, pushing a lone infantry battalion across the road on the 4th. To the east, however, other division elements were thrown out of Wingen-sur-Moder on the night of 3–4 December by a German counterattack in which one American rifle company was surrounded and eventually forced to surrender. German troops continued to hold the Wingen area and parts of Route N–419 through the 4th, thereby making it difficult to supply the 100th Division forces and delaying the longer drive toward the corps' Siersthal-Bitche objectives.

East of the Vosges, Haislip also sent the 45th and 79th Divisions northward with what forces were ready to attack, trying to keep their advance roughly parallel to the 44th and 100th Divisions in the Vosges. Advancing on a much broader front, the units headed for an artificial line, eighteen miles wide, between Rothbach on the west, at the base of the Vosges, and Bischwiller on the east, with the boundary line of the two divisions at Mertzwiller, about eight miles southeast of Rothbach.[14]

Their progress was slow but not as painful as in the Vosges because of the open terrain and the late arrival of defending German forces. On the left, Eagles' 45th Division took Ingwiller on the 28th, Rothbach on the 29th, and most of what was left of the

objective line by the 30th. Only on the far right, around Mertzwiller, did its units encounter any serious difficulties. There the 180th Infantry was unable to force a crossing of the Moder River southwest of Mertzwiller until 30 November, and even then the Germans managed to keep the regiment at arm's length from the town.

Despite the delay at Mertzwiller, Haislip was heartened by the advance of the 45th Division and directed it to continue north and northeast to a new objective line—a railroad running between Niederbronn-les-Bains, six miles northeast of Rothbach, and Mertzwiller.[15] As the division resumed its attack on 1 December, however, it finally began to encounter heavier resistance, marking the arrival of the *245th Volksgrenadier Division*'s leading elements into the *LXXXIX Corps'* sector. Additional factors that slowed the advance included an increase in prepared defensive measures—minefields, roadblocks, demolitions, and so forth—and, most important, the growing difficulty of the terrain as the 45th Division pushed into the Low Vosges foothills. Nevertheless, the division was within a few miles of its objective by 4 December, actually pushing across the railway at Gundershoffen in the division center. Mertzwiller, however, remained in German hands. Eyeing its location on the boundary between the 45th and 79th Divisions, Haislip suspected that the Germans were attempting to develop the town into an assembly area and strongpoint that might threaten the flank of either division.

---

[14] XV Corps FO 13, 27 Nov 44.

[15] XV Corps OI 57, 1 Dec 44; XV Corps FO 14, 2 Dec 44.

SOLDIER AND PACK MULE MAKE THEIR WAY IN HEAVY SNOWFALL, *Vosges, 1944.*

On the XV Corps' far right, the objectives of Wyche's 79th Division were more modest. With the *256th Volksgrenadier Division* beginning to close the Haguenau area on 26 November and with strong German forces occupying the Gambsheim area on the division's right flank, Haislip directed the 79th to undertake only strong reconnaissance to the north and northeast without becoming seriously engaged. Wyche, the 79th Division commander, posted both the 313th Infantry and the attached 94th Cavalry Squadron on his right, facing Gambsheim; on the 29th he began probing toward the south bank of the Moder River with the 314th and 315th regiments. Encountering some artillery and mortar fire but only

small German infantry forces, both units approached the southern banks of the Moder between Schweighausen and Haguenau on the following evening, only to discover that the Germans had evacuated most of their forces across the river. There the regiments halted, waiting for further orders.

An Evaluation

Advancing in two different directions on two widely separated fronts had greatly dissipated the combat power of the Seventh Army, as everyone should have expected. Eisenhower's decision on 24 November to turn the 6th Army Group's main effort north had not only halted Patch's plans for a drive into Germany northeast of Strasbourg, but had also prevented him from applying more pressure against the northern edge of the Colmar Pocket. Although the German decision to reinforce and hold the bridgehead came as a surprise to all the Allied commanders, Eisenhower clearly believed that the Seventh Army's new mission of supporting the Third Army's advance toward the Saar industrial region was far more important than clearing the southern Alsatian plains. The Allied Supreme Commander had forcefully communicated this point of view to Devers in November. Eisenhower had never attached much importance to the extreme southern sector of the Allied front, and might understandably have been upset that Devers and Patch had not chosen to redeploy the VI Corps sooner. Having the VI Corps attack northwards in the greatest strength possible and at the earliest possible date would force the German *First Army* to divert even more of its forces that opposed the U.S. Third Army. Of course, a crossing in the Rastatt area and a subsequent drive north up the east bank of the Rhine might have accomplished the same result, but without giving any immediate assistance to the effort against the Colmar Pocket. There both Eisenhower and

Devers had underestimated the German ability to strengthen the bridgehead and overestimated de Lattre's ability to keep his basically colonial army moving against suddenly renewed and greatly strengthened German resistance. Of course, SHAEF still had the option of ignoring the Colmar Pocket, ringing it with defensive units, postponing Operation INDEPENDENCE, outposting the Franco-Italian border with FFI units, and sending the better part of de Lattre's army north to assist Patch and Patton in forcing the Saar. Both the terrain in the south and the operational goals of Eisenhower would seem to suggest that such measures would have at least been considered. But politico-military constraints as well as German unpredictability probably made this course of action unlikely. The German high command had often been quick to take advantage of gambles made by Allied commanders in the past, and a major setback on the western Allied front might threaten the entire alliance. Like Jellicoe, commander of the British battle fleet in World War I, Eisenhower could also have lost the war in the space of an afternoon, and the Allied Supreme Commander remained understandably cautious in his operational deployments.

CHAPTER XXVI

On the Siegfried Line

The opening days of December 1944 found General Devers increasingly disturbed over the Seventh Army's slow progress northward as well as the even slower advance of both the Seventh and the First French Armies toward the city of Colmar.[1] After conferring with General de Lattre on 1 December, Devers once again postponed French redeployments for Operation INDEPENDENCE, thereby hoping to accelerate the elimination of the Colmar Pocket. Now the French 1st Infantry Division was to start westward on 9 December instead of the 7th, and the French 1st Armored Division on the 17th instead of the 10th. For similar reasons the 6th Army Group commander decided to transfer operational control of the U.S. 36th Infantry Division and the French 2d Armored Division from the Seventh to the First French Army, effective 5 December. As a corollary, Devers also moved the boundary be-

tween the two armies north to Plobsheim, seven miles below Strasbourg. These changes relieved both Patch and Brooks of any further responsibility for the Colmar area, although the Seventh Army continued to provide logistical support for the two transferred divisions. With these reinforcements and the continued deferral of Operation INDEPENDENCE, Devers wanted the First French Army to renew its offensive as soon as possible and finish the job of clearing southern Alsace.

Having presumably settled matters concerning the Colmar Pocket and INDEPENDENCE, General Devers turned his attention to the Seventh Army's attack northward. At its current rate of advance, Haislip's XV Corps would be unable to protect and support the right of Patton's Third Army. In fact, by 2 December, the 4th Armored Division of the Third Army's XII Corps was already waiting impatiently for the XV Corps' 44th Division to come up on its right before continuing its advance northward.[2] To speed up the advance of the 44th and his other forces toward the German border and

---

[1] The basic sources for this section are 6th Army Gp LI 3, 26 Nov 44; 6th Army Gp LI 4, 2 Dec 44; Ltr, CG, 6th Army Gp, to CG, First French Army, sub: Movement of Units Scheduled for Operation INDEPENDENCE, 1 Dec 44, in 6th Army Gp Doc File, Nov–Dec 44; Devers Diary, 2 Dec 44; Seventh Army FO 7, 2 Dec 44; *Seventh Army Rpt*, II, 453–62; XV Corps FO 14, 2 Dec 44; VI Corps OI 21, 2 Dec 44; VI Corps FO 9, 5 Dec 44; de Lattre, *History*, pp. 285–87; and Seventh Army OI 27, 3 Dec 44.

[2] The 4th Armored Division was also waiting for XII Corps' 26th Infantry Division to come up on its left.

the West Wall, Devers estimated that he would need the full power of Patch's Seventh Army, including both the XV and VI Corps, and on 2 December he issued orders to that effect.

With Devers' instructions in hand, Patch quickly published implementing directives the same day, outlining new corps boundaries, deployments, and missions. Brooks' VI Corps was to move north and position itself to the right of Haislip's XV Corps. The new boundary between XV and VI Corps would run from the vicinity of Saverne north and northeast along the crest of the Low Vosges Mountains, which was essentially the same boundary that Haislip had previously established between the 100th and 45th Divisions. West of the new boundary the XV Corps, now consisting of the 44th and 100th Infantry Divisions, would continue the attack northward on a narrower sector approximately ten to fifteen miles wide. To the east, the VI Corps would push northward across a much broader front of about thirty miles with the 45th, 79th, and 103d Infantry Divisions, leaving the 3d Division behind to secure the Strasbourg area. To strengthen the offensives of both corps, Patch gave each an armored division: the 14th Armored Division, now united under Brig. Gen. Albert C. Smith, went to Brooks; and a fresh unit, the recently arrived 12th Armored Division, commanded by Maj. Gen. Roderick R. Allen, went to Haislip. In addition, Devers wanted to have elements of the new 42d, 63d, and 70th Infantry Divisions, scheduled to begin disembarking at Marseille in early December, brought

BRIG. GEN. ALBERT C. SMITH

north as quickly as possible relieving the 3d Division of its static mission and making another experienced division available for the drive north.

A final arrangement involved the XV Corps' new 12th Armored Division. As December opened, General Eddy, the XII Corps commander, informed General Patton, in charge of the Third Army, that the worn 4th Armored Division was no longer capable of making any substantive contribution to XII Corps operations, and suggested that Haislip's XV Corps, with a much narrower front, could spare a division to relieve the tired unit temporarily. The 12th Armored Division was the obvious candidate for the proposed substitution.

Patton put the question to Patch, who
agreed in principle, but was understandably reluctant to lose control of
the unit. However, Devers, Patch, and
Haislip realized that the proposition
was sensible. The 12th Armored Division would find the hilly but generally
open terrain of the 4th Armored Division's sector more suitable than the
rough, forested ground of the Low
Vosges over which the XV Corps infantry divisions were advancing.
Moving slightly to the west, the new
armored division would have a much
easier time breaking in its various
components, while giving the 4th Armored Division—which had given a
good account of itself earlier during
the *Panzer Lehr Division*'s counterattack
against the XV Corps—a well-earned
rest. In the end, the involved commanders worked out a compromise:
the 12th Armored would move into
the XII Corps' sector to relieve the
4th, but would not pass to General
Eddy's command and instead would
remain under General Haislip's "tactical control." Subsequently CCA of
the 12th Armored Division began relieving forward elements of the 4th
Armored on the morning of 7 December, and the last of its units were out
of the line by evening of the next
day.[3]

The German Situation

While the Seventh Army was reorganizing for its December offensive,
Army Group G and the *First Army* were
taking what measures they could to

MAJ. GEN. RODERICK R. ALLEN

halt or at least delay the advance of
the Third and Seventh Armies to the
West Wall.[4] As December opened,
leadership and morale within the *First
Army* was low. What had once been
considered an excellent organization
had fallen on hard times. Both von
Rundstedt at *OB West* and Balck at
Army Group G felt that the headquarters had developed a withdrawal psy-
chosis; at the same time, its units had
run up a sobering total of defections,
desertions, and surrenders in the face
of continuous pressure from the
American Third and Seventh Armies.
Furthermore, von Rundstedt and

---

[3] Cole, *The Lorraine Campaign*, pp. 525, 533–34;
Seventh Army OI 30, 6 Dec 44; XV Corps OI 62, 6
Dec 44.

[4] This section is based on von Luttichau,
"German Operations," ch. 26; and CMH MS C–003,
Col. Kurt Reschke, Chief of Staff, *LXXXIX Corps*, 26
Jun 48.

Balck were increasingly dissatisfied with the conduct of the *First Army*'s commander, General von Knobelsdorff, and a series of events soon resulted in his relief. On 1 December von Rundstedt warned Balck that *Army Group G* would have to redeploy even more units to *Army Group B* for the Ardennes offensive, specifically the *Panzer Lehr Division, 11th Panzer Division,* and the *401st* and *404th Volks Artillery Corps*—all *First Army* units. After learning of the impending transfers, von Knobelsdorff informed Balck that he could not accept responsibility for stabilizing his front if these forces were withdrawn, nor could he hold his section of the West Wall with the forces that would remain. The following morning, 2 December, von Knobelsdorff reported being ill, and von Rundstedt immediately replaced him with Lt. Gen. Hans von Obstfelder.

Von Obstfelder took command of a rather demoralized army that consisted of three corps: the *LXXXII* on the far right, or west; the *XIII SS* in the center, with its southeastern flank in the vicinity of Sarre-Union; and the *LXXXIX Corps,* which occupied a front of over forty-five linear miles from Sarre-Union east to the Rhine. The *LXXXII Corps* and the *XIII SS Corps* faced Patton's Third Army, as did *LXXXIX Corps* units in the Sarre-Union area, while the rest of the *LXXXIX Corps* held the German front opposite the Seventh Army.

During the first week of December the German high command made several changes in these arrangements. First, von Obstfelder moved the right, or western, boundary of the *LXXXIX Corps* east to Bitche, thereby narrowing the corps front by about ten miles. Next, von Rundstedt decided to transfer the *XC Corps* headquarters from the *Nineteenth Army*'s center to the *First Army,* inserting it between the *XIII SS* and the *LXXXIX Corps;* initially the transferred corps would control little more than the *25th Panzer Grenadier Division.* This action ultimately pushed the *LXXXIX Corps'* western boundary farther east to the Camp de Bitche, a large prewar French Army installation.[5] For the Seventh Army, these boundary adjustments meant that Haislip's XV Corps would face both Petersen's *XC* and Hoehne's *LXXXIX Corps,* while, from the crest of the Low Vosges east to the Rhine, Brooks' VI Corps would meet only *LXXXIX Corps* forces.

Increasingly concerned over American advances east of the Low Vosges and apparently doubting the ability of *First Army* headquarters to supervise and coordinate the operations of four corps, von Rundstedt, on 8 December, raised the *LXXXIX Corps* headquarters to the status of an independent command, directly under Balck's *Army Group G* and on the same echelon as the *First* and *Nineteenth Army* headquarters. Designated *Group Hoehne,* the new command consisted mainly of the *361st, 245th,* and *256th Volksgrenadier Divisions* and had an effective strength of about 9,000 troops, of which some 5,500 could be considered infantry combat effectives. On 8 December *Group Hoehne* also picked up *Division Raessler* and the *21st Panzer Division.* The panzer division

---

[5] The *XC Corps,* formerly the *IV Luftwaffe Field Corps,* did not become fully operational in the new zone until 10 December.

was greatly understrength at the time, with no more than 2,200 combat effectives, and would need several days to redeploy to Hoehne's sector. *Division Raessler,* with about 4,700 troops, was responsible for preparing the West Wall defenses in *Group Hoehne*'s sector; however, a standing directive from Hitler forbade the employment of any West Wall troops forward of the fortification line, so the acquisition was of no immediate advantage.

Both General Hoehne and his neighbor, General Petersen, had the mission of holding the area in front of the West Wall until 16 December, the scheduled date for the start of the Ardennes offensive. While accomplishing this task, Balck also instructed both commanders to preserve the integrity of their units so that they could fall back on the West Wall reasonably intact and contribute to its defense. Von Rundstedt agreed to this additional guidance, but made it clear to all concerned that the West Wall was to be a final line from which no further German withdrawals could be countenanced.

The XV Corps Offensive North

Late on 4 December, as the reorganized XV Corps prepared to continue its drive north, the German forces in front of Haislip's command began a limited withdrawal. As a result, the XV Corps' attack on the 5th at first encountered little resistance. Quickly elements of the 100th Division's 397th and 398th Infantry regiments cleared the Wingen-Ingwiller section of Route N–419 through the Low Vosges, thus placing the entire east-west mountain road under American

control *(Map 32).* On the corps' left, the 44th Division's 324th and 114th Infantry secured the Ratzwiller area on the 5th and seized Montbronn on the 6th. Although operating in more rugged and more forested terrain, the 100th Division easily kept pace, moving up from N–419 to the area east of Montbronn and occupying Mouterhouse, all against negligible German resistance. The 106th Cavalry Group, meanwhile, initiated an extensive mountain patrolling program east of the 100th Division to protect XV Corps' right flank.

The initial gains of 5 and 6 December made Haislip optimistic, and he urged both divisions to push on rapidly to their current objectives: Siersthal and nearby high ground for the 44th Division, and Bitche and associated fortifications for the 100th. The divisions would then drive on to "develop" the German West Wall defenses.[6] At the time, forward elements of the 44th Division were only four miles short of Siersthal, and the leading 100th Division units were about the same distance from Bitche. Haislip also expected that operations by the fresh 12th Armored Division on the XV Corps' left, or western, flank would assist the advance of both units.

On 7 December, however, the German defenses in front of Haislip's two divisions suddenly became more active. Infantry resistance stiffened markedly, and advancing American troops came under heavy and accurate mortar and artillery fire, which forced several local withdrawals. De-

---

[6] XV Corps OI 62, 6 Dec 44; XV Corps OI 63, 7 Dec 44.

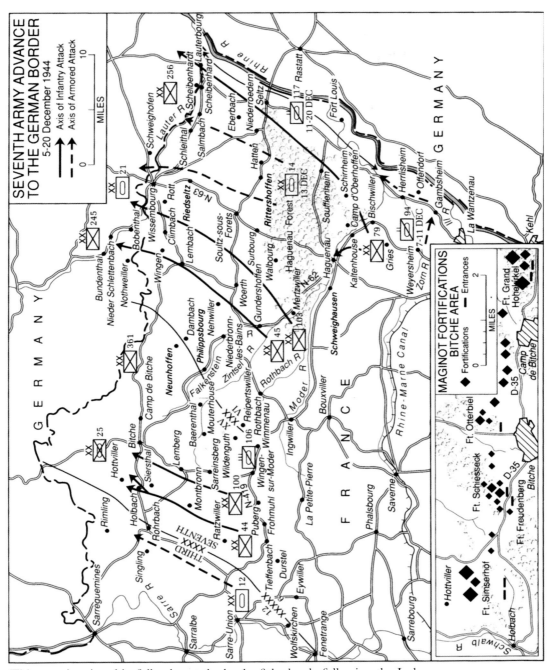

SEVENTH ARMY ADVANCE
TO THE GERMAN BORDER
5-20 December 1944

Axis of Infantry Attack
Axis of Armored Attack

MILES
0   10

MAGINOT FORTIFICATIONS
BITCHE AREA

Fortifications   Entrances
♦   ▬

MILES
0   2

Ft. Grand
Hohekirkel

Camp
de Bitche

D-35

Ft. Otterbiel

Ft. Schiesseck

D-35

Ft. Freudenberg   Bitche

Hottviller

Ft. Simserhof

Schwalb R

Holbach

This map is printed in full color at the back of the book, following the Index.

MAP 32

laying German forces clung to hamlets and towns and turned isolated stone farmhouses into minor strongholds that slowed American progress. The retreating units had destroyed or damaged all bridges, left craters in roads, and blocked almost all routes of advance with booby traps and mines including many made of plastic and clay, which the American troops found hard to detect. The terrain, especially in the 100th Division's sector, became more rugged as the advance moved north, and its difficulty was increased by hasty field fortifications that went up wherever the Germans chose to make a stand. Rain, fog, and occasionally snow and ice now added to the discomfort of the XV Corps' infantrymen, while the heavily overcast skies continued to limit air support. From 5 to 20 December the XII Tactical Air Force supporting the 6th Army Group was able to provide significant air support on only four days, and on three of those days poor visibility curtailed the planned missions.

On the same day that German resistance stiffened, the 12th Armored Division's CCA moved into forward positions west of Ratzwiller and, on the 9th, launched an attack over open terrain toward Singling and Rohrbach near the 6th Army Group boundary. Passing through undefended or lightly manned Maginot Line positions, the American armor secured Singling on 9 December and Rohrbach on the 10th and then continued to push northward. Above Rohrbach, however, mines and later accurate German antitank fire and armored counterattacks halted CCA on the 10th and 11th, forcing several withdrawals. This series of actions cost the 23d

Tank Battalion eight medium tanks as well as many casualties, including the life of its commander, Lt. Col. Montgomery C. Meigs.[7] Like the 14th Armored Division, the 12th was acquiring its experience the hard way.

On 12 December the German forces facing the 12th Armored Division, apparently exhausted, withdrew, and CCA, now reinforced by CCR, had little trouble consolidating its previous gains. On 16 December the XII Corps' veteran 80th Infantry Division began taking over the 12th Armored Division's sector, and on the 17th the armored division reverted to XV Corps reserve. The division's introduction to combat between 7 and 15 December had cost approximately 5 officers and 40 enlisted men killed and 15 officers and 140 enlisted men wounded.

While Allen's 12th Armored Division was operating in the Rohrbach area, Spragins' 44th Division took another five hard days—7 through 11 December—to battle its way northward to Siersthal. This town finally fell to the 71st Infantry late on the 11th, just as the 324th Infantry was coming up on the west between Siersthal and Rohrbach. But on the XV Corps' right, the 100th Division, fighting its way across rough, forested country, found the going tougher; at dusk on the 11th it was still over two miles short of Bitche.

---

[7] Colonel Meigs, USMA 1940, was a descendant of Dr. John F. Meigs, brother of Maj. Gen. Montgomery C. Meigs, the Quartermaster General of the Union Army.

COMMANDING GENERALS CONTEMPLATE THE NEXT MOVE. *Generals Allen and Spragins are on the left.*

The Fortresses of Bitche

The capture of Siersthal opened a potential route, through the valley of the Schwalb River, bypassing the German-held Maginot Line installations in the Bitche area on the west. By the end of 11 December, however, it was evident that the Germans had chosen to hold the forts around Bitche, threatening the flank of any American advance that ignored these strongholds. Reluctantly, Haislip thus ordered both of his infantry divisions to prepare assault operations against the western and central fortresses. Both he and his division commanders hoped that the Germans would not defend the fortresses in any great strength and would abandon the area after only token resistance.

In deciding to make a stand at the Ensemble de Bitche, the Germans had chosen well. Unlike most Maginot Line forts, which were positioned primarily against attacks from the north and east, many of the installations in the Bitche area could also defend and fire effectively against an assault from the south. The Ensemble stretched eastward about eight miles from the vicinity of Hottviller past Bitche and the Camp de Bitche to Fort Grand Hohekirkel. The major works lay on rising ground north of Route D–35, the east-west road running through the valley in which the town of Bitche was located.

Westernmost of the larger fortifications was Fort Simserhof with ten separate fortified complexes, or "units," all situated on commanding ground south of Hottviller and approximately two miles north of Route D–35. About a mile and a half east of Simserhof was Fort Schiesseck with eleven units, the most extensive of all Bitche area installations; just on the south side of D–35 from Fort Schiesseck was the much smaller Fort Freudenberg, with only a single major unit. Another mile and a half east of Schiesseck and centered half a mile north of Bitche spread Fort Otterbiel with four or five larger units; and, continuing east, several rather isolated installations dominated Route D–35 for the two miles between Bitche and the Camp de Bitche. The Ensemble ended in the east with Fort Grand Hohekirkel, which had five major units all located about a mile east of the Camp de Bitche.

The units of the main installations were each formidable fortifications built of reinforced concrete, with walls and overheads that were three to ten feet thick. Some had as many as five underground levels, while others had no ground-level entrances and could be reached only through long tunnels. Barbed-wire entanglements surrounded most of the fortifications, supplemented by elaborate antitank obstacles. Most of the installations were mutually supporting and provided broad, clear fields of fire in all directions. Gaps between the major units were covered by hasty field fortifications, and many of the German troops initially occupied such positions rather than the interiors of the larger installations.

The Germans were able to employ some French artillery, including a few disappearing guns, while German field artillery and mortars emplaced north of the fortresses added to the defense. Although the latter could be neutralized by counterbattery fire, American artillery, up to 8-inch and 240-mm., would find the fortifications themselves nearly impervious except at entrances, escape hatches, and open gun emplacements; the ordnance delivered by XII Tactical Air Force fighter-bombers would fare no better. In the end, the reduction of the massive forts would depend largely on teams of infantry and combat engineers.

The *XC Corps' 25th Panzer Grenadier Division* was responsible for defending Forts Simserhof, Schiesseck, and Otterbiel, and *Group Hoehne's 361st Volksgrenadier Division* for Fort Grand Hohekirkel and the installations in the Camp de Bitche area. However, with the rapid changes in the German boundaries during this period, many of the troop reassignments could not be put into effect before the American attack, and the defensive responsibilities for the central fortresses were somewhat blurred.

From the American point of view, the lay of the land and the positioning of the major installations dictated that the Ensemble de Bitche forts should be taken out sequentially, from west to east. Thus, on 13 December the 44th Division led off the XV Corps' effort with an attack on Fort Simserhof, the westernmost fortification. While the 71st Infantry made the main assault from the Holbach area south of the installation, General Spragins sent the 324th In-

71ST REGIMENT, 44TH DIVISION, FORT SIMSERHOF, NOVEMBER 1944

fantry east across the Schwalb River to seize high ground north of the fort in the vicinity of Hottviller in order to secure the flank of the attack. The 324th's effort met little opposition, but the 71st Infantry's advance on the fort proved painfully slow. On the left, the 71st was subject to intense German artillery and mortar fire; on the right, a German counterattack from the Freudenberg Farm area, half a mile west of Fort Freudenberg, frustrated attempts by the regiment to outflank Simserhof on the east. The 44th Division ended the first day of the assault with little to show for its efforts.

On 14 December the 71st Infantry regained some lost ground and secured Freudenberg Farm. In addition, the regiment captured some minor positions between Forts Simserhof and Schiesseck and, reinforced with combat engineers, began pushing northward in another attempt to invest Simserhof on the east. Progress, however, was again slow. During the next four days, 14 through 18 December, Spragins put all the artillery, tank, and tank destroyer fire that he could marshal against the major installations of Simserhof, while the 71st, fighting off numerous small counterattacks, focused its infantry-engineer assault teams against the fort's ammunition and personnel entrances, which were all about 1,500 yards south of the main units. By evening of the 17th, troops of the 71st Infantry, with engineer support, had entered the underground portions of Simserhof, while other elements of the regiment on the surface had penetrated a number of the strongest fortifications. On the morning of 19 December, the 71st launched a final attack to clear the last Germans from the installations, only to find that the remaining defenders had withdrawn northward during the night. On the same day, the 44th Division's 114th regiment moved into the town of Hottviller without opposition. With the fall of Simserhof and Hottviller, the division began regrouping for an attack north to the West Wall, gratefully leaving the rest of the Ensemble de Bitche to the 100th Division.

On 14 December General Burress, commanding the 100th Infantry Division, had sent the 398th Infantry directly toward Forts Freudenberg and Schiesseck without any extensive preliminary bombardment, about the same time that the 44th Division was beginning to invest Simserhof. Like the 71st Infantry, the 398th quickly learned that the Germans intended to present more than token resistance. Moving north out of the wooded hills south of Bitche and Route D–35, the advancing American infantry was met by accurate artillery fire from both Forts Schiesseck and Otterbiel and was forced to pull back almost immediately. Burress then brought up his corps and division artillery, including some heavy 240-mm. pieces, to begin a two-day bombardment, supplemented when possible by air strikes. Although a later investigation would show that the firepower exercise caused no significant damage to the installations themselves (the French

had built well), it did appear to shake the morale of the defenders. Equally important, Burress' infantry commanders used the two days to plan their approaches to the fortifications more carefully.

Resuming the attack on 17 December, the 398th Infantry recaptured small Fort Freudenberg[8] and secured the two southern entrances to Fort Schiesseck. The strong German opposition lessened somewhat on the 18th, allowing the 398th Infantry, with engineer support, to begin closing on the main units of the fort. As each unit was reached, infantry-engineer teams engaged any Germans remaining on the ground level, and then dropped explosives down elevator shafts, stairwells, and ventilating conduits to isolate the lower levels. The American troops generally made no attempt to descend into the depths of the fortifications, satisfied with sealing off the lower sections of each installation and interring any Germans that remained.

On 20 December the 398th secured the last of Fort Schiesseck's eleven major units, and the regiment, with the rest of the Century Division, prepared to push on toward the German border, roughly eight miles north of Bitche. A few forces stayed behind in the Simserhof-Schiesseck area to protect the division's right flank. Bitche itself remained in German hands, as did Forts Otterbiel and Grand Hohekirkel and the entire Camp de Bitche area. Haislip may have hoped that the

---

[8] Both the 44th and 100th Divisions claimed the capture of Fort Freudenberg. Elements of the 44th Division reportedly found the fort empty on 14 December, but German troops may have reoccupied the position later.

Germans occupying the Ensemble de Bitche would leave once they were no longer in a position to delay his advance to the West Wall and their own escape routes to the north were threatened. Unknown to the XV Corps commanders, events occurring outside of their area of operation had already made the question academic.

The 398th Infantry's operations against the Ensemble de Bitche from 14 through 20 December cost the regiment approximately fifteen men killed and eighty wounded; the low casualties stemmed in part from the decision to use firepower instead of potentially costly infantry assaults against the prepared positions. Heavy artillery and air bombardments, supplemented as often as possible by direct tank and tank destroyer fire, at least kept the German defenders under cover, unable to man weapons or maneuver above the ground, and allowed American infantry and engineers to infiltrate the approaches to the individual blockhouses in order to do their work.

Of at least equal importance was von Rundstedt's guidance to the field commanders directing the defense of the Bitche area: to prepare to withdraw to the West Wall once the Ardennes offensive was under way and to preserve unit integrity during that withdrawal. Both Generals Petersen and Hoehne thus regarded the Ensemble de Bitche as no more than a delaying position. Had they manned these installations with greater strength, the seizure of Simserhof and Schiesseck would have been a much more expensive affair for the American forces.

The VI Corps Offensive North

On 5 December General Brooks, the VI Corps commander, assumed operational control of the 45th and 79th Infantry Divisions, which were spread across a front of about thirty miles from the Low Vosges to the Rhine. During the following days he bolstered these units with the 14th Armored and 103d Infantry Divisions, inserting the 103d between the 45th and 79th and assembling the 14th Armored in the rear, ready to move up on command. Temporarily O'Daniel's 3d Infantry Division, still assigned to the VI Corps, would remain around Strasbourg.

Brooks' offensive plans called for the 103d and 79th Divisions to undertake the main effort in the strengthened Seventh Army drive north to the West Wall.[9] Wyche's 79th, on the corps' right, or eastern, sector, was initially to lead the main attack, moving north up the right bank of the Rhine with Haffner's 103d on its left. The 79th Division was to attack on 9 December, and the 103d Division on the 10th. When Brooks decided the time was right, Smith's 14th Armored Division would pass through the 103d and head for Wissembourg, about seventeen miles north of Haguenau. There the armored division would secure crossings over the Lauter River, which marked the German border in the Wissembourg area, and prepare to exploit northward through the West Wall.

The 45th Division, in a supporting role, would conduct limited objective

---

[9] See VI Corps FO 9, 5 Dec 44; Seventh Army FO 7, 2 Dec 44; VI Corps OI 22, 6 Dec 44.

attacks on the VI Corps' left wing until 10 December; it would then strike northeast from the vicinity of Niederbronn-les-Bains, the division's current objective, to support the main effort. The 45th would have a new commander for the December offensive. General Eagles had been wounded on 30 November when his jeep hit a mine, and Maj. Gen. Robert T. Frederick, formerly the commander of the 1st Airborne Task Force, took command of the division on 4 December.

The VI Corps confronted the bulk of *Group Hoehne*'s forces. On General Hoehne's right, or western, sector the *361st Volksgrenadier Division* held the Low Vosges area from the Camp de Bitche southeast about twelve miles to the vicinity of Niederbronn-les-Bains.[10] The weak *245th Volksgrenadier Division* occupied the zone from Niederbronn southeast about ten miles to the Moder River at Schweighausen, covering a gap of generally open, rolling ground between the Low Vosges and the Haguenau forest. The sector from Schweighausen to the Rhine, over fifteen miles, was the responsibility of the stronger *256th Volksgrenadier Division*.

In preparation for the main series of attacks on 9 and 10 December, the 45th and 79th Divisions conducted several preliminary operations to secure their lines of departure. On 5 December the 45th Division's three regiments continued their push up to the Niederbronn-Mertzwiller railway line, but progress was slow. The division's axis of advance was beginning to take Frederick's forces deep into the broadening Low Vosges Mountains, where heavily wooded hills and valleys channeled and constricted forward movement. Every village and hamlet became a German delaying position difficult to outflank; roadblocks, demolitions, and mines abounded; nearly every bridge was destroyed or damaged; and German artillery and mortar fire seemed to intensify with each step American troops took toward the West Wall. On the division's right, the 180th regiment, still operating in reasonably open terrain, cleared most of Mertzwiller on the 5th; but the next day a German infantry-armor counterattack drove the Americans south, back across the Zintsel du Nord Brook, which bisected the town.[11] The Germans chose not to follow up their success, and on 7 December a battalion of the 410th Infantry, 103d Division, coming from the High Vosges front, relieved the 180th Infantry, thus allowing Frederick to pull the regiment back for the main attack three days away.

Meanwhile, the 45th Division's 157th regiment was able to slowly outflank German defenses at Niederbronn on the west and north, and finally occupied the town on 9 December. However, the 179th regiment, in the division's center, made little headway, and the area around Gundershoffen, between Niederbronn and Mertzwiller, remained in German

---

[10] Subsequent information on German forces in this chapter comes from von Luttichau, "German Operations," ch. 26.

[11] VI Corps AAR, Dec 44, p. 13; 45th Div AAR, Dec 44, p. 8. The division report estimated the German force at 200 infantry and 4 tanks; the corps report put it at 75 infantry and 3 tanks—discrepancies that were common in such documentation.

hands. Although it had defended its sector fairly well, the *245th Volksgrenadier Division*, one of *Group Hoehne's* weakest units, had taken severe losses from the continued 45th Division attacks and would have difficulty carrying on the fight.

The preparatory actions of the 79th Infantry Division were more crucial. Both Brooks and the division commander, General Wyche, were concerned with the corps' right flank. As long as the Germans held the Gambsheim area on the west bank of the Rhine, Wyche felt obliged to secure the sector between Gries and Weyersheim with the 313th regiment and to post the attached 94th Cavalry Squadron below Weyersheim as well.[12] In the south, the 117th Cavalry Squadron, temporarily attached to the 3d Infantry Division, screened the Gambsheim area from La Wantzenau, just north of Strasbourg. This entire effort, all because of a small German bridgehead west of the Rhine, was absorbing too many units, and the 79th Division commander wanted Gambsheim secured before he moved his division north.

Wyche gave the task of clearing Gambsheim to the 94th Cavalry Squadron, which had been reinforced by a platoon of medium tanks, two companies of armored infantry, and a battery of 105-mm. self-propelled artillery. After a thirty-minute artillery preparation early on 7 December, the squadron attacked, at first meeting stiff resistance. Automatic weapons and well-directed mortar and artillery fire, some from positions east of the

Rhine, slowed the light armor down somewhat, but by evening the leading cavalry units had reached the western edge of Gambsheim. The following day, 8 December, resistance faded. By noon, after twenty-five soldiers from the *256th Volksgrenadier Division* surrendered, the 94th Cavalry cleared the town and surrounding area, thus ending the threat to the 79th Division's flank and allowing Wyche to use all three of his infantry regiments for the main attack.

VI Corps Attacks (10–20 December)

For Brooks, the 79th Division's initial assault across the Moder River and through Haguenau was the most critical phase of the offensive. A delay here would have repercussions all along the front, while a successful crossing could set a good pace for the entire advance. Located on VI Corps' right wing, the 79th had two infantry regiments—the 315th and the 314th—facing the Haguenau area, west to east, and a third—the 313th— in reserve securing the division's right flank. Initially Wyche planned to attack north on 9 December, directing his main effort east of Haguenau. He wanted his forces to cross the Moder River in the vicinity of Bischwiller, some four miles southeast of Haguenau, and then drive north for about fifteen miles to Seltz, a mile or so west of the Rhine. To screen the left flank of the projected Moder River crossing, he wanted to pull the entire 315th regiment out of his left wing and have it swing behind and through the 314th to seize Kaltenhouse, about two miles northwest of Bischwiller. To screen the right side,

---

[12] The 94th Cavalry Squadron was on loan from the 14th Armored Division.

he ordered the 94th Cavalry Squadron to advance northward from Gambsheim. The 313th regiment, currently in reserve, would undertake the main effort, striking north for the Moder River at Bischwiller, as the 314th moved up to the Moder around Haguenau, keeping the German defenders occupied and ready to reinforce any of the principal attacking forces on Wyche's order.[13]

The 79th Division faced *Group Hoehne*'s *256th Volksgrenadier Division*, which was understrength as well as weak in supporting armor, antitank weapons, and some type of artillery. Although it was occupying good defensive terrain and had been receiving some reinforcements from east of the Rhine, the *256th* had no designated reserves, and *Group Hoehne* could supply none. Neither Brig. Gen. Gerhard Franz, commanding the *256th*, nor Generals Hoehne and Balck expected the unit to hold back a general attack.

With the Gambsheim area secured by 8 December, the 79th Division launched its attack on the 9th as planned. The *256th Volksgrenadiers* appeared to have concentrated their defenses around Haguenau, and the direction of the 79th Division's main effort took them by surprise. Although the 314th reached the Moder only with great difficulty and the 315th was stopped about a mile short of Kaltenhouse, the advance of the 313th on Bischwiller was only lightly opposed. Striking north at 0645 without any preliminary artillery bombardment, the 313th managed to cap-

ture intact a major bridge over the Moder. By the end of the day the regiment had cleared Bischwiller, crossed the river, and pushed northward another mile.

The breakthrough at Bischwiller opened up many possibilities for Wyche. On 10 December, with the 314th and 315th Infantry still stalled in the Haguenau-Kaltenhouse area, Wyche had a battalion of the 315th sidestep to the east, cross the Moder at Bischwiller, then strike out west along the northern side of the Moder, hitting the German defenders on their flanks and occupying Camp d'Oberhoffen, a former French Army training center. Meanwhile the 313th Infantry consolidated its bridgehead and continued to push north, advancing to Schirrhein, four miles north of Bischwiller, while elements of the 94th Cavalry Squadron reached Herrlisheim, three miles north of Gambsheim, on the 79th Division's right.

While German attention was focused on the Haguenau area, the 45th and 103d Infantry Divisions began their offensives in the west. On 10 December the 157th Infantry, leading the 45th Division's attack on the corps' extreme left wing, gained over two miles north and northeast of Niederbronn, while the 180th Infantry, coming back into the line, passed through the 179th regiment to cross the railway line and Route N–62 at Gundershoffen, three miles south of Niederbronn. The 180th then swung off to the northeast as the 411th Infantry of the 103d Division came up on its right to push two miles east of Gundershoffen against diminishing resistance. Another three miles to the south the 103d Division's 410th In-

313TH REGIMENT, 79TH DIVISION, IN THE VICINITY OF BISCHWILLER. *M5 light tanks are on the road, December 1944.*

fantry recaptured Mertzwiller after bitter house-to-house fighting, an action that included the recovery of about eighty men of the 180th Infantry who had been hiding out in the town since 6 December.

After Mertzwiller, the 410th advanced over a mile eastward into the western fringes of the vast Haguenau forest, which extended east about twenty miles. Laced by minor roads and logging trails, the forest lay on generally flat land cut by numerous small streams that in wet weather could severely curtail troop and vehicle movements. In addition there were several Maginot Line installations in the eastern third of the forest, and a determined German de-

fense of the forest could have caused serious trouble. Now, however, the full weight of the VI Corps' assault as well as the earlier offensives of the XV Corps began to have a decided effect on the weary German defenders, and by evening of the 10th the entire German line had begun to give way.

The attacks of the 45th and 103d Divisions on 10 December had caught the weak *245th Volksgrenadier Division* unprepared to conduct an organized defense, and by the end of the day the unit had begun to fall apart. Hoehne was quick to appreciate that its collapse would threaten the flanks of both his other divisions; as a partial remedy, he narrowed the *245th's* sector somewhat, forcing the *256th* to extend its right flank to the northwest. But with the continued penetration into the *256th Volksgrenadier Division*'s front by the 79th Division along the Rhine, the measure was obviously unsatisfactory. Sometime that night, therefore, with the approval of *Army Group G*, Hoehne directed both the *245th* and *256th* to withdraw two to six miles north to a secondary defensive line. The new line was to begin at Nehwiller, a little over two miles east of Niederbronn, and extend twenty miles eastward to the Rhine at Fort Louis. The decision meant that *Group Hoehne* would abandon both Haguenau city and most of the Haguenau forest without further fighting, but given his strength as well as his instructions to preserve the integrity of his forces, General Hoehne felt that he had little choice. At *Army Group G*, General Balck reluctantly acquiesced to the withdrawal.

During 11 December all three of Brooks' attacking infantry divisions made considerable progress. On the corps' right, the 79th Division's 314th regiment moved into Haguenau unopposed in the morning, and the 315th secured the area between Bischwiller and Haguenau, uncovering large stocks of unused German supplies and equipment in Camp d'Oberhoffen. Still pushing northward, the 313th Infantry met strong resistance at Soufflenheim, but reconnaissance patrols probing the eastern portion of the Haguenau forest detected no enemy presence. Along the Rhine other patrols advanced the lines three miles north from Herrlisheim. During the day most of the 94th Cavalry Squadron rejoined the

14th Armored Division, and the 117th Cavalry Squadron, with one troop of the 94th attached, took over the right flank security mission.[14]

In the west, the 157th Infantry, 45th Division, secured Nehwiller on 11 December against little opposition, breaking through Hoehne's projected defensive line before it could be established. The 157th then pushed northeastward through the Low Vosges another mile or so, while the 180th Infantry, on the 45th Division's right, gained about three miles. But the terrain facing the 45th was now becoming increasingly difficult. In the 103d Division's sector, the 411th and 409th Infantry advanced nearly three miles, piercing the planned German line near the road junction town of Woerth; on the division's right, the 410th Infantry seized Walbourg on the northeastern border of the Haguenau forest. Neither of the two divisions encountered any significant German opposition.

On the 12th the German rout continued. In the Vosges the 45th Division seized Philippsbourg on the corps' far left and outflanked a German strongpoint at Lembach, only about four miles short of the border. To the east the 103d Division kept pace, reaching Surbourg on the northern edge of the Haguenau forest; along the Rhine, the 79th Division occupied Soufflenheim and advanced eight miles farther north to Niederroedern and Seltz. Wyche, the 79th Division commander, expected

---

[14] With control of the 117th Squadron passing from the 3d to the 79th Division, a battalion of the 3d Division's 7th regiment assumed responsibility for the Rhine area around Gambsheim.

German counterattacks from the eastern section of the Haguenau forest, but his patrols there found only damaged bridges, abandoned roadblocks, and empty Maginot Line installations. The *256th Volksgrenadier Division* was no longer trying to contest his division's advance.

By 12 December Brooks had become convinced that the Germans would not stand and fight, but would instead attempt a series of delaying actions as they fell slowly back to the German border and the West Wall. The cold weather plus the rain, rough terrain, demolitions, mines and roadblocks of all types, mortar and long-range artillery fire, and tactical supply problems were more responsible for retarding American progress than any ground combat action on the part of the Germans. As for *Group Hoehne's* forces, 12 December was a disaster. Hoehne's small staff was no longer able to keep pace with the tempo of changing events nor could it direct its subordinate units in any coherent manner. In the center the *245th Volksgrenadier Division* finally collapsed, and the *256th* along the Rhine was not in much better shape. Deep in the Vosges the failing *361st Volksgrenadiers,* under increasing pressure from Haislip's XV Corps around Bitche, could do little to assist their neighbors. Only the emergency arrival of the *192d Panzer Grenadiers* of the *21st Panzer Division* forestalled a complete breakthrough in Hoehne's front.

Drive to the West Wall

With the Germans reeling, Brooks was now ready to commit Smith's 14th Armored Division. Believing that

at best only a weak shell of defenders confronted his forces, he reviewed his plans for the commitment of the armored unit on the evening of the 12th. Originally he had intended to have the armored division pass through the 103d Division and strike for Wissembourg. However, after the *256th Volksgrenadier Division* put up a respectable defense in front of the 79th Division on 9 and 10 December, he considered passing the 14th Armored through the right flank of the 103d, swinging it north of the Haguenau forest and east to the Rhine, thus striking the German defenses around Haguenau from the rear. However, with the *256th* now rapidly retreating, Brooks decided to insert the 14th Armored Division between the 103d and 79th Divisions. This action would allow both infantry divisions to concentrate on narrower fronts for a continuing push north and would provide the armored division with a sector of its own without masking the advance of the others. Brooks therefore directed the armored division to move up to the Haguenau forest area and attack northward at daylight on 13 December across a nine-mile-wide front between Surbourg and Niederroedern. Still aiming for Wissembourg, the division was to secure crossings over the Lauter River southeast of the town, while the 103d and 79th Divisions, their sectors of advance substantially narrowed, would continue northward abreast of the armored forces to the German border.[15] For the second

---

[15] See VI Corps FO 9, 5 Dec 44; VI Corps OI 23, 9 Dec 44; VI Corps OI 25, 12 Dec 44; 14th Armd

time since taking command of the VI Corps, General Brooks had ordered what amounted to a general pursuit.

Leading off for the 14th Armored Division on 13 December, CCB quickly reached Surbourg and then swung east six miles along the northern edge of the Haguenau forest to Hatten before encountering significant opposition. CCA followed CCB to Surbourg and continued northeast about two miles to Soultz-sous-Forets, where the armor linked up with the 103d Division's 409th Infantry coming in from the west. On 14 December CCA gained another five miles along the axis of Route N–63, the Haguenau-Wissembourg road, and wound up the day in a fire fight three miles south of Wissembourg. CCB, on the same day, pushed northeast seven miles from Hatten to Salmbach, about one mile short of the Lauter River and the German border. As armored patrols approached the small river, they found it flooded, measuring up to eighty feet across in some areas and not easily fordable.

Meanwhile, the VI Corps' infantry divisions continued their steady advances during 13 and 14 December. On the 13th, the 79th Division resumed its drive northward just east of the armored division, clearing Seltz and Niederroedern after much house-to-house fighting; it then advanced another two miles north to Eberbach and reached the Lauter River near Scheibenhard and Lauterbourg on the 14th.

In the far west the 45th Division, struggling through the Low Vosges,

finally took isolated Lembach and reached Wingen on 14 December. On its right flank, the 103d Division continued northward, meeting heavy resistance at Climbach, a road junction town two miles east of Wingen. There the 3d Platoon of Company C, 614th Tank Destroyer Battalion (towed), a black unit of a 411th Infantry task force, lost three of its four guns and suffered 50 percent casualties, but threw back a strong armor-supported counterattack by the *21st Panzer Division*.[16] Elsewhere the 103d's advance met less resistance, and division elements reached Rott on the 13th and the Wissembourg area the following day.

Into Germany

By the morning of 15 December, Brooks' VI Corps was ready to move across the German border in strength. In the broadening Low Vosges, the 45th and 103d Infantry Divisions prepared to push through a rough, wooded axis of advance, five to six miles wide, with four regiments on line and two in reserve. In the VI Corps center, the 14th Armored Division concentrated against Wissembourg and Schleithal, aided by the right wing of the 103d Division. To the east the 79th Infantry Division focused on Lauterbourg and the Lauter

---

Div FO 1, 11 Dec 44; 14th Armd Div FO 2, 12 Dec 44.

[16] The platoon received a Presidential Unit Citation for the action, and 1st Lt. Charles L. Thomas of Company C was awarded the Distinguished Service Cross for heroic action and outstanding leadership. For an account, see Ralph Mueller and Jerry Turk, *Report After Action: The Story of the 103d Infantry Division* (Innsbruck, 1945), pp. 48–49; and Mary Penick Motley, ed., *The Invisible Soldier: The Experience of the Black Soldier, World War II* (Detroit: Wayne State U Press, 1975), pp. 166–77.

River, still using armored cavalry units to screen its right flank on the Rhine. The final drive north would take all of the units directly into the vaunted West Wall, the defensive works that the German Army had been preparing for several months a few miles inside the German border.

Facing the center of the VI Corps was the weak *21st Panzer Division* intermixed with remnants of the *245th Volksgrenadier Division* and filled in here and there by yet a few more rear-echelon units turned infantry. To the west the *361st Volksgrenadier Division* still had a precarious hold on its mountain defensive line from the Camp de Bitche to the area just northwest of Wingen; to the east the *256th Volksgrenadier Division* was attempting to make a final delaying stand on the Lauter River. Meanwhile, behind all of *Group Hoehne's* flagging forces, *Division Raessler* and the other designated fortress units were preparing to make their first defense of the West Wall.

During the morning of 15 December, the 14th Armored Division's CCA cleared Riedseltz, but ran into intense artillery fire and a German tank-supported counterattack while attempting to move farther north, probably indicating the arrival of additional *21st Panzer Division* units to reinforce the *256th Volksgrenadiers.* CCA repulsed the assault, destroying two tanks, but gained little more ground. Elsewhere VI Corps units were at first more successful. Although harassed by artillery and mortar fire, the 45th Division's 157th Infantry gained almost two miles of rugged terrain on the division's left; meanwhile the 180th Infantry, more

than keeping pace, reached the German border north of Wingen and at 1245 sent a patrol into Germany. On the 45th Division's right, the 411th Infantry of the 103d Division, after cleaning up the Climbach area, crossed the German border at 1305 and continued north. To the east, in the Lauter River area, the 79th Division's 315th regiment cleared the southern half of Scheibenhard and sent patrols across the river into the German half of the town (Scheibenhardt). In the meantime, the 313th Infantry had come up on the right and, after more house-to-house fighting, had forced the Germans out of Lauterbourg, placing the southern bank of the Lauter firmly in the hands of the 79th Division.

By late afternoon of 15 December, VI Corps forces had thus reached or crossed the German border at half a dozen locations. At this point General Hoehne, having committed all his forces and realizing that a stand at the border itself was impossible, decided that the moment had finally come for a complete withdrawal into the West Wall defenses. Accordingly he informed Balck of his decision, emphasizing that an immediate withdrawal was necessary if he was to preserve the integrity of his remaining forces and use them to strengthen the fortified line. At *Army Group G* headquarters Balck had learned that the long-awaited Ardennes offensive was definitely to be launched on 16 December and concluded that *Group Hoehne* had fulfilled its stated mission: to hold in front of the West Wall until the Ardennes operation began. At 2045 on 15 December, he therefore approved the withdrawal of *Group*

Hoehne into the West Wall defenses.[17]

Balck's decision was not well received at *OB West.* Von Rundstedt at first refused to condone the withdrawal and severely criticized Balck for the conduct of operations in Hoehne's area. The field marshal wanted to halt the withdrawal, but *Group Hoehne* had already begun pulling back and there was little he could do to reverse the movement. Von Rundstedt insisted, however, that the *361st Volksgrenadier Division* continue to hold across the Vosges and that the *25th Panzer Grenadier Division* of *XC Corps* continue to defend the Maginot Line positions west of the Camp de Bitche where the XV Corps was attacking. Balck relayed these directives to Hoehne at midnight, allowing *Group Hoehne* to withdraw everything except the *361st Volksgrenadier Division*, but warned him that the West Wall was to be the final German position— "there you die."[18]

Between 16 and 20 December VI Corps units found that German resistance would slacken, but then stiffen remarkably as the units bumped into the West Wall defenses. In the Vosges the 45th Division seized the German mountain village of Nothweiller and the town of Bobenthal on the upper reaches of the Lauter River on the 16th, and reached Bundenthal and Nieder Schlettenbach a few miles farther north by 18 December. There its advance ended, and on the 18th and 19th German counterattacks and intense artillery and mortar fire forced a general withdrawal back across the Lauter. The experience of the 103d Division was much the same. On the 14th Armored Division's front in the VI Corps' center, American armor occupied Wissembourg and Schleithal on the 16th and reached out to Schweighofen, a mile or so into Germany; but by the 19th Smith's armored units were able to hang on to only a few precarious bridgeheads in the face of German counterattacks and increased artillery fire. In the east, combat engineers had erected some bridges over the Lauter unmolested, which allowed 79th Division units to push several miles into Germany, but this advance also stalled by the 19th.[19] The VI Corps had now reached the outer works of the West Wall and would need a respite before attempting a major penetration of the somewhat overrated defensive line.

Stalemate at Colmar (5–20 December)

By 5 December General Devers had turned almost the entire Seventh Army north, still expecting that General de Lattre's First French Army could finish off the Colmar Pocket assisted by Dahlquist's 36th Infantry Division and Leclerc's armor. At the time de Lattre assigned both units to the French II Corps, although they would still be supported logistically by the Seventh Army. Devers and de Lattre were accordingly surprised when the German defensive effort

---

[17] See ULTRA Msg HP9500, 152157 Dec 44, ULTRA Collection, MHI.

[18] Von Luttichau, "German Operations," ch. 26, p. 42, citing the Army Group G War Diary for 15–16 December 1944.

[19] For heroic action near Berg, Germany, on 19 December, Technical Sergeant Robert E. Gerstung, Company H, 313th Infantry, 79th Division, was awarded the Congressional Medal of Honor.

TROOPS OF THE 45TH DIVISION MAKE HOUSE-TO-HOUSE SEARCH, *Bobenthal, Germany, 1944.*

continued to solidify and, rather than meekly withdrawing across the Rhine, the *Nineteenth Army* held in place. Once again Wiese attempted to fill up the depleted combat battalions of his now ten infantry divisions [20] with a variety of military personnel from all branches and services. On the 10th, Hitler's determination to hold the trans-Rhine enclave was sharply underscored by the appointment of

police chief Heinrich Himmler to oversee the task. Himmler was to command *Army Group Oberrhein*, a new headquarters controlling Wiese's *Nineteenth Army* in the Colmar region as well as a mixture of defensive formations on the east bank of the Rhine south of Lauterbourg. *Oberrhein* would be a semi-independent headquarters and treated as a separate theater command; thus Himmler reported not to von Rundstedt's *OB West*, but directly to *OKW*, and in practice answered only to Hitler himself. Himmler, in turn, replaced Wiese on 15 December with Lt. Gen. Siegfried Rasp, apparently finding the long-time commander of the *Nineteenth Army* less than enthusiastic regarding his new mission.

[20] These ten included, approximately clockwise from the south, the *30th SS Division;* the *338th, 189th,* and *159th Infantry Divisions;* the *269th, 16th,* and *708th Volksgrenadier Divisions;* the *716th* and *198th Infantry Divisions;* and *Division Burke;* all were controlled by the *LXIV* and *LXIII Corps,* with some of the divisions initially able to marshal perhaps no more than a few thousand men or the equivalent of one or two combat battalions.

For the next few weeks the command changes proved effective. However questionable his military abilities, Himmler was able to accelerate the infusion of replacements into both the Colmar area and the east bank defenses by having the immediate German interior scoured more thoroughly for supplies, equipment, and manpower. In addition, the direct presence of the head of the dreaded secret police undoubtedly ensured that no unauthorized withdrawals occurred and inspired local German troop commanders to defend each village, water crossing, and road intersection more vigorously.

At the time of the VI Corps' redeployment northward, its attacks in the north had reduced the base of the Colmar Pocket from about fifty to forty miles—from the town of Rhinau in the north to Kembs in the south—but the pocket still extended about thirty miles to the west, reaching the upper Thur River valley deep in the High Vosges (*Map 33*). On the southern border of the pocket, the *Nineteenth Army* had managed to secure the Harth forest area between Mulhouse and the Rhine and to form a solid defensive line from St. Amarin in the Vosges to Cernay and the Thur River. To the west, in the High Vosges, German units continued to defend the mountain passes in the area that once marked the gap between the First French and U.S. Seventh Armies. On the northern edge of the pocket, between Selestat and the Rhine, Wiese and his successor, Rasp, had gradually reinforced the area with mainly infantry units of all types, so that each Alsatian hamlet and crossroads had become a defensive strong point.

To crack this defensive enclave, de Lattre planned a full-scale offensive. Bethouart's I Corps would attack north through Cernay on 13 December, and de Monsabert's II Corps, with the U.S. 36th Infantry and the French 2d Armored Divisions attached, would push south from the Selestat region on the 15th.[21] But de Lattre's mid-December offensive probably never had the strength necessary for success. The November fight through the southern portion of the High Vosges and the Belfort-Mulhouse drive had been more difficult than Haislip's advance to Strasbourg, and had exhausted French manpower and materiel resources. Furthermore, with their weaker logistical and personnel support systems, the French units always took longer to recuperate than their American counterparts. In December Devers regarded the endemic French shortage of infantry replacements as de Lattre's most immediate problem, followed by the shortage of line officers with experience handling African colonial troops. Efforts to attach militia elements to regular units continued to have serious drawbacks, and the recruiting and training of new personnel, especially officers and technicians, could not be accomplished overnight.

From the French commander's point of view, the need to commit strong forces to Operation INDEPENDENCE in western France was his greatest frustration. Ordered again to begin redeploying major troop units for an endeavor entirely unrelated to his current mission, he could only rue

---

[21] This section is based primarily on *Seventh Army Rpt*, II, 503–27, and de Lattre, *History*, pp. 287–300.

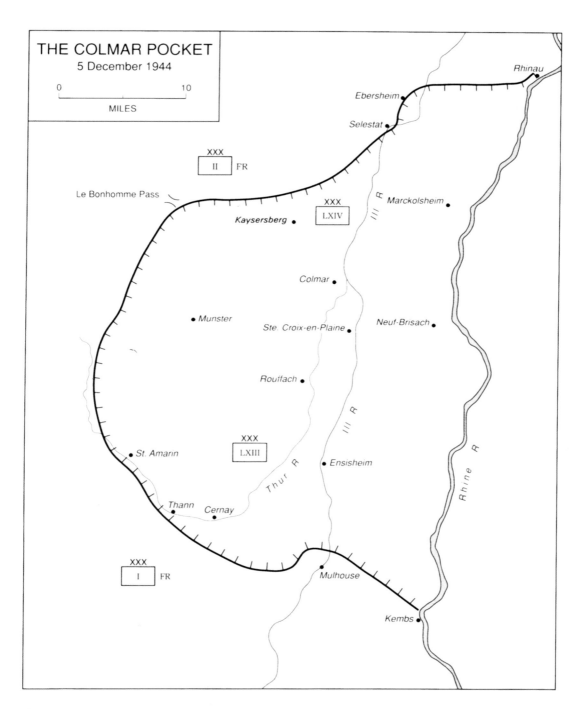

THE COLMAR POCKET
5 December 1944

0 — 10
MILES

XXX
II FR

Le Bonhomme Pass

Rhinau

Ebersheim

Selestat

Marckolsheim

XXX
LXIV

Kaysersberg •

Ill R

Colmar •

• Munster

Ste. Croix-en-Plaine •

Neuf-Brisach •

Rouffach •

Ill R

XXX
LXIII

• St. Amarin

• *Ensisheim*

Thur R

Thann • • Cernay

Rhine R

XXX
I FR

Mulhouse •

Kembs •

MAP 33   This map is printed in full color at the back of the book, following the Index.

his misfortune. On 5 December the French 1st Infantry Division had begun moving west; by the 18th, the main body of the division had closed on western France, and major units of the 1st Armored Division were preparing to follow. Suddenly, SHAEF agreed to yet another postponement.[22] Although the infantry division quickly turned around and headed back to the main front, it could obviously play no part in the renewed offensive against Colmar. To Devers and de Lattre, the entire redeployment affair was a waste of effort.

Meanwhile, the tired 36th Division and the roadbound French 2d Armored Division had continued to plug their way south. Between the Rhine and the Ill rivers, Leclerc's armor had difficulty penetrating the canal-laced, water-soaked Alsatian plains without more infantry. West of the Ill, Dahlquist's 36th Division, initially strung out between the Bonhomme Pass in the High Vosges and the Selestat region on the plains, managed only to clean out a portion of the Kaysersberg valley during ten days of heavy fighting, taking one small village after another while fending off almost continuous German counterattacks. Progress was agonizingly slow, but from their observation posts in the mountains, 36th Division troops could see German soldiers walking the streets of Colmar.[23] So near, yet so far. In almost constant combat

since it first began to push through the Vosges in October, the 36th was exhausted, and Dahlquist finally requested the division's immediate relief. With Devers' approval, Patch replaced it with O'Daniel's rested 3d Infantry Division on 15 December. Recalling his promise at the Vittel conference in November to clear southern Alsace, Devers hoped that de Lattre's renewed offensive, with the help of one of the Seventh Army's strongest units, would finally complete the task.[24] Provisionally American engineer units assumed responsibility for the Strasbourg area, and the 36th Division went into a reserve status.

At the same time that Dahlquist was having problems pushing the 36th Division farther, Devers began having serious difficulties with Leclerc. The commander of the French 2d Armored Division was extremely unhappy with his new orders and had gone to Paris to plead his case with de Gaulle, later arguing that the mission of clearing the Alsatian plains between the Rhine and Ill rivers was more appropriate for an infantry division. He also requested that his armored unit be returned to American control immediately, even though, like the 3d and 36th Divisions, it was still supported logistically by the Seventh Army. Angry, Devers personally mediated the altercation and privately considered for a short time either disbanding the unit or having Eisenhower ship it off somewhere else. He kept his misgivings to himself, however, feeling that the real problem was the

---

[22] The operation was postponed officially on 14 December. See 1st (French) Infantry Division Movement Order, 4 Dec 44; 1st Inf Div Jnl de Marche, 5 and 19 Dec 44; Fr Forces of the West Jnl de Marche, 13, 18, and 22 Dec 44; Vigneras–de Camas Intervs; *La Premiere Division Blindee au Combat*, p. 102.

[23] Adams Interv, pp. 21–22.

[24] See Ltr, Devers to Eisenhower, 18 Dec 44 (copy CMH).

"bitter hatred" between Leclerc, de Monsabert, and de Lattre over past political differences. Avoiding any open discussion of such matters, Devers informed Leclerc that the mission was necessary and that he had no infantry to spare. The justifiably famous "deuxieme division blindee" would have to make the best of a difficult situation. The problem with Leclerc and the hostility among the various French elements would nag Devers throughout the rest of the war.[25]

On 15 December, shortly after the arrival of O'Daniel's 3d Division, de Lattre renewed his offensive against the pocket, with de Monsabert's II Corps striking through the Kaysersberg-Selestat area for Colmar city and Bethouart's I Corps again heading for Cernay. For the first few days, however, the attacks went nowhere; neither the American division nor the French forces were able to make more than a few dents in the now strengthened German defenses. As elsewhere throughout the Allied front, offensive operations continued to be slowed by increasingly cold, wet, and overcast weather. In the flooded southern Alsatian plains, especially in the area between the Ill and Rhine rivers, vehicles of all types found it impossible to operate off the narrow roads,

which nullified de Lattre's numerical superiority in tanks and other armored vehicles. In addition, German control of the Ill-Rhine area exposed the flank of de Monsabert's offensive to infantry counterattacks from the east, thus blunting the strength of the Franco-American attack toward Colmar.[26]

On 22 December, after more than one week of fruitless attacks against the Colmar Pocket, Devers finally ordered a halt to the effort. Developments to the north, on the front of General Bradley's 12th Army Group, now began to have a major effect on Allied military operations throughout western Europe. This concern led Eisenhower to order the 6th Army Group to adopt a defensive posture, and de Lattre's forces once again broke off the action against Colmar.

Epilogue

News of the German Ardennes attack had spread rapidly through the staffs of the Seventh Army and the 6th Army Group during the evening of 16 December. Initially there was some jubilation. Not believing at first that the assault would pose any severe difficulties for Bradley's forces, many of Devers' commanders hoped that the German effort in the north might correspondingly weaken German strength in the south, thereby offer-

[25] See Devers Diary, 13–15 and 22 Dec 44, and also entries for 17 and 31 Jan and 11 Feb 45; Ltrs, A. Diethelm (French War Minister) to Devers, 13 Dec 44; Devers to Diethelm, 18 Dec 44; Devers to Leclerc, 18 Dec 44 (copies CMH); and Henry Maule, *Out of the Sand: The Epic Story of General Le Clerc and the Fighting Free French* (London: Odhams, 1966), pp. 230–31, 259–75. Ultimately, the French 2d Armored Division, with Leclerc still in command, was sent to western France for operations against the German Atlantic pockets and did not return to the main front until May.

[26] For heroic action in the Kaysersberg area northeast of Colmar between 16 and 18 December 1944, Congressional Medals of Honor were awarded to T. Sgt. Bernard Bell, Company I, 142d Infantry, 36th Infantry Division; 1st Lt. Charles P. Murray, Jr., Company C, 30th Infantry, 3d Infantry Division; and S. Sgt. Gus Kefurt, Company K, 3d Battalion, 15th Infantry, 3d Infantry Division.

ing the Seventh Army a unique opportunity to break through the West Wall defenses into the German interior.[27] But such wishful thinking did not last far beyond 18 December as the strength of the German offensive became more evident. A successful German offensive in the north, threatening Antwerp and the entire Allied rear, would be a disaster for all.[28]

Once again the weight of Allied combat strength began to shift north, although this time for different reasons. Late on the 18th, SHAEF ordered the Third Army's 80th Infantry and 4th Armored Divisions to redeploy northward for the Ardennes, which forced Haislip to quickly recommit the 12th Armored to the vacated sector. At the same time, Bradley instructed Patton, the Third Army commander, to halt all preparations for his own offensive, then scheduled for the following day, and prepare to send more of his divisions northward. Patton complied but was disgruntled, feeling that the Seventh Army's drive into the West Wall had loosened up the German defenses in the Third Army's sector. However, he rapidly recovered both his composure and his enthusiasm after learning of the grave situation in the north and the importance of his new mission.

These changes were only the first signs of a rapid Allied reorientation

toward the threatened front. The next day, 19 December, General Eisenhower held a major command conference at Verdun with Devers, Bradley, Patton, and various high-ranking staff officers. There the Allied Supreme Commander's primary concern was the Ardennes sector, and the urgent need to prepare counterattacks against the northern and southern shoulders of the German penetration. Eisenhower and Bradley put Patton's Third Army in charge of the southern counterattack, changing its direction of advance from east to north. To support the effort, Devers' 6th Army Group was to halt all offensive operations and be ready to yield ground if necessary. Furthermore, the 6th Army Group would be responsible for most of the sector vacated by the Third Army. Priority in supplies, equipment, and manpower would go to the forces fighting in the Ardennes.

With this guidance, Devers ordered the offensives against the West Wall and the Colmar Pocket abruptly ended. He also directed the Seventh Army to undertake responsibility for the extended front, spreading out to the west and northwest over twenty-five miles. The increased frontage meant that even without Eisenhower's instructions, the Seventh Army would have to cease offensive operations, reorganize its forces, and adopt a defensive posture by straightening out its front lines and echeloning its troops in depth.[29]

Privately General Devers was hardly pleased with the new orders. Recalling Eisenhower's decision on 24 No-

---

[27] See messages cited in the VI Corps War Room Journal for 16 December.

[28] Following section is based on Pogue, *The Supreme Command*, pp. 374–77; SCAF–151, 20 Dec 44; Blumenson, *The Patton Papers, 1940–1945*, p. 598; Patton, *War As I Knew It*, pp. 188–89; Hugh Cole, *The Ardennes: Battle of the Bulge*, United States Army in World War II (Washington, 1965), pp. 484–88; and Ladislas Farago, *Patton: Ordeal and Triumph* (New York: Ivan Obolensky Inc., 1964), pp. 703–04.

---

[29] SCAF–151, 20 Dec 44; 6th Army Gp LI 5, 21 Dec 44.

vember halting the Seventh Army's Rhine crossing in the Rastatt area, he felt that his command was once again being called on to bail out the northern army groups "just as we are about to crack the Siegfried Line by infiltration . . . which would permit us to turn both east and west, threatening Karlsruhe to the east and loosening up the entire Siegfried Line in front of the Third Army to the west." Although recognizing the necessity of turning the Third Army north against the German Ardennes offensive, Devers believed it a "tragedy" that the Allied high command "has not seen fit to reinforce success on this flank."[30]

Once the territorial adjustments were made, the new boundary between the 12th and 6th Army Groups would be located near St. Avold, roughly twenty-seven miles west of the old 26 November line.[31] Patch's

Seventh Army would have to absorb the new frontage. To accomplish this, Patch decided to leave his corps boundary intact, but to transfer the 103d Infantry Division from the center of the VI Corps line to the left of the XV Corps. There, with elements of the 12th Armored Division and the 106th Cavalry Group, it would be responsible for almost all of the new sector. As a precaution, he also pulled the 14th Armored Division back into reserve.

South of Strasbourg, General Devers made no changes in the boundary between the U.S. Seventh and the First French Armies. Although calling off the current effort against Colmar, he directed the First French Army to be prepared to resume its offensive no later than 5 January by which time he expected the emergency in the north to be over.[32]

[30] Quotes from Devers Diary, 19 Dec 44.

[31] SCAF–151, 20 Dec 44; 6th Army Gp LI 5, 21 Dec 44.

[32] 6th Army Gp LI 6, 21 Dec 44.

CHAPTER XXVII

Northwind

When the Germans began their Ardennes offensive on 16 December 1944, the 6th Army Group was preparing for a new thrust into German territory and making another try at the Colmar Pocket. At first Devers had hoped that the German focus in the north would facilitate his own offensives. But this expectation was quickly dispelled by Eisenhower's decision on the 19th to have the 6th Group halt all offensive operations and assume a significant portion of the Third Army's area of responsibility. The subsequent realignment placed Devers' forces in an awkward position. For the moment the front of the 6th Army Group remained stable, but resembled a reverse letter *S* with its double bulge—a northern one between Saarbrucken and Strasbourg, with the Haguenau forest and the town of Lauterbourg at its apex, and a southern one north of Mulhouse around the city of Colmar. Eisenhower's order froze Patch's Seventh Army in the upper portion of the reverse *S* and de Lattre's First French Army in the lower half. In the north, the U.S. XV Corps held a narrow alley across the Sarre River valley between Saarbrucken and Bitche, and the U.S. VI Corps occupied the Lauterbourg

bulge, or salient—a large, rolling plain bounded by the Franco-German border, with the small Lauter River on the north and the larger Rhine River on the east. South of Strasbourg, the Colmar Pocket bowed the front of the First French Army inward, forcing it to disperse its units in a semicircle around the German-held salient. The French II Corps occupied the northern perimeter of the pocket from the Rhine to the High Vosges, and the French I Corps held the southern sector above the Belfort Gap. As the army group slowly made the transition from offensive to defensive operations, its commanders recognized that their long curving front lines were particularly unsuited for the new mission.

In mid-December the 6th Army Group could muster roughly eighteen divisions: two armored and six infantry in the U.S. Seventh Army and three armored and seven infantry in the French First.[1] Although all were

[1] These included the U.S. 12th and 14th Armored Divisions and the 36th, 44th, 45th, 79th, 100th, and 103d Infantry Divisions in the Seventh Army, and the French 1st, 2d (Leclerc), and 5th Armored Divisions, the 1st and 16th (a new unit) Infantry, 3d Algerian, 2d Moroccan, 4th Moroccan Mountain, and 9th Colonial Divisions, and the U.S. 3d Infantry Division in the First French Army.

combat effective, many had been worn thin by the heavy winter campaigning, and others were still relatively new and untested. Only two of the armored divisions, the French 1st and 2d, could be considered experienced, and the U.S. 12th had just recently arrived. In addition, all were suffering severe shortages in supplies, equipment, and manpower because of the increased demands of the northern armies and the still limited logistical support available to the Allied ground combat forces throughout the theater. A new corps headquarters, the U.S. XXI, had also recently arrived in the 6th Army Group's area, but was likewise inexperienced with few supporting forces.

Initially the opposing German forces were in worse condition. Most of the German Army's better-equipped and better-manned units were in Field Marshal Walter Model's *Army Group B,* which was fighting in the Ardennes; the offensive there had diverted German supplies, equipment, and manpower away from the Vosges-Alsace sector. The creation of *Army Group Oberrhein* on 10 December had further encumbered German operations in the south.[2] The new headquarters was completely independent of von Rundstedt's *OB West,* and its creation had divided command and control of the German forces that were opposite the 6th Army Group between von Obstfelder's *First Army,* under *Army Group G* and *OB West,* which was above the Lauterbourg salient, and Rasp's *Nineteenth Army,* under *Army Group Oberrhein,* which was below it. Altogether these forces amounted to about twenty divisions, but many were at half strength and some could field only a few thousand combat troops. Although Himmler's political influence gradually increased the manpower, supplies, and materiel available to the upper Rhine front, the Ardennes battlefield continued to receive the largest share of German military resources for the moment. Once the main German offensive began to bog down, however, the eyes of Hitler and *OKW* turned south.

Planning Operation Northwind
(21–27 December 1944)

By 21 December the German high command had begun to examine its operational alternatives on the battlefield. The momentum of *Army Group B's* attack in the Ardennes had begun to dissipate, the important road junction at Bastogne was still in American hands, and pressure on the southern flank of the German advance was steadily mounting as Patton wheeled his Third Army north.[3] However, both Hitler and von Rundstedt realized that the Allies had greatly weakened their southern army group to meet the Ardennes thrust and believed that a fresh German offensive in the south could exploit this weakness. At the very least it would bring some relief to Model's hard-pressed

---

[2] *Army Group Oberrhein* ("Upper Rhine") controlled the *Nineteenth Army* in the Colmar Pocket as well as the *XIV SS Corps* and a variety of military and paramilitary units east of the Rhine.

[3] German planning information is based on von Luttichau, "German Operations," ch. 27; "Operation Northwind" file, Box 1, William W. Quinn Papers, MHI; and Paul Rigoulot, "Operation Northwind: 1–26 janvier 1945" (unpublished MS, ca. 1988), pp. 1–70 (copy CMH).

forces in the Ardennes.

Von Rundstedt's staff at *OB West* initially proposed an attack north of Saarbrucken by *Army Group G* toward Metz, threatening to envelop either Patton's Third Army to the north or Patch's Seventh in the south. But Hitler and von Rundstedt quickly concluded that they lacked the resources for such an ambitious undertaking. Instead Hitler, who had moved his headquarters from Berlin to Command Post *Adlerhorst* near Bad Nauheim in early December in order to keep a close watch over the entire campaign, approved an attack south of the Saarbrucken area toward the Saverne Gap, with the goal of splitting the U.S. Seventh Army and clearing northern Alsace. If successful, the German high command intended to launch a second series of attacks from the Sarre valley–Saverne area toward Luneville, Metz, and the rear of Patton's Third Army, tentatively code-named Operation *ZAHNARZT* ("Dentist").[4] Von Rundstedt ordered General Blaskowitz, who had returned to replace Balck as the *Army Group G* commander on 22 December, to begin planning immediately and authorized the rehabilitation of two mobile divisions (panzer or panzer grenadier) to form the core of the attacking force.

In the days that followed, the German military leaders debated several operational plans. Hitler favored a main effort southeast of Saarbrucken along the Sarre River valley to Phalsbourg and the Saverne Gap.

The attacking forces could be concentrated fairly easily using the road and rail net around Saarbrucken, and the axis of advance was relatively flat with enough roads to support a rapid armored thrust. But von Rundstedt and Blaskowitz were uneasy over their shortage of armor and lack of air support, and argued that the open nature of the Sarre River valley made it too dangerous for a successful offensive. Instead, they favored a main effort farther east, from the Bitche sector in the Vosges, judging that the heavily forested hills and mountains would offer the attackers cover from Allied air observation and interdiction during the critical first phase of the attack. In addition, about half of the large Maginot Line fortresses around Bitche were still in German hands, providing cover and concealment for the assembly areas. Although road communications into the Bitche area and along the projected Vosges line of advance were more limited, the two generals believed that swiftly moving infantry could exploit what they suspected was a weakly defended gap in the American lines between the Seventh Army's two corps; with their infantry units gradually pushing south to the Saverne Gap, they could send their mobile panzer reserves into either the Sarre River valley on the west or the Alsatian plains on the east.

Both plans had serious disadvantages. A Sarre River offensive would have to pass through the American-occupied portion of the Maginot Line and would be open to Allied air attacks during daylight hours. A drive from Bitche through the Vosges Mountains, on the other hand, would

---

[4] For a discussion of *ZAHNARZT* alternatives, see von Luttichau, "German Operations," ch. 28, pp. 21–24.

leave the XV Corps and the bulk of the American armored forces free to counterattack the western flank of the advance. In addition, both plans assumed supporting attacks by *Army Group Oberrhein* to keep the U.S. VI Corps occupied, actions over which *OB West* had no control or authority.

On 27 December Hitler, von Rundstedt, and Blaskowitz approved a rough compromise. Under the operational control of the *First Army,* one panzer grenadier and one infantry division would punch a hole in the American Sarre River valley defenses, while four refitted infantry divisions would push off from the Bitche area along a southwest axis of advance through the Vosges. Blaskowitz would keep his strongest units, the equivalent of two panzer divisions, in reserve to exploit any breakthrough. However, on Hitler's instructions, the reserve units were to remain in the Saarbrucken area in the expectation that the main effort would develop along the Sarre River valley. In addition, Blaskowitz's request that units of *Army Group Oberrhein* launching supporting attacks be placed under *Army Group G's* jurisdiction was disapproved, as was his proposal to delay the start of the offensive until more troops and materiel could be assembled. Hitler informed Blaskowitz that *Army Group Oberrhein* would launch supporting attacks north and south of Strasbourg, but only *after* the main effort down the Sarre River valley corridor had been successful. He also felt that speed was essential, and he scheduled the beginning of the *First Army's* two northern attacks—one down the Sarre valley and the other through the Low Vosges—for New

Year's Eve 1944. Code-named *NORDWIND* ("Northwind"), these attacks would begin the last major German offensive of the European war.

The Defense of Strasbourg
(26 December 1944–1 January 1945)

In the Allied camp the rapid shift from offensive to defensive operations had created both military and political problems for the 6th Army Group.[5] Initially Eisenhower had directed Devers to cease all offensive operations while the Ardennes battle remained unresolved and to shorten his own defensive lines in order to make more forces available for the struggle in the north. Elaborating on these guidelines on 26 December, he ordered the 6th Army Group to pull its "main line of defense" back to the Vosges Mountains, compressing its elongated front and making one corps headquarters, with one armored and one infantry division, immediately available for theater reserve. Despite Allied successes in the Ardennes, Eisenhower judged the final outcome still in doubt; he had also become alarmed at new intelligence reports pointing to another German military buildup opposite the Seventh Army. As a result, he wanted Devers to pull the VI Corps completely out of the Lauterbourg salient as soon as possible. A meeting between Eisenhower and Devers the following day in Paris confirmed the directive and the new Allied intelligence. Devers, however,

---

[5] Material relating to the defense of Strasbourg is based primarily on John W. Price, "The Strasbourg Incident" (1967), CMH MS; and de Lattre, *History,* pp. 301–13.

was convinced that this second German offensive would most likely come down the Sarre River valley, well north of the exposed salient, and did not attach any urgency to the projected withdrawal. In fact, the 6th Army Group commander came away from the conference impressed with the need to hold Strasbourg as well as other significant urban centers in northern Alsace.[6]

On returning to his headquarters on 28 December, General Devers instructed Patch to have the VI Corps prepare three intermediate withdrawal positions to be occupied only "in the face of heavy attack," as well as a final defensive line on the eastern slopes of the Vosges. The first intermediate position was to follow the trace of the American-held portions of the Maginot Line just inside the Franco-German border; the second was to lie between Bitche, Niederbronn, and Bischwiller (on the Falkenstein, Zintsel, and Moder rivers); and the third would be between Bitche, Ingwiller, and Strasbourg. A final defensive position would pull the VI Corps all the way back to the Vosges. But Devers saw no need to carry out any of these withdrawals until a more specific threat presented itself and therefore indicated no execution dates for them. Instead he transferred Leclerc's 2d Armored Division from the First French Army to the American Seventh to further beef up Patch's command and make up for the projected loss of an American armored division to the SHAEF reserve.[7]

General Eisenhower's concern over

the ability of Brooks' VI Corps to hold the exposed Lauterbourg salient against a determined German attack was understandable. The terrain occupied by the Seventh Army was difficult to defend. The lower Vosges mountain range bisected its front, greatly limiting lateral movement between the XV and VI Corps to several easily interdicted mountain roads. A German drive southwest, either through the Low Vosges or along its eastern or western slopes, would threaten the flanks of both American corps; and if the Saverne Gap area, just twenty miles inside the American lines, fell, the entire VI Corps within the Lauterbourg salient would be trapped. The threat of a complementary German attack from the south by forces from the Colmar Pocket only made SHAEF more nervous, as did the Allied failure to predict the Ardennes offensive. Perhaps the Allied high command had been relying too heavily on ULTRA and other sophisticated intelligence sources and had now simply given up attempting to second-guess German intentions. Whatever the case, Eisenhower continued to insist that Devers withdraw his forces from the salient as quickly as possible and pull his defensive lines all the way back to the eastern slopes of the Vosges Mountains. The shift would greatly reduce the defensive responsibilities of the Seventh Army, making it easier to concentrate forces in the Sarre River valley or, if necessary, dispatch more reinforcements to the Ardennes.

Once again Devers questioned the wisdom of Eisenhower's operational guidance. Despite the Supreme Commander's clear-cut instructions on the

[6] Devers Diary, 27 Dec 44.
[7] 6th Army Gp LOI 7, 28 Dec 44.

matter, the 6th Army Group chief remained reluctant to make such a
major withdrawal without cause.
Patch supported him, regarding it as
"a terrifically difficult proposition to
give up a strong defensive position
when you feel confident that you can
hold it," and both dragged their feet
in executing the order.[8] The delay finally led to an angry call by Eisenhower's chief of staff, General Bedell
Smith, on New Year's Day, relaying
the Supreme Commander's displeasure over the Seventh Army's failure
to carry out the withdrawal and ordering Devers to issue the necessary
instructions at once.[9] But Devers had
more than one reason to put off the
matter. As Patch had pointed out to
him earlier, Eisenhower's more extensive withdrawal concept would uncov-
er the entire northern Alsatian plains,
including the city of Strasbourg, and
would have great political ramifica-
tions for the Allied alliance.

Violent French objections to any
hint of abandoning Strasbourg or
northern Alsace without a fight were
predictable. De Gaulle had learned of
the withdrawal planning almost immediately on 28 December; two days
later he had General Alphonse Juin,
his chief of staff in the Ministry of National Defense, send a strong protest
to SHAEF, accompanied by an offer
of three newly formed FFI divisions
to help defend Strasbourg city if necessary. De Gaulle personally restated
the French position on 1 January
1945, conceding that it might be necessary to abandon the salient but demanding that Strasbourg be defended

at all costs. Believing Allied forces
could use the city to anchor a defensible east-west line along the Rhine-
Marne Canal, he warned that French
forces would defend Strasbourg "no
matter what comes." On the same day
he also sent a direct communication
to de Lattre, outlining his stand and
ordering the First French Army commander, "in the eventuality that the
Allied Forces retire from their present
positions to the north . . . to take in
hand and assure the defense of Strasbourg." The Free French leader was
prepared to challenge the Allied high
command in order to spare the city
an almost certainly vengeful German
reoccupation. Finally, on the night of
2–3 January, Juin had a long conference with Eisenhower's chief of staff
over the matter and relayed de
Gaulle's threat to withdraw the First
French Army from SHAEF control if
Strasbourg was abandoned.[10] Simultaneously de Lattre began making unilateral plans to pull the 3d Algerian
Division out of the High Vosges to
defend the city.[11] The controversy
thus threatened to disrupt the entire
Allied chain of command and greatly
complicate the Allied response to a
fresh German offensive in Alsace.

*Preparations for the Attack
(27–31 December 1944)*

As the Allied leaders debated the

---

[8] Devers Diary, 29 Dec 44.
[9] Devers Diary, 1 Jan 45.

---

[10] For an account of the conference, see Ltr,
David G. Barr to Devers, 5 Sep 67 (copy CMH).
Barr, who was Devers' chief of staff at the time, was
present at the meeting and related that de Gaulle's
threat was communicated by a French draft memo
that was somehow passed on to the American generals toward the end of the session.
[11] Vigneras Intervs, pp. 35–36.

fate of Strasbourg, the two contenders prepared for a final struggle in northern Alsace. Between 27 and 30 December the *First Army* withdrew the designated assault divisions from their defensive sectors, which stretched the fronts of the remaining divisions thin, and attempted to cover the many gaps with fortress units and a miscellany of odd formations, especially recently formed *Volkssturm* militia. While the signal elements of the departing units remained temporarily in place to give the impression of normalcy, the German staffs shunted scarce supplies, equipment, and replacements into anemic units and moved artillery into supporting positions. Opposite the U.S. XV Corps, which was defending the Sarre River valley area, General Max Simon's *XIII SS Corps* readied *NORDWIND*'s primary assault force, consisting of the *17th SS Panzer Grenadier* ("Gotz von Berlichingen") and the *36th Volksgrenadier Divisions*, the *404th* and *410th Volks Artillery Corps*, the *20th Volks Werfer* (rocket-launcher) *Brigade*, two armored flame-thrower companies, two army artillery battalions, and one observation battalion. In the Bitche area the second attacking force consisted of General Petersen's *XC Corps* on the right, or western, wing, controlling the strengthened *559th* and *257th Volksgrenadier Divisions*, and General Hoehne's *LXXXIX Corps* on the left, or eastern, wing, with the refitted *361st* and *256th Volksgrenadier Divisions*. The Vosges forces were also beefed up by additional self-propelled and assault guns, supported by two army artillery battalions and an army engineer battalion, and later reinforced by the experienced *6th SS Mountain Divi-*

sion as it arrived from the defunct Finnish front. In reserve, temporarily under the direct control of *Army Group G*, lay the *XXXIX Panzer Corps*, under Lt. Gen. Karl Decker, with the re-quipped *21st Panzer* and *25th Panzer Grenadier Divisions*—the former with 18 medium (Mark IV) and 31 heavy (Mark V) Panther tanks, and the latter with 9 medium and 20 heavies, with about 20 additional Panthers and more assault and self-propelled guns en route, which had been temporarily delayed by Allied air attacks on the German transportation network. To further strengthen the reserve forces and serve as a basis for Operation *ZAHNARZT*, *OB West* began preparations for assembling the *10th SS Panzer Division*, the *7th Parachute Division*, and other units behind the lines of the *First Army*. [12]

Blaskowitz obviously would have preferred assembling all of these units first and giving the initial assault forces more time to train replacements and break in new equipment. But further delays threatened to end what was clearly a fleeting tactical opportunity to penetrate the weakened Seventh Army lines. Not even his "Arrow Flash" convoys—the equivalent of the American "Red Ball Express"—were able to negotiate the maze of tangled lines and broken bridges behind the front lines with any speed. Just prior to the offensive, Blaskowitz thus agreed to strengthen the attacking *17th SS Panzer Grenadiers*

[12] Von Rundstedt had also considered the *11th Panzer Division* for *ZAHNARZT*, but later committed it on 18 January in a minor attack north of the main Alsatian battlefield. See CMH MS R–91, Magna E. Bauer, "*Army Group G*, January 1945" (December 1956).

with a company of Panthers (ten heavy tanks) from the *21st Panzers* to ensure the success of the initial assault. By that time he had also received one company of the *653d Superheavy Antitank Battalion* with a few monstrous seventy-ton, 128-mm.-gunned *Jagdtigers* (turretless assault guns based on the Mark VI "Royal Tiger" chassis). This gave him about eighty tanks, mostly heavies, in reserve to exploit any breakthrough at the beginning of the operation, with more armor on the way.[13]

On the morning of 28 December Blaskowitz brought his attacking corps and division commanders to *OB West* headquarters at Ziegenberg and then, after a twenty-minute bus ride, to Hitler's *Adlerhorst* for a personal pep talk by the Fuhrer. For most of the participants, it was the first time that they had ever seen their supreme commander in person. Although physically in poor condition, Hitler led off with a fifty-minute speech that showed he had lost none of his personal magnetism. Despite tremendous sacrifices, he conceded, the Ardennes offensive had failed. Perhaps no one was to blame. With the Russians threatening in the east, however, he impressed on them that defeat in the forthcoming offensive was unthinkable. The Western Allies had to be stopped and their offensive capabili-

ties so badly damaged that most of Germany's military strength could be devoted to the eastern front in the months ahead. To accomplish this the German Army had to keep the initiative, attacking the Allied forces wherever they were weak and using speed to avoid being crushed by Allied materiel superiority. Hitler discussed the details of the forthcoming operation individually with each commander, continually emphasizing both its necessity and its possibility for success. To all he stressed that the objective of *NORDWIND* was neither terrain nor prestige, but "manpower . . . the destruction of enemy forces."[14]

Preparations for the Defense (19–31 December 1944)

For the American soldiers in the Seventh Army, the last two weeks of December were also busy as commanders reoriented their units from offensive to defensive postures.[15] Between 19 and 26 December, Patch's forces took over large portions of the Third Army's front, thus allowing Patton to shift more forces into the Ardennes sector. As a result, the Seventh Army found itself holding a front of about 126 miles—84 miles from the Saarbrucken area east to Lauterbourg, and another 42 miles south along the Rhine—with only six infantry divisions. This worked out to about twenty miles of front per division, six miles per regiment, or two per battalion—with the two armored

---

[13] *Army Group G*'s constantly changing order of battle and its equipment situation during this period make it difficult to ascertain the exact number and type of tanks and assault guns committed. In fact, many units and machines entered the battle as they arrived on the front. Neither the *6th Mountain SS Division* nor the *XXXIX Panzer Corps* headquarters, for example, was available at the start of *NORDWIND*, both arriving a day or two later. See Rigoulot, "Operation Nordwind," pp. 51–53.

[14] Quoted in von Luttichau, "German Operations," ch. 27.

[15] For general information on American actions before and during *NORDWIND*, see Hist, 6th Army Gp, pp. 106–58; *Seventh Army Rpt*, II, chs. 22–23.

divisions in reserve. Patch believed he had no choice but to use the Low Vosges as a dividing line between his two corps and placed his own headquarters at Saverne, directly behind the middle of his defenses. Expecting the main German attack down the Sarre River corridor, he concentrated the bulk of his strength in General Haislip's XV Corps, west of the Vosges, with three infantry divisions—the 103d, 44th, and 100th—on line covering about thirty-five miles of total frontage, backed by the new 12th Armored Division. East of the Vosges, General Brooks' VI Corps held the upper, open portion of the salient, from Bitche to Lauterbourg, with the 45th and 79th Divisions, while using the 36th Division to cover its Rhine River front from Lauterbourg south to Strasbourg; the 14th Armored Division was his reserve. Although not enthusiastic about abandoning the Lauterbourg salient, both Devers and Patch agreed that Brooks should start pulling his forces back at the first sign of a major German attack.

Even before these dispositions could be finalized, Devers passed SHAEF's requirements for two divisions down to the Seventh Army. Although he could ill afford to spare them, Patch promptly nominated the 36th Infantry and 12th Armored Divisions for the SHAEF reserve. Their departures left his defensive lines paper thin. As a partial remedy, Devers brought Leclerc's 2d Armored Division back and began rushing elements of three new infantry divisions—the 42d, 63d, and 70th—into the battle area. All three were untested units that had recently disem-

BRIG. GEN. HENRY H. LINDEN

barked at Marseille and arrived at the front with little besides their infantry regiments. Without waiting for their attached artillery, armor, and other supporting elements, Patch organized them into task forces, each consisting of the three infantry regiments and a small command group led by the designated assistant division commander. Task Force Linden controlled the 42d Division's regiments, Task Force Harris those of the 63d, and Task Force Herren those of the 70th.[16]

---

[16] The task forces were commanded by Brig. Gens. Henry H. Linden, Frederick M. Harris, and Thomas W. Herren. For a detailed account of the operations of Task Force Herren's 275th Infantry regiment during NORDWIND, see Donald C. Pence and Eugene J. Petersen, *Ordeal in the Vosges* (Sanford, N.C.: Transition Press, 1981); for the 274th regiment, see Wallace R. Cheves, ed., *Snow Ridges and*

BRIG. GEN. FREDERICK M. HARRIS

These three formations together with Leclerc's armor would have to fill in the many gaps in the Seventh Army's lines.

With these additions and losses, Patch reorganized his defenses, initially placing the inexperienced infantrymen of Task Forces Linden, Harris, and Herren along the Rhine River front under the VI Corps. He later transferred two of Task Force Harris' regiments as well as the entire French 2d Armored Division north to the Sarre River valley area to bolster Haislip's XV Corps. In his center,

---

Pillboxes (privately published, n.d.) (copy MHI); and for all three, the 70th Infantry Division official records for December 1944–January 1945 at the WNRC.

southeast of Bitche, Patch inserted a small mechanized screening force to cover the Vosges area between Haislip's 100th Infantry Division in the north and Brooks' 45th Division in the south. This element, Task Force Hudelson, consisted of two cavalry squadrons, a detached armored infantry battalion, and a few supporting detachments. A similar screening force held the extreme left, or northeastern, flank of the Seventh Army, in the crease separating the XV Corps from the Third Army's XII Corps. In reserve was the bulk of the 14th Armored Division in the VI Corps zone, while the French 2d Armored Division performed the same function for the XV Corps. The withdrawn 12th Armored and 36th Infantry Divisions remained uncommitted, but were also in the Seventh Army's rear area around Sarrebourg and available in an emergency. Still expecting a major German thrust down the Sarre River valley but unsure of the location and magnitude of secondary offensives, Devers moved his own advance headquarters from Phalsbourg in the Saverne Gap area to Luneville, forty miles to the rear. Nevertheless, he allowed de Lattre to retain control of the U.S. 3d Infantry Division in the Colmar Pocket region and even reinforced it with a regiment from Task Force Harris. The 6th Army Group commander remained optimistic and still saw no need for a precipitous withdrawal from the Lauterbourg salient or from anywhere else. After steadily pushing enemy forces back for the past five months, Devers and his fellow generals were confident that the Seventh Army could stop any German attack, and they had no in-

BRIG. GEN. THOMAS W. HERREN

tention of voluntarily surrendering the ground their troops had painfully taken during the past several months.

Aware of the impending German offensive, American infantrymen on line prepared as best they could. Foxholes and trenches had to be excavated in the frozen earth, fields of fire planned and cleared, minefields and other obstacles constructed, prearranged artillery and mortar barrages plotted, and telephone lines laid to replace the less-reliable radio communications system used in the offense. Slightly to the rear, staffs and supporting units brought up and stocked supplies—ammunition, fuel, and food—worked replacements into understrength units, and prepared con-

tingency plans for all possible aspects of the coming battle. SHAEF levies on the newly arrived regiments further exacerbated the shortage of infantry, forcing Patch to begin converting some of his Army service personnel into foot soldiers and engineer units into rifle battalions, even before the expected offensive began.[17] Regardless, the line units continued to mask their weaknesses by aggressive patrolling against the German lines, at times conducting raids across the Rhine, gathering information on enemy preparations, and giving some combat experience to the new infantry units in the process.

On 29 December, three days before Hitler had scheduled NORDWIND to begin, specific German intentions were still unclear to the American defenders. Allied analyses of enemy rail and road traffic, radio intercepts, prisoner-of-war reports, and air reconnaissance over the battlefield indicated major German troop buildups in the Saarbrucken area, beyond the Rhine, and in the Colmar Pocket. Intelligence at the 6th Army Group headquarters placed the 21st Panzer Division and the 17th SS and 25th Panzer Grenadier Divisions somewhere in the Zweibruecken area, about ten miles behind the Sarre River line; American patrols had identified elements of these units and nine German infantry divisions on their fronts. The Seventh Army G–2, Colonel Quinn, believed that the total strength of opposing German infantry was equal to about twenty-four or twenty-five American battalions, but

---

[17] The conversion program is discussed in Seventh Army Diary, pp. 460–61, 465–66.

BUILDING DEFENSIVE WORKS IN THE SNOW. *111th Engineer Battalion, 36th Division, in Weibruch area.*

the size of the armored forces was a question mark. He estimated that the enemy would either launch a major attack with three mobile divisions down the Sarre River valley or "with forces currently in contact and in immediate reserve . . . launch a series of limited objective attacks." The latter alternative, he believed, was the most likely.[18] The Seventh Army ULTRA officer, Maj. Donald S. Bussey, disagreed, feeling that current information on the German

order of battle and an analysis of *Luftwaffe* air reconnaissance orders pinpointed the Sarre River valley as the major area of attack. However, ULTRA remained mute on specific German intentions.[19]

Patch's evaluation of intelligence estimates was strongly influenced by the tactical situation. In his judgment, the Sarre River corridor approach still represented the gravest threat to the Seventh Army; a penetration there could split his forces and leave the VI

[18] "G-2 History: Seventh Army Operations in Europe," V (1–31 December 44), Box 2, William W. Quinn Papers, MHI.

[19] Bussey Interv, 19 Aug 87; Bussey, ULTRA Report; Hinsley et al., *British Intelligence in the Second World War*, III, 2, p. 664.

GENERALS DEVERS AND PATCH
CONFER *at Luneville.*

Corps stranded on the Alsatian
plains. In fact, the Germans had already signaled a preference for the
region's offensive possibilities with
the *Panzer Lehr Division*'s counterattack
back in November; obviously the
same route promised the Germans
their best chance of tactical success,
especially since any offensive there
could be easily supported from the
Saarbrucken road nets. For these reasons Patch, with Devers' blessing,
continued to build up his forces west
of the Low Vosges and, despite continued SHAEF pressure for a complete VI Corps withdrawal to the
Vosges, planned only a partial and
gradual retirement from the Lauter-

bourg salient—one that would plac(
the VI Corps' main line of resistanc(
on an east-west, Bitche-Strasbour{
line (as later suggested by de Gaulle
by 5 January.

As New Year's Day approached
Devers and Patch increasingly regard
ed the Sarre River valley as the prin
cipal danger point. On 30 Decembe
Devers even authorized Patch to us(
elements of the SHAEF-designate(
reserve units in his area, the 12th Ar
mored and 36th Infantry Divisions, t(
establish a secondary line of defens(
behind the XV Corps. The following
day Patch ordered the 14th Armore(
Division, the only reserve in the V
Corps area, north to Phalsbourg
where it could provide even more re
inforcements for the XV Corps
Clearly the American commanders ex
pected the main German effort woul(
take place west of the Vosges and ha(
prepared an appropriate reception.

On New Year's Eve, a Sunda'
evening, Patch met with both hi:
corps commanders at Fenetrange, th(
XV Corps headquarters, and warne(
them to expect a major enemy attacl
during the early morning hours o
New Year's Day. Late afternoon ai
reconnaissance had reported Germar
troop movements all across the north
ern front.[20] Local festivities for th(
holiday would have to be postponed
Haislip's forces, he predicted, woul(
bear the brunt of the impending of
fensive, but Patch was confident tha
his units were up to the task. Stil
there was no definite knowledge o
specific German intentions or th(
scope and size of the predicted at
tacks. Inclement weather had cur

---

[20] Cited in Bussey Interv, 19 Aug 87.

tailed further aerial reconnaissance, and signal intercepts had revealed little. Outside the American command post, a new snowfall covered the woods and forests of the Low Vosges Mountains east of Fenetrange with a deceptively innocent coating of white, giving little hint of the coming struggle.

The New Year's Eve Attacks (31 December 1944–5 January 1945)

The German *First Army* launched its initial attacks on schedule a few hours before New Year's Day, with Simon's *XIII SS Corps* pushing south over the Sarre River valley and Petersen's *XC* and Hoehne's *LXXXIX Corps* heading in the same general direction through the woods of the Low Vosges (*Map 34*).[21] In both cases the leading German echelons began to hit the main American lines about midnight. In the Sarre valley the assault force was met by determined resistance from the 44th and 100th Infantry Division troops, who were well dug in and deployed in depth. Expecting the major attack in this area, Patch and Haislip had jammed the XV Corps zone with three infantry divisions buttressed by the two regiments of Task Force Harris and—if the theater reserve units are counted—two armored and another infantry division in reserve, with a third armored division arriving. The German attack barely made a dent in the beefed-up Allied line. In some cases the *SS* troopers

advanced in suicidal open waves, cursing and screaming at the American infantrymen who refused to be intimidated. The infantry of the *36th Volksgrenadier* did little better. Although Simon's forces finally managed to poke a narrow hole, about two miles in depth, at Rimling on the right wing of the 44th Division, the 100th Infantry Division held firm. In the days that followed the Germans saw their small advances continuously eroded by repeated counterattacks from the 44th, 100th, and 63d (TF Harris) Division infantry supported by elements of the French 2d Armored Division.[22] Allied artillery and, when the weather broke, Allied air attacks, together with the bitter cold, also sapped the strength of the attackers. On 4 January the German high command formally called off the effort. As General Simon, the attacking corps commander, caustically observed, the Sarre assault had shown only that the German soldier still knew how to fight and how to die, but little else. Blaskowitz, with Hitler and von Rundstedt's approval, obviously chose not to throw the German armored reserves into the battle there, as planned, and sought weaker links in the American lines.

The second attack, launched from the Bitche area south through the Low Vosges, was more successful. Believing that the major German effort would be

---

[21] This section is based on official U.S. Army records; von Luttichau, "German Operations," ch. 28; and Rigoulot, "Operation Nordwind," pp. 71–128.

[22] For heroic action in defense of his unit's perimeter on 1 January 1945, Sgt. Charles A. Gillivary, Company I, 71st Infantry, 44th Infantry Division, was awarded the Congressional Medal of Honor, as was Tech. Sgt. Charles F. Carey, Jr., 379th Infantry, 100th Infantry Division (posthumously), several days later for action on the night of 8–9 January 1945, in which he commanded an antitank platoon near Rimling.

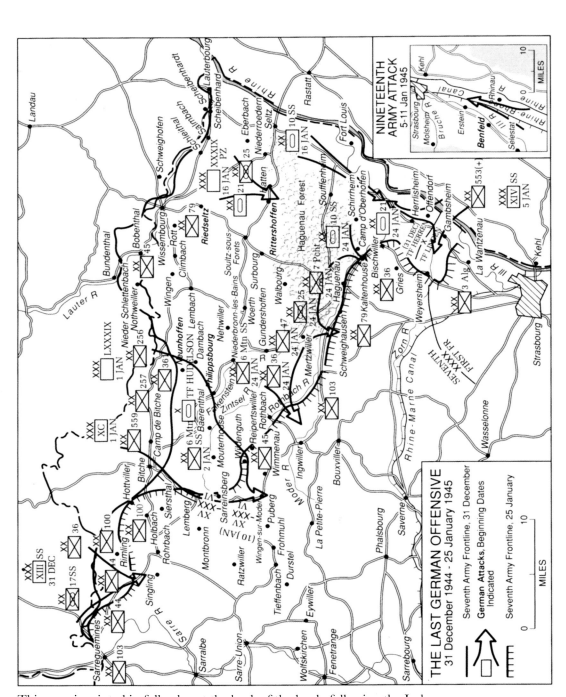

THE LAST GERMAN OFFENSIVE
31 December 1944 - 25 January 1945

Seventh Army Frontline, 31 December

German Attacks, Beginning Dates
Indicated

Seventh Army Frontline, 25 January

0   10
MILES

NINETEENTH
ARMY ATTACK
5-11 Jan 1945

0   10
MILES

MAP 34

This map is printed in full color at the back of the book, following the Index.

MEN OF THE 100TH DIVISION MAINTAIN HEAVY MACHINE-GUN POSITION, *near Rimling, 1945.*

west of the mountains—or more concerned with the thin VI Corps lines in the Lauterbourg salient to the east— the American generals had not expected an enemy drive through such rough terrain, where snowy, narrow roads bisected rather than paralleled the southward German axis of advance. The assembly areas of the attacking infantry on New Year's Eve had been hidden in the Maginot Line bunkers still in German hands; there had been no preattack artillery bombardment to warn the defenders; and the overcast sky and thick mountain forests had provided cover for the assault throughout the first day of the offensive.

On 31 December Task Force Hudelson held a roughly defined mountain front from the Bitche area on the west to the vicinity of Neunhoffen on the east. This *ad hoc* group, commanded by Col. D. H. Hudelson, consisted of the 94th and 117th Cavalry Squadrons, with mostly jeeps and light armored cars, and the half-tracks of the 62d Armored Infantry Battalion, reinforced only by a tank destroyer company.[23] To screen the area Hudelson had established a series of strongpoints on the mountain roads

[23] The task force was built around CCR of the 14th Armored Division, with the divisional and corps cavalry squadrons substituting for the combat command's organic tank battalion. Also attached were Company B, 645th Tank Destroyer Battalion; Company B, 83d Mortar Battalion; Company A, 125th Armored Engineer Battalion; and 1st Battalion, 540th Engineers.

that entered his sector from the east and west, supplementing them with small patrols and checkpoints. Rather than stopping a determined attack, his job was to delay and channel it until reinforcements could arrive. But Hudelson's delaying power proved limited during the early hours of 1 January. Moving south through the dark forests, leading elements of the *559th, 257th, 361st,* and *256th Volksgrenadier Divisions* easily penetrated the positions of the small American mechanized force, bypassing strongpoints and scattering the roadbound armored units as they withdrew and tried to regroup.[24] Hudelson's local counterattacks were hampered by the snow—both wheeled and tracked vehicles losing traction on the icy mountain roads—and were too minor to have any effect on the general progress of the German offensive. Quickly the various components of the light mechanized unit found themselves retreating to the east and west, abandoning many of their snowbound vehicles in the process.

During the next four days the attacking infantry divisions pushed south through the Vosges for about ten miles; but the real contest for control of the vital mountain exits began almost immediately, as reinforcing American units tried to keep the German *volksgrenadiers* bottled up in the Low Vosges forests. On the western edge of the advance, the U.S. 100th Infantry Division held firm, strengthening its right shoulder first

with an additional regiment from Task Force Harris (63d Division) and then with the 36th Division's 141st regiment, which Patch released to Haislip late on 1 January. Together these units, with an assist from the 14th Armored Division, channeled the advancing German infantry away from the Sarre River valley to the south and east.

Across the Vosges, with fewer forces at his immediate disposal, Brooks was forced to make major changes in the dispositions of his corps. First he withdrew two inexperienced infantry regiments of Task Force Herren (70th Division) from the Rhine front and moved them across the interior of the VI Corps area to plug up the eastern exits to the Vosges, under the direction of Frederick's 45th Infantry Division. In the center, blocking the way to Phalsbourg and Saverne, Brooks and Frederick inserted two regiments of the 45th Division as well as another on loan from Wyche's 79th Division; they backfilled the 45th's northern front with a combat engineer regiment, the 36th C, temporarily converted to infantry, and backstopped all of these forces with parts of the 14th Armored Division still under VI Corps control. Such complex switching completely entangled the 45th, 79th, and 70th Division forces. By 4 January, for example, the 45th Division had crossed its extended front, from east to west, parts of the 179th and 180th Infantry (organic to the 45th) and elements of the 276th Infantry (Task Force Herren) in the Vosges; the 313th Infantry (reinforced with battalions of the 314th and 315th Infantry, all from the 79th Division), elements of the

---

[24] No records from Task Force Hudelson survived, and the above information is based on a Seventh Army Historical Officer interview report, "Task Force Hudelson, 14th Armored Division, 21 December 1944–1 January 1945" (ca. 1945), MHI.

274th and 275th Infantry (Task Force Herren), and the 157th Infantry (organic) along the eastern exits to the Vosges; and the 36th C Engineers together with leftovers from the 179th and 180th Infantry on its regular northern front. Very quickly Frederick found himself trying to control eight different regiments, half of which had commanders and staffs that had never been in combat before. Although these hasty measures contained the advance of the German infantry divisions at least temporarily, they left very few troops to defend the Lauterbourg salient farther east.

As American reinforcements met German attackers, the battle quickly turned into a bitter winter infantry fight focusing on the towns that lay along the snow-covered mountain roads. Here at Lemberg, Sarreinsberg, Wildenguth, Wingen, Wimmenau, Reipertswiller, Mouterhouse, Baerenthal, Philippsbourg, Dambach, and a host of other tiny Alsatian mountain villages and hamlets, the Americans finally began to hold their ground. Yet, even before the four attacking *volksgrenadier* divisions began to flag, Blaskowitz and von Obstfelder, the *First Army* commander, started feeding elements of the *6th SS Mountain Division* ("Nord") into the battle. The *SS* division, an experienced unit trained and equipped for cold-weather warfare, fresh and at full strength, began to deploy on the battlefield sometime on 2 January and was soon spearheading a renewed drive south.[25] Nevertheless, elements

of the 45th and 79th Divisions, reinforced by more battalions from Task Force Herren as well as units of the 540th Engineers, which also served as infantry, continued to protect the vital Vosges exits, constantly counterattacking the now overextended German forces.

At this point Patch decided to move the entire 103d Infantry Division, now unengaged, from the far northwestern wing of the XV Corps over to the eastern shoulder of the German Vosges advance, thus relieving Task Force Herren elements that had begun to wear thin and beginning his own counteroffensive against the flanks of the German penetration.[26] On the other side, the German commanders, to guard against such a threat, had begun to deploy the *36th Volksgrenadier Division* from Simon's *XIII SS Corps* in the Sarre area to Hoehne's *LXXXIX Corps* in the Vosges in order to strengthen the base of the salient. Hemmed in on three sides, however, the German offensive through the Low Vosges seemed to be coming to a complete standstill by the 5th. Brooks had been able to move his forces over to the Vosges faster than any of the German commanders had thought possible, and the green troops of Task Force Herren along with the converted engineers had fought with an enthusiasm that belied their inexperience. Without possession of the exits to the Vosges, Hitler refused to commit the mobile reserves, and as long as the

---

[25] The *SS* division had been fighting on the Finnish front until the autumn of 1944, when it retreated into northern Norway and returned to Germany via Oslo and Denmark in November and December.

[26] Its place was taken first by a regiment of the 36th Division and then by the new XXI Corps, which supervised a miscellaneous collection of units.

Americans controlled the Saverne Gap and the road networks on either side of the Vosges, they could bring reinforcements into the area faster than the attackers. With nowhere to go, *NORDWIND* was essentially a failure. Blaskowitz and von Obstfelder, however, still had their uncommitted armor reserves—but so did Patch and Devers. The struggle was far from over.

Command and Control

Both German and American post-battle autopsies of the *NORDWIND* offensive severely criticized the planning and conduct of the Sarre River valley attack. The *XIII SS Corps* had put the assault together hastily, and even the American commanders were surprised by its poor execution. The division-level leadership and staff work of the *17th SS Panzer Grenadier Division* in particular proved marginal. The unit was unable even to bring its armor up to the battle area until the third day because of icy road conditions and limited engineer support; the German demolition effort had been too thorough when they had vacated the area in early December. Artillery support had also been badly coordinated, as had just about everything else. In fact, during the battles for northern Alsace the *SS* division went through about five division commanders, mostly *SS* colonels with comparatively little military experience.[27] Given the means at

---

[27] Rigoulot, "Operation Nordwind," p. 53. On American evaluations of its performance, see "G–2 History: Seventh Army Operations in Europe (1–31 Dec 44)," V, William W. Quinn Papers, MHI.

Blaskowitz's disposal and the strength of the Allied forces west of the Low Vosges, however, perhaps the failure of what Hitler hoped would be the main German effort was inevitable.

The inability of the successful Vosges attacking forces to break out of the mountain exits was another matter entirely. Here the divided German command structure on the Alsatian front clearly contributed heavily to the ultimate lack of success. Had *Army Group Oberrhein* launched supporting attacks across the Rhine at the start of the offensive, Brooks might not have been able to transfer the three regiments of Task Force Herren from the Rhine to the Vosges so readily, and at least some of the eastern mountain exits might have fallen to the advancing *volksgrenadiers*. Although Blaskowitz might still have elected not to employ his panzer reserves through the Vosges, the results would have greatly increased his options. But as future events would show, Himmler had his own objectives in mind, and the lack of coordination between *Army Group G* and *Army Group Oberrhein* during *NORDWIND* and in the ensuing campaign was remarkable.

The Allied commanders had their own serious command and control problems. For example, General Leclerc's extreme reluctance to place his 2d Armored Division under de Lattre's control was well known. Although publicly emphasizing the better logistical support available from American corps and army commands, he privately harbored strong feelings against many senior officers of the First French Army, whose loyalty to the Allied cause and the Free French in particular had come relatively late in the war. The ghost of Marshal Petain's Vichy regime had already begun to cast its long shadow over France. However, both the Ardennes and *NORDWIND* attacks temporarily made the matter academic, as Leclerc's armor was needed more in the north and, for the moment, was better employed supporting Patch's thinly spread forces.

The defense of Strasbourg was another matter and demanded immediate resolution. Devers himself was still reluctant to pull his entire line back to the Vosges, preferring to reinforce Brooks with the three proto-infantry divisions, and was probably content to let de Lattre buck the decision on Strasbourg up to their political and military superiors. The entire concept of abandoning all of northern Alsace was fraught with danger. Such a major withdrawal would have surrendered much of the easily defensible Rhine front, exposed the northern flank of the French II Corps above the Colmar Pocket, and placed the entire Saverne Gap under German artillery fire, while making it highly unlikely that the Allies could regain the territory in the near future. After being surprised in the Ardennes, Eisenhower may have simply become too cautious, overreacting to the smaller threat posed by the initial *NORDWIND* assault forces and then unwilling to reverse the order when the offensive came well to the west of the Lauterbourg salient.

Eisenhower's decision to press on with the withdrawal continued to place Devers in a dilemma. On 1 January, as *NORDWIND* began, he informed General Touzet du Vigier, an emissary of Juin, that SHAEF had re-

quired the 6th Army Group to fall back to the Vosges, thus temporarily relinquishing Strasbourg to German control. Yet, on the same day, he also requested that SHAEF "clarify" its instructions on the matter. At the time, the VI Corps had just begun planning for the first phase of the withdrawal, pulling back from the Bitche-Lauterbourg trace to the Maginot Line, but had made no concrete preparations for anything further. The following day, 2 January, de Gaulle reviewed Juin's report, sent orders confirming de Lattre's responsibility for the defense of the city, and dispatched Juin to SHAEF headquarters to argue the matter with Eisenhower's chief of staff. Juin's meeting with General Smith, related earlier, fully alerted Eisenhower to the weight that the French political leader gave to the safety of the French city. Massive reprisals against Strasbourg's citizens by vengeful German military, paramilitary, or police units were likely, and a belated defense of the city by French forces bereft of American support might have severe implications regarding future Franco-American relations. On the other hand, a decision to surrender Strasbourg to the Germans out of hand might well have adverse repercussions on de Gaulle's own political plans, strengthening the Communist leadership centered in the resistance movement. For these reasons, de Gaulle asked Churchill and Roosevelt to intervene in the dispute. Churchill quickly concurred, and at a SHAEF staff conference held the following day, 3 January, and attended by Churchill, de Gaulle, Eisenhower, Smith, Juin, and their assistants, the Allied commander in chief agreed to

suspend the withdrawal. Actually, Eisenhower appears to have reversed
the order just prior to the conference
and passed down the change to
Brooks. With the situation in the Ardennes stable and the initial German
NORDWIND attacks confined to the
areas above the Lauterbourg salient, a
complete withdrawal was less pressing. Allied unity was thus preserved,
and cooperation between American
and French soldiers in the field remained undisturbed. But events that
followed soon proved that Eisenhower's concern over Brooks' position
was not completely unwarranted.

CHAPTER XXVIII

The Battle of Alsace

Operation *NORDWIND* proved only the first in a series of German attacks against the 6th Army Group, which American soldiers dubbed collectively the New Year's Eve offensive. Altogether, between 5 and 25 January, the German Army undertook four additional multidivision offensives against the U.S. Seventh Army and another against the First French Army just above the Colmar Pocket. Although most of these attacks were hastily planned and executed with little finesse, some caught the Americans by surprise, and together they threatened to overwhelm the tired units of the Seventh Army. Having already been greatly weakened by the massive diversion of military supplies and replacements to the Ardennes, Patch's forces somehow had to find the means from their own strength and resources to turn back the multiple German threats.

On 5 January, as Patch began deploying the 103d Division east of the Vosges, Himmler's *Army Group Oberrhein* began its *NORDWIND* "supporting" attack.[1] Under the direction of

General Otto von dem Bach's *XIV SS Corps*, the *553d Volksgrenadier Division*, reinforced with armor and commando units, spearheaded the main effort, which fell on the right, or eastern, flank of Brooks' VI Corps across the west bank of the Rhine at Gambsheim, just ten miles north of Strasbourg. Two days later, on 7 January, Rasp's *Nineteenth Army* initiated another attack south of the city near Rhinau, on the northern edge of the Colmar Pocket. Code-named Operation *SONNENWENDE* ("Winter Solstice"), the southern offensive included attacks by Thumm's *LXIV Corps*, with the *198th Volksgrenadier Division*, the *106th Panzer Brigade*, and other armored elements (with forty to fifty heavy tanks and assault guns). The new series of attacks at Rhinau and Gambsheim not only threatened the southern flank and rear of the VI Corps, but also the city of Strasbourg. If Hitler could not take Antwerp in the north, then Himmler was determined to present him with Strasbourg in the south. The two attacks quickly

---

[1] Information in this chapter is from von Luttichau, "Southern France," ch. 29; Rigoulot, "Operation Nordwind," pp. 128–225; and U.S. Army unit records. *Army Group Oberrhein* had four corps head-

quarters in its zone: the *LXIV* and *LXIII* under the *Nineteenth Army* in the Colmar Pocket, with about four divisions each, and the *XIV SS* and *XVIII SS* as well as *Wehrkreis V*, all with various forces on the east side of the Rhine.

GAMBSHEIM–RHINE RIVER AREA

forced Patch to shelve any plans for an offensive by the 103d Division in the Vosges or any expectations of immediate relief from the French in the south.

The VI Corps

North of Strasbourg, the departure of first Task Force Harris and then Task Force Herren had stretched the three inexperienced regiments of Task Force Linden (42d Division) thin over a broad, marshy 42-mile Rhine front. To ease matters, Devers had finally approved an immediate VI Corps withdrawal south from the Lauter River to the Maginot Line by 2 January and the transfer of responsibility for the defense of the Strasbourg area to the French II Corps by the 6th. However, before these arrangements could be completed, Himmler's forces had attacked at Gambsheim and Rhinau, preventing de Lattre from moving any strength up to the Strasbourg area to provide immediate relief.[2] Thus, almost single-handedly, with its units scattered along the Rhine front, Task Force Linden tried to counter the

[2] At the time Brooks was also in the process of extending the boundary of the 79th Division westward to relieve the 45th Division of its northern responsibilities, but the Gambsheim attack on his eastern flank caused him to rescind the change.

penetration. But with no organic signal, artillery, or transportation units of its own and with only a few platoons of 79th Division armor in direct support, the scattered rifle battalions of the task force were overmatched. Ferrying troops and armored vehicles across the Rhine as quickly as possible, the initial assault force was able to brush aside the weak American counterattacks and rapidly expand the width of the bridgehead to about ten miles. Meanwhile in the west, fresh units of the *6th Mountain SS Division* bulled through the 45th Division's patchwork defensive line in the Vosges and captured the town of Wingen, which represented the southernmost penetration of the initial *NORDWIND* offensive. The VI Corps was now heavily engaged on both its flanks, and Brooks was just about out of reserves.

Devers and Patch reacted quickly. On 6 January, with the uncommitted 36th and 103d Infantry Divisions headed for the Vosges front, they transferred the rest of the 14th Armored Division to Brooks, urged de Lattre to push additional forces up to the Strasbourg area as quickly as possible, and began deploying the army group's final reserve, the inexperienced 12th Armored Division, to the VI Corps area as well. The busy VI Corps commander tried to counter the Gambsheim threat, first, by reinforcing the area with a few more infantry battalions from the 79th Division's now greatly weakened northern front, and second, on 8 January, by committing a recently arrived combat command of the 12th Armored Division against the bridgehead.

In the Vosges, Brooks' forces continued to hold the mountain exits, and the 276th Infantry (TF Herren), led by a battalion of the recently committed 274th, even managed to clear Wingen of SS troops by the afternoon of the 7th after several days of bitter fighting.[3] On VI Corps' eastern flank, however, the canals, streams, and destroyed bridges made it difficult for either side to advance; Brooks' counterattacks were no more successful than the German efforts to expand their foothold across the Rhine, which now centered around the towns of Gambsheim, Herrlisheim, and Offendorf.

On 8 January, Combat Command B (CCB) of the 12th Armored Division, consisting mainly of the 56th Armored Infantry Battalion and the 714th Tank Battalion, attempted to seize Herrlisheim at the center of the German bridgehead by a direct attack. The ensuing action typified the experiences and frustrations of armored units fighting in built-up areas. Unable to put its vehicles across a series of waterways just west of the town, the unit ultimately had to assault the northern outskirts of Herrlisheim with its dismounted infantry. The lone battalion remained overnight, locked in combat with tank-supported German grenadiers, and could make no further progress. On the 9th, when the American medium tanks attempted to move up to the edge of a nearby canal in support, they were picked off one by one, "like ducks in a shooting gallery," by high-

---

[3] For action in the Wingen area, 5–7 January 1945, the 2d Battalion, 274th Infantry, 70th Infantry Division, received the Presidential Unit Citation. For treatment of the action, see Cheves, *Snow Ridges and Pill Boxes*, pp. 47–86.

714TH TANK BATTALION, 12TH ARMORED DIVISION, NEAR BISCHWILLER, FRANCE. *Guns point to Drusenheim, January 1945.*

velocity German antitank cannons; the remaining armored vehicles quickly withdrew.

During the 10th, several supporting M8 self-propelled guns also tried to move up closer to the town using different approaches, but they ended up crashing through the thick ice covering the local canals and could not be extracted until nightfall. Just about the only American armor able to reach Herrlisheim, the 714th's light tanks, proved useless in combat, but they were able to bring up supplies and evacuate the wounded—one tank serving only to cast a beam on the operating table of a nearby first-aid station. Although reinforced during the day by a company of engineers used as infantry fillers, the battalion finally had to withdraw on the night of 10–11 January, feeling fortunate that it had not been cut off and completely destroyed. Herrlisheim was not a good place for a new armored division.[4]

The French II Corps

Fortunately for Brooks, the German attack south of Strasbourg never became a serious threat. Well before

---

[4] Account based on 12th Arm Div AAR, Jan 45; and Seventh Army Historical Office, Interv Rpt, "Initial Assault on Herrlisheim by the 56th Armored Infantry Battalion of the 12th Armored Division during the Period 8–11 January 1945" (ca. 1945), MHI.

RIFLEMAN OF 70TH DIVISION *searching for snipers, Wingen, January 1945.*

the offensive, de Lattre had replaced Leclerc's departing armor with units of the French 5th Armored Division and the French 1st Infantry Division, as the latter deployed back from its abortive mission on the Atlantic coast. With these units in place, de Monsabert was in the process of pulling the 3d Algerian Division out of the Vosges and moving it up to Strasbourg when the German Colmar-based attacks began at Rhinau.[5]

The initial objectives of *SONNEN-WENDE* were limited and consisted of a triangular zone between the Ill and Rhine rivers fom Selestat to Erstein, representing about a fourth of the

[5] See de Lattre, *History*, pp. 313–23.

territory that the 2d Armored Division had secured back in December. The extension of German control north to Erstein, which would include a small logistical bridgehead at Rhinau, was then to serve as a springboard for an advance to Molsheim, another ten miles northward, until eventually Strasbourg was invested. Both Rasp and the *LXIV Corps* commander, General Thumm, had misgivings about the operation from the beginning, recognizing that ultimate success would depend on the *Nineteenth Army* receiving reinforcements and on the main attacking forces north of Strasbourg doing most of the work. Nevertheless, spurred by Himmler, the two generals did what they could.

Charged with the initial assault, Thumm concentrated his attacking forces on the west side of the Rhone-Rhine Canal, believing that the French forces between the canal and the Rhine would simply fall back if Erstein could be taken quickly enough. This proved the case when, on 7 January, the bulk of the German armor and one regiment of the *198th Volksgrenadier Division* drove north, reached Erstein during the first day of the attack, and then swung back to the southwest along the Ill River to trap French units engaging the rest of the *198th*'s forces. Although most of the surrounded French troops managed to escape across the Ill that night, Thumm's forces, reinforced by one regiment of the *269th Volksgrenadier Division*, currently in reserve on the east side of the Rhine, cleared the entire west side of the Ill River by the 11th and secured the west bank of the Rhine as far as Erstein. There, on 13

January, Operation *SONNENWENDE* formally ended. Although Hitler had previously directed Himmler to continue his attack northward with the entire *269th Division*, he later canceled the order, and a renewal of the offensive from Colmar never occurred. By 18 January the *269th Volksgrenadier Division* was on its way to the eastern front, but its scheduled replacement, the *2d Mountain Division*, had yet to arrive. Thumm was thus left with an even larger perimeter to defend with fewer units, supplies, and equipment than he had had at the beginning.

The XXXIX Panzer Corps Attacks

The fourth German assault against the Seventh Army began in earnest on 7 January along the vulnerable northern portion of the Lauterbourg salient. On the previous day Blaskowitz had finally obtained permission from Hitler to commit the panzer reserve units in this area, and Decker's *XXXIX Panzer Corps* arrived to control the operation, with both armored divisions and the *245th Volksgrenadier Division* in support. Carefully monitoring the progress of the offensive, the *Army Group G* commander was convinced that American redeployments from the Lauter River area had greatly reduced American defenses in the zone and that a quick strike all the way to Saverne was possible. By that time Brooks had withdrawn his defending forces five to ten miles back to the American-held portions of the Maginot Line—the first of his planned three-phase withdrawals—and the VI Corps defenses that remained were indeed extremely weak, consisting of a few infantry bat-

talions and support troops of the 45th and 79th Divisions and some elements of Task Force Linden (242d regiment). As a result Brooks' right wing and right flank were as jumbled as his left, with Wyche's 79th Division trying to control the following forces: from east to west, elements of the 222d (TF Linden), 315th, 313th, and 232d (TF Linden) Infantry occupying mainly Maginot Line positions; and, from north to south along the Rhine and around the Gambsheim bridgehead, elements of the 314th Infantry, CCB of the 14th Armored Division, the 232d Infantry, and finally elements of the 3d Algerian Division, which had begun to trickle in from the Vosges—all with a variety of tank, tank destroyer, engineer, and cavalry units mixed in.

Suddenly, with the commitment of the *21st Panzer* and *25th Panzer Grenadier Divisions* in the north, the entire American defensive effort appeared to be in grave danger. Nevertheless, for a time the Americans were able to hang on. In the center of the Lauterbourg salient, the heterogeneous collection of American units occupying old Maginot Line fortifications put up an energetic defense against somewhat listless German armor. Lack of proper reconnaissance as well as 79th Division minefields and artillery stalled the German tanks as did the weather, icy terrain, and the unexpected presence of Task Force Linden (42d Division) units. Meanwhile the remainder of Brooks' corps tried to hold the flanks at Gambsheim and in the Vosges, keeping the salient from caving in. Disturbed by the lack of progress on the 7th, Blaskowitz personally visited the Lauterbourg

48TH TANK BATTALION, 14TH ARMORED DIVISION, OUTSIDE OF RITTERSHOFFEN, *January 1945.*

front to find out what was holding up his panzer units, threatening to court-martial all of the principal armor commanders for their lack of aggressiveness. Finally, on 9 January, Decker's armor pierced the VI Corps center, driving it back to the Haguenau forest and forcing Brooks to commit his final reserve, the 14th Armored Division, near the towns of Hatten and Rittershoffen. Here American tanks met German armor in towns, fields, and roads, and the bitter fighting continued. The VI Corps was battling for its life on three sides.

The battleground now began to resemble a general melee. Between 10 and 20 January General Smith's 14th Armored Division, which assumed operational control of assorted infantry units of the 242d and 315th Infantry above the Haguenau forest and was supported by most of its own artillery plus that of the 79th Division, fought a sustained action with Decker's panzers. The German commanders, in turn, reinforced the attacking troops on the night of 13–14 January with the *20th Parachute Regiment (7th Parachute Division)*, and on the 16th with the *104th Infantry Regiment (47th Volksgrenadier Division)*, thereby steadily raising the stakes of the contest. But along the entire front of the VI Corps, division and regimental commanders gradually lost control over the battle, and the struggle devolved into a fierce tactical conflict between opposing battalions, companies, platoons, and smaller combat units.

The heaviest fighting was concentrated in the two small Alsatian towns of Rittershoffen and Hatten, both just north of the Haguenau forest and a mile or so apart.[6] Chance and circumstance had led the Germans to seize the eastern sections of both towns and the Americans to occupy the western parts, making the fields and roads in between a no-man's land of artillery, antitank, and small-arms fire. Efforts by each party to cut the resupply routes of the other by armored sweeps continually failed in the face of strong tank, antitank, and artillery fire from both sides. The battle thus boiled down to a desperate infantry fight within the towns, with dismounted panzer grenadiers and armored infantrymen fighting side by side with the more lowly foot infantry.[7] Almost every structure was hotly contested, and at the end of every day each side totaled up the number of houses and buildings it controlled in an attempt to measure the progress of the battle. Often in the smoke, haze, and darkness, friendly troops found themselves firing at one another, and few ventured into the narrow but open streets, preferring to advance or withdraw through the blown-out interior walls of the gutted homes and businesses. Both sides employed armor inside the town, but the half-blind tank crews had to be protected by a moving perimeter of infantrymen and could only play a limited supporting role. In Hatten, even with strong infantry and artillery support, no German or American tanker dared push his vehicle around "the bend"— a slight turn in the town's marginally wider main street that was covered by several antitank weapons from both sides.

By 15 January, as the German commitment of infantry in the two towns escalated, the Americans found themselves increasingly on the defensive; resupply and the evacuation of casualties became major operations, as did the continual reorganization of their shrinking perimeters to consolidate the territory they were able to hold. As elsewhere the cold weather kept bodies from deteriorating, and the troops reached a consensus among themselves that no one would be evacuated for shock, since everyone who was left fell into that dubious category. Nevertheless, the American armored division and the attached infantry managed to hang on, completely stalling the Germans' main effort, but in the process they lost perhaps one-third of their combat strength in men and equipment.

An equally desperate fight took place in the Vosges between Mouterhouse and Baerenthal involving the 45th Division's 157th regiment and additional units of the *6th SS Mountain Division*. Although the struggle lasted seven days, from 14 to 21 January, it began in earnest on the 15th when one of the 157th Infantry's battalions managed to penetrate the German

---

[6] Following account based on the 14th Arm Div AAR, Jan 45; and Seventh Army Historical Office, Interv Rpt, "Hatten, 14th Armored Division, 10–20 Jan 45," MHI. For a German view, see Hans von Luck, *Panzer Commander* (New York: Praeger, 1989), pp. 181–92.

[7] For combat leadership and heroic action inside Hatten on 9–10 January, the Congressional Medal of Honor was awarded to M. Sgt. Vito R. Bertoldo, Company A, 242d Infantry, 42d Infantry Division.

defensive positions and the other battalions were unable to follow. During the next two days the German defenders, after unsuccessfully trying to push the battalion back, managed to surround it and cut it off from its sister units. This isolated force, made up of five companies (L, I, C, K, and G), hung on for three days while various elements of the 45th and 103d Divisions and the 36th Engineers tried unsuccessfully to break through the German blockade, continually hampered by sleet and blinding snowstorms as well as by severe shortages of artillery ammunition and other supplies. With food running low and their own small-arms and mortar ammunition growing short, the remaining soldiers of the 157th's trapped force formed a small defensive perimeter, placing the wounded in foxholes so that they could be cared for by those who were still fighting. On the 20th, the end was near. With only about 125 able-bodied soldiers left, the trapped infantrymen tried to infiltrate out. News of the Malmedy Massacre in the Ardennes had spread throughout the Seventh Army, and few wished to surrender to the *SS* troops. But in the end only two enlisted men reached Allied lines. Shortly thereafter the remainder of the regiment was withdrawn from the front for rest and refitting; the *SS* mountain unit was equally battered, however, and had to be taken out of the line several days later.[8]

---

[8] 157th Rgt AAR, Jan 45. The survivors were PFC Benjamin Melton and Private Walter Bruce; regimental casualties for the month included 32 killed, 244 wounded, 472 missing, and 70 known prisoners of war. For a popular account, see Leo V. Bishop et al., eds., *The Fighting Forty-Fifth: The Combat Report of*

The Panzer Assault

Since the beginning of the *XXXIX Panzer Corps'* offensive in the north on 7 January, the German high command had debated incessantly over the role of the final German reserves, including the *10th SS* and *11th Panzer Divisions* and the *7th Parachute*, *47th Volksgrenadier*, and *2d Mountain Divisions*, many of which were beginning to arrive at the front in strength. On the evening of the 8th, Blaskowitz proposed using the parachute, *volksgrenadier*, and mountain units now assembling in the *First Army* area to assist the infantry units in capturing the eastern exits to the Vosges and from there striking west with the two additional panzer divisions toward Haguenau and Gambsheim, while Decker's forces kept the Americans busy in the north. With the exception of the *11th Panzer Division*, Hitler agreed to commit all of the *ZAHNARZT* forces to Alsace, but insisted that the *10th SS Panzer Division* be employed east of the Haguenau forest, along the Rhine, to link up with *Army Group Oberrhein's* forces in the Gambsheim bridgehead; the remainder of the reserves could be used in whatever way the field commanders thought best. However, by the time these decisions had been made and communicated to the front, Decker's breakthrough to Hatten and Rittershoffen, about noon on the 9th, together with the failure of both Hoehne in the Vosges and von dem Bach at Gambsheim to move out of their respective enclaves, appeared to support the immediate

---

an Infantry Division (Nashville, Tenn.: The Battery Press, 1978), pp. 142–46.

commitment of the reserves in the center, behind the *XXXIX Panzer Corps*.

The problems inherent in the awkward command and control arrangements of the Germans again became apparent, making it difficult for them to implement any of the proposals rapidly or to take advantage of the tactical situation on the battlefield. Hitler issued his instructions regarding the reserve forces sometime on the 9th, but Blaskowitz did not receive them until about twenty-four hours later, probably about the same time that *OKW* was passing the news of Decker's breakthrough on to Hitler. Meanwhile, leading elements of the 14th Armored Division had arrived in the Hatten-Rittershoffen area on the 10th, temporarily blocking any further German drive south. Although Decker might have attempted to bypass the Haguenau forest on the east or west, he could not afford to have an entire enemy armored division on his lines of communication, at least not until additional reinforcements arrived to free his mobile units from the embattled area. However the *ZAHNARZT* reserves reached the front in bits and pieces, forcing Blaskowitz and von Obstfelder to feed them into the battle in small increments, as they had done with the *6th SS Mountain Division*. Thus, on 10 and 11 January, units of the *7th Parachute* entered the struggle at Hatten and Rittershoffen, but Blaskowitz, in accordance with Hitler's orders, began assembling the *10th SS Panzer Division* northeast of what he considered the critical battle area for a drive along the water-soaked west bank of the Rhine. Later in the day Blaskowitz re-turned to his headquarters, apparently giving up the idea of a rapid breakthrough; about the same time Hitler, judging that the *XXXIX Panzer Corps* was again completely bogged down, decided to transfer responsibility for continuing the offensive east of the Vosges to *Army Group Oberrhein*. The decision became effective on 12 January, with the *XXXIX Panzer Corps* headquarters and the *10th SS Panzer* and *7th Parachute Divisions* going to Himmler; with the *21st Panzer*, *25th Panzer Grenadier*, and *47th Volksgrenadier Divisions* (upon arriving) coming under Hoehne's *LXXXIX Corps*, moving out of the Vosges; and with almost all of the Vosges assault forces taken over by Petersen's *XC Corps*.[9] While the Germans proceeded to shift their commands in order to comply with these changes, the *10th SS Panzer Division* continued to assemble in the Lauterbourg area for the main drive south.

Patch and Brooks also used the next few days to reorganize their forces and strengthen their defenses. The end of the *Nineteenth Army*'s offensive in the Rhinau-Erstein area on 13 January allowed de Lattre to accelerate the deployment of the 3d Algerian Division to Strasbourg, and the arrival of the U.S. 103d Infantry Division in the VI Corps zone had given Brooks an opportunity to begin pulling some the exhausted TF Herren regiments out of the line. Even

---

[9] The *LXXXIX* and *XC Corps* remained under the *First Army*, with the *XC Corps* now controlling the *6th Mountain SS Division* and the *36th*, *256th*, *257th*, and *361st Volksgrenadier Divisions*, and the *559th Volksgrenadier Division* going to Simon's *XIII SS Corps* (which still controlled the *17th SS Panzer Grenadier* and *19th Volksgrenadier Divisions*).

SHAEF had begun to pay some attention to the southern battlefield, informing Devers several days later that it would make the 101st Airborne Division and additional artillery available to the Seventh Army as soon as possible.[10] Patch now transferred both the 36th Infantry Division and the rest of the 12th Armored Division to Brooks, who quickly directed them to begin closing the Gambsheim area in order to relieve units of the 79th Infantry Division and TF Linden, which were equally tired.[11] Except in the Hatten-Rittershoffen area and in some sections of the eastern Vosges, the front appeared relatively quiet for a few days, with the notable exception of incessant strafing attacks by *Luftwaffe* aircraft, many of them reportedly jet fighters that were easier heard than seen. Both sides took the opportunity to rest and resupply their forces, contending with the freezing temperatures as best they could and preparing to renew the contest once again.

The Final Attack

On 16 January the *XXXIX Panzer Corps*, with the *10th SS Panzer Division*, the *7th Parachute Division*, the *384th* and *667th Assault Gun Brigades*, and even the *Reichsfuehrer's Escort Battalion*,

---

[10] Devers Diary, 18 Jan 45.

[11] From its reserve location at Sarrebourg, the 36th Division had first sent its 141st regiment to aid the 100th Division on 1 January and began following with the rest of the division on the 3d; the 142d regiment had been temporarily diverted west to cover the gap left by the departing 103d Division. The 36th Division thus initially arrived at the Gambsheim area with only one regiment, the 143d, but the 142d soon followed, allowing the division to assume responsibility for the area on 19 January.

spearheaded a final German drive from Lauterbourg south down the west bank of the Rhine River, scattering the defenders from Task Force Linden and the 79th Division and linking the northern attacking forces with those in the Gambsheim bridgehead. Some *10th SS* units had even been ferried directly into the bridgehead from the east bank of the Rhine. From there, the German commanders hoped to continue south and then drive west, behind the VI Corps' main line of resistance, striking for the Saverne Gap. Both Patch and Brooks had expected a resumption of the offensive, but the main axis of the German attack came as something of a surprise. The American unit that took the brunt of the attack was thus not Wyche's worn 79th Division or Smith's embattled 14th Armored, but Allen's new 12th Armored Division operating on the western flank of the Gambsheim bridgehead.

On 16 January the 12th Armored had begun another effort to seize Herrlisheim, the possession of which would have cut the principal German north-south communication line within the Gambsheim bridgehead. This time CCB was to renew its efforts north of Herrlisheim, again attacking east over the Zorn River; meanwhile CCA, with two armored infantry battalions and a reinforced tank battalion, made an administrative crossing of the Zorn south of the objective area at Weyersheim, still in American hands, and moved up on Herrlisheim from the opposite direction. General Allen hoped his two units could encircle and isolate the town, which current intelligence indicated was being held only by about

HERRLISHEIM

500 to 800 disorganized German infantrymen. Once Herrlisheim was surrounded and the Germans found
themselves unable to reinforce the
town, Allen felt that his three organic
infantry battalions could clear the interior relatively easily. Obviously the
mission was more suited to an infantry division, but until either the U.S.
36th or the French 3d Algerian
moved up to the area in strength,
Allen's unit was the only uncommitted force left to Brooks for the task.

The attack went badly from the
start. CCB was again unable to span
all the water crossings in the north,
where German artillery interfered
with bridging efforts; and a night

attack by the 43d Tank and 66th Armored Infantry Battalions south of
Herrlisheim met determined resistance. CCA quickly discovered that the
Germans had positioned antitank and
assault guns in the woods south of
Herrlisheim as well as in another
town, Offendorf, about a mile southeast of the command's objective. At
daylight on the 17th, Allen ordered
both of his combat commands to
renew the attack, with CCA pushing
two fresh companies of the 17th Armored Infantry Battalion, under Maj.
James W. Logan, into the southern
outskirts of Herrlisheim; while the
43d Tank Battalion, commanded by
Lt. Col. Nicholas Novosel, skirted east

of the town; and the 66th Armored Infantry Battalion, reinforced by elements of the 23d Tank Battalion and more artillery, made another attempt at the woods to the south. Logan's force subsequently advanced on foot, reaching the southern edge of Herrlisheim without incident, while Novosel's force of twenty-eight whitewashed Sherman tanks moved off to the east.

By noon both units had reported meeting heavy opposition, as did other CCA elements still trying to clear the area south of Herrlisheim. What occurred thereafter remains somewhat hazy. By late afternoon the 17th Battalion's infantrymen appeared to have consolidated their positions in the southern section of the town, and Allen decided to leave them there for the night. No trace, however, could be found of the 43d Tank Battalion. The battalion S–3 had reported taking German antitank fire at 0849 that morning; Logan's 17th Armored Infantry had lost radio contact with the 43d about 1000, and shortly thereafter Novosel had given his unit's location as somewhere in the eastern section of Herrlisheim. Around 1330, a final radio message sent by someone in the 43d indicated only that the battalion commander's tank had been knocked out and that the unit was now east of the town.

That night the rest of CCA together with the supply trains of the 43d Tank Battalion searched in vain for some sign of the missing armored unit. Meanwhile, inside the town, Logan noted a steadily increasing number of enemy probes throughout his lines, and about midnight he reported large-scale infantry attacks

supported by armor and artillery against all of his positions. The division immediately responded with concentrations of artillery fire to support the isolated infantrymen, but from his central command post Logan relayed that his units were constantly being forced to give ground. A final message—"I guess this is it"—about 0400 told Allen that the battalion had been overrun. Only a few of the surrounded infantrymen survived to escape in the darkness of the early morning hours. But of the tank battalion there was still no clue.

As later intelligence reports would show, CCA had unexpectedly run into the leading elements of the *10th SS Panzers*, which had linked up with von dem Bach's hard-pressed Gambsheim forces and evidently continued their drive south. Regarding the fate of the 43d, an American artillery observer flying over Herrlisheim on the 18th ended some of the mystery. He reported several destroyed tanks in the eastern section of Herrlisheim and, flying east of the town, spotted 4 or 5 more and then 12 to 15 others, dug in and deployed in a circle for all-around defense, some painted white and others burned black. At once Allen began preparations for a rescue mission with his entire division; however, further air reconnaissance revealed German troops and vehicles around the motionless American tanks, and the effort was abandoned. That evening German radio broadcasts boasted that an American lieutenant colonel and 300 of his men had been taken prisoner at Herrlisheim and 50 American tanks captured or destroyed. The 12th Division officers could only speculate that the

43d had run into an extensive anti-tank ambush between Herrlisheim and Offendorf early on the 17th, had taken refuge in the eastern section of Herrlisheim, and had been forced out into the open by infantry attacks for a final stand. Like many of the other armored units, the 12th was paying a steep price for its introduction to sustained combat.[12]

Outflanked by this new attack on his right, and with both of his attached armored divisions exhausted, Brooks finally elected to withdraw. On the night of 20–21 January those units of the VI Corps north of the Haguenau forest pulled back, moving southwest toward the Moder River. The movement took the attacking Germans by surprise and prevented them from pursuing the retreating Americans, giving Brooks time to organize new positions along the Zorn, Moder, and Rothbach rivers with little interference.

---

[12] The 12th Armored Division Graves Registration Report of 23 February indicated that the tanks inside the town had been destroyed by *panzerfausts*—infantry antitank rockets—and the tanks to the east by high-velocity cannons, a conclusion that was buttressed by the many antitank positions later found in the area littered with 75-mm. and 88-mm. shell casings. Some twenty-eight destroyed tanks of the 43d Tank Battalion were later recovered, as were the bodies of the battalion commander and many of his men; furthermore, tank tracks through the snow indicated that the Germans had evacuated four American tanks across the Rhine when they withdrew from the area. The account of the action is based on the following sources: Seventh Army Historical Office, Interv Rpts, "12th Armored Division at Herrlisheim" (interviews with members of the 17th AIB and the 43d Tank Bn, 12th AD); ibid., "Weyersheim-Herrlisheim Area: CCA, 12th Armored Division, 16–21 Jan 45" (both ca. 1945); and Ltr, HQ, 12th Armored Division, 1 Feb 45, sub: Investigation of Circumstances in the Action of the 17th Armored Infantry Battalion and the 43d Tank Battalion, both of the 12th Armored Division, 17–18 January 1945," all at MHI.

The new VI Corps positions behind the Moder River greatly reduced the frontage Brooks' units would have to hold, but surrendered no great advantage to the advancing Germans. In fact, it took another four days for Hoehne, Decker, and von dem Bach to bring all the attacking German units with their supplies and equipment up to the new American positions. By that time, Brooks had the 45th, 103d, 79th, and 36th Infantry Divisions on line (west to east), and had moved the survivors of the 12th and 14th Armored Divisions and Task Force Linden back into reserve. In addition, stronger French forces were in place north of Strasbourg, and Maj. Gen. Maxwell D. Taylor's 101st Airborne Division was en route to the front. With these forces the VI Corps was able to contain a final series of German attacks, undertaken during the night of 24–25 January during a driving snowstorm. The attacking forces briefly managed to penetrate the new VI Corps lines in three places, but were promptly ejected by 14th Armored and 42d Infantry Division counterattacks. The following day Patch's forces began counterattacking across the German line, with the 100th and 45th Divisions on the west and the U.S. 36th and the French 3d Algerian on the east, forcing the Germans to protect their gains and putting them on the defensive again. Repulsed once more and with the Americans still game, the German high command had had enough and on 26 January, with their reserves exhausted, finally called a halt to what had clearly become a battle of attrition. As suddenly as it had begun, the German offensive was over. By the end of the month Hitler had replaced Blaskowitz with Lt. Gen. Paul Hauser, an *SS* officer, and had sent most of the better German formations to the Eastern Front, leaving those forces opposite the 6th Army Group weaker than they had been at the beginning of the offensive.

An Analysis

In the end, the Germans expended much strength for little gain. Seventh Army casualties for the month of January numbered about 14,000, while the attacking German forces lost almost 23,000 officers and men.[13] Moreover, the Allied losses could be replaced; the German casualties could not. From the beginning, the division of authority between *OB West, Army Group G,* and *First Army* in the north and *Army Group Oberrhein* and *Nineteenth Army* in the south greatly hindered German chances for success. *Army Group G*'s initial *NORDWIND* at-

---

[13] As elsewhere, casualty figures are only rough estimates, and the figures presented are based on the postwar "Seventh Army Operational Report, Alsace Campaign and Battle Participation, 1 June 1945" (copy CMH), which notes 11,609 Seventh Army battle casualties for the period, plus 2,836 cases of trench foot and 380 cases of frostbite, and estimates about 17,000 Germans killed or wounded with 5,985 processed prisoners of war. But the VI Corps AAR for January 1945 puts its total losses at 14,716 (773 killed, 4,838 wounded, 3,657 missing, and 5,448 nonbattle casualties); and Albert E. Cowdrey and Graham A. Cosmas, "The Medical Department: The War Against Germany," draft CMH MS (1988), pp. 54–55, a forthcoming volume in the United States Army in World War II series, reports Seventh Army hospitals processing about 9,000 wounded and 17,000 "sick and injured" during the period. Many of these, however, may have been returned to their units, and others may have come from American units operating in the Colmar area but still supported by Seventh Army medical services. Von Luttichau's "German Operations," ch. 29, pp. 39–40, puts German losses at 22,932.

tacks eased *Army Group Oberrhein*'s assault across the Rhine at Gambsheim rather than the reverse. But by the time Hitler agreed to give one headquarters, in this case *Army Group Oberrhein,* operational control over the primary attacking forces on 13 January, surprise had been lost as well as much of the German offensive punch. Although badly battered by this date, the Seventh Army and its two corps were still intact and functioning well. Allied success in the Ardennes had allowed Devers to retain both the 12th Armored and 36th Infantry Divisions and throw them into the battle. Further assistance came as the rest of the 42d, 63d, and 70th Infantry Divisions and, from the SHAEF reserve, the 101st Airborne Division arrived, and as SHAEF increased the priority of supplies, equipment, and manpower allocated to the 6th Army Group. The timely arrival of the 103d Division allowed Patch to pull Task Force Herren into reserve, while the 36th Division performed the same service for Task Force Linden and the 12th Armored Division; the 101st Airborne Division, slated to replace the battered 79th Division, was never really needed. The withdrawal of the VI Corps out of the Lauterbourg salient and behind the Moder River greatly improved its defensive posture and tightened up the front of the Seventh Army in general, while the arrival of the 3d Algerian Division safeguarded Strasbourg city. In addition, the commanders, staffs, and combat troops of Patch's three new divisions were, by the end of *NORDWIND*, undoubtedly more experienced and more confident.

The Americans had good reasons

for their confidence. For many Seventh Army soldiers, this had been their first real engagement with attacking German forces whose strength was equal or superior to their own. In the contest, their leaders—Devers, Patch, and the corps, division, and regimental commanders—had done well, proving more than adept at switching large American units back and forth to meet the wide variety of German threats, and had little difficulty keeping pace with the German-orchestrated tempo of operations. Devers' decision to rush the nine brand-new infantry regiments into the line before the attacks had even begun was perhaps his most important contribution, while Patch's plan to reinforce the Sarre valley area and to rely elsewhere on defense in depth proved sound. The Seventh Army could not be strong everywhere, and the Germans probably could have penetrated Brooks' lines almost anywhere on the long VI Corps front without, however, achieving decisive results. Good use of interior lines of communications, especially the lateral road networks through the Vosges, more than made up for the VI Corps' thin lines and its exposed position in the Lauterbourg salient. But Devers was probably accurate when he stated that "Ted Brooks . . . fought one of the great defensive battles of all times with very little."[14]

In the field, American officers and men at the tactical level performed well, especially considering the general confusion that resulted from the rapid movement of units back and forth across the battlefield. Often

with little support and even less direction from higher headquarters, regiments, battalions, and companies stubbornly clung to key towns, waterways, and road junctions, while corps and divisional artillery and service units desperately tried to see that each unit was given at least enough support to enable it to survive. Officers stayed awake by loading themselves with Benzadrine, while NCOs tried to stave off the effects of bitter cold on their men with fires and hot coffee.[15] For all of them, it was their first experience at conducting a sustained defensive effort.

Neither Devers nor Patch relied excessively on their exceptional intelligence capabilities, which may have told the Allied leaders that the German high command had the ability to attack in their sector, but not where and when the major assaults would actually occur. In fact, both commanders were still concerned over the possibility of a new German offensive slightly west of the Sarre River valley area, where the withdrawal of the 103d Division had temporarily weakened the boundary zone between the Seventh and Third Armies.[16] For this reason Patch continued to retain Leclerc's 2d Armored Division—arguably the 6th Army Group's best armored force—in reserve west of the Vosges behind Haislip's XV Corps.

In the air, poor flying conditions prevented the defenders from making full use of their tactical air superiori-

[14] Devers Diary, 17 Jan 45.

[15] Interv, Clarke with Theodore C. Mataxis (former commander, 2d Battalion, 274th Infantry, Task Force Herren), 3 Aug 88.
[16] Devers Diary, 8–9 Jan 45.

ty. During January alone, Allied aircraft were grounded nearly half the month. But the German Air Force high command failed to take full advantage of the weather. Although the start of Operation *NORDWIND* had been accompanied by a massive *Luftwaffe* attack of about 700 aircraft against Allied air bases, which destroyed over 150 planes and damaged many more, the strikes had been directed almost totally against airfields in Belgium and the Netherlands and had no impact on the campaign in Alsace. Moreover, German losses during the strike were also high, and the *Luftwaffe* was unable to sustain such efforts, normally flying no more than 125 to 150 sorties per day across the entire Western Front. Although briefly sending 150–175 sorties into the Alsace area to support the final attacks in the Lauterbourg salient, the effort had a negligible effect on the battlefield.[17] American commanders reported numerous strafing attacks by German aircraft during the period, but no sustained effort to disrupt their lines of communication.

For the 6th Army Group, the supporting 1st Tactical Air Command concentrated its air strikes north and east of the Saar, Lauter, and Rhine rivers in the German communications zone behind the battlefield, especially in the railway marshaling areas, thus making it difficult for the German ground forces to move supplies and reinforcements up to the front lines or to move troop units laterally behind the battlefield. Poor visibility limited the command's effect on the battlefield, but the threat of Allied air attacks greatly influenced German deployments. Equally important, air reconnaissance had tracked the general German buildup opposite the XV Corps, when ULTRA intercepts gave no warning of a German attack.

ULTRA itself was of marginal use during the battle, and the information it supplied was often many days out of date. For example, on 31 December ULTRA intelligence officers believed that the *6th Mountain SS Division* had started to leave Norway in early December, but had no information regarding its destination. A decrypt of 4 January reported that the last elements of the division had departed Norway a week earlier; a decrypt available on 6 January of a 28 December message referred to large movements by rail to *Army Group G;* a decrypt on the following day, 7 January, disclosed that the mountain *SS* division was in the Kaiserslautern area on the 5th; and a decrypt of 10 January finally placed it on the battlefield under Hoehne's *LXXXIX Corps.*[18] Actually the unit had entered the battle on 2 January, eight days earlier, where it had been promptly identified by opposing Seventh Army units.

ULTRA, nevertheless, performed a valuable function, enabling its users to verify the welter of often conflicting information that poured in during the battle from POW reports and other conventional sources. In these matters, experience and common

---

[17] According to Bussey's ULTRA Report, ULTRA intercepts had warned the Allies of the main air attack, and ULTRA Msg BT 2834 200541 Jan 45 alludes to the final air support activities against the VI Corps.

[18] ULTRA information provided by Hinsley et al., *British Intelligence in the Second World War*, III, 2, pp. 665–66.

sense were more valuable to intelligence officers than exotic sources of information. For example, no one at SHAEF headquarters or anywhere else was taken in by information apparently planted on 26 January indicating that the entire *II SS Panzer Corps,* with its divisions, had been transferred from the Ardennes to *Army Group G* for commitment to the Alsatian campaign.[19]

On the German side, order-of-battle information concerning Seventh Army's dispositions was often hazy, especially in regard to the location of Patch's armored divisions behind the battlefield. *OB West* and the *First Army,* for example, expected to find the 36th Division in the Vosges instead of Task Force Hudelson, and the shallowness of the American defenses there may have been a welcome surprise. Less pleasing, however, was the appearance of Leclerc's 2d Armored Division instead of the inexperienced 12th in the Sarre River valley, as was the discovery that the Seventh Army had not deployed more formations north to the Ardennes. The stiff resistance from some of the green American units must also have been unexpected.

On the ground most American soldiers, from new privates to seasoned veterans, had little idea of the scope or magnitude of the successive offensives. According to many participants, the average infantryman had only two concerns, "not letting his buddies down and surviving." Often it was the weather, in one of the coldest winters of the decade, rather than the Germans that gave American foot soldiers the most problems. In general they may have performed better than their German opponents, many of whom, according to a wide variety of American reports, appeared intoxicated during the initial phase of the attacks, shouting a variety of slogans and epithets at the defenders and advancing in successive waves over open terrain. The average American GIs, always somewhat cynical, were notably unimpressed by the German performance and, in effect, by the whole Nazi military mystic.

Shortages of personnel and equipment could not completely explain the marginal German showing. Given the scarcity of ammunition, transportation, and radio communications, German artillery support was understandably poor at times, but was not critical to German success. Their best efforts were consistently the result of surprise attacks without artillery preparation and quick infantry penetrations through gaps in the American lines. In contrast, German armor, the exploiting component, was technically impressive but tactically disappointing. American officers reported that the heavier German armored vehicles slipped on the icy roads, were continually hampered by mines and destroyed bridges, and were too easily separated from their supporting infantry. The attackers' well-armored but turretless assault guns were better suited to the defense, and the large Panther and Tiger tanks did not do much better. Perhaps they never had much of a chance. Finally, the superheavy German tanks like the Royal Tigers and *Jagdtigers* were extremely powerful machines, but their weight and high fuel consumption made

---

[19] Hinsley, p. 668.

their positioning on the battefield difficult, and they may have only wasted the limited supplies and trained manpower available to the attackers.

American combat support was superior, and the prompt availability of adequate artillery, engineer, signal, and logistical support may have been decisive in many tactical engagements. Combat engineers often found themselves in the forefront of the battle, building or destroying bridges, constructing obstacles and minefields, or serving as infantry alongside of artillery forward observers, medical personnel, radio operators, truck drivers, and other rear-echelon soldiers. Others, whose tasks kept them farther in the rear, worked around the clock at supply depots, repair facilities, and artillery sites, and many crowded the daily religious services to pray for those on the front lines.

Some materiel and logistical failings were difficult to overcome. Artillery munitions still had to be carefully rationed, and even the newer tanks and tank destroyers, equipped with higher-velocity guns, were inferior in many ways to their German counterparts. All had greater speed, mobility, and range than their opponents, but they were still outclassed in armored protection and firepower. Devers himself judged the American tank equal to the average German machine, but even before the battle he had been concerned over the readiness of his two American armored divisions.[20] Like the German panzer divisions, they were organized and equipped primarily for mobile warfare and had

no business throwing themselves into built-up areas like Hatten, Rittershoffen, and Herrlisheim. But Brooks, a former armored division commander himself, had no choice in this matter, and both the 12th and 14th Armored were at least able to enter the battle arena rapidly, reinforcing critical areas and blunting the final German drives south. Yet, like Blaskowitz, Devers would have liked his armored units to have had more training and experience.

Not surprisingly, armor losses on both sides were high, because the critical fighting was centered around key crossroads and river crossings in built-up areas where armored vehicles became easy prey for mines and infantry antitank weapons. Here both sides were relatively strong: the standard American 57-mm. antitank cannons were buttressed by 75-mm. and 76-mm. pieces, and the Germans fielded similar high-velocity artillery; the American bazooka rocket-launchers were matched by the German *panzerfaust*. On the defense, the German antitank gunners had a distinct advantage over the American crews because of the comparatively light frontal armor of the Allied tanks. Nevertheless, good cooperation between U.S. tank-infantry teams and supporting artillery usually compensated for such technical disadvantages within the more experienced American divisions. Experience, not armor plating, was the key; accordingly, Smith's 14th Armored Division, having received its initiation in street fighting the previous November in southern Alsace, did much better at Hatten and Rittershoffen than Allen's inexperienced 12th did at Herrlisheim.

---

[20] See Devers Diary, 9 and 16 Jan 45.

As in other campaigns, the entire battle underlined the continued importance of well-trained infantry and experienced tactical commanders and staffs as well as the need for a command system that delegated the proper amount of authority to the implementing echelons. In the case of the controversial withdrawal from the Lauterbourg salient, it was Eisenhower, Devers, and the Allied political leaders who discussed the overall implications of the proposal; Patch, the army commander, who brought the VI Corps back to the Maginot Line; and Brooks, the corps commander, who ordered the final tactical withdrawal to the Moder. But in the field where the battles were fought, neither the vast Allied fleets of flying machines nor the heavily armored German land battleships had much of an effect. Success in battle thus came down to the ability of infantry forces on both sides to attack and defend and the ability of their corps, division, regiment, and battalion commanders to position them effectively on the battlefield and make the best use of supporting manpower and machinery. In the end it was the capability of the machine to serve the foot soldier in the field, rather than the reverse, that proved decisive.

CHAPTER XXIX

The Colmar Pocket

By the end of the German winter offensives, the battered Western Front traced a ragged line across Belgium, France, and Germany from the North Sea down to the Swiss border. The first Allied order of business was to straighten this line, pulling it taut and reducing its length as much as possible. Shorter lines would mean fewer troops at the front, thus allowing the commanders of the three army groups to move more units back to the rear for rest and recuperation and, ultimately, to concentrate them for a final thrust into the German interior. In northern Alsace, the German attack, which forced the VI Corps out of the Lauterbourg salient and onto the more defensible Moder River line, had partially solved this problem, reducing the VI Corps front by more than half. To the south, however, the Colmar Pocket still created a large fifty-mile gap in the Rhine front of the First French Army, an enemy-held salient that threatened the flanks of any future French advance eastward into Germany.

In early December de Lattre had tried to eliminate the pocket, but his renewed offensive had been undermined by the demands of Operation INDEPENDENCE and by the constant attrition of men and materiel throughout the winter fighting in the Vosges. The French commander continued to have difficulty in overcoming his weak support organization and in turning FFI militia and local draftees into conventional soldiers. The Ardennes emergency finally forced him to call off the effort. For the Germans, maintaining the pocket also presented severe problems. French aggressiveness had kept almost the entire *Nineteenth Army* busy in defense of the salient, greatly limiting its ability to assist German attacks in the north. The northern offensives, in turn, had siphoned off any reserves that might have been committed to the pocket, making Operation SONNEN-WENDE, the *Nineteenth Army*'s contribution to the battle of Alsace, a limited affair that only lengthened the vast 130-mile defensive perimeter around the city of Colmar.

Planning the Colmar Offensive

Even as the German attacks in northern Alsace reached their peak, Devers was preparing for a new major offensive against the 850-square-mile Colmar Pocket.[1] Allied intelligence

---

[1] General information on Allied planning and operations in this chapter is based on the following

sources, including ULTRA, showed that the Germans did not intend to transfer the rest of their armored forces to the Alsatian front and indicated that de Lattre's headquarters may have greatly overestimated the size of the German forces now remaining in the pocket. Nevertheless, the 6th Army Group commander was prepared to reinforce the French with considerable American support to ensure that the southern Alsatian plains were swept clean. Devers wanted the Colmar Pocket eliminated once and for all, preferably in January or early February before rainfall and warmer temperatures turned the frozen farming area into a quagmire. The weather was critical for the timing of the attack. The 6th Army Group expected that, after the heavy snowfalls of December and early January, the weather would break in the latter half of January, giving the French some clear skies and clear roads for the offensive, an expectation that agreed with official SHAEF weather predictions. But once slightly warmer weather began to melt the accumulated snowfall, military operations would again become extremely difficult.

On the afternoon of 11 January, Devers and de Lattre conferred at Vittel regarding a renewal of the Colmar offensive. Although both men were eager to begin the effort as soon

as possible, they were also concerned about the ground the French had recently been forced to relinquish around Erstein and about the possibility of having to make a last-ditch defense of Strasbourg. For the moment, Devers thought the First French Army was too weak to see the operation through alone and promised to seek additional units from the SHAEF reserve.

Two days later, during a visit by Eisenhower's chief of staff to the 6th Army Group, Devers put the question to Bedell Smith, asking for two American divisions—an infantry division to reinforce O'Daniel's 3d Division at Colmar and an armored division to replace Leclerc's unit, which he also intended to return south. Smith apparently convinced Eisenhower that the request was justified and cabled a favorable response to Devers the following day, 14 January; he promised the 6th Army Group both the 10th Armored and 28th Infantry Divisions, but warned Devers that the 28th, still badly battered from the Ardennes fighting, was capable of only limited offensive action.

Meanwhile, Devers had already ordered his own staff to put together a general operational plan for de Lattre based on the expected reinforcements and the employment of the U.S. XXI Corps headquarters, which Devers had temporarily placed in charge of Patch's northern flank.[2] Dubbed Op-

---

sources: Hist, 6th Army Gp, ch. 6; *Seventh Army Rpt*, ch. 24; HQ, II Corps, Report on the Offensive Operations by II Corps for the Reduction of the Colmar Pocket, 28 Feb 45; HQ, I Corps, Chronological Report on the Operations from 20 January to 9 February 1945 to Reduce the Colmar Pocket, 24 Feb 45; XXI Corps AAR, Jan 45; de Lattre, *History*, pp. 334–401; and "The 5th French Armored Division at Colmar," *Military Review*, XXIX, No. 9 (December 1949), 77–83 (reprinted from the *Revue historique de l'armee*).

[2] On 6th Army Group planning, see Jonathan O. Seaman, "Reduction of the Colmar Pocket: A 6th Army Group Operation," *Military Review*, XXXI, No. 7 (October 1951), 45–46. (Seaman served in the 6th Army Group G–3 section during World War II and later commanded a U.S. corps-level force in South Vietnam.)

eration CHEERFUL by the Americans, the basic concept was a simultaneous attack on both sides of the pocket toward the major surviving Rhine River bridge near Neuf-Brisach, about seven miles east of Colmar city. The French I Corps was to lead off in the south with a drive from Mulhouse directly to the bridge area, conducting a secondary attack in the mountains north of Thann in order to tie down German forces. After the German reserves had hopefully moved to the south, Maj. Gen. Frank W. Milburn's XXI Corps was to direct the main effort; while Milburn sent two American infantry divisions and Leclerc's armored division against the Neuf-Brisach area, assisted perhaps by an airborne assault, the French II Corps would seize Colmar itself. The 6th Army Group planners estimated that Operation CHEERFUL would take about one week and, after studying weather and flood records, recommended that it begin in early February, certainly before the 20th.

Devers accepted the general operational concept, but was more worried about rising temperatures than cloudy skies and insisted that the operation begin much earlier, without either Milburn's corps or Leclerc's armor if necessary. De Monsabert's French corps would have to direct the main effort, which, he agreed, should not be toward Colmar but against Neuf-Brisach. SHAEF's negative response regarding the availability of airborne forces, an unnecessary complication, did not disturb Devers. He ordered de Lattre to begin the effort by attacking from the south on 20 January and from the north on the 22d, with the U.S. 28th Infantry Divi-

sion supporting the northern effort in accordance with its limited capabilities as it arrived on the scene. Despite the rather precarious situation of the VI Corps in the north, Devers was confident that Patch could handle the situation there and wanted to move against the Colmar Pocket while the Germans were still overextended and the weather prognosis was good.

De Lattre accepted the 6th Army Group's planning concept to use the southern attack to draw off German reserves and concentrate the main effort against the Neuf-Brisach bridge, trapping as many Germans inside the pocket as possible.[3] In the north, de Monsabert's II Corps, already consisting of the U.S. 3d, the French 1st, and the 3d Algerian Divisions, would be reinforced with both the French 5th Armored Division and the U.S. 28th Infantry Division, under Maj. Gen. Norman D. Cota. Cota's weak division was to take over the northwestern perimeter of the pocket, along the Kaysersberg valley just above Colmar city, while the 3d Algerian Division screened the extreme northern perimeter south of Strasbourg. O'Daniel's 3d and the two other French divisions would be concentrated in between, just south of Selestat, for the thrust at Neuf-Brisach and the Rhine. To provide more combat power, Devers also agreed to begin deploying Leclerc's 2d Armored Division south to the Strasbourg area as quickly as he could and to move the U.S. 12th Armored Division into the Kaysersberg-Selestat area

---

[3] First Fr Army, Personal and Secret Directive 7, 15 Jan 45 (Annex VII of de Lattre, *Histoire*, French language edition).

by the 22d as a reserve for the French.[4]

With these additions, de Monsabert decided that the American 3d Division, reinforced by one infantry regiment from Task Force Harris (63d Infantry Division) and supported by one combat command of the French 5th Armored Division, would make the main effort, pushing southeast from the area between Selestat and Kaysersberg. On its left, the French 1st Infantry Division, with some of Leclerc's armor attached, would push east, covering the northern flank of the American unit. The extreme flanks of the offensive would, in turn, be screened by the rest of de Monsabert's French units in the north and by Cota's 28th Division in the south. Once the U.S. 3d Division had secured bridgeheads over the Colmar Canal, about halfway to the Rhine, the French commander was prepared to commit the rest of the 5th Armored Division to seize the objective area, leaving Leclerc and some attached FFI forces to mop up any Germans left in the Erstein salient north of Neuf-Brisach. At the beginning, however, the main attacking forces would ignore both the Erstein salient and Colmar itself and would advance southeast, between these two more obvious objectives. The projected route of advance would take them across four major water barriers: the Fecht and Ill rivers, the Riedwiller Brook, and the Colmar Canal. Each was critical, and de Monsabert hoped that, with speed and surprise, all four

could be breached quickly before the Germans could react.

On the southern edge of the pocket, General Bethouart's I Corps prepared to support the main effort by beginning its attack two days earlier than de Monsabert and striking north with two divisions, the 4th Moroccan Mountain and the 2d Moroccan Infantry, using the 9th Colonial Infantry Division at the base of the pocket as a pivot. The French 1st Armored Division would provide some tank support to the attacking formations, but the bulk of du Vigier's armored command would initially remain in reserve. Departing from the 6th Army Group's planning concept, Bethouart wanted his Moroccan divisions to make the main effort on the left (west) between Thann and Cernay over the Thur River toward Ensisheim, while the 9th Colonial pushed into the suburbs and woods north of Mulhouse. Once these forces had cleared a roughly triangular shape of territory between Cernay, Ensisheim, and Mulhouse and had secured bridges over the Ill River at Ensisheim, the 1st Armored Division would pass through the French lines and drive for Neuf-Brisach.

North of Thann, in the High Vosges, de Lattre had replaced the 3d Algerian Division with the new French 10th Infantry Division, which had been assembled primarily from FFI resources, and expected the unit only to guard the western boundaries of the pocket on the slopes of the Vosges.

As everyone now realized, the Colmar terrain presented many challenges to the Allied forces, both north and south. Because of innumerable

---

[4] The French 2d and the U.S. 12th Armored Divisions were temporarily replaced by the U.S. 10th Armored Division, which began arriving in the Seventh Army area on 17 January.

streams, brooks, small rivers, and canals on the projected routes of advance of both corps, considerable bridging equipment was required. To make the maximum amount available, the French replaced many of the existing Bailey bridges in their areas with timber structures, and Devers managed to obtain a bridge company from the Third Army to provide direct support for the U.S. 3d Division. But bridging remained scarce and had to be carefully rationed; ultimately much more had to be made available to the French from Seventh Army and theater reserves during the course of the operation. Other shortages existed throughout the First French Army: initially only ten days' worth of ammunition and one day's reserve of gasoline were available at forward depots; large numbers of vehicles were deadlined and awaiting repair due to a lack of spare parts; and the manpower losses suffered during the November offensive had not yet been replenished. O'Daniel's 3d Division was in better shape, having been relieved by Cota's 28th on 19 January, but had been fighting a fierce seesaw battle for control of the Kaysersberg valley since its arrival on the northern approaches to Colmar.[5] Before the offensive and during the days that followed, the 6th Army Group staff endeavored to satisfy

de Lattre's most pressing supply and equipment shortages, aided by the quiet that had finally descended on Patch's Seventh Army front to the north.

The German Defense

In mid-January 1945 the mission of General Rasp's *Nineteenth Army* was to tie down the largest possible number of Allied forces west of the Rhine, giving *OKW* more time to redeploy German units to the Eastern Front and reorganize the defenses of those that remained. In addition, on 22 January *Army Group Oberrhein* ordered Rasp to be prepared to renew his attacks in the northern corner of the pocket in support of what was to be the final German effort against Brooks' VI Corps along the Moder River. At the time, Rasp and his two corps commanders would have preferred to conduct a gradual, fighting withdrawal to the east bank of the Rhine and eventually to deploy the bulk of the *Nineteenth Army* north of the Black Forest, where the major Allied offensives were expected to occur.[6] But the abrupt termination of the offensive in northern Alsace on the 26th at least freed them from any further supporting requirements.

Inside the Colmar Pocket the *Nineteenth Army* controlled two corps headquarters, eight infantry divisions, and one armored brigade. General Thumm's *LXIV Corps* held the northern half of the pocket with the *189th* and *198th Infantry Divisions* and the *16th* and

---

[5] For heroic action during these generally unheralded skirmishes, Congressional Medals of Honor were awarded to three 3d Division soldiers: Lt. Col. Keith L. Ware, Commanding Officer, 1st Battalion, 15th Infantry, for action on 26 December 1944; 1st Lt. Eli Whiteley, Company L, 15th Infantry, also for action on the 26th; and T. Sgt. Russell E. Dunham, Company I, 30th Infantry, for action on 8 January 1945. Colonel Ware, later promoted to major general, was killed in action in Vietnam while commanding the 1st Infantry Division in 1969.

[6] German information in this chapter is based primarily on Magna E. Bauer, "The German Withdrawal from the Colmar Pocket," CMH MS R–56.

708th Volksgrenadier Divisions.[7] Operation *SONNENWENDE* had left the *198th* in the Erstein salient and the *708th Volksgrenadiers* holding a north-south line along the Ill River from Selestat south to Colmar, supported by the *280th Assault Gun Battalion.* At Colmar, the *189th Infantry Division* took over the defensive perimeter, which stretched westward into the Vosges where the *16th Volksgrenadiers* outposted the mountainous western section of the pocket. In the south Lt. Gen. Erich Abraham, who had replaced Schack as commander of the *LXIII Corps* on 13 December, had the *338th, 159th,* and *716th Infantry Divisions,* with the weak *338th* in the mountains northwest of Thann, the *159th* centered around Cernay, and the *716th* opposite Mulhouse. In army reserve were the *106th Panzer Brigade* and the *269th Infantry Division;* however, the latter unit was currently in the process of deploying to the Eastern Front, and its replacement, the *2d Mountain Division,* was still nowhere in sight.

All of the line divisions were understrength, undertrained, and underequipped, having only about 30 to 40 percent of their antitank weapons and little ammunition for their more numerous artillery pieces. Armor was even scarcer, totaling perhaps sixty-five operational tanks and assault guns, and was concentrated generally in the armored brigade and two mobile antitank units, the *280th Assault Gun Battalion* and the *654th Tank*

Destroyer *(Panzerjaeger) Battalion.* Experienced infantry was also in short supply, with most of the line battalions fleshed out with hastily trained fillers and recruits. By now, such conditions must have seemed almost normal to the *Nineteenth Army* staff, which could still count on many advantages that made it difficult for the Allies to summarily eject its forces from the area. Rasp had some 22,500 effectives (versus an Allied estimate of 15,000); short interior lines of communication; good wire communications down to at least the battalion level; ample rations and stocks of mines and small-arms ammunition; and a secure rear area. The weather and terrain heavily favored the defense, as did the Alsatian network of small towns, each of which could be turned into a tiny fortress; together they provided a ready-made strong-point defensive system that enabled Rasp to make the best use of his poorly trained but highly motivated troops. The failure of the French and Americans to make any vital penetrations in this system during the past month attested to its effectiveness, but Rasp's fixed defensive arrangements also made it difficult to concentrate his forces for local counterattacks of any significance.

Key to Rasp's defensive effort was his ability to secure two major bridges over the Rhine, which, because of their sturdy construction, had proved impossible to destroy by air attacks. The first was a single-track, reinforced railway bridge at Brisach (two miles east of Neuf-Brisach), which the German soldiers had already awarded an honorary Iron Cross for surviving massive Allied bombing assaults; the

---

[7] The U.S. XV Corps had destroyed the *708th Volksgrenadier Division* during the November offensive, but the German high command had reconstituted the unit sometime in December and moved it to the Colmar front.

second was the Neuenburg bridge just opposite the French town of Cha-lampe, which de Lattre had consid-ered seizing back in November. In ad-dition the *Nineteenth Army* maintained numerous permanent ferry sites along the Rhine capable of handling 8-, 16-, 40-, and even a few 70-ton loads. Near Brisach alone were four 10-ton, six 16-ton, and one 70-ton ferry sites, two cable ferries, and one fuel pipe-line; furthermore, all road networks on the German side of the Rhine were in good condition. But the two bridge sites were critical for the sur-vival of the *Nineteenth Army,* and the German commanders predicted that the Allies would eventually try to seize them. No one at either *Nineteenth Army* headquarters or at *Army Group Oberrhein,* however, expected that the attempt would be made before the battles in the north had ended and the Allied forces had taken some time to recover.

The Initial Attacks

As scheduled, the French I Corps attack jumped off in the south on 20 January with Bethouart's two Moroc-can divisions undertaking the main effort from Cernay to Ensisheim, the 9th Colonial Division making a sec-ondary foray north of Mulhouse, and other units conducting a small diver-sionary maneuver north of Thann (*Map 35*). Unhappily for the southern French forces, Allied weather predic-tions proved incorrect, and the offen-sive began in the middle of a driving snowstorm. Bethouart's forces easily achieved tactical surprise, driving for-

ward several miles during the first day of the attack and striking hard at the boundary between the German *159th* and *716th Divisions.* But the adverse weather and terrain together with the elastic German defenses broke the tempo of the advance during the night. Throughout the 21st, the Ger-mans launched a series of small armor-supported counterattacks and managed to hold on to Cernay and limit French gains above Mulhouse. Although failing to achieve the deep penetration that the I Corps com-mander had hoped for, the attacks at least succeeded in drawing the *Nine-teenth Army's* scant armor reserves southward. *Army Group Oberrhein* ap-proved the immediate commitment of the *654th Tank Destroyer Battalion* and also ordered the *106th Panzer Brigade* and later arriving elements of the *2d Mountain Division* southward to the threatened area. Initially, however, neither Himmler nor Rasp attached any great significance to the actions, which, they believed, represented no more than a limited diversionary effort to reduce pressure on Stras-bourg in the north.

Despite the attention that Rasp would direct to his northern sector sev-eral days later, the I Corps attack re-mained stalled in the south for the rest of the month. Bethouart shifted his main effort slightly east, where the 9th Colonial had done a bit better, but the results were the same. German resist-ance was stubborn and their defenses were organized in depth, with the French attacks channeled by roads, for-ests, streams, and small towns through a series of heavily defended choke points. Furthermore, the slow pace of the French advance allowed bypassed

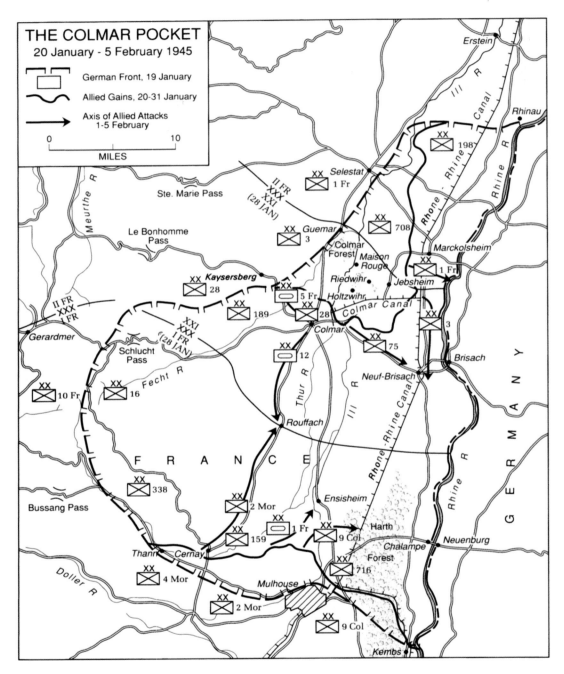

THE COLMAR POCKET
20 January - 5 February 1945

German Front, 19 January

Allied Gains, 20-31 January

Axis of Allied Attacks
1-5 February

0   10
MILES

Erstein

Rhinau

Selestat
1 Fr

Ste. Marie Pass

II FR
XXX
XXI
(28 JAN)

708

Guemar
3

Colmar
Forest

Maison
Rouge

Markolsheim

Le Bonhomme
Pass

1 Fr

Kaysersberg
28

Riedwihr

Jebsheim

Holtzwihr

Colmar Canal

189

5 Fr

28

3

II FR
XXX
1 FR

Gerardmer

XXI
XXX
1 FR
(28 JAN)

12

Colmar

75

Neuf-Brisach

Brisach

Schlucht
Pass

Fecht R

Thur R

III R

Rhone-Rhine Canal

Rhine R

G E R M A N Y

10 Fr

16

Rouffach

F   R   A   N   C   E

338

Ensisheim

Bussang Pass

2 Mor

1 Fr

Harth

Neuenburg

Thann

159

9 Col

Chalampe
Forest

Cernay

Doller R

4 Mor

716

Mulhouse

9 Col

2 Mor

Kembs

MAP 35   This map is printed in full color at the back of the book, following the Index.

defenders to pull back in an orderly manner, aided by the heavy snowfall and overcast skies that limited Allied air support and vehicle mobility. At the end of the month, after eleven days of fighting, the *159th Division* maintained its hold on Cernay, and the I Corps forces were still a disappointing five or six miles short of Ensisheim, their intermediate objective. At the time, Bethouart reported that his infantry was exhausted, his stocks of artillery ammunition almost depleted, and two of his armored division's three tank battalions reduced to between sixteen and eighteen operable armored vehicles apiece. CC1 alone had lost thirty-six tanks during the offensive to German mines.

In the north de Monsabert's II Corps attack began on 22 January, also on schedule, and initially achieved more success. General Thumm, the *LXIV Corps* commander, had noted the Allied buildup between Colmar and Selestat as well as the reinforcement of the U.S. 3d Division by what he assumed was the entire American 63d Infantry Division (actually it was one TF Harris regiment). Since he was under orders to hold the entire Erstein salient, however, the German commander had no opportunity to consolidate his defending forces or to strengthen those facing the American units. Instead, he instructed the *708th Volksgrenadier Division* to maintain only a thin defensive screen west of the Ill River, keeping enough forces to the rear for strong, local counterattacks in order to prevent its front from being pierced by a single concentrated attack. He also attached the *280th Assault Battalion,* with a dozen or so heavy Mark V *jagd-*

panthers and some tanks and assault guns, to the division to give it reserve muscle, but he lacked the infantry strength in the area to give the defense more substance and depth.

General O'Daniel, still commanding the experienced 3d Division, fully understood the difficulties that would face his troops. The arrival of the U.S. 28th Division in the Kaysersberg area had at least given him the opportunity to rest his infantry for a few days while he concentrated them for the attack. With the French 1st Infantry Division supporting his advance on the left, and with both units substantially reinforced with experienced armored units, O'Daniel was confident that a rapid breakthrough could be achieved. Specifically he planned to begin the 3d Division's attack with a successive series of assaults by his four infantry regiments (the 7th, 15th, and 30th and the attached 254th). Each was to push directly east for a few miles and then drive south for another five to ten miles; the next attacking regiment would pass through the rear lines of the first and then attack east for a few miles before turning south as the first had done. In this way O'Daniel hoped to sidestep the entire division southeast to the Colmar Canal and beyond, opening a path for a final drive by the French 5th Armored Division on Neuf-Brisach. At that point the 28th Division could extend its front westward, allowing most of the 3d Division to support the final push. The maneuver might also deceive the Germans into believing that the Americans were trying either to outflank Colmar city or threaten the Erstein salient, when their real objective was the Neuf-Brisach bridge and ferry sites.

The Bridge at Maison Rouge

Successful river crossings were vital to the Allied attack. On the first two days of de Monsabert's offensive, 22 and 23 January, all went according to the 3d Division plan, Operation GRANDSLAM.[8] The division's 7th Infantry regiment, commanded by Col. John A. Heintges, crossed the Fecht River at Guemar, which was already in Allied hands, around 2100 on the 21st and proceeded south. There it would spend the next four days clearing the forests and towns between the Fecht and Ill rivers for about ten miles, rolling up Thumm's thin screening forces in the process.[9] Following in the footsteps of the 7th, the 30th Infantry, under Col. Lionel C. McGarr, was also to cross the Fecht at Guemar during the night of 22–23 January. McGarr planned to have his unit march east through the Colmar forest, previously cleared by the 7th regiment, secure crossing points over the Ill, and then push south, paralleling the advance of the 7th, clearing the towns of Riedwihr and Holtzwihr, and finally seizing crossing points over the Colmar Canal. O'Daniel had attached one tank and one tank destroyer company to the regiment to screen its open, eastern flank until the next attacking regiment, the 15th Infantry, could swing into position

behind and to the east of the others.

McGarr's regiment set out from Guemar around midnight, trudging through the deep snow. In addition to his semiautomatic M1, each rifleman carried four bandoleers of ammunition, three fragmentation and one white phosphorous grenade, one day's worth of K-rations, one blanket and one shelter half, and inevitably cigarettes, toilet articles, and other miscellaneous personal items, including letters and pictures from home. The temperature was well below freezing, but the dark Colmar forest cut the wind somewhat, which made the foot march more bearable. The unit's initial objective was the Maison Rouge bridge, a medium-sized wooden span over the Ill River opposite the southeastern corner of the forest. Once this crossing site had been secured, along with a road junction a few miles beyond the Ill, the engineers were to bring up bridging equipment early on the 23d, enabling the entire force to move across the Ill for its advance south.

Shortly after entering the Colmar forest, McGarr split the regiment into two attacking forces; he sent the 3d Battalion southeast directly for the bridge and the 1st Battalion east with instructions to cross the Ill about 1,500 yards above the bridge site and move down to the crossing site from the north. Subsequently, the 1st Battalion managed to cross the Ill in rubber boats during the night unopposed and sweep down the east bank of the river, surprising a small detachment of Germans at the bridge. By 0530 the next morning, McGarr's unit thus found itself in possession of a fairly large but worn timber bridge

---

[8] Information presented in the following section is based on the 3d Inf Div AAR, Jan 45; and the small-unit accounts taken from the Seventh Army Historical Office, Interv Rpts, "Operation Grand-slam, 30th Infantry Regt., 3rd Infantry Division," and "La Maison Rouge: The Story of an Engagement," MHI.

[9] For heroic action during a German counterattack on 25 January 1945, Pfc. Jose F. Valdez, Company B, 7th Infantry, 3d Infantry Division, was posthumously awarded the Congressional Medal of Honor.

over the Ill as well as the crossroads located about a mile or so east of the bridge and the small farm complex of Maison Rouge in between.[10]

During the early morning hours of the 24th, McGarr consolidated the bridgehead, bringing the rest of his forces up to the area as quickly as possible, organizing defensive positions for the expected German counterattack, and pushing patrols out to the east, southeast, and south. Outside of several strands of trees along the Ill River and a small parallel stream, the troops found little natural cover in the area, with broad, snow-covered Alsatian fields stretching off to the east of the river for several miles. About two miles to the southeast stood the Riedwihr woods and, beyond the small forest, the towns of Riedwihr and Holtzwihr, both intermediate regimental objectives. With apparently no German response to the crossing immediately forthcoming, McGarr decided to continue the advance as quickly as possible. He directed the 1st Battalion to move through the Riedwihr woods toward Riedwihr; the 3d to pass behind the 1st and advance on Holtzwihr, a mile or so farther south; and the 2d to follow the 1st into the Riedwihr woods as a reserve. O'Daniel had already radioed McGarr at 0755 that morning, impressing on him the need for speed and the necessity of pushing across the Colmar Canal by the following night.

The bridge at Maison Rouge presented a problem for the attacking force. The Americans had not expected to find the structure intact and had planned to begin constructing an armored treadway bridge to the north later in the day. The capture of the span, however, changed these plans, and McGarr judged that his accompanying vehicles could use the bridge after engineers reinforced it. Division engineer officers confirmed McGarr's estimate around 1330, but could not guarantee completion of the work until early the next morning. The river at the crossing site was about 90 feet wide; the bridge was about 100 feet long, consisting of two 30-foot approach ramps and two 20-foot center spans. One of the attached thirty-ton Sherman tanks had been run up and down the west ramp, causing the structure to shake and sway violently, which ended any ideas the tankers might have had of charging across.

Throughout the day McGarr became increasingly nervous about his lack of armor or antitank support east of the river. As early as 1142, leading elements of the 1st Battalion had reported hearing enemy armor around Riedwihr and later, from the eastern edge of the Riedwihr woods, had seen a few German armored vehicles running through the town. Concerned, McGarr pressed the engineers for immediate assistance with the bridge; they decided that, as an expedient, strengthening the center spans somewhat and reinforcing the surface with treadway bridging would enable it to hold the heavier vehicles. However, when the treadway sections finally arrived around 1500, the engineers found that too little had been brought forward to cover the entire

---

[10] The 30th Inf AAR, Jan 45, gives two different times for the specific seizure of the bridge, 0530 and 1130, but does not explain the discrepancy.

bridge and warned that the arrival of additional sections might be delayed several hours because of the heavy traffic on the 3d Division's supply routes. Informed of the difficulty, O'Daniel again called McGarr at 1555 and instructed him to continue his advance south without the armor. Speed was essential if the momentum of the attack was to continue.

At 1630 McGarr ordered his units to begin their assaults on Riedwihr and Holtzwihr. Almost immediately both attacking battalions ran into trouble. The 3d Battalion moved into Holtzwihr sometime between 1630 and 1700, but was counterattacked by strong infantry-tank teams and reported having difficulty holding on. The 1st Battalion met heavy enemy fire as soon as it approached Riedwihr and was barely able to reach the outskirts of town. Both units requested immediate assistance to deal with the enemy armor.

Impressed by the need to bring some tanks across the Ill at once, the engineers took a calculated risk. Without waiting for additional bridging supplies, they decided to overlay both of the unsteady bridge ramps with treadway sections and hoped that the shorter center spans could take about ten medium tanks. About 1700, after running three of the regiment's towed 57-mm. antitank guns and movers and a large ten-ton truck across the bridge, Lt. John F. Harmon drove the lead tank up the reinforced ramp and onto the center span. Almost immediately, as soon as the thirty-ton Sherman had cleared the eight-inch high treadway and hit the wooden surface, the bridge gave way, with tank and lieutenant falling "like an elevator"

into the icy Ill River. Harmon escaped with a few bruises, but obviously no more American vehicles would be attempting to cross the river for many hours, and the 30th Infantry would have to fight on alone. The crews of the remaining tanks and tank destroyers could do little more than place their machines in supporting positions along the opposite bank of the river.

What occurred during the next several hours is unclear. Apparently all three of McGarr's battalions suddenly found themselves in the midst of a general German counterattack from elements of the *708th Volksgrenadier Division* and the *280th Assault Gun Battalion*. The 30th Infantry's antitank forces, bazookas and 57-mm. cannons, had no chance against the heavily armored *jagdpanzers* and *jagdpanthers* (assault guns on Mark IV and V tank chassis). Around 1800 one of the American tank officers, after crossing the damaged bridge on foot to reconnoiter the opposite side, reported streams of panicked soldiers from the 30th pouring back from the Riedwihr woods in complete disorder, abandoning weapons and attempting to climb over the damaged bridge. In the background he noted white tracers from German automatic weapons mingled with the red tracers of American arms—someone was still fighting—but most of the regiment appeared to be taking refuge along the stream and riverbanks or braving the cold waters of the Ill to reach the opposite shore. There, frustrated tank and tank destroyer crews watched the debacle, and shortly thereafter, as the sunlight began to fade, they spotted the squat German assault guns moving up two by two, each section covering the advance of the other. Antitank and artillery fire kept the counterattacking force at bay for a while, but sometime after dark the bridgehead appeared to be in German hands, though no one could tell for sure.[11]

At 2030 that night, as the 30th Infantry collected itself on the west side of the Ill, O'Daniel ordered Lt. Col. Hallett D. Edson, commanding the 15th Infantry, to secure the bridgehead, see to the repair of the structure, and resume the 3d Division's attack as soon as possible. Loss of momentum had to be avoided at all costs. Edson alerted his 3d Battalion and immediately sent two of its rifle companies, I and K, directly through Guemar and the Colmar woods and over the Ill, following the trail that the 30th Infantry's 1st Battalion had taken twenty-four hours earlier. Descending on the Maison Rouge area from the north, as their predecessors had done, the two companies scattered a small German holding force around 0500 on 24 January, rounded up a number of 30th regiment infantrymen who had somehow survived the night on the east bank, and proceeded to secure the area as best they could. Instructed to defend both the bridge area and the crossroads, the battalion commander gave Company K the responsibility for the crossing site and sent Company I out to occupy the crossroads. As dawn came, the Company I commander, finding the crossroads completely exposed and without any cover, requested permission to pull the unit back to the tree line, but was instructed to hold in place: division engineers were just completing a new treadway bridge to the north, and armored support could be expected shortly.

For the next several hours the men of Company I frantically chipped away at the frozen ground, digging up at best a few inches of dirt, ice, and snow and wondering when the tanks would arrive. They finally came about three hours later, but from the wrong side. At 0800 on the 24th, the Germans launched their second counterattack against the bridgehead with thirteen heavy assault guns and a company or more of infantry. As the enemy machines began pushing through the mile or so of fields between Company I and the Riedwihr woods, the American soldiers scrambled into their makeshift foxholes and watched and waited, lying flat on the frozen ground. Friendly artillery soon caused the attacking infantry, barely visible at first, to disperse and lag behind; but the assault guns, accompanied by a few tanks and lighter armored vehicles, continued toward them at a steady pace. The company commander and his forward observer ticked off the German progress for many to hear—800 yards away, then 600, and then 500. A few panicked and fled, and others asked their officers, "Can we go?" The rest stayed, although, as one sergeant later recalled, "we all practically had one foot out of the foxhole," and when the company commander finally made the decision to pull back, "we didn't have to give the order very loud."

---

[11] Initial German reports indicated that 145 prisoners had been taken during the counterattack. Bauer, "The German Withdrawal from the Colmar Pocket," p. 38.

That morning, shortly after 0800, the company was overrun. Some soldiers were crushed under the German tank treads or machine-gunned where they lay; others managed to fall back into the Company K area closer to the river; still others were shot while trying to surrender. Most of the 3d Platoon was thought to have been captured.

The success of the German counterattack again proved brief. As it swept through Company I and moved on against Company K, direct American tank and tank destroyer fire from across the river forced the German assault guns back, and the German infantry was unable to budge the defenders by themselves. In the north, however, two American tanks and a tank destroyer, which had finally managed to cross the new treadway bridge, charged south and rolled into the battle area "bumper-to-bumper," where they were promptly picked off by the German tank gunners. The battle for the bridgehead thus continued throughout the rest of the morning and into the early afternoon, with neither side able to completely secure the area. At last, around 1430 that afternoon, the 1st Battalion, 15th Infantry, counterattacked from the north with more armor, finally relieving those at the bridge site: "here they come . . . if that ain't a beautiful sight . . . strictly a Hollywood finish . . . just like the movies." The rest of the regiment soon followed.

Edson's regiment continued south, advancing on Riedwihr, Holtzwihr, and the Colmar Canal, while the German forces pulled back east, still unsure of the 3d Division's specific axis of advance. West of the Ill the

30th Infantry, rather dazed but also embarrassed and angry, regrouped and reorganized. The average strength of its rifle companies had fallen to seventy-two or seventy-three men, and the survivors later added a new verse to the regimental ditty:

> But we have our weaker moments
> Even when success is huge
> 'Cause the outfit took a licken
> at the bridge at Maison Rouge.

But three days later, on 27 January, after only a brief respite, the 30th Infantry went back into action as if nothing had happened. O'Daniel's high opinion of the unit and his equally high expectations of its performance remained unchanged.

The fighting at Maison Rouge typified the back-and-forth flow of the Allied advance in the north and south. In both areas the attackers found the Germans deployed in depth, counterattacking whenever possible but lacking the strength or mobility to do more than wear down the advancing forces. As the 15th Infantry entered Riedwihr on the night of 25–26 January, O'Daniel was slipping the 254th Infantry regiment behind the 15th and directing it at the next 3d Division objective, Jebsheim. On the 26th and 27th, the Germans made a spirited defense of the town, a key north-south communications junction, while launching repeated armor-supported counterattacks in the Riedwihr area, but to no avail. On 26 January 1945, in the much-contested Riedwihr woods, 2d Lt. Audie Murphy, one of the most decorated U.S. soldiers of the war and later a popular film star, earned the Congressional Medal of Honor for turning back several German attacks from the turret of a burning tank destroyer.[12] With equal determination, the 254th secured Jebsheim by the 28th and continued east.

O'Daniel recommitted the 30th Infantry south of Riedwihr on the 27th. McGarr's unit again took Holtzwihr and drove south, reaching its original objective, the Colmar Canal, on the 29th. Meanwhile, de Monsabert extended the front of the U.S. 28th Division eastward, freeing Heintges' 7th regiment for employment elsewhere; furthermore, to the north the French 1st Infantry Division, which had also encountered difficulties maintaining a bridgehead over the Ill, began making substantial progress, securing the 3d Division's northern flank. With the 30th Infantry on the canal and the 28th Division moving east, O'Daniel finally sidestepped both the 7th and 15th regiments between Riedwihr and Jebsheim, putting them over the Colmar Canal on the night of 29–30 January, abreast of the 30th Infantry. The following day all three regiments drove south several miles, securing the canal crossing sites for the French 5th Armored Division. By the 30th therefore, O'Daniel had pushed a fairly substantial wedge into the German lines, with the 30th Infantry outflanking Colmar city on the east; the 254th advancing out of Jebsheim toward the Rhone-Rhine Canal and the Rhine River; and the 7th and 15th regiments, supported by French armor, facing south and southeast toward Neuf-Brisach. Here the advance halted. The 3d Division was exhausted at least temporarily and,

with some of its rifle companies now down to about thirty able-bodied men, its offensive capabilities were greatly reduced.

Reorganization

From the beginning of the effort Devers had been concerned about de Lattre's strength as well as the vagaries of weather and terrain. Despite the advances by American troops, the progress of the French forces north and south had not been encouraging. As early as the 27th the slow forward movement of both attacks and the heavy expenditure of ammunition had convinced the 6th Army Group commander that more American assistance was needed. Assessing the situation on that day, Devers was dissatisfied, feeling that the French units lacked "the punch or the willingness to go all out," but he also noted that, contrary to expectations, "the weather, with three feet of snow, has been abominable," and had slowed progress everywhere on the Allied front. He was, however, proud of the 3d Division's accomplishments, describing the earlier Maison Rouge episode as "one of those unpredictable things in war." He noted that O'Daniel, "sound, sober . . . but just as determined as ever to carry on," took full responsibility for the tactical mistakes made there.[13]

At the time, SHAEF had already promised Devers two more American infantry divisions, the 35th for Patch and the 75th for de Lattre; furthermore, Devers was now ready to

---

[12] At the time, Lieutenant Murphy commanded Company B, 15th Infantry, 3d Infantry Division.

[13] Above quotes from Devers Diary, 24 and 27 Jan 45.

commit Milburn's XXI Corps and Allen's 12th Armored Division to the Colmar struggle. Basically Devers wanted the XXI Corps to control the three American infantry divisions, the 3d, 28th, and 75th, for a final drive on Neuf-Brisach, with the 12th Armored in reserve. De Lattre agreed and also assigned the French 5th Armored Division entirely to Milburn, leaving Leclerc's 2d Armored Division with de Monsabert. General Milburn, who had been alerted to the mission well before the start of the offensive, intended to continue using O'Daniel's 3d to spearhead the attack, but now reinforced it with most of the 5th Armored Division in order to beef up the tired American regiments. Cota's 28th Division, assisted by Maj. Gen. Ray E. Porter's 75th, another worn-out veteran of the Ardennes, would continue to fill in the southern flanks of the advance, while de Monsabert's II Corps forces secured the northern flank. The 12th Armored Division, still recovering from its ordeal at Herrlisheim, would temporarily remain in reserve north of Colmar. With these forces plus additional allocations of artillery ammunition from the 6th Army Group, de Lattre planned to renew the dual offensive on 1 February.

Significant changes had also occurred on the opposing side. On 29 January General Paul Hauser, a combat-experienced *SS* officer, assumed command of *Army Group G*, including all forces formerly assigned to *Army Group Oberrhein*. At the same time Hitler dissolved *Army Group Oberrhein*, assigned Himmler a command on the Eastern Front, and appointed Blaskowitz commander of *Army Group*

H in Holland. The German armies on the Western Front were thus once again united under von Rundstedt's *OB West*.

In preparation for the command change, *Army Group G* had already reviewed the situation of the *Nineteenth Army* in the Colmar Pocket and, as early as the 25th, had concluded that the enclave was no longer important to the German defensive effort in the west. The current Allied attacks were threatening to isolate and destroy the German divisions in the Erstein salient, and their evacuation seemed the first order of business. In sum, the staff recommended that either the entire pocket should be abandoned or, at the very least, the northern extension at Erstein should be evacuated and the forces used to strengthen the northern shoulder. On the night of 28–29 January Hitler finally agreed to the partial withdrawal in the north, but insisted that the pocket be defended as long as possible. Von Rundstedt was of the same opinion, mistakenly believing that a renewed Allied offensive against the Saar basin was imminent and that a continued diversion of Allied resources against Colmar would significantly delay the start of this endeavor.

German intelligence in the Colmar area was faulty. The German commanders generally remained ignorant of American reinforcements until the troops actually appeared on the battlefield, and they continued to believe that the primary Franco-American objective in the north was a drive directly east from Selestat to Marckolsheim, which would reach out to the Rhine River and both isolate the forces in the Erstein salient and secure a springboard for a later offensive against the Neuf-Brisach bridge. At no time did they appear to discern de Lattre's intention of attempting a double envelopment from north and south; instead they judged that de Lattre's forces in the west and south would simply try to exert pressure on all sides of the pocket until something gave way.

Inside the pocket the defensive situation of the *Nineteenth Army* was also becoming muddled. To assist in the defense of both Cernay and Ensisheim in the south and Marckolsheim in the north, Rasp had authorized his corps commanders, Thumm and Abraham, to begin withdrawing several battle groups from the Vosges. As a result, units from the *16th Volksgrenadier* and the *189th* and *338th Infantry Divisions* had become hopelessly mixed with those of the other divisions in a helter-skelter fashion; these mixtures were then further infused with a miscellany of service and support forces turned into infantry as well as with units of the *2d Mountain Division*, which had begun arriving in the pocket sometime after the 20th and were being fed piecemeal into the battle. For the American and French commanders, the German tactical situation was often equally confusing, with many of the 3d Division's regiments identifying elements of four or five different German divisions on their front. The net result was the fragmentation of the entire German defensive effort. On the 29th, for example, Thumm had tried to counter the surprise American assault south over the Colmar Canal with a few battalions of the *189th Division*, one from the *198th* (currently deploying from

the Erstein salient), and another from the *2d Mountain Division*. Not surprisingly, the counterattacks were uncoordinated and ineffective. Elsewhere similar situations were common, and the German commanders remained unable to discern the main axis of de Lattre's offensive or even to predict the next objective of O'Daniel's sidestepping division.

Only on 30 January, with the entire 3d Division pouring over the Colmar Canal, did Rasp, Hauser, and von Rundstedt begin to perceive that the Allied drive was headed directly for the bridge at Neuf-Brisach and not Marckolsheim; at the same time they concluded—again mistakenly—that the objective of the French drive in the south was the Neuenburg bridge at Chalampe. Yet almost all of their "reserves"—forces from the Erstein salient and those from the Vosges—had been committed elsewhere, and they had no means of stopping a renewed Allied drive or reinforcing those units that appeared to lie in its path. As a result, on the night of the 30th, *Army Group G* sent new orders to Rasp, specifying that his main mission was to "assure the survival" of the German pocket across the Rhine for as long as possible and authorizing him to withdraw most of his forces from the Vosges front, leaving only reconnaissance detachments to hold the mountain passes. The *Nineteenth Army* was henceforth to concentrate all of its combat power on the northern and southern shoulders of the bridgehead. Rasp, in turn, ordered the immediate evacuation of all forces in the Vosges that had no organic transportation as well as the transfer of all heavy equipment and support installations to and

RAILWAY BRIDGE AT NEUF-BRISACH FINALLY DESTROYED

across the Rhine, while sending what reinforcement he could from the west to protect his two major bridge sites. How much time he had to shuffle his units around was a question mark, especially since *OKW* had so far refused to authorize the withdrawal of any of his forces across the Rhine.

The February Offensive

The second Franco-American surge against the Colmar Pocket proved successful. Although the Germans still tried to jam the Allied advance at key road and water junctions, especially those on their own lines of communication, the Allied penetration of their initial strongpoint defense system was too deep; their secondary and tertiary positions had too many gaps that were easily exploited; and they continued to be unable to move adequate reinforcements to threatened areas. The U.S. 75th Infantry Division had begun moving into the First French Army area on 27 January and by the evening of the 31st started to relieve O'Daniel's 3d Division regiments south of the Colmar Canal for the final push. Again O'Daniel attacked east and then south, first slipping the 30th Infantry behind the others and moving it east to the Rhone-Rhine Canal for a drive south with units of the French 5th Armored Division. Next, with the arrival of Porter's 75th Division on the battlefield, he transferred both the 7th and 15th Infantry to the far side of the Rhone-Rhine

Canal, turning them south as well. The 254th Infantry brought up the rear. By 3 February elements of all three 3d Division regiments were approaching Neuf-Brisach, and the Germans began a last-ditch defense of the bridgehead with all available manpower.[14] On the 5th, with the old fortress town nearly surrounded, the Germans started to evacuate the area, and by noon of the following day, 6 February, the entire sector was under Allied control.

Inside the pocket the German defenses around the city of Colmar had already collapsed. While the 3d Division attacked toward Neuf-Brisach, first the attached 254th regiment and then the regiments of the 28th Division steadily pushed against the northern approaches to Colmar in the Kaysersberg valley. By 2 February Cota's units had cleared the city's suburbs against diminishing resistance, allowing units of the French 5th Armored Division to drive into the heart of Colmar nearly unopposed. Immediately de Lattre agreed to commit the U.S. 12th Armored Division through the 28th Division for a drive south; two days later American armored task forces, moving south along two parallel axes, met French I Corps elements at Rouffach during the early morning hours of 5 February. By that date the bulk of Bethouart's southern forces had finally bypassed German emplacements around Ensisheim and, finding enemy de-

fenses crumbling elsewhere, raced to Rouffach from the south. The drives split the Colmar Pocket wide open.

Between 5 and 9 February, as the supporting American divisions redeployed northward, French forces finished cleaning out the pocket. In the north de Monsabert's forces swept the west side of the Rhine from Erstein to Marckolsheim, while in the west units of the new French 10th Infantry Division and the 4th Moroccan Mountain Division policed up the interior of the pocket. To the south, Bethouart directed his main effort against the last German bridgehead at Chalampe, using the 1st Armored and the 2d Moroccan and 9th Colonial Divisions. Here German resistance remained fierce for a few days, but the French managed to penetrate across the Ill River on 5 February, secure Ensisheim on the 6th, and reach the Rhone-Rhine Canal by the 7th. There they were joined by Leclerc's armor on the 8th; the next morning, elements of the 9th Colonial reached the Rhine at Chalampe, forcing the Germans to destroy the remaining bridge at 0800. This final act marked the end of the Colmar Pocket and the German presence in upper Alsace as well.

Tactics and Techniques

For the troops on the ground, the fighting rivaled the harshness of the earlier advance through the Vosges. Here the French were at a disadvantage: the ranks of their specialized colonial troops were stretched precariously thin, and many Caucasian infantry replacements had little more than a few months of military training at best. They were good enough for

---

[14] For heroic action on 3 February while serving as a forward observer around Biesheim, about two miles north of Neuf-Brisach, T5g. Forrest E. Peden, Battery C, 10th Field Artillery Battalion, 3d Infantry Division, was posthumously awarded the Congressional Medal of Honor.

NEUF-BRISACH (OLD FORTRESS TOWN)

static defensive operations, but less able to perform the tactically more complicated mission of attacking. Only the stubbornness of their own officers and the assistance of the Americans finally gave them the edge. In this area, the U.S. 3d Infantry Division showed everyone why it was considered one of the finest units in the American Army. Shrugging off the Maison Rouge bridge incident, the division's stellar performance was clearly vital to the First French Army's overall success. Although it was an "old" division that theoretically had been "fought out"—exhausted—by the end of its Italian campaigning, its small units, especially the infantry-

tank teams, seemed to rise to the occasion as they approached each of the fortified Alsatian towns on their route of advance.[15]

By this time, experienced units like the 3d Division had almost unconsciously perfected their combined arms teamwork to a fine art, enabling them to overcome the physical fatigue that most of the soldiers, officers and enlisted men alike, must have felt. In the Colmar campaign, the American armor-supported infantry units sent out small patrols to scout each town

[15] Information in this section on the 3d Division is based primarily on Seventh Army Historical Office, Interv Rpt, "The Colmar Pocket, 7th Regiment, 3d Division, 22 Jan–8 Feb 45," MHI.

FRENCH INFANTRY ADVANCES INTO COLMAR

briefly, while the main attacking forces prepared to assault the area. If the town was defended, the infantry moved forward covered by the direct fire of supporting tanks and tank destroyers; stronger resistance merited additional support from mortars and artillery and perhaps even tactical air strikes if available. Once foot soldiers reached the outskirts of town, a few tanks might move up to support deeper penetrations, but the rest stayed clear of the built-up areas, covering the flanks of the attacking force and maybe shifting their position to one side of the town or the other in order to prevent reinforcements from arriving. Inside, infantrymen searched each house deliberately from top to bottom, tossing grenades in the cellars where the defenders usually congregated and greeting survivors with the traditional "Hindy Ho" (*Hande Hoch,* or literally "hands up"). Meanwhile, American artillery shells destined for "Krautland" streamed overhead, striking the opposite side of the town or interdicting the roads beyond that might carry German reinforcements, or perhaps only "softening up" the unit's next objective down the line.

The American troops were brave, but not foolhardy. As elsewhere, the 3d Division combat soldiers had an abiding fear of the German flat-trajectory, high-velocity cannons—the so-called 88s (although most were 75-mm. pieces)—as well as German mortar fire (for its accuracy) and the buzz-saw-like German machine guns (with a higher rate of fire than the American equivalents).[16] In the eyes of the average soldier, however, the German tanks presented the most serious problem. Because of the better armor protection of the heavier German vehicles, tanks and assault guns alike (foot troops tended to identify all as Tigers), the bazookas and 57-mm. antitank guns organic to the infantry battalions and regiments were relatively ineffective, as were the 37-mm. cannons of the cavalry units; even the 75-mm. and 76-mm. (3-inch) guns of the tanks and tank destroyers had to close to within 300 yards or less to do any damage to the frontal armor of the German machines.[17] Contemporary American military doctrine regarded the tank primarily as an anti-infantry rather than an anti-tank weapon and, in the infantry-tank team, expected supporting tanks to engage enemy automatic weapons, while infantry dealt with opposing antitank gun crews, and artillery and tank destroyers handled enemy armor. In practice, however, even the self-propelled, turreted American tank destroyers found it difficult to close within effective firing range of German armor, while American artillery often had only a limited effect on such moving targets. Fighter-bombers were one answer, but they were af-

fected by the weather, limited to the daytime, and dependent on good air-ground communications—something still lacking at the tactical unit level. As a result, small-unit commanders in the 3d Division and other Allied infantry elements often could do little more than direct artillery and mortar fire on German armored units, at least keeping the German machines on the move and separating them from supporting infantry. Even bazooka fire could force the largest German tanks to keep their distance; although direct hits from any of the available American weapons might not destroy such machines, they often caused damage to treads, periscopes, radios, and other ancillary equipment, or at least shook up the German crews enough to make them leave. For the half-blinded German panzer troops, friendly infantry support was as vital to them as it was to the American tankers, for at close range even the smallest antitank weapons could immobilize the heaviest tank of the battlefield.

Fighting below the Colmar Canal on 30 January, for example, one 7th regiment private managed to KO ("knock out") an advancing armored *panzerjaeger* by arcing his bazooka rocket high in the air, about 200 yards out, somehow hitting the vehicle on top and destroying it, a rather extraordinary feat—or tale. Later the same day, another 7th Infantry bazookaman inflicted similar damage on a Mark IV medium, firing at it point-blank from a window as it passed through a town the unit was attempting to secure. However, in this case a second German tank, obviously wiser, elected to withdraw about 1,000 yards

---

[16] For discussion, see Samuel A. Stouffer et al., *The American Soldier: Combat and its Aftermath*, II (N.Y.: Wiley, 1949), 231–41 (1965 edition) (studies based on data collected by the Research Branch, Information and Education Division, War Department, during World War II).

[17] See Christopher R. Gabel, *Seek, Strike, and Destroy: U.S. Army Tank Destroyer Doctrine in World War II*, Leavenworth Paper 12 (Fort Leavenworth, Kans.: Combat Studies Institute, 1985), pp. 52–54.

to the side of the town, content to pump high-explosive shells and machine-gun fire into the American positions despite their best efforts to chase it away with rocket and artillery fire. Fortunately for the 3d Division, the *Nineteenth Army* had few such machines, partly because of the difficulty in fielding them. As the Americans already knew, the terrain of southern Alsace was not conducive to the employment of large armored formations.

For the 12th Armored Division, one of the least-experienced units in the American Army, which was still recovering from its initiation at Herrlisheim, the push from Colmar to Rouffach marked its transition to a veteran unit.[18] Here the division's mobile tank-infantry task forces had greater success, duplicating the combined arms tactics used by the 3d Division units to the north. Dismounted infantry cleared the outskirts of each town before tanks and tank destroyers moved forward, with the tanks taking enemy automatic weapon positions under fire and the infantry probing for antitank mines and gun positions. Inside the town, infantry skirmish lines preceded each tank by twenty-five yards or more, attempting to secure all of the entrances to the town first (to prevent the arrival of reinforcements) before completely clearing the town itself. On the road, armored commanders led off with their latest model Shermans, with

higher-velocity guns and more armor, and with their newer TDs (tank destroyers) in direct support, equipped with the very effective 90-mm. antitank cannons. Experience had taught them to leave wider gaps between vehicles and to stagger the gaps as well, allowing individual drivers to vary their speeds, thus preventing German antitank gunners from "leading" their target effectively. Placing artillery and even direct fire on possible enemy antitank sites also cut down on losses, as did switching the point, or lead, position between the most experienced crews. In this way the 12th Armored leapfrogged from town to town—one task force passing through an area secured by the other—until the junction was made with southern French forces, suffering relatively few casualties in the process. The experiences here would soon be put to good use in the final campaign to come.

In Retrospect

The struggle for the Colmar Pocket had few immediate implications for either Allied or German operations elsewhere. The formation of the pocket itself was almost an accident, a product of two factors: Eisenhower's eagerness to have Patch's Seventh Army turn north, and Hitler's determination to hold on to at least a portion of southern Alsace at all costs. The resulting inability of the 6th Army Group to eliminate the pocket in December was perhaps inevitable. De Lattre's First French Army was clearly superior to the German *Nineteenth* in terms of materiel and supplies but, when all was said and done,

---

[18] Information on the 12th Armored Division is based on Seventh Army Historical Office, Interv Rpts, "Colmar Pocket Cut Off by the 66th Armored Infantry Battalion and the 43d Tank Battalion of the 12th Armored Division during the Period 4–7 February 1945," MHI.

probably greatly inferior in terms of trained manpower. The French lacked the command and control and the logistical apparatus to conduct a sustained offensive in the face of determined opposition, and even their combat leadership lacked the depth to sustain heavy losses on the battlefield within the ranks of junior officers and NCOs. Furthermore, the terrain and weather repeatedly dulled the cutting edge of their combat formations, making a repeat of the quick penetration that they had achieved south of Belfort (and at Saverne) in November extremely unlikely on the southern Alsatian plains. Perhaps it would have been better to leave a defensive holding force around Colmar in November and turn the bulk of the First French Army north along with Patch's Seventh.

Eisenhower continued to hold Devers responsible for the Colmar Pocket, describing it during a visit to the 6th Army Group headquarters on 27 January as the only "sore" on his entire front and emphasizing the need to eliminate the enclave as soon as possible.[19] The Supreme Commander was now more than willing to send assistance to both Patch and de Lattre, ultimately providing five American combat divisions (the 24th, 35th, and 75th Infantry, 10th Armored, and 101st Airborne) and 12,000 service troops to Devers by the end of the month. As might be expected, General Bradley, commanding the 12th Army Group, was upset by the transfer of combat forces south, feeling that Devers was "using up" all of his rested divisions, that the defensive ef-

forts of the Seventh Army had been "poorly handled," and that Eisenhower was probably trying to do too many things at once with the limited resources available.[20] Devers, aware of the opinions of the 12th Army Group commander, noted only that his own forces had repeatedly supported the northern army groups when they were in trouble and that it was unfair to begrudge the 6th a few divisions when they were desperately needed.[21]

The cost of the Colmar battle was heavy on both sides. The 6th Army Group staff estimated American casualties around 8,000 and French losses about twice that number, but only some 500 American soldiers were killed in action; in both national components, disease and noncombat injuries accounted for almost a third of the losses and probably even more.[22] The deep snow, freezing temperatures, and numerous water crossings caused a marked increase in trench foot and frostbite, and the mixed Franco-American casualty evacuation flow prevented medical services from keeping a precise tally of the toll taken by the weather. German casualty records are even more sparse than usual. During the operation, the 6th Army Group recorded 16,438 Germans taken prisoner in the Colmar area and obviously thousands more were killed or wounded, while nonbattlefield casualties from the weather may also have been high. On 10 Feb-

---

[19] Devers Diary, 27 Jan 45.

[20] HQ, 12th Army Gp, Bradley MFR, 23 Jan 45, Bradley Papers, MHI.

[21] Devers Diary, 16 Jan 45.

[22] For example, between 22 January and 6 February 1945, the 3d Division's 7th Infantry recorded 134 dead, 584 wounded, and 249 nonbattle casualties.

ruary the *Nineteenth Army* recorded over 22,000 permanent (killed or missing) casualties, and Rasp probably saved no more than 10,000 troops of all types.[23] Certainly no more than 400 to 500 combat effectives from each of the eight divisions managed to escape across the Rhine. Allied losses of combat vehicles because of enemy action and mechanical breakdown were also high, but most were recoverable, while the German defenders lost most of what they had permanently. As an effective fighting force the *Nineteenth Army* had ceased to exist.

The high German losses were a direct result of the decision by Hitler and von Rundstedt to maintain the pocket as long as possible. By 1 February, despite standing orders to the contrary, General Rasp, the *Nineteenth Army* commander, had at least begun to deploy most of his forces out of the Vosges and to move service troops and damaged equipment east of the Rhine in expectation of a withdrawal order. The order never came. Hitler's directions to stand fast in the pocket arrived at *Army Group G* headquarters at 1719 that night and were immediately passed on by telephone to the *Nineteenth Army*. Von Rundstedt fully supported the decision and, while approving a limited withdrawal from the Vosges, personally informed Rasp that he was to defend the northern and southern shoulders of the

pocket with every man at his disposal.

Renewed Allied attacks on the 1st only increased the confusion in the German high command, as the appearances of first the U.S. 75th Infantry Division and then the 12th Armored Division were suddenly noted on the battlefield. On 3 February, as Allied forces were investing Neuf-Brisach and simultaneously driving south out of Colmar, *Army Group G* began proposing various contingency plans for a greatly reduced salient across the Rhine and at least a partial *Nineteenth Army* withdrawal to Germany. Hauser could not afford to lose all these forces, which would be desperately needed north of Alsace where the main Allied attack would inevitably come. Nevertheless, at 1940 that evening *OKW* again informed the German field commanders that the pocket was to be maintained at all costs and that the *Nineteenth Army* was to defend the shoulders of the pocket to the last man. There would be no withdrawal.

These final instructions from *OKW* remained unaltered to the end. By the 5th, neither Rasp nor his corps commanders could influence the battle or organize an orderly withdrawal. On the night of 5–6 February, *OB West* approved the *Nineteenth Army*'s plan for a final stand in the southeast corner of the pocket along the Rhone-Rhine Canal, but instructed it to delay any evacuation until the last possible minute. Nevertheless, between 6 and 9 February, Rasp took responsibility for starting to evacuate at least some of his equipment over the Rhine, either by ferry or over the Neuenburg bridge, while the bulk of what combat forces remained at-

---

[23] Bauer, "The German Withdrawal from the Colmar Pocket," p. 110, notes that *Army Group G* put *Nineteenth Army* losses between 20 January and 5 February at only 800 dead, 2,596 wounded, and 3,129 missing, but also points out, as an example, that a postwar report placed casualties in the *2d Mountain Division* alone at approximately 7,500.

tempted to fall back on Chalampe.[24] On the night of 7–8 February the German high command again insisted that the bridgehead be held without thought of retreat; *OKW* had interpreted the redeployment of American forces from the battlefield after the fall of Neuf-Brisach as the end of the Allied offensive there. At that point, however, the *Nineteenth Army* had no control over the conduct of the battle, and what remained of the Colmar Pocket was no more than an enclave seven miles wide and two miles deep. Hitler's permission to withdraw finally arrived at *Army Group G* headquarters at 1445 on the 8th and was transmitted to the *Nineteenth Army* by telephone shortly thereafter. But by that time the order served no purpose. The *Nineteenth Army* had been sacrificed for no appreciable gain.

Toward the Final Offensive

The battles of northern Alsace and those in the Colmar Pocket had seriously depleted the fighting capabilities of the German Army. During the last weeks of February and the first weeks of March, the 6th Army Group made final preparations to exploit this weakness during its forthcoming drive into Germany. In the First French Army zone, de Lattre's forces swept the entire Colmar area, from the Vosges to the Rhine, and moved up to the more easily defensible Franco-German river border. Outposting the river with FFI units and a few regular formations, the French units finally had a chance to rest, recovering and repairing equipment that had begun to wear thin and absorbing new recruits into their units in much the same way as the Germans had been doing.

In the north, Patch's Seventh Army made several limited attacks to improve its posture for future offensive operations. While the bulk of the VI Corps remained in place on the east-west Moder River line, the U.S. 36th Infantry Division on Brooks' right, or eastern, wing pushed into the Gambsheim bridgehead area on 31 January to close up the slight indentation in the corps' front line, finally retaking Rohrwiller, Herrlisheim, Offendorf, and Gambsheim itself. Although assisted by CCB of the 14th Armored Division, flood conditions continued to limit the use of armor, and a shortage of munitions throughout the army group greatly reduced artillery support, thus turning what had been planned as a rapid, concentrated drive against weak units of the *XIV SS Corps* into a series of small, hard-fought infantry engagements that only ended on 11 February.[25]

To the north, the XV Corps also conducted a number of limited offensives in the Sarre valley region with the U.S. 70th, 63d, and 44th Infantry

---

[24] German records indicate that by 7 February 6,997 motor vehicles, 37,000 horse-drawn vehicles, and 488 artillery pieces and antitank guns had been brought back across the Rhine; but the figures are suspect, and the implication that this equipment was evacuated only after 5 February as part of a planned withdrawal effort is incorrect.

[25] For their actions at Oberhoffen, two soldiers of the 142d regiment of the 36th Infantry Division were awarded Congressional Medals of Honor: Sgt. Emile Deleau, Jr., of Company A, posthumously, for heroism during the division's initial assault on the town on the night of 1–2 February 1945; and Sgt. Edward C. Dahlgren, for bravery during the final German counterattack on 11 February 1945.

Divisions, seizing the heights above Saarbrucken as well as key terrain between Saarbrucken and Bitche. German forces opposite Haislip's units offered only minimal resistance when engaged, briefly defending a few prepared strongpoints, such as the old Schlossberg fortress in the 70th Division's zone of attack and the Bliesbrucken and Bellevue farm complexes in the zones of the 63d and 44th. However, on both the Sarre valley and Gambsheim fronts, mines and booby traps took a high toll of American soldiers, as did the cold, wet weather.

For most of the 6th Army Group, the last days of winter were spent reorganizing and retraining, stocking supplies and equipment, improving local defensive positions, and planning for future operations across the German border. Unit commanders conducted formal training programs for new recruits in basic weaponry, map reading and use of the compass, and squad- and platoon-level tactics and worked new soldiers into their seasoned units; even veterans in rear areas performed range firing to resight weapons, while those on the front lines conducted periodic raids into German territory. The logistical buildup was critical. Food and, with the reduction in mobile operations, fuel supplies were adequate, but the general shortage in munitions forced Devers to drastically curtail almost all expenditures of large-caliber weapons and urgently request supplemental supplies from SHAEF. At the same time, to avoid a complete deterioration of the local French road network, the 6th Army Group had to place severe restrictions on vehicle speeds

and loading, minimize the lateral movement of large units, and, whenever possible, rely more heavily on the French rail system. As the Riviera-based armies grew ever larger and plunged ever deeper into the European heartland, logistics remained critical. The Franco-American forces under Devers, Patch, and de Lattre had come a long way since the relatively simple landings in the sunny south and the heady drive up the Rhone River valley.

Properly fueled and supplied, the 6th Army Group was now a powerful fighting force and one that was still growing steadily in size and combat power. By the end of February all major American participants in the Colmar struggle had returned north, including the XXI Corps, the three infantry divisions, and the 12th Armored Division. In the ensuing reorganization, the Seventh Army returned the 10th Armored Division to the U.S. Third Army, the 101st Airborne Division to the SHAEF reserve, and eventually the 28th, 35th, and 75th Divisions to the 12th Army Group. For the moment at least, de Lattre retained control of the French 2d Armored Division, while Patch kept the 3d Algerian, and also received a new unit, the 6th Armored Division, to replace Leclerc's force. In early March, after further shuffling and resting of these tired units, the Seventh Army had three corps with eight infantry divisions and one armored division on line as well as three infantry divisions and two armored divisions in reserve.[26] South of

---

[26] From roughly north to south, the XXI Corps with the 70th and 63d Infantry Divisions; the XV

Strasbourg the First French Army could put two corps with three armored and four infantry divisions—all

French—in the field. The 6th Army Group, now stronger than ever, was ready for the final offensive in Western Europe.[27]

Corps with the 44th, 100th, and 79th Infantry Divisions; and the VI Corps with the 42d and 103d Infantry Divisions, the 14th Armored Division, and the French 3d Algerian Division. In reserve were the 3d, 36th, and 45th Infantry Divisions—Truscott's "old divisions"—and the 6th and 12th Armored.

[27] For the final operations of the Allied 6th, 12th, and 21st Army Groups from March to May 1945, see Charles B. MacDonald, *The Last Offensive*, United States Army in World War II (Washington, 1973).

CHAPTER XXX

Riviera to the Rhine: An Evaluation

The operations of the Seventh Army and the 6th Army Group constituted one of the most successful series of campaigns during World War II. Although opposed by many Allied political and military leaders from its inception and largely ignored by historians of the war, the campaign in southern France, including the ANVIL landings, the seizure of Toulon and Marseille, and the battles for the lower Rhone valley, set the stage for the more significant ventures to the north. The subsequent pursuit north up the Rhone and Saone valleys, the drive northeast of Lyon to the Belfort Gap, the difficult Vosges campaign that followed, and the ultimate conquest of Alsace were critical to Allied military fortunes on the Western Front. Perhaps the greatest contribution of the southern invasion was placing a third Allied army group—one with two army headquarters, three corps, and the equivalent of ten combat divisions—with its own independent supply lines, in northeastern France at a time when the two northern Allied army groups were stretched to the limit in almost every way. Whether a third army group could have been supported by the Atlantic ports without an exceedingly

lengthy struggle is doubtful, and without such a force Bradley's 12th Army Group would have had great difficulty holding the additional frontage from the Luneville-Saverne area to the Swiss border. With the added strength of German units retreating unscathed from the Atlantic and Mediterranean, the German counterattack against the Third Army's exposed southern flank in September 1944 might have been far more effective, drastically retarding the initial Allied drive to the German border in the north. More important, Allied strength in northeastern France would have been much diluted without the forces of the 6th Army Group, and the Ardennes counteroffensive—or something similar—might have had a better chance of success or, at the very least, done more damage. In such a case the starting date for the final invasion of Germany might have been greatly delayed with unforeseen consequences.

The Campaigns

The significance of the ANVIL landings themselves is difficult to evaluate. An earlier invasion date would undoubtedly have meant much stiffer

opposition, but could also have diverted German reinforcements from
the OVERLORD invasion area in Normandy and possibly resulted in an
earlier Allied breakout there from the
beachhead. Allowing the ANVIL forces
to remain on the Italian front, however, would have given no immediate
assistance to OVERLORD and only
eased additional German deployments
to Normandy. In Italy Allied success
in the rugged Italian peninsula north
of Rome would have, at best, forced
the German defenders back into even
more defensible terrain along the
Alps, while lengthening Allied supply
lines and dispersing Allied ground
combat strength. But even a successful march across the Po and over the
Alps to the borders of Austria and
Hungary would have profited the
Allied cause little if the campaign in
northern France had been indefinitely
stalled. Moreover, without the southern invasion the Germans might have
retained strong forces in southern
France. The Allied breakout at St. Lo
never isolated the German forces in
the south, and certainly they would
have been able to survive more easily
than the smaller German forces in the
Channel and Atlantic ports. In such a
scenario the bulk of the *Nineteenth
Army* might well have been transferred
to Italy, more than matching the
strengthening of Allied forces there if
ANVIL had been permanently canceled.

Although the landings themselves
were eminently successful, Allied logistical limitations, specifically the
shortage of amphibious shipping,
made the ANVIL campaign plan somewhat inflexible and prevented Patch
and Truscott from taking full advan-

tage of German weaknesses in the
south. Had more fuel and vehicles
been available, Truscott would have
been able to bring more pressure to
bear on Montelimar and other locations along the German route of withdrawal and could have done more
damage. In the same vein, the demands of security and invasion time-
tables made it difficult for the ANVIL
commanders to make full use of the
strong FFI organization in southern
France. Had more coordination between the two components been possible, Allied combat power during the
Riviera-Rhone campaign would have
been significantly increased.

In balance, Blaskowitz and Wiese
were fortunate to escape from the
south with any forces at all. In this respect the German tactical commanders deserve no more than an average
grade for their performance during
the early campaign. It was not the
weakness of their forces, but their inability to best use what they had that
made the ANVIL landings such a success and made the German withdrawal north such a harrowing one. From
beginning to end, the southern
France campaign and the operations
that immediately followed were characterized by the aggressiveness of the
American and French commanders
and their ruthless pursuit across the
coast and hinterlands of southern
France and then north up the Rhone
valley. If the aggressive personality of
Lucian Truscott, the American VI
Corps commander, seemed to dominate the drive north, certainly he was
well matched by the enthusiastic, dy-
namic Devers, the competent but
more taciturn Patch, and the fiery de
Lattre, all of whom pushed with equal

determination for early seizure of the great French ports, without which the northern campaign could not have been supported. The German leaders, in contrast, appeared to be confused and indecisive. Rarely did they try to take the initiative, even at the local level. There was no organized defense of the critical ports, and German forces in Italy did not even attempt to pose a threat to the vulnerable Allied eastern flank. Only the Allied shortage of fuel and vehicles saved Wiese's forces from a worse disaster. The later stubborn German resistance in the Vosges by forces that were less well trained and equipped only underlined the poor initial performance of the *Nineteenth Army* in the Riviera campaign.

Despite Truscott's judgments regarding the state of the German *Nineteenth Army* in mid-September and the VI Corps' ability to force the Belfort Gap, the Seventh Army would have had extreme difficulty in achieving more than a local tactical success in this area. Given the army's precarious logistical situation and the ever-growing distance between the southern ports and the front lines, both Patch and Truscott probably would have been unable to exploit an early penetration of the Belfort Gap, despite the more favorable weather conditions that prevailed. The subsequent campaign showed how easily the Vosges-Rhine area could be held by relatively weak infantry forces, which were often hard to dislodge without a major attack. Devers warned Patch at the time that the VI Corps was "living with just one day's supplies ahead of the game," [1] and Truscott

---

[1] Devers Diary, 16 Sep 44.

was, in effect, grabbing what territory he could before his inevitable supply problems made further advances impossible.

Two months later, however, the situation had changed dramatically, and Eisenhower's November decision not to exploit in some way the Belfort and Saverne penetrations to the Rhine is difficult to understand. Although long gone, Truscott would have been the first to remonstrate the call. At the time, the Seventh Army might have moved south in strength to help the First French Army clear the Alsatian plains around Colmar. Or it could have moved north, advancing up either the west or east banks of the Rhine through Rastatt, Lauterbourg, and beyond, thereby unhinging the German Saar basin defenses and achieving significant operational (destruction of the German *First Army*) and strategic (the Saar industries) goals. Instead, both Eisenhower and Bradley sought to have Devers' American forces go directly to the aid of Patton's stalled Third Army, taking over portions of the Third Army's front and transferring two divisions from the Seventh to the Third Army. Yet, at the time, Patch's Seventh Army had no more than two armored divisions (one French division and one completely inexperienced American unit) and seven infantry divisions, four of which were nearly exhausted. Giving up any of these forces would have made it even more difficult for Patch to push north on both sides of the Vosges (in direct support of the Third Army) and simultaneously hold Strasbourg in the center and assist the French in the south. Devers later blamed himself for overestimating the ability of de Lattre's forces to clear the Colmar area, but it is doubtful that he could have given the French any more assistance without ignoring Eisenhower's instructions to support Patton in the north. Eisenhower's later criticism of Dever's inability to eliminate the Colmar Pocket thus appears both unfair and unjustified.[2] In any case, the Germans surely wasted as much manpower holding the awkward wedge of terrain—primarily for political reasons—as the Allies did surrounding it, and in the process *Army Group G* was never able to use the better defensive terrain along the upper Rhine River and in the Black Forest, or to put much of an effort into its final West Wall defenses. More to the point, a Seventh Army crossing of the Rhine at Rastatt or its penetration of the German West Wall immediately west of the Rhine would have made the German defensive buildup in the Colmar region extremely unlikely and, at best, a waste of the *Wehrmacht*'s declining manpower resources.

NORDWIND proved a true test of the 6th Army Group, the Seventh Army, and the associated American—and French—corps, divisions, and regiments. Although the attacking panzer, panzer grenadier, and infantry divisions may have been fewer in number than the German forces sent into the Ardennes counteroffensive, and decidedly less well equipped,

they clearly outnumbered their Allied opponents who were also defending less favorable terrain than the Americans in the north. During the campaign, the American soldiers fought well, but it was good intelligence analysis and effective defensive deployments that gave the Seventh Army troops, including nine new infantry regiments that were rushed to the front with no combat experience, a distinct edge over the American defenders in the Ardennes. Patch, Brooks, and Haislip, making good use of their interior lines of communication, were able to checkmate almost every German initiative and, when the pressure became too great, conduct a rapid, orderly withdrawal that the Germans were unable to exploit.

Nevertheless, the German offensive was a close call. Had the attackers been able to articulate their units with the speed and, most important, with the unity of purpose that characterized the movements of their opponents, the results might have been far different. The capture of Saverne would have threatened the survival of the VI Corps, greatly strengthened the position of the Germans in the Colmar Pocket, isolated the First French Army in the south, and opened the rear of Patton's Third Army to German armor just when his forces were directing their main effort to the Ardennes in the north. Although perhaps neither the Ardennes counteroffensive nor the *NORDWIND* attacks ever had the chance of decisively reversing German fortunes in the west, greater success in either offensive would have assuredly delayed the end of the war in Europe.

If the actions of the American gen-

---

[2] See also Russell Weigley, *Eisenhower's Lieutenants* (Bloomington: Indiana University Press, 1981), pp. 550–51; and F. W. von Mellenthin (former *Army Group G* chief of staff), *Panzer Battles*, trans. H. Betzler, and ed. L. C. F. Turner (Norman: University of Oklahoma Press, 1951), p. 334.

erals were critical in halting *NORD-WIND*, credit for the victory in the Vosges must go to the American and French small-unit commanders and their unheralded infantrymen. The campaign in the High Vosges from late September to early December was one of the bitterest contests of the war. There the American army, corps, and divisional commanders had little room for maneuver, and their direct influence on the battles was limited. Waged in wet, cold, and then frozen mountain jungles where the materiel superiority of the Allied forces had little impact, the mountain battles continually tested the skill and determination of the average soldiers and their small-unit leaders. Despite the advantages that the terrain conferred on the German defenders, the constant fighting steadily sapped the strength of the *Nineteenth Army*, forcing the German high command to throw ever greater numbers of their precious infantry into the mountain forests in a losing war of attrition. The war in the Vosges ultimately made the relatively rapid penetrations of the Belfort and Saverne gaps possible and reduced the manpower available for the battlefields in the north. Nevertheless, for the Allied troops, the Vosges campaign was an uphill struggle all the way, with success depending on a policy of almost constant pressure. Attacking French and American infantry, supported by armor and artillery when feasible, continually exploited small gaps in the German lines, always pushing the defenders back and wearing them down bit by bit. Although weather and terrain largely canceled out Allied air, armor, and firepower supe-

riority (as did Allied munitions shortages [3]), the German commanders, again conducting a rather unimaginative defense at the division and corps levels, were rarely able to use the terrain and their interior lines of communication to stem the steady Allied advance by force of arms.

The Soldier

From the sunny beaches of the Riviera to the frozen forests of the Vosges, the campaign gave the average American soldier a tour of the European heartland that he would not soon forget. As one later exclaimed as he returned home, "I wouldn't trade the experience for a million dollars—but I wouldn't give a nickel to do it all over again." [4] Recalling his reactions going into combat for the first time, one former infantryman described his emotions as "taciturn; diffident; frightened, almost meek; mechanically going forward," as his unit moved up to the line, where, surrounded by "an alien landscape," he contemplated his situation. [5] Closer to the front, he recalled, conversation languished and tension steadily mounted. Rifles, ammunition belts, and hand grenades were mechanically checked and rechecked; helmets clamped down a bit snugger; chin straps tightened. The sudden sound of small-arms fire and artillery electrified each man, paralyzing him for a few sec-

---

[3] For a comprehensive treatment, see Ruppenthal, *Logistical Support of the Armies,* II, 269–73.

[4] Interv, Clarke with Robert Stuart, Seventh Army veteran, 25 Jun 88.

[5] The following description is based on a draft manuscript prepared by Ralph M. Morales regarding his experiences as a rifleman in the 254th Infantry during the Colmar campaign in January 1945.

AMERICAN INFANTRYMEN

onds as he automatically hunched closer to the ground. Then, as the unit moved forward to "the objective," the noise of exploding shells grew deafening, each one causing the earth to shake and pieces of dirt, metal, and wood to whine overhead. The tangy smell of burnt powder filled the air and the sounds of men screaming and officers cursing and yelling were quickly lost in the general din. Then suddenly the attack was over—the goal reached, the objective secured. At that point, he recalled, "the fear we had felt descended on us like an avalanche, leaving us only cold and wet and exhausted."

Later, attacking at Jebsheim in the Colmar Pocket, he could only remember "the incessant, unrelenting noise . . . the fellows attacking, our artillery fire, my rifle jerking with every shot . . . [and] the German fire pouring into us, and how, at any instant, a bullet might smash into me." His emotions in battle alternated between a kind of detachment—"a state neither easily achieved nor easily defined"—and "a feeling of fear, stark, cold fear . . . [that he] fought to control."

At rest, the foot soldier's lot was little better. Far from the amenities of the rear bases, he explained:

An infantryman has to fashion means for his comfort. He has to resort to expediencies to ameliorate some of the harshness of field living for he becomes filthy by tramping for days without washing; his hair becomes matted, dirty and stiff with the constant wearing of the metal helmet, and as he tries to comb it, it falls in tufts, and his scalp pains to the touch. He picks up ticks, fleas, and body lice from sleeping in hay stacks, on open fields, holes in the ground, with animals in barns, and in demolished, filth-spewed hovels. And he just might conceive, as we once did, of dousing his clothes and body with gasoline in order to rid himself of lice.

The severe cold weather was another constant problem. Feet quickly became wet either with perspiration or from tramping through the snow or fording small streams and brooks. With more experience the infantryman learned to carry extra socks close to his body, either to dry them or keep them dry while on the move. But feet inevitably became wet and cold in the field, growing alternately numb and then sore as more skin was rubbed raw. Most soldiers continued to hobble on, attempting to dry or at least air their feet at every momentary halt; both trench foot and frostbite were gnawing concerns.

Disease took a measured toll of the 6th Army Group infantrymen, as it had in all combat formations during the war. Because of the weather and terrain during the Vosges and Alsatian campaigns, trench foot and frostbite were the primary causes of nonbattle casualties. Both were the result of extensive tissue damage due to prolonged exposure to cold and dampness, conditions that were common in the front lines throughout the long winter.[6]

Trench foot reached epidemic proportions in mid-November throughout the American front lines and increased sharply during the next four months whenever units were in prolonged action. The problem quickly received command attention in all units: dry socks went forward with daily rations; and the availability of shoe-pacs, insulated rubber boots, increased. Trench-foot control officers, teams, and committees were created to discuss, formulate, and enforce preventive measures, and a SHAEF-sponsored press campaign was launched to encourage them. But the only reliable solution was the regular rotation of units from the field, and American manpower policies as well as the general combat situation on the Western Front rarely allowed such measures to be taken on a large scale. In the end, solutions to the problem depended primarily on the ingenuity of small-unit leaders and the infantryman himself. Yet, even in a highly disciplined unit such as O'Daniel's 3d Division, the incidence of cold injuries rose dramatically a few days after each major operation began. The Seventh Army's rate of these injuries was almost always substantially less than that of the neighboring Third Army throughout the winter, reflecting either greater command attention or the experience absorbed by the VI Corps and its three veteran divisions during the preceding winter in Italy.[7]

Neuropsychiatric disorders—shock and combat exhaustion—also deplet-

---

[6] Information on cold weather casualties is drawn from Tom F. Whayne and Michael E. DeBakey, *Cold Injury, Ground Type*, Medical Department, United

States Army in World War II (Washington: Office of the Surgeon General, 1958), pp. 7–28, 127–210.

[7] See tables, ibid., pp. 411, 450.

ed the ranks of the combat infantrymen, and testimonies of the hollow,
blank faces of the young soldiers
coming out of the line were
common.[8] Again, rotation of units
was the best solution, but could rarely
be done. Between 15 August and 31
December 1944, a period of four and
a half months, the Seventh Army suffered over 10,000 psychiatric cases, of
which about one-third were returned
to duty; between 1 January and 31
March 1945, a three-month period
but with double the number of forces,
the army sustained over 3,700 more
cases, of which two-thirds were returned to their units. Contemporary
analyses of these statistics showed
that the high rate in 1944 was attrib-
utable to the larger number of veterans in the three "older" divisions; the
rate steadily shrank as attrition reduced their number, while the high
return rate of 1945 was mainly due to
the inability of inexperienced medical
personnel in the newer divisions to
diagnose such cases properly. Further
studies showed that frequent changes
in leadership also resulted in higher
psychiatric casualty rates—a result
that could easily be seen in the 36th
Division's three regiments—while, not
unexpectedly, the rates for all units
increased during prolonged combat
operations. How such problems affected the majority of soldiers, officers and men alike, was not analyzed
at the time, but the general wear and
tear of combat, especially offensive
operations, must have worn away the

fresh edges of many new American
combat units—an acceptable trade-off
for the experience acquired in learning to survive.

The rapid campaign put a terrific
burden on combat commanders at all
levels. Most had done surprisingly
well on the battlefield with a new
army, and from Montelimar to the
Vosges and on to the Alsatian campaigns, few were relieved, although
many, especially in the lower ranks,
were casualties. At the tactical level,
the indirect attack became the hall-
mark of the American commanders;
even their opponents noted that the
Americans rarely attempted a frontal
assault, feeling perhaps that in always
striking for their enemy's flanks or
rear they had become predictable.[9]
But despite their superiority in materiel and firepower, Seventh Army officers were hesitant to use their infantry in direct assaults against even
hastily prepared defensive positions.

Speaking for the career officers,
General Dahlquist noted the intense
psychological pressure on the regimental, divisional, and corps commanders as well as the difficulties of
maintaining control over all their di-

---

[8] This section is based on Alfred O. Ludwig's
"Seventh U.S. Army," a section in *Neuropsychiatry in
World War II*, II, Medical Department, United States
Army in World War II (Washington: Office of the
Surgeon General, 1973), pp. 334–66.

[9] For German evaluations of American performance, see, for example, World War II German officer debriefings (copies at NARA and MHI), especially Lt. Gen. Walter Botsch, Chief of Staff, Nineteenth Army, B–213, pp. 11–12, and B–515, pp. 58–
64; and Drews, "Remarks Regarding the War History of the Seventh Army," John Dahlquist Papers,
MHI; and comments on 36th Division in Martin
Blumenson, *Salerno to Cassino*, United States Army in
World War II (Washington, D.C., 1969), p. 289. But
newer American divisions had a harder time, as
chronicled in Romie L. Brownlee and William J.
Mullen III, *Changing an Army: An Oral History of General William E. DePuy, USA Retired* (MHI/CMH joint
publication, GPO, n.d.), pp. 43–66, 78–79, 85–87,
90–91.

verse subordinate elements, whether in the pursuit or deep in the French mountains.[10] During the Alsatian campaign he brushed off the matter of physical danger as the "least worry" of a division commander, explaining that the most "terrible strain" was "the responsibility for the men you have committed to an action—the ever-present gnawing wonder if you have taken the right step because usually, once deployed, the decision is irrevocable." Partly to escape such pressures, Dahlquist found himself visiting the front-line battalions whenever he could, where, he found, "confidence is usually the highest."[11]

From a higher perspective, General Patch, the Seventh Army commander, was most concerned over the effects of the campaign on the junior leadership in combat units. Although in November 1944 SHAEF had lifted previous restrictions limiting the number of direct officer appointments to twenty per division every ninety days, and had given division commanders unlimited authority in this area, no new officers from outside the theater were expected until March 1945; furthermore, the massive use of direct commissions was risky. Patch estimated that the older divisions, the 3d, 36th, and 45th, had just about used up their leadership resources from the enlisted ranks through attrition; and, despite the slightly more elaborate training programs for direct appointment candidates, there seemed no satisfactory way to make up for the high number of losses among small-unit officers and NCOs that his units suffered in the Vosges.[12]

Such difficulties undoubtedly contributed to the disciplinary problems that afflicted many American combat units in the European theater—AWOLs, desertions, stragglers, combat refusals, and so forth. But the troubles experienced here were, in balance, minor and fairly commonplace. In this regard French officers had a much harder time controlling their African troops recruited in the colonies who had perhaps a lesser stake in the war than their American counterparts, and even the *Wehrmacht* had its special disciplinary battalions (*sonderbataillons*) composed of unruly German soldiers whose enthusiasm for battle was unsatisfactory. In other areas the surrender of small units and the refusal of some to advance reflected the nature of the war: the inability of conventionally armed troops to continue fighting when cut off from their sources of supply, especially ammunition and fuel, and the growing ineffectiveness of both troops and troop leaders when isolated or when simply left in the field too long. Tactical commanders on both sides and at all levels were well aware of these conditions and constantly sought to use them to their advantage, outmaneuvering their opponents, rather than overrunning them with frontal assaults, and wearing them down through continuous attack and harassment activities of all kinds.

In the French colonial units cultural and linguistic differences between of-

---

[10] Dahlquist Ltr, 25 Aug 44, John E. Dahlquist Papers, MHI.

[11] Dahlquist Ltr, 2 Jan 45, John E. Dahlquist Papers, MHI.

[12] For discussion, see Seventh Army Diary, pp. 376, 520A–521.

ficers and men made it difficult to replace experienced cadre, and de Lattre's *blanchiment* ("whitening") of his tropical African units proceeded slowly.[13] American military leaders, in contrast, had no such excuse for the poor treatment often given to black American soldiers whose cultural and intellectual background was essentially no different from that of their Caucasian troops. Although black combat units had compiled an excellent history in the regular Army since the American Civil War, the Army made its own segregationist policies worse by relegating blacks mainly to support units. After its successful action at Climbach, the black 614th Tank Destroyer Battalion continued to perform well; after proving itself in combat, its members later related that they quickly developed close ties with the white regiments of the 103d Division. Although disappointed that their unit had never been reequipped with the new self-propelled guns, they bragged that even with their towed pieces, the 614th "could still split trail, beat them to the draw, and hit the target." [14] In March 1945 another black unit, the 761st Tank Battalion, joined the 103d Division, and in the ensuing campaign across Germany the two units often led the advance of the division. But in this area the Seventh Army had not learned its lessons well. Patch later chose to dissolve another black tank destroyer battalion— an inexperienced and poorly led unit

that Brooks had thrown into the general Hatten-Gambsheim area with mixed results—and he had a difficult time persuading his two armored divisions to accept platoons of black volunteer riflemen to bolster their depleted infantry ranks. Had more black volunteers been used in this manner, the combat strength of all Seventh Army units would have been measurably improved and the shortage of infantry greatly alleviated.[15]

In both black and white units, African and European, the quality of leadership often determined whether or not a unit fought well. Nevertheless, the postwar conclusions reached in S. L. A. Marshall's *Men Against Fire* were unsettling. Based on his extensive field research of American troops in the European and Pacific theaters, Marshall charged American troops with a widespread lack of aggressiveness in combat, citing the low percentage of riflemen that claimed to have fired their weapons in combat.[16]

---

[13] For some discussion, see Rita Headrick, "African Soldiers in World War II," *Armed Forces and Society*, IV, No. 3 (Spring 1978), 501–26.

[14] Quotes from Motley, ed., *The Invisible Soldier*, p. 170.

[15] For further treatment, see Ulysses Lee, *The Employment of Negro Troops*, United States Army in World War II (Washington, 1966), especially pp. 667–87, 700–704.

[16] S. L. A. Marshall, *Men Against Fire* (New York: Morrow, 1947), p. 56. Based on his interviews, the author noted that the rate of soldiers firing their weapons in battle was never greater than 25 percent and generally closer to 15 percent, but with a very high participation rate by those equipped with automatic weapons. For a repeat of the charge during the Korean War, see George Juskalian, "Why Didn't They Shoot More?" *Army Combat Forces Journal*, V, No. 2 (September 1954), 35. For recent challenges to Marshall's research, see Roger J. Spiller, "S. L. A. Marshall and the Ratio of Fire," *Journal of the Royal Service Institute*, XXXIII, No. 4 (Winter 1988), 63–71; Fredric Smoler, "The Secret of the Soldiers Who Didn't Shoot," *American Heritage*, XL, No. 2 (March 1989), 36–45; and Russell W. Glenn, "Men and Fire in Vietnam," *Army*, XXXIX, No. 4 (April 1989), 18–26.

Most U.S. soldiers, he concluded, relied too much on armor, artillery, or airpower to push back or destroy the enemy. However, as one former infantryman of the 7th Infantry regiment (3d Division) recalled, American small units generally did not advance in linear formations (abreast), but attacked in small groups of infiltrating columns led by officers and NCOs and, if available, supported by automatic weapons, tanks, and artillery. Skirmish lines could be built up when engaged, but were difficult to control for any length of time, and attacking in open waves, as the Germans had done at the beginning of *NORD-WIND*, was often suicidal. Under such conditions, he noted, it was sometimes difficult and even dangerous to fire one's rifle during the attack, especially when other friendly soldiers were all around and the enemy was difficult to locate.[17] In defensive positions the situation was often quite different, but then American soldiers, especially those interviewed by Marshall in the latter part of the war, were rarely on the defensive.

Despite these explanations, the alleged reticence of American infantry has merited considerable attention since World War II, and Marshall's accusations seem to have been fueled by the performance of the U.S. soldier in subsequent conflicts. Evolution of the criticism is somewhat complex. Postwar American scholars, seeking explanations for German military successes during the war, concluded that the German Army consist-

ently produced better soldiers than did their Allied counterparts.[18] Implied was the assumption that German officers and men fought longer, harder, and better than their opponents, despite vastly inferior resources, and that their ultimate failure on the battlefield was primarily due to overwhelming Allied materiel and manpower superiority. Their success, critics believed, lay in two factors: the superior leadership of the German officer corps and the strong interior "cohesion" of the German small-unit combat formations. The former was the product of good training, sound doctrine, and a military tradition that emphasized leadership on the battlefield; the latter, strong unit cohesion, was the result of a training and replacement system that attached the German soldier to the unit in which he would be fighting from the time of his induction into the *Wehrmacht* until the moment he entered the battle-

---

[17] Reitan, "The Seventh Infantry Crosses the Meurthe," MS, p. 13.

[18] For general clinical background, see Edward A. Shils and Morris Janowitz, "Cohesion and Disintegration in the German Wehrmacht in World War II," *Public Opinion Quarterly* (Summer 1948), 280–315; Samuel Stouffer et al., *Studies in Social Psychology in World War II;* and Herbert Spiegel, "Psychiatry with an Infantry Battalion in North Africa," *Neuropsychiatry in World War II,* II, 111–26. For the controversy, see Martin van Creveld, *Fighting Power: German and U.S. Army Performance, 1939–45* (Westport, Conn.: Greenwood, 1982); and Trevor N. Dupuy, *A Genius for War: The German Army and General Staff, 1807–1945* (Englewood Cliffs, N.J.: Prentice-Hall, 1977); Richard A. Gabriel and Paul Savage, "Cohesion and Disintegration in the American Army: An Alternative Perspective," *Armed Forces and Society,* II, No. 3 (Spring 1976), 340–76, and their subsequent *Crisis in Command: Mismanagement in the Army* (New York: Hill and Wang, 1978), both deal essentially with a later period; and, in a more popular vein, Max Hastings, "Their Wehrmacht Was Better Than Our Army," *Washington Post* (and others), 5 May 85, C1–4.

field.[19] Taking up where S. L. A. Marshall left off, these critics have contended that the American infantrymen lacked such advantages and thus made poorer soldiers in the field. The impersonal American replacement system, which assigned soldiers solely according to the immediate needs of the combat units, was often cited as the primary reason behind the supposedly low cohesion in American fighting units and their correspondingly lower performance on the battlefield. One military researcher even constructed elaborate models, or equations, showing that even in defeat German units outperformed American units and inflicted more casualties on the Americans than should have been expected, given the general situation and the manpower and materiel available to both forces at the time of the battle. The American soldier was good, but the German soldier was better.[20]

A complete examination of these charges is clearly beyond the scope of this book; however, since they obviously impinge on many aspects of the Seventh Army's campaigns, some discussion is needed. Not surprisingly other writers have challenged many of the assumptions and conclusions made by these authors, deeming them either erroneous or irrelevant.[21] Some

have pointed out that the German territorial recruitment and replacement system, hardly unique, was inefficient and unable to keep German units up to strength or ensure a uniform quality of training. The lack of combat effectives, especially in the German infantry battalions, may have made their actual ratios of enlisted men to officers and combat to noncombat ("tooth to tail") even lower than those of the American Army, which has often been criticized in this regard (higher ratios indicating a lean, or efficient, military force; lower ratios signifying one with supposedly excess "fat," that is, too many officers or support units). Other historians have directly challenged the battlefield performance models, pointing out, for example, that the Americans faced a much higher proportion of the better German formations, the panzer and panzer grenadier divisions, while the *Wehrmacht* posted most of its neglected infantry divisions to the Eastern Front, where mass was more important than quality. Still others have noted that German inability to sustain their supposedly high combat power on the battlefield made claims of superior military prowess irrelevant. An army is the measure of many things, and, for example, General Erwin Rommel's successes in the western desert must be balanced by his failure to expand the Libyan ports and thereby ease his

[19] See Samuel J. Newland, "Manning the Force German-Style," *Military Review*, LXVII, No. 5 (May 1987), 36–45, and other related articles in this issue.

[20] See Trevor N. Dupuy, *Numbers, Predictions, and War* (New York: Bobbs-Merrill, 1979).

[21] For example, see the various critiques of Gabriel and Savage in "Commentary on 'Cohesion and Disintegration in the American Army,' " *Armed Forces and Society*, III, No. 3 (Spring 1977), 457–90; Roger A. Beaumont, "On the Wehrmacht Mystic," *Military*

Review, LXVI, No. 7 (July 1986), 44–56; and John Sloan Brown, "Colonel Trevor N. Dupuy and the Mythos of Wehrmacht Superiority: A Reconsideration," *Military Affairs*, L, No. 1 (January 1986), 16–20, and the ensuing rejoinders by Dupuy and Brown in subsequent issues.

continual logistical problems.[22] What good did it do the *Wehrmacht* to put its best formations and impressive war machines on the battlefield, if it failed to provide the means to support and sustain them?

In southern France and during the campaigns in the Vosges and Alsace, the discussion is still ambiguous, and judgments are amply colored by national and personal prejudices. Were new troops to be considered "fresh," or were they to be judged "green" and liable to panic or make mistakes on entering the battlefield? Were older units "worn out" or "experienced"? Poor logistical capabilities curtailed the mobility of German panzer divisions just as inclement weather reduced the impact of Allied airpower on the battlefield, and unit cohesion was of little use to anemic infantry battalions that could obtain no replacements. In the 6th Army Group, perhaps all that can be said is that the American and French infantrymen did the job that had to be done, and it is doubtful that even with better small-unit leadership or cohesion they could have accomplished their missions sooner or suffered fewer casualties in the process. As the *Wehrmacht* discovered time and time again, too much focus on one aspect of an army only caused serious difficulties elsewhere, which ultimately affected the entire organism. Sorting out and mathematically weighing all of the variables on the battlefield is probably an impossible task. Nevertheless, at least the ongoing debate

has placed more attention on the capabilities and accomplishments of the average foot soldier, whose exploits are often undocumented and forgotten.

Allied Strategy and Operations

Allied "strategy" in western Europe and the relationship between General Eisenhower and General Devers have also been subjects of much debate. Ironically, the British and American positions on Allied ground strategy seem to have reversed themselves between 1943 and 1944. At first, Prime Minister Winston Churchill and his British commanders leaned heavily toward a peripheral operational strategy that took advantage of the superior mobility (seapower) of Allied military forces in order to attack the German-held Continent at many points, thereby eroding Germany's military strength. (The RAF bombing campaign against Germany fit into this category, as did Britain's early economic blockade of the Continent.) The Americans, on the other hand, led by General Marshall and the U.S. Joint Chiefs of Staff, favored a more direct approach and championed a war-winning ground strategy involving the concentration of all Allied resources for the OVERLORD cross-Channel invasion, followed by a direct strike into the German heartland over the north European plains. (The land strategy had its counterpart in the U.S. Army Air Force's strategic bombing campaign.) Eisenhower's position in the debate seems ambiguous, but once charged with the Allied campaign in northern France, he appears to have supported a "broad front," or

---

[22] See Martin van Creveld, *Supplying War: Logistics from Wallenstein to Patton* (New York: Cambridge University Press, 1977), pp. 181–201.

flexible, operational strategy, aimed at destroying German military forces west of the Rhine and then pushing into Germany itself. The British, however, led by Field Marshal Montgomery, advocated a war-winning ground strategy involving either a knife-like thrust deep into the German heartland or at least the immediate seizure of the Ruhr industrial area, thereby ending Germany's war-making capabilities. Lacking the logistical resources for a broad front campaign, Eisenhower adopted the British point of view, but seems to have compromised somewhat by giving Bradley's southern force, Patton's Third Army, the task of seizing the Saar basin— also a "strategic" industrial region— which kept his American generals in Bradley's center army group occupied along with many German divisions. But this operational plan allowed the Germans to concentrate their inferior defensive resources against two relatively narrow and easily recognizable Allied axes of advance, and it denied Eisenhower the flexibility to shift his attacks elsewhere once his main offensives were halted.

In this regard, Eisenhower's plans were undoubtedly influenced by national considerations—keeping the Allied coalition intact—and by his evaluations of the various Allied commanders. His personal dislike for General Devers was well known, as was his supposedly low opinion of Devers' military abilities. In 1943, when Eisenhower commanded the Allied forces in the Mediterranean theater, Devers, who was Eisenhower's senior in age and also a protege of General Marshall, occupied a somewhat analogous position in Eng-

land, where he was charged with the buildup for the OVERLORD attack; the two were often at odds over the distribution of resources between the two theaters. Then, when Eisenhower came to England in early 1944 to head the invasion force, he recommended that Devers be made deputy to General Wilson, Eisenhower's successor in the Mediterranean theater. At the time, Marshall felt that Eisenhower was trying to ship out his potential rivals for the post of Supreme Allied Commander, and he was disturbed that Eisenhower rejected Devers for any high command positions in the invading forces. Nevertheless, Marshall approved the transfer, feeling that Eisenhower would be more at ease with generals who had served under him during the recent campaigns in the Mediterranean. As a result, Devers and Eisenhower were again at opposite ends of the Allied European military effort, competing for a limited number of military resources. Thus, Eisenhower may have been unpleasantly surprised in July 1944 when he learned that Marshall intended to appoint Devers to head the new army group moving up from southern France. Although acquiescing to the appointment, he may have retained serious reservations regarding the capability of the newly designated army group commander. On the other hand, the politically astute Eisenhower must have realized that the appointment of Devers would ensure the survival of ANVIL, a vital consideration given the difficulties Eisenhower was personally facing in Normandy at the time.

The success of ANVIL and the subsequent drive north apparently did not change the Supreme Commander's feelings toward General Devers. In the end, his misgivings may have only reflected personality differences between the two high-ranking officers. Such differences, however, can have a direct effect on an individual's actions and may explain, in part, Eisenhower's reluctance to assign additional forces to the 6th Army Group when it was established in September or even to consider allowing it to exploit the Saverne Gap penetration in November 1944. On 1 February of the following year, in preparing an evaluation of American generals requested by Marshall, Eisenhower's low estimation of Devers was striking. Rating him twenty-fourth of thirty-eight—far below all of the other principal Army commanders—he described him as "loyal and energetic" and "enthusiastic, but often inaccurate in statements and evaluations." He added that, despite the fact that Devers' accomplishments were "generally good, sometimes outstanding . . . he has not, so far, produced among the seniors of the American organization here that feeling of trust and confidence that is so necessary to continued success." Devers was still not part of the team.[23]

Eisenhower's low assessment of Devers is highly questionable. Cer-

tainly the forces under the 6th Army Group had chalked up an impressive record of military successes during the November offensive, the Alsatian battles, and the reduction of the Colmar Pocket. His record prior to November had been equally impressive. The success of ANVIL had led directly to the acquisition of Marseille and other Riviera ports, opening up a major Allied logistical gateway to France for Eisenhower's hungry armies. By September the southern ports were accounting for over one-fourth of the Allied supplies arriving in France and over one-third during October and November; they were not surpassed by Antwerp until sometime in March 1945 (*Table 1*). Moreover, going back further, Devers had always been a proponent of both OVERLORD and ANVIL and, on becoming deputy commander of the Mediterranean theater, was one of the principal officers who kept ANVIL alive. As the Commanding General, NATOUSA, he continued logistical preparations for the southern France invasion throughout early 1944, even after the operation had been temporarily canceled. In this respect, the Allies probably could not have undertaken ANVIL without the attention that Devers had devoted to it.

Once securely installed as the 6th Army Group chief, Devers took issue with Eisenhower's operational guidance. Initially he viewed the Supreme Commander as more concerned with the acquisition of territory—the Saar and the Ruhr—than with the destruction of the German Army. Although fully accepting Eisenhower's decision to concentrate on destroying the German Army west of the Rhine,

---

[23] Quotes from Eisenhower Memo, 1 Feb 45, in *Eisenhower Papers*, IV, 2466–69. Eisenhower rated Bradley and Spaatz tied for first; Smith, his chief of staff, third; Patton, fourth; Clark (in Italy), fifth; and Truscott, sixth. See also Pogue, *Marshall: Organizer of the Victory*, pp. 372–75; Omar N. Bradley, *A General's Life: An Autobiography* (New York: Simon and Schuster, 1983), pp. 210, 217; Dwight D. Eisenhower, *Crusade in Europe* (Garden City: Doubleday, 1948), p. 216; and Weigley, *Eisenhower's Lieutenants*, p. 580. None of these sources, however, sheds any direct light on the matter.

TABLE 1—TONNAGES DISCHARGED AT CONTINENTAL PORTS: JUNE 1944–APRIL 1945

[Long Tons^a]

Year and Month	Total	OMAHA Beach	UTAH BEACH	Cher-bourg	Norman-dy Minor Ports [b]	Brittany Ports	Le Havre	Rouen	Antwerp	Ghent	Southern France
1944											
June............	291,333	182,199	109,134								
July..............	621,322	356,219	193,154	31,658	40,291						
August	1,112,771	348,820	187,955	266,644	125,353	9,499					174,500
September	1,210,290	243,564	150,158	314,431	100,126	75,198					326,813
October.........	1,309,184	120,786	72,728	365,603	58,816	77,735	61,731	26,891			524,894
November	1,402,080	13,411	12,885	433,301	48,707	64,078	148,654	127,569	5,873		547,602
December	1,555,819			250,112	50,749	27,327	166,038	132,433	427,592		501,568
1945											
January.........	1,501,269			262,423	47,773		198,768	157,709	433,094	15,742	385,760
February	1,735,502			286,591	41,836		195,332	173,016	473,463	69,698	495,566
March............	2,039,778			261,492	39,691		192,593	268,174	558,066	172,259	547,503
April.............	2,025,142			181,043	47,542		165,438	240,708	628,227	277,553	484,631

^a Exclusive of bulk POL and vehicles.
^b Including Granville.
Source: Historical Report of the Transportation Corps, ETO, Vol. VII, April–June 1945, App. 7, Table 8A.

Devers obviously favored a more flexible "operational" strategy for SHAEF, one that would allow the 6th Army Group to exploit its successes on the battlefield. Even before taking over the army group, Devers had observed that it was "not cracking the line or pushing the enemy back to a line or river" that was important, "but the destruction of the enemy itself that counts"; he emphasized that "we must capture the German army or what exists of it and take our minds off terrain." [24] He did agree that Antwerp was an exception, but judged that the port and the Schelde approaches should have been secured before Montgomery continued his advance; he labeled the British commander "a prima donna who thinks more of himself than he does of winning the war." [25] His own attitude toward Eisenhower was equivocal. According to the Seventh Army operational chief (G–3), Col. John S. Guthrie, Devers was often openly critical of Eisenhower's judgments when such matters came up in 6th Army Group or Seventh Army staff meetings. [26] Since Devers expressed his misgivings publicly, Guthrie thought it inevitable that Eisenhower would have learned of them and that Maj. Gen. David G. Barr, the affable 6th Army Group chief of staff, played a vital role in smoothing out the difficulties between the two commanders. Eisenhower was certainly stung by Devers' criticism of his operational strategy during their 24–25 November meeting and was surely angered by

[24] Devers Diary, 11–12 Sep 44 (Devers was primarily addressing the Italian compaign in this entry).

[25] Devers Diary, 5 Oct 44; see also 16 Oct 44 entries.

[26] See Guthrie's comments on draft MS; Telecon, Clarke-Guthrie, 11 Aug 88.

his almost open refusal to withdraw the Seventh Army from the Lauterbourg salient in December. The cancellation of Operation INDEPENDENCE, whatever its merit, on the pretext that de Lattre's forces were on the verge of eliminating the Colmar Pocket, must also have been annoying. Although Eisenhower may have overrated Devers' political influence within the upper echelons of the American high command, the persistent differences between the Supreme Commander and Field Marshal Montgomery may have made Eisenhower even less forgiving of Devers' independent attitudes. Not surprisingly then, Eisenhower continued to be more comfortable dealing with Bradley, a longtime subordinate and friend, than with more demanding commanders such as Montgomery, Truscott, or Devers. In the upper reaches of the Allied high command, there was room for only a few mavericks, like the irascible Patton.

Within his own headquarters, Devers, was less controversial. If some of his verbal directives were vague at times, he delegated enough authority to enable subordinates, such as Barr, Maj. Gen. Reuben Jenkins (his G–3), and even the young liaison officer, Lt. Col. Henry Cabot Lodge, to clarify his wishes to Patch, de Lattre, and others.[27] In general, he ran the 6th Army Group as an operational rather than a strategic or tactical command, assigning general objectives to his two army commanders and preferring to let the corps commanders fight the battles. Although

allowing the two large subordinate army headquarters to run their own logistical and administrative affairs, he also had his own staff serve as a link between the armies and the theater headquarters and the theater communications zone logistical and personnel agencies. Consistent with U.S. Army doctrine of the time, his army group headquarters thus performed a minimal amount of administrative functions and, except for engineer and signal services, had none of the special staff sections that were normally found at the army headquarters level.[28]

Patch, the Seventh Army commander, proved more enigmatic than Devers, Truscott, or any of the other major commanders in the 6th Army Group. Rarely did his hand appear on the battlefield. Yet, it was Patch and not Truscott who had made almost all of the critical planning decisions for ANVIL and had kept a tight rein on the U.S. VI Corps until de Lattre's Army B forces were well on their way into Toulon and Marseille; thereafter he did his best to keep his rather jumbled Franco-American army on the road to Lyon and Belfort. Unlike his German opponents, however, Patch rarely stepped into the daily fighting arena and was more concerned with seeing that the combat forces under his command, both French and American, received the men, equipment,

---

[27] Telecon, Clarke-Guthrie, 11 Aug 88; Ltr, Guthrie to Clarke, 22 Oct 88.

[28] Headquarters, 6th Army Group, had a total strength of only 311 officers and 1,221 enlisted men. On the functions of the 6th Army Group, see Hist, 6th Army Gp, ch. 1, "Concept and Organization"; G–3, 6th Army Group, Final Report (July 1945), p. 3; Ltr, Maj Gen Reuben E. Jenkins to Col Robert N. Young, 28 Jan 47, Reuben E. Jenkins Papers, MHI.

and supplies necessary to accomplish their missions. This task was, in fact, the primary textbook responsibility of an American army headquarters; furthermore, given the compartmentalized nature of the Vosges campaign, there was little else for him to do once the mountain barrier had been reached. But during the German offensives in Alsace, Patch quickly changed his role and became an active tactical commander, juggling forces between his two corps and the army reserve and keeping close track of the course of the battle, current intelligence on enemy dispositions and intentions, and the status and plans of his own forces. Still he allowed his two corps commanders the freedom to fight their own battles within their assigned zones, backstopping them with advice and assistance. In this regard, his actions continued to reflect his quiet, almost paternal style of command. Although sometimes regarding the antics of Patton as both "greatly amusing" and beneficial to Third Army morale, he never attempted to emulate his well-known neighbor, who would later come to symbolize the entire American combat effort in northern France.[29]

De Lattre, whose First French Army headquarters was more tactically oriented, did not see the role of his army headquarters in this light and kept a much closer rein on his corps and division commanders than Patch did. In many nontactical areas, however, de Lattre's authority was more limited, and Devers and his staff often had to assist the French in such mat-

ters as ammunition stockage and expenditures, backing up the understandably weak French logistical and administrative support organizations. Although French commanders generally regarded many of the administrative and logistical elements that supported U.S. combat forces as luxury items, American commanders gave even their lowly laundry units a high degree of respect: dry socks and uniforms were vital to the health of their army and could not be ignored.

Like Eisenhower, Devers also found himself arbitrating, or at least attempting to mediate, between Allied military needs and national (French) political concerns regarding such matters as Operation INDEPENDENCE, the defense of Strasbourg, the security of the Franco-Italian border, and the supply of FFI units in the First French Army. Here his diplomatic skills were sorely tested, but he was generally able to iron out the many difficulties among his various constituents, minimizing their impact on military operations. Although having been forced to listen to de Lattre's temper on many occasions (as had Patch and Truscott in the past) and viewing him as "difficult to handle," Devers regarded the French commander as a man of "great courage [who] . . . will fight the 1st French Army realistically and effectively," and he went on to make good use of his sometimes troublesome ally.[30]

Devers, Patch, and de Lattre had two additional concerns that often went unnoticed: the Franco-Italian front and the German pockets on the

[29] Quote related in Wyant Interv, 20 Jun 88.

[30] Devers Diary, 7 Nov 44; see also 8 Oct 44.

Atlantic coast of France.[31] Both areas threatened to divert important combat resources from the 6th Army Group throughout the entire campaign. Initially, Eisenhower had decided to generally ignore the German enclaves at Lorient, St. Nazaire, and La Rochelle as well as those on either side of the Gironde Estuary blocking the approaches to Bordeaux. At the insistence of de Gaulle, however, in early November the Supreme Commander had made Devers responsible for clearing the Gironde Estuary. Thus began Devers' long struggle with SHAEF, the French provisional government, and the First French Army over the deployment of forces to support Operation INDEPENDENCE, always a somewhat questionable effort. Ultimately, General de Larminat's French Forces of the West headquarters launched the often-postponed endeavor in mid-April 1945 and, with the assistance of Leclerc's 2d Armored Division and a U.S. artillery brigade, completed the affair in about one week. But by then the Allies had no need for additional ports, and the entire operation, essentially an internal French political effort to boost the legitimacy of de Gaulle's provisional government, represented a waste of both 6th Army Group and First French Army military strength.

The Italian border was another matter entirely. From the beginning of ANVIL, Patch had no choice but to maintain strong holding forces along the Franco-Italian frontier despite the general inactivity of the German forces there. After taking command of the 6th Army Group in September, Devers would have preferred to deploy both the French 4th Moroccan Mountain Division and General Frederick's airborne–Special Services task force to the Vosges area as quickly as possible, replacing them with FFI forces; but he judged that the French militia was not up to the task. Not until the end of November was Devers able to exchange the Moroccans for a newly created French Alpine division along the northern frontier, and not until March 1945 were enough additional French forces available to fill in along the southern sector. By then Devers had replaced Frederick's task force first with the 442d (Japanese-American) Regimental Combat Team, then with elements of the 14th Armored Division, and finally with bits and pieces of other American units that were arriving in southern France, placing them under the control of the U.S. 44th Antiaircraft Artillery Brigade. But with several weak German divisions stationed opposite the frontier, constantly posing a threat to the 6th Army Group's line of communications, neither Patch nor Devers could afford to ignore this area. Moreover, they were never able to employ any of Frederick's elite forces in the north, and Eisenhower ultimately incorporated the airborne units into the SHAEF reserve and reorganized the Special Service units into an infantry brigade under Bradley's 12th Army Group.[32]

---

[31] For a full treatment, see Robert Ross Smith, "The German Pockets on the Atlantic" and "The Franco-Italian Border: Protecting the Southeast Flank," CMH MSS.

[32] The airborne units began departing the Alpine front on 15 November, the 1st Airborne Task Force

After World War II, German officers, when asked about the possibility of conducting an attack against the Riviera-Rhone area from northern Italy, cited a host of difficulties that precluded even the consideration of such an operation. Most important were *OB Southwest*'s lack of transportation to make and support a shift of forces; the Alpine terrain and weather that any offensive would have to face; the lack of air support to protect such an extended movement; and, above all, the constant pressure exerted by Wilson's forces on the main Italian front.[33] On the other hand, the ability of the *Wehrmacht* to secretly mass and support a small number of mobile forces along the Alpine front was never beyond its scope—as the much larger concentration of divisions for the Ardennes offensive demonstrated. Even the remote possibility of such an attack was enough to keep the Allied high commands concerned. If greater economy of force was necessary, then those units stationed by Bradley and Devers on the Atlantic coast were the most likely candidates for redeploy-

ment elsewhere; but such movements depended more on the ability of Roosevelt and de Gaulle to iron out their political differences and make greater use of the FFI.

Finally, the role of ULTRA in the Seventh Army and the 6th Army Group operations should be noted. The availability of the German withdrawal orders on 17 and 18 August represented a rare intelligence coup. Normally individual ULTRA intercepts revealed only mundane information that had to be collated with thousands of other intercepts and intelligence reports from other sources before any value could be attached to it. Truscott's overreaction to the reported presence of the *11th Panzer Division* east of the Rhone on 22 August illustrates the danger of depending too greatly on these sources; in any case, German commanders rarely discussed specific operational plans over the radio, and tactical commanders often altered plans prepared by higher headquarters because of changing situations in the field. In many other areas ULTRA was mute—such as the direction of the German withdrawal north of Lyon or the establishment of the Colmar Pocket. Therefore, those who relied too heavily on these sources, such as Bradley's 12th Army Group before the Ardennes offensive, sometimes suffered unpleasant surprises.[34] As noted in the official British history of the intelligence effort, if the Germans had attacked in the Aachen sector, instead of in the Ardennes, "the [available] intelligence would have been quite

---

headquarters was dissolved around the 25th, and the 1st Special Service Force was relieved shortly thereafter. The Special Service Force units were formally disbanded on 6 January 1945. The Canadian troops returned to their national command, and the American components formed the nucleus of the 1st and 2d Battalions of the newly organized 474th Infantry Brigade, along with the independent Norwegian-American 99th Infantry Battalion. On the Special Service Force transfer, see *Eisenhower Papers*, IV, 2232n.

[33] Ltr, Lt Gen Walter Warlimont (former deputy chief of staff for operations at *OKW*) to CMH (n.d., recvd 12 Oct 57); Ltr, Lt Gen Siegfried Westphal (former chief of staff at *OB Southwest*) to CMH, 23 Oct 57. Both letters were in reply to a questionnaire sent to the generals by CMH historians on 17 Sep 57 (copies CMH).

[34] See Bradley, *A General's Life*, pp. 350–52.

compatible with that outcome." [35] *NORDWIND* was another case in point. Although ULTRA order-of-battle information, together with other intelligence sources, may have suggested the possibility of a German thrust down the Sarre River corridor, it was unable to predict the German infantry assault south of Bitche, the switch of the German mobile divisions to the Lauterbourg salient, or the double offensive of Himmler's *Army Group Oberrhein*—although it is doubtful whether even von Rundstedt could have predicted the place or date of these last attacks. [36] Nevertheless, ULTRA played a major role in confirming other intelligence information acquired by more conventional means, and was one of many factors that promoted the success of the Allied forces from the Riviera coast and their decisive contribution to the Allied campaigns in northeastern France during the fall and winter of 1944–45.

[35] Hinsley, *British Intelligence in the Second World War*, III, 2, 430–31.

[36] See Ltr, Bussey to Smith, 27 Nov 79.

Bibliographical Note

Representing the final campaign volume of the United States Army in World War II series published by the U.S. Army Center of Military History (CMH) (formerly the Office of the Chief of Military History), this work is based primarily on the official records of U.S. Army units and commands. These sources contain monthly operational reports submitted by each headquarters, from army through regiment and separate battalion, and retired unit records, including journals, message and correspondence files, planning documents and operational orders, maps and overlays, and special reports, studies, and similar memoranda, the volume of which is roughly proportional to the size of the concerned headquarters. Also of vital interest are the personal papers and diaries of leading participants, as well as special after action interview reports done by Army historians in the field and a wide variety of semiofficial unit histories whose distribution has been extremely limited. Most combat records are on file at the National Archives under the numerical military designation of the retiring unit, and citations to such material have been made only when specific reference to them occurs within the text.

Official Records

Over the years the official records of the U.S. Army during World War II have migrated to the National Archives and Records Administration (NARA) and are currently housed at the National Archives in Washington, D.C., and at the Washington National Records Center in nearby Suitland, Maryland. Under the direct control of the Military Field Branch and the Military Reference Branch, both sections of NARA's Military Archives Division, these records can be found in a few key "record groups" (RG). Most combat unit records are located in RG 338 ("U.S. Army Commands"—records retired by units) or RG 407 ("Unit Records"—required reports such as monthly operational, or after action, reports). Material relating to both the Supreme Headquarters, Allied Expeditionary Force (SHAEF), and Allied Forces Headquarters (AFHQ) is contained in RG 331 ("Allied Operations Headquarters"), while RG 165 ("War Department General and Special Staffs") includes significant message traffic between Washington agencies and the overseas commands.

Naval records cited in the text are still under the control of the Department of the Navy and managed by the Operational Archives section of the Naval Historical Center. Other official records, or at least copies of them, can also be found at CMH, or at the archives maintained by the U.S. Army's Military History Institute (MHI) at Carlisle Barracks, Pennsylvania; the Marshall Library in Lexington, Virginia; the Devers Collection in York, Pennsylvania; and the Eisenhower Library in Abilene, Kansas. Records used by the authors from these institutions have been noted in the text citations.

Unofficial Records

Personal papers and related material of Generals Marshall, Eisenhower, and Devers are held by the institutions noted above. Other papers of participants can also be found at MHI together with a number of transcribed interviews that have proved useful. In addition, large collections of unit histories, of widely varying length and quality, exist at MHI, CMH, and other military libraries. For this volume the most important studies of this nature are the three-volume *Seventh Army Report of Operations,* prepared by Army historians in Europe using primary documents; the *History of the Headquarters Sixth Army Group,* a short narrative with many documents appended; and the three-volume "diary" of General Patch, actually an official journal prepared by the Seventh Army staff. Copies of all three works are located at CMH. Also at CMH are a number of supporting files for this project, including smaller monographs, interviews, and other material prepared or gathered by CMH historians. A final

but invaluable document extensively used is the three-volume diary kept by General Devers, one copy of which is currently located at CMH and another at the Devers Collection in York. Upon completion of this volume, most of the supporting material at CMH will be retired and the Center's copy of the "Devers Diary" will be transferred to MHI.

Foreign Records

The account of German operations in this volume is based primarily on monographs prepared within CMH by Charles V. P. von Luttichau and several other German-language historians, as cited in the text. These authors, in turn, based their studies on official German records captured or seized during the war and on a series of postwar manuscripts written by former German commanders under the auspices of the U.S. Army. Copies of the monographs prepared by Mr. von Luttichau and his colleagues are available at CMH and MHI. The official German war records have been returned to Germany, but microfilm copies are held at NARA and are available to researchers. Also on file at NARA are the German-authored manuscripts, numbering over two thousand studies, cataloged and indexed in the *Guide to Foreign Military Studies, 1945–54,* and under the supervision of the Military Reference Branch.

ULTRA documents, including the raw transcripts of decoded and translated German message traffic during World War II, are located in the NSA/CSS Cryptologic Documents Collection in RG 457 ("National Security Agency/Central Security Service") at NARA. Copies of the intercepts and associated studies are also available at MHI, where their significance can be further clarified by Col. Donald S. Bussey, the former Seventh Army ULTRA officer who retired to the Carlisle area.

French records include a nearly complete collection of daily journals, situation reports, and operations orders for all French divisions, corps, and higher headquarters for the campaigns in Tunisia, Italy, France, and Germany. These documents, together with large numbers of French Army plans, reports, and other special studies were microfilmed by CMH historians in 1948 and later supplemented by additional records and information supplied by the Service Historique de l'Armee. The microfilm has now been retired and is in the custody of NARA's Military Reference Branch in RG 319 ("Army Staff").

Basic Military Map Symbols

Symbols within a rectangle indicate a military unit, within a triangle an observation post, and within a circle a supply point.

Military Units—Identification

Antiaircraft Artillery . . . .

Armored Command . . . .

Army Air Forces . . . .

Artillery, except Antiaircraft and Coast Artillery . . . .

Cavalry, Horse . . . .

Cavalry, Mechanized . . . .

Chemical Warfare Service . . . .

Coast Artillery . . . .

Engineers . . . .

Infantry . . . .

Medical Corps . . . .

Ordnance Department . . . .

Quartermaster Corps . . . .

Signal Corps . . . .

Tank Destroyer . . . .

Transportation Corps . . . .

Veterinary Corps . . . .

Airborne units are designated by combining a gull wing symbol with the arm or service symbol:

Airborne Artillery . . . .

Airborne Infantry . . . .

Size Symbols

The following symbols placed either in boundary lines or above the rectangle, triangle, or circle inclosing the identifying arm or service symbol indicate the size of military organization:

Squad	●
Section	●●
Platoon	●●●
Company, troop, battery, Air Force flight	I
Battalion, cavalry squadron, or Air Force squadron	I I
Regiment or group; combat team (with abbreviation CT following identifying numeral)	I I I
Brigade, Combat Command of Armored Division, or Air Force Wing	X
Division or Command of an Air Force	XX
Corps or Air Force	XXX
Army	XXXX
Group of Armies	XXXXX

EXAMPLES

The letter or number to the left of the symbol indicates the unit designation; that to the right, the designation of the parent unit to which it belongs. Letters or numbers above or below boundary lines designate the units separated by the lines:

Company A, 137th Infantry	A ⊠ 137
8th Field Artillery Battalion	● 8
Combat Command A, 1st Armored Division	A ⊡ I
Observation Post, 23d Infantry	△ 23
Command Post, 5th Infantry Division	⊠ 5
Boundary between 137th and 138th Infantry	—‖‖‖— 137 / 138

Weapons

Machine gun	●→
Gun	●
Gun battery	⊔
Howitzer or Mortar	●|
Tank	◇
Self-propelled gun	▣

Index

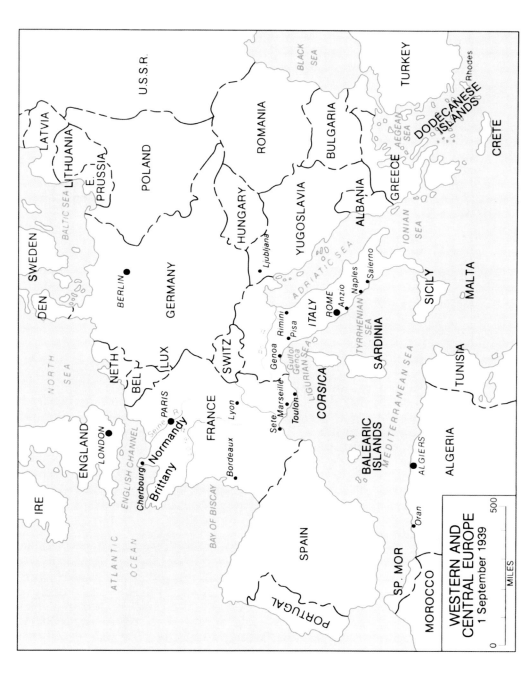

WESTERN AND
CENTRAL EUROPE
1 September 1939

0   MILES   500

MAP 1

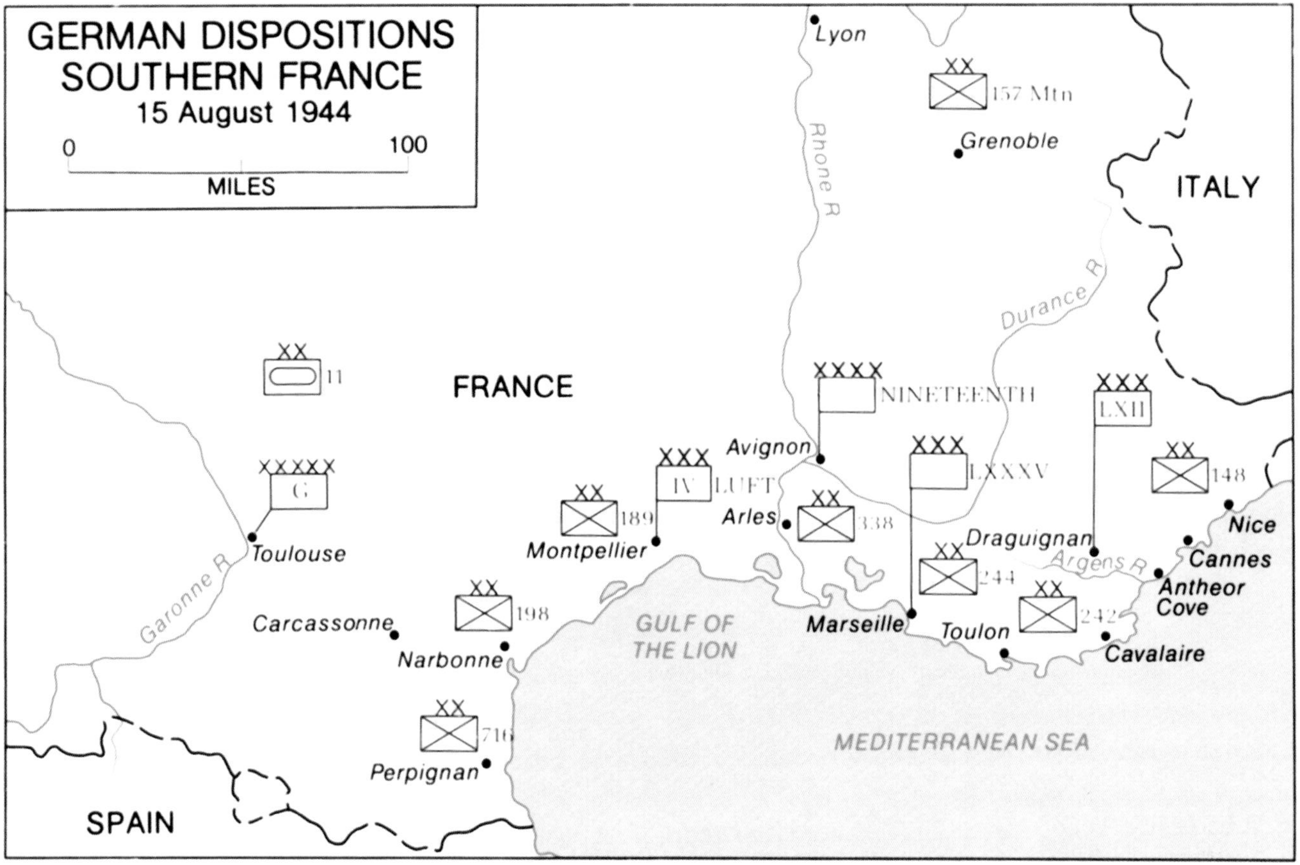

MAP 2

GERMAN DISPOSITIONS
SOUTHERN FRANCE
15 August 1944

MILES

0   100

SPAIN

FRANCE

ITALY

Garonne R.

Toulouse

Carcassonne

Narbonne

Perpignan

Montpellier

GULF OF
THE LION

Arles

Avignon

Marseille

MEDITERRANEAN SEA

Toulon

Draguignan

Cavalaire

Antheor
Cove

Cannes

Nice

Argens R.

Durance R.

Rhone R.

Grenoble

Lyon

G

11

711

198

189

IV LUFT

338

NINETEENTH

LXXXV

244

242

148

LXII

157 Mtn

NORTH
SEA

ENGLAND

NETHERLANDS

GERMANY

LONDON

Antwerp

BELGIUM

Rhine R

ENGLISH CHANNEL

LUX

Cherbourg

Normandy

Seine R

PARIS

Strasbourg

Brest

FRANCE

Brittany

Lorient

Loire R

Tours

Dijon

Saone R

SWITZERLAND

St. Nazaire

Geneva

La Rochelle

ITALY

BAY OF
BISCAY

GIRONDE
ESTUARY

Lyon

Grenoble

Bordeaux

Massif
Central

Alps

Rhone R

Garonne R

Nice

Cannes

Toulouse

Montpellier

Marseille

Toulon

SPAIN

GULF OF
THE LION

FRANCE

Highground

0   100

MILES

Pyrenees

MAP 3

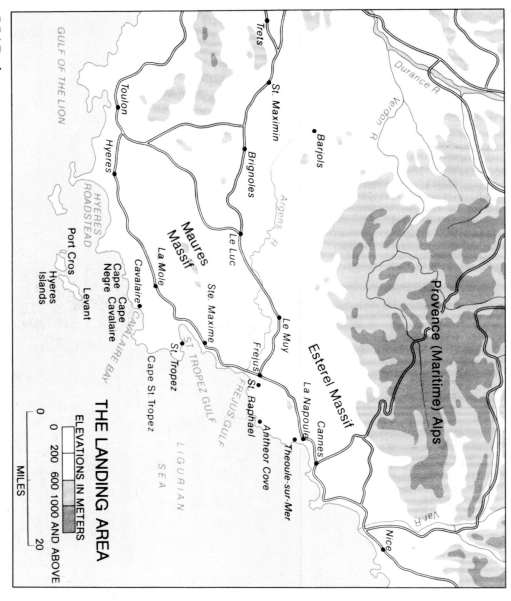

MAP 4

THE LANDING AREA

ELEVATIONS IN METERS

0   200   600 1000 AND ABOVE

0   20
MILES

GULF OF THE LION

Toulon

Trets

St. Maximin

Barjols

Hyeres

Brignoles

Durance R

Verdon R

Argens R

Le Luc

Maures
Massif

Provence (Maritime) Alps

HYERES
ROADSTEAD

Port Cros

Hyeres
Islands

Levant

Cape
Negre

Cape
Cavalaire

Cavalaire

CAVALAIRE BAY

La Mole

Ste. Maxime

Cape St. Tropez

St. Tropez

ST TROPEZ GULF

FREJUS GULF

Frejus

St. Raphael

Antheor Cove

Le Muy

La Napoule

Esterel Massif

Cannes

Theoule-sur-Mer

Var R

Nice

LIGURIAN

SEA

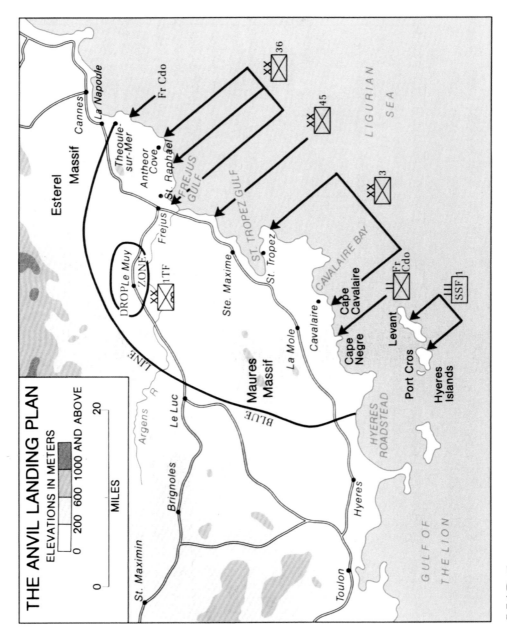

THE ANVIL LANDING PLAN

ELEVATIONS IN METERS

0   200   600   1000 AND ABOVE

MILES
0   20

MAP 5

MAP 6

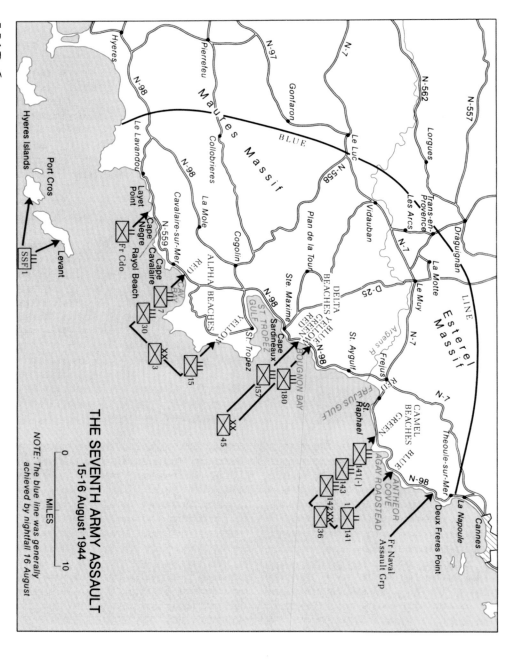

THE SEVENTH ARMY ASSAULT
15-16 August 1944

NOTE: The blue line was generally
achieved by nightfall 16 August

MILES
0 ____ 10

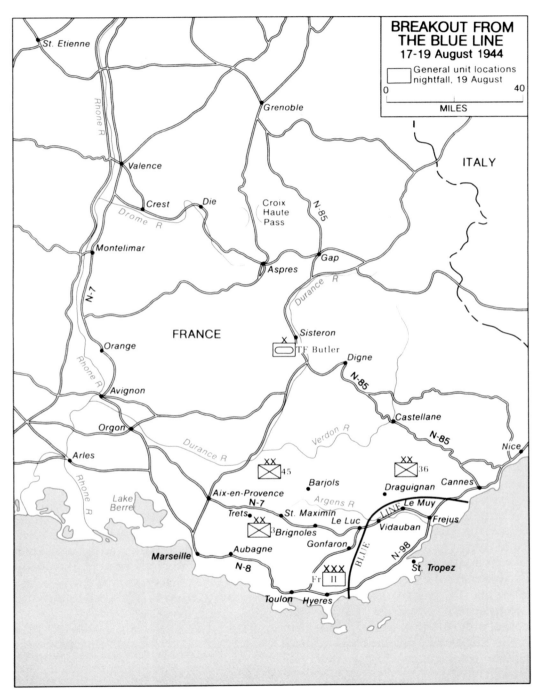

**BREAKOUT FROM
THE BLUE LINE**
17-19 August 1944

General unit locations
nightfall, 19 August

0   40

MILES

St. Etienne

Grenoble

ITALY

Valence

Crest   *Die*

Drome R.

N-85

*Croix
Haute
Pass*

Montelimar

Aspres

Gap

N-7

Durance R.

FRANCE

Sisteron

TF Butler

Digne

Orange

N-85

Avignon

Castellane

N-85

Orgon

Durance R.

Verdon R.

Nice

Arles

XX 45

Barjols

XX 36

Draguignan

Cannes

Rhone R.

*Lake
Berre*

Aix-en-Provence

N-7

Argens R.

Le Muy

LINE

Trets

XX 3 *Brignoles*

St. Maximin

Le Luc

Vidauban

Frejus

Marseille

Aubagne

Gonfaron

BLUE

N-98

St. Tropez

N-8

XXX
Fr   II

Toulon   *Hyeres*

MAP 7

MAP 8

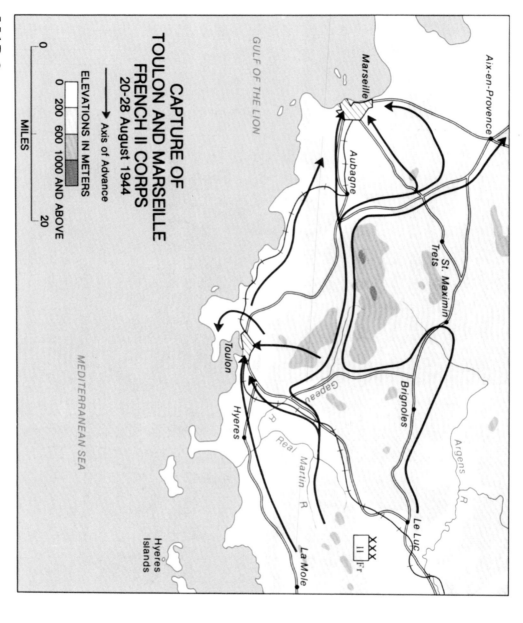

CAPTURE OF
TOULON AND MARSEILLE
FRENCH II CORPS
20-28 August 1944

Axis of Advance

ELEVATIONS IN METERS

| 0 | 200 | 600 | 1000 AND ABOVE |

0   20
MILES

GULF OF THE LION

MEDITERRANEAN SEA

Aix-en-Provence

Marseille

Aubagne

Trets

St. Maximin

Brignoles

Argens R.

Le Luc

Toulon

Gapeau R.

Hyeres

Real

Martin R.

La Mole

Hyeres Islands

XXXX
II Fr

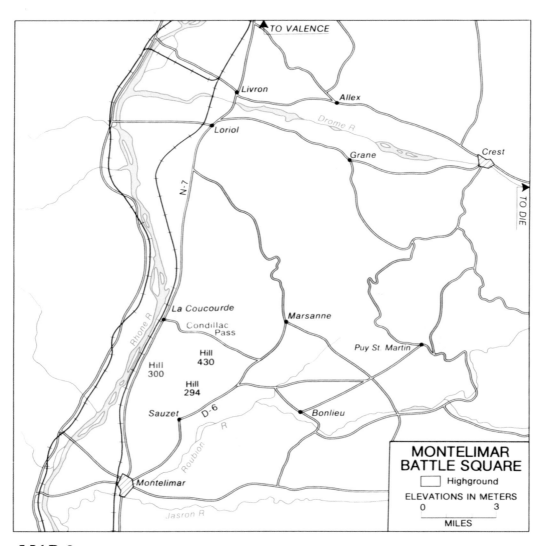

MAP 9

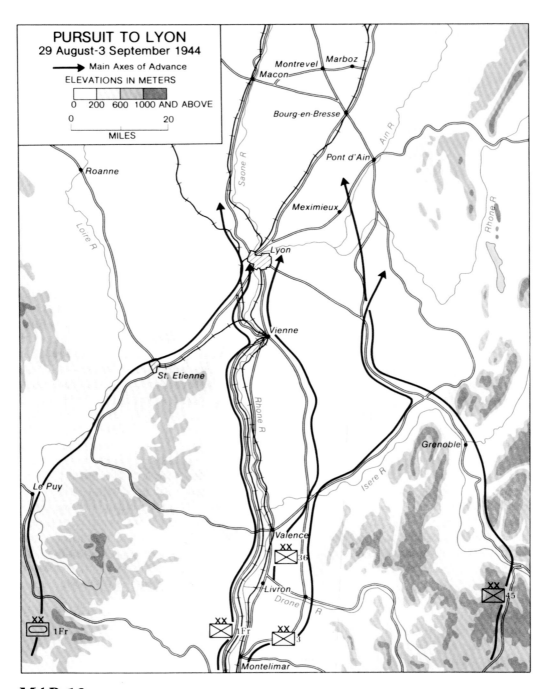

PURSUIT TO LYON
29 August-3 September 1944

Main Axes of Advance

ELEVATIONS IN METERS

0   200   600   1000 AND ABOVE

0   20

MILES

Roanne

Loire R

Saone R

Montrevel   Marboz
Macon

Bourg-en-Bresse

Ain R

Pont d'Ain

Meximieux

Rhone R

Lyon

Vienne

St. Etienne

Rhone R

Grenoble

Le Puy

Isere R

Valence

XX
36

Livron

Drone   R

XX
45

XX
1Fr

XX
Fr

XX
3

Montelimar

MAP 10

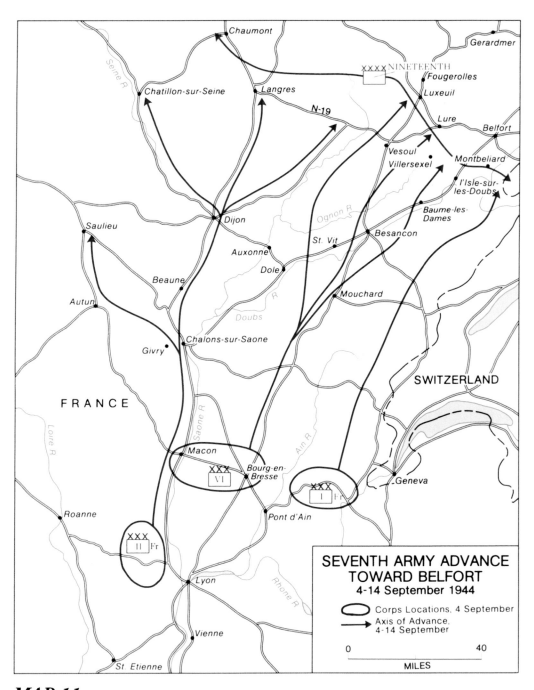

Chaumont

Gerardmer

XXXX NINETEENTH

Fougerolles

Chatillon-sur-Seine

Langres

Luxeuil

N-19

Lure

Belfort

Seine R.

Vesoul

Villersexel

Montbeliard

l'Isle-sur-
les-Doubs

Saulieu

Dijon

Ognon R.

Baume-les-
Dames

St. Vit

Besancon

Auxonne

Dole

Beaune

R

Autun

Mouchard

Doubs

Chalons-sur-Saone

SWITZERLAND

Givry

FRANCE

Loire R.

Saone R.

Ain R.

Macon

XXX
VI

Bourg-en-
Bresse

XXX
I Fr

Geneva

Roanne

Pont d'Ain

XXX
II Fr

Lyon

Rhone R.

**SEVENTH ARMY ADVANCE
TOWARD BELFORT**
4-14 September 1944

⬭ Corps Locations, 4 September
→ Axis of Advance,
4-14 September

Vienne

0   40

St. Etienne

MILES

MAP 11

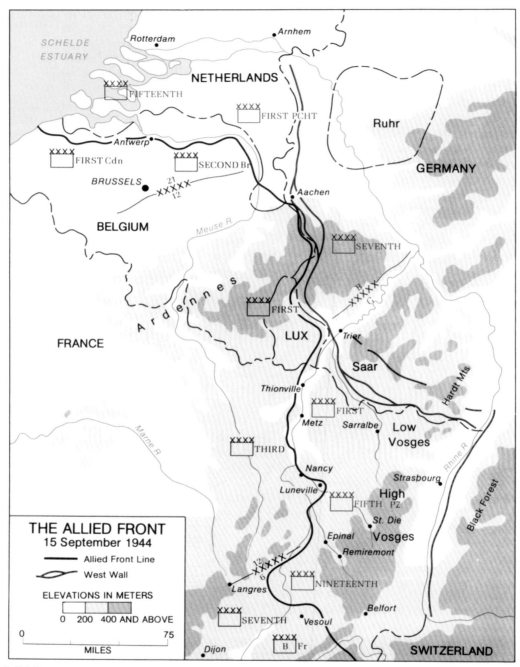

SCHELDE
ESTUARY

Rotterdam

Arnhem

NETHERLANDS

XXXX
FIFTEENTH

XXXX
FIRST PCHT

Ruhr

Antwerp

XXXX
FIRST Cdn

XXXX
SECOND Br

GERMANY

BRUSSELS

21
XXXXX
12

Aachen

BELGIUM

Meuse R

XXXX
SEVENTH

FRANCE

A r d e n n e s

XXXX
FIRST

B
XXXXX
C

LUX

Trier

Thionville

Saar

XXXX
FIRST

Metz

Sarralbe

**Low
Vosges**

Hardt Mts

Marne R

XXXX
THIRD

Nancy

Strasbourg

Luneville

XXXX
FIFTH PZ

**High
PZ**

Rhine R

St. Die

THE ALLIED FRONT
15 September 1944

Epinal

Vosges

Black Forest

Allied Front Line

Remiremont

West Wall

ELEVATIONS IN METERS

2
XXXXX
6

Langres

XXXX
NINETEENTH

0   200   400 AND ABOVE

XXXX
SEVENTH

Belfort

0   75

Vesoul

MILES

XXXX
B   Fr

Dijon

SWITZERLAND

MAP 12

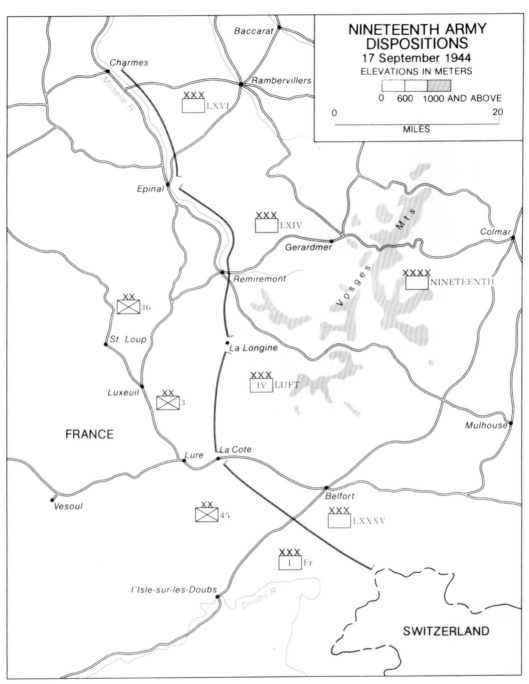

NINETEENTH ARMY
DISPOSITIONS
17 September 1944
ELEVATIONS IN METERS

0   600   1000 AND ABOVE

0   20
MILES

Baccarat

Charmes

Rambervillers

XXX
LXVI

Moselle R

Epinal

XXX
LXIV

Gerardmer

Colmar

Vosges Mts

Remiremont

XXXX
NINETEENTH

XX
36

St. Loup

La Longine

Luxeuil

XX
3

XXX
IV LUFT

FRANCE

Mulhouse

Lure

La Cote

Belfort

Vesoul

XX
45

XXX
LXXXV

XXX
I Fr

l'Isle-sur-les-Doubs

Doubs R

SWITZERLAND

MAP 13

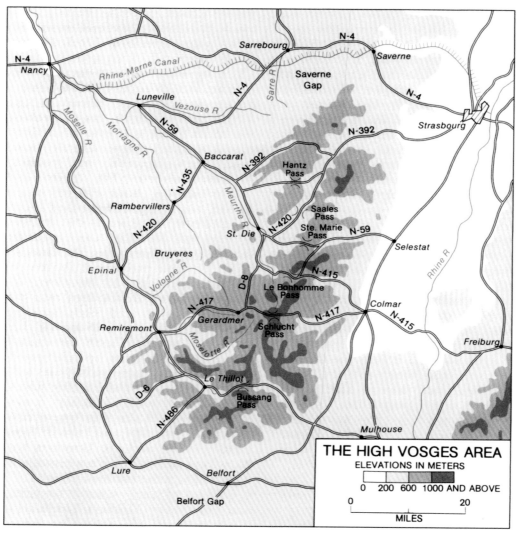

THE HIGH VOSGES AREA

ELEVATIONS IN METERS

0 200 600 1000 AND ABOVE

0   20

MILES

MAP 14

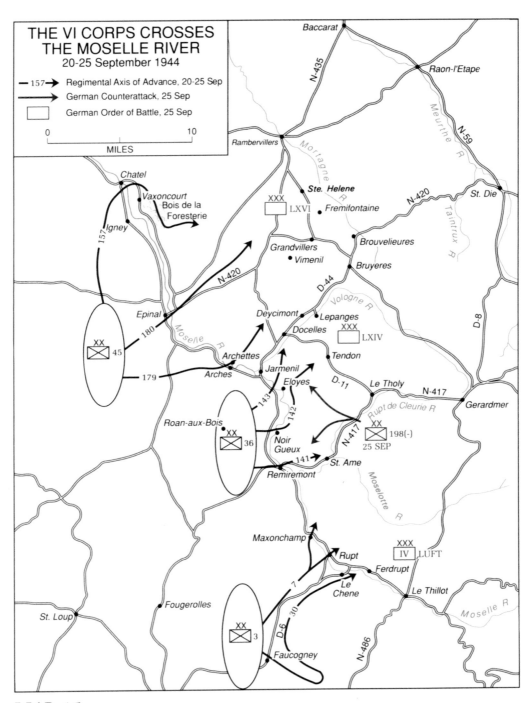

**THE VI CORPS CROSSES
THE MOSELLE RIVER**
20-25 September 1944

- 157→ Regimental Axis of Advance, 20-25 Sep
→ German Counterattack, 25 Sep
▭ German Order of Battle, 25 Sep

0   10
MILES

Baccarat

Raon-l'Etape

N-435

Meurthe R.

N-59

Rambervillers

Mortagne R.

Ste. Helene

Fremifontaine

N-420

St. Die

LXVI

Taintrux R.

Chatel

Vaxoncourt
Bois de la
Foresterie

Igney

157

Grandvillers

Vimenil

Brouvelieures

Bruyeres

D-44

Vologne R.

D-8

N-420

Epinal

Moselle R.

180

Deycimont

Lepanges

Docelles

LXIV

XX 45

Archettes

Arches

179

Jarmenil

Eloyes

Tendon

D-11

Le Tholy

N-417

Gerardmer

Rupt de Cleurie R.

143

142

N-417

XX 198(-)
25 SEP

Roan-aux-Bois

XX 36

Noir
Gueux

141

St. Ame

Moselotte R.

Remiremont

Maxonchamp

Rupt

LUFT
IV

Ferdrupt

Le
Chene

Le Thillot

Moselle R.

Fougerolles

St. Loup

7

D-6 30

XX 3

N-486

Faucogney

MAP 15

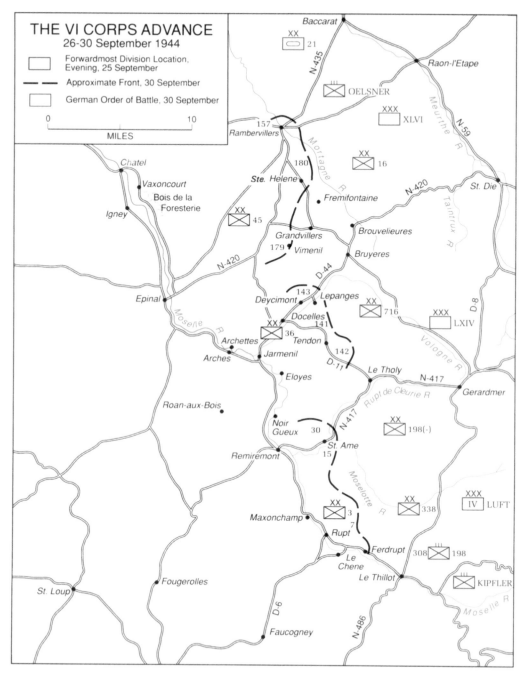

THE VI CORPS ADVANCE
26-30 September 1944

Forwardmost Division Location,
Evening, 25 September

Approximate Front, 30 September

German Order of Battle, 30 September

0   10
MILES

Baccarat

21

Raon-l'Etape

OELSNER

XLVI

157
Rambervillers

16

St. Die

Chatel

Vaxoncourt

Bois de la
Foresterie

Igney

180

Ste. Helene

Fremifontaine

45

Grandvillers

179   Vimenil

Brouvelieures

Bruyeres

N-420

Epinal

143
Deycimont   Lepanges

716

LXIV

Docelles
141

36
Archettes   Tendon

Arches   Jarmenil

142
D-11

Le Tholy   N-417

Gerardmer

Eloyes

Roan-aux-Bois

Noir
Gueux   30

N-417

198(-)

St. Ame
15

IV   LUFT

Remiremont

Maxonchamp

3
7

338

Rupt

Le
Chene

Ferdrupt   308   198

Le Thillot

KIPFLER

St. Loup

Fougerolles

Faucogney

MAP 16

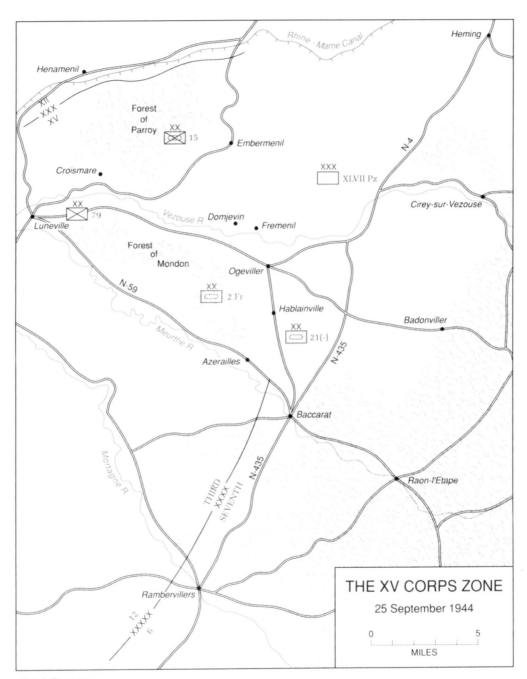

MAP 17

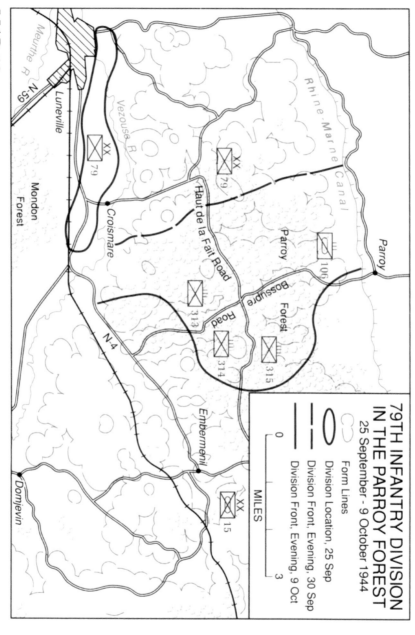

MAP 18

79TH INFANTRY DIVISION
IN THE PARROY FOREST
25 September - 9 October 1944

○   Form Lines
     Division Location, 25 Sep
|| Division Front, Evening, 30 Sep
| Division Front, Evening, 9 Oct

0   MILES   3

Meurthe R.

N-59

Luneville

Mondon Forest

Vezouse R.

XX 79

Croismare

Haut de la Fait Road

Rhine-Marne Canal

XX 79

Parroy Forest

Bossupre Road

106

Parroy

313

314

315

N-4

Embermenil

Domjevin

XX 15

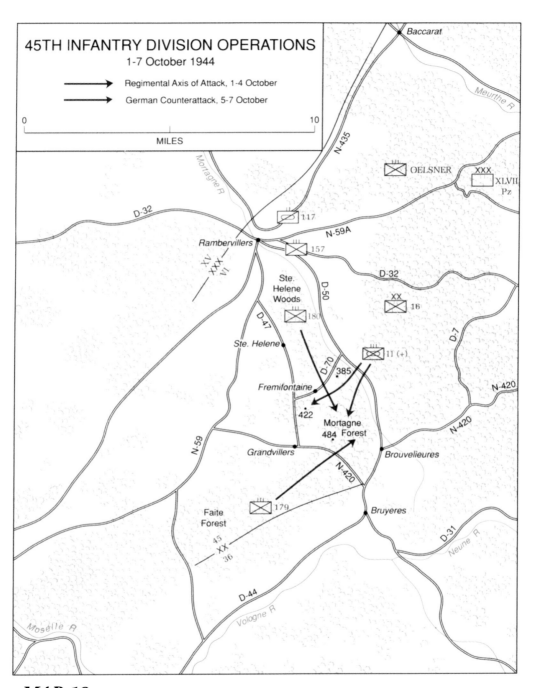

MAP 19

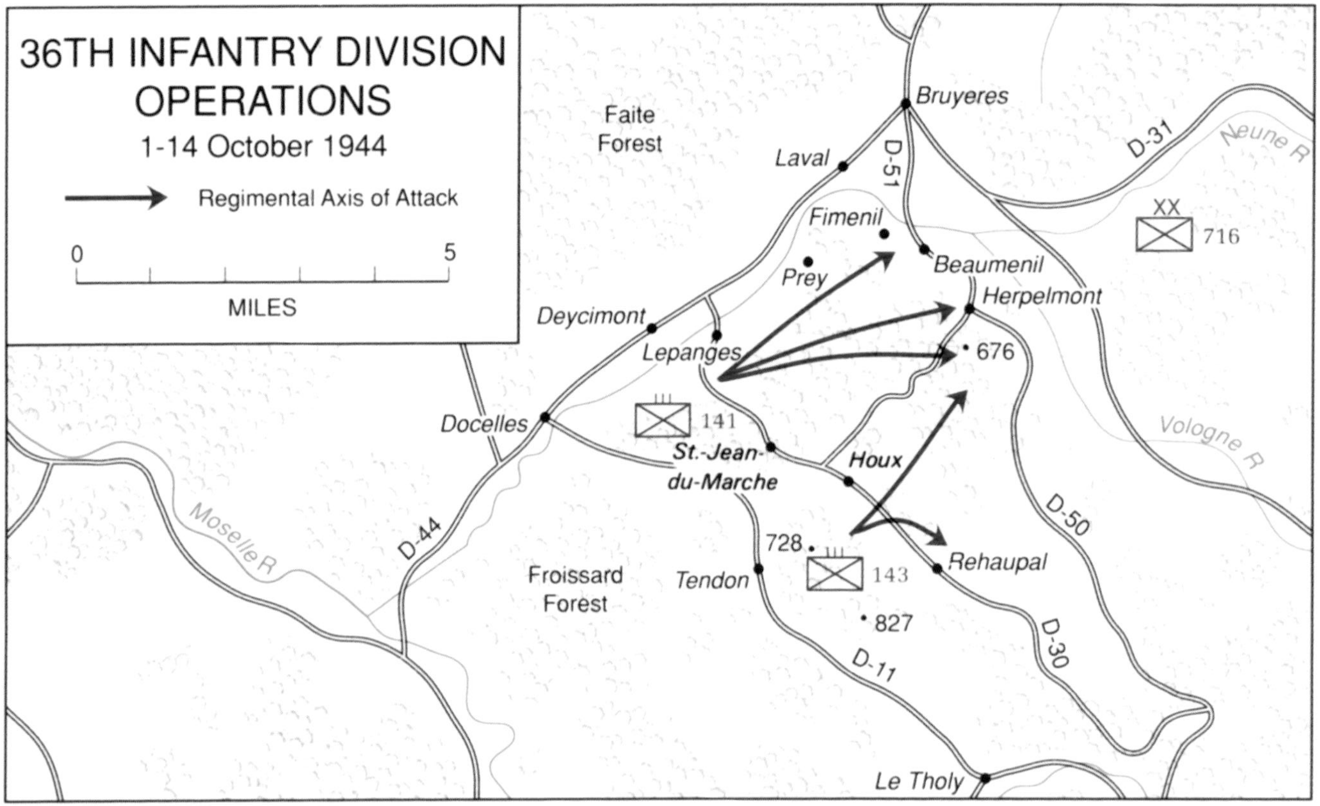

MAP 20

36TH INFANTRY DIVISION
OPERATIONS
1–14 October 1944

→ Regimental Axis of Attack

MILES
0 5

Moselle R.

D-44

Docelles

Froissard Forest

Deycimont

Faîte Forest

Lepanges

St.-Jean-du-Marche

Tendon

728

141

Prey

Fimenil

Laval

D-51

Bruyeres

143

827

Houx

676

Beaumenil

Herpelmont

Le Tholy

D-11

Rehaupal

D-30

D-50

Vologne R.

716

D-31

Neune R.

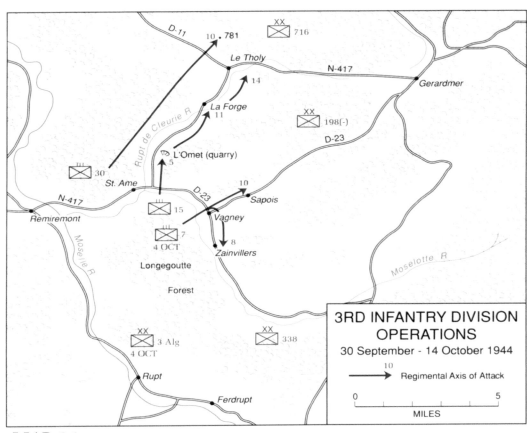

MAP 21

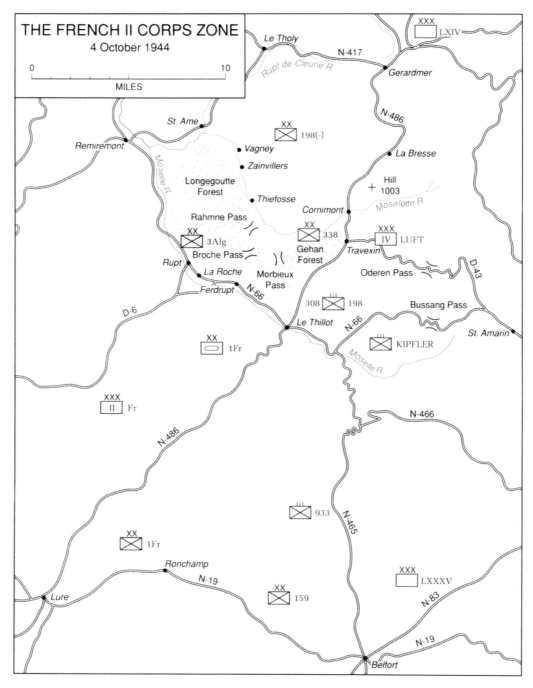

THE FRENCH II CORPS ZONE
4 October 1944

0   10

MILES

Le Tholy

N-417

Rupt de Cleurie R

Gerardmer

XXX
LXIV

N-486

St. Ame

XX
198(-)

Remiremont

Vagney

La Bresse

Zainvillers

Moselle R

Longegoutte
Forest

Hill
1003

Thiefosse

Moselotte R

Cornimont

Rahmne Pass

XX
338

XXX
IV   LUFT

XX
3Alg

Gehan
Forest

Travexin

Broche Pass

Rupt

La Roche

Morbieux
Pass

Oderen Pass

D-43

Ferdrupt

N-66

308   XX
198

Bussang Pass

D-6

Le Thillot

N-66

St. Amarin

XX
KIPFLER

XX
1Fr

Moselle R

XXX
II   Fr

N-466

N-486

XX
933

N-465

XX
1Fr

Ronchamp

XXX
LXXXV

N-19

N-83

Lure

XX
159

N-19

Belfort

MAP 22

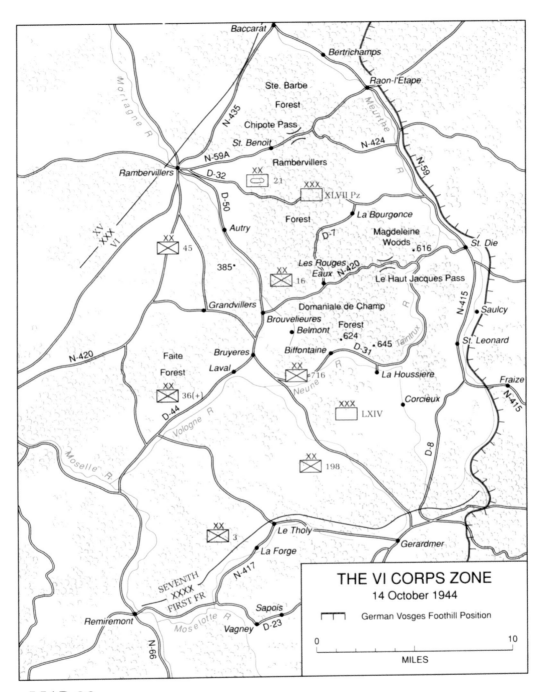

Baccarat

Bertrichamps

Ste. Barbe
Forest

Raon-l'Etape

N-435

Chipote Pass

St. Benoit

N-424

Meurthe R

N-59

N-59A

Rambervillers

D-32

Rambervillers

D-50

XX 21

XXX XLVII Pz

Forest

La Bourgonce

D-7

Magdeleine
Woods

St. Die

XV
XXX
VI

XX 45

Autry

385·

·616

XX 16

Les Rouges
Eaux

N-420

Le Haut Jacques Pass

N-415

Saulcy

Grandvillers

Domaniale de Champ

Brouvelieures

Belmont

Forest
·624

St. Leonard

N-420

Faite
Forest

Bruyeres

Biffontaine

D-31

·645

Tainrux R

·716

Laval

XX 716

La Houssiere

Fraize

N-415

XX 36(+)

XXX LXIV

Corcieux

D-8

D-44

Vologne R

Neune R

Moselle R

XX 198

XX 3

Le Tholy

La Forge

Gerardmer

SEVENTH
XXXX
FIRST FR

N-417

Sapois

THE VI CORPS ZONE
14 October 1944

German Vosges Foothill Position

Remiremont

Moselotte R

Vagney

D-23

0   MILES   10

N-66

MAP 23

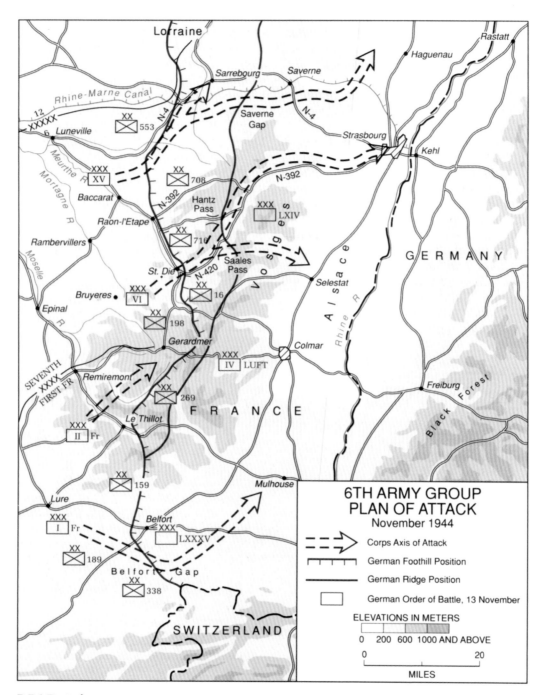

Lorraine
Rastatt
Haguenau
Sarrebourg   Saverne
Rhine-Marne Canal
12
XXXXX
6   Luneville   XX 553
N-4
Saverne
Gap   N-4   Strasbourg
Kehl

Meurthe R
Mortagne R
XXX
XV   XX 708
N-392   N-392
Baccarat   Hantz
Pass
Raon-l'Etape   XXX   LXIV
Rambervillers   XX 716
Moselle R
St. Die   N-420   Saales
Pass   GERMANY
Bruyeres   XXX
VI   XX 16   Selestat
Epinal   XX 198
Gerardmer   Colmar
SEVENTH   XXX
XXXX   IV LUFT
FIRST FR   Remiremont   XX 269   Rhine R
F R A N C E   Freiburg
Le Thillot   Black Forest
XXX
II Fr   XX 159
Lure   Mulhouse
XXX   Belfort   **6TH ARMY GROUP**
I Fr   XXX LXXXV   **PLAN OF ATTACK**
XX 189   November 1944
B e l f o r t   Gap   Corps Axis of Attack
XX 338   German Foothill Position
German Ridge Position
SWITZERLAND   German Order of Battle, 13 November
ELEVATIONS IN METERS
0   200 600 1000 AND ABOVE
0   20
MILES

MAP 24

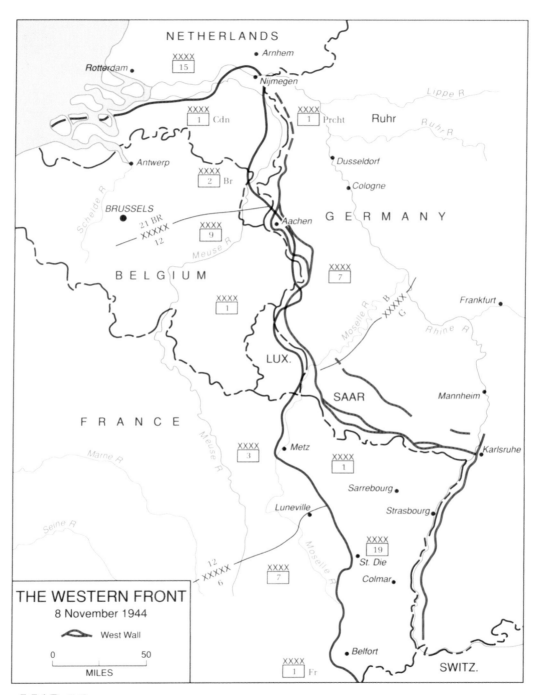

NETHERLANDS

Arnhem

Rotterdam

XXXX
15

Nijmegen

Lippe R.

Ruhr

Ruhr R.

XXXX
1 Cdn

XXXX
1 Prcht

Antwerp

Dusseldorf

Cologne

XXXX
2 Br

Scheide R.

BRUSSELS

21 BR
XXXXX
12

XXXX
9

Aachen

G E R M A N Y

B E L G I U M

Meuse R.

XXXX
1

XXXX
7

Moselle R.

B
XXXXX
G

Frankfurt

Rhine R.

LUX.

SAAR

Mannheim

F R A N C E

Meuse R.

Marne R.

XXXX
3

Metz

XXXX
1

Karlsruhe

Sarrebourg

Seine R.

Luneville

Strasbourg

Moselle R.

XXXX
19

St. Die

12
XXXXX
6

XXXX
7

Colmar

THE WESTERN FRONT
8 November 1944

West Wall

0   50

MILES

Belfort

SWITZ.

XXXX
1 Fr

MAP 25

MAP 26

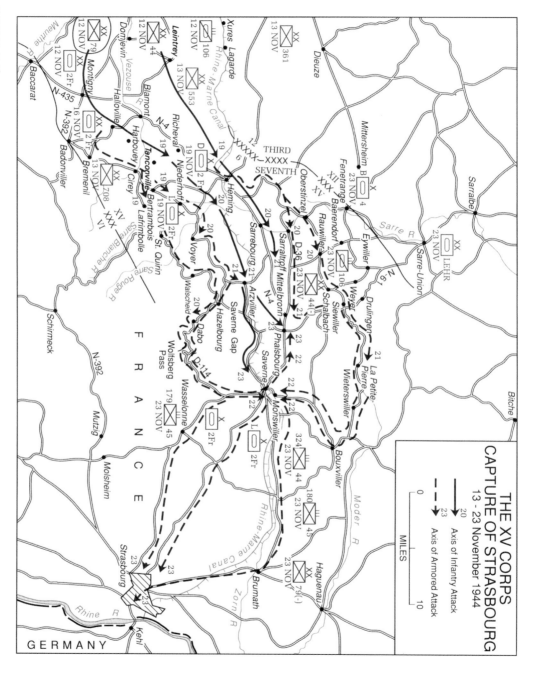

THE XV CORPS
CAPTURE OF STRASBOURG
13 - 23 November 1944

Axis of Infantry Attack

Axis of Armored Attack

0   10

MILES

GERMANY

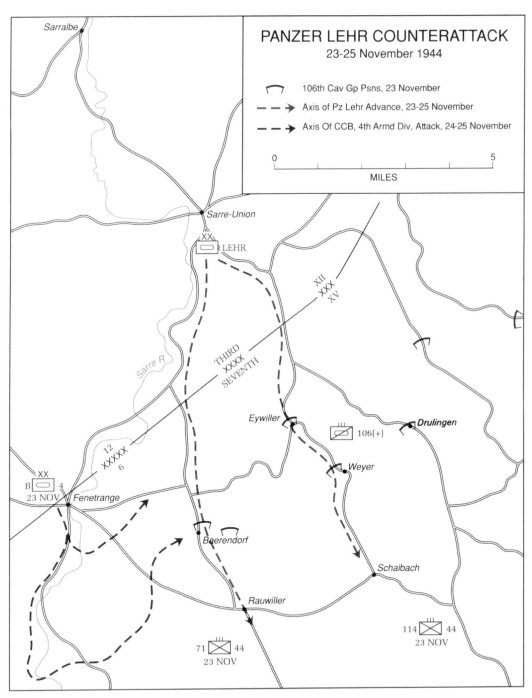

PANZER LEHR COUNTERATTACK
23-25 November 1944

106th Cav Gp Psns, 23 November

Axis of Pz Lehr Advance, 23-25 November

Axis Of CCB, 4th Armd Div, Attack, 24-25 November

0   5

MILES

Sarralbe

Sarre-Union

LEHR

XII
XXX
XV

Sarre R

THIRD
XXXX
SEVENTH

Eywiller

106(+)

Drulingen

12
XXXXX
6

Weyer

B
XX
4
23 NOV

Fenetrange

Baerendorf

Schalbach

Rauwiller

114
44
23 NOV

71
44
23 NOV

MAP 27

MAP 28

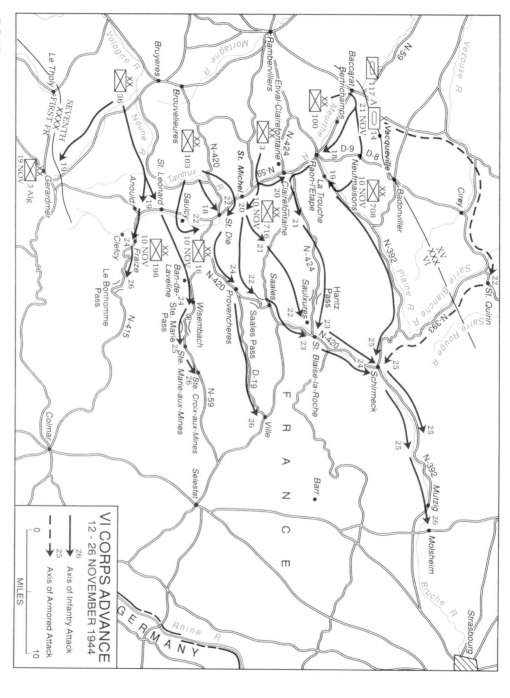

VI CORPS ADVANCE
12 - 26 NOVEMBER 1944

Axis of Infantry Attack

Axis of Armored Attack

0   MILES   10

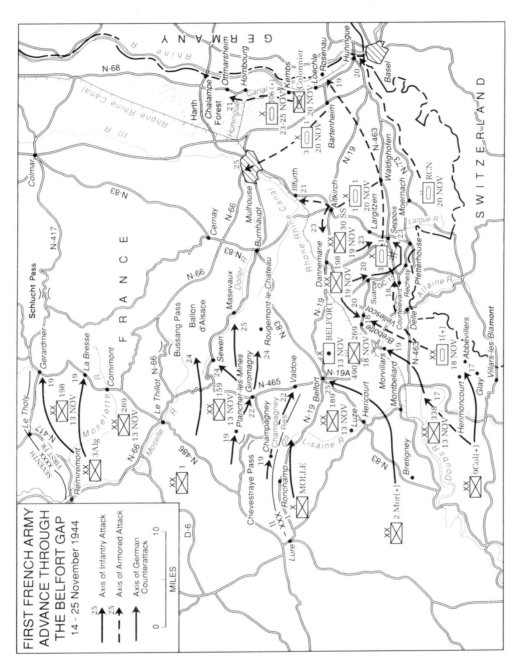

FIRST FRENCH ARMY
ADVANCE THROUGH
THE BELFORT GAP
14 - 25 November 1944

25 — Axis of Infantry Attack
25 --- Axis of Armored Attack
Axis of German Counterattack

MILES
0   10

MAP 29

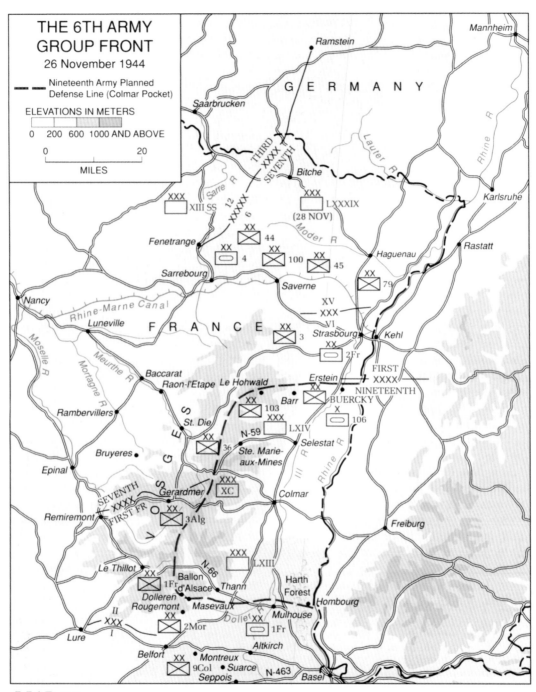

THE 6TH ARMY
GROUP FRONT
26 November 1944

- - - Nineteenth Army Planned
Defense Line (Colmar Pocket)

ELEVATIONS IN METERS

0   200 600 1000 AND ABOVE

0   20
MILES

GERMANY

Mannheim

Ramstein

Saarbrucken

Lauter R.

Rhine R.

Karlsruhe

THIRD
XXXX
SEVENTH

Bitche

Sarre R.

LXXXIX
(28 NOV)

Moder R.

Rastatt

XIII SS

12
XXXX
6

Fenetrange

44

4

100

45

Haguenau

Sarrebourg

Saverne

79

Nancy

Rhine-Marne Canal

FRANCE

XV
XXX

Strasbourg

Kehl

Luneville

Moselle R.

Mortagne R.

Meurthe R.

Baccarat
Raon-l'Etape

Le Hohwald

3

VI

2Fr

Erstein

FIRST
XXXX
NINETEENTH

BUERCKY

Rambervillers

St. Die

Barr

103

N-59

LXIV

106

Bruyeres

Epinal

V
O
S
G
E
S

36

Ste. Marie-
aux-Mines

Selestat

III

Rhine R.

SEVENTH
XXXX
FIRST FR

Gerardmer

XC

Colmar

Remiremont

3Alg

Freiburg

Le Thillot

LXIII

N-66

Ballon
d'Alsace

1Fr

Thann

Harth
Forest

Dolleren
Rougemont

Masevaux

Mulhouse

Hombourg

II
XXX
I

Lure

2Mor

Dolle R.

1Fr

Altkirch

Belfort

Montreux

9Col

Suarce

Seppois

N-463

Basel

MAP 30

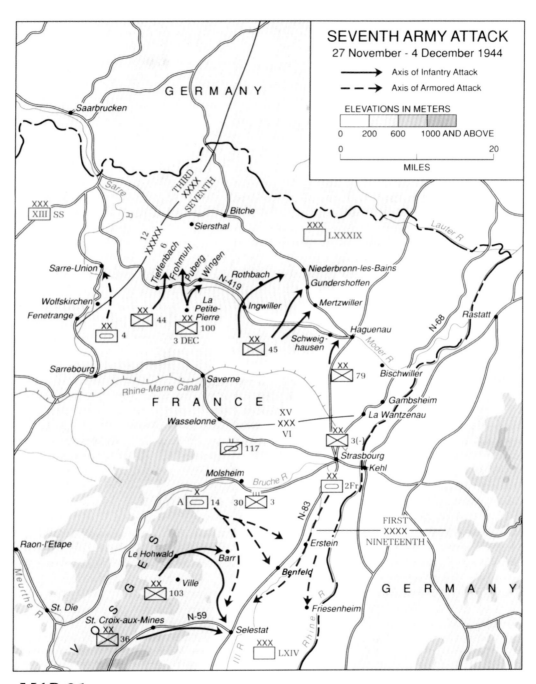

SEVENTH ARMY ATTACK
27 November - 4 December 1944

→ Axis of Infantry Attack

--→ Axis of Armored Attack

ELEVATIONS IN METERS

0   200   600   1000 AND ABOVE

0   20

MILES

GERMANY

Saarbrucken

Sarre R

THIRD XXXX SEVENTH

XXX
XIII SS

Bitche

Siersthal

XXX
LXXXIX

12 XXXXX 6
XXXXX
Tieffenbach
Frohmuhl
Puberg
Wingen

Sarre-Union

Rothbach
N-419

Niederbronn-les-Bains
Gundershoffen

Lauter R

Wolfskirchen

La Petite-Pierre

Ingwiller

Mertzwiller

N-68

Rastatt

Fenetrange

XX
4

XX
44

XX
100
3 DEC

XX
45

Schweig-hausen

Haguenau

Moder R

Sarrebourg

Saverne

Rhine-Marne Canal

F R A N C E

Wasselonne

XX
79

Bischwiller

Gambsheim

XV
XXX
VI

La Wantzenau

Molsheim

XX
117

Bruche R

XX
3(-)

Strasbourg
Kehl

A
14

X
30

XX
3

XX
2Fr

N-83

FIRST
XXXX
NINETEENTH

Raon-l'Etape

Le Hohwald

Barr

Erstein

Benfeld

V O S G E S

Ville

XX
103

G E R M A N Y

Meurthe R

St. Die

St. Croix-aux-Mines

XX
36

N-59

Selestat

Friesenheim

Rhine R

Ill R

XXX
LXIV

MAP 31

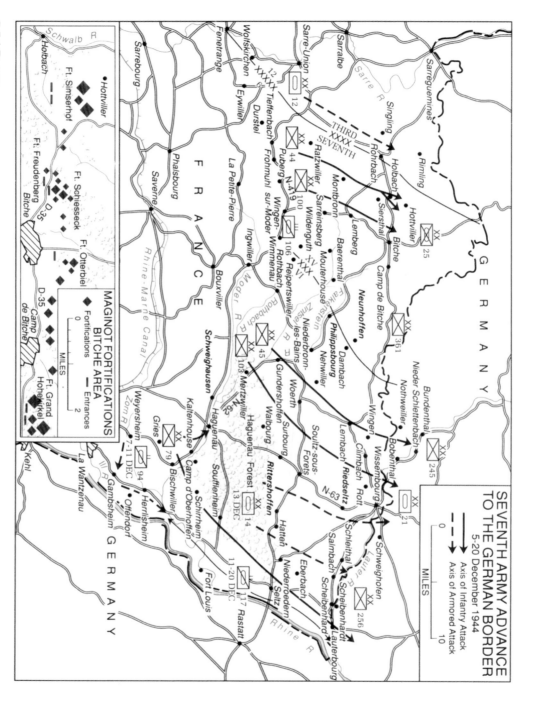

MAP 32

SEVENTH ARMY ADVANCE
TO THE GERMAN BORDER
5-20 December 1944

→ Axis of Infantry Attack
⇢ Axis of Armored Attack

0 MILES 10

MAGINOT FORTIFICATIONS
BITCHE AREA

◆ Fortifications
— Entrances

0 MILES 2

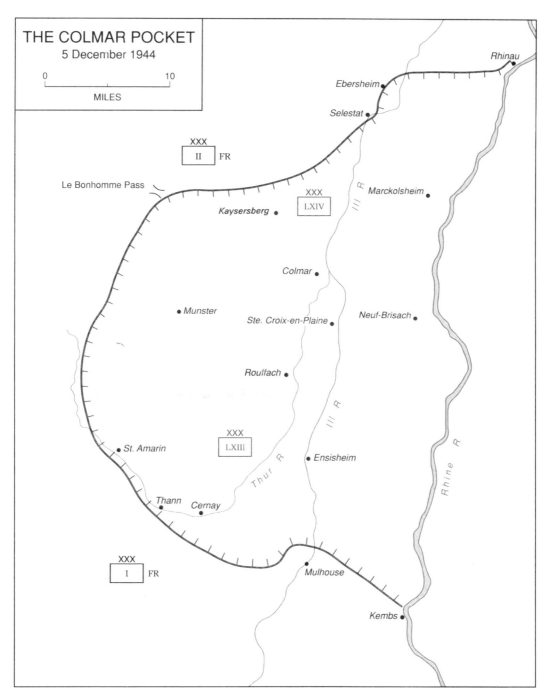

THE COLMAR POCKET
5 December 1944

0   10

MILES

XXX
II   FR

Rhinau

Ebersheim

Selestat

Le Bonhomme Pass

XXX
LXIV

Marckolsheim

Kaysersberg

Colmar

Munster

Ste. Croix-en-Plaine

Neuf-Brisach

III R

Rouffach

III R

XXX
LXIII

St. Amarin

Ensisheim

Thann   Cernay

Thur R

Rhine R

XXX
I   FR

Mulhouse

Kembs

MAP 33

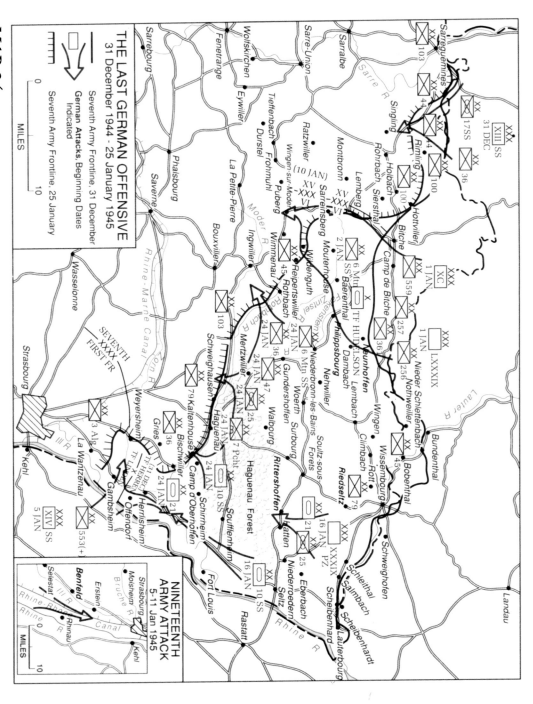

MAP 34

THE LAST GERMAN OFFENSIVE
31 December 1944 - 25 January 1945

Seventh Army Frontline, 31 December
German Attacks, Beginning Dates
Indicated
Seventh Army Frontline, 25 January

MILES

0   10

NINETEENTH
ARMY ATTACK
5-11 Jan 1945

MILES

0   10

Sarreguemines
31 DEC
XIII SS
17SS
36
100
44
Rimling
Holbach
Singling
Rohrbach
Siersthal
Bitche
Camp de Bitche
Hottviller
Sarre-Union
Saralbe
Sarre R.
Woelfskirchen
Fenetrange
Eywiller
Sarrebourg
Tieffenbach
Frohmuhl
Durstel
Montbronn
Ratzwiller
Lemberg
Wingen-sur-Moder
(10 JAN)
XV
XXX
VI
Puberg
Phalsbourg
La Petite-Pierre
Bouxviller
Ingwiller
Moder R.
Wimmenau
Wildenguth
Reipertswiller
Rothbach
45
Mouterhouse
21 JAN
6 Mtn SS Baerenthal
Philippsbourg
TF HUDSON
Munhoffen
Dambach
Lembach
Nehwiller
Wingen
Climbach
Rott
Niederbronn-les-Bains
6 Mtn SS
Woerth
Gundershoffen
Soultz-sous-Forets
Wissembourg
Bobenthal
Bundenthal
1 JAN
XC
559
257
Nieder Schlettenbach
256
Notnwiller
45
LXXXIX
Lauter R.
Landau
Rhine-Marne Canal
Saverne
Ion R.
Rhine R.
Strasbourg
Wasselonne
SEVENTH
FIRST FR
103
Schweighausen
Kaltenhouse
Mertzwiller
24 JAN
24 JAN
Haguenau
Metzwiller
24 JAN
24 JAN
36
47
24 JAN
25
Walburg
Surbourg
Rittershoffen
Riedseltz
79
Schleithal
Salmbach
Scheibenhardt
Lauterbourg
Schweighofen
24 JAN
Weyersheim
3 Alg
Gries
Bischwiller
36
Herrlisheim
Offendorf
Gambsheim
31 DEC
TF HERREN
31 DEC
24 JAN
24 JAN
24 JAN
Camp d'Oberhoffen
Schirrheim
Souffelnheim
10 SS
7 Pcht
Haguenau Forest
Hatten
21
16 JAN
Niederroedern
25
Eberbach
Seltz
10 SS
16 JAN
Fort Louis
Rastatt
16 JAN
21
XXX
XXXIX
PZ
Kehl
La Wantzenau
XIV SS
5 JAN
553(+)
16 JAN
PZ
Rhine R.
Strasbourg
Mutzig
Molsheim
Bruche R.
Ill R.
Erstein
Benfeld
Selestat
Rhinau
Rhine R.
Rhine R.
Rhine-Rhone Canal
Kehl

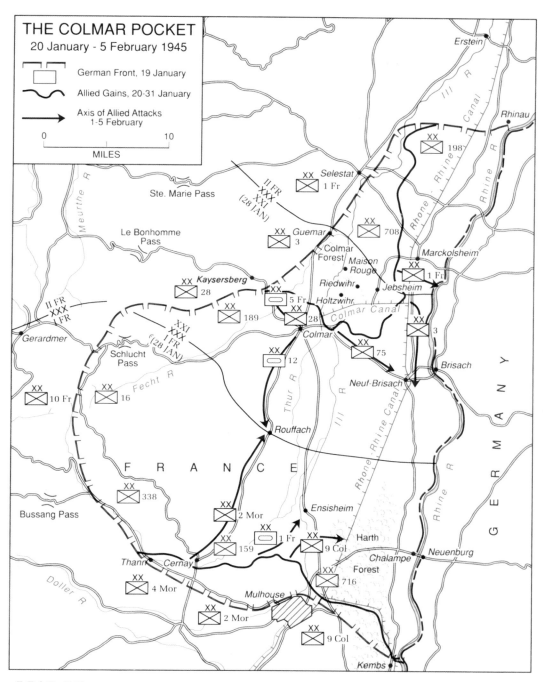

THE COLMAR POCKET
20 January - 5 February 1945

German Front, 19 January

Allied Gains, 20-31 January

Axis of Allied Attacks
1-5 February

0   10

MILES

Erstein

Rhinau

III R

Rhine Canal

Rhine R

Selestat

1 Fr

198

Ste. Marie Pass

II FR
XXX
XXI
(28 JAN)

Le Bonhomme
Pass

Guemar

3

708

Rhone

Colmar
Forest

Maison
Rouge

Marckolsheim

Kaysersberg

28

Riedwihr

1 Fr

Jebsheim

II FR
XXX
1 FR

189

5 Fr

Colmar Canal

Holtzwihr

28

3

Gerardmer

XXI
XXX
1 FR
(28 JAN)

Schlucht
Pass

Fecht R

Colmar

75

Neuf-Brisach

Brisach

10 Fr

16

Thur R

III R

Rouffach

Rhone-Rhine Canal

Rhine R

G
E
R
M
A
N
Y

F R A N C E

338

Bussang Pass

2 Mor

Ensisheim

159

1 Fr

9 Col

Harth

Chalampe
Forest

Neuenburg

Thann   Cernay

Doller R

4 Mor

716

Mulhouse

2 Mor

9 Col

Kembs

MAP 35